Asheville-Buncombe
Technical Community College
Learning Resources Center
340 Victoria Rd.
Asheville, NC 28801

The United Nations and Human Rights, 1945-1995

For Reference

Not to be taken from this room

Discarded
Date SEP 1 3 2021

D1495393

The United Nations
Blue Books Series, Volume VII

The United Nations and
Human Rights
1945-1995

**With an introduction by
Boutros Boutros-Ghali,
Secretary-General of the United Nations**

Department of Public Information
United Nations, New York

Published by the United Nations
Department of Public Information
New York, NY 10017

Editor's note:

Each of the United Nations documents and other materials reproduced in this book ("Texts of documents", pages 143-510) has been assigned a number (e.g. Document 1, Document 2, etc.). This number is used throughout the Introduction and other parts of this book to guide readers to the document texts. For other documents mentioned in the book but not reproduced, the United Nations document symbol (e.g., E/CN.14/714) is provided. With this symbol, such documents can be consulted at the Dag Hammarskjöld Library at United Nations Headquarters in New York, at other libraries in the United Nations system or at libraries around the world which have been designated as depository libraries for United Nations documents. The information contained in this volume is correct as at 1 July 1995.

Copyright © 1995 United Nations

The United Nations and Human Rights, 1945-1995
The United Nations Blue Books Series
Volume VII
ISBN 92-1-100560-4
United Nations Publication
Sales No. E. 95.I.21

Printed by the United Nations Reproduction Section
New York, NY

Contents

Section One
Introduction

I Overview

1   Modern human rights law emerged at the end of the Second World War in response to the atrocities and massive violations of these rights witnessed during the conflict. In 1945, when the Charter of the United Nations[1] was drafted in San Francisco, States laid the conceptual and legal foundations for the future development of international measures to protect human rights. Accordingly, Article 1 of the Charter establishes respect for human rights as the basis and the primary vehicle for achieving the purposes of the Organization, and Articles 55 and 56[2] pledge Member States and the United Nations itself to promote "universal respect for, and observance of, human rights and fundamental freedoms".

1/Document 1
See page 143

2/Document 1
See page 143

2   This work, part of the "United Nations Blue Books Series", is designed to provide succinct analysis and documentation regarding the main aspects of United Nations activities in the field of human rights. It is divided into two sections. Section One is a framework for analysis, Section Two for documentation. Section One contains seven Parts.

3   Part I is a general overview. Part II is a historical account of the establishment of the system from 1945 to 1948, during which period the Organization adopted the Universal Declaration of Human Rights.

4   Part III of Section One is devoted to the development of the system, the lengthy interval between the proclamation in 1948, by the General Assembly, of the Universal Declaration of Human Rights,[3] and the adoption in 1966 of the International Covenants on Human Rights.

3/Document 8
See page 153

5   Part IV describes the working of the system. In particular, it discusses the implementation of the International Covenants, the development of United Nations standard-setting activities, and the creation of mechanisms for monitoring human rights violations which are outside the purview of the conventions.

6   Part V describes the upheavals brought about by the end of the cold war and the resulting new phase in the evolution of the universal protection of human rights. These changes have clearly had an effect on how the various United Nations organs view their mandates and have enabled the system to expand.

7   In this respect, the 1993 World Conference on Human Rights marked a critical stage in United Nations policy in the field of human rights. First of all, by adopting the Vienna Declaration by consensus, it encouraged the United Nations to pursue and strengthen its activities to make respect for human rights a priority objective, on the same level as development and democracy, to which they are intrinsically related, and to work for the concurrent achievement of these three objectives.

8   Part VI describes the new guarantees established in the human rights field in recent years. Basically, these guarantees cover two areas: operational guarantees, related to the human rights component in the framework of peace-keeping operations; and jurisdictional guarantees, which concern international tribunals (the former Yugoslavia and Rwanda).

9   Part VII is the general conclusion of Section One of the book. It emphasizes that today, more than ever in human history, the conditions are close to being met for translating a great hope into reality: to devote all of humanity's energy to attaining the highest and most valued goal of the rights and freedoms of the human person.

10   Section Two of the book provides the reader with a basic set of United Nations documentation on human rights and fundamental freedoms within the Organization. First of all, a brief chronology describes the major stages in the establishment of international human rights law, particularly through the adoption of the major resolutions of the General Assembly and the Economic and Social Council, and the declarations and conventions referred to in Section One of the book. Second, it provides a list of widely known reference documents which the reader will easily be able to obtain, either in libraries or through United Nations Information Centres. Finally, the most important documents are reproduced *in extenso*.

11   It should be noted that this work is not intended to be exhaustive. It has been deliberately designed as a tool for the general presentation of United Nations activities in the field of human rights. Its purpose is to make this documentation widely available. Furthermore, its field is limited to the United Nations in the narrow sense; it does not touch on the often important activities of the specialized agencies.

II Establishing the system:
From the Charter to the Universal Declaration of Human Rights (1945-1948)

12   The United Nations system in the field of human rights was set up in a mere three years. On the institutional level, the signing of the Charter was followed by the creation of the principal organs and specialized agencies with competence in the human rights field. The defence and promotion of human rights by those organs were complemented by the establishment of conventions.

Human rights in the Charter

13   The Charter of the United Nations, signed in San Francisco on 26 June 1945, is the first international treaty whose aims are expressly based on universal respect for human rights.

14   The idea of international protection for human rights by an international organization originated in philosophical, social and political movements and diverse legal doctrines, born several centuries ago, in a number of different parts of the world. However, for various reasons, including the conflicting interests of States, it was for many years limited to simple declarations of intent.

15   Among the rare examples in history are the formal prohibition of the slave trade by the Treaty of Vienna (1815) and the General Act of Brussels, as well as the protection of the wounded and the sick in wartime laid down by the first Geneva Conventions in 1864. Respect for these standards was safeguarded by the "concert" of States parties to the treaties, meeting in periodic congresses.

16   After the First World War, in 1919, the Covenant of the League of Nations emphasized the principle of the primacy of human dignity over the interests of States in a number of areas such as the situation of the inhabitants of trust territories. In addition, the practice of the League of Nations gave rise to a system of protection whose purpose was to guarantee certain basic rights to members of minority groups.

17   The Constitution of the International Labour Organization (ILO), also adopted in 1919, established as one of its main objectives the promotion of social justice and respect for the dignity of workers. These

principles were further developed in 1944 in the Declaration of Philadelphia, later incorporated into the organization's Constitution.

18   These instruments marked important steps; however, they did not protect human dignity in the overall sense.

4/Document 1
See page 143

19   The United Nations Charter, however, in its Article 1, paragraph 3, and Article 55,[4] expressly places the Organization under an obligation to encourage "respect for human rights and for fundamental freedoms for all without distinction as to race, sex, language, or religion" and makes that respect the very foundation for the achievement of its goals.

20   It was the horror of the Second World War, and the consequent awareness of the close connection between respect for human dignity and peace, which motivated the Charter's qualitative leap towards the promotion of human rights "for all". The traces of that awareness can be found in the Charter's immediate predecessors, such as the Atlantic Charter of 14 August 1941, the Declaration by United Nations of 1 January 1942 and the Dumbarton Oaks Proposals of September and October 1944.

5/Document 1
See page 143

21   The innovative nature of the Charter is not limited to the simple proclamation of goals. Article 55 (c),[5] written in imperative terms, obliges the United Nations to act in such a way as to promote "universal respect for, and observance of, human rights". To enable it to fulfil that mission, the Charter gives the United Nations certain powers and prescribes certain methods. These powers and methods essentially come under three concepts: "study", "examination" and "recommendation". Reference should be made, in this context, to Article 13,[6] concerning the General Assembly; Article 60,[7] concerning the implementation of international cooperation in the economic, social and human rights fields; Article 62,[8] which defines the functions of the Economic and Social Council; and Articles 76[9] and 87,[10] which concern the trusteeship system.

6/Document 1
See page 143

7/Document 1
See page 143

8/Document 1
See page 143

9/Document 1
See page 143

10/Document 1
See page 143

11/Document 1
See page 143

22   These powers and methods enable the United Nations, in particular, to recommend to States the ratification of human rights treaties drafted within the Organization. As a result of the systematic use of this procedure, as set forth in Article 62, paragraph 3,[11] about 200 United Nations human rights instruments are currently in force.

23   The recommendation is the main weapon of the United Nations in the area of human rights. Unlike treaties, recommendations do not create a legal obligation for States. They are not, however, mere exhortations. It has often been considered that Article 56[12] creates a duty to examine recommendations carefully and in good faith, and even presupposes that there is a positive attitude towards them. This Article indeed obliges Member States "to take joint and separate action in cooperation with the Organization for the achievement of the purposes [including respect for human rights] set forth in Article 55".[13]

12/Document 1
See page 143

13/Document 1
See page 143

At the very least, there is general agreement that the practices of systematic obstruction and of total rejection of United Nations recommendations are contrary to Article 56.[14] In particular, this clause was invoked in order to condemn the system of apartheid for its grave, massive and systematic rejection of the relevant United Nations resolutions.

14/Document 1
See page 143

24   It should also be emphasized that certain United Nations human rights standards, presented in the form of recommendations, have taken on such authority that they are widely considered to constitute or to strengthen a rule of customary international law. This has been said, in particular, of a number of parts of the Universal Declaration of Human Rights.

25   The duties of Member States, based on Article 56,[15] are not limited to giving positive consideration to recommendations of the United Nations. It is also considered that these duties include a general obligation to take initiatives, in accordance with each country's distinct priorities and methods, to bring about progress in national legislation and practices in the field of human rights, even where there is no clear United Nations guidance.

15/Document 1
See page 143

26   Article 56[16] also encourages "joint" actions by States in order to promote international cooperation, including cooperation in the human rights field. Accordingly, some aspects of the activities of several major regional institutions, such as the Council of Europe, the Organization of American States (OAS) and the Organization of African Unity (OAU), concern the promotion and protection of human rights.

16/Document 1
See page 143

27   The Charter does not seem to exclude the possibility of the adoption by the United Nations of legally binding measures bearing on human rights, but it subjects them to strict conditions which limit them to special cases. Such measures might be incorporated into a Security Council resolution under Chapter VII of the Charter, in cases of "threats to the peace, breaches of the peace, and acts of aggression". Massive human rights violations can, in fact, be a contributory cause of "threats to the peace" and the Security Council seems in several instances to have decided that such had been the case. Similarly, the decisions of the International Court of Justice, which are legally binding under Article 94 [17] of the Charter, might also concern human rights even if, in practice, the Court has been seized of only a very small number of disputes concerning human rights.[18]

17/Document 1
See page 143

18/Document 100
See page 510

28   These innovative provisions of the Charter were adopted in response to the general wish of the States present at the San Francisco Conference and due also to the efforts of non-governmental human rights organizations, which were represented by consultants in some governmental delegations. This constructive momentum also made possible the adoption of Article 71 [19] of the Charter, which permits competent non-governmental organizations to participate in a non-voting

19/Document 1
See page 143

capacity in the work of the Economic and Social Council, the Commission on Human Rights and other subsidiary bodies after being granted consultative status by the Council.

20/Document 1
See page 143

21/Document 1
See page 143

22/Document 1
See page 143

23/Document 1
See page 143

29   Nevertheless, the Governments that drafted the Charter also attempted to balance these new powers of the Organization by a dual reaffirmation: that of national sovereignty, for example, in Article 2, paragraph 1;[20] and that of "friendly relations" and "cooperation" among States, goals to which Article 1, paragraph 2,[21] and Article 1, paragraph 3,[22] attach a high priority. According to Article 1, paragraph 4,[23] the United Nations should be a "centre for harmonizing the actions of nations in the attainment of these common ends", including respect for human rights.

30   It is in this spirit that, from the beginning, United Nations activities in the field of human rights have most often been defined in such terms as "debate", "study" and "report" rather than "inquiry" and "investigation". As we have seen, the concept of "recommendation" is at the heart of the Organization's rules of procedure, largely in order to avoid any drift towards a restrictive system.

24/Document 1
See page 143

31   This prudent and balanced approach is, moreover, reflected in another provision: Article 2, paragraph 7,[24] of the Charter. Taken in substance from the Covenant of the League of Nations, it stipulates that "Nothing contained in the present Charter shall authorize the United Nations to intervene in matters which are essentially within the domestic jurisdiction of any State or shall require the Members to submit such matters to settlement under the present Charter; but this principle shall not prejudice the application of enforcement measures under Chapter VII".

32   Although human rights are not explicitly mentioned, this statement could lend itself to an extremely restrictive interpretation of United Nations powers in that field. The weight of the past seems to count heavily here: What is more "essentially national" for a State, according to some, than its treatment of its own inhabitants?

33   In practice, in the first decades following the creation of the United Nations, several States considered that draft resolutions referring to particular countries or situations, and even at times the mere mention of such matters in agenda items, were in violation of Article 2, paragraph 7.

34   From 1948 on, the reappearance of major tensions, and, in particular, the cold war, led to the strong politicization of some United Nations discussions of human rights and to a certain inertia.

35   The powerful dynamics of large-scale movements, such as the emancipation of colonial peoples and the international struggle against colonialism and apartheid and for self-determination, have triggered a greater liberalization of this system.

36 Little by little, the Organization has broadened its competence in the field of human rights, where it has developed an extensive body of norms. Moreover, by making maximum use of the Charter's potential while respecting its principles, the United Nations has instituted an international system of implementation—governmental reports, individual communications, studies and special reports—through its treaties and resolutions. As will be seen below, the non-binding nature of these procedures does not preclude a significant degree of efficacy.

37 This remarkable evolution is the result of numerous sociological and political factors: first and foremost, growing public awareness of human rights as a result of such factors as progress in communications and education, democratization, decolonization, the public nature of United Nations debates, the role of non-governmental organizations and emulation among States.

38 At the same time, an increasing number of legal experts have been taking a second look at the Charter. Article 56,[25] concerning Member States' duty to "cooperate" with the United Nations, has taken on a broader meaning, becoming, for example, the basis of Governments' obligation to facilitate missions of inquiry, even those created merely by means of a resolution. Article 2, paragraph 7,[26] concerning the domestic jurisdiction of States, has been interpreted as excluding only expressly coercive "interventions", thus permitting proceedings which lead to recommendations.

25/Document 1
See page 143

26/Document 1
See page 143

39 Above all, following the example of the principal United Nations organs, the organizations created by or based on the Charter and entrusted with matters relating to human rights and fundamental freedoms have increasingly and intentionally been involved in first the promotion and then the protection of human rights.

The institutional framework

40 The structure and procedures instituted by the Charter of the United Nations are quite different from those in force under the League of Nations. This difference is perhaps most evident in the field of human rights.

41 Among the most important of these differences is the pluralist and flexible nature of the United Nations system. The Charter granted fairly broad responsibilities, including the right to consider various aspects of human rights, to a large number of bodies and organizations rather than to a single committee. Thus, all of the principal United Nations bodies have been given a direct or indirect role in the field of human rights.

42   In addition to the principal organs, a network of subsidiary bodies specializing in human rights was created.

43   If the complexity of the organizational structure which results from this plurality of organs and other bodies is difficult to grasp and requires a coordination as necessary as it is difficult, it must be recognized that this institutional pluralism has the advantage of taking into account the many-sided nature of human rights questions.

The principal organs and human rights

The General Assembly

27/Document 1
See page 143

28/Document 1
See page 143

44   The General Assembly's competence *ratione materiae* is almost unlimited, since Article 10 [27] allows it to "discuss any questions or any matters within the scope of the present Charter" and to make "recommendations" to the Member States on these subjects. Specifically, in the words of Article 13, paragraph 1 (*b*),[28] of the Charter, it can "initiate studies and make recommendations" for the purpose of "assisting in the realization of human rights and fundamental freedoms for all without distinction as to race, sex, language, or religion".

29/Document 1
See page 143

45   On the technical level, the General Assembly's recommendations are not legally binding on States. Nevertheless, in order to appreciate the degree of authority of Assembly resolutions, one must keep in mind the general obligation of Member States, under Articles 55 and 56 [29] of the Charter, to act "in cooperation" with the United Nations. In this regard, the impact of a General Assembly recommendation may be particularly strong in the case of a text adopted unanimously, by consensus or without dissenting vote. Since the early days of the Organization, this has been true of several resolutions, including the one proclaiming the Universal Declaration of Human Rights in 1948.

46   Noteworthy among the numerous other resolutions on human rights adopted by the General Assembly between 1946 and 1948 are those "affirming", as early as 1946, "the principles of international law" with regard to war crimes and crimes against humanity, which were included in the Charter and Judgement of the International Military Tribunal at Nuremberg in 1945 and which charge the International Law Commission with explaining these principles and developing a Code of Offences Against the Peace and Security of Mankind.

47   Also in 1946, the General Assembly affirmed that genocide was a crime against international law and began the normative process which culminated in 1948 with the adoption of a convention against this crime.

48   In addition, the General Assembly launched the efforts of the Economic and Social Council which led to the organization of the 1948

United Nations Conference on Freedom of Information at Geneva and to the preparation of draft conventions on that subject. Other General Assembly recommendations concerned, for example, the question of equality between men and women, particularly with regard to political rights, the protection of trade union rights and the prohibition of forced labour. These last two questions, which fall under the competence of the International Labour Organization (ILO), have been considered by the General Assembly at the request of, and in cooperation with, this specialized agency.

The Security Council

49   The Security Council is the United Nations organ to which Article 24 [30] of the Charter entrusts the primary responsibility for the maintenance of international peace and security.

30/Document 1
See page 143

50   Article 34 [31] of the Charter stipulates that the Security Council "may investigate any dispute, or any situation which might lead to international friction or give rise to a dispute, in order to determine whether the continuance of the dispute or situation is likely to endanger the maintenance of international peace and security". Such "situations" too often stem in part from, or are accompanied by, massive and persistent human rights violations. It is primarily from this perspective that the Council may find itself concerned with human rights problems. In extreme cases, moreover, the Council may "determine" that a situation characterized by particularly serious human rights violations constitutes a "threat to the peace" under Article 39 [32] of the Charter, leading if necessary to enforcement measures on the part of the United Nations.

31/Document 1
See page 143

32/Document 1
See page 143

51   The Council has the final voice in these matters. It is especially with regard to apartheid, and, in particular, massacres under the apartheid regime, that the Security Council has invoked international human rights standards.

The Economic and Social Council

52   The Economic and Social Council, established by the Charter as an intergovernmental body under the authority of the General Assembly, makes studies and recommendations on a broad spectrum of issues, encompassing not only "respect for, and observance of, human rights . . . for all", but also "economic, social, cultural, educational, health and related matters". In addition, it is responsible for the crucial task of coordinating, rationalizing and, to some extent, programming the activities of the United Nations, its autonomous organs and the specialized agencies in all of these sectors.

53   Such an institution, conceived in these terms, represents an innovation *vis-à-vis* the League of Nations, whose economic, social and human rights components were fragmentary and dispersed. Moreover, the Council and its subsidiary bodies provide a forum for the participation of non-governmental organizations in consultative status.

33/Document 1
See page 143

34/Document 2
See page 146

54   Between 1946 and 1948, the Council took a number of key institutional decisions concerning human rights. In 1946, pursuant to Article 68 [33] of the Charter, it established the Commission on Human Rights,[34] whose first priority was to elaborate an international bill of rights. That same year, responsibility for issues concerning the status and rights of women, which initially had been assigned to a subcommission of experts, was transferred to an intergovernmental Commission that reports directly to the Council.

55   The Economic and Social Council has also addressed a variety of other problems, including genocide, prevention of statelessness, discrimination, protection of minorities, the organization of the 1948 Conference on Freedom of Information, the establishment of the *Yearbook on Human Rights* and, in cooperation with the International Labour Organization (ILO), the protection of the right to form trade unions and the prevention of forced labour.

The Trusteeship Council

35/Document 1
See page 143

56   Under Article 75 [35] of the Charter, the United Nations established "an international trusteeship system for the administration and supervision of such territories as may be placed thereunder by subsequent individual agreements". One of the basic objectives of the trusteeship

36/Document 1
See page 143

system, as set forth in Article 76,[36] is "to encourage respect for human rights and for fundamental freedoms for all without distinction as to race, sex, language or religion". The system is also intended to promote economic and social equality, as well as "equal treatment . . . in the administration of justice".

The International Court of Justice

57   The International Court of Justice, made up of 15 independent judges elected by the General Assembly and the Security Council, is the judicial organ of the United Nations, established by the Charter and

37/Document 1
See page 143

governed by its Statute, which is annexed to the Charter.[37]

58   According to Article 34, paragraph 1, of the Statute of the

38/Document 1
See page 143

Court,[38] "only States may be parties in cases before the Court". This means that individuals, juridical persons and international or non-governmental organizations may not be parties in litigation before the Court.

59   Since neither of the two International Covenants on Human Rights specifically provides for adjudication by the Court, the latter has dealt with only a few cases concerning human rights. However, each of its decisions in such cases has laid down fundamental principles.

60   From time to time, the Court has taken decisions, in either an adjudicatory or an advisory capacity, on questions regarding the existence or protection of human rights. The Court's deliberations on these issues are of considerable interest, since its decisions have played a significant role in defining international human rights law. In this respect, the judicial practice of the International Court of Justice is consistent with the decisions handed down by its predecessor, the Permanent Court of International Justice.[39]

39/Document 100
See page 510

The Secretariat

61   The Charter provides that "the Secretariat shall comprise a Secretary-General and such staff as the Organization may require". It further stipulates that the Secretary-General, as the "chief administrative officer of the Organization", shall "act in that capacity in all meetings of the General Assembly, of the Security Council, of the Economic and Social Council, and of the Trusteeship Council, and shall perform such other functions as are entrusted to him by these organs". The Secretary-General is also required to "make an annual report to the General Assembly on the work of the Organization".

62   At a very early stage, the Secretary-General set up, within the Secretariat, an entire administrative structure (described in subsequent sections) entrusted with protecting, promoting and disseminating information on the respect for human rights. Over the years, the Secretariat has fine-tuned its management of this vital issue. It continues to do so as the international community makes progress in the field of human rights, as witnessed by the recent establishment of a United Nations High Commissioner for Human Rights.

Specialized bodies in the field of human rights

The Commission on Human Rights

63   Article 68 [40] of the Charter requests the Economic and Social Council to set up specialized commissions in a number of subject areas, including human rights.

40/Document 1
See page 143

64   Consequently, at its first session, the Council established the Commission on Human Rights.[41] Originally, the Commission consisted of nine core members acting in their individual capacity; hence the

41/Document 2
See page 146

designation "nuclear Commission". In its report to the Council (E/38/Rev.1), the nuclear Commission recommended that all the members of the Commission on Human Rights should act as non-governmental representatives. The Council did not approve this recommendation, deciding instead, at its second session, that the Commission on Human Rights should consist of one representative from each of 18 Members of the United Nations selected by the Council. However, it made a small concession to those who felt that the Commission should consist of individuals acting in their personal capacity and not as representatives by providing that, "with a view to securing a balanced representation in the various fields covered by the Commission, the Secretary-General shall consult with the Governments so selected before the representatives are finally nominated by these Governments and confirmed by the Council".

65   Pursuant to the decisions taken at the first and second sessions of the Economic and Social Council, in 1946, the Commission has the mandate of submitting proposals, recommendations and reports to the Council regarding:

(a)   An international bill of rights;

(b)   International declarations or conventions on civil liberties, the status of women, freedom of information and similar matters;

(c)   The protection of minorities;

(d)   The prevention of discrimination on grounds of race, sex, language or religion;

(e)   Any other matter concerning human rights not covered by the other items.

66   The Council specifically empowered the Commission on Human Rights to formulate recommendations, provide information and perform other services at the Council's request. It also authorized the Commission "to call in ad hoc working groups of non-governmental experts in specialized fields or individual experts, without further reference to the Council, but with the approval of the President of the Council and the Secretary-General". This mandate has been flexible enough to enable the Commission to initiate numerous projects and to establish, as discussed below, a number of new mechanisms for international implementation, with the subsequent approval of the Council. The Commission, which originally comprised 18 members, now has 53, designated by the Council according to the rules of geographical distribution governing election to the Council.

67   Since that early stage, and especially during the drafting of the Universal Declaration of Human Rights and the International Covenants on Human Rights, the input of non-governmental organizations has had a significant impact on the Commission's work.

68   The Commission meets once a year. Its sessions now last six

weeks, although since 1990 it has had the option of calling special sessions as well, provided a majority of its members so agree. It submits annual reports to the Economic and Social Council, which may issue instructions or guidelines to the Commission.

69   Initially, the Commission's highest priority was to prepare a draft Universal Declaration of Human Rights. That essential task was speedily completed between January 1947 and June 1948.

70   Furthermore, the Commission took the initiative of proposing the simultaneous preparation of a far-reaching international convention or "covenant" on human rights whose provisions would be legally binding. It began work on the covenant in 1947. The decision to elaborate the covenant—which was later divided into two separate treaties—was subsequently approved by the Council and the General Assembly. These Covenants will be discussed in subsequent sections.

71   The Commission has also dealt with such issues as discrimination, the status of women, the protection of minorities and the procedure for dealing with individual complaints (called "communications") of human rights violations.

72   The Commission's actions with regard to individual communications, which the United Nations receives in enormous quantities, have been limited by various factors, such as uncertainty about the status of international law on the subject and, especially, the fear of political exploitation during the cold-war years. The Commission therefore declared unanimously, in 1947, that it had no power to take any action on complaints relating to human rights. Under the rules proposed by the Commission and adopted by the Council in 1947, individual communications have been dealt with through a very simple procedure consisting essentially of the distribution, in camera, of confidential lists to members of the Commission.

The Commission on the Status of Women

73   In February 1946, the Economic and Social Council initially decided to establish this body as one of the subcommissions of the Commission on Human Rights consisting of experts acting in their personal capacity. However, at its second session, in June 1946, the Council gave this body the status of an intergovernmental commission reporting directly to the Council. The suggestions of interested non-governmental organizations played an important role in raising the Commission's status, but most of those organizations felt that the Commission should have remained non-governmental in nature.

74   Economic and Social Council resolution 11 (II)[42] mandated the Commission to "prepare recommendations and reports to the Economic

42/Document 3
See page 147

and Social Council on promoting women's rights in political, economic, social and educational fields" and to "make recommendations to the Council on urgent problems". In accordance with a recommendation made by the Commission on the Status of Women at its first session (1947), the Economic and Social Council expanded the Commission's mandate to include the promotion of women's civil rights. The Council expressly stated that recommendations on "urgent" aspects of women's rights should be aimed at achieving de facto observance of the principle of equality between men and women and that the Commission should propose ways of implementing such recommendations.

75   The members of the Commission are government experts elected by the Council. The membership, which was originally 15, is now 45; the members are chosen according to criteria of geographical representation similar to those that govern election to the Council and to the Commission on Human Rights.

76   It was provided that the Commission should meet in regular session once a year. Between 1971 and 1989, these sessions were held every two years. Beginning in 1989 and until the year 2000, the Commission will again meet annually.

77   From the outset, observers from non-governmental organizations in consultative status have played at least as active a role in this body as they have in the Commission on Human Rights.

78   At its first meetings in 1947 and 1948, the Commission began to draw up its programme of work, especially concerning the issue of the nationality of married women (a topic which the Commission had been studying since the beginning of 1948), the political rights of women and consent in marriage.

79   With regard to individual communications, the confidential procedure proposed by the Commission on the Status of Women and adopted by the Economic and Social Council on 5 August 1947 was very similar to that used in the Commission on Human Rights. In contrast to the decision of the Commission on Human Rights, however, the Commission on the Status of Women declined to say that it had "no power" in this regard.

The Subcommission on Prevention of Discrimination and Protection of Minorities

80   In 1946, the Council had intended to authorize the Commission on Human Rights to create, among others, a subcommission on the prevention of discrimination and a separate subcommission on the protection of minorities.[43] However, after extensive discussion, it was decided that the two functions were in reality closely related. Accordingly,

43/Document 2
See page 146

at its first session in January and February 1947, the Commission elected to create a single body dedicated to both functions, and this was subsequently approved by the Council.

81 As set forth in a resolution adopted by the Commission at its fifth session (see E/1371) in 1949, the functions of the Subcommission are as follows:

(a) To undertake studies, particularly in the light of the Universal Declaration of Human Rights, and to make recommendations to the Commission on Human Rights concerning the prevention of discrimination of any kind relating to human rights and fundamental freedoms and the protection of racial, national, religious and linguistic minorities;

(b) To perform any other functions which may be entrusted to it by the Economic and Social Council or the Commission on Human Rights.

82 The unrestricted character of this mandate allowed the Commission and the Council to gradually expand the competence of the Subcommission beyond problems of discrimination and of minorities. For the past decade, the Subcommission has essentially come to concern itself with human rights in general.

83 The Subcommission meets once yearly and submits a report to the Commission. It should be emphasized that the members of the Subcommission (initially 12, now 26) are elected by the Commission in their personal capacity as experts and not as representatives of States. Their candidacies must nevertheless be presented by Governments and their election is governed by specific rules of geographical distribution.

84 The non-governmental membership of the Subcommission distinguishes it from all other human rights bodies previously described. In fact, for a long time it was the only such institution in the United Nations system. It may be recalled that initial attempts to make the Commission on Human Rights itself—as well as the Commission on the Status of Women—non-governmental in composition failed very early on.

85 Non-governmental organizations in consultative status have the right to participate in the work of the Subcommission and these organizations have gradually expanded the scope of their influence therein.

The Subcommission on Freedom of Information and of the Press

86 As with the Subcommission on the Prevention of Discrimination and Protection of Minorities, the Subcommission on Freedom of Information and of the Press was established by the Commission on

Human Rights in 1947 and was composed of 12 members serving in their personal capacity. Its duties were, primarily, to study what rights, obligations and practices should constitute the concept of freedom of information, to report to the Commission on Human Rights on all questions that this study might entail and to perform any other functions which might be entrusted to it by the Council or the Commission.

87   The Subcommission held only five sessions: May to June 1947, January to February 1948, May to June 1949, May 1950 and March 1952.

88   The first session of the Subcommission was devoted in large part to the preparation of the 1948 United Nations Conference on Freedom of the Press. At its second session, the Subcommission drafted provisions on freedom of expression and of information to be included in the draft universal declaration and in the draft covenant on human rights. The third session was dedicated to the preparation of studies on freedom of information. At its fourth session, the Subcommission undertook to draw up a draft international code of ethics for everyone engaged in the gathering, transmission and dissemination of information. This body also deliberated on various specific issues concerning freedom of information.

89   In 1951, the Economic and Social Council decided to disband the Subcommission as soon as it completed a draft code of ethics at a final session called for that purpose. This goal was accomplished and the draft of the code was submitted to the Council at the Subcommission's final session in March 1952.

The Convention on the Prevention and Punishment of the Crime of Genocide

90   Genocide can essentially be defined as the intentional extermination of distinct human groups—national, ethnic, racial, religious or other—as such. Though the term may be recent, the acts it designates are, unfortunately, as old as the human race itself.

91   It has taken many centuries for such acts to be condemned, first by the human conscience and then, much later, by the law. The struggle against slavery that began in the late eighteenth century may be cited as a step on the path towards this realization.

92   However, the profound horror evinced in 1944 by the discovery of Nazi crimes, committed in accordance with a systematic plan of extermination, was decisive in laying the foundations for the condemnation of genocide on moral and legal grounds.

93   The Indictment of 10 October 1945, drawn up against the major Nazi war criminals brought before the Nuremberg Tribunal, was

the first official proceeding at the international level in which the term "genocide" was used. It charged the accused with "deliberate and systematic genocide, *viz.*, the extermination of racial and national groups, against the civilian populations of certain occupied territories in order to destroy particular races and classes of people and national, racial or religious groups". Without using the word "genocide" or referring directly to that concept, the Judgement of the Nuremberg Tribunal nevertheless included a description of the atrocious crimes committed by the Nazis against groups, stating that the acts of cruelty and mass executions were part of a plan designed to remove entire indigenous populations by expelling them so that their territories could be colonized by the Germans. Subsequently, the word "genocide" was used at various trials of Nazi war criminals carried out before the national tribunals of the Allies.

94   On 11 December 1946, during the second part of its first session, the General Assembly, whose agenda included an item entitled "Prevention and punishment of the crime of genocide", adopted resolution 96 (I),[44] in which it affirmed that genocide "is a crime under international law". It invited the Member States "to enact the necessary legislation for the prevention and punishment of this crime" and then requested "the Economic and Social Council to undertake the necessary studies, with a view to drawing up a draft convention on the crime of genocide to be submitted to the next regular session of the General Assembly".

44/Document 4
See page 148

95   On 28 March 1947, the Economic and Social Council requested the Secretary-General to undertake, "with the assistance of experts in the fields of international and criminal law, the necessary studies with a view to drawing up a draft convention . . . [and] to submit [it] to the next session of the Economic and Social Council" (E/RES/47 (IV)). Consultations of the Member States with the Committee on the Development and Codification of International Law and the Commission on Human Rights were also provided for. The Secretary-General had a preliminary draft of the convention drawn up with the contribution of experts in the field and he submitted it to the Council in 1947.

96   In March 1948,[45] the Council set up an ad hoc committee responsible for drawing up a draft convention based on the text prepared by the Secretariat as well as on the comments of the Member States and the Commission on Human Rights. The Council submitted the ad hoc committee's draft to the summer session of the General Assembly in August 1948. By its resolution 260 A (III)[46] of 9 December 1948, the General Assembly unanimously approved the text of the Convention on the Prevention and Punishment of the Crime of Genocide. As indicated by this chronology, the legislative process was as rapid as that for the Universal Declaration described below. This was even more remarkable

45/Document 7
See page 151

46/Document 7
See page 151

in view of the fact that it involved a treaty entailing legal obligations. The bitter memories throughout the world of the atrocities of the Second World War, together with the exceptional dedication of several experts and the appeals of many non-governmental organizations, were largely responsible for this result.

97   The Convention entered into force on 12 January 1951, having received the minimum requirement of 20 ratifications.

47/Document 7
See page 151

98   The first article of the Convention[47] condemns genocide "whether committed in time of peace or in time of war", thereby giving the definition of this crime a new precision. Punishment of it is not subject to the limitations of time and place set by the Statute of the Nuremberg Tribunal.

48/Document 7
See page 151

99   In article II,[48] genocide is defined as "any of the following acts committed with intent to destroy, in whole or in part, a national, ethnical, racial or religious group, as such:

"(*a*) Killing members of the group;

"(*b*) Causing serious bodily or mental harm to members of the group;

"(*c*) Deliberately inflicting on the group conditions of life calculated to bring about its physical destruction in whole or in part;

"(*d*) Imposing measures intended to prevent births within the group;

"(*e*) Forcibly transferring children of the group to another group."

100   Protected groups—national, ethnic, racial or religious—are defined in a limited manner, a formula that was criticized as too restrictive at the time the Convention was drawn up as well as after it came into force. General clauses were therefore proposed, condemning all threats to life aimed at a human group or an individual as a member of a human group, particularly on the grounds of his nationality, race, religion or opinions. Wording of this kind had prevailed in the Statute of the Nuremberg Tribunal and was also used later for various articles of the International Covenants and other conventions. The General Assembly had rejected these amendments, however, judging them too vague to serve as the basis for a criminal accusation.

101   At the very least, proposals were made to add certain other groups to the list of protected entities, especially those grouped around a single "opinion", even a non-religious one, as well as socio-economic categories and political groupings.

102   In favour of their inclusion, it was held that political groups should be treated in the same way as religious groups, as both were characterized by a common ideal uniting their members. Concrete examples taken from the recent history of nazism proved that political groups were completely identifiable and that, in view of the persecutions to

which they could be subjected in times of ideological struggle, the need of such groups for protection could be imperative. But after a long debate, the Assembly decided to reject these amendments. In substance, the arguments against the inclusion of political groups were that such groups are not made up of elements that are, objectively speaking, sufficiently stable or permanent, since they are based mainly on the voluntary participation of their members and not on factors independent of that choice; moreover, the inclusion of political groups would prevent a great many States from accepting the Convention or an international criminal court on the grounds that such an inclusion would lead to the intervention of the United Nations in the internal political struggles of each country. It would also create difficulties for legally constituted Governments acting in self-defence against subversive elements.

103   Acts that constitute genocide are also enumerated on a restrictive list in subparagraphs (*a*) to (*e*) of the above-mentioned article II.[49] Once again, there were numerous calls for this clause to be broadened. For instance, the original texts proposed that various acts such as forbidding the use of a certain group's language, destroying schools and other cultural institutions or forcibly transferring the children of one group to another group should be condemned as "cultural genocide". Of these drafts, only the last type of crime was retained by the Assembly. The majority considered that cultural genocide fell within the scope of the protection of minorities and that the notion was too vague to be a subject of law.

49/Document 7
See page 151

104   The specific "intent" to destroy a group, in whole or in part, is a fundamental element which must be proved in order to reach a conclusion of genocide and not homicide under general law. It is difficult to prove such an intent, as was later seen in the United Nations during consideration of various situations of massive human rights violations.

105   Article III[50] provides for punishment not only for acts of genocide but also for preparatory acts, namely, conspiracy to commit genocide, direct and public incitement to commit genocide, attempt to commit genocide and complicity in genocide.

50/Document 7
See page 151

106   The principle of individual criminal responsibility of the "constitutionally responsible rulers", "public officials" or "private individuals" is set forth in article IV.[51] The Convention thus conforms to the standards of the Nuremberg Judgement rejecting immunity of persons acting on behalf of the State in crimes under international law. The innovation in the Convention on genocide is that it extends the scope of this principle beyond the circumstances of the Second World War.

51/Document 7
See page 151

107   In the Nuremberg texts, orders from higher-ranking officials were expressly excluded as grounds for immunity. However, the Convention on the Prevention and Punishment of the Crime of Genocide does not address this issue. The General Assembly seems to have preferred to

leave the judge free to rule in each case in accordance with the circumstances.

52/Document 7
See page 151

108   In article V,[52] the States parties undertake to "provide effective penalties" for persons guilty of genocide.

53/Document 7
See page 151

109   Article VI [53] deals with important questions relating to the competence of tribunals on genocide. First, it establishes the traditional principle granting jurisdiction to the State on whose territory the act was committed. However, this principle is often thought to be largely illusory, since the crime of genocide is often committed by the State itself.

110   It had therefore been proposed, during the preparatory phase, that the jurisdiction of the State on whose territory the persons suspected of genocide were physically present should be recognized, irrespective of the nationality of those persons or the place where the crime was committed. The proposal was for this rule to be applied, at least on a subsidiary basis, when extradition has not been requested by the State availing itself of its territorial competence. It is the principle of the universal punishment of crime as applied to the traffic in women and children, piracy and counterfeiting and, more recently, through different conventions dealing with terrorism on board aircraft, the protection of diplomats, torture and apartheid. The General Assembly rejected these proposed amendments, however, citing various problems of a legal or political character that could arise from the universal suppression of genocide.

54/Document 7
See page 151

111   None the less, in addition to territorial jurisdiction, article VI [54] of the Convention provides for the possibility of having persons accused of genocide brought before "such international penal tribunal as may have jurisdiction with respect to those Contracting Parties which shall have accepted its jurisdiction". This is a highly innovative provision since no international criminal tribunal nor indeed any United Nations proposal for one existed at the time, after the Nuremberg Tribunal had completed its mandate.

55/Document 7
See page 151

56/Document 7
See page 151

112   The Convention also contains provisions for facilitating the extradition of persons accused of genocide (article VII).[55] Article IX[56] confers jurisdiction on the International Court of Justice, at the request of any of the parties, for all legal disputes between the contracting parties, "including those relating to the responsibility of a State for genocide".

57/Document 11
See page 164

113   On 28 May 1951, the International Court of Justice rendered an advisory opinion[57] to the General Assembly on the question of reservations concerning the Convention in which it stated that "the principles underlying the Convention are principles which are recognized by civilized nations as binding on States, even without any conventional obligation".[58]

58/Document 11
See page 164

114   Notwithstanding the entry into force of the Convention and

the numerous appeals by the United Nations for respect of its principles, acts of genocide on a massive scale in a number of countries have been denounced since 1948. Several calls were made for strengthening international action to prevent and suppress this scourge.

115   It was proposed that the scope of the Convention should be enlarged or other instruments developed to cover, for example, genocide against political groups, cultural genocide and "ecocide" (the massive destruction of the environment to the detriment of human, animal or plant life). Another proposal was for the establishment of a permanent international monitoring body on genocide. These concerns were discussed especially by the Subcommittee. On two occasions, special rapporteurs were appointed on the matter with the approval of the Commission on Human Rights and the Economic and Social Council.

116   The ideas aimed at combating genocide more effectively were used again indirectly in certain United Nations instruments, such as the Conventions against torture and apartheid, and in certain international monitoring mechanisms, such as the Working Group on Enforced or Involuntary Disappearances of the Commission on Human Rights and the special rapporteurs on summary or arbitrary executions and on the human rights situation in some countries. Recently, the mandates of the ad hoc international criminal tribunals instituted by the Security Council to judge war crimes committed in the former Yugoslavia and in Rwanda reveal a significant potential for progress in this area, as will be explained in a later section.

117   Thus far, however, no overall review of the international system for combating genocide has been carried out.

The Universal Declaration of Human Rights

118   Since 1941, a vast number of preliminary studies on human rights have been drafted by academic institutions, non-governmental human rights organizations, certain States and a few intergovernmental organizations that had survived the war. On 10 May 1944, the Declaration of Philadelphia, adopted unanimously by the International Labour Organization, proclaimed the need for social justice for all, without discrimination, in freedom and dignity.

119   However, the San Francisco Conference, in the interests of avoiding dilatory controversies, did not attempt to propose a definition of human rights. It was understood, as emphasized by the presiding officer at the closing session, that such a declaration would be drafted by the new world Organization.

120   The preparatory work on the Universal Declaration of Human

Rights is a remarkable example of normative efficiency at the international level. The text was drafted in less than three years—between February 1946, the date of the original relevant mandate of the Commission on Human Rights, and 10 December 1948, when it was adopted by the General Assembly. The Commission on Human Rights started work at its first plenary session in January and February 1947, in compliance with Economic and Social Council resolution 5 (I) of February 1946, which mandated it to submit recommendations, as a priority, regarding "an international bill of rights".

121   A considerable number of drafts—governmental and non-governmental—had been submitted to the Commission, including a text that one Government had submitted to the General Assembly at its first session, in 1946, which the Assembly had decided not to consider at that stage.

59/Document 5
See page 149

122   The working method adopted by the Commission and endorsed by the Council[59] was to appoint a drafting committee, consisting of eight members chosen on the basis of geographical distribution, to prepare a preliminary text using a detailed model prepared by the Secretariat and other documents that it would collect.

123   At its second session, in December 1947, the Commission, on the basis of the report from the drafting committee as revised by a working group, produced a draft declaration, which was then submitted to Member States for comment. In May 1948, the drafting committee revised the draft in the light of replies from Governments.

124   At its third session, from 24 May to 16 June 1948, the Commission further revised the draft declaration before submitting it to the Economic and Social Council, which submitted it once more to the General Assembly in August 1948.

60/Document 8
See page 153

125   At its third session (September to December 1948), in Paris, the General Assembly subjected this text to very thorough scrutiny, voting a total of 1,400 times, on practically every word and every clause. On 10 December 1948, the Assembly proclaimed the Universal Declaration of Human Rights[60] by 48 votes to none, with 8 abstentions. This was hailed as a triumph uniting very diverse, even conflicting, political regimes, philosophical and religious systems and cultural traditions. The fundamental principles on which the Declaration was based are summarized in the following paragraphs.

126   First, human rights are based on the "inherent dignity" of every human person. This dignity, and the rights to freedom and equality which derive therefrom, are inalienable and imprescriptible. They have precedence over all powers, including that of the State, which may regulate but may not abrogate them.

127   The dignity of the human person exists and should be recognized

"without distinction of any kind". It follows that human rights are by nature universal, acquired at birth by "all members of the human family" whatever "the political, jurisdictional or international status of the country or territory to which a person belongs".

128   The growing "recognition" among human beings of their equal dignity, which is their common heritage, is such that it gradually promotes a "spirit of brotherhood" in their relations.

129   The Declaration recognizes the need for a social "order", both domestic and international, so that human rights "can be fully realized". The individual has "duties" to the community "in which alone the free and full development of his personality is possible". These duties impose certain limitations on the exercise of human rights, provided they are "determined by law" and are "solely for the purpose of securing due recognition and respect for the rights" of others and of meeting "the just requirements of morality, public order and the general welfare in a democratic society".

130   These last clauses, which were drafted after long debate, express the idea embodied in the Declaration of relations among human beings, society and the State, namely, that each should yield to the requirements of the general welfare as defined by the organized community, whose *raison d'être* remains, in any case, the promotion of human rights through democracy.

131   A number of criticisms have been made of this philosophy underlying the Declaration, alleging, in particular, that its universalism is too abstract and reductive and that it fails to recognize cultural differences. It should be noted, however, that the essential concepts and principles of the Declaration, including universalism, have been clearly reaffirmed in subsequent international instruments, including many United Nations conventions and declarations adopted unanimously by the international community.

132   Article 2 [61] sets forth the essential principle of equality and non-discrimination, recalling Article 55 of the Charter, which provides that the United Nations should encourage respect for human rights and freedoms "for all without distinction as to race, sex, language, or religion", and conferring on this principle an unlimited scope by prohibiting distinctions made on the basis of any other "status".

61/Document 8
See page 153

133   Article 3 [62] proclaims three interrelated fundamental rights, namely, the right to life, the right to liberty and the right to security of person. This article serves as the first pillar of the Declaration, introducing a series of articles (articles 4 to 21)[63] in which civil and political rights are developed. These articles provide that "no one shall be held in slavery or servitude"; that "no one shall be subjected to torture or to cruel, inhuman or degrading treatment or punishment"; that "everyone has the right to recognition everywhere as a person before the law"; that

62/Document 8
See page 153

63/Document 8
See page 153

"everyone has the right to an effective remedy by the competent national tribunals"; that "no one shall be subjected to arbitrary arrest, detention or exile"; that "everyone is entitled in full equality to a fair and public hearing by an independent and impartial tribunal"; that "everyone charged with a penal offence has the right to be presumed innocent until proved guilty"; that "no one shall be subjected to arbitrary interference with his privacy, family, home or correspondence"; that "everyone has the right to freedom of movement"; that "everyone has the right to seek . . . asylum from persecution"; that "everyone has the right to a nationality"; that "men and women of full age . . . have the right to marry and to found a family"; that "everyone has the right to own property", to "freedom of thought, conscience and religion", to "freedom of opinion and expression" and to "freedom of peaceful assembly and association"; and that "everyone has the right to take part in the government of his country" and to "equal access to public service".

64/Document 8
See page 153

134   Article 22,[64] the second basic element of the Declaration, introduces articles 23 to 27, which set forth the economic, social and cultural rights of everyone, "as a member of society". This article states that the rights in question are indispensable for the individual's dignity and "the free development of his personality" and provides that everyone is entitled to realization of these rights "through national effort and international cooperation". The article recognizes that the effective enjoyment of these rights depends on the resources of each State and of the international community.

65/Document 8
See page 153

135   Articles 23 to 27 [65] recognize a number of economic, social and cultural rights, such as the right to social security, to work, to rest and leisure, to a standard of living adequate for a person's health and well-being, to education, to participate in the cultural life of the community and to share in scientific advancement.

136   Lastly, articles 28 to 30 define everyone's "duties to the community".

137   The Universal Declaration is not a "lowest common denominator". It proclaims, on the contrary, "a common standard of achievement". Its progressive and even innovative tone is evident in many of its articles.

138   It was one of the very first international instruments to recognize the ethical and juridical value of economic, social and cultural rights and to affirm their equal and interdependent relationship with civil and political rights. The 1944 Declaration of Philadelphia of the International Labour Organization (ILO) and subsequently the constitutions of the Food and Agriculture Organization of the United Nations (FAO) (1945), the World Health Organization (WHO) (1946) and the United Nations Educational, Scientific and Cultural Organization (UNESCO) (1946) recognize certain economic, social or cultural rights as fundamental,

but deal only peripherally with civil and political freedoms. Some instruments of the Organization of American States (OAS), adopted shortly before the Universal Declaration, refer to some economic, social and cultural rights. Except for certain 1944 and 1945 Allied conventions on war crimes and crimes against humanity committed during the Second World War, the Declaration was the first international instrument to condemn all "torture" and "cruel, inhuman or degrading treatment or punishment". Similarly, the right to "a nationality" had previously been recognized by only a small minority of States. These are but a few examples of the innovative nature of the Declaration.

139   The Declaration appears to us today to have some gaps, including the lack of explicit articles on the right to petition, the right to self-determination, the right to development and the rights of minority groups and indigenous people. It touches only peripherally on human rights problems caused by scientific and technical developments. It might be said, however, that it addressed the great majority of the current or foreseeable issues of its time.

140   The problem of the juridical nature of the Declaration has been the subject of many studies. The Declaration was adopted in the form of a General Assembly resolution and it is not, in principle, legally binding. Many delegates, during the voting in 1948 and thereafter, have drawn attention to its merely programmatic nature. On the other hand, frequent references to the authority of the Declaration in multilateral debates in the United Nations and elsewhere, and the fact that it is mentioned as a fundamental source in many international treaties and in the growing legislative and judicial practice in many States, have been interpreted by some as a possible indication that the Universal Declaration, at least in some of its articles, has been a powerful factor in the establishment or more rapid advancement of customary international human rights law.

141   A considerable number of international human rights instruments affirm the obligation to implement the Declaration. Among these are the United Nations International Covenants (1966),[66] the three great regional conventions—European (1950),[67] American (1969)[68] and African (1981)[69]—and the great majority if not all of the treaties in the United Nations treaty series. Practically all of the international human rights declarations by the United Nations adopted since 1948 refer to the Declaration. This is true, in particular, of the Vienna Declaration adopted by the World Conference on Human Rights in 1993.[70]

142   Similarly, it is striking to note that many concepts first enunciated in the 1948 Universal Declaration of Human Rights[71] were textually reproduced in later international juridical instruments and that, at the national level, constitutions and laws concerning civil liberties in

66/Document 31
See page 229;

Document 32
See page 235

67/Document 10
See page 256

68/Document 36
See page 248

69/Document 47
See page 284

70/Document 85
See page 448

71/Document 8
See page 153

many countries, especially those that have gained their independence since 1948, incorporate all or part of the Declaration.

143   None the less, the Universal Declaration does not have a direct impact on government machinery. Its preamble deals for the most part with "peoples" and "individuals" and its inspiring message provides encouragement to the excluded and the persecuted in their daily struggles. Their cry for justice and freedom, amplified by human rights groups, resonates louder each day in the corridors of power.

III Improving the system:
Towards the adoption of the International Covenants on Human Rights (1949-1966)

144 Since 1949, the United Nations has made considerable efforts to ensure the protection and promotion of human rights. The work of the Commission on Human Rights, the Subcommission on Prevention of Discrimination and Protection of Minorities and other bodies in both the standard-setting and the procedural fields should be underscored, as should be the adoption of the two International Covenants on Human Rights, a landmark in the activities of the international community to promote human rights.

Activities of the Commission on Human Rights, the Subcommission on Prevention of Discrimination and Protection of Minorities and other bodies

145 The United Nations achieved a substantial body of work during this period in both standard-setting and procedures, overcoming serious political difficulties resulting, in particular, from cold-war tensions, and in spite of inhibitions with regard to the "domestic jurisdiction" of States under Article 2, paragraph 7, of the Charter.[72]

72/Document 1
See page 143

Standard-setting instruments

146 After the adoption of the Universal Declaration of Human Rights, the Commission on Human Rights, beginning in 1949, attached the highest priority to drawing up the two Covenants on Human Rights.[73] This mission prevented it from considering other draft instruments until 1955, when the draft covenants were transmitted to the General Assembly. Nevertheless, during this period, other bodies—the General Assembly, the Economic and Social Council and specialized conferences—elaborated other international instruments.

73/Document 31
See page 229;
Document 32
See page 235

147 In 1949, for instance, with regard to slavery and similar practices, the United Nations adopted the Convention for the Suppression of the Traffic in Persons and of the Exploitation of the Prostitution of Others, which developed and reinforced earlier instruments of the

74/Document 18
See page 198

nineteenth century and the League of Nations. The 1926 Slavery Convention was adapted to United Nations institutions through the Protocol of 23 October 1953. In addition, a Supplementary Convention, which was broader in scope and more restrictive in its injunctions, was concluded in 1956 against slavery, the slave trade and "institutions and practices similar to slavery".[74] This Convention contains clauses on international implementation with regard to the communication by States of information on its implementation to the Secretary-General (article 8).

148   Important international norms concerning women's rights were drawn up by the Commission on the Status of Women and adopted by the General Assembly: the Convention on the Political Rights of Women of 20 December 1952,[75] the Convention on the Nationality of Married Women of 29 January 1957 [76] and the Convention on Consent to Marriage, Minimum Age for Marriage and Registration of Marriages of 7 November 1962.[77]

75/Document 13
See page 180

76/Document 19
See page 202

77/Document 23
See page 210

149   The last-mentioned treaty requires that a minimum age should be set for marriage but does not specify any. A subsequent recommendation of 1 November 1965 sets a minimum of 15 years of age in principle.

150   On 20 November 1963, before the adoption of the Convention on racial discrimination (see paragraphs 164 to 182), the General Assembly adopted the United Nations Declaration on the Elimination of All Forms of Racial Discrimination.

151   The human rights of persons deprived of their liberty were the subject of the "Standard Minimum Rules for the Treatment of Prisoners", adopted by the First United Nations Congress on the Prevention of Crime and the Treatment of Offenders in 1955 and approved by the Economic and Social Council on 31 July 1957.[78] The scope of the rules was expanded in 1977, *inter alia*, in order to cover persons held in preventive detention before trial.

78/Document 15
See page 187

152   The scale and urgent nature of the problems concerning refugees and stateless persons had come to public attention after the Second World War. This awareness led to establishment of the office of a United Nations High Commissioner for Refugees on a temporary but renewable basis and the subsequent adoption of several multilateral treaties: the Convention relating to the Status of Refugees[79] of 28 July 1951, the Convention relating to the Status of Stateless Persons[80] of 28 September 1954 and the Convention on the Reduction of Statelessness[81] of 30 August 1961.

79/Document 12
See page 172

80/Document 14
See page 181

81/Document 22
See page 206

82/Document 60
See page 334

153   On 20 November 1959, well before the elaboration of the Convention on the subject,[82] the United Nations adopted the Declaration on the Rights of the Child.

First initiatives in the field of crime prevention and the treatment of offenders

154 Efforts to protect human rights and fundamental freedoms go hand in hand with vigorous action relating to crime prevention and criminal justice. In this regard, at least two objectives must be pursued: reducing the social and material costs of crime and its impact on socio-economic development and encouraging respect for international norms relating to criminal justice. This last aspect is of direct interest to us within the framework of this study.

155 In order to provide a body where all questions concerning these two phenomena could be given adequate consideration, in 1950 the General Assembly authorized the convening every five years of the United Nations Congress on the Prevention of Crime and the Treatment of Offenders. The participants in the Congress are criminologists, specialists from various penitentiary systems and high-level police officers as well as specialists in criminal law and human rights. Three such Congresses were organized during the time period covered by Part III. The documents emerging from the Congresses had a profound influence on the history of contemporary law relating to the administration of justice and the treatment of persons deprived of liberty. They served, in many respects, as the forerunner of numerous initiatives organized subsequently within the framework of the Commission on Human Rights and, more generally, the competent United Nations bodies in the field of human rights. Conversely, it can also be said that several of the concerns expressed during the Congresses were obviously inspired by the philosophy underlying the Universal Declaration of Human Rights and, therefore, problems or concepts considered by the human rights bodies, either the Commission on Human Rights or the Subcommission. The following commentary will describe the results achieved by each of the various Congresses held since 1955, stressing their impact on the work and activities carried out by the United Nations in the field of human rights.

156 The Standard Minimum Rules for the Treatment of Prisoners[83] were adopted at the First United Nations Congress on the Prevention of Crime and the Treatment of Offenders, held in Geneva in 1955. The document was approved by the Economic and Social Council in 1957. The rules seek to set out good principle and practice in the treatment of prisoners and the management of penal institutions. In view of the great variety of legal, social, economic and geographical conditions of the world, it is clearly understood that the rules cannot be applied in all places and at all times. They are designed to stimulate an endeavour to ensure their implementation, in the knowledge that they represent, as a whole, the minimum conditions which are accepted as suitable by the United Nations. It is interesting to note that the text is

83/Document 15
See page 187

based on a progressive concept of protection of the rights of prisoners and prison management, since specific reference is made to the constantly developing thought in the field and new experiments and practices.

157 Various principles govern the treatment of prisoners. The basic principle of non-discrimination already included in the Universal Declaration is recalled as the basic principle applicable to all prisoners. It is also necessary to note the requirement to separate prisoners taking account of their age, sex, criminal record, the legal reason for their detention and the necessities of their treatment. Thus, men and women must be detained in separate institutions, untried prisoners must be kept separate from convicted prisoners and young prisoners must be kept separate from adults. It will be noted that these rules were subsequently codified in article 10 of the International Covenant on Civil and Political Rights.[84]

84/Document 32
See page 235

158 Various rules apply, for example, to places of detention, personal hygiene, clothing and bedding, food, exercise and discipline and punishment of prisoners. The instruments of restraint are specified, as well as information which absolutely must be communicated to prisoners concerning the authorized methods of seeking information and making complaints. Lastly, the rules stress that qualified and experienced inspectors must carry out a regular inspection of penal institutions and services.

159 A number of guiding principles are set forth and indicate the philosophy underlying any deprivation of liberty. Since imprisonment and other measures which result in cutting off an offender from the outside world are afflictive by nature, the prison system must not aggravate the suffering inherent in such a situation. Furthermore, since the ultimate purpose of a sentence of imprisonment or a similar measure deprivative of liberty is to protect society against crime, the period of imprisonment must be used to ensure, so far as possible, that upon his return to society the offender is able to lead a law-abiding and self-supporting life. All remedial, educational, moral and spiritual forces should be made available to this end.

160 Persons arrested but not yet tried and sentenced must be presumed to be innocent. This presumption, which was subsequently codified in article 9 of the Covenant, involves appropriate treatment and specific rights, the first of which is the housing of those prisoners in separate rooms away from convicted prisoners.

161 The Second Congress, held in London in 1960, considered measures for preventing juvenile delinquency and questions concerning prison labour, conditional release and post-penitential assistance.

162 The Third Congress, held in Stockholm in 1965, adopted measures concerning preventive action by communities against crime as well as measures against repeated offences.

163   The subsequent Congresses, which are described in detail in paragraphs 336 to 340, led to the adoption of innovative and basic texts that had an undeniable impact on both the codification of human rights and their implementation at the national level.

The International Convention on the Elimination of All Forms of Racial Discrimination

164   The International Convention on the Elimination of All Forms of Racial Discrimination,[85] which was adopted on 21 December 1965 and entered into force on 4 January 1969, was the first United Nations human rights instrument to set up an international monitoring system including, in particular, a procedure for individual complaints.

85/Document 27
See page 219

165   The memory of the Nazi atrocities during the Second World War, profound indignation at the continued existence of racism and the development of the institutionalized racial segregation in South Africa under the name of apartheid led to the creation of the most effective possible international legal weapon against those abhorrent practices. The conclusion of such a convention was one of the priority objectives, in particular, of the new Member States which had just acceded to independence in the early 1960s.

166   The Convention was essentially the work of the General Assembly itself, in consultation with various other bodies. Article 1 [86] defines the term "racial discrimination" broadly as "any distinction, exclusion, restriction or preference based on race, colour, descent or national or ethnic origin which has the purpose or effect of nullifying or impairing the recognition, enjoyment or exercise, on an equal footing, of human rights and fundamental freedoms . . .". It nevertheless stipulates that the Convention does not prohibit distinctions between citizens and non-citizens.

86/Document 27
See page 219

167   The preamble succinctly sets forth the philosophy of the Convention.[87] It expresses the view: (*a*) "that any doctrine of superiority based on racial differentiation is scientifically false, morally condemnable, socially unjust and dangerous"; (*b*) "that there is no justification for racial discrimination, in theory or in practice"; and (*c*) "that the existence of racial barriers is repugnant to the ideals of any human society". The preamble reaffirms "that discrimination between human beings on the grounds of race, colour or ethnic origin is an obstacle to friendly and peaceful relations among nations and is capable of disturbing peace and security among peoples and the harmony of persons living side by side even within one and the same State".

87/Document 27
See page 219

168   In article 2, paragraph 1,[88] the States parties "condemn racial discrimination and undertake to pursue by all appropriate means and

88/Document 27
See page 219

without delay a policy of eliminating racial discrimination in all its forms and promoting understanding among all races". They undertake in particular "to take effective measures to review governmental, national and local policies, and to amend, rescind or nullify any laws and regulations which have the effect of creating or perpetuating racial discrimination wherever it exists" and "to encourage, where appropriate, integrationist multiracial organizations and movements and other means of eliminating barriers between races, and to discourage anything which tends to strengthen racial division".

169 The Convention was the first international instrument, and one of the first legal texts in the world, to provide for differential measures to benefit certain disadvantaged racial groups. Thus, article 1, paragraph 4,[89] provides that "Special measures taken for the sole purpose of securing adequate advancement of certain racial or ethnic groups or individuals requiring such protection as may be necessary in order to ensure such groups or individuals equal enjoyment or exercise of human rights and fundamental freedoms shall not be deemed racial discrimination, provided, however, that such measures do not, as a consequence, lead to the maintenance of separate rights for different racial groups and that they shall not be continued after the objectives for which they were taken have been achieved".

89/Document 27
See page 219

90/Document 27
See page 219

170 In article 4,[90] the States parties "condemn all propaganda and all organizations which are based on ideas or theories of superiority of one race or group of persons of one colour or ethnic origin, or which attempt to justify or promote racial hatred and discrimination in any form, and undertake to adopt immediate and positive measures designed to eradicate all incitement to, or acts of, such discrimination". In particular, the States parties are required to "declare an offence punishable by law all dissemination of ideas based on racial superiority or hatred, incitement to racial discrimination, as well as all acts of violence or incitement to such acts against any race or group of persons of another colour or ethnic origin, and also the provision of any assistance to racist activities, including the financing thereof"; to "declare illegal" and to "prohibit organizations, and also organized and all other propaganda activities, which promote and incite racial discrimination"; to "recognize participation in such organizations or activities as an offence punishable by law"; and not to "permit public authorities or public institutions, national or local, to promote or incite racial discrimination".

171 This article was extensively debated, some delegates feeling that it entailed the risk of improper applications contravening the freedom of expression proclaimed by the Universal Declaration of Human Rights. The majority maintained, however, that history had amply proved the extreme harmfulness of all forms of racist propaganda. This prohibition of all forms of racist propaganda was in keeping with the criteria for limitations laid down in article 29 of the Universal Declaration for the purpose of safeguarding human rights.

172   In article 5,[91] the Convention specifies the areas in which the State must eliminate racial discrimination and guarantee equality before the law. This list, which is not exhaustive, includes even certain rights which are not expressly recognized by the Covenants, for example, the right to own property, the right to inherit and the right of access to any place or service intended for use by the general public.

91/Document 27
See page 219

173   Under article 6,[92] the States parties "shall assure to everyone within their jurisdiction effective protection and remedies, through the competent national tribunals and other State institutions, against any acts of racial discrimination which violate his human rights and fundamental freedoms contrary to this Convention, as well as the right to seek from such tribunals just and adequate reparation or satisfaction".

92/Document 27
See page 219

174   Under article 7,[93] they "undertake to adopt immediate and effective measures, particularly in the fields of teaching, education, culture and information, with a view to combating prejudices which lead to racial discrimination and to promoting understanding, tolerance and friendship among nations and racial or ethnical groups".

93/Document 27
See page 219

175   Articles 8 to 16 of the Convention are concerned with international monitoring procedures. A Committee on the Elimination of Racial Discrimination, consisting of 18 independent experts elected by the States parties after being nominated by one such State, receives and studies the periodic reports of States (article 9) describing measures which they have adopted and which give effect to the provisions of the Convention. The Committee is also competent to perform the role of organ of inquiry and conciliation for complaints about one State by another (articles 11 to 13).[94]

94/Document 27
See page 219

176   The Convention is innovative in the United Nations system by virtue of its article 14,[95] which contains an optional clause about individual complaints. It provides for a first review at the domestic level by a national body designated or specially established to consider such complaints. Should this fail, the case is considered by the Committee, which, after declaring the complaint admissible, may make "suggestions and recommendations" to the State concerned.

95/Document 27
See page 219

177   In addition, article 15 assigns the Committee responsibility for making recommendations on petitions concerning racial discrimination received by the United Nations bodies concerned with Trust and Non-Self-Governing Territories.

178   The Committee was established on 10 July 1969.

179   The Committee sends to the General Assembly annually a report on its activities containing a summary of the explanations of the

States parties concerned and of its own suggestions and recommendations on the complaints.

180 In short, the Convention establishes a potentially vigorous system of international monitoring. This system depends, however, on financing by the States parties (article 8(6)), which determine the expenses of the members of the Committee while they are in performance of Committee duties. The regular budget of the United Nations can be drawn upon only on a subsidiary basis. This was, from the outset, a source of practical difficulties for the Committee.

181 A second source of difficulty for the Committee was the delay, varying from a few months to four years, of a number of States parties in submitting both their initial and their periodic reports. This situation was aggravated later with the entry into force of several other conventions which also required separate national reports.

182 Nevertheless, the Convention played a pioneering role in the United Nations programme, in respect of both standard-setting and implementation.

Procedural innovations

The system of periodic reports

96/Document 17
See page 198

183 On the proposal of the Commission on Human Rights, the Economic and Social Council, in its resolution 624 B (XXII) of 1 August 1956,[96] established a system of periodic reports on human rights. The Council requested States Members of the United Nations and of the specialized agencies "to transmit to the Secretary-General, every three years, a report describing developments and the progress achieved during the preceding three years in the field of human rights, and measures taken to safeguard human liberty in their metropolitan area and Non-Self-Governing and Trust Territories; the report to deal with the rights enumerated in the Universal Declaration of Human Rights and with the right of peoples to self-determination".

97/Document 25
See page 213

184 In its resolution 1074 C (XXXIX) of 28 July 1965,[97] the Council reviewed the reporting system. It requested the Secretary-General to forward the information received from Member States and specialized agencies under the terms of the resolution in full, together with a subject and country index, to the Commission on Human Rights, to the Commission on the Status of Women and to the Subcommission on Prevention of Discrimination and Protection of Minorities. The comments received from non-governmental organizations in consultative status, as well as any comments which might be made on them by the Member State concerned, were also to be made available by the Secretary-General to the two Commissions and the Subcommission.

185 The Council requested the Subcommission on Prevention of

Discrimination and Protection of Minorities to undertake the initial study of the materials, to report thereon to the Commission on Human Rights and to submit comments and recommendations for consideration by the Commission. It invited the Commission on the Status of Women to inform the Commission on Human Rights of its comments and of any recommendations it might wish to make.

186   To complete this account, a few words should be said about subsequent developments. After considering the periodic reports at regular intervals, from 1957 to 1977, the Commission on Human Rights, in 1977 and at several subsequent sessions, deferred consideration of the question. In its resolution 35/209 of 17 December 1980,[98] the General Assembly decided to terminate certain activities which the Secretary-General had identified as obsolete, ineffective or of marginal usefulness, including the system of periodic reports on human rights.

98/Document 46
See page 283

187   In certain other areas, the United Nations established mechanisms for specific study and investigation, on a temporary basis, by means of resolutions. This was the case, for example, with slavery. In this area, an ad hoc committee of independent experts, appointed by the Secretary-General in accordance with Economic and Social Council resolution 238 (IX)[99] of 20 July 1949, was established. Then, in 1954, the Council appointed a Special Rapporteur, who submitted a report in 1955. The Rapporteur's recommendations, which were accepted by the Council, led to the convening of a conference of plenipotentiaries which adopted, in 1956, the Supplementary Convention on the Abolition of Slavery, the Slave Trade, and Institutions and Practices Similar to Slavery,

99/Document 9
See page 156

188   Modern-day problems with respect to forced labour were considered *in concreto* by a joint United Nations/ILO committee of experts established jointly by the Economic and Social Council and the Governing Body of ILO.

189   The Committee concluded that there existed forced labour systems of an extremely serious nature, necessitating a strengthening of international law in that respect. The Council and then the General Assembly approved the Committee's report.

190   It was towards the end of this period, in 1965-1966, that a movement developed at the United Nations for the adoption of effective monitoring measures to prevent human rights violations. By itself, the procedure of the confidential list, adopted in 1947 under Economic and Social Council resolution 75 (V)[100] (see paragraph 72), was increasingly regarded as grossly inadequate to deal with grave and systematic violations such as apartheid.

100/Document 6
See page 150

191   Thus, in its resolution 1102 (XL) of 4 March 1966,[101] on the initiative of the Special Committee on decolonization, the Economic and Social Council invited the Commission on Human Rights to "consider as a matter of importance and urgency the question of the violation of

101/Document 28
See page 226

human rights and fundamental freedoms, including policies of racial discrimination and segregation and of apartheid in all countries, with particular reference to colonial and other dependent countries and territories, and to submit to the Council . . . its recommendations on measures to halt those violations". The Commission on Human Rights, in its resolution 2 (XXII), informed the Council that, in order to deal completely with the question of violations of human rights in all countries, it would be necessary for the Commission to consider fully the means by which it might be more fully informed of such violations. The

102/Document 29
See page 226

103/Document 30
See page 228

Economic and Social Council, in its resolution 1164 (XLI)[102] of 5 August 1966, concurred with the Commission's view, and shortly afterwards the General Assembly, in its resolution 2144 A (XXI) of 26 October 1966,[103] invited the Council and the Commission "to give urgent consideration to ways and means of improving the capacity of the United Nations to put a stop to violations of human rights wherever they may occur".

192   On the basis of these resolutions, as proposed by the Commission on Human Rights, the Economic and Social Council, in its

104/Document 34
See page 246

resolution 1235 (XLII) of 6 June 1967,[104] expressly authorized the Commission on Human Rights and the Subcommission to examine information relevant to gross violations of human rights in all countries.

193   Furthermore, the Commission on Human Rights was authorized, after careful consideration, to make a "thorough study" of situations which "reveal a consistent pattern of violations of human rights", and to report, with recommendations, to the Economic and Social Council.

194   Lastly, it was during this period, in 1955, that the General Assembly, on the proposal of the Commission on Human Rights and the

105/Document 16
See page 196

Council, instituted the programme of advisory services in the field of human rights.[105]

The International Covenants on Human Rights

195   The two International Covenants on Human Rights, one on economic, social and cultural rights, the other on civil and political

106/Document 31
See page 229;
Document 32
See page 235

rights,[106] were adopted in 1966 and entered into force in 1976. The Covenants constitute the most extensive corpus of international treaty law on the subject, both in terms of the areas covered and in terms of their geographical scope. More than 120 States, on all continents, are today parties to the Covenants.

196   The legislative history of these instruments, which goes back to the early years of the Organization, has been complex and relatively long. A detailed analysis can be found in other United Nations publications. The Commission on Human Rights played a leading role in this major undertaking from the very beginning. Whereas the General Assembly and the Economic and Social Council had envisaged a general "instrument" or "charter" on human rights, the Commission took the initiative, as early as 1947, in proposing specifically that, in addition to a Declaration, there should be a binding multilateral treaty on human rights.

197   A lengthy debate was held on the need for a convention and on the issue of harmonization of the two strategies, declaration and treaty. It was concluded that the two strategies were complementary and that adoption of the Covenants would not in any way rule out the possibility of drawing up non-binding instruments that might perhaps deal with broader areas.

198   In its work on the Covenants, the Commission took into account various recommendations of the General Assembly and of the Economic and Social Council. It consulted States again and again. The organs and specialized agencies—including the Office of the United Nations High Commissioner for Refugees, the International Labour Organization, the World Health Organization and the United Nations Educational, Scientific and Cultural Organization—gave their views and participated in the drafting of important articles in the areas within their competence. Non-governmental organizations with consultative status played an active role within the Council, the Commission on Human Rights and the Subcommission.

199   The complete text of the two Covenants and of the two Optional Protocols to the International Covenant on Civil and Political Rights can be found in Section Two of this book.[107] We shall limit ourselves here to summarizing the broad outlines of the substantive provisions.

200   The two Covenants contain some identical or similar provisions. The preambles stress their common view regarding the inherent dignity of the human person and of the inalienable rights to freedom and to equality.

201   Article 1 of the International Covenant on Civil and Political Rights[108] is identical to article 1 of the International Covenant on Economic, Social and Cultural Rights. Both reaffirm the principle that the right of self-determination is universal, and both call upon all States to undertake two obligations: (1) "to promote the realization of the right to self-determination" in all their territories; and (2) to respect that right in conformity with the provisions of the United Nations Charter. Both Covenants state that "all peoples have the right of self-determination", and add that "by virtue of that right they freely determine their political status and freely pursue their economic, social and cultural development". Both further provide that "all peoples may, for their own ends, freely dispose of their natural wealth and resources".

107/Document 31
See page 229;
Document 32
See page 235;
Document 33
See page 244;
Document 61
See page 344

108/Document 32
See page 235

109/Document 31
See page 229;
Document 32
See page 235

202 Under article 3 of both Covenants,[109] States parties undertake to ensure the equal right of men and women to the enjoyment of all economic, social and cultural rights, and of all civil and political rights, set out in the respective instruments. The article not only reaffirms the principle of equality of men and women as regards human rights, but also enjoins States to make that principle a reality. The article carries out the General Assembly's instruction in part E of its resolution 421 (V) of 4 December 1950 that the Covenants should include "an explicit recognition of equality of men and women in related rights, as set forth in the Charter of the United Nations".

110/Document 31
See page 229;
Document 32
See page 235

203 Article 5 of both Covenants[110] contains safeguard clauses to prevent the destruction or limitation of the rights recognized in other articles, and to safeguard rights recognized independently of the Covenants. Paragraph 1 of this article, derived from article 30 of the Universal Declaration of Human Rights, provides protection against misinterpretation of the Covenants to justify infringement of a right or freedom, or restriction of such a right or freedom to a greater extent than provided for in the Covenants. Paragraph 2 covers possible conflicts between the Covenants in question and the laws, regulations and customs of contracting States, or agreements other than the Covenants binding upon them, and prevents States from limiting rights already enjoyed within their territories on the ground that such rights are not recognized, or are recognized to a lesser extent, in the Covenant.

204 The International Covenant on Economic, Social and Cultural

111/Document 31
See page 229

Rights contains 15 normative articles.[111]

205 In article 6, the States parties recognize the right to work—work which has been freely chosen or accepted—and agree that they will take appropriate steps to safeguard this right.

206 In article 7, the States parties recognize the right of everyone to the enjoyment of just and favourable conditions of work, which are to some degree spelt out.

207 Article 8 recognizes the right of everyone to form trade unions "and join the trade union of his choice, subject only to the rules of the organization concerned, for the promotion and protection of his economic and social interests"; the right of trade unions to function freely subject to "no limitations other than those prescribed by law and which are necessary in a democratic society in the interests of national security or public order or for the protection of the rights and freedoms of others"; and "the right to strike, provided that it is exercised in conformity with the laws of the particular country".

208 In article 9, the States parties "recognize the right of everyone to social security, including social insurance".

209 In article 10, the States parties recognize that "the widest possible protection and assistance should be accorded to the family", that "special protection should be accorded to mothers during a reasonable period before and after childbirth" and that "special measures of protection and assistance should be taken on behalf of all children and young persons".

210   In article 11, the States parties recognize "the right of everyone to an adequate standard of living for himself and his family, including adequate food, clothing and housing, and to the continuous improvement of living conditions" and further recognize "the fundamental right of everyone to be free from hunger".

211   In article 12, the States parties recognize "the right of everyone to the enjoyment of the highest attainable standard of physical and mental health" and agree on the steps to be taken "to achieve the full realization of this right".

212   Article 13 deals with "the right of everyone to education", which "shall be directed to the full development of the human personality and the sense of its dignity, and shall strengthen the respect for human rights and fundamental freedoms". "Education shall enable all persons to participate effectively in a free society, promote understanding, tolerance and friendship among all nations and all racial, ethnic or religious groups, and further the activities of the United Nations for the maintenance of peace". The Covenant guarantees the liberty of parents "to choose for their children schools, other than those established by the public authorities, which conform to such minimum educational standards as may be laid down or approved by the State and to ensure the religious and moral education of their children in conformity with their own convictions".

213   In article 14, the States parties undertake to adopt "a detailed plan of action" to provide "compulsory [primary] education free of charge for all".

214   Finally, in article 15, the States parties recognize the right of everyone "to take part in cultural life", "to enjoy the benefits of scientific progress and its applications" and "to benefit from the protection of the moral and material interests resulting from any scientific, literary or artistic production of which he is the author".

215   The International Covenant on Civil and Political Rights contains 27 normative articles. They provide for protection of the "right to life" (article 6) and stipulate that "no one shall be subjected to torture or to cruel, inhuman or degrading treatment or punishment" (article 7); that "no one shall be held in slavery", that "slavery and the slave trade" shall be prohibited and that "no one shall be held in servitude" or "required to perform forced or compulsory labour" (article 8); that "no one shall be subjected to arbitrary arrest or detention" (article 9); that "all persons deprived of their liberty shall be treated with humanity" (article 10); and

that "no one shall be imprisoned merely on the ground of inability to fulfil a contractual obligation" (article 11).

216   These articles further provide for "liberty of movement and freedom to choose" a residence (article 12) and place limitations on the expulsion of aliens lawfully in the territory of a State party (article 13). They make provision in considerable detail for equality before the courts and tribunals and for guarantees in criminal and civil procedure (article 14). They also prohibit retroactive criminal legislation (article 15); establish the right of everyone to "recognition everywhere as a person before the law" (article 16); and call for the prohibition of arbitrary or unlawful interference with an individual's privacy, family, home or correspondence (article 17).

217   The Covenant also provides for protection of the "right to freedom of thought, conscience and religion" (article 18) and to "freedom of expression" (article 19). It calls for the prohibition by law of "any propaganda for war" and of "any advocacy of national, racial or religious hatred that constitutes incitement to discrimination, hostility or violence" (article 20). It recognizes the "right of peaceful assembly" (article 21) and the right to "freedom of association" (article 22). It also recognizes "the right of men and women of marriageable age to marry and to found a family", and the principle of "equality of rights and responsibilities of spouses as to marriage, during marriage and at its dissolution" (article 23). It sets forth measures to protect the rights of children (article 24) and recognizes the right of every citizen "to take part in the conduct of public affairs" of his country (article 25). It provides that "all persons are equal before the law and are entitled . . . to the equal protection of the law" (article 26) and it provides measures for the protection of members of such ethnic, religious or linguistic minorities as may exist in the territories of States parties to the Covenant (article 27).

218   Certain general questions regarding the Covenants as a whole were discussed in detail and were the subject of basic decisions by the Commission on Human Rights, the Economic and Social Council and the General Assembly.

219   These questions were the following: Should there be one or two covenants? Should the substantive provisions be drafted in general terms or in very specific terms? Should the covenants provide for international monitoring measures or mechanisms and, if so, what should they be?

The decision to create two covenants

220   In its resolution 303 I (XI), the Economic and Social Council asked the General Assembly, *inter alia*, to take a basic decision on "the desirability of including [in the Covenant] articles on economic, social

and cultural rights". In its resolution 421 E (V), the General Assembly decided "to include in the draft Covenant a clear expression of economic, social and cultural rights in a manner which relates them to the civic and political freedoms proclaimed by the draft Covenant".

221   In its resolution 543 (VI) of 5 February 1952, the General Assembly opted in the end for two covenants, "one to contain civil and political rights and the other to contain economic, social and cultural rights". In order that they might be approved and opened for signature simultaneously in order to emphasize the unity of the aim, they were to include as many similar provisions as possible.

222   Both those who were in favour of, and those who opposed, the idea of having two covenants generally agreed that the enjoyment of civic and political freedoms and the enjoyment of economic, social and cultural rights are interconnected and interdependent and that when an individual is deprived of economic, social and cultural rights, he does not represent the human person whom the Universal Declaration regards as the ideal of the free man. They disagreed not about the goal but rather about how to achieve it.

223   Those favouring a single covenant maintained that no clear distinction could be made between the different categories of human rights, nor could those rights be ranked in order of importance. Consequently, all rights should be promoted and protected together. Indeed, without economic, social and cultural rights, there was a danger that civil and political rights would be no more than nominal; and without civil and political rights, it would be impossible to guarantee economic, social and cultural rights. Accordingly, a single covenant should be drafted to encompass all human rights.

224   Those who favoured two covenants contended that civil and political rights could be protected through the courts, whereas economic, social and cultural rights were not or could not be so protected; that the former rights were immediately applicable, whereas the latter were to be established gradually; and that, in general, the former corresponded to the individual's rights *vis-à-vis* unlawful or unjust action by the State, whereas the latter represented rights which the State would be called upon to promote through positive action. Since civil and political rights and economic, social and cultural rights were different in nature, as were the obligations of the State in relation to those rights, two separate instruments were desirable.

225   The question of whether there should be one or two covenants was closely linked to the question of monitoring. In general, civil and political rights were considered to be within the realm of positive law. Hence, the best way to protect such rights appeared to be to establish a fact-finding body. Economic, social and cultural rights, on the other hand, were viewed rather as practical objectives, more suited to monitor-

ing on the basis of periodic reports. Given the existence of these two major categories of rights, which called for different monitoring arrangements, it seemed both logical and convenient to draft two separate covenants. However, the objection was raised that the delimitation of the two categories of rights could vary from one country or territory to another and that it was consequently preferable to draft a single covenant providing that, upon ratification, States could make a declaration specifying how they intended to categorize the various civil, political, economic, social and cultural rights and accordingly to identify appropriate arrangements for monitoring in each case.

The debate over the provisions and limitations of the Covenants

226   Those favouring a broad approach believed that within an all-encompassing instrument it would be impossible to set forth in great detail the scope and content of each right. Some concepts enjoyed very widespread acceptance, but acceptance of others varied considerably from one legal system to another. For example, it seemed preferable to affirm that "the States Parties to the present Covenant recognize the right of everyone to social security, including social insurance", rather than to attempt to define precisely the content of that right. In their view, it was best left to each country to spell out in its own legislation the scope and content of each right.

227   As regards the obligations of States, those favouring a broad approach felt that the Covenants should call upon States parties to guarantee civil and political rights in accordance with the law and to recognize and gradually promote economic, social and cultural rights. There was no question, however, of expressly presenting in the Covenants the list of actions which States could take to protect civil and political rights or of determining *a priori* the measures to be taken to promote economic, social or cultural rights.

228   The question of limitations on the exercise of rights was even more delicate. Thus, during the discussion of the right to liberty and security of person, some 30 restrictions were suggested. It was considered preferable to provide that "no one shall be subjected to arbitrary arrest or detention"—the word "arbitrary" being used to mean both "unlawful" and "unjust"—rather than to include in the Covenant a catalogue of some 30 limitations. A similar number of limitations was suggested for freedom of information and, once again, it was argued that it would be better to have a simple limitations clause rather than to present an inventory of 30 restrictions.

229   Lastly, it was argued that the Covenants would not be the only, or the last, instruments to deal with human rights. The rights set forth in these instruments could be developed in specific conventions.

Thus, a convention on slavery and servitude, on freedom of information, on social security or on political rights could be more precise and detailed than the articles dealing with these rights in the Covenants.

230   Those who favoured a more specific approach felt that the Covenants should not duplicate the Universal Declaration of Human Rights, which had already set forth the general principles of human rights and fundamental freedoms. To their way of thinking, there was not much point in repeating word for word the articles of the Declaration or merely reproducing their substance.

231   Clearly, each of these two positions had some influence on the drafting of the substantive provisions. Some articles are couched in very general terms, whereas others are quite detailed. Naturally, it was realized that there was a need to find a middle ground between the two extremes: the Covenants should be neither a recasting of the Universal Declaration of Human Rights nor a compendium of all civil and penal codes and all social or education legislation.

The problem of derogations based on a state of emergency

232   This critical problem is linked to the question of limitations. There are, however, some aspects that are peculiar to it. The need to provide for the possibility of derogations was invoked during the discussion of both Covenants. However, only the International Covenant on Civil and Political Rights contains a disabling clause, namely, article 4.[112] This article recognizes the need for exceptions in times of emergency. But it is also intended to limit the scope of any exceptions and establish certain safeguards.

112/Document 32
See page 235

233   It is the notion of a threat to public order, the seriousness of which must be such that it "threatens the life of the nation", that defines the scope of the disabling clause. The state of emergency must be officially proclaimed. Measures may be taken when "required by the exigencies of the situation". The measures must not be inconsistent with international law and must not involve any discrimination on the ground of race, colour, sex, language, religion or social origin.

234   It was agreed that the disabling clause could not apply to certain rights. However, the list of imprescriptible rights includes only "the right to life" (article 6), the prohibition of torture and ill-treatment (article 7), the prohibition of slavery and servitude (article 8, paragraphs 1 and 2), the prohibition of imprisonment for failure to fulfil a contractual obligation (article 11), the non-retroactivity of criminal law (article 15), the right of everyone to recognition as a person before the law (article 16) and "freedom of thought, conscience and religion" (article 18). Various proposals for expanding this list are under consideration today.

235   Moreover, article 4 requires that a State which derogates from human rights in time of emergency should immediately inform the other

States parties, through the intermediary of the Secretary-General, of the provisions from which it has derogated, the reasons by which it was actuated and the date on which it terminates the derogation.

International monitoring mechanisms

236 All the participants recognized that the provisions of the Covenants should be implemented primarily at the national level, by means of legislative, administrative and other measures. On the other hand, opinions differed widely with regard to the introduction and the nature of international monitoring measures.

113/Document 1
See page 143

237 For a long time, and especially during the cold war, the question as to whether article 2, paragraph 7, of the Charter,[113] concerning "domestic jurisdiction", allowed for international monitoring, was the subject of some controversy. In the end, the Assembly entrusted the Commission on Human Rights with the task of developing provisions for implementation.

238 From the time the decision was made to have two Covenants, it was felt that separate international monitoring machinery should be developed for each instrument.

239 A Human Rights Committee, composed of independent experts selected by a meeting of the States parties, was established pursuant to articles 28 to 45 of the International Covenant on Civil and Political Rights.[114] The Committee's mandate was to consider the periodic reports which all States were required to submit in accordance with article 40. Following its consideration of a periodic report, the Committee was to confine itself to formulating general, objective observations.

114/Document 32
See page 235

240 In addition, it was agreed following lengthy discussion that, in accordance with the optional provisions of article 41, the Committee could make available its good offices in the case of complaints by one State against another.

241 On the other hand, all the proposals made within the Commission for the establishment of a procedure for dealing with complaints from individuals, in various forms, were rejected.

242 It was only at the final meeting of its session in 1966 that the United Nations General Assembly adopted a proposal providing for the possibility of consideration in the Committee of complaints (or "communications") from individuals against States parties. This proposal was adopted following a vote and took the form of an Optional Protocol to the Covenant. It was patterned on article 25 of the European Convention on Human Rights and had been sponsored by both developed and developing countries.

243 However, the protocol dealing with communications from individuals limited the powers of the Human Rights Committee to establishing the facts and formulating recommendations. It contained no provision analogous to those contained in the European and inter-American conventions on human rights, in accordance with which an international human rights court could be asked to consider the Committee's report and hand down binding judgements. The establishment of such a court was proposed on numerous occasions during the Commission's discussions, but was never agreed to.

244   With regard to the International Covenant on Economic, Social and Cultural Rights,[115] it was agreed, in article 16, that the periodic reports of States would be transmitted to the Economic and Social Council, which would have the option of establishing an expert body to which the task of considering such reports would be entrusted.

115/Document 31
See page 229

245   It was emphasized that the Economic and Social Council should bear in mind the gradual nature of the obligations of States and take duly into account the constraints imposed by the resources available to each State.

246   At the time it was believed that, owing to its gradual character, the International Covenant on Economic, Social and Cultural Rights did not lend itself to any kind of fact-finding procedure. This position was challenged by several delegations and by non-governmental organizations, which pointed out that the International Labour Office, the secretariat of the ILO, had for years used fact-finding machinery set up in response to requests from both workers' and employers' representatives.

247   Today the idea of a protocol establishing a procedure for dealing with communications to supplement the International Covenant on Economic, Social and Cultural Rights is increasingly gaining support.

IV   Operating the system:
From the International Covenants to the Vienna World Conference on Human Rights (1967-1993)

248   The first step in examining the way in which the system operates is to look at the implementation of the International Covenant on Economic, Social and Cultural Rights and the International Covenant on Civil and Political Rights. In that regard, the following aspects are particularly important: the functions of the Committees, actions taken by the Committees, the system for reporting by States and the procedures for individual communications. In addition, there are other procedures which, though not as common, still play an important role in the overall system of monitoring human rights. Finally, mention should be made of the standard-setting activities that led up to the Vienna World Conference on Human Rights.

Implementation of the International Covenants

249   The International Covenant on Economic, Social and Cultural Rights and the International Covenant on Civil and Political Rights entered into force on 3 January and 23 March 1976, respectively, nearly 10 years after the General Assembly opened the Covenants for signature, ratification and accession. As the legal expression of the moral principles underlying the Universal Declaration of Human Rights, these two Covenants were seen as instruments that would encourage States to give greater impetus to their human rights commitments.

250   As might have been expected, the Human Rights Committee and the Committee on Economic, Social and Cultural Rights are similar in terms of composition and mandates. Each consists of 18 members who must be persons of high moral character and recognized competence in the field of human rights. The members of both Committees serve in their personal capacity rather than as representatives of their Governments. Only States parties may nominate qualified candidates to the Human Rights Committee, the treaty-monitoring body for the International Covenant on Civil and Political Rights, whereas all members of the Economic and Social Council may vote in elections of the members of the Committee on Economic, Social and Cultural Rights, whether or not they are parties to the Covenant. Those who vote to elect members to

either Committee must give consideration to the fact that each Committee may include no more than one national of the same State and that membership must represent the different forms of civilization and the principal legal systems, as well as equitable geographical distribution.

Functions of the Committees

251   The Human Rights Committee fulfils four main functions: to study reports from States, to formulate general comments, to consider complaints from a State party regarding another State party (called communications from States) and to consider complaints from individuals against a State party (called individual complaints or communications). The States parties to the International Covenant on Civil and Political Rights undertake to submit reports on human rights on a regular basis for consideration by the Committee (article 40). The Human Rights Committee studies the reports submitted by States and formulates general comments (article 40, paragraph 4) which, until the present time, have always been transmitted to the States parties rather than to a particular State. The Committee carries out these two functions for all States parties to the Covenant. On the other hand, a State party may choose to recognize the competence of the Committee to receive communications from another State party (article 41) or individual (Optional Protocol to the International Covenant on Civil and Political Rights). The functions of the Committee on Economic, Social and Cultural Rights duplicate those of the Human Rights Committee with regard to the consideration of reports and formulation of general comments on the content of the rights recognized in the relevant instrument. On the other hand, the International Covenant on Economic, Social and Cultural Rights does not provide for the possibility of receiving communications from States or individuals. However, plans to introduce an optional mechanism to allow individuals to submit communications are currently under way.

252   The Human Rights Committee has characterized its role in carrying out its four main functions as an "advisory and monitoring" body (in the consideration of reports from States and the formulation of general comments), as a "conciliatory" body (with respect to communications from States) and as an "inquiring and investigative" body (with respect to complaints from individuals). The key concept that applies to all these functions is cooperation between the Committee and States parties, the objective being to give effect to the rights recognized in the Covenant. The same principle guides the activities of the Committee on Economic, Social and Cultural Rights.

253   It is within the competence of the treaty bodies to monitor compliance in giving effect to existing fundamental rights; it is not within their competence to propose new ones. Be that as it may, all human rights instruments are the result of compromise and, because of this, they usually contain general or vague wording which creates difficulties for States parties who wish to fulfil their obligations in good faith. In order to begin to address this problem, the Human Rights Committee, followed by the Committee on Economic, Social and Cultural Rights, introduced the practice of preparing "general comments". Formulated for the first time by the Human Rights Committee in 1980, general comments aim to summarize the Committee's experience gained through the examination of reports from States. In practice, although this is not specifically stated, general comments were to be transmitted to States parties as a group, rather than to individual States.

254   The first general comments of the Human Rights Committee and of the Committee on Economic, Social and Cultural Rights dealt essentially with two aspects of States' reporting obligations. They articulated what both Committees expected from State reports, such as the purpose and format of the reports, and developed both Committees' understanding of the nature of States' obligations to implement the rights recognized in the Covenants in their national legislation, practices and policies. This related to particularly important questions regarding the Covenant on Economic, Social and Cultural Rights, whose language, at least in part, seemed to reflect aspirations rather than indicating a specific direction to follow.

255   In certain respects, the Committee on Economic, Social and Cultural Rights encountered a greater number of specific difficulties than the Human Rights Committee, owing primarily to the different content of the rights recognized in the two Covenants. The International Covenant on Civil and Political Rights protects a set of rights which have been recognized for some time in a majority of the world's national legal systems and which have been the subject of extensive examination and discussion by jurists and academics. The International Covenant on Economic, Social and Cultural Rights, on the other hand, relates to a series of rights that, for the most part, reflect more recent concepts of rights for which legislation, practice and theory are much less developed. Therefore, the Committee on Economic, Social and Cultural Rights has the onerous task of defining the normative content of the rights recognized in the Covenant. It was thought this work would be done using the mechanisms that the two Committees have in common: the consideration of periodic reports and the formulation of general comments. However, the Committee on Economic, Social and Cultural Rights introduced an innovation of its own, a day of general discussion devoted to a particular right or group of rights to be decided upon in advance.

Actions taken by the Committees

256 In the sense that they emanate from the Universal Declaration of Human Rights, the two International Covenants constitute the cornerstone of the legal protection of human rights recognized by the United Nations. The Human Rights Committee and the Committee on Economic, Social and Cultural Rights, aware of the importance of their activities in establishing this legal protection on solid ground, act as role models for other United Nations organs created under more specialized instruments. The methods they have worked out to identify both the standards for the rights themselves and the obligations of States parties not only to report to the treaty bodies on compliance with their obligations under the Covenants, but also to respect these rights effectively in their own territory, have served as models for similar methods that are used by other United Nations human rights treaty-monitoring bodies.

257 Even if they are drawn up in somewhat broad terms, the general comments of both Committees provide important interpretations of the Covenants. As such, they enjoy a wide audience within the United Nations system. In addition, and more significantly, both Committees have affirmed that States parties must consider general comments when preparing the periodic reports that they submit to those two Committees.

258 The working methods of the Human Rights Committee and of the Committee on Economic, Social and Cultural Rights have also inspired new types of innovative approaches to monitoring the implementation of more recent human rights instruments. In some cases, these instruments themselves contain provisions that appear only in the internal rules of procedure of the two Committees or are raised only in their practice. The introduction of thematic considerations as part of a Committee's daily activities and participation and contribution by specialists from non-governmental organizations and United Nations specialized agencies are two examples of methods that have been adopted by other treaty bodies.

259 Finally, both Committees have elaborated a dynamic, rather than merely procedural, process for considering reports by States. In part, this evolution occurred naturally, by virtue of the inherent diversity of the mandates of the two Committees, whose members contribute varying viewpoints and experiences. This evolution also resulted from an innovative and dynamic approach to the system of monitoring adopted by both Committees to question representatives of States regarding national legislation, practices and policies described in the periodic reports and to request that States provide more specific details when answers are incomplete. The combination of both elements has made it possible to enrich the consideration of reports submitted by States parties to a degree that the drafters of the Covenants had perhaps never imagined.

System for the submission of reports by States

260 Six of the seven major international human rights instruments drawn up by the United Nations provide for the establishment of a monitoring and follow-up mechanism. These are the International Covenant on Civil and Political Rights, the International Convention on the Elimination of All Forms of Racial Discrimination, the Convention on the Elimination of All Forms of Discrimination against Women, the Convention against Torture and Other Cruel, Inhuman or Degrading Treatment or Punishment, the Convention on the Rights of the Child and the International Convention on the Protection of the Rights of All Migrant Workers and Members of Their Families. Although the seventh such instrument—the International Covenant on Economic, Social and Cultural Rights—has a monitoring mechanism similar to those of the other conventions, the latter was established pursuant to a resolution of the Economic and Social Council, not under the Covenant itself.

261 The monitoring and follow-up of the implementation of the above-mentioned human rights instruments are entrusted to committees of independent experts chosen by the States parties to each instrument or, in the case of the International Covenant on Economic, Social and Cultural Rights, by the members of the Economic and Social Council. Each of these committees is named after the instrument it monitors, except the Human Rights Committee, which is the body established under the International Covenant on Civil and Political Rights.

262 Of the many human rights monitoring procedures applied under the auspices of the United Nations, the only one common to all of the aforementioned instruments is the submission of reports. This system is based on the principle that States which ratify international human rights instruments do so in good faith and are willing to subject their national legislation and human rights record to international monitoring. None the less, it is important to recognize that ensuring respect for human rights is first and foremost a national responsibility: States have an obligation to take effective measures to safeguard the human rights of all individuals within their territory or subject to their jurisdiction. In this sense, then, the international monitoring procedures instituted under the various human rights instruments should be considered to play an auxiliary role *vis-à-vis* national procedures.

263 One or two years after ratifying a treaty, a State must furnish the body established thereunder with a report on the treaty's implementation and on the exercise of the rights set forth therein. This initial report must provide detailed background information, *inter alia*, on the nature and structure of domestic law and on the population (size, ethnic composition etc.), and must also give an overview of how the Government puts each of the treaty's provisions into practice. Since the basic purpose of the reporting system is to provide as complete a picture as possible of the human rights situation in a given country, the reports may not merely list the constitutional provisions, laws and regulations in force. They must also specify how these texts are implemented in practice and describe the country's actual situation. Subsequent reports, known as periodic reports, must be submitted three or four years after each previous report. They may provide a general update of the previous reports, indicating what changes have taken place in the country's legislation, practice or situation, or they may focus on only a few of the rights dealt with in the relevant treaty. Each Committee determines its preferences in this regard. Treaty bodies may also request additional information from a State at any time, even before the date on which the next periodic report must be submitted.

Guidelines for the preparation of reports

264   Each of the above-mentioned human rights instruments contains general guidelines on the information that should be included in States' reports. States parties to five of these instruments—the two Covenants, the Convention on the Elimination of All Forms of Discrimination against Women, the Convention on the Rights of the Child and the International Convention on the Protection of the Rights of All Migrant Workers and Members of Their Families—must submit information both on the measures they have adopted to give effect to the rights recognized therein and on any factors and difficulties that hinder their efforts to ensure the full exercise of those rights. Only the Convention against Torture and Other Cruel, Inhuman or Degrading Treatment or Punishment and the International Convention on the Elimination of All Forms of Racial Discrimination require States parties to report solely on the measures taken to give effect to the rights concerned, without asking for explanations of the difficulties affecting the full and immediate enjoyment of those rights. In addition to the general reporting requirements laid down in each instrument, each treaty body has developed reporting guidelines and work methods adapted to the types of rights or population groups concerned, in order to give the clearest possible guidance to the government representatives who prepare these reports or present them before the Committee.

265   With the proliferation of increasingly detailed and technical human rights instruments, the preparation, presentation and consideration of reports have become a burdensome if not impossible task for many States. This task is particularly problematic for countries that do not always have the resources they need to prepare reports that meet the quality standards demanded by treaty bodies. In order to facilitate their work and avoid duplication of effort, the persons chairing the treaty bodies introduced the idea of "consolidated guidelines" that briefly

indicate what basic information each State should include in a single "core document", prepared only once and updated as needed, to be submitted to the United Nations Secretariat for distribution to each of the treaty bodies, along with the substantive report on the implementation of the relevant instrument. Under the consolidated guidelines, countries must provide information on their legal system and political structure and on the main features of their territory and population. They are also asked to specify what efforts they have made to familiarize government authorities and the public with the rights proclaimed in human rights instruments.

Work methods of treaty bodies

266   The work methods of a treaty body differ according to whether it is considering an initial or a periodic report. The initial report gives the Committee in charge of monitoring a State's fulfilment of its obligations under the relevant instrument a general idea of the human rights situation in that State. This initial report paves the way for the Committee's consideration of all of the subsequent reports submitted by that State under the instrument in question and serves to establish its first contact with that State. All of the Committee members carefully review the initial report, which is submitted in writing. The Committee then holds a meeting at which the report is considered orally, with the active participation of representatives of the State party concerned. The fact that an initial report is often considered in the course of several meetings gives an idea of the seriousness with which all of the parties concerned approach this task.

267   The work methods for the consideration of the periodic reports that follow the initial report vary from one Committee to another. The Committee on the Elimination of Racial Discrimination and the Committee against Torture choose country rapporteurs from among their members to review all available information on the countries under consideration and to draw up a list of questions for their representatives. The Human Rights Committee, the Committee on Economic, Social and Cultural Rights, the Committee on the Elimination of Discrimination against Women and the Committee on the Rights of the Child set up working groups for that purpose. To promote still closer cooperation with States and to obtain a complete picture of the human rights situation in the countries under consideration, the working groups established by the Human Rights Committee and the Committee on Economic, Social and Cultural Rights prepare lists of questions which are likely to be raised during the examination of each report and send them in advance to the Governments of the States parties concerned.

268   In reviewing the reports, the members of the competent Com-

mittee may address questions to the government representatives concerned and may ask them or the Governments themselves for additional information. In general, they try to establish an ongoing dialogue with the various States parties in order to promote and facilitate respect for human rights. All of the meetings at which treaty bodies examine reports of States parties and question the representatives of those States are public.

269   The guiding principle underlying the reporting system is that of "constructive dialogue" between the treaty bodies and the representatives of the States whose reports are examined. As explained earlier, the authorities of each State have primary responsibility for ensuring respect for human rights, but the exercise of that responsibility goes hand in hand with the international monitoring carried out by the treaty bodies. The main purpose of considering the reports of States parties is, therefore, to establish cooperation between the Committee members and the representatives of the States concerned in order to guarantee the exercise of the rights protected under the instrument in question. Thus, the review process is not intended as a forum for accusing or criticizing Governments. However, when a State party furnishes too little information or when the Committee concerned has good reason to believe that the information provided diverges considerably from the country's real situation, the Committee members are entitled to be very frank in questioning that State's representatives. The Committee may also ask for more information or details on the points at issue.

Other participants in the reporting system

270   Some United Nations human rights instruments provide for the participation of specialized agencies in considering the reports of States parties. The most detailed stipulations in this regard are found in the International Convention on the Protection of the Rights of All Migrant Workers and Members of Their Families, which provides for the participation of the International Labour Office (the secretariat of the International Labour Organization) throughout the review process and allows its designated representatives to take part, in a consultative capacity, in the meetings of the competent body. Pursuant to the provisions of the International Covenant on Economic, Social and Cultural Rights, the specialized agencies receive copies of the reports of States parties to the Covenant or of parts therefrom that relate to any matters which fall within their responsibilities. The relevant Committee may also receive information from the specialized agencies on the progress made in achieving the observance of the rights which it monitors, including particulars of decisions and recommendations adopted by the competent organs of those agencies. The specialized agencies may also submit

comments on any general recommendation of the Committee. The Convention on the Rights of the Child contains provisions similar to those of the International Covenant on Economic, Social and Cultural Rights. However, the Committee on the Rights of the Child may also "invite the specialized agencies, the United Nations Children's Fund and other competent bodies" to provide "expert advice" on the implementation of the Convention. In contrast, the Convention on the Elimination of All Forms of Discrimination against Women limits the specialized agencies' participation in the examination of States parties' reports, only allowing them to be represented "at the consideration of the implementation of such provisions of the present Convention as fall within the scope of their activities". The relevant Committee may also invite the specialized agencies to submit reports on the implementation of the Convention in their respective areas of competence.

271   Non-governmental human rights organizations often make direct or indirect contributions to the treaty bodies' reviews of the reports of States parties. They may usefully contribute to the work of the Committees by providing independently gathered factual information or by proposing different interpretations of government policies—in other words, by offering an alternative view of the human rights situation in a given country. However, the nature and degree of their involvement, and in some cases their participation in the oral review, are controversial issues. The primary objection to non-governmental organizations' participation in the reporting process is that it seems incompatible with the system's basic purpose. Specifically, most non-governmental human rights organizations act as "watchdogs" by scrutinizing the activities and policies of Governments in order to detect and report violations of the rights that concern them. Consequently, giving them too important a role in the consideration of States' reports runs the risk of turning the process of cooperation and "constructive dialogue" into an opportunity for indicting the reporting States and could create the impression that the treaty bodies act as prosecutors, thereby overstepping the bounds of their mandates.

Role of the reporting system at the international level

272   As stated elsewhere in this book, the Committee on Economic, Social and Cultural Rights indicated in its first general comment the nature of the role played by States' reports in the global realization of human rights. In line with the principle whereby the responsibility for giving effect to these rights devolves first and foremost on national authorities, this general comment stresses ways to encourage States parties to discharge this responsibility with the following objectives: (1) ensuring that a comprehensive review is undertaken with respect to national legislation, administrative rules, procedures and practices;

(2) ensuring that the State party monitors the actual situation with respect to each of the rights on a regular basis (raising awareness); (3) providing the basis for the elaboration of clearly stated and carefully targeted policies, including the establishment by the Government of priorities which demonstrate the State's good faith; (4) facilitating public scrutiny of government policies and encouraging the involvement of various sectors of society in their formulation; (5) providing a basis on which the State party itself, as well as the Committee, can effectively evaluate the progress it has made; (6) enabling the State party to develop a better understanding of the problems and shortcomings encountered in efforts to progressively realize human rights; and (7) enabling the Committee and the States parties as a whole to facilitate the exchange of information among States and to develop a better understanding of the common problems faced by States and a fuller appreciation of the type of measures which might be taken to promote effective realization of the rights contained in the Covenant. As well as encouraging States to bear in mind their human rights obligations in the policies and procedures they elaborate, the text also places emphasis on the idea of cooperation which underpins States' reporting arrangements, since the role of States is to formulate programmes and priorities and to evaluate them in relation to human rights. The role of treaty-monitoring bodies is to assess the extent to which States have met human rights objectives and to advise them on any changes that might be necessary or useful in meeting those objectives.

273   At the international level, the reporting system is the only framework in which senior officials can be called to account for the laws and policies applied by their Governments in the field of human rights. However, the obligation to submit a report to a treaty-monitoring body is not linked to the obligation to remedy any violation which may be brought to light during the consideration of such a report. It is therefore encouraging to note that a number of States have demonstrated that they are serious about their obligations under human rights instruments by modifying their legislation or their policy in response to the concerns expressed by the relevant treaty-monitoring bodies. This attitude exemplifies the good faith on which the entire reporting system is based.

Procedures relating to individual communications

274   Individuals who claim that their human rights have been violated may address "communications"[116] or complaints to the Secretary-General of the United Nations.

Admissibility procedure and conditions of admissibility

275   Pursuant to Economic and Social Council resolution 1503 (XLVIII),[117] communications may refer to any Member State of the

116/Document 98
See page 501

117/Document 38
See page 262

United Nations. Communications are processed by the Secretariat. They are then submitted for examination to a specialized working group of the Subcommission on Prevention of Discrimination and Protection of Minorities. If communications satisfy the criteria for admissibility, they are examined by the Subcommission in plenary meeting, which may refer the question back to the specialized working group of the Commission or to the Commission on Human Rights itself, in plenary meeting, for a more thorough examination. Pursuant to resolution 1503 (XLVIII), the examining body shall determine whether or not a systematic human rights violation has taken place; in this connection the resolution refers to "situations" which appear to reveal "a consistent pattern of gross and reliably attested violations of human rights". Individual or isolated violations are not examined under this procedure. These "situations" are examined in closed meetings by the various bodies and the explanations by the parties remain confidential. The examination generally concludes with the adoption by the Commission of an appropriate resolution which may provide for the appointment of a Special Rapporteur or a representative for the country concerned.

276   Communications may also be examined by three expert committees of the United Nations which were established pursuant to certain international instruments. These expert committees do not, however, possess a universal competence and can only examine communications referring to States which have recognized their competence to examine communications received from individuals. In July 1995, a total of 84 States had recognized the competence of the Human Rights Committee (established in 1976) by ratifying or acceding to the Optional Protocol to the International Covenant on Civil and Political Rights (130 States parties; entry into force on 23 March 1976);[118] 28 States had recognized the competence of the Committee against Torture (established in 1987) by making the declaration envisaged in article 22 of the Convention against Torture and Other Cruel, Inhuman or Degrading Treatment or Punishment (entry into force on 26 June 1987);[119] and 14 States had recognized the competence of the Committee on the Elimination of Racial Discrimination (established in 1969) by making the declaration envisaged in article 14 of the International Convention on the Elimination of All Forms of Racial Discrimination (entry into force on 4 January 1969).[120] Communications referring to States which have not officially recognized the competence of expert committees cannot be examined by these committees and may only be examined under the procedure outlined in the above-mentioned resolution 1503 (XLVIII).

277   The examination of communications by these three expert committees may be compared with the work of international regional bodies of inquiry, such as the Inter-American Commission on Human Rights and Court of Human Rights and the European Commission of

118/Document 33
See page 244

119/Document 50
See page 294

120/Document 27
See page 219

Human Rights and Court of Human Rights. The most extensive body of case law arises from the Human Rights Committee, which was set up to examine communications from individuals who claim violations of their rights as set out in the International Covenant on Civil and Political Rights.[121]

121/Document 32
See page 235

278   The three committees examine communications in closed meetings. The parties, non-governmental organizations and other persons concerned cannot participate in the committees' work. Only the final decisions are published, namely, those whereby communications are declared inadmissible and those by which the committees determine whether or not the provisions of the treaties have been violated. Contrary to the arrangements pertaining in regional systems, there are no hearings in United Nations expert committees. Although the procedure is based solely on written communications from the parties, it is nevertheless the case that the applicants may submit communications themselves and are not obliged to submit them through lawyers. The discussions of the expert committee members are reflected in the confidential summary records of closed meetings.

279   The criteria governing the admissibility of communications, outlined below, are the same for all three expert committees:

1)   *Competence.* The victim or his representative may submit a communication to the relevant expert committee. No committee is entitled to examine the compatibility of national laws with the relevant instrument in the abstract. There must have been a "victim" whose rights have been violated or at least an individual whose rights appear to have been violated as a result of a specific action or dereliction on the part of the State. The right of a citizen to sue for a penalty is not admissible unless the victims have been mentioned individually.

2)   *Exhaustion of domestic remedies.* Applicants should have exhausted all national judicial and/or administrative remedies before addressing a complaint to the United Nations, the aim being to obtain reparation at the national level and not through international mediation. The expert committees may, however, examine communications if they conclude that, in practice, domestic remedies are unavailable or ineffective or if the implementation of domestic remedies has been unnecessarily delayed by the State party.

3)   *Evidence that the "same case" is not being examined simultaneously under other international procedures.* The Human Rights Committee may examine cases that have already been the subject of a resolution of the Inter-American Commission on Human Rights, a decision of the European Commission of Human Rights or a judgement of the European Court of Human Rights. But a number of States, in ratifying the Optional Protocol, have formulated reservations which rule

out the Committee's ability to re-examine a case that has already been settled elsewhere.

4) *Relation to the field covered by the relevant instrument.* Each committee is competent to examine communications relating to the relevant instrument. Committees may and do take account of the general principles of international law and of other instruments, but they do not have the competence to state whether a provision of another instrument has been violated. Applicants should therefore invoke the specific provisions of the instrument whose implementation is being monitored by the expert committee. A communication addressed to the Human Rights Committee which invokes the right to own property set forth in article 17 of the Universal Declaration of Human Rights or the right to asylum set forth in article 14 of the same Declaration[122] would normally be declared inadmissible by reason of the matter involved because these rights are not protected under the Covenant. The Human Rights Committee could, however, examine these questions if the applicants simultaneously invoked other provisions of the Covenant, for example, those in article 26 which set forth a clear-cut right to non-discrimination. Thus a complaint arising from discriminatory confiscation could be examined on the basis of a violation of the right to equality.

122/Document 8
See page 153

5) *Posteriority of the violation in relation to the application of the procedure as regards the State party concerned.* Expert committees cannot exercise their competence retroactively. A complaint relating to a human rights violation which allegedly occurred before the entry into force of the relevant instrument would normally be declared inadmissible by reason of time, unless the violation has continuing repercussions which themselves violate the instrument in question. Contrary to other international procedures, United Nations expert committees do not have to receive complaints within a precisely defined period following the exhaustion of domestic remedies. Expert committees have thus examined cases three or more years after a final judgement has been handed down at the national level.

Interim protection measures

280   United Nations procedures allow emergencies to be dealt with rapidly. In cases where the victim is at risk of suffering irreparable damage if immediate action is not taken, the expert committees generally request the use of interim protection measures. Article 86 of the rules of procedure of the Human Rights Committee reads as follows: "The Committee may, prior to forwarding its views on the communication to the State party concerned, inform that State of its views as to whether interim measures may be desirable to avoid irreparable damage to the victim of the alleged violation. In doing so, the Committee shall inform the State party concerned that such expression of its views on interim

measures does not imply a determination on the merits of the communication." The Committee has invoked this article with increasing frequency, for example, to obtain a stay of execution when an individual sentenced to death claims that he has not received a fair trial.

281   When a communication has been declared admissible, States parties have six months to respond to the substance of the complaint. The State party's explanations are transmitted to the complainant for comment, and the complainant's comments are transmitted to the State party for information.

282   From the time the Human Rights Committee began to consider communications, at its second session, held in 1977, to its fifty-third session, held in March-April 1995, more than 630 communications have been registered and the Committee has concluded its consideration of 202 of them by adopting "views", or final decisions on the substance. Thirty-eight such decisions were adopted in 1994 (compared to 21 in 1992 and 1993). In 73 per cent of cases, the Committee concluded that there were violations of various provisions of the Covenant. In 54 cases, it found that the facts submitted to it did not indicate any violation of any article of the Covenant. Compared with regional human rights bodies, the proportion of complaints leading to a finding of a violation is extremely high. It is also interesting to note that, while the first decisions adopted in the early 1980s dealt mainly with the right to life and the prohibition of torture, the decisions recently handed down are increasingly sophisticated and involve most of the rights set out in the Covenant.

283   The body of case law that the Human Rights Committee is establishing through its decisions on admissibility and its "views" is vast and covers many aspects of the protection of the "right to life" and the "death penalty" (article 6 of the Covenant), the prohibition of torture (article 7), the "right to liberty and security of person" (article 9), inhuman treatment during detention (article 10), "liberty of movement" (article 12), all aspects of the right of everyone to a fair and public hearing in civil and criminal matters (article 14), the right to privacy (article 17), freedom of religion (article 18), freedom of opinion and expression (article 19), protection of the family (articles 23 and 24), equal treatment (article 26) and minority rights (article 27).

Implementation in good faith

284   The decisions of bodies established under international instruments do not have binding force, but the States which have recognized the competence of the expert committees to receive communications from individuals are called on to implement the Committee's recommendations in good faith.

123/Document 33
See page 244

285 If, after its consideration of the substance of the communications submitted by individuals under the Optional Protocol,[123] the Committee concludes that the provisions of the International Covenant on Civil and Political Rights have been violated, it presents specific proposals to the State party which might include, for example, a suggestion to amend legislation found to be incompatible with the Covenant, to commute a death sentence, to release a detainee or to compensate victims of human rights violations.

286 Thus, even though the international instruments do not establish mechanisms aimed at ensuring their implementation, the expert committees rely on, and generally receive, the cooperation of States parties in giving effect to their recommendations.

287 In order to determine the extent to which the recommendations contained in committee views are carried out, follow-up procedures have been established. In 1990, after years of discussion, the Human Rights Committee decided to create the post of Special Rapporteur for follow-up of views. His first action was to determine the extent to which States were in conformity with the Committee's recommendations. Next, he initiated a dialogue with the representatives of Governments which had not fully complied with the Committee's views and personally visited countries where a failure to observe commitments had been reported. None of the three expert bodies currently has the ability to impose sanctions for failure to meet commitments.

288 Over the past 20 years, the United Nations expert committees have established a rich body of case law which is cited more and more often by lawyers and judges in many regions of the world. They have established their credibility as qualified, quasi-judicial bodies and have demonstrated that they were not relying on one particular legal system, but strongly desired to establish a universal body of case law.

124/Document 71
See page 383

289 Finally, in addition to the three already mentioned, there will soon be three other expert committees to which individual complaints can be addressed: article 77 of the International Convention on the Protection of the Rights of All Migrant Workers and Their Families[124] provides for such a procedure. It could be implemented, as soon as the Convention enters into force, by the Committee on the Protection of the Rights of All Migrant Workers and Members of Their Families. In addition, the Committee on Economic, Social and Cultural Rights and the Committee on the Elimination of Discrimination against Women are currently studying optional protocols that would provide mechanisms for receiving communications.

Other procedures

290   Other less well-known procedures have played a role in the general system of monitoring human rights under United Nations human rights instruments. Some of these procedures are spelt out in the instruments themselves, while others have arisen from the evolving practice of some treaty-monitoring bodies.

Disputes between States parties

291   All the major United Nations human rights instruments, with the exception of the two Covenants, include a provision under which States parties which disagree on the interpretation or implementation of one or more of the rights stipulated by the instrument in question may have recourse to negotiations, conciliation or arbitration to settle the dispute. Moreover, if the dispute has not been settled within a certain amount of time, any of the States parties involved can submit it to the International Court of Justice for an opinion. Each of the instruments allows a State party to make a declaration, at the time of ratification, that it is not subject to this procedure.

292   Both the International Convention on the Elimination of All Forms of Racial Discrimination and the International Covenant on Civil and Political Rights have established their own mechanisms for dealing with any complaint submitted by a State party claiming that another State party is not fulfilling its obligations under the relevant instrument. It is noteworthy that this mechanism differs from the above-mentioned litigation concerning the interpretation or application of the Convention on a more theoretical level. Under article 41 of the International Covenant on Civil and Political Rights, a State party to the Covenant must make a separate declaration recognizing the competence of the Human Rights Committee to consider any complaints against it. Under the International Convention on the Elimination of All Forms of Racial Discrimination, this competence automatically falls to the Committee on the Elimination of Racial Discrimination (article 11).

293   The two procedures take the same basic approach: they give the States parties involved in a dispute the option to resolve it among themselves through an exchange of information on the issue under consideration. Only if the States parties cannot come to an agreement do the Committees intervene directly. Under the International Covenant on Civil and Political Rights, the Human Rights Committee first offers its "good offices" to the States parties concerned, in order to reach an amicable settlement. If that is impossible, the Committee can agree with the two parties to set up an ad hoc Conciliation Commission, still with the mandate to find an amicable solution, after further contacts with the

States parties and often after gathering more information. If, on completion of this process, there is still no solution, the Conciliation Commission issues a report containing its evaluation of the "possibilities of an amicable solution of the matter". After receiving the report, the States parties have three months to decide whether or not they accept the Commission's conclusions.

294 In examining complaints among States which have not been resolved through negotiations between the States parties concerned, the Committee on the Elimination of Racial Discrimination first sets up an ad hoc Conciliation Commission among its members. This Commission, like the one under the International Covenant on Civil and Political Rights, makes efforts to arrive at an amicable solution. However, unlike the one established under the Covenant, the Commission of the Committee on the Elimination of Racial Discrimination publishes a report "containing such recommendations as it may think proper for the amicable solution of the dispute". After three months, during which the States parties can decide whether to accept or reject those recommendations, the Chairman of the Committee communicates the report of the Conciliation Commission and the declarations of the States parties concerned to all other States parties to the Convention. Not only are the prerogatives of the ad hoc Conciliation Commission under the International Convention on the Elimination of All Forms of Racial Discrimination broader than those of the Commission established under the Covenant, but its documentation is more widely distributed.

Procedures under the Convention against Torture and Other Cruel, Inhuman or Degrading Treatment or Punishment

125/Document 50
See page 294

295 The Convention against Torture and Other Cruel, Inhuman or Degrading Treatment or Punishment[125] is the first United Nations human rights instrument which explicitly authorizes its Committee to conduct an inquiry on the situation existing in a State party. Under article 20 of this Convention, the Committee against Torture can invite a State party to cooperate in the examination of "reliable information which appears to it to contain well-founded indications that torture is being systematically practised in the territory of a State party". Taking into account any information received from this State party or from other sources, the Committee may designate one or more of its members to make a confidential inquiry on the situation and to report to the Committee urgently. Such an inquiry may include a visit to the territory of the State party, but only with its agreement. Once the Committee as a whole has examined the findings of such an inquiry, it transmits its findings together with any comments or suggestions to the State party concerned. The entire procedure is confidential, and at all stages the cooperation of the State party whose practices are under examination is sought. After the inquiry is completed, the Committee may, after consultation with the State party concerned, decide to include a summary account of the results of the proceedings in its annual report to States parties and to the General Assembly. To date, the Committee has used this procedure only once.

296   Discussions are under way on the introduction of an optional protocol to this Convention in order to enhance the Committee's monitoring capability. Based on the working methods established under the European Convention for the Prevention of Torture and Inhuman or Degrading Treatment or Punishment (an instrument implemented by the Council of Europe, a regional intergovernmental organization), this protocol would allow the Committee against Torture to travel to any State party at any time to visit detention centres, meet with police officials and prison staff, interview detainees and generally observe at first hand how the Convention is being implemented. The important element of this approach is that it intends to be preventive rather than reactive. In other words, the Committee's visits are viewed as another facet of the "constructive dialogue" between the Committee and the State party and carry no connotation of suspicion or accusation on the part of the Committee.

Mechanisms outside the purview of the Conventions

297   It was not until the mid-1960s that States empowered the United Nations to monitor the implementation of the Conventions and, more generally, to take steps to remedy gross and systematic violations of human rights. Nevertheless, every year the United Nations has received a considerable number of petitions and communications from individuals and non-governmental organizations reporting human rights violations. The victims of human rights violations, whose complaints are forwarded by human rights advocacy organizations, have rightly considered the United Nations as the competent body in the field. Economic and Social Council resolution 728 F (XXVIII) of 30 July 1959 [126] instituted a procedure which to a certain extent allowed these petitions to be dealt with while respecting the principle of non-interference in States' internal affairs. Under this resolution, the Secretariat was instructed to compile a confidential list containing a brief indication of the substance of each communication and any replies from the Governments concerned. This list was then to be circulated to the Commission on Human Rights and the Subcommission. These bodies could not, however, take any action pursuant to these communications, which were to be treated with the strictest confidentiality.

126/Document 20
See page 204

298   On 6 June 1967, the Economic and Social Council adopted resolution 1235 (XLII)[127] following a recommendation from the Commission on Human Rights. This resolution establishes the procedures for examining human rights violations. The resolution authorized the Com-

127/Document 34
See page 246

mission to "examine information relevant to gross violations of human rights and fundamental freedoms", and to "make a thorough study of situations which reveal a consistent pattern of violations of human rights", as exemplified by the situations in the Republic of South Africa, the Territory of South West Africa and Southern Rhodesia.

299   Following the adoption of resolution 1235 (XLII), the Commission initiated a study of the mechanisms that the Commission and Subcommission should use to deal with the various communications sent by individuals and non-governmental organizations notifying them of serious human rights violations. This study initially culminated in the adoption by the Economic and Social Council of resolution 1503 (XLVIII) of 27 May 1970.[128]

128/Document 38
See page 262

300   The confidential procedure established by resolution 1503 (XLVIII) is the first to have been implemented. By authorizing the Subcommission to appoint a select working group to examine all communications received by the United Nations "which appear to reveal a consistent pattern of gross and reliably attested violations of human rights and fundamental freedoms", and by stating that "all actions envisaged in the implementation of the present resolution" by the Subcommission and the Commission "shall remain confidential until such time as the Commission may decide to make recommendations to the Economic and Social Council", this resolution makes possible an appropriate method of dealing with the many cases of human rights violations all over the world.

301   Alongside the procedure laid down in resolution 1503 (XLVIII), and on the basis of the procedure outlined in resolution 1235 (XLII), the Commission gradually developed a consistent practice in its public meetings of closely studying human rights violations in certain countries and then examining certain specific human rights violations in States Members of the United Nations as a whole. This public procedure enables the Commission freely to examine any case that exhibits flagrant and systematic human rights violations.

302   The first case examined was that of Chile following the violent overthrow in September 1973 of the constitutional Government of President Salvador Allende. The revulsion felt by people all over the world at the methods used during this troubled period (widespread murder, enforced disappearances and torture) led the Commission, following a recommendation by the Subcommission, to set up a working group to launch an inquiry into the situation. In 1978, the working group was replaced by a Special Rapporteur. The Special Rapporteur's mandate lasted until 1990 and was only terminated by the Commission once a constitutional Government had been democratically elected.

303   On the basis of the Chilean example, the Commission went on to formulate a general position on the procedures to be followed in

certain "situations". The changes on the international scene and the easing of the cold war would provide opportunities for the increasingly effective implementation of the procedures outlined in resolutions 1235 (XLII) and 1503 (XLVIII). A number of special rapporteurs, working groups and representatives of the Secretary-General would gradually be appointed and take vigorous steps to eliminate the most blatant human rights violations.

304   In all cases, the appointed Special Rapporteurs compile a report using all the resources at their disposal. Generally speaking, they examine communications sent by individuals or non-governmental organizations and, if the Governments concerned agree, they visit the country in question to verify the facts which have been reported to them, meet representatives of the authorities, gather evidence, visit detention centres, and so forth. The reports thus compiled are submitted to the Commission on Human Rights, which examines, publishes and circulates them without restrictions. The Special Rapporteurs also play an increasingly important role in initiating measures to prevent or remedy violations of certain rights in urgent cases.

305   Alongside investigation of cases in specific countries, the Commission established a mechanism for examining certain particularly grave human rights violations in countries all over the world under so-called "thematic" mandates. The first such mechanism was the Working Group on Enforced or Involuntary Disappearances, established by the Commission in 1980. The political context in which this mandate was established was characterized by concern at the development of a phenomenon whereby suspected "subversive elements" were arrested, often by persons who were not clearly connected with the legal authorities of the country, and then detained at an unknown location, mistreated and often killed without their families being informed. Allegations that several thousand people had been victims of such practices made this issue one of highest priority. The reports prepared by the Working Group have gone far beyond the scope of a single State to embrace a number of countries where such phenomena have been observed.

306   Once this initial thematic mechanism had been put in place, it became possible to address other human rights violations. The next step was the appointment in 1982 of a Special Rapporteur on questions related to summary or arbitrary executions. This mandate was established to study the significant increase in the number of executions taking place in various parts of the world without the protection of elementary guarantees, including that of a fair trial. The Commission therefore decided to recommend that the Economic and Social Council appoint a Special Rapporteur on this question and the Council acted on this recommendation in its resolution 1982/35 of 7 May 1982. In 1985, the Special Rapporteur on questions relating to torture was appointed. It

was obvious that torture merited careful study owing to its close connection with the problems already mentioned.

307 Since 1986, the Commission has gone far beyond the scope of violations of the rights of the natural person to address the topic of fundamental freedoms by appointing a Special Rapporteur on the implementation of the Declaration on the Elimination of All Forms of Intolerance and of Discrimination Based on Religion and Belief. In 1990, with a view to protecting a special category of potential victims of human rights violations, namely children, the Commission appointed a Special Rapporteur on the sale of children, child prostitution and child pornography.

308 An increasingly intricate structure of special procedures has thus gradually been established in order to deal with various kinds of human rights violations. This development could only be described as fragmentary in so far as the appointment of thematic rapporteurs depends entirely on the nature of the human rights violations concerned and the importance which the international community attaches to them at a given moment in time. It remains a fact that just as the potential for human rights violations is unfortunately almost unlimited, so are the opportunities for creating new mandates. Working groups and special rapporteurs have thus been instructed to examine questions relating to the use of mercenaries, unlawful imprisonment, internally displaced persons, freedom of opinion and expression, racism, racial discrimination and xenophobia, impartiality of the judiciary and violence against women.

Activities of the Centre for Human Rights

309 The United Nations Centre for Human Rights plays an important role in the framework for monitoring respect for human rights. It has been the principal instrument of the Secretariat in the field of human rights since 1982. In 1993, an Assistant Secretary-General was appointed Director of the Centre for Human Rights. The Assistant Secretary-General reports directly to the Secretary-General of the United Nations.

310 The functions of the Centre include providing assistance in the field of human rights to the General Assembly and its Third Committee, the Economic and Social Council, the Commission on Human Rights, the Subcommission on Prevention of Discrimination and Protection of Minorities, the Committee on the Elimination of Racial Discrimination, the Committee against Torture and the Committee on the Rights of the Child. The Centre also compiles reports on the implementation of international human rights instruments.

Further standard-setting activities

311   The United Nations undertook standard-setting activities in the human rights sphere following the adoption of the two Covenants on Human Rights. Viewed in this light, the Teheran Conference provided the opportunity to set goals for the years ahead. A series of new conventions was adopted which served to define and develop the rights set out in the two Covenants. The standard-setting activity undertaken by the United Nations was particularly important in the spheres of crime prevention, the right to development, the rights of the child and the rights of women.

The Teheran International Conference on Human Rights (22 April–13 May 1968)

312   To mark the twentieth anniversary of the adoption of the Universal Declaration of Human Rights, the General Assembly decided to designate the year 1968 as the International Year for Human Rights and to convene an International Conference on Human Rights (resolution 2081 (XX) of 20 December 1965).[129]

129/Document 26
See page 215

313   This Conference was held in Teheran from 22 April to 13 May 1968 and was attended by delegations from 84 States. Its objective was to reaffirm the will of the international community to put a stop to gross denials of human rights and step up both national and international efforts and initiatives in the human rights field.

314   The Conference adopted 29 resolutions and a proclamation;[130] in addition, 18 other resolutions were transmitted to the competent bodies of the United Nations for examination. The Conference evaluated the effects of the Universal Declaration of Human Rights on national constitutions, laws and, in some cases, judicial decisions. It also took note of the fact that certain important documents had made reference to the Declaration, for example, the 1950 European Convention on Human Rights,[131] the Caracas Declaration adopted by the Inter-American Conference of 1954 and the Declaration of the Bandung Asian-African Conference of 1955.

130/Document 35
See page 247

131/Document 10
See page 156

315   While stressing that the Universal Declaration was binding on all States, the Conference urged all members of the international community to redouble their efforts to apply the principles set out in the Universal Declaration of Human Rights, the International Covenant on Civil and Political Rights,[132] the International Covenant on Economic, Social and Cultural Rights,[133] the Declaration on the Granting of Independence to Colonial Countries and Peoples,[134] the International Convention on the Elimination of All Forms of Racial Discrimina-

132/Document 32
See page 235

133/Document 31
See page 229

134/Document 21
See page 205

135/Document 27
See page 219

tion[135] and other conventions and declarations in the human rights sphere.

316 A major opportunity was thus presented to review the progress that had been made in protecting human rights since the adoption of the Universal Declaration, to evaluate the effectiveness of the methods and techniques that had been used and to take stock of the principal obstacles to be faced. It was clear that even though substantial progress had been made in setting standards, there was an urgent need to find new ways of pursuing the constant struggle for the protection of human rights, which was considered to be closely linked to the struggle for peace, prosperity and the other fundamental purposes of the United Nations.

317 During the Teheran Conference, particular attention was paid to the problems of racial discrimination, apartheid, illiteracy and the protection of the family and of the child.

318 Furthermore, concerning the application of international human rights standards, the Conference recommended that the Commission on Human Rights should stipulate procedures relevant to the examination of violations of such rights.

136/Document 35
See page 247

319 The Proclamation of Teheran,[136] adopted on 13 May 1968, addressed various problems or achievements relating to the activities of the United Nations for the promotion and encouragement of respect for human rights and fundamental freedoms, and formulated a programme for the future.

320 It noted that the Universal Declaration of Human Rights stated the "common understanding of the peoples of the world concerning the inalienable and inviolable rights of all members of the human family" and constituted "an obligation for the members of the international community". The creation of new standards and obligations was also noted in the light of the adoption, shortly before, of the International Covenant on Civil and Political Rights, the International Covenant on Economic, Social and Cultural Rights, the Declaration on the Granting of Independence to Colonial Countries and Peoples and the International Convention on the Elimination of All Forms of Racial Discrimination, as well as other conventions and declarations on human rights adopted under the auspices of the United Nations.

321 The international community was urged to use all possible means to eradicate problems related to the policy of apartheid, which was condemned as a "crime against humanity". States were also requested to apply the principle of non-discrimination at the international and national levels as a matter of urgency.

322 With regard to the problem of colonialism, States were urged to cooperate with the appropriate organs of the United Nations so that measures would be taken towards the full implementation of the General Assembly's Declaration on the Granting of Independence to Colonial Countries and Peoples.

323   The Proclamation of Teheran also emphasized that "since human rights and fundamental freedoms are indivisible, the full realization of civil and political rights without the enjoyment of economic, social and cultural rights is impossible". Thus, sound and effective national and international policies of economic and social development were considered essential to the implementation of human rights.

324   The Proclamation further stated that the requisite attention should be given as a matter of urgency to the problem of illiteracy. The existence of more than 700 million illiterate persons throughout the world was an enormous obstacle to all efforts at realizing the aims and purposes of the Charter of the United Nations and the provisions of the Universal Declaration of Human Rights.

325   In addition, the Proclamation highlighted the need to eliminate discrimination against women, to improve the protection of the family and of the child and to continue efforts aimed at disarmament. Finally, the International Conference urged all peoples and Governments to dedicate themselves to increasing respect for human rights and promoting their implementation.

The new conventions

326   Beginning in the 1970s, additional conventions, which anticipated the establishment of systems for monitoring standard-setting texts, began to be adopted. These conventions restated and developed a number of the principles defined in the International Covenants which deserved special attention. Each dealt with one specific type of right and articulated in more detail than possible in the Covenants the preventive measures and sanctions to which the contracting parties should have recourse.

327   The International Convention on the Suppression and Punishment of the Crime of Apartheid[137] entered into force on 18 July 1976. It is monitored by a Group of Three consisting of three members of the Commission on Human Rights, who are also representatives of States parties to the Convention, under article IX of the Convention. The mechanism for implementing this Convention was recently put in abeyance, as a result of the favourable developments in southern Africa.

137/Document 40
See page 264

328   The Convention on the Elimination of All Forms of Discrimination against Women,[138] which entered into force on 3 September 1981, established the Committee on the Elimination of Discrimination against Women.

138/Document 45
See page 277

329   The Convention against Torture and Other Cruel, Inhuman or

139/Document 50
See page 294

Degrading Treatment or Punishment,[139] which entered into force on 26 June 1987, established the Committee against Torture. The Convention imposes on States parties the obligation to make torture a crime and to prosecute and punish those found guilty of it. An order from a superior officer or a public authority may not be invoked as a justification of torture. Furthermore, torturers may be tried by the courts of any State party, no matter where the offences were committed. An international inquiry may be instituted if there is reliable information, within the meaning of article 20 of the Convention, indicating that torture is being practised in the territory of a State party.

140/Document 61
See page 344

330   The Second Optional Protocol to the International Covenant on Civil and Political Rights,[140] aimed at the abolition of the death penalty, was adopted by the General Assembly on 15 December 1989. Its monitoring body is the Human Rights Committee.

141/Document 60
See page 334

331   The Convention on the Rights of the Child,[141] which was adopted by the General Assembly on 20 November 1989 and entered into force on 2 September 1990, established the Committee on the Rights of the Child, consisting of 10 independent experts. The Committee's activities are described below.

142/Document 71
See page 383

332   Lastly, the International Convention on the Protection of the Rights of All Migrant Workers and Members of Their Families[142] was adopted by the General Assembly on 18 December 1990 but has not yet entered into force. The intention of this instrument, which applies to a difficult area, is to protect a group of people who are particularly vulnerable and susceptible to any upsurge in the spread of xenophobic or nationalistic ideas. It establishes a number of rights on their behalf and imposes obligations on the host States. It is to be hoped that the members of the international community will undertake to accede to this important instrument without delay.

333   Other instruments which were drafted during this period did not anticipate the establishment of a monitoring mechanism. The most notable of these are the Convention on the Non-Applicability of Statutory Limitations to War Crimes and Crimes against Humanity (1968), the Convention concerning Protection and Facilities to Be Afforded Workers' Representatives (1971), the International Convention against

143/Document 54
See page 315
144/Document 79
See page 414

Apartheid in Sports (1985)[143] and the Declaration on the Rights of Persons Belonging to National or Ethnic, Religious and Linguistic Minorities (1992).[144]

334   Parallel to these efforts to establish international standards in the field of human rights, the General Assembly and the Economic and Social Council, going beyond the strict framework laid down by Council resolution 728 (XXVIII), decided to set up appropriate procedures for the investigation of allegations of human rights violations in certain specific situations. Of particular note are the Special Committee to Investi-

gate Israeli Practices Affecting the Human Rights of the Population of the Occupied Territories, set up by the General Assembly in 1970, and the Committee on the Exercise of the Inalienable Rights of the Palestinian People, established in 1975. These Committees originated in Assembly resolutions 2535 B (XXIV)[145] of 10 December 1969, 3236 (XXIX)[146] of 22 November 1974 and 3376 (XXX)[147] of 10 November 1975.

145/Document 37
See page 261

146/Document 41
See page 268

147/Document 42
See page 268

335 Finally, during the same period, the General Assembly and the Economic and Social Council continued to sensitize the international community to human rights issues. This was achieved through a series of declarations, the most notable of which were the Declaration on the Elimination of All Forms of Intolerance and of Discrimination Based on Religion or Belief, proclaimed by the General Assembly on 25 November 1981;[148] the Safeguards guaranteeing protection of the rights of those facing the death penalty, approved by the Economic and Social Council on 25 May 1984;[149] the Body of Principles for the Protection of All Persons under Any Form of Detention or Imprisonment, adopted by the General Assembly on 9 December 1988;[150] the Principles on the Effective Prevention and Investigation of Extra-legal, Arbitrary and Summary Executions, recommended by the Economic and Social Council on 24 May 1989;[151] and the Declaration on the Protection of All Persons from Enforced Disappearance, adopted by the General Assembly on 18 December 1992.[152]

148/Document 48
See page 291

149/Document 49
See page 293

150/Document 58
See page 327

151/Document 59
See page 332

152/Document 78
See page 410

Crime prevention and the treatment of offenders

336 As noted in the description of the period 1949 to 1966 (see paragraphs 154 to 163), links were gradually established between the programmes developed in the field of human rights and those relating to crime prevention and criminal justice.

337 The Fifth United Nations Congress on the Prevention of Crime and the Treatment of Offenders, held in Geneva in 1975, adopted the Declaration on the Protection of All Persons from Being Subjected to Torture and Other Cruel, Inhuman or Degrading Treatment or Punishment, which was to open the way to adoption of the Convention of the same name some years later. That Congress also laid down the basis for the Code of Conduct for Law Enforcement Officials,[153] which the General Assembly adopted in 1979. This code has been designed to be inserted directly into the national regulations applying to law enforcement officials, particularly members of the police force and other security forces, and it is thus a primary means of directly incorporating the injunctions contained in article 7 of the International Covenant on Civil and Political Rights and in the Convention against Torture and Other Cruel, Inhuman or Degrading Treatment or Punishment.[154]

153/Document 44
See page 274

154/Document 50
See page 294

338 The Seventh Congress, held in Milan in 1985, adopted a plan of action to strengthen international cooperation in the field of crime

155/Document 53
See page 313;
Document 52
See page 312

156/Document 51
See page 300

157/Document 62
See page 346;
Document 63
See page 348;
Document 64
See page 351

158/Document 66
See page 364

159/Document 67
See page 368

160/Document 68
See page 369

161/Document 69
See page 374

prevention and criminal justice. It also adopted a series of Basic Principles on the Independence of the Judiciary[155] and the United Nations Standard Minimum Rules for the Administration of Juvenile Justice (the Beijing Rules).[156]

339   The Eighth Congress, held in Havana in 1990, adopted a number of very important instruments,[157] including the United Nations Standard Minimum Rules for Non-Custodial Measures (the Tokyo Rules),[158] the Basic Principles for the Treatment of Prisoners,[159] the United Nations Guidelines for the Prevention of Juvenile Delinquency (the Riyadh Guidelines)[160] and the United Nations Rules for the Protection of Juveniles Deprived of Their Liberty.[161]

340   In the context of strengthening international cooperation in the field of crime prevention and criminal justice, a Commission on Crime Prevention and Criminal Justice was established by the Economic and Social Council in February 1992. In 1995, the Ninth Congress on the Prevention of Crime and the Treatment of Offenders was held in Cairo and adopted a resolution urging States to explicitly extend criminal justice and criminal sanctions to a number of specific acts of violence towards women.

The Declaration on the Right to Development

162/Document 56
See page 322

163/Document 85
See page 448

341   After 10 years of drafting, the Declaration on the Right to Development was adopted by the General Assembly, following a vote, in 1986.[162] In 1993, the World Conference on Human Rights reaffirmed by consensus that the right to development is an integral part of human rights and fundamental freedoms.[163]

342   Today, almost 10 years after the adoption of the Declaration, the Commission on Human Rights has still to determine the means to implement it. To this end, an open-ended working group of governmental experts met from 1982 to 1989. In 1990, on the Working Group's recommendation, the Secretary-General organized the Global Consultation on the Realization of the Right to Development, which dealt mainly with the basic problems encountered in implementing the Declaration, the criteria which could be used to identify progress and possible mechanisms for evaluating that progress. In 1993, the Commission on Human Rights decided to establish, for three years initially, another expert Working Group on the Right to Development. This Group had a dual mandate: to identify obstacles to the implementation and realization of the Declaration, and to recommend ways of enabling all States to give effect to the right to development. The recommendations of the Working Group will be submitted to the United Nations General Assembly in 1995, in the context of the fiftieth anniversary of the Organization.[164]

164/Document 91
See page 476

343   The adoption of the Declaration on the Right to Development marked a turning-point in that it expressed a new way of regarding the very concept of "development" following the failure of national and international development policies, a failure attested to, on the one hand, by the growing poverty of most human beings and, on the other hand, by the increasing concentration of wealth and power in the hands of a few. In fact, with the adoption of the Declaration on the Right to Development, the international community for the first time questioned the idea that the primary objective of economic activity was to improve economic and financial indicators. Instead it placed human beings, individually and collectively, at the centre of all economic activity, making them both the central subject and principal beneficiary of development. In that connection the Declaration defined development as "a comprehensive economic, social, cultural and political process, which aims at the constant improvement of the well-being of the entire population and of all individuals on the basis of their active, free and meaningful participation in development and in the fair distribution of benefits resulting therefrom".

344 The Declaration redefined the objective of economic activity, which was no longer geared towards growth and profit but towards the attainment of human and social objectives through the improvement of the social, economic, political and cultural well-being of individuals, groups and peoples. It also provided that those objectives must be determined by people themselves and that their benefits must be equally distributed. The meaning of development was thus subjective and required effective participation by all in the decisions affecting people's lives. In a study dating from 1981 (E/CN.4/Sub.2/404/Rev.1), the United Nations Special Rapporteur on the right to self-determination stressed that development must be defined in each specific context and must be based on popular participation. Thus, "development can be neither exported nor imported. It presupposes taking into consideration numerous economic, technical and social parameters and establishing priorities and setting growth rates on the basis of knowledge of needs, conditions and external possibilities. It presupposes the participation of the entire people inspired by a common ideal, and individual and collective creativity in devising the most adequate solutions to problems arising from local conditions, needs and aspirations."

345 Similarly, the Working Group on the right to development stressed that "States have primary responsibility to ensure the conditions necessary for the enjoyment of the right to development, as both an individual and a collective right. Development cannot be seen as an imported phenomenon or one that is based on the charity of developed countries" (E/CN.4/1995/27). Implementation of the right to development could only be the result of national policy and strategy, taking due account of the specific situation of each country, without thereby ignoring economic realities. There was no ready-made universal solution available for all States in implementing the right to development. Its realization could only reflect the outcome of a long and laborious process undertaken in accordance with the conditions prevailing in each country.

346   Thus, the aim of development is not only economic and financial efficiency and improvement of the principal macroeconomic indicators, such as gross national product, the balance of trade and the balance of payments. The aim of this complex process is, in substance, through the active participation of the population as a whole, to promote social change centred on people, leading to a democratically controlled system of production designed to satisfy human and social needs. The desired progress must be measured in terms of social justice, equality, well-being and respect for the fundamental dignity of all individuals, groups and peoples.

347   The key concepts of the Declaration on the Right to Development reflecting this new way of thinking include recognition of reciprocal relations and the interdependence of respect for human rights and development, as well as the indivisibility and interdependence of civil and political rights and economic, social and cultural rights. In a report dated 31 December 1981 (E/CN.4/1488) on the regional and national dimensions of the right to development as a human right, the then Secretary-General stressed that an approach that gave priority to economic growth over the goals of human development (including such concepts as equity, non-discrimination, social justice and self-sufficiency) was incompatible with the human rights obligations of States. In that regard the report was quite definite: "Any development strategy which directly involves the denial of fundamental human rights, in whatever name or cause it may be undertaken, must be deemed to be a systematic violation of the right to development". The report went on to state that the persistence of conditions of underdevelopment, in which millions of human beings were denied access to such essentials as food, water, clothing, housing and medicine in adequate measure, and were compelled to live in conditions that were incompatible with human dignity, clearly represented a flagrant mass violation of human rights.

348   The Declaration insists on a certain number of fundamental human rights principles on which development must be based, including non-discrimination, equality, equity, social justice, self-sufficiency and solidarity. These principles may not be renounced even in the short run. The concept of short-term sacrifices, to be made by people in the name of economic growth and balance-of-payments equilibrium, is essentially a violation of these fundamental principles, which date back at least as far as the League of Nations and the Declaration of Philadelphia, adopted in 1944 and incorporated into the ILO Constitution in 1946. They have subsequently been reformulated and developed in various studies and in legal instruments adopted by United Nations organs.

It is against these principles that the realization or non-realization of development must be measured, and it is they which must inspire and guide the formulation of appropriate policies.

349　The right of peoples to self-determination in its economic, political, social and cultural dimensions lies at the heart of recognition of the right to development. A development approach mindful of human rights must recognize that all peoples have the universal right to determine their own economic, social, political and cultural system and to formulate their own policies, adapted to their situation and their particular needs, without external interference, coercion or threats.

350　Over the first two years of its mandate, the Working Group on the Right to Development identified a certain number of obstacles to implementation of the right to development. At the international level, particular emphasis was placed on the implementation of unilateral coercive measures, the imposition of conditions, the prolongation of denial of self-determination and the reverse transfer of resources. United Nations human rights bodies have drawn attention to the way in which the globalization of the economy affects the ability of peoples living in developing countries to make their own economic, social and political choices. The Special Rapporteur on the realization of economic, social and cultural rights and the Working Group on the Right to Development have clearly shown that as a result there is less latitude for Governments in formulating social, economic, monetary and fiscal policy in terms of their own economic and social objectives.

351　The Committee on Economic, Social and Cultural Rights and the Special Rapporteur have expressed concern over the negative impact on these rights caused by the lack of financial resources in debtor countries owing to debt repayment, structural adjustment programmes and deterioration in the terms of trade. The Special Rapporteur has also drawn attention, in his second interim report, to certain negative consequences of privatization for giving effect to these rights. In that regard, he emphasized the impact which the privatization of the basic services provided by Governments had had on the poorest segments of the population as a result of the increase in the price of such services as well as the role of the State *vis-à-vis* those segments.

352　The Working Group identified a certain number of other obstacles arising from the globalization of the economy that specifically affect the operation of the United Nations system. These include a lack of transparency and responsibility, particularly in the allocation of resources; the overall inadequacy of resources allotted to multilateral cooperation as compared to those made available in a bilateral context or through private transfers; the unequal distribution of resources within international agencies, with social goals being at a disadvantage in comparison with economic goals; the generalization of a sectoral approach favouring economic growth; the tendency to separate macroeconomic policies from social objectives; and inadequate coordination within the United Nations system.

353   The right to development implicitly supposes that States will mutually assist each other when external factors impede the effective implementation of human rights. The Declaration on the Right to Development stresses that States have the duty to cooperate in order to ensure development and to eliminate obstacles to its realization. They must exercise their rights and discharge their duties in such a way as to promote a new international economic order based on sovereign equality, interdependence, mutual interest and cooperation. The principle of self-determination requires democratization and the establishment of equitable and appropriate international structures open to effective and significant participation by all peoples and all States. This is particularly important in the case of decision-making structures dealing with economic, financial and monetary issues.

354   The Working Group stressed the fact that, in the context of increasing globalization, developed countries had a particular responsibility to create a world economic environment conducive to accelerated and sustainable development. It stressed in particular that the most powerful States and international agencies bore the primary responsibility for the coordination of macroeconomic policies to create a stable and predictable international environment and to encourage, stimulate and promote viable human development.

355   The multidimensional nature of a concept of development mindful of human rights also implies collective responsibility on the part of the United Nations system as a whole, which demands greater coordination of strategies and programmes, more effective cooperation in the field, ongoing consultation between specialized agencies and improved circulation of information between them.

356   The Declaration on the Right to Development also attests to the existence of reciprocal relations and interdependence between social justice at the national and at the international levels. The attainment of international social justice would require structural changes at the international level aimed at remodelling economic relations on a basis of cooperation and solidarity rather than competition. It stressed that to ensure effective promotion of fundamental human rights and economic, social and cultural development, it was essential to establish "a new international economic order based on the sovereign equality" of States and respect for the rights of all peoples, an international order able to guarantee the comprehensive economic, social and cultural development of all peoples and States, in accordance with their aspirations for progress and well-being.

357   At a recent session the Working Group on the Right to Development reaffirmed that realization of the right to development required

not only firm political will, but also far-reaching changes in national and international structures and institutions involved in the realization of the right to development. Stressing that States could not abdicate their responsibility and submit to market forces, it recalled that it was up to them to ensure that international institutions operated in a transparent, responsible and coordinated manner. It further noted that it was necessary to establish a framework of rules and economic instruments able to ensure transparency in the interplay of market forces and compensate for shortcomings in that domain; implement human resources development policies; and ensure equitable distribution of resources and income. With particular reference to international financial institutions, the Working Group recommended that the international community should ensure greater transparency in their activities and the strengthening of consultations between such agencies and the Governments of Member States.

358   The international community has given increasing priority to implementation of the right to development. In that connection the Vienna World Conference on Human Rights stressed that the Working Group on the Right to Development should, in consultation and cooperation with other organs and agencies of the United Nations system, speedily formulate, for submission at the earliest opportunity to the General Assembly for its consideration, comprehensive and effective measures aimed at eliminating the obstacles to the implementation and realization of the Declaration on the Right to Development and recommend means of promoting the enjoyment of that right in all States.

359   At its fifty-first session, held from 30 January to 10 March 1995 in Geneva, the Commission on Human Rights welcomed the efforts made by the Working Group, which are increasingly oriented towards the establishment of a permanent evaluation mechanism to follow up the implementation of the Declaration on the Right to Development. It decided that the reports of the Working Group and other relevant documentation should be made available to the General Assembly in the context of the celebration of the fiftieth anniversary of the United Nations.

360   The importance the international community attaches to the implementation of the right to development is referred to also in the mandate of the United Nations High Commissioner for Human Rights, who is given the responsibility of promoting and protecting the realization of the right to development. In that regard, the High Commissioner engaged in a dialogue with United Nations agencies and organs with a view to increasing the coordination of system-wide activities for the promotion and implementation of the right to development. On behalf of the Secretary-General, he also initiated a process of high-level consultations with heads of State or Government, the multilateral financial

institutions, the specialized agencies and intergovernmental and non-governmental organizations in order to find a durable solution to the developing countries' debt crisis.

361 The international community took a further step in assigning increasing priority to the implementation of the right to development in February 1995, when the Commission on Human Rights adopted resolution 1995/17 calling on the Centre for Human Rights to give priority to the right to development by making it a subprogramme of its programme of activities for the years 1992-1997 and of its future programme of activities. In addition, with a view to strengthening the capacity of the Centre for Human Rights, the Commission requested the Secretary-General to provide the Centre with a focal unit with the specific task of following up on the Declaration on the Right to Development and its implementation.

The Convention on the Rights of the Child

165/Document 60
See page 334

362 The adoption of the Convention on the Rights of the Child[165] on 20 November 1989 was the culmination of long-standing United Nations concern for this aspect of human rights. Indeed, the well-being, protection and rights of children have been at the core of the Organization's concerns since its founding in 1945. Its interest in questions concerning the child led the United Nations to establish, on 11 December 1946, the United Nations Children's Fund (UNICEF), which remains today the primary organization of the United Nations system responsible for international assistance to children.

363 Two years later, on 10 December 1948, the Universal Declaration of Human Rights was adopted. Its provisions and those of the 1966 International Covenants on Human Rights recognize that children's rights must be protected.

364 The first standard-setting United Nations instrument exclusively devoted to the rights of children was the 1959 Declaration of the Rights of the Child. Affirming that "mankind owes to the child the best it has to give" and that the principle of "the best interests of the child" should guide the actions of those responsible for them, this Declaration offered a moral framework for the rights of the child.

365 The United Nations chose to commemorate the twentieth anniversary of the adoption of this Declaration by proclaiming the year 1979 the International Year of the Child. Many activities were organized to celebrate this Year, and a number of different initiatives were undertaken. In 1978, for instance, the Government of Poland submitted a draft convention on the rights of the child to the Commission on Human Rights.

366 The Commission on Human Rights, which had been assigned the task of drafting the text of the convention, completed its work in

1989, and the General Assembly adopted the Convention on the Rights of the Child[166] the same year, or 30 years after the adoption of the Declaration of the Rights of the Child.

166/Document 60
See page 334

367   Both before and after the adoption of the Convention, a number of meetings were organized to draw attention to this instrument and increase public awareness of it. United Nations organizations, bodies and specialized agencies participated actively in these meetings, and 61 countries—a record number—signed the Convention on the first day it was opened for signature, 26 January 1990.

368   The organization of the World Summit for Children provided considerable impetus to the signing and ratification of the Convention. Held in New York on 29 and 30 September 1990 and attended by many heads of State and Government, the Summit bore witness to the fact that the international community was resolved to improve the fate of children and that it had the political will to do so. One of the stated goals of the Declaration and Plan of Action,[167] adopted by the Summit and signed the same day by 163 heads of State and Government, is to achieve ratification of the Convention by all countries. In September 1990, when 20 States had become parties to the Convention, it was possible to undertake the procedures leading to the establishment of the Committee on the Rights of the Child and the election of 10 independent experts to serve on the Committee. Pursuant to the provisions of the Convention, the Committee has the task of considering the reports to be submitted by States parties to the Convention.

167/Document 65
See page 354

369   The United Nations and the Committee were very aware at that stage of the keen interest aroused by the Convention and of the great hopes that had been placed in their work.

370   The Committee held its first session from 30 September to 18 October 1991. During these three weeks, it considered a number of questions relating to the organization of its work and undertook a serious study of how to proceed in order to best fulfil its mandate to consider the reports of States parties. In the initial report, which must be submitted within the two years following the date of the entry into force of the Convention for the State party concerned, States parties are required to indicate the degree of fulfilment of the more than 40 substantive articles of the Convention.

371   To assist States parties in fulfilling this obligation, the Committee adopted general guidelines for preparing the reports. The guidelines state that the preparation of the report affords an important opportunity to bring national law and policies into line with the Convention and to monitor progress made in the enjoyment of the rights set forth in this instrument. In addition, "the process should be one that encourages and facilitates popular participation and public scrutiny of government policies". In its guidelines, the Committee also notes that these reports

should also include information on existing or planned mechanisms at the national or local level for coordinating policies relating to children and for monitoring the implementation of the Convention.

372 Since the Convention provides that the rights of children should be made widely known, the Committee requested States parties to describe those measures taken or foreseen to make the principles and provisions of the Convention widely known to adults and children alike, and to make their reports on the implementation of the Convention available to the public at large in their own countries.

373 The Convention on the Rights of the Child is the most recent in a series aimed at enshrining the protection of human rights in international law. Its provisions therefore take into account existing standards relating to the rights of the child and the way their interpretation has evolved. It derives from the Convention that the child is a subject of law and that all human rights—civil, cultural, economic, political and social—necessary to his or her survival, development, protection and participation are interdependent and indivisible.

374 The Convention is particularly aimed at protecting the child against sexual and economic exploitation, emergency situations, abandonment and ill treatment. It is also meant to protect children involved in armed conflicts and to provide assistance to those seeking refugee status. The Convention prohibits the practice of torture. It also provides that neither capital punishment nor life imprisonment may be imposed for offences committed by persons below 18 years of age.

375 In other provisions, the Convention provides that children should have the right to health care, education and leisure, and that disabled children should receive special care. It recognizes the right of the child to have a name and nationality from birth, and to preserve his or her identity. It also provides that both parents have the primary responsibility for the upbringing of the child, that children should not be separated from their parents except when the competent authorities so determine and that, where children are separated from their parents for whatever reason, they have the right to maintain personal relations with the parents.

376 The Convention on the Rights of the Child has also paved the way for the recognition of the right of the child to respect for his or her views. The Convention provides that children have the right to express their views in matters affecting them, and that these views should be given due weight in accordance with the age and maturity of the child.

377 Non-discrimination is another important principle embodied in the Convention. The Convention expressly provides that children shall enjoy all the rights set forth therein without discrimination of any kind, irrespective of the child's or his or her parent's or legal guardian's race, colour, sex, language, religion, political or other opinion, national,

ethnic or social origin, property, disability, birth or other status. More-over, the principle that "the best interests of the child" should be a primary consideration in all decisions affecting him or her is reaffirmed in the Convention. Another important point in this instrument is that it mandates that States Parties shall ensure to the maximum extent possible the survival and development of the child. Importantly, article 41 of the Convention stipulates that nothing in the Convention should affect any provisions which are more conducive to the realization of the rights of the child and which may be contained in the law of a State party or international law in force for that State.

378   The Convention recognizes the importance of international cooperation and technical assistance to help ensure respect for the rights of the child, special account being taken of the needs of developing countries. To date, the Committee has held eight sessions and considered reports submitted by more than 30 States parties. The Committee's views on each of the reports it has considered are set forth in the final observations of the Committee. These include various sections, namely, an introduction, positive aspects, principal subjects of concern and rec-ommendations and suggestions concerning steps to be taken.

379   An analysis of the content of these observations reveals that the philosophy and spirit of the Convention, as interpreted by the Committee on the Rights of the Child, not only consist of recognizing the value and validity of each of the rights set forth in the Convention, but also of stressing the importance of the principles of non-discrimination and the best interests of the child, as well as the right of children to freedom of expression for the purposes of the implementation of the other rights recognized in this instrument. The Committee also feels that these principles, especially that of the "best interests of the child", should underlie the decisions and measures taken in the design of policy, to ensure that resources are allocated "to the maximum extent" to the realization of the rights of the child. It is generally recognized that the Convention and the Committee's work have aroused a great deal of interest throughout the United Nations system. They have done much to encourage cooperation and action at the international, regional and national levels.

380   At this stage, special mention should be made of the extremely useful role played by UNICEF. Not only has this body worked actively for the universal ratification of the Convention, but it has also made a strong effort to promote its implementation. As UNICEF has begun to integrate the rights set forth in the Convention into its planning activities, its country offices are in turn incorporating the Committee's suggestions and recommendations in their programmes. UNICEF has also taken the initiative to encourage and facilitate studies on subjects relating to the rights of the child, some of which have been carried out and compiled by

the UNICEF research institute in Florence, better known as Centre Innocenti.

381 The Convention on the Rights of the Child, which establishes international standards for promotion and protection of the rights of the child, has been ratified by more countries than any other human rights instrument. As of July 1995, 176 States were parties to the Convention. The exceptional nature of this Convention is evidenced not only by the unprecedented speed with which it has been accepted, but also by the degree of cooperation and coordination achieved, particularly within the United Nations system, to ensure its implementation. Clearly, in the context of the celebration of the fiftieth anniversary of the United Nations, it would be a noteworthy achievement if the Convention could become the first human rights instrument to be universally ratified.

Women's fundamental rights

382 The United Nations has always affirmed that women's rights are fundamental rights, that women should be guaranteed full participation on an equal footing in all aspects of political, civil, economic, social and cultural life and that the elimination of all forms of gender-related discrimination is one of the international community's highest priorities. Based on this position, a number of initiatives have been taken over the years for the advancement of women, both by bodies created under the Charter and by others created under international instruments.

Promotion of the rights of women by bodies created under the Charter

383 Since the mid-1970s, the United Nations has taken several important initiatives in the field of women's rights, including the drafting of the Convention on the Elimination of All Forms of Discrimination against Women. In 1974, the Economic and Social Council established a voluntary fund in relation to the International Women's Year. This fund later became the United Nations Development Fund for Women (UNIFEM), whose mandate is to identify and study trends and attitudes which present obstacles for women and to suggest promotional, educational and other measures designed to mitigate those problems. The Fund has also been active in questions concerning refugees, of whom a high proportion are poor women from developing countries who are responsible for their families' survival. It works closely in this field with the Office of the United Nations High Commissioner for Refugees (UNHCR). In 1985, UNIFEM became a part of the United Nations Development Programme (UNDP), reaffirming the close links between the advancement of women and economic development.

384 In 1976, the General Assembly endorsed the Economic and

Social Council decision to create an International Research and Training Institute for the Advancement of Women (INSTRAW). The essential role of the Institute is to research ways of monitoring and appraising the effects of programmes and projects on women's integration into development activities. In some respects, the Institute acts as an early-warning system for development strategies which appear to have an adverse effect on women's economic situation. The Institute works closely with the Commission on the Status of Women.

385   The Institute also works with UNIFEM for the empowerment of women. The two bodies play a particularly important role in the advancement of the status of women and of women's basic rights. In its resolution 49/163 of 23 December 1994,[168] the General Assembly, recalling that it had "urged the International Research and Training Institute for the Advancement of Women to continue to strengthen its activities in the areas of research, training and information aimed at mainstreaming gender in development strategies and giving women greater visibility through recognition of their contribution to social and economic development", "emphasized the unique function of the Institute as the only entity within the United Nations system devoted exclusively to research and training for the integration of women in development". It also "stressed the importance of making its research findings available for policy purposes and for operational activities".

168/Document 95
See page 496

386   Referring to the Economic and Social Council decision in which the Council agreed to the recommendation of the Secretary-General to merge the International Research and Training Institute for the Advancement of Women and the United Nations Development Fund for Women, subject to proper analysis of the legal, financial and administrative implications of the merger, the General Assembly requested the Secretary-General to report on this question to the General Assembly at its fiftieth session under the item entitled "Advancement of women".

387   The United Nations Decade for Women (1976-1985) was proclaimed following the World Conference of the International Women's Year, held in Mexico City in 1975. Among other resolutions and decisions, the Conference adopted the Declaration of Mexico on the Equality of Women and Their Contribution to Development and Peace. The Declaration and the World Plan of Action for the Implementation of the Objectives of the International Women's Year, appended to the Declaration, dealt with a number of important issues. They focused essentially, however, on the underdevelopment of socio-economic structures in most areas of the world as the major cause of women's inferior position. The Plan outlined nine specific areas for national action, focusing primarily on equality of opportunity in education and employment and equality of remuneration and social benefits. Recommendations

were also made as to various policies which could usefully be implemented at the regional and international levels.

388   The World Conference of the United Nations Decade for Women, held in Copenhagen in 1980 around the themes of "equality, development and peace", adopted a Programme of Action which stressed even more strongly the links between economic development and improvement in the status of women. In the same year, the General Assembly adopted the International Development Strategy for the Third United Nations Development Decade, in which it emphasized the importance of women as both agents and beneficiaries of the development process.

389   The United Nations Decade for Women concluded with the World Conference to Review and Appraise the Achievements of the United Nations Decade for Women: Equality, Development and Peace, held in Nairobi. The Conference culminated in the formulation of the Nairobi Forward-looking Strategies for the Advancement of Women.[169] The General Assembly subsequently endorsed the Strategies and entrusted their monitoring and implementation to the Commission on the Status of Women. The Strategies constitute the principal instrument of overall policy of the United Nations in the promotion of the rights of women.

169/Document 55
See page 319

390   The Nairobi Forward-looking Strategies were based on the principle that an essential contribution to the strengthening of international peace and security would be made by the elimination of all forms of inequality between women and men and by the integration of women into the development process. Great weight was given to the fundamental importance of national means of implementing the proposed policies, and Governments were requested to allocate resources and to establish or reinforce mechanisms to promote the full integration of women in all aspects of civil life in their countries.

391   The Economic and Social Council approved both the contents of the programme and the thrust of the implementation measures. It entrusted the practical application of the programme to United Nations bodies, specialized agencies and other intergovernmental and non-governmental organizations. The Council also established within the United Nations system a reporting mechanism with the aim of monitoring, reviewing and appraising the implementation of the Nairobi Forward-looking Strategies.[170] By this mechanism, the Secretary-General was requested to produce two series of reports, one every two years and the other every five years. The biennial report, which addresses the progress made within the United Nations system to implement the Strategies, is to contain information on the integration of the Strategies in each of the programmes carried out under United Nations auspices and on the progress made towards meeting the targets for the participation of women in these programmes. The quinquennial report is to deal with the

170/Document 57
See page 325

progress achieved at the national level by the States Members of the United Nations and include an appraisal of the effectiveness of the measures and programmes of action employed in their implementation of the Strategies. The States are to provide the Secretary-General with this information themselves, indicating the situation with regard to ratification of international instruments concerning women's rights and their implementation at the national level. Non-governmental organizations may also submit to the Secretary-General information to be used in drawing up the quinquennial report. The Commission on the Status of Women uses the consolidated quinquennial report as a basis for appraising the progress made in areas regarding women over the previous five years and for selecting priority themes for the future.

392   In its review and appraisal of the implementation of the Nairobi Forward-looking Strategies (E/1990/25), the Commission on the Status of Women noted a number of serious obstacles hindering the advancement of women and recommended steps to be taken to remove them. In relation to the *de jure* and de facto inequality which continued to exist between men and women, it recommended that countries should make efforts to make women more aware of their rights. Teachers should receive training on gender issues and textbooks should be revised to eliminate negative stereotypes of women. The proportion of women involved in economic decision-making and the number of women in paid employment should be increased. The proportion of women involved in political decision-making should reach 30 per cent by 1995 and they should achieve equal representation in this area by the year 2000. The Commission put forward other suggestions relating to women and development. Extreme poverty was seen as a serious threat to the status of a great number of women in many countries. Access to education and training, especially in technical fields, were among the issues considered, together with the question of women's involvement in decisions concerning economic reform, development initiatives affecting the environment and improvements in health and family planning services. The Commission also suggested setting two deadlines for certain targets: the year 2000 for the elimination of gender-related differences in adult literacy, and 1995 for the establishment of social measures to allow women to combine family responsibilities with paid employment. The Commission also urged that greater attention should be paid to the problem of violence against women, in the family, in the workplace and in society.

393   The Commission on the Status of Women is also responsible for preparations for the Fourth World Conference on Women to be held in Beijing in September 1995. The theme of this Conference is Action for Equality, Development and Peace. Preparations include activities at the local, regional and international levels, with particular emphasis being placed on activities which will publicize the Conference as

widely as possible and encourage and facilitate the participation of non-governmental organizations, both in the preparations and at the Conference itself. The aim of the Conference is to deal with basic questions which have arisen from studies and preparatory meetings and which are recognized as forming the principal obstacles to the advancement of the status of the majority of women and to draw up a programme of action and timetable for the achievement of targets in these areas, with the aim of implementing the Nairobi Strategies more fully.

394   A draft platform for action (A/CONF.177/L.1) has been drawn up by the Commission on the Status of Women acting as the Preparatory Committee for the Fourth World Conference on Women. The Platform for Action upholds the Convention on the Elimination of All Forms of Discrimination against Women and builds upon the Nairobi Forward-looking Strategies for the Advancement of Women, as well as relevant resolutions adopted by the Economic and Social Council and the General Assembly. The formulation of the Platform for Action is aimed at establishing a basic group of priority actions that should be carried out during the next five years.

395   Governments, the international community and civil society, including non-governmental organizations and the private sector, are called upon to take strategic action in the following critical areas of concern:

      — The persistent and increasing burden of poverty on women;

      — Unequal access to or inadequate educational and training opportunities of good quality at all levels;

      — Inequalities in health care and related services;

      — All forms of violence against women;

      — Effects of persecution and armed or other kinds of conflict on women;

      — Inequality in women's access to and participation in the definition of economic structures and policies and the productive process itself;

      — Inequality between men and women in the sharing of power and decision-making at all levels;

      — Insufficient mechanisms at all levels to promote the advancement of women;

      — Promotion and protection of all the fundamental human rights of women;

      — Women and the media;

      — Lack of adequate recognition and support for women's contribution to managing natural resources and safeguarding the environment;

      — The girl-child.

All the parties must devise mechanisms to ensure that responsibility will be taken for all these critical areas of concern and to ensure the functioning of those mechanisms.

396   The Platform for Action is an agenda for women's empowerment. It aims at accelerating the implementation of the Nairobi Forward-looking Strategies for the Advancement of Women and at removing all the obstacles to women's active participation in all spheres of public and private life through a full and equal share in economic, social, cultural and political decision-making. This means that the principle of shared power and responsibility should be established between women and men at home, in the workplace and in the wider national and international communities. Equality between women and men is a matter of human rights and a condition for social justice and is also a necessary and fundamental prerequisite for equality, development and peace.

Protection of women's rights by the organs established under international instruments

397   Most of the principal international human rights instruments have been drafted based on the model of the Charter of the United Nations and the Universal Declaration of Human Rights, pursuant to which human rights must be guaranteed "without distinction of any kind, such as . . . sex". Thus, all the bodies established to monitor the implementation of these instruments are authorized to consider questions of discrimination on the basis of sex which arise in the exercise of the rights guaranteed. The Human Rights Committee, the monitoring body established under the International Covenant on Civil and Political Rights, has examined numerous complaints from individuals claiming to be victims of sex discrimination. The issue of discrimination against women was mentioned in the guidelines for the submission of reports under the International Covenant on Economic, Social and Cultural Rights and in several of the general comments of the Committee on Economic, Social and Cultural Rights. The Committee on the Rights of the Child has, for its part, devoted one of its first daylong sessions of general debate to the topic of the rights of the girl-child.

398   There are a number of international instruments devoted to specific aspects of the rights of women, but, in fact, the international community became aware of some of the most serious problems even before the establishment of the United Nations. Other instruments, in particular the conventions of the International Labour Organization, led to the implementation of important measures of protection against discriminatory labour practices which placed women in an inferior position in the workforce.

399   As an additional measure to ensure equal rights for women, in 1979, the General Assembly adopted the Convention on the Elimination

of All Forms of Discrimination against Women,[171] which entered into force on 3 September 1981. As with the other major international human rights instruments, the Convention provides for the establishment of a Committee to consider the progress made in the implementation of the Convention. The Committee on the Elimination of Discrimination against Women consists of 23 independent experts, elected by the States parties from among their nationals. At present, the Committee is authorized only to consider reports submitted by States parties, as no mechanism exists for the consideration of complaints from States or from individuals, although the World Conference on Human Rights, held at Vienna in 1993, had proposed the adoption of an optional protocol authorizing it to receive communications from individuals.

400 In its annual report submitted to the General Assembly through the Economic and Social Council, the Committee can request the United Nations to conduct studies either directly or indirectly on important aspects of women's rights. The Committee's reports are also transmitted for information to the Commission on the Status of Women.

401 The definition of discrimination against women as found in the Convention on the Elimination of All Forms of Discrimination against Women is more detailed than the definitions found in other instruments which are more general in scope. The Convention forbids any distinction, exclusion or restriction made on the basis of sex which has the effect or purpose of impairing or nullifying the recognition, enjoyment or exercise by women, irrespective of their marital status, on a basis of equality by men and women, of human rights and fundamental freedoms in the political, economic, social, cultural, civil or any other field. The importance of this definition lies in the fact that the States which have ratified the Convention are required to evaluate the results of their measures and policies on the basis of the progress made in the prevention of discrimination. None the less, inequalities can persist in practice despite the existence of laws and regulations intended to guarantee equality under the law. Therefore, the States parties to the Convention are invited to take special measures to establish de facto equality, while ensuring that these measures are non-discriminatory. The States parties are required to establish education programmes aimed at eliminating gender bias and stereotypes and to take other measures to eliminate practices which are detrimental to women or place them at a disadvantage in relation to men. In its General Recommendation No. 5, the Committee on the Elimination of Discrimination against Women reaffirmed the importance of special measures to advance women's integration into all aspects of civil society. For education, politics, the economy and employment in particular, these measures may be temporary according to the degree of equal access. But as far as pregnancy and motherhood are concerned, special measures should be applied on an ongoing basis to protect that equality.

402 Since 1986, the Committee on the Elimination of Discrimination against Women has formulated general recommendations on such issues as equal pay, equal rights for disabled women, the elimination of the practice of genital mutilation and other issues relating to women's rights. Many of these recommendations were purely formal, but in recent years the Committee has begun to adopt more specific "general comments", following the model of the Committees established under the two Covenants. For example, in its general recommendation on violence against women, it declared that gender-based violence was a form of discrimination that might breach specific provisions of the Convention, regardless of whether those provisions expressly mentioned it. Finally, since 1991, the Committee has decided to hold thematic debates, following the example of the Committee on Economic, Social and Cultural Rights and the Committee on the Rights of the Child.

V   Expanding the system:
The Vienna World Conference on Human Rights and its follow-up (1993-1995)

172/Document 84
See page 441

403   The World Conference on Human Rights, held in Vienna from 14 to 25 June 1993, provided the opportunity to reaffirm the equality and interdependence of all human rights. In my address at the opening meeting of the Conference, I stressed the importance of the question of the interdependence of all human rights.[172] The Vienna Conference emphasized that action for the promotion and protection of economic, social and cultural rights is as important as action for civil and political rights. This Conference should be regarded both as the culmination of a long process and as the point of departure for a new adventure on behalf of human rights.

The Vienna Declaration and Programme of Action

173/Document 70
See page 381

404   The United Nations decided to hold a world conference on human rights in 1993, pursuant to General Assembly resolution 45/155 of 18 December 1990.[173] Forty-five years after the adoption of the Universal Declaration of Human Rights and 25 years after the Teheran International Conference on Human Rights, the United Nations organized the World Conference to review and assess the progress that had been made in the field of human rights and to identify obstacles to further progress in this area and ways in which they could be overcome.

General context and preparatory work

405   In the overall United Nations human rights programme, a link has been established between development, democracy and all the different categories of rights—economic, social, cultural, civil and political—embodied in the Universal Declaration. The problem of how these three issues are related was one of the central themes of the Vienna Conference agenda. The mandate of this Conference was to evaluate the effectiveness of the United Nations in all fields of activity dealing with human rights in order to formulate recommendations for ensuring the full enjoyment by all men and women of their rights. The objective was also to recommend improvements in the work methods and mechanisms used by the

Organization and in the allocation of financial resources, while maintaining respect for the universality, objectivity, non-selectivity and interdependence of all rights.

406   During the period preceding the Conference, States Members of the United Nations, intergovernmental organizations and nongovernmental organizations, both international and national, participated in the preparatory activities, which were oriented towards the agenda itself and the final document and programme of action. The Preparatory Committee established by the United Nations had the task of coordinating these activities and reconciling, to the extent possible, the often diametrically opposed points of view expressed in the various forums. To focus efforts on common objectives and to defuse some of the tension that was causing discord, three large preparatory meetings were held, in Tunis, San José and Bangkok, which adopted declarations on the most important aspects of human rights in the regions concerned.

407   The role of non-governmental organizations during the preparatory stage and at the Conference itself should not be underestimated. As groups working closely with persons whose rights are constantly being gravely threatened, thousands of non-governmental organizations participated in meetings prior to the above-mentioned regional meetings, and in the regional meetings themselves. They also played an active part in the work of the Preparatory Committee and at the Vienna Conference itself. Thus, a good number of recommendations from the non-governmental organization forum held outside the Conference were incorporated into the Vienna Declaration and Programme of Action adopted following the work of the Conference. A number of independent experts conducted useful studies in the period immediately preceding the Conference and made individual contributions to the preparatory process.

Human rights and fundamental freedoms

408   The issues at stake and the significance of the Vienna Conference were in every way exceptional.[174] The Vienna Declaration and Programme of Action[175] reaffirmed the human rights principles which constitute the very foundation of the United Nations, in particular the universality, objectivity, non-selectivity, interdependence and equality of these rights. They also reaffirmed the dignity and worth inherent in the human person, whose preservation and promotion are the basis of all human rights and fundamental freedoms. As the subject of these rights and liberties, the individual is the principal beneficiary and should participate actively in their realization. At the same time, the international community, acting under the auspices of the United Nations, has the collective responsibility to ensure the conditions necessary for the enjoyment of human rights and fundamental freedoms.

409   The United Nations cannot vigorously pursue its human rights

174/Document 84
See page 441

175/Document 85
See page 448

objectives unless Member States contribute to its efforts and do not thwart them. From the standpoint of the common objectives of individuals, of the State and of the international community in the field of human rights, the main actor is necessarily the State. On the one hand, it operates together with other States with a view to setting the standards governing human rights and agreeing on ways to monitor the international implementation of these standards. On the other hand, it acts unilaterally to ensure respect for human rights at the national level.

410   One of the important ways that Member States can demonstrate their support for the United Nations and its ideals in the field of human rights is to sign the major United Nations instruments which enshrine the fundamental principles based on human rights: equal rights, self-determination, democracy, the rule of law, economic and social progress and the whole range of related rights and freedoms. One of the ways that Member States can show that they accept in good faith the instruments they have ratified is to take seriously the obligation to implement them at the national level. The community of nations should set itself the following goals: ratification, accession or succession of all States to United Nations human rights instruments; limitation of the scope of their reservations, and eventually the withdrawal of these reservations; and recognition of the jurisdiction of the competent bodies established under human rights instruments to consider individual complaints against the State.

411   While reaffirming the attachment of the United Nations to the universal enjoyment of human rights and fundamental freedoms, the Vienna Declaration and Programme of Action notes several key areas on which the Organization should focus its efforts in the years to come. The document reaffirms the right to development as a universal and inalienable right and the interdependence of the right to development, democracy and other fundamental human rights. It stresses that economic development in the poorest nations is the collective responsibility of the international community and, in particular, that the least developed countries, which are struggling to achieve democracy and implement reforms for the well-being of their people, deserve the support of that community. Equitable economic relations among States and a favourable economic environment at the international level are of crucial importance from the standpoint of sustainable development. It is equally important to implement effective development policies at the national level which involve the participation of the populations concerned. To attain these objectives, the Declaration considers that the heavy external debt burden must be alleviated and that the widespread poverty and illiteracy in various countries must be combated. Moreover, the countries with flourishing economies and high standards of living should refrain from injuring the populations of other countries by exporting

hazardous substances and waste and from endangering their own population.

412   The Vienna Declaration and Programme of Action[176] also contains important measures to ensure better protection of the rights of women and children. With regard to women's rights, the Declaration notes that discrimination and violence are the daily lot of many women, and that girl-children, in particular, are among those most vulnerable to human rights violations in many regions of the world. Some of the most serious issues are the near absence of women in decision-making positions at the national and international levels, the insufficiency of health care and family planning services and the violation of rights specific to women. The Conference also recommends, within the framework of the Programme of Action, that a special rapporteur on violence against women be appointed. (This recommendation was accepted by the Economic and Social Council and, in November 1994, the Special Rapporteur proposed an optional protocol to the Convention on the Elimination of Discrimination against Women to provide women victimized by violence with the right of petition, a proposal endorsed by the Commission on the Status of Women in 1995.) The Vienna Declaration and Programme of Action encourages all States to ratify the Convention on the Elimination of All Forms of Discrimination against Women by the year 2000. As for the rights of the child, the Declaration reiterates the principle of "First Call for Children" and urges all States to ratify the Convention on the Rights of the Child by 1995 to make it a universal instrument. It also called on States to make every effort to ensure the effective implementation of this Convention, devoting particular attention to non-discrimination, the best interests of the child and the need to take the child's views into account in all questions concerning him or her.

176/Document 85
See page 448

413   The Vienna Declaration and Programme of Action also stresses the rights of indigenous populations, affirming the international community's commitment to their economic, social and cultural well-being and their participation in all aspects of the political and social life in the communities and States where they live.

414   The rights that the Conference felt deserved special attention included the right to request and be granted asylum and the rights of disabled persons, vulnerable groups and migrant workers. Moving from individual to collective rights, the Declaration notes that States are responsible for creating favourable conditions to ensure their enjoyment. For example, States are chiefly responsible for developing strategies to address the root causes of mass migrations, internal displacement of persons and extreme poverty and to incorporate human rights education programmes in educational curricula at all levels. In this regard, special emphasis is placed on the importance of promoting and protecting the right to development as an inalienable human right.

415 In addition, States are urged to act immediately to put an end to flagrant and systematic violations of human rights, including torture, summary and arbitrary execution and disappearances, genocide, collective rape and other heinous crimes, and States are responsible for ensuring that the perpetrators of such crimes are punished. International humanitarian law and the laws of war should be reactivated and their principles inculcated in members of the armed forces through intensive training.

416 The persistence of discrimination is a constant theme in the Vienna Declaration and Programme of Action. While welcoming the dismantling of apartheid, the Conference takes note of the sombre reality of the increase in intolerance, xenophobia, racism and racial discrimination in many countries, and urges Governments to combat the attitudes and prohibit the activities which nourish such ideologies. Finally, an entire section of the Vienna Declaration and Programme of Action deals with the rights of women from the point of view of both the violation of these rights and the ways and means of ensuring their effective and central promotion and protection through activities and programmes of the United Nations and individual States.

Future United Nations action on the universal enjoyment of human rights

417 None of the participants in the World Conference on Human Rights harboured any illusions with regard to the grave difficulties the United Nations would face in taking up the challenges of protecting human rights in the years to come. This realism permeates the Vienna Declaration and Programme of Action, which contains concrete recommendations to strengthen the technical-assistance and monitoring activities of the United Nations and to improve the coordination of the many United Nations activities in this field. In this connection, the General Assembly was formally invited to consider, as a matter of priority, the question of the establishment of a United Nations High Commissioner for Human Rights. On the other hand, the Conference frankly recognized that the lack of financial and other resources constituted a significant obstacle to United Nations human rights activities. The Declaration therefore urges the United Nations and Member States to study methods of improving the support they can contribute in this essential domain. Taking into account the material obstacles that prevent the United Nations from fully carrying out all aspects of its human rights mandate, some of the proposals formulated in the Vienna Declaration and Programme of Action are aimed at improving current human rights programmes while launching new initiatives to promote the enjoyment of human rights in all States.

418 The Declaration invites the United Nations to strengthen, rationalize and simplify its activities, so as to avoid redundancies and conflicts among the human rights initiatives undertaken by its different divisions. The Centre for Human Rights is asked to centralize and coordinate these efforts at both the administrative and technical levels. The Centre will not only coordinate system-wide attention to human rights, but also support the Organization's system of rapporteurs, experts, working groups and treaty bodies. Consequently, it will be necessary to provide it with sufficient resources to carry out these tasks. The Declaration and Programme of Action recommends, *inter alia*, that human rights officers be assigned if and when necessary to regional offices of the United Nations for the purpose of disseminating information and offering training and other technical assistance in the field of human rights upon the request of concerned Member States. The manner in which the Commission on Human Rights and other United Nations bodies have reacted to recent emergency situations indicates a positive trend, which should be encouraged through the search for other means of dealing with grave human rights violations. Regional organizations, international financial institutions and specialized agencies have been earnestly invited to make human rights a top priority in the carrying out of their policies and mandates.

419 As formulated in the Vienna Declaration and Programme of Action, the implementation of the United Nations human rights programme requires various measures tailored to its objectives. In order to provide States with the means they require to ensure respect for human rights, diligent long-term work is needed to put in place the infrastructure of a society capable of guaranteeing democracy and the rule of law. It is often necessary to create the very foundations of civil society, without which it is impossible to consolidate the advances made in the field of human rights. In this regard, it is noted in the Vienna Declaration that non-governmental organizations and the media contribute in large measure to anchoring the principles of human rights in the national consciousness. Having taken note of the role played by the United Nations within the framework of these efforts, the States that are working for the realization of the above-mentioned goals can request the assistance of the Centre for Human Rights, whose consultative and technical cooperation programmes and services are aimed at establishing national institutional mechanisms for the protection of human rights.

420 With the Vienna Declaration and Programme of Action, the human rights programme of the United Nations has at its disposal the appropriate goals, guidelines and work programmes for the twenty-first century. However, the implementation of this programme requires not only action on the part of the United Nations, but also a commitment at the regional, national and local levels. For its part, the United Nations General Assembly approved the Vienna Declaration and Programme of Action, thereby making it the reference document for policy and the activities of the international community for the future. It also implemented a pivotal provision of the Vienna Declaration by creating the post of United Nations High Commissioner for Human Rights.

Universal accession to human rights conventions

421   One of the most fundamental aspects of the Vienna Declaration and Programme of Action is its affirmation of the universality of human rights. In past decades, there has been constant controversy about the relative importance of one type of right over another. It is therefore particularly opportune that the Vienna Conference especially emphasizes that "human rights are universal, indivisible and interdependent and interrelated". Civil, economic, cultural, political and social rights must consequently be treated in a fair and equal manner, and with the same emphasis. It follows from this affirmation that while the significance of national and regional particularities and various historical, cultural and religious backgrounds must be borne in mind, it is the duty of States to promote and protect all human rights and fundamental freedoms. It is consequently no less important that human rights issues be considered in a spirit of universality, objectivity and non-selectivity.

422   This fundamental affirmation, contained in paragraph 5 of the Vienna Declaration, constitutes one of the pillars of the new international structure for the protection of human rights. It refers to the unity of thought that characterized the adoption of the Universal Declaration of Human Rights, but was lost during the preparatory work for the adoption of the International Covenant on Economic, Social and Cultural Rights on the one hand, and the International Covenant on Civil and Political Rights on the other.

423   Understood in this manner, universality of human rights also implies that the international community is clearly and vigorously committed to the unequivocal adoption of all international human rights instruments. It follows from the Vienna document that States should endeavour to support all of these treaties while avoiding, in so far as possible, recourse to reservations.

424   The Vienna Programme of Action clearly reflects these imperatives. It calls for measures ensuring ratification of the Convention on the Rights of the Child by 1995 and also encourages States to ratify the Convention on the Elimination of All Forms of Discrimination against Women by the year 2000. Finally, special efforts are called for regarding the International Convention on the Rights of All Migrant Workers and Members of Their Families, which has yet to enter into force, and the Convention against Torture and Other Cruel, Inhuman or Degrading Treatment or Punishment.

425   It should be noted that this solemn and urgent appeal, accom-

panied by a definitive timetable, falls within the purview of the many tasks undertaken by the General Assembly, the Commission on Human Rights and the various treaty bodies. Moreover, the Subcommission on Prevention of Discrimination and Protection of Minorities has undertaken specific efforts and continues to carry out special studies aimed at analysing the problems hindering the universal ratification of international instruments in the area of human rights.

426 As a direct follow-up to the recommendations of the World Conference, I have personally invited heads of State and Government to consider all the means available to them for working towards this common goal of universality of human rights. I have the pleasure of noting in this regard that the goal of universal recognition of the Convention on the Rights of the Child has every chance of being attained on schedule.

427 Nevertheless, it is important to underline that the universalizing of human rights conventions should not be accompanied by systematic recourse to reservations, which would diminish the commitment of States and impair the consistency of the conventions. For that reason, all appeals for universalizing have been accompanied by mention of the hope that States will commit themselves to international human rights instruments, if possible without reservations, as members of the community of States parties to the various conventions.

428 The World Conference contributes to these efforts by calling upon States to withdraw the reservations they have formulated, which are contrary to the objectives and purposes of the conventions. Besides the fact that such reservations are considered incompatible with international treaty law, it is important to recall that international human rights law is specific by nature in that it entails fundamental rights and liberties benefiting individuals in addition to obligations on States. The rules of the Vienna Convention on the Law of Treaties should be read in the light of this specificity. The Human Rights Committee, created under the International Covenant on Civil and Political Rights, has recently emphasized these elements in demonstrating the existence of particular rules for this type of international treaty. The Commission and the Subcommission have also constantly urged the States to demonstrate self-discipline in issuing reservations or declarations.

429 The Vienna Conference assigned to the Secretary-General the specific task of engaging in a dialogue with the Governments concerned precisely because of the dual awareness of the sovereign right of States to accompany their accession to international human rights treaties with reservations or declarations, on the one hand, and, on the other, of the danger such reservations or declarations present for the unity and universality of human rights, and the need to make them compatible with the objectives and purposes of these treaties. The goal is to examine the

reasons for such reservations, as well as ways and means to reduce or withdraw them, in order to safeguard universal accession to the conventions and the very universality of human rights to which they are dedicated.

430   It is my firm intention to carry out this task in the light of studies and preliminary investigations that are being carried out to isolate the obstacles to universal accession and the reasons for them.

The new Decades

431   At present, several interesting initiatives are aimed at strengthening the already impressive list of rights of the individual or at envisioning new mechanisms to protect human rights. An important current initiative is the draft optional protocol to the Convention against Torture and Other Cruel, Inhuman or Degrading Treatment or Punishment, aimed at establishing a torture-prevention system based on visits of independent experts to the territories of States that have accepted such a procedure. Two other drafts are being prepared relative to the Convention on the Rights of the Child: one concerning the sale of children, child prostitution and child pornography and one concerning the participation of children in armed conflicts. Also under study is a draft declaration on the right and responsibility of individuals, groups and organs of society to promote and protect universally recognized human rights and fundamental freedoms.

432   These initiatives will soon reach a stage of development that will allow for the further evolution of international human rights law. Specific and intrinsic by nature, this law protects the individual against all forms of violation and permits that individual full self-realization in a society of which he or she is the foundation and an essential participant. This law should be seen not as a fixed framework incapable of any evolution, but rather as a new law, open to change and enrichment, flexible by nature and able to evolve in order to better protect those whom it is designed to protect: the human person.

The Third Decade to Combat Racism and Racial Discrimination

433   Judicial and political activities designed to combat racism and racial discrimination have taken the form of decades for action to combat racism and racial discrimination. Two such decades have already been organized, the first covering the period from 1973 to 1982 and the second from 1983 to 1992. The United Nations obtained significant results in the course of those two Decades, as illustrated by the independence of Namibia and the ending of the racist policies practised in that country by South Africa, the dismantling of apartheid in South Africa, the ratification of the International Convention on the Elimination of All Forms of Racial Discrimination and the development of new international instruments aimed at protecting the rights of migrant workers, minorities and indigenous peoples.

434 Recently, the international community has been concerned by the rise of racism, racial discrimination, xenophobia and other demonstrations of intolerance such as inter-ethnic conflicts and "ethnic cleansing". At the World Conference on Human Rights, the international community adopted as a "priority task" the need for "speedy and comprehensive elimination of all forms of racism and racial discrimination, xenophobia and related intolerance". It strongly urged groups, institutions, intergovernmental and non-governmental organizations and individuals to intensify their efforts in cooperating and coordinating their activities against these evils.

435 As part of this new crusade against the scourge of racism and racial discrimination, the United Nations General Assembly, on 20 December 1993, adopted resolution 48/91,[177] in which it proclaimed the Third Decade to Combat Racism and Racial Discrimination and adopted a Programme of Action, which was amended the following year. This Programme, which must be implemented by the United Nations, Governments and intergovernmental organizations over the next 10 years, contains five essential elements:

177/Document 86
See page 464

— Action at the international level;
— Action at the national and regional levels;
— Basic research and studies;
— Coordination and reporting;
— Regular system-wide consultations.

436 In addition to the adoption of this multidimensional Programme by the General Assembly, the United Nations Commission on Human Rights appointed a Special Rapporteur on contemporary forms of racism, racial discrimination, xenophobia and related intolerance who will constitute another important mechanism for realizing the goals of the Third Decade to Combat Racism and Racial Discrimination.

437 Appointed as an independent expert by the Commission in 1993 for a three-year term, the Special Rapporteur is mandated to study both institutionalized and indirect forms of racism and racial discrimination against national, racial, ethnic, linguistic and religious minorities and migrant workers throughout the world. He is also required to report on racist acts of violence against minorities and migrant workers and to "examine incidents of contemporary forms of racism, racial discrimination, any form of discrimination against Blacks, Arabs and Muslims, xenophobia, negrophobia, anti-Semitism and related intolerance".

The International Decade of the World's Indigenous People

178/Document 60
See page 334

438 There are more than 300 million indigenous people throughout the world. Yet neither the Universal Declaration of Human Rights nor the two International Covenants on Human Rights contain any reference to indigenous people. Similarly, the International Conference on Human Rights, held in Teheran in 1968, made no mention of this particular group. With the entry into force of the Convention on the Rights of the Child[178] in 1990, the notion of indigenous populations was expressly included for the first time in the text of a United Nations human rights instrument.

439 Indigenous populations have been absent from part of the history of the United Nations because of national policies which, until very recently, were more concerned with integration, on the assumption that indigenous populations would be slowly absorbed into the wider society.

440 Today, assimilationist policies have been discarded by most States and by indigenous populations. The United Nations has begun work on the drafting of an international instrument which—in its current form—seeks to promote the different cultures of indigenous populations and recognizes their right to development in accordance with their own priorities. Moreover, at its forty-ninth session, in 1994, the General Assembly launched the International Decade of the World's Indigenous People (1995-2004) to seek solutions to the problems of indigenous populations in such areas as health, education, development, the environment and human rights.

441 The United Nations has taken the first steps towards a better understanding of the growing movement of indigenous people through the decision of the Subcommission on Prevention of Discrimination and Protection of Minorities to authorize a study on discrimination against indigenous populations, the results of which were published in 1982. One of its recommendations was the establishment of a working group on indigenous populations. The first session of this Working Group in 1982 marks the beginning of formal contacts between the United Nations and indigenous populations.

442 As for the results achieved since 1982, the Working Group on Indigenous Populations has become the principal forum for discussion of the concerns of indigenous people. Participants at the July 1994 session of the Working Group included 161 indigenous organizations, 42 Governments and nearly 800 individuals. In just over 10 years, the Working Group has become the third largest United Nations human rights forum, after the Commission on Human Rights and the Subcommission on Prevention of Discrimination and Protection of Minorities.

443 The Working Group's mandate is to devote attention to the elaboration and development of norms for the protection of the rights of indigenous populations. In the past few years, the Working Group has prepared a draft United Nations declaration on the rights of indigenous peoples, which was adopted in August 1994 by the Subcommission and is currently being considered by the Commission on Human Rights. The Subcommission has also begun consideration of two studies prepared by special rapporteurs, one on treaties between indigenous populations and States, and the other on principles and guidelines for the protection of the cultural and intellectual patrimony of indigenous populations. Expert workshops have been held on the subject of racism, autonomy and sustainable development. A further workshop devoted to land rights will be held during the first year of the Decade.

444   In 1993, the General Assembly launched the International Year of the World's Indigenous People.[179] The Year provided an opportunity for the international community to recognize indigenous populations. Rigoberta Menchú, winner of the 1992 Nobel Peace Prize and an advocate of indigenous rights, was appointed Goodwill Ambassador for the Year. A month later, various officials were invited to address the Commission on Human Rights and, in June, a dozen or so representatives spoke in plenary meeting at the Vienna World Conference on Human Rights. Such public access to high-level forums would not have been possible four or five years earlier. Through the Voluntary Fund for the Decade, indigenous organizations were given financial assistance for such projects as the establishment of a cultural centre, a legal advisory centre for indigenous populations, human rights training programmes and cultural programmes.

179/Document 87
See page 469

445   The International Year also provided an opportunity to raise the question of indigenous populations and their rights in regions with limited awareness of this internationally important subject. Perhaps more importantly, the Year underscored the urgent need to adopt norms for the protection of the rights of indigenous populations. It also demonstrated that the United Nations system as a whole, including the specialized agencies, could and should play a role in the development of programmes geared towards indigenous populations. Lastly, the International Year should provide inspiration for the activities to be undertaken within the framework of the International Decade of the World's Indigenous People.[180]

180/Document 97
See page 498

446   Indeed, this Decade creates a wealth of opportunities for States, the United Nations system, non-governmental organizations and indigenous populations. The General Assembly adopted the theme "Indigenous people: partnership in action" and decided that the Decade would have an operational focus. International action is required in two areas. First, priority must be given to reaching consensus on the rights of indigenous populations. The challenge of the next few years is to reach agreement as soon as possible on the principles to be applied to the

partnership proposed by the General Assembly. Second, the international community must mobilize its resources to improve the living conditions of indigenous populations.

447   The programmes and projects to be developed should be integrated—linking such concerns as development, the environment, human rights, health and education—and managed by indigenous people. The challenge of the years ahead will be to convince the international community to devote more funding to the development of indigenous peoples and the United Nations agencies to lend their expertise to indigenous peoples for the planning and execution of effective projects and programmes.

448   Although the General Assembly resolution on the Decade identifies a precise goal, the United Nations system needs to establish clear priorities and policy objectives. In consultation with Governments and indigenous populations, and through the mechanism of national committees, specific programmes and objectives should be elaborated.

Technical cooperation in the field of human rights

449   Since 1955, the United Nations programme of advisory services and technical assistance in the field of human rights has been devoted to helping States, at their request, to build and strengthen national structures which have a direct impact on general respect for human rights and on the defence of the rule of law.

450   Some 10 years after the entry into force of the Charter, and after some initial ad hoc assistance programmes in the field of human rights, the General Assembly officially established the United Nations programme of advisory services in the field of human rights and authorized the Secretary-General to make arrangements to provide requesting Governments with such assistance as expert advisory services, scholarships for training and advanced training, and study courses. The General Assembly later expanded the services provided under the programme by including regional and national training courses in human rights. Pursuant to these resolutions, the programme has been conducting activities for some 40 years now in numerous countries in every region of the world.

451   The programme was expanded yet again when the voluntary fund for advisory services and technical assistance in the field of human rights (later renamed Voluntary Fund for Technical Cooperation in the Field of Human Rights) was created by my predecessor, on 16 November 1987, pursuant to Commission on Human Rights resolution 1987/38 of

10 March 1987 and to Economic and Social Council resolution 1987/147 of 29 May 1987. The goal of the Voluntary Fund is to provide additional financial support for practical activities focused on the implementation of international conventions and other international instruments on human rights promulgated by the United Nations, its specialized agencies or regional organizations.

452   The elements of the programme emphasize the integration of international human rights standards into national legislation and policies and the creation or strengthening of national institutions to protect and promote human rights and democracy based on the rule of law. Today, this assistance takes various forms: expert advisory services, training courses, workshops and seminars, scholarships, awards, information and documentation, and evaluation of national needs in the field of human rights.

453   For its part, throughout the Vienna Declaration and Programme of Action, the World Conference on Human Rights stressed the importance of advisory services and technical assistance for human rights and called for the strengthening of the programme.

454   With regard to technical assistance, the Vienna Declaration calls for the implementation of coherent and comprehensive country-based plans of action for the promotion and protection of human rights through the implementation of an overall United Nations programme. According to the Declaration, the programme of advisory services and technical assistance is to be strengthened. The Declaration also stipulates that the Centre for Human Rights should provide States with technical and financial assistance upon request, including the elaboration and attainment of coherent and comprehensive plans of action. These plans of action would regroup activities (*a*) to strengthen institutions that advocate human rights and democracy; (*b*) to reform penal and correctional institutions; (*c*) to provide legal protection for human rights; (*d*) to provide theoretical and practical training in the field of human rights for officials, lawyers, judges, officers of security forces and others; (*e*) to educate and inform the public at large with a view to promoting respect for human rights; and (*f*) to give preference to other activities which contribute to the smooth functioning of a rule-of-law society.

Funding and administration of the programme of advisory services and technical assistance in the field of human rights

455   The programme of advisory services and technical assistance in the field of human rights is to be funded from the regular budget of the United Nations and by the United Nations Voluntary Fund for Technical Cooperation in the Field of Human Rights, which came into

operation in 1988. At the present time contributions of more than $15 million have been pledged or received. Specific projects may also be funded by the Centre's partners in the United Nations system.

456 Whatever the source of funding, projects are implemented within the framework of a single comprehensive programme administered by the Centre for Human Rights. Although in accordance with the resolutions of the Commission on Human Rights a distinction is made between projects financed under the regular budget and projects financed under the Voluntary Fund, both as regards accountability obligations and the compilation of reports and as regards budgetary information, the substance and general policy lines of the programme are not affected.

457 The elaboration and execution of the programme, as well as support for its activities and follow-up, are conducted by the Technical Cooperation Unit of the Centre for Human Rights, headed by the Assistant Secretary-General for Human Rights. The United Nations High Commissioner for Human Rights, under the authority of the Secretary-General of the United Nations, provides advisory services and technical assistance through the Centre for Human Rights at the request of the State concerned and, where appropriate, regional human rights organizations with a view to supporting actions and programmes in the field of human rights and of coordinating the human rights promotion and protection activities throughout the United Nations system.

Overview of the programme

458 Advisory services and technical cooperation activities are regarded by the United Nations as a complement to, but never a substitute for, the monitoring and investigative activities of the human rights programme. As stated in previous reports by the Secretary-General on the topic and in Commission on Human Rights resolution 1994/69, the provision of advisory services and technical assistance does not in any way reduce a Government's responsibility for accountability on the human rights situation in its country and, wherever applicable, would not exempt it from scrutiny through the various monitoring procedures established by the United Nations.

459 The Centre usually responds to a request from a Government by undertaking a careful study of the country's specific requirements. Assistance programmes are then formulated to address these needs in a comprehensive and coordinated manner. The Centre for Human Rights executes its own projects. I outlined this comprehensive approach for the first time in the report on advisory services in the field of human rights which I delivered at the Commission on Human Rights in 1993. It was subsequently elaborated in my 1994 report.

Contents of the programme

460 In much the same way as the programme, the areas of assistance on which the programme's activities are focused have changed. In keeping with successive resolutions of the General Assembly and the Commission on Human Rights, and taking account of the nature of the requests submitted by States themselves, the programme has gradually been endowed in a number of areas with assistance capabilities which currently provide a useful framework for national efforts to consolidate human rights and the rule of law.

461 Some of the most noteworthy constitutional questions which the Centre is addressing are the formulation of legislative and constitutional provisions; declarations of rights; remedies that can be used in courts of law; the allocation and separation of the powers of State; the independence of the judicial system; the role of the judicial system in monitoring police and penal services; states of emergency in constitutional law; the incorporation of economic, social and cultural rights in constitutional law; nationality, citizenship and the right of asylum; constitutional protection for national minorities; national human rights institutions, including national commissions and mediation services; trade union freedoms; the constitutional protection of human rights in the administration of justice; the incorporation of international standards in domestic law and their implementation by courts of law; and constitutional mechanisms relating to equality and non-discrimination.

462 Awareness-raising, information and education are the key elements in establishing a society which respects human rights and fundamental freedoms. This explains why the United Nations is conducting a broad range of activities in this field, from training law officers at national level to publishing appropriate material designed for students, educators, the mass media and the public at large. The World Public Information Campaign for Human Rights launched in 1988 has thus aimed to raise the awareness of people throughout the world with regard to human rights questions and, in particular, to raise the profile of international human rights machinery. Information and education activities fit into a universal culture of human rights in which the fundamental precepts recognized by the Universal Declaration of Human Rights, enshrined in the Covenants and amplified by the body of international human rights instruments, will act as a keystone for societies irrespective of their level of development.

463 Human rights education and the publication of appropriate material play a particularly important role in the creation of this kind of culture. This fact needs to be borne in mind in education policies at both national and international levels. It is therefore entirely logical that the Vienna Declaration and Programme of Action should contain a number of provisions on human rights education, which is a direct extension of the principles set forth in the Universal Declaration and the International Covenant on Economic, Social and Cultural Rights, both of which require States to ensure that education shall be directed to the strengthening of respect for human rights and fundamental freedoms.

181/Document 96
See page 417

464   By its resolution 49/184 of 23 December 1994, the General Assembly officially proclaimed the ten-year period beginning on 1 January 1995 the United Nations Decade for Human Rights Education.[181] This decade should give new impetus to the task of addressing the many efforts that have already been initiated in the field of human rights education and to supplementing effectively the numerous efforts that have been made to achieve the widest possible dissemination of human rights material.

465   The five main objectives of the decade are the assessment of needs and the formulation of education strategies at all levels, the strengthening of programmes and capacities for education, the development of suitable education materials, the strengthening of the role of the mass media in the furtherance of human rights education and, finally, the global dissemination of the Universal Declaration of Human Rights in the maximum possible number of languages.

466   It is essential for the smooth functioning of the rule of law that armed forces should be bound by the constitution and laws in force, that they should be accountable to a democratic government and that they should be trained to respect the principles of human rights and humanitarian law in the performance of their legitimate functions in society.

467   The United Nations has conducted a number of training activities designed for security officers. Traditionally, such training has been offered as part of more general programmes intended for police officers, penal institutions and the army. The United Nations is currently targeting its military training activities on armed forces considered as a distinct professional category. It is directly adapting the content and methods of the training to the needs and specific tasks of the modern soldier.

468   National and international non-governmental organizations which operate in the field of human rights play a key role in the programme of advisory services and technical assistance. Non-governmental organizations are involved in providing such assistance and they benefit from it as well. In line with the programme's objective of strengthening civil society, Governments and other parties are increasingly asking the United Nations to assist national non-governmental organizations. The programme helps to expand the resources available to them, thus enabling them more effectively to perform the crucial role which they have to play in a democratic society.

469   The programme also aims to establish a human rights infrastructure at the regional level. This task is basically performed through

regional workshops and seminars and through assistance provided to regional human rights institutions.

470   The United Nations also uses the Voluntary Fund for Technical Cooperation in the Field of Human Rights to assist regional institutions which are involved in promoting and protecting human rights and are active in the field of education. For example, it directly supports the African Commission on Human and Peoples' Rights, the Arab Institute for Human Rights and the African Centre for Democracy and Human Rights Studies.

471   Since the United Nations continues to be geared towards a policy of long-term assistance to countries which are emerging from a crisis or which are undergoing a period of democratic transition, an increase in the number of long-term technical assistance projects in the field of human rights seems likely, as demonstrated by the policy of integrated country programmes adopted by the Centre. In order to meet the challenges posed by this development, the programme has in some cases begun to consolidate its presence in the field by setting up regional or national field offices. This is the context in which the overall technical assistance programme is being implemented, from the definition of needs to the execution of the various stages of projects and the compilation of reports on completed projects. The programme has established offices in Burundi, Cambodia, Guatemala, Malawi, Romania and Rwanda, and there are plans to set up other offices elsewhere.

The Role of the United Nations High Commissioner for Human Rights

472   More than 40 years after the idea of appointing a United Nations High Commissioner to deal with matters related to human rights was first raised, the 1993 World Conference on Human Rights recommended to the General Assembly that "when examining the report of the Conference at its forty-eighth session, it begin, as a matter of priority, consideration of the question of the establishment of a High Commissioner for Human Rights for the promotion and protection of all human rights" (The Vienna Declaration, section II, paragraph 18). In the autumn of 1993, the General Assembly reached consensus on the draft resolution providing for the creation of the post of United Nations High Commissioner for Human Rights (resolution 48/141 of 20 December 1993).[182]

182/Document 88
See page 471

473   In accordance with this resolution, the United Nations High Commissioner for Human Rights, holding the rank of Under-Secretary-General, is the United Nations official with principal responsibility for

United Nations human rights activities, under the direction and authority of the Secretary-General within the framework of the overall competence, authority and decisions of the General Assembly, the Economic and Social Council and the Commission on Human Rights. The High Commissioner must perform his duties in an impartial, objective, non-selective and effective manner and must be guided by the recognition that all human rights—civil, cultural, economic, political and social—are universal, indivisible, interdependent and interrelated.

474 Appointed by the Secretary-General, the High Commissioner, whose four-year term may be renewed once, must also have the confidence of the General Assembly, which must approve his appointment. His office is located in Geneva. On 14 February 1994, the General Assembly confirmed my decision to appoint Mr. José Ayala Lasso as the first United Nations High Commissioner for Human Rights. Mr. Ayala Lasso took office in Geneva on 5 April 1994.

475 The mandate of the High Commissioner was formulated so that the United Nations human rights machinery could respond to the new problematic situation given prominence in the Vienna Declaration and Programme of Action. It covers six broad areas, namely the promotion and protection of human rights throughout the world, the reinforcement of international cooperation in the field of human rights, the establishment of a dialogue with Governments with a view to ensuring respect for human rights, the coordination of efforts made in this area by the different United Nations organs, the adaptation of the United Nations machinery in this area to current and future needs and the supervision of the Centre for Human Rights.

476 Pursuant to his mandate and in the context of the Vienna Declaration and Programme of Action, the High Commissioner has oriented his activities towards the following areas: promotion of international cooperation in the field of human rights; reinforcement of all human rights; reaction to cases of serious human rights violations and prevention of human rights violations; provision of advisory services and technical assistance in the field of human rights, including assistance to nations in transition to democracy; coordination of activities related to human rights in the United Nations system; adaptation of the United Nations human rights machinery to current and future needs; promotion of the right to development and the enjoyment of cultural, economic and social rights; the fight against racial discrimination; promotion of the rights of persons belonging to particularly vulnerable groups, including women, children, minorities and indigenous peoples; the fight against particularly heinous human rights violations such as torture and enforced disappearances; promotion of education and public information programmes in the field of human rights; and implementation of the Vienna Declaration and Programme of Action.

477   The United Nations High Commissioner for Human Rights is responsible for the supervision of the Centre for Human Rights. The High Commissioner and the Centre, which is the principal Secretariat service for human rights issues, work together; the former sets policies and the latter implements them. The organization of the Centre must also be adapted to the new goals and functions defined first in the Vienna Declaration and Programme of Action and later in the General Assembly resolution which created the post of United Nations High Commissioner for Human Rights.

VI Towards new guarantees in the field of human rights

478   While continuing to intensify the standard-setting work in which it has been involved since the outset, the United Nations is at present taking new initiatives in order to better guarantee human rights and make their protection ever more effective. It is both in the operational sphere and in the jurisdictional sphere that the United Nations now wants to make innovations. Thus, at the operational level, since the end of the cold war the mandates of peace-keeping forces have increasingly included a "human rights" component. Among the 22 operations deployed since 1988, seven operations should be noted in which the concern for human rights occupies a particularly important place: the United Nations Transition Assistance Group (UNTAG) in Namibia; the United Nations Observer Mission in El Salvador (ONUSAL); the United Nations Transitional Authority in Cambodia (UNTAC); the United Nations Operation in Mozambique (ONUMOZ); the United Nations Protection Force (UNPROFOR) and the United Nations Confidence Restoration Operation in Croatia (UNCRO) in the former Yugoslavia; and the United Nations Mission for the Verification of Human Rights and of Compliance with the Commitments of the Comprehensive Agreement on Human Rights in Guatemala (MINUGUA). At the jurisdictional level, the International Law Commission adopted the final version of the draft statute for an international criminal court in 1994. Most noteworthy is the establishment of the international tribunals for the former Yugoslavia and for Rwanda, which were set up in 1993 and 1994, respectively, to prosecute persons responsible for war crimes and human rights violations.

New operational guarantees: human rights in peace-keeping operations

479   Initially, peace-keeping operations were simply observation or interposition missions. Progressively, these missions grew larger and became more diversified, particularly after the end of the cold war.

480   For several years, peace-keeping missions have been composed increasingly of civilian personnel, including police officers, whose task is to promote the reconstitution of society and of civilian institutions. Thus, in *An Agenda for Peace*, I stressed that in peace-keeping operations,

civilian political officers, human rights monitors, electoral officials, refugee and humanitarian aid specialists and police play as central a role as the military.

481   At the same time, it has become clear to the international community that there is an essential link between peace-keeping and human rights. The first paragraph of the preamble to the Universal Declaration of Human Rights acknowledges that recognition of the inalienable rights of all individuals is the foundation of freedom, justice and peace in the world. According to the second paragraph of the preamble to the Universal Declaration of Human Rights, "disregard and contempt for human rights have resulted in barbarous acts which have outraged the conscience of mankind". The third paragraph of the preamble states that "it is essential, if man is not to be compelled to have recourse, as a last resort, to rebellion against tyranny and oppression, that human rights should be protected by the rule of law". In my 1994 annual report on the work of the Organization, I stressed that "poverty, human rights abuses and underdevelopment are critical factors contributing to the breakdown of societies and the outbreak of violence".

482   Under these conditions, the concept of peace, in the global sense of the term, is closely linked with respect for human rights, and any process whose goal is one of peace-keeping must take into account the human rights situation and aim to ensure the effective promotion and protection of those rights. Today, more than ever before, human rights are an essential component of peace-keeping operations. The United Nations established 13 peace-keeping operations between 1948 and 1987, and 22 between 1988 and 1994. With respect to the seven operations which include an essential human rights component (UNTAG in Namibia, ONUSAL in El Salvador, UNTAC in Cambodia, ONUMOZ in Mozambique, UNPROFOR and UNCRO in the former Yugoslavia and MINUGUA in Guatemala), each mandate is different and is designed to take into account the specific characteristics of each situation. Even so, three major fields of action in the area of human rights can be identified: contribution to respect for human rights, technical assistance and protection of the rights of displaced persons and refugees.

Contribution to respect for human rights

Respect for international human rights standards

483   In El Salvador, the first significant agreement in the negotiating process was achieved on 26 July 1990, when the Government and the Frente Farabundo Martí para la Liberación Nacional (FMLN) signed the San José Agreement on Human Rights. The parties undertook to respect international laws and standards in the field of human rights and called upon the United Nations to play an essential role in verifying that

undertaking. The powers accorded to the United Nations Verification Mission made it possible to undertake systematic action to promote human rights. This was also a decisive element in the Salvadorian Legislative Assembly's recognition, on 30 March 1995, of the jurisdiction of the Inter-American Court of Human Rights, and its ratification of the main international instruments, whose adoption had been recommended by the Commission on the Truth, namely, the Optional Protocol to the International Covenant on Civil and Political Rights and the Additional Protocol to the American Convention on Human Rights in the area of economic, social and cultural rights.

484   In Cambodia, the human rights component of UNTAC encouraged the Supreme National Council (SNC) to accede to the applicable international human rights instruments and to undertake a study of the provisions of existing judicial and criminal regimes. On 20 April 1992, the SNC ratified the International Covenant on Civil and Political Rights and the International Covenant on Economic, Social and Cultural Rights. On 10 September, it decided to accede to the Convention against Torture and Other Cruel, Inhuman or Degrading Treatment or Punishment, the Convention on the Elimination of All Forms of Discrimination against Women, the Convention on the Rights of the Child and the Convention and Protocol relating to the Status of Refugees.

485   In the context of the conflict in the former Yugoslavia, the Security Council has repeatedly stressed that the parties involved must respect the human rights conventions. Thus, in its resolution 941 (1994) of 23 September 1994,[183] the Security Council emphasized that "ethnic cleansing" constituted a violation of international humanitarian law and reaffirmed that all parties to the conflict were bound to comply with the Geneva Conventions of 12 August 1949.

183/Document 93
See page 488

486   In one instance, even before the establishment by the Security Council of a peace-keeping mission—the United Nations Mission in Haiti (UNMIH) —the General Assembly, in its resolution 47/20 B of 20 April 1993,[184] authorized United Nations participation in the International Civilian Mission to Haiti (MICIVIH), jointly with the Organization of American States. The mandate of MICIVIH is to verify respect for human rights as set forth in the Haitian Constitution and in the international instruments to which Haiti is a party, in particular, the International Covenant on Civil and Political Rights and the American Convention on Human Rights.

184/Document 81
See page 417

Monitoring of the police

487   In Namibia, one of the main tasks of the United Nations Transition Assistance Group (UNTAG) was to monitor the activities of the South West Africa Police (SWAPOL) and other security forces under

the command of the South African Administrator-General. In this regard, the United Nations Plan for the Independence of Namibia made possible the deployment of United Nations civilian police forces (CIVPOL) in the territory of Namibia. In the elections of November 1989, about 1,500 members of CIVPOL from 26 countries were deployed in Namibia. Their mission consisted mainly of patrolling the towns and rural areas and investigating human rights violations perpetrated by SWAPOL or by the counter-terrorism unit in the territory.

488   In Mozambique, it was proposed in December 1992 that a force consisting of police officers should form part of the United Nations Operation in Mozambique (ONUMOZ). In September 1993, after lengthy negotiations, the Government and the Resistência Nacional Moçambicana (RENAMO) agreed to request the United Nations to monitor all police activities in Mozambique. The first civilian police (CIVPOL) observers were deployed at Maputo and in the provincial capitals in the following month. The mandate of CIVPOL was, in particular, to ensure the neutrality of the Mozambican police.

489   In Croatia, UNPROFOR was deployed in certain United Nations Protected Areas (UNPAs) in which the Security Council deemed it necessary to establish special interim arrangements designed to ensure that a lasting cease-fire be maintained and that these areas remain demilitarized, and to monitor the activities of the local police in them in order to guarantee non-discrimination and the protection of human rights.

Investigation of human rights violations

490   The initial mandate of the United Nations Observer Mission in El Salvador (ONUSAL), established on 20 May 1991 by Security Council resolution 693 (1991),[185] was to verify the compliance by the parties with the Agreement on Human Rights signed at San José. The task of ONUSAL was to register objectively all information relating to human rights violations and also to use its good offices to put an end to human rights violations. Responsibility for those tasks passed to the Human Rights Division when, after the signing of the Chapultepec Peace Agreement on 16 January 1992, the mandate of ONUSAL was enlarged to allow for a multi-functional peace-keeping operation.

185/Document 72
See page 402

491   In Cambodia, UNTAC investigated complaints of human rights violations, deciding to take corrective measures as needed.

492   In Mozambique, the CIVPOL personnel verified complaints of violations of political and human rights, including those committed against the Mozambican police forces and the other State security forces. By December 1994, CIVPOL had investigated 511 complaints, including 61 relating to human rights violations. These duly documented complaints

were transmitted to the Mozambican police so that it could take disciplinary or preventive measures.

493 In Haiti, MICIVIH has the objective of devoting special attention to the observance of the right to life, to the integrity and security of the person, to personal liberty, to freedom of expression and to freedom of association. Its mandate provides that it is entitled to receive communications relating to alleged human rights violations. MICIVIH therefore registered complaints concerning human rights.

494 In Guatemala, the Comprehensive Agreement on Human Rights, signed by the parties on 29 March 1994, stipulates that MINUGUA should receive, consider and follow up complaints of possible human rights violations and establish whether the competent national institutions have carried out the necessary investigations autonomously, effectively and in accordance with Guatemalan and international human rights norms. The Mission is also asked to determine whether the armed confrontation has given rise to human rights violations.[186]

186/Document 92
See page 487

495 The United Nations Mission for the Verification of Human Rights and of Compliance with the Commitments of the Comprehensive Agreement on Human Rights in Guatemala (MINUGUA), which employs 245 people located in eight regional offices and five subregional offices, represents a significant effort by the United Nations to monitor and strengthen human rights institutions. To date, this has been the most tangible outcome of the negotiations between the Government of Guatemala and the Unidad Revolucionaria Nacional Guatemalteca (URNG). The first report of the Director of MINUGUA (A/49/856) was prepared following the first three months of the Mission's operation. During that period, the Mission registered about 1,000 complaints, of which 288 were received for verification.

187/Document 90
See page 475

496 In the case of Rwanda, the Security Council, in its resolution 935 (1994)[187] of 1 July 1994, requested the Secretary-General to establish an impartial Commission of Experts to investigate violations of human rights committed after 6 April 1994. The mandate of the Commission, established in late July 1994, is to obtain and analyse information and to provide conclusions regarding actual human rights violations, including the occurrence of acts of genocide.

Technical assistance

Elections and human rights

497 In Namibia, the civilian police played an important role in the organization of elections and in ensuring that they were free and fair.

498 In the case of Cambodia, the Agreement on a Comprehensive Political Settlement of the Cambodia Conflict, signed in Paris on

23 October 1991, entrusted the United Nations Transitional Authority in Cambodia (UNTAC) with promoting a climate that would ensure respect for human rights and fundamental freedoms and the holding of free and fair elections during the period of transition.

499   In Mozambique, it was also agreed that the codes of conduct for political activities, especially the electoral process, should be verified in order to protect the fundamental freedoms of individuals and those of political groups and organizations during electoral campaigns. In that regard, the Security Council, in its resolution 898 (1994) of 23 February 1994[188] authorized the establishment of a police component as an integral part of the United Nations Operation in Mozambique (ONUMOZ) to carry out those functions.

188/Document 89
See page 473

Education in the field of human rights

500   The human rights component of UNTAC organized a widespread campaign to raise awareness about human rights in Cambodia. After elections were held in the spring of 1993, the United Nations continued to provide assistance to Cambodia in the field of human rights. During that same period, the Centre for Human Rights opened an office in Cambodia with a mandate to provide technical and educational assistance in human rights issues.

501   In Mozambique, with the assistance of the Centre for Human Rights, members of the civilian police benefited from a training course in human rights issues, the first of its kind to be provided by the United Nations to a police force. Training courses were also given to local police to familiarize them with international concepts of rights, civil liberties and fundamental freedoms and with the codes of conduct that the parties had agreed to follow during the electoral process.

502   In Haiti, MICIVIH made a series of recommendations to the Haitian authorities regarding the introduction of programmes in civic studies.

Strengthening of national human rights institutions

503   In El Salvador, the establishment of the Commission on the Truth was a significant event that set an important precedent. It was composed of three individuals appointed by the Secretary-General, and its task was to investigate serious acts of violence that occurred since 1980. The Commission, which began its work on 13 July 1992, received more than 22,000 complaints of "acts of violence". On 15 March 1993, the Commission published a report, entitled *From madness to hope: the 12-year war in El Salvador* (S/25500), which indicated that 95 per cent of all acts of violence were committed by members of the armed forces, security forces and death squads, while the Frente Farabundo Martí para

la Liberación Nacional (FMLN) was responsible for 5 per cent of all acts of violence. Moreover, in reports published during the latter part of the United Nations Observer Mission in El Salvador (ONUSAL), the ONUSAL Human Rights Division repeatedly stressed that impunity was a main cause of human rights violations. Therefore, and in preparation for the withdrawal of ONUSAL, the Division worked to consolidate the various institutions that had been entrusted with defending and protecting human rights. Specifically, it directed these efforts at the office of the national council for the defence of human rights. ONUSAL departed from the country on 30 April 1995, leaving the Office of Political Affairs of the United Nations Mission in El Salvador (MINUSAL) to carry out the functions of verification and good offices, in accordance with decisions adopted by the Security Council upon my recommendations. The result is that the population and institutions of El Salvador are now responsible for monitoring and guaranteeing respect for human rights, while technical assistance is being provided by the United Nations Centre for Human Rights.

504   In Cambodia, UNTAC, as part of its efforts to promote the establishment of an independent judiciary, introduced an important training programme for judges and lawyers. Training programmes for civil servants in existing administrative structures and for members of occupational associations or activist groups were set up in nearly all provinces.

505   In Haiti, MICIVIH also contributed to the strengthening of human rights institutions, in particular in cooperation with the National Commission for Truth and Justice. Moreover, MICIVIH continued to cooperate with the police component of the United Nations Mission in Haiti (UNMIH). In addition to the efforts of MICIVIH and UNMIH, an independent expert in human rights matters, working within the Commission on Human Rights, will soon provide advice and technical assistance to the Haitian Government.

506   In Guatemala, the mission of MINUGUA is to strengthen national governmental and non-governmental human rights agencies. MINUGUA also verifies compliance with commitments regarding illegal security forces and secret organizations, regulations for carrying weapons and the elimination of conscription. In general, the Mission's first conclusions indicate that impunity is a major obstacle to respect for human rights in Guatemala. Under the circumstances, the Mission recommended more governmental control over the security forces.

Re-establishment of the rights of displaced persons and refugees

507 In Namibia, the plan for independence contained provisions for the appointment of an independent judge to settle disputes that might arise with regard to political prisoners. Discriminatory and restrictive laws were also removed and full and unconditional amnesty was given to Namibian exiles. The United Nations Transition Assistance Group (UNTAG) played an essential role in these areas as part of its overall responsibilities to ensure the implementation of the plan for independence.

508 In the territory of the former Yugoslavia, the mandate of UNPROFOR is also to facilitate the return of civilians who were deported from their homes in UNPAs.

New jurisdictional guarantees: special tribunals

509 Faced with a situation characterized by widespread violations of international humanitarian law occurring within the territory of the former Yugoslavia, including the existence of concentration camps and the continuance of the practice of "ethnic cleansing", the Security Council adopted a series of resolutions[189] requesting that all parties concerned in the conflict comply with the obligations under international humanitarian law, in particular the Geneva Conventions, and desist from all breaches of international humanitarian law. The Council reaffirmed the principle of individual criminal responsibility of persons who commit or order the commission of grave breaches of the Geneva Conventions or other breaches of international humanitarian law.

510 In its resolution 808 (1993) of 22 February 1993,[190] the Security Council decided that an international tribunal would be established for the prosecution of persons responsible for serious violations of international humanitarian law committed in the territory of the former Yugoslavia since 1991 and requested the Secretary-General to prepare a report on this matter.[191] The report of the Secretary-General containing the statute of the International Tribunal was submitted to the Security Council, which, acting under Chapter VII of the Charter of the United Nations, adopted it in its resolution 827 (1993) of 25 May 1993.[192]

511 When it specified the competence *ratione materiae* of the International Tribunal, the Security Council was aware that because it was not a legislative body, it could not legislate or claim to establish a new international law to be imposed on the parties concerned in the conflict. Therefore, it limited the right of the International Tribunal to apply rules of international humanitarian law which are irrefutably part of customary international law, independent of their codification in any

189/Document 73
See page 403;
Document 74
See page 403;
Document 75
See page 407;
Document 76
See page 407;
Document 77
See page 410

190/Document 80
See page 416

191/Document 82
See page 418

192/Document 83
See page 440

international instrument, in order to avoid the problem of whether or not the relevant State or States had acceded to such instruments or had introduced them into their domestic legislation. It also limited violations of international humanitarian law which are unequivocally part of customary international law to those acts which normally involved individual criminal responsibility; under articles 2 to 5 of the statute, these include grave breaches of the Geneva Conventions, violations of the laws or customs of war, the crime of genocide and crimes against humanity.

512 It must be pointed out that the practice of so-called "ethnic cleansing", one of the crimes that is most frequently mentioned in relation to the conflict in the former Yugoslavia, is not specifically named in the statute of the International Tribunal. "Ethnic cleansing", a new name for an old crime, is a serious violation relating to the "deportation" or illegal transfer of a civilian or the "deportation" of civilian populations under article 5 of the statute. In so far as "ethnic cleansing" includes murder, extermination, rape and so on, it pertains to the crimes in question, which are qualified as war crimes or crimes against humanity.

513 By limiting the competence *ratione materiae* of the International Tribunal, the Security Council reaffirmed the well-established principle of individual criminal responsibility for serious violations of international humanitarian law. Under article 7 of the statute, the principle of individual criminal responsibility applies to all persons who participate, from the one who made the decision down to the soldiers themselves and to paramilitary forces and civilians. A person who planned, instigated, ordered or committed a crime within the jurisdiction of the International Tribunal is individually criminally responsible, either as the perpetrator of, or as an accomplice to, the crime.

514 Article 7 of the statute excludes so-called "head of State" immunity and specifies that obedience to the order of a superior does not relieve an accused person of his "criminal responsibility", but may be considered "in mitigation of punishment". The statute considers a superior as criminally responsible for the acts committed by a subordinate, reflecting the principle of "hierarchical responsibility" in customary international law that developed following the Second World War.

193/Document 83
See page 440

515 In 1993, the Security Council adopted resolution 827 (1993)[193] on the establishment of an international tribunal for the former Yugoslavia. Eighteen months later, in a similar situation in Rwanda characterized by systematic and widespread violations of international humanitarian law, including the unpunished massacre of tens of thousands of civilians, the Security Council adopted resolution

194/Document 94
See page 489

955 (1994).[194] In this resolution, it decided "to establish an international tribunal for the sole purpose of prosecuting persons responsible for genocide and other serious violations of international humanitarian law committed in the territory of Rwanda and Rwandan citizens responsible

for genocide and other such violations committed in the territory of neighbouring States".

516   When it was decided to establish a tribunal for Rwanda, the fact that the International Tribunal for the former Yugoslavia already existed made it possible to use a similar legal approach. The statute of the International Tribunal for Rwanda, which was drafted by members of the Security Council, was essentially an adaptation of the statute of the International Tribunal for the former Yugoslavia.

517   However, unlike the conflict in the territory of the former Yugoslavia, which had elements of both international and internal conflicts, the conflict in Rwanda is internal in character. Given the nature of the conflict in Rwanda, only those violations of internal humanitarian law that could be committed as part of international armed conflicts were considered to fall within the competence of the International Tribunal for Rwanda. Thus, articles 2 to 4 of the statute of the International Tribunal for Rwanda mention the crime of genocide, which may be committed in times of peace and in times of war, crimes against humanity, which may be committed in armed international conflicts as well as in internal conflicts, and violations of article 3 common to the four Geneva Conventions and of Additional Protocol II, as they are more fully enumerated in article 4 of the Additional Protocol II of 8 June 1977[195] to the Geneva Conventions which applies to armed conflicts of an internal nature.

195/Document 43
See page 269

518   Like the statute of the International Tribunal for the former Yugoslavia, the statute of the International Tribunal for Rwanda excludes the death sentence from the list of penalties. However, unlike the former Yugoslavia, where most of the republics have abolished capital punishment, Rwanda still applies the death sentence. It was due in part to the fact that the death penalty had been excluded from the list of penalties which could be pronounced by the Tribunal that the Government of Rwanda voted against Security Council resolution 955 (1994), despite having initially requested the creation of an international tribunal. The Government of Rwanda felt that the exclusion of the death penalty from the list of sentences that could be passed by the International Tribunal, when it still existed in the country's domestic legislation, could give rise to a situation in which leaders would be judged by the International Tribunal for having planned and organized the crime of genocide and would be sentenced to life imprisonment, whereas thousands of ordinary civilians, most of whom had been manipulated by their leaders, would be subject to the death penalty. Indeed, that dilemma has still not been resolved.

VII   Conclusion

519   On the occasion of the celebration this year of the fiftieth anniversary of the United Nations, it seems useful and timely to ponder the ways that the protection of human rights worldwide might be assured at the dawn of the twenty-first century. Admittedly, more than any other component of international law and policy, human rights are highly dependent on variables whose nature and scope are extremely difficult to define at any given point in time. The state of international society, the changes which it will undergo and the frictions or even divisions that will occur a few decades hence are all issues which we cannot readily foresee. Nevertheless, based on the experience acquired since the Organization was established, we can present a general picture of what the major trends in the universal protection of human rights will be in the next century.

520   We are not suggesting that the failures and difficulties which have been and continue to be experienced should be ignored. On the contrary, they should be included in a comprehensive debate on this subject. In the preceding chapters, it was essential to try to give an overview, however incomplete, of how the protection of human rights has evolved at the global level during the last 50 years in order to be able to put forward some fundamental ideas on how it will continue to evolve over the next few decades.

521   In this regard, it should be noted that while over the last 50 years the emerging international community has permitted the establishment of a carefully developed, intricate and substantial mechanism for the protection and promotion of human rights, the resulting overlaps and inconsistencies have made the current system for the protection of those rights less than transparent. It must also be recognized that there are many factors which make it difficult to have a clear interpretation of these mechanisms and which prevent them from being fully effective. Rapporteurs and special representatives for individual countries coexist with thematic procedures, advisory-service programmes and work carried out by treaty bodies.

522   Similarly, it appears that consideration will have to be given at some point to harmonizing the various human rights conventions as a necessary corollary to the streamlining of the treaty-monitoring bodies.[196] Under the current treaty-monitoring system, the main responsibility of States parties to individual treaties is to submit periodic reports at regular intervals to several committees outlining what steps they have taken to implement the rights protected by the various instruments.

196/Document 99
See page 509

However, many of the subjects dealt with are similar in nature, since a number of the relevant conventions were designed to elaborate on obligations already provided for under the International Covenants on Human Rights. Since each monitoring body has its own procedures for reviewing these reports, recalling where necessary the specific nature of the relevant instrument, one of the direct consequences of such burdensome obligations on Governments is the extremely high rate of delinquency in the submission of reports. There is also a loss of interest on the part of human rights advocacy groups, not to mention the public at large, in the very useful work done by the committees. Moreover, even some States have considerable difficulties in understanding the precise purpose of the treaty-monitoring mechanism. Lastly, the sheer number of procedures, in addition to the fact that it takes a relatively long time to implement them, serve to heighten the sense of confusion of victims and all those who support them in their attempts to secure respect for their rights.

523   It therefore seems appropriate to consider the possibility of reforming the entire international human rights treaty-monitoring system. The aim of such reform would be to streamline procedures and reduce the number of monitoring bodies. As a first step, States should be allowed to submit a comprehensive report covering all the treaties to which they are parties. Such an approach would in no way endanger the principle of the specific nature of individual conventions, since each report would have to contain a separate section on each convention to which the submitting State was a party; each section would deal with the rights and freedoms provided for in the relevant convention. This would make it easier for the reporting State to refer, where certain individual rights are concerned, to comments made in other parts of the report. For example, a State party to both the International Covenant on Civil and Political Rights and the Convention against Torture and Other Cruel, Inhuman or Degrading Treatment or Punishment could, in reporting on its application of article 7 of the Covenant, refer to developments presented under the heading of the Convention.

524   Thus, the State party's reporting obligations would be considerably simplified. Those States parties to all the above-mentioned instruments would submit a single report instead of the five or six reports presently required. While the amount of information to be included would undoubtedly be substantial, the procedure would be carried out only once and, since the report would be submitted once every four or five years, there would be more than enough time to prepare it. This would also facilitate the establishment of interministerial committees responsible for drafting government reports. Similarly, such comprehensive reports would highlight the complementarity between conventions, thereby serving as a powerful incentive for States to accede to those treaties to which they are not yet parties.

525   In addition to such reform, consideration might be given to instituting by the turn of the century a single review procedure for international human rights instruments. As the sole interlocutor with semi-permanent status, the technical body entrusted with the monitoring of treaties would have a dual mandate of considering not only reports submitted by States parties but also complaints filed by individuals. It would become the alter ego of the Commission on Human Rights and would benefit from having a technical, systematic, comprehensive and global approach to the situation of human rights.

526   In the medium term, such reforms would require a review of certain technical provisions of the human rights conventions.

527   Parallel with this debate on the overall reform of mechanisms for monitoring the implementation of international treaties and stream-lining treaty procedures, it would also seem useful to consider possible ways of improving the work done by and on behalf of the Commission on Human Rights. This debate outside the purview of the conventions is all the more thought-provoking since the Commission is the framework within which the international community puts in place the different structures and mechanisms under consideration. The Commission necessarily reflects the inconsistencies and difficulties encountered by the international community.

528   A number of improvements can be contemplated. There is no doubt that the work of the Commission and consequently that of the rapporteurs, special representatives and working groups must be streamlined. Such an exercise involves a number of improvements which we can attempt to outline. The dialogue between the community of non-governmental organizations and Governments could be given a substance and form more in consonance with the ideal which underlies this fruitful partnership. Similarly, the procedure whereby the Commission considers the work of experts responsible for preparing reports on individual countries or specific topics could be reviewed and improved.

529   The Commission, as the main political body of the new system for the protection of human rights at the global level, could also stream-line its work by making it more flexible and introducing increased transparency into its deliberations. Ultimately, the plenary sessions should be shorter and less cumbersome. In between plenary sessions, special sessions or meetings of an inter-sessional body with the power to act in case of emergency would make it easier to keep in touch with the reality of human rights violations in the world.

530   The sometimes highly politicized and arcane discussions could give way to more attractive meetings of sessional working groups, plenary sessions being reserved for official statements and the formal adoption of the deliberations of subsidiary bodies. The role of rapporteurs and special representatives as well as that of non-governmental organizations might be reviewed in such subsidiary bodies.

531   Moreover, the rapporteurs and special representatives, as well as the working groups, should continue to harmonize their methods of work in order to enable them to carry out to the best of their abilities the burdensome tasks flowing from the mandates given by the Commission. Thus, they would also enhance considerably their preventive action in the defence of human rights in coordination with the United Nations High Commissioner for Human Rights.

532   Lastly, human rights activities and those undertaken within the framework of the advisory services programme should be strengthened within the context of the relevant policy guidelines established by the World Conference on Human Rights and as part of a comprehensive approach to technical assistance in the field of human rights, incorporating the technical assistance recommendations made by treaty bodies, rapporteurs, United Nations bodies and agencies, development institutions and regional international organizations under the overall guidance of the United Nations High Commissioner for Human Rights.

533   I believe that it is in this way that the international community will continue to give the most effective service to the cause of human rights throughout the world. We have entered a new period of history, but the post-cold-war period has not given rise to the new political order of which some had dreamed, no doubt prematurely. The fight for human rights remains, more than ever before, a top priority for the international community. The United Nations must continue to mobilize its efforts, so that human rights may one day emerge at last as the common language of humanity.

BOUTROS BOUTROS-GHALI

Section Two
Chronology and Documents

I   Chronology of events

26 June 1945
Signing of the Charter of the United Nations and Statute of the International Court of Justice, in San Francisco.
See Document 1, page 143

21 June 1946
Establishment of the Commission on Human Rights under Economic and Social Council resolution 9 (II). At its first session, in 1947, the Commission establishes the Subcommission on Prevention of Discrimination and Protection of Minorities on the basis of that resolution.
See Document 2, page 146

21 June 1946
Establishment of the Commission on the Status of Women under resolution 11 (II) of the Economic and Social Council.
See Document 3, page 147

9 December 1948
Adoption by the General Assembly of the Convention on the Prevention and Punishment of the Crime of Genocide.
See Document 7, page 151

10 December 1948
Adoption by the General Assembly of the Universal Declaration of Human Rights.
See Document 8, page 153

2 December 1949
Adoption by the General Assembly of the Convention for the Suppression of the Traffic in Persons and of the Exploitation of the Prostitution of Others.

4 November 1950
Adoption by the members of the Council of Europe of the Convention for the Protection of Human Rights and Fundamental Freedoms (European Convention on Human Rights).
See Document 10, page 156

1 December 1950
Creation of the Committee on Crime Prevention and Control under General Assembly resolution 415 (V). The Committee is responsible for preparing the United Nations Congresses on the Prevention of Crime and the Treatment of Offenders. It is institutionalized in the

form of the Commission on Crime Prevention and Criminal Justice by the Economic and Social Council on 6 February 1992.

28 July 1951
Adoption by a United Nations Conference of Plenipotentiaries of the Convention relating to the Status of Refugees.
See Document 12, page 172

20 December 1952
Adoption by the General Assembly of the Convention on the Political Rights of Women.
See Document 13, page 180

23 October 1953
Adoption by the General Assembly of the Protocol amending the Slavery Convention signed at Geneva on 25 September 1926.

28 September 1954
Adoption by a Conference of Plenipotentiaries of the Convention relating to the Status of Stateless Persons.
See Document 14, page 181

30 August 1955
Adoption by the First United Nations Congress on the Prevention of Crime and the Treatment of Offenders of the Standard Minimum Rules for the Treatment of Prisoners.
See Document 15, page 187

7 September 1956
Adoption by a Conference of Plenipotentiaries of the Supplementary Convention on the Abolition of Slavery, the Slave Trade, and Institutions and Practices Similar to Slavery.
See Document 18, page. 198

29 January 1957
Adoption by the General Assembly of the Convention on the Nationality of Married Women.
See Document 19, page. 202

25 June 1957
Adoption by the General Conference of the International Labour Organization of the Convention on the Abolition of Forced Labour.

30 July 1959
Adoption by the Economic and Social Council of resolution 728 F (XXVIII), giving the Commission on Human Rights certain responsibilities with regard to the treatment of communications dealing with human rights.
See Document 20, page 204

20 November 1959
Adoption by the General Assembly of the Declaration of the Rights of the Child.

14 December 1960
Adoption by the General Assembly of the Declaration on the Granting of Independence to Colonial Countries and Peoples.
See Document 21, page 205

30 August 1961
Adoption by a Conference of Plenipotentiaries of the Convention on the Reduction of Statelessness.
See Document 22, page 206

7 November 1962
Adoption by the General Assembly of the Convention on Consent to Marriage, Minimum Age for Marriage and Registration of Marriages.
See Document 23, page 210

14 December 1962
Adoption by the General Assembly of resolution 1803 (XVII) on permanent sovereignty over natural resources.
See Document 24, page 211

20 November 1963
Adoption by the General Assembly of the United Nations Declaration on the Elimination of All Forms of Racial Discrimination.

21 December 1965
Adoption by the General Assembly of the International Convention on the Elimination of All Forms of Racial Discrimination. This Convention provides for the establishment of the Committee on the Elimination of Racial Discrimination.
See Document 27, page 219

16 December 1966
Adoption by the General Assembly of the International Covenant on Economic, Social and Cultural Rights. Adoption of the International Covenant on Civil and Political Rights and of the corresponding Optional Protocol. This Covenant provides for the establishment of the Human Rights Committee.
See Document 31, page 229; Document 32, page 235; and Document 33, page 244

6 June 1967
Adoption by the Economic and Social Council of resolution 1235 (XLII), authorizing the Commission on Human Rights and the Subcommission on Prevention of Discrimination and Protection of Minorities to examine information relevant to gross violations of human rights and fundamental freedoms.
See Document 34, page 246

7 November 1967
Adoption by the General Assembly of the Declaration on the Elimination of Discrimination against Women.

13 May 1968
Proclamation by the International Conference on Human Rights of the Proclamation of Teheran.
See Document 35, page 247

26 November 1968
Adoption by the General Assembly of the Convention on the Non-Applicability of Statutory Limitations to War Crimes and Crimes against Humanity.

22 November 1969
Adoption of the American Convention on Human Rights.
See Document 36, page 248

11 December 1969
Adoption by the General Assembly of the Declaration on Social Progress and Development.

27 May 1970
Adoption by the Economic and Social Council of resolution 1503 (XLVIII), establishing procedures allowing the Commission on Human Rights and the Subcommission on Prevention of Discrimination and Protection of Minorities to hold private meetings to consider communications relating to violations of human rights and fundamental freedoms.
See Document 38, page 262

13 August 1971
Adoption by the Subcommission on Prevention of Discrimination and Protection of Minorities of resolution 1 (XXIV), concerning procedures for the implementation of Economic and Social Council resolution 1503 (XLVIII).
See Document 39, page 263

30 November 1973
Adoption by the General Assembly of the International Convention on the Suppression and Punishment of the Crime of Apartheid. The Convention provides for the establishment of the Group of Three, which is to monitor its implementation.
See Document 40, page 264

9 December 1975
Adoption by the General Assembly of the Declaration on the Protection of All Persons from Being Subjected to Torture and Other Cruel, Inhuman or Degrading Treatment or Punishment.

8 June 1977
Adoption by the Diplomatic Conference on the Reaffirmation and Development of International Humanitarian Law applicable in Armed Conflicts of the Protocol Additional to the Geneva Conventions of 12 August 1949, and relating to the Protection of Victims of Non-International Armed Conflicts (Protocol II).
See Document 43, page 269

27 November 1978
Adoption by the General Conference of UNESCO of the Declaration on Race and Racial Prejudice.

17 December 1979
Adoption by the General Assembly of the Code of Conduct for Law Enforcement Officials.
See Document 44, page 274

18 December 1979
Adoption by the General Assembly of the Convention on the Elimination of All Forms of Discrimination against Women. The Convention provides for the establishment of the Committee on the Elimination of Discrimination against Women.
See Document 45, page 277

June 1981
Adoption of the African Charter on Human and Peoples' Rights, by the Eighteenth Conference of Heads of State and Government of the Organization of African Unity.
See Document 47, page 284

25 November 1981
Adoption by the General Assembly of the Declaration on the Elimination of All Forms of Intolerance and of Discrimination Based on Religion or Belief.
See Document 48, page 291

25 May 1984
Approval by the Economic and Social Council of the Safeguards guaranteeing protection of the rights of those facing the death penalty.
See Document 49, page 293

12 November 1984
Adoption by the General Assembly of the Declaration on the Right of Peoples to Peace.

10 December 1984
Adoption by the General Assembly of the Convention against Torture and Other Cruel, Inhuman or Degrading Treatment or Punishment. The Convention provides for the establishment of the Committee against Torture.
See Document 50, page 294

28 May 1985
Adoption by the Economic and Social Council of resolution 1985/17 establishing the Committee on Economic, Social and Cultural Rights, responsible for monitoring the implementation of the International Covenant on Economic, Social and Cultural Rights.

29 November 1985
Adoption by the General Assembly of the United Nations Standard Minimum Rules for the Administration of Juvenile Justice (The Beijing Rules).
See Document 51, page 300

29 November 1985
Adoption by the General Assembly of the Declaration of Basic Principles of Justice for Victims of Crime and Abuse of Power.
See Document 52, page 312

29 November 1985
Adoption by the Seventh United Nations Congress on the Prevention of Crime and the Treatment of Offenders of the Basic Principles on the Independence of the Judiciary.
See Document 53, page 313

10 December 1985
Adoption by the General Assembly of the International Convention against Apartheid in Sports. The Convention provides for the establishment of the Commission against Apartheid in Sports.
See Document 54, page 315

13 December 1985
Adoption by the General Assembly of a resolution on the implementation of the Nairobi Forward-looking Strategies for the Advancement of Women.
See Document 55, page 319

4 December 1986
Adoption by the General Assembly of the Declaration on the Right to Development.
See Document 56, page 322

9 December 1988
Adoption by the General Assembly of the Body of Principles for the Protection of All Persons under Any Form of Detention or Imprisonment.
See Document 58, page 327

24 May 1989
Adoption by the Economic and Social Council of the Principles on the Effective Prevention and Investigation of Extra-legal, Arbitrary and Summary Executions.
See Document 59, page 332

20 November 1989
Adoption by the General Assembly of the Convention on the Rights of the Child. The Convention provides for the establishment of the Committee on the Rights of the Child.
See Document 60, page 334

15 December 1989
Adoption by the General Assembly of the Second Optional Protocol to the International Covenant on Civil and Political Rights, aiming at the abolition of the death penalty. The Human Rights Committee is the monitoring body for the Protocol.
See Document 61, page 344

7 September 1990
Adoption by the Eighth United Nations Congress on the Prevention of Crime and the Treatment of Offenders of the Basic Principles on the Use of Force and Firearms by Law Enforcement Officials.
See Document 62, page 346

7 September 1990
Adoption by the Eighth United Nations Congress on the Prevention of Crime and the Treatment of Offenders of the Basic Principles on the Role of Lawyers.
See Document 63, page 348

7 September 1990
Adoption by the Eighth United Nations Congress on the Prevention of Crime and the Treatment of Offenders of the Guidelines on the Role of Prosecutors.
See Document 64, page 351

30 September 1990
Adoption by the World Summit for Children of the World Declaration on the Survival, Protection and Development of Children and of the Plan of Action for Implementing the World Declaration.
See Document 65, page 354

14 December 1990
Adoption by the General Assembly of the United Nations Standard Minimum Rules for Non-custodial Measures (The Tokyo Rules); Basic Principles for the Treatment of Prisoners; the United Nations Guidelines for the Prevention of Juvenile Delinquency (The Riyadh

Guidelines) and the United Nations Rules for the Protection of Juveniles Deprived of their Liberty.
See Document 66, p. 364; Document 67, p. 368; Document 68, p. 369; and Document 69, page 374

18 December 1990
Adoption by the General Assembly of a resolution deciding to convene a World Conference on Human Rights in 1993.
See Document 70, page 381

18 December 1990
Adoption by the General Assembly of the International Convention on the Protection of the Rights of All Migrant Workers and Members of Their Families. The Convention provides for the establishment of the Committee on the Protection of the Rights of All Migrant Workers and Members of Their Families.
See Document 71, page 383

20 May 1991
Adoption by the Security Council of a resolution establishing the United Nations Observer Mission in El Salvador (ONUSAL).
See Document 72, page 402

7 April 1992
Adoption by the Security Council of a resolution deciding to deploy the United Nations Protection Force (UNPROFOR) in the former Yugoslavia.
See Document 73, page 403

30 May 1992
Adoption by the Security Council of a resolution demanding that the parties to the conflict in Bosnia and Herzegovina allow the unimpeded delivery of humanitarian supplies.
See Document 74, page 403

14 September 1992
Adoption by the Security Council of a resolution authorizing the enlargement of the mandate of UNPROFOR.
See Document 75, page 407

16 November 1992
Adoption by the Security Council of a resolution condemning "ethnic cleansing" in Bosnia and Herzegovina.
See Document 76, page 407

18 December 1992
Adoption by the Security Council of a resolution demanding that the detention camps in Bosnia and Herzegovina should be closed.
See Document 77, page 410

18 December 1992
Adoption by the General Assembly of the Declaration on the Protection of All Persons from Enforced Disappearance.
See Document 78, page 410

18 December 1992
Adoption by the General Assembly of the Declaration on the Rights of Persons Belonging to National or Ethnic, Religious and Linguistic Minorities.
See Document 79, page 414

22 February 1993
Adoption by the Security Council of a resolution establishing an International Tribunal for the prosecution of persons responsible for serious violations of international humanitarian law committed in the territory of the former Yugoslavia since 1991.
See Document 80, page 416

20 April 1993
Adoption by the General Assembly of a resolution authorizing the participation of the United Nations jointly with the Organization of American States in an International Civilian Mission to Haiti (MICIVIH).
See Document 81, page 417

25 May 1993
Adoption by the Security Council of a resolution adopting the statute of the International Tribunal for the Prosecution of Persons Responsible for Serious Violations of International Humanitarian Law Committed in the Territory of the Former Yugoslavia since 1991.
See Document 82, p.418; and Document 83, page 440

14 June 1993
The Secretary-General, at the opening of the World Conference on Human Rights in Vienna, describes human rights as "the quintessential values through which we affirm together that we are a single human community".
See Document 84, page 441

25 June 1993
Adoption of the Vienna Declaration and Programme of Action at the closing of the World Conference on Human Rights.
See Document 85, page 448

20 December 1993
Adoption by the General Assembly of resolution 48/91, proclaiming the Third Decade to Combat Racism and Racial Discrimination.
See Document 86, page 464

20 December 1993
Adoption by the General Assembly of resolution 48/163, proclaiming the International Decade of the World's Indigenous People.

20 December 1993
Adoption by the General Assembly of resolution 48/141, establishing the post of United Nations High Commissioner for Human Rights.
See Document 88, page 471

23 February 1994
Adoption by the Security Council of a resolution establishing the civil police component of the United Nations Operation in Mozambique (ONUMOZ).
See Document 89, page 473

1 July 1994
Adoption by the Security Council of a resolution establishing a Commission of Experts to investigate violations of human rights in Rwanda.
See Document 90, page 475

19 September 1994
Adoption by the General Assembly of a resolution establishing the United Nations Mission for the Verification of Human Rights and of Compliance with the Commitments of the Comprehensive Agreement on Human Rights in Guatemala (MINUGUA).
See Document 92, page 487

23 September 1994
Adoption by the Security Council of a resolution re-emphasizing that "ethnic cleansing" constitutes a clear violation of international humanitarian law.
See Document 93, page 488

8 November 1994
Adoption by the Security Council of resolution 955 (1994), establishing an International Tribunal for Rwanda.
See Document 94, page 489

23 December 1994
Adoption by the General Assembly of resolution 49/184, proclaiming the United Nations Decade for Human Rights Education.
See Document 96, page 497

3 March 1995
Adoption by the Commission on Human Rights of a resolution establishing a working group to elaborate a draft declaration on the rights of indigenous people (resolution 1995/32).

II List of reproduced documents

The documents reproduced on pages 143 to 510 include the Charter of the United Nations and the Statute of the International Court of Justice; Conventions, Declarations, Covenants, Protocols and other instruments relating to human rights; resolutions of the General Assembly, the Security Council and the Economic and Social Council; reports by the Secretary-General, and other documents.

Document 1
Articles 1, 2, 10, 13, 24, 34, 39, 55, 56, 60, 62, 68, 71, 75, 76, 87, 94 and 98 of the Charter of the United Nations and Article 34 of the Statute of the International Court of Justice.
26 June 1945
See page 143

Document 2
Economic and Social Council resolution establishing the Commission on Human Rights.
E/RES/9 (II), 21 June 1946
See page 146

Document 3
Economic and Social Council resolution establishing the Commission on the Status of Women.
E/RES/11 (II), 21 June 1946
See page 147

Document 4
General Assembly resolution on the crime of genocide.
A/RES/96 (I), 11 December 1946
See page 148

Document 5
Economic and Social Council resolution concerning the drafting of the Universal Declaration of Human Rights.
E/RES/46 (IV), 28 March 1947
See page 149

Document 6
Economic and Social Council resolution on communications concerning human rights.
E/RES/75 (V), 5 August 1947
See page 150

Document 7
Convention on the Prevention and Punishment of the Crime of Genocide.
A/RES/260 A (III), 9 December 1948
See page 151

Document 8
Universal Declaration of Human Rights.
A/RES/217 A (III), 10 December 1948
See page 153

Document 9
Economic and Social Council resolution on the problem of slavery.
E/RES/238 (IX), 20 July 1949
See page 156

Document 10
Convention for the Protection of Human Rights and Fundamental Freedoms (European Convention on Human Rights) signed in Rome by the members of the Council of Europe.
4 November 1950
See page 156

Document 11
Advisory Opinion of the International Court of Justice (Reservations to the Convention on the Prevention and Punishment of the Crime of Genocide).
28 May 1951
See page 164

Document 12
Convention relating to the Status of Refugees, adopted by the United Nations Conference of Plenipotentiaries on the Status of Refugees and Stateless Persons convened pursuant to General Assembly resolution 429 (V) of 14 December 1950.
28 July 1951
See page 172

Document 13
Convention on the Political Rights of Women.
A/RES/640 (VII), 20 December 1952
See page 180

Document 93

Security Council resolution emphasizing that the practice of "ethnic cleansing" is a clear violation of international humanitarian law.
S/RES/941 (1994), 23 September 1994
See page 488

Document 94

Security Council resolution containing the decision to establish an international tribunal for the prosecution of persons responsible for genocide and other serious violations of international humanitarian law committed in Rwanda or in the territory of neighbouring States.
S/RES/955 (1994), 8 November 1994
See page 489

Document 95

General Assembly resolution on the International Research and Training Institute for the Advancement of Women.
A/RES/49/163, 23 December 1994
See page 496

Document 96

General Assembly resolution proclaiming the ten-year period beginning on 1 January 1995 the United Nations Decade for Human Rights Education.
A/RES/49/184, 23 December 1994
See page 497

Document 97

General Assembly resolution on the International Decade of the World's Indigenous People.
A/RES/49/214, 23 December 1994
See page 498

Document 98

Model communication for information concerning alleged victims of human rights violations.
See page 501

Document 99

Status of international human rights instruments; oversight bodies, international human rights instruments, basic information.
See page 503

Document 100

List of judgments and opinions of the International Court of Justice on the subject of human rights
See page 510

The list of documents broken down by category is reproduced below.

Charter of the United Nations and Statute of the International Court of Justice
Document 1

Universal Declaration of Human Rights
Document 8

International Covenant on Economic, Social and Cultural Rights
Document 31

International Covenant on Civil and Political Rights and Protocols thereto
Documents 32-33, 61

General Assembly resolutions
Documents 4, 16, 24, 26, 30, 37, 41-42, 46, 55, 70, 81, 86-88, 92, 95-97

Security Council resolutions
Documents 72-77, 80, 83, 89-90, 93-94

Economic and Social Council resolutions
Documents 2-3, 5-6, 9, 18, 20, 25, 28-29, 34, 38, 57

Resolution of the Subcommission on Prevention of Discrimination and Protection of Minorities
Document 39

International Court of Justice
Document 11

Conventions
Documents 7, 10, 12-14, 17, 19, 22-23, 27, 36, 40, 45, 47, 50, 54, 60, 71

Declarations
Documents 21, 48, 52, 56, 65, 78-79

International Conference on Human Rights (Teheran, 1968)
Document 35

World Conference on Human Rights (Vienna, 1993)
Document 85

Reports and statements by the Secretary-General
Documents 82, 84

Other documents
Documents 15, 43-44, 49, 51, 53, 58-59, 62-64, 66-69, 91, 98-100

III Other documents

Readers wishing additional information on human rights may consult the following documents, which are available in the Dag Hammarskjöld Library at United Nations Headquarters, New York, in the libraries of United Nations agencies, and in libraries throughout the world which have been designated as depositaries of United Nations documents.

Slavery Convention, of 25 September 1926, United Nations

Convention concerning Forced or Compulsory Labour, of 28 June 1930, United Nations

General Assembly resolutions 3 (I) of 13 February 1946, 95 (I) of 11 December 1946 and 170 (II) of 31 October 1947 affirming the principles of international law relating to war crimes and to crimes against humanity

Trial of the major war criminals, Nürnberg International Military Tribunal

Economic and Social Council resolution 11 (II), dated 21 June 1946, on the role of the Commission on Human Rights

Economic and Social Council resolution 76 (V), dated 5 August 1947, concerning the treatment of individual communications by the Commission on the Status of Women

Convention for the Suppression of the Traffic in Persons and of the Exploitation of the Prostitution of Others, of 2 December 1949, United Nations

Protocol amending the Slavery Convention signed at Geneva on 25 September 1926, dated 23 October 1953, United Nations

Supplementary Convention on the Abolition of Slavery, the Slave Trade, and Institutions and Practices Similar to Slavery, of 7 September 1956, United Nations

Convention on the Non-Applicability of Statutory Limitations to War Crimes and Crimes against Humanity, of 26 November 1968, United Nations

Principles of international cooperation in the detection, arrest, extradition and punishment of persons guilty of war crimes and crimes against humanity, of 3 December 1973, United Nations

Recommendation concerning Education for International Understanding, Cooperation and Peace and Education relating to Human Rights and Fundamental Freedoms, of 19 November 1974

Declaration on Race and Racial Prejudice, of 27 November 1978, United Nations

Declaration on Fundamental Principles concerning the Contribution of the Mass Media to Strengthening Peace and International Understanding, to the Promotion of Human Rights and to Countering Racialism, Apartheid and Incitement to War, of 28 November 1978

Principles of Medical Ethics relevant to the role of health personnel, particularly physicians, in the protection of prisoners and detainees against torture and other cruel, inhuman or degrading treatment or punishment, of 18 December 1982, United Nations

Guidelines for the regulation of computerized personal data files, of 14 December 1990, United Nations

Report of the Secretary-General to the Security Council on "An Agenda for Peace". Document A/47/277-S/24111 of 17 June 1992

Readers may also consult the five-volume general human rights bibliography published by the United Nations: *Human Rights Bibliography: United Nations Documents and Publications, 1980-1990*, New York 1993.

IV Texts of documents

The texts of the 100 documents listed on the preceding pages are reproduced below. The appearance of ellipses (. . .) in the text indicates that portions of the document have been omitted. A subject index to the documents begins on page 511.

Document 1

Articles 1, 2, 10, 13, 24, 34, 39, 55, 56, 60, 62, 68, 71, 75, 76, 87, 94 and 98 of the Charter of the United Nations and Article 34 of the Statute of the International Court of Justice

26 June 1945

Charter of the United Nations

CHAPTER I

PURPOSES AND PRINCIPLES

Article 1

The Purposes of the United Nations are:

1. To maintain international peace and security, and to that end: to take effective collective measures for the prevention and removal of threats to the peace, and for the suppression of acts of aggression or other breaches of the peace, and to bring about by peaceful means, and in conformity with the principles of justice and international law, adjustment or settlement of international disputes or situations which might lead to a breach of the peace;

2. To develop friendly relations among nations based on respect for the principle of equal rights and self-determination of peoples, and to take other appropriate measures to strengthen universal peace;

3. To achieve international cooperation in solving international problems of an economic, social, cultural, or humanitarian character, and in promoting and encouraging respect for human rights and for fundamental freedoms for all without distinction as to race, sex, language, or religion; and

4. To be a centre for harmonizing the actions of nations in the attainment of these common ends.

Article 2

The Organization and its Members, in pursuit of the Purposes stated in Article 1, shall act in accordance with the following Principles.

1. The Organization is based on the principle of the sovereign equality of all its Members.

2. All Members, in order to ensure to all of them the rights and benefits resulting from membership, shall fulfil in good faith the obligations assumed by them in accordance with the present Charter.

3. All Members shall settle their international disputes by peaceful means in such a manner that international peace and security, and justice, are not endangered.

4. All Members shall refrain in their international relations from the threat or use of force against the territorial integrity or political independence of any state, or in any other manner inconsistent with the Purposes of the United Nations.

5. All Members shall give the United Nations every assistance in any action it takes in accordance with the present Charter, and shall refrain from giving assistance to any state against which the United Nations is taking preventive or enforcement action.

6. The Organization shall ensure that states which are not Members of the United Nations act in accordance with these Principles so far as may be necessary for the maintenance of international peace and security.

7. Nothing contained in the present Charter shall authorize the United Nations to intervene in matters which are essentially within the domestic jurisdiction of any state or shall require the Members to submit such matters to settlement under the present Charter; but this principle shall not prejudice the application of enforcement measures under Chapter VII.

CHAPTER IV

THE GENERAL ASSEMBLY

Functions and Powers

Article 10

The General Assembly may discuss any questions or any matters within the scope of the present Charter or relating to the powers and functions of any organs provided for in the present Charter, and, except as provided in Article 12, may make recommendations to the Members of the United Nations or to the Security Council or to both on any such questions or matters.

Article 13

1. The General Assembly shall initiate studies and make recommendations for the purpose of:

(a) promoting international cooperation in the political field and encouraging the progressive development of international law and its codification;

(b) promoting international cooperation in the economic, social, cultural, educational, and health fields, and assisting in the realization of human rights and fundamental freedoms for all without distinction as to race, sex, language, or religion.

2. The further responsibilities, functions and powers of the General Assembly with respect to matters mentioned in paragraph I (b) above are set forth in Chapters IX and X.

CHAPTER V

THE SECURITY COUNCIL

Functions and Powers

Article 24

1. In order to ensure prompt and effective action by the United Nations, its Members confer on the Security Council primary responsibility for the maintenance of international peace and security, and agree that in carrying out its duties under this responsibility the Security Council acts on their behalf.

2. In discharging these duties the Security Council shall act in accordance with the Purposes and Principles of the United Nations. The specific powers granted to the Security Council for the discharge of these duties are laid down in Chapters VI, VII, VIII, and XII.

3. The Security Council shall submit annual and, when necessary, special reports to the General Assembly for its consideration.

CHAPTER VI

PACIFIC SETTLEMENT OF DISPUTES

Article 34

The Security Council may investigate any dispute, or any situation which might lead to international friction or give rise to a dispute, in order to determine whether the continuance of the dispute or situation is likely to endanger the maintenance of international peace and security.

CHAPTER VII

ACTION WITH RESPECT TO THREATS TO THE PEACE, BREACHES OF THE PEACE, AND ACTS OF AGGRESSION

Article 39

The Security Council shall determine the existence of any threat to the peace, breach of the peace, or act of aggression and shall make recommendations, or decide what measures shall be taken in accordance with Articles 41 and 42, to maintain or restore international peace and security.

CHAPTER IX

INTERNATIONAL ECONOMIC AND SOCIAL COOPERATION

Article 55

With a view to the creation of conditions of stability and well-being which are necessary for peaceful and friendly relations among nations based on respect for the principle of equal rights and self-determination of peoples, the United Nations shall promote:

(a) higher standards of living, full employment, and conditions of economic and social progress and development;

(b) solutions of international economic, social, health, and related problems; and international cultural and educational cooperation; and

(c) universal respect for, and observance of, human rights and fundamental freedoms for all without distinction as to race, sex, language, or religion.

Article 56

All Members pledge themselves to take joint and separate action in cooperation with the Organization for the achievement of the purposes set forth in Article 55.

Article 60

Responsibility for the discharge of the functions of the Organization set forth in this Chapter shall be vested in the General Assembly and, under the authority of the General Assembly, in the Economic and Social Council, which shall have for this purpose the powers set forth in Chapter X.

CHAPTER X

THE ECONOMIC AND SOCIAL COUNCIL

Functions and Powers

Article 62

1. The Economic and Social Council may make or initiate studies and reports with respect to international

economic, social, cultural, educational, health, and related matters and may make recommendations with respect to any such matters to the General Assembly, to the Members of the United Nations, and to the specialized agencies concerned.

2. It may make recommendations for the purpose of promoting respect for, and observance of, human rights and fundamental freedoms for all.

3. It may prepare draft conventions for submission to the General Assembly, with respect to matters falling within its competence.

4. It may call, in accordance with the rules prescribed by the United Nations, international conferences on matters falling within its competence.

Procedure

Article 68

The Economic and Social Council shall set up commissions in economic and social fields and for the promotion of human rights, and such other commissions as may be required for the performance of its functions.

Article 71

The Economic and Social Council may make suitable arrangements for consultation with non-governmental organizations which are concerned with matters within its competence. Such arrangements may be made with international organizations and, where appropriate, with national organizations after consultation with the Member of the United Nations concerned.

CHAPTER XII

INTERNATIONAL TRUSTEESHIP SYSTEM

Article 75

The United Nations shall establish under its authority an international trusteeship system for the administration and supervision of such territories as may be placed thereunder by subsequent individual agreements. These territories are hereinafter referred to as trust territories.

Article 76

The basic objectives of the trusteeship system, in accordance with the Purposes of the United Nations laid down in Article I of the present Charter, shall be:

(a) to further international peace and security;

(b) to promote the political, economic, social, and educational advancement of the inhabitants of the trust territories, and their progressive development towards self-government or independence as may be appropriate to the particular circumstances of each territory and its peoples and the freely expressed wishes of the peoples

concerned, and as may be provided by the terms of each trusteeship agreement;

(c) to encourage respect for human rights and for fundamental freedoms for all without distinction as to race, sex, language, or religion, and to encourage recognition of the interdependence of the peoples of the world; and

(d) to ensure equal treatment in social, economic, and commercial matters for all Members of the United Nations and their nationals, and also equal treatment for the latter in the administration of justice, without prejudice to the attainment of the foregoing objectives and subject to the provisions of Article 80.

CHAPTER XIII

THE TRUSTEESHIP COUNCIL

Functions and Powers

Article 87

The General Assembly and, under its authority, the Trusteeship Council, in carrying out their functions, may:

(a) consider reports submitted by the administering authority;

(b) accept petitions and examine them in consultation with the administering authority;

(c) provide for periodic visits to the respective trust territories at times agreed upon with the administering authority; and

(d) take these and other actions in conformity with the terms of the trusteeship agreements.

CHAPTER XIV

THE INTERNATIONAL COURT OF JUSTICE

Article 94

1. Each Member of the United Nations undertakes to comply with the decision of the International Court of Justice in any case to which it is a party.

2. If any party to a case fails to perform the obligations incumbent upon it under a judgment rendered by the Court, the other party may have recourse to the Security Council, which may, if it deems necessary, make recommendations or decide upon measures to be taken to give effect to the judgment.

CHAPTER XV

THE SECRETARIAT

Article 98

The Secretary-General shall act in that capacity in all meetings of the General Assembly, of the Security Council, of the Economic and Social Council, and of the Trusteeship Council, and shall perform such other functions as are entrusted to him by these organs. The Secretary-General shall make an annual report to the General Assembly on the work of the Organization.

Statute of the International Court of Justice

CHAPTER II

COMPETENCE OF THE COURT

Article 34

1. Only states may be parties in cases before the Court.

2. The Court, subject to and in conformity with its Rules, may request of public international organizations information relevant to cases before it, and shall receive such information presented by such organizations on their own initiative.

3. Whenever the construction of the constituent instrument of a public international organization or of an international convention adopted thereunder is in question in a case before the Court, the Registrar shall so notify the public international organization concerned and shall communicate to it copies of all the written proceedings.

Document 2

Economic and Social Council resolution establishing the Commission on Human Rights

E/RES/9 (II), 21 June 1946

The Economic and Social Council, having considered the report of the nuclear Commission on Human Rights of 21 May 1946 (document E/38/Rev.1)

Decides as follows:

1. *Functions*

The functions of the Commission on Human Rights shall be those set forth in the terms of reference of the Commission, approved by the Economic and Social Council in its resolution of 16 February 1946, with the addition to paragraph 2 of that resolution of a new sub-paragraph (e) as follows:

(e) any other matter concerning human rights not covered by items (a), (b), (c), and (d).

2. *Composition*

(a) The Commission on Human Rights shall consist of one representative from each of eighteen members of the United Nations selected by the Council.

(b) With a view to securing a balanced representation in the various fields covered by the Commission, the Secretary-General shall consult with the governments so selected before the representatives are finally nominated by these governments and confirmed by the Council.

(c) Except for the initial period, the term of office shall be for three years. For the initial period, one-third of the members shall serve for two years, one-third for three years, and one-third for four years, the term of each member to be determined by lot.

(d) Retiring members shall be eligible for re-election.

(e) In the event that a member of the Commission is unable to serve for the full three-year term, the vacancy thus arising shall be filled by a representative designated by the Member Government, subject to the provisions of paragraph (b) above.

3. *Working groups of experts*

The Commission is authorized to call in *ad hoc* working groups of non-governmental experts in specialized fields or individual experts, without further reference to the Council, but with the approval of the President of the Council and the Secretary-General.

4. *Documentation*

The Secretary-General is requested to make arrangements for:

(a) the compilation and publication of a year-book on law and usage relating to human rights, the first edition of which should include all declarations and bills on human rights now in force in the various countries;

(b) the collection and publication of information on the activities concerning human rights of all organs of the United Nations;

(c) the collection and publication of information concerning human rights arising from trials of war criminals, quislings, and traitors, and in particular from the Nuremberg and Tokyo trials;

(d) the preparation and publication of a survey of the development of human rights;

(e) the collection and publication of plans and declarations on human rights by specialized agencies and non-governmental national and international organizations.

5. Information groups

Members of the United Nations are invited to consider the desirability of establishing information groups or local human rights committees within their respective countries to collaborate with them in furthering the work of the Commission on Human Rights.

6. Human rights in international treaties

Pending the adoption of an international bill of rights, the general principle shall be accepted that international treaties involving basic human rights, including to the fullest extent practicable treaties of peace, shall conform to the fundamental standards relative to such rights set forth in the Charter.

7. Provisions for implementation

Considering that the purpose of the United Nations with regard to the promotion and observance of human rights, as defined in the Charter of the United Nations, can only be fulfilled if provisions are made for the implementation of human rights and of an international bill of rights, the Council requests the Commission on Human Rights to submit at an early date suggestions regarding the ways and means for the effective implementation of human rights and fundamental freedoms, with a view to assisting the Economic and Social Council in working out arrangements for such implementation with other appropriate organs of the United Nations.

8. Sub-Commission on Freedom of Information and of the Press

(a) The Commission on Human Rights is empowered to establish a Sub-Commission on Freedom of Information and of the Press.

(b) The function of the Sub-Commission shall be, in the first instance, to examine what rights, obligations, and practices should be included in the concept of freedom of information, and to report to the Commission on Human Rights on any issues that may arise from such examination.

9. Sub-Commission on Protection of Minorities

(a) The Commission on Human Rights is empowered to establish a Sub-Commission on the Protection of Minorities.

(b) Unless the Commission otherwise decides, the function of the Sub-Commission shall be, in the first instance, to examine what provisions should be adopted in the definition of the principles which are to be applied in the field of protection of minorities, and to deal with the urgent problems in this field by making recommendations to the Commission.

10. Sub-Commission on the Prevention of Discrimination

(a) The Commission on Human Rights is empowered to establish a Sub-Commission on the prevention of discrimination on the grounds of race, sex, language, or religion.

(b) Unless the Commission otherwise decides, the function of the Sub-Commission shall be, in the first instance, to examine what provisions should be adopted in the definition of the principles which are to be applied in the field of the prevention of discrimination, and to deal with the urgent problems in this field by making recommendations to the Commission.

Document 3

Economic and Social Council resolution establishing the Commission on the Status of Women

E/RES/11 (II), 21 June 1946

The Economic and Social Council, having considered the report of the nuclear Commission on Human Rights and the nuclear Sub-Commission on the Status of Women of 21 May 1946 (document E/38/Rev.1),

Decides to confer upon the Sub-Commission the status of a full commission to be known as the Commission on the Status of Women.

1. *Functions*

The functions of the Commission shall be to prepare recommendations and reports to the Economic and Social Council on promoting women's rights in political, economic, social and educational fields. The Commission shall also make recommendations to the Council on urgent problems requiring immediate attention in the field of women's rights.

The Commission may submit proposals to the Council regarding its terms of reference.

2. *Composition*

(a) The Commission on the Status of Women shall consist of one representative from each of fifteen Members of the United Nations selected by the Council.

(b) With a view to securing a balanced representation in the various fields covered by the Commission, the Secretary-General shall consult with the governments so selected before the representatives are finally nominated by these governments and confirmed by the Council,

(c) Except for the initial period, the term of office shall be for three years. For the initial period, one-third of the members shall serve for two years, one-third for three years, and one-third for four years, the term of each member to be determined by lot.

(d) Retiring members shall be eligible for re-election.

(e) In the event that a member of the Commission is unable to serve for the full three-year term, the vacancy thus arising shall be filled by a representative designated by the Member Government, subject to the provisions of paragraph (b) above.

3. *Policy and Programme*

Sections I and II of the report of the Sub-Commission, concerning policy and programme, shall be referred for study to the Commission on the Status of Women.

4. *Documentation*

In order to assist the Commission on the Status of Women, the Secretary-General is requested to make arrangements for a complete and detailed study of the legislation concerning the status of women and the practical application of such legislation.

Document 4

General Assembly resolution on the crime of genocide

A/RES/96 (I), 11 December 1946

Genocide is a denial of the right of existence of entire human groups, as homicide is the denial of the right to live of individual human beings; such denial of the right of existence shocks the conscience of mankind, results in great losses to humanity in the form of cultural and other contributions represented by these human groups, and is contrary to moral law and to the spirit and aims of the United Nations.

Many instances of such crimes of genocide have occurred when racial, religious, political and other groups have been destroyed, entirely or in part.

The punishment of the crime of genocide is a matter of international concern.

The General Assembly, therefore,

Affirms that genocide is a crime under international law which the civilized world condemns, and for the commission of which principals and accomplices—whether private individuals, public officials or statesmen, and whether the crime is committed on religious, racial, political or any other grounds—are punishable;

Invites the Member States to enact the necessary legislation for the prevention and punishment of this crime;

Recommends that international cooperation be organized between States with a view to facilitating the speedy prevention and punishment of the crime of genocide, and, to this end,

Requests the Economic and Social Council to undertake the necessary studies, with a view to drawing up a draft convention on the crime of genocide to be submitted to the next regular session of the General Assembly.

Document 5

Economic and Social Council resolution concerning the drafting of the Universal Declaration of Human Rights

E/RES/46 (IV), 28 March 1947

The Economic and Social Council,

Pursuant to resolution No. 43 (I) of the General Assembly of 11 December 1946, 1/

Transmits the Declaration on Fundamental Human Rights and Freedoms, presented by the delegation of Panama, and any other draft declarations received from Member States, to the Drafting Committee of the Commission on Human Rights and to the Commission on Human Rights for consideration in their preparation of an international bill of human rights.

International Conference on Freedom of Information

The Economic and Social Council

Requests the Sub-Commission on Freedom of Information and of the Press to prepare, guided by resolution No. 59 (I) of 14 December 1946 of the General Assembly 2/, a draft documented agenda for the Conference on Freedom of Information, and to submit this along with proposals concerning preparations for the Conference to the Commission on Human Rights and to the Council. These proposals shall include suggestions concerning the invitation of States not Members of the United Nations, and plans whereby appropriate specialized agencies, such as the United Nations Educational, Scientific and Cultural Organization, and appropriate non-governmental organizations may assist in the preparation of the Conference and attend it; and

Transmits to the Sub-Commission on Freedom of Information and of the Press the draft agenda for the Conference on Freedom of Information presented by the delegation of France (documents E/355 and E/355/Corr.1) and any other similar communications received from Member States; and

Recommends to the Sub-Commission to invite a representative of the International Organization of Journalists to be present as an observer at its meetings for purpose of consultation; and further

Resolves that the decision on the date and place of the Conference be deferred to its fifth session.

Report of the Commission on Human Rights

A. Draft international bill of human rights

B. Sub-Commission on Freedom of Information and of the Press

C. Sub-Commission on Prevention of Discrimination and Protection of Minorities

D. Consideration of Communications concerning human rights deferred

The Economic and Social Council,

Taking note of chapter II, paragraph 10 of the report of the Commission on Human Rights. 3/

A. *Requests* the Secretariat to prepare a documented outline concerning an international bill of human rights; and

Having noted with approval the letter of the Chairman of the Commission on Human Rights to the President of the Economic and Social Council, dated 24 March 1947, including her statement of intention to appoint immediately a drafting committee of the Commission on Human Rights consisting of the members of the Commission on Human Rights representing Australia, Chile, China, France, Lebanon, United States of America, United Kingdom, and the Union of Soviet Socialist Republics, which will be convened prior to the second session of the Commission on Human Rights and prepare, on the basis of documentation supplied by the Secretariat, a preliminary draft of an international bill of human rights,

Decides

(a) That the draft prepared by the above-mentioned drafting committee be submitted to the second session of the Commission on Human Rights; and

(b) That the draft as developed by the Commission on Human Rights be submitted to all States Members of the United Nations for their observations, suggestions and proposals; and

(c) That these observations, suggestions and proposals then be considered as a basis of a re-draft, if necessary, by the drafting committee; and

(d) That the resulting draft then be submitted to the Commission on Human Rights for final consideration; and

(e) That the Council consider the proposed international bill of human rights as submitted by the Commission on Human Rights with a view to recommending

---

1/ See Resolutions adopted by the General Assembly during the second part of its first session, page 68.
2/ Ibid., page 95.
3/ See document E/259.

an international bill of human rights to the General Assembly in 1948; and further

(f) That the Commission on Human Rights invite the officers of the Commission on the Status of Women, the Chairman, the Vice-Chairman and the Rapporteur, to be present and participate without vote in its deliberations when sections of the draft of the international bill of human rights concerning the particular rights of women are being considered;

B. *Resolves* that, subject to the consent of their Governments, the Sub-Commission on Freedom of Information and of the Press be composed of the following persons:

Mr. George V. Ferguson (Canada)
Mr. P. H. Chang (China)
Mr. Lev Sychrava (Czechoslovakia)
Mr. André Géraud (France)
Dr. G. J. van Heuven Goedhart (Netherlands)
Mr. A. R. Christensen (Norway)
Mr. Jose Isaac Fabrega (Panama)
Mr. Salvador López (Philippine Republic)
Mr. J. M. Lomakin (Union of Soviet Socialist Republics)
Mr. R. J. Cruikshank (United Kingdom)
Mr. Z. Chafee (United States of America)
Mr. Roberto Fontaina (Uruguay)

and further
Resolves that the functions of the Sub-Commission be:

(a) In the first instance, to examine what rights, obligations and practices should be included in the concept of freedom of information, and to report to the Commission on Human Rights on any issues that may arise from such examination;

(b) To perform any other functions which may be entrusted to it by the Economic and Social Council or by the Commission on Human Rights;

C. *Resolves* that, subject to the consent of their Governments, the Sub-Commission on Prevention of Discrimination and Protection of Minorities be composed of the following persons:

Mr. William Morris Jutson McNamara (Australia)
Mr. Joseph Nisot (Belgium)
Mr. C. F. Chang (China)
Mr. Arturo Meneses Pallares (Ecuador)
Mr. Samuel Spanien (France)
Mr. Herard Roy (Haiti)
Mr. M. R. Masani (India)
Mr. Rezazada Shafaq (Iran)
Mr. Erik Enar Ekstrand (Sweden)
Mr. A. P. Borisov (Union of Soviet Socialist Republics)
Miss Elisabeth Monroe (United Kingdom)
Mr. Jonathan Daniels (United States of America)

D. *Resolves* that consideration of chapter V of the report of the Commission on Human Rights, entitled "Communications concerning human rights", be deferred until its fifth session.

Document 6

Economic and Social Council resolution on communications concerning human rights

E/RES/75 (V), 5 August 1947 1/

The Economic and Social Council,

Having considered chapter V of the report of the first session of the Commission on Human Rights concerning communications (document E/259),

Approves the statement that "the Commission recognizes that it has no power to take any action in regard to any complaints concerning human rights";

Requests the Secretary-General:

(a) To compile a confidential list of communications received concerning human rights, before each session of the Commission, with a brief indication of the substance of each;

(b) To furnish this confidential list to the Commission, in private meeting, without divulging the identity of the authors of the communications;

(c) To enable the members of the Commission, upon request, to consult the originals of communications dealing with the principles involved in the promotion of universal respect for and observance of human rights;

(d) To inform the writers of all communications concerning human rights, however addressed, that their communications have been received and duly noted for consideration in accordance with the procedure laid down

1/ See document E.505.

by the United Nations. Where necessary, the Secretary-General should indicate that the Commission has no power to take any action in regard to any complaint concerning human rights;

(e) To furnish each Member State not represented on the Commission with a brief indication of the substance of any communication concerning human rights which refers explicitly to that State or to territories under its jurisdiction, without divulging the identity of the author;

Suggests to the Commission on Human Rights that it should at each session appoint an *ad hoc* committee to meet shortly before its next session for the purpose of reviewing the confidential list of communications prepared by the Secretary-General under paragraph (a) above and of recommending which of these communications, in original, should, in accordance with paragraph (c) above, be made available to members of the Commission on request.

Document 7

Convention on the Prevention and Punishment of the Crime of Genocide

A/RES/260 A (III), 9 December 1948

The Contracting Parties,

Having considered the declaration made by the General Assembly of the United Nations in its resolution 96 (I) dated 11 December 1946 that genocide is a crime under international law, contrary to the spirit and aims of the United Nations and condemned by the civilized world,

Recognizing that at all periods of history genocide has inflicted great losses on humanity, and

Being convinced that, in order to liberate mankind from such an odious scourge, international cooperation is required,

Hereby agree as hereinafter provided:

Article I

The Contracting Parties confirm that genocide, whether committed in time of peace or in time of war, is a crime under international law which they undertake to prevent and to punish.

Article II

In the present Convention, genocide means any of the following acts committed with intent to destroy, in whole or in part, a national, ethnical, racial or religious group, as such:

(a) Killing members of the group;

(b) Causing serious bodily or mental harm to members of the group;

(c) Deliberately inflicting on the group conditions of life calculated to bring about its physical destruction in whole or in part;

(d) Imposing measures intended to prevent births within the group;

(e) Forcibly transferring children of the group to another group.

Article III

The following acts shall be punishable:

(a) Genocide;

(b) Conspiracy to commit genocide;

(c) Direct and public incitement to commit genocide;

(d) Attempt to commit genocide;

(e) Complicity in genocide.

Article IV

Persons committing genocide or any of the other acts enumerated in article III shall be punished, whether they are constitutionally responsible rulers, public officials or private individuals.

Article V

The Contracting Parties undertake to enact, in accordance with their respective Constitutions, the necessary legislation to give effect to the provisions of the present Convention, and, in particular, to provide effective penalties for persons guilty of genocide or any of the other acts enumerated in article III.

Article VI

Persons charged with genocide or any of the other acts enumerated in article III shall be tried by a competent tribunal of the State in the territory of which the act was committed, or by such international penal tribunal as may have jurisdiction with respect to those Contracting Parties which shall have accepted its jurisdiction.

Article VII

Genocide and the other acts enumerated in article III shall not be considered as political crimes for the purpose of extradition.

The Contracting Parties pledge themselves in such cases to grant extradition in accordance with their laws and treaties in force.

Article VIII

Any Contracting Party may call upon the competent organs of the United Nations to take such action under the Charter of the United Nations as they consider appropriate for the prevention and suppression of acts of genocide or any of the other acts enumerated in article III.

Article IX

Disputes between the Contracting Parties relating to the interpretation, application or fulfilment of the present Convention, including those relating to the responsibility of a State for genocide or for any of the other acts enumerated in article III, shall be submitted to the International Court of Justice at the request of any of the parties to the dispute.

Article X

The present Convention, of which the Chinese, English, French, Russian and Spanish texts are equally authentic, shall bear the date of 9 December 1948.

Article XI

The present Convention shall be open until 31 December 1949 for signature on behalf of any Member of the United Nations and of any non-member State to which an invitation to sign has been addressed by the General Assembly.

The present Convention shall be ratified, and the instruments of ratification shall be deposited with the Secretary-General of the United Nations.

After 1 January 1950, the present Convention may be acceded to on behalf of any Member of the United Nations and of any non-member State which has received an invitation as aforesaid.

Instruments of accession shall be deposited with the Secretary-General of the United Nations.

Article XII

Any Contracting Party may at any time, by notification addressed to the Secretary-General of the United Nations, extend the application of the present Convention to all or any of the territories for the conduct of whose foreign relations that Contracting Party is responsible.

Article XIII

On the day when the first twenty instruments of ratification or accession have been deposited, the Secretary-General shall draw up a procès-verbal and transmit a copy thereof to each Member of the United Nations and to each of the non-member States contemplated in article XI.

The present Convention shall come into force on the ninetieth day following the date of deposit of the twentieth instrument of ratification or accession.

Any ratification or accession effected, subsequent to the latter date shall become effective on the ninetieth day following the deposit of the instrument of ratification or accession.

Article XIV

The present Convention shall remain in effect for a period of ten years as from the date of its coming into force.

It shall thereafter remain in force for successive periods of five years for such Contracting Parties as have not denounced it at least six months before the expiration of the current period.

Denunciation shall be effected by a written notification addressed to the Secretary-General of the United Nations.

Article XV

If, as a result of denunciations, the number of Parties to the present Convention should become less than sixteen, the Convention shall cease to be in force as from the date on which the last of these denunciations shall become effective.

Article XVI

A request for the revision of the present Convention may be made at any time by any Contracting Party by means of a notification in writing addressed to the Secretary-General.

The General Assembly shall decide upon the steps, if any, to be taken in respect of such request.

Article XVII

The Secretary-General of the United Nations shall notify all Members of the United Nations and the non-member States contemplated in article XI of the following:

(a) Signatures, ratifications and accessions received in accordance with article XI;

(b) Notifications received in accordance with article XII;

(c) The date upon which the present Convention comes into force in accordance with article XIII;

(d) Denunciations received in accordance with article XIV;

(e) The abrogation of the Convention in accordance with article XV;

(f) Notifications received in accordance with article XVI.

Article XVIII

The original of the present Convention shall be deposited in the archives of the United Nations.

A certified copy of the Convention shall be transmitted to each Member of the United Nations and to each of the non-member States contemplated in article XI.

Article XIX

The present Convention shall be registered by the Secretary-General of the United Nations on the date of its coming into force.

Document 8

Universal Declaration of Human Rights

A/RES/217 A (III), 10 December 1948

PREAMBLE

Whereas recognition of the inherent dignity and of the equal and inalienable rights of all members of the human family is the foundation of freedom, justice and peace in the world,

Whereas disregard and contempt for human rights have resulted in barbarous acts which have outraged the conscience of mankind, and the advent of a world in which human beings shall enjoy freedom of speech and belief and freedom from fear and want has been proclaimed as the highest aspiration of the common people,

Whereas it is essential, if man is not to be compelled to have recourse, as a last resort, to rebellion against tyranny and oppression, that human rights should be protected by the rule of law,

Whereas it is essential to promote the development of friendly relations between nations,

Whereas the peoples of the United Nations have in the Charter reaffirmed their faith in fundamental human rights, in the dignity and worth of the human person and in the equal rights of men and women and have determined to promote social progress and better standards of life in larger freedom,

Whereas Member States have pledged themselves to achieve, in cooperation with the United Nations, the promotion of universal respect for and observance of human rights and fundamental freedoms,

Whereas a common understanding of these rights and freedoms is of the greatest importance for the full realization of this pledge,

Now, therefore,

The General Assembly,

Proclaims this Universal Declaration of Human Rights as a common standard of achievement for all peoples and all nations, to the end that every individual and every organ of society, keeping this Declaration constantly in mind, shall strive by teaching and education to promote respect for these rights and freedoms and by progressive measures, national and international, to secure their universal and effective recognition and observance, both among the peoples of Member States themselves and among the peoples of territories under their jurisdiction.

Article 1

All human beings are born free and equal in dignity and rights. They are endowed with reason and conscience and should act towards one another in a spirit of brotherhood.

Article 2

1. Everyone is entitled to all the rights and freedoms set forth in this Declaration, without distinction of any kind, such as race, colour, sex, language, religion, political or other opinion, national or social origin, property, birth or other status.

2. Furthermore, no distinction shall be made on the basis of the political, jurisdictional or international status of the country or territory to which a person belongs, whether it be independent, trust, non-self-governing or under any other limitation of sovereignty.

Article 3

Everyone has the right to life, liberty and security of person.

Article 4

No one shall be held in slavery or servitude; slavery and the slave trade shall be prohibited in all their forms.

Article 5

No one shall be subjected to torture or to cruel, inhuman or degrading treatment or punishment.

Article 6

Everyone has the right to recognition everywhere as a person before the law.

Article 7

All are equal before the law and are entitled without any discrimination to equal protection of the law. All are entitled to equal protection against any discrimination in violation of this Declaration and against any incitement to such discrimination.

Article 8

Everyone has the right to an effective remedy by the competent national tribunals for acts violating the fundamental rights granted him by the constitution or by law.

Article 9

No one shall be subjected to arbitrary arrest, detention or exile.

Article 10

Everyone is entitled in full equality to a fair and public hearing by an independent and impartial tribunal, in the determination of his rights and obligations and of any criminal charge against him.

Article 11

1. Everyone charged with a penal offence has the right to be presumed innocent until proved guilty according to law in a public trial at which he has had all the guarantees necessary for his defence.

2. No one shall be held guilty of any penal offence on account of any act or omission which did not constitute a penal offence, under national or international law, at the time when it was committed. Nor shall a heavier penalty be imposed than the one that was applicable at the time the penal offence was committed.

Article 12

No one shall be subjected to arbitrary interference with his privacy, family, home or correspondence, nor to attacks upon his honour and reputation. Everyone has the right to the protection of the law against such interference or attacks.

Article 13

1. Everyone has the right to freedom of movement and residence within the borders of each State.

2. Everyone has the right to leave any country, including his own, and to return to his country.

Article 14

1. Everyone has the right to seek and to enjoy in other countries asylum from persecution.

2. This right may not be invoked in the case of prosecutions genuinely arising from non-political crimes or from acts contrary to the purposes and principles of the United Nations.

Article 15

1. Everyone has the right to a nationality.

2. No one shall be arbitrarily deprived of his nationality nor denied the right to change his nationality.

Article 16

1. Men and women of full age, without any limitation due to race, nationality or religion, have the right to marry and to found a family. They are entitled to equal rights as to marriage, during marriage and at its dissolution.

2. Marriage shall be entered into only with the free and full consent of the intending spouses.

3. The family is the natural and fundamental group unit of society and is entitled to protection by society and the State.

Article 17

1. Everyone has the right to own property alone as well as in association with others.

2. No one shall be arbitrarily deprived of his property.

Article 18

Everyone has the right to freedom of thought, conscience and religion; this right includes freedom to change his religion or belief, and freedom, either alone or in community with others and in public or private, to manifest his religion or belief in teaching, practice, worship and observance.

Article 19

Everyone has the right to freedom of opinion and expression; this right includes freedom to hold opinions without interference and to seek, receive and impart information and ideas through any media and regardless of frontiers.

Article 20

1. Everyone has the right to freedom of peaceful assembly and association.

2. No one may be compelled to belong to an association.

Article 21

1. Everyone has the right to take part in the government of his country, directly or through freely chosen representatives.

2. Everyone has the right to equal access to public service in his country.

3. The will of the people shall be the basis of the authority of government; this will shall be expressed in periodic and genuine elections which shall be by universal and equal suffrage and shall be held by secret vote or by equivalent free voting procedures.

Article 22

Everyone, as a member of society, has the right to social security and is entitled to realization, through national effort and international cooperation and in accordance with the organization and resources of each State, of the economic, social and cultural rights indispensable for his dignity and the free development of his personality.

Article 23

1. Everyone has the right to work, to free choice of employment, to just and favourable conditions of work and to protection against unemployment.

2. Everyone, without any discrimination, has the right to equal pay for equal work.

3. Everyone who works has the right to just and favourable remuneration ensuring for himself and his family an existence worthy of human dignity, and supplemented, if necessary, by other means of social protection.

4. Everyone has the right to form and to join trade unions for the protection of his interests.

Article 24

Everyone has the right to rest and leisure, including reasonable limitation of working hours and periodic holidays with pay.

Article 25

1. Everyone has the right to a standard of living adequate for the health and well-being of himself and of his family, including food, clothing, housing and medical care and necessary social services, and the right to security in the event of unemployment, sickness, disability, widowhood, old age or other lack of livelihood in circumstances beyond his control.

2. Motherhood and childhood are entitled to special care and assistance. All children, whether born in or out of wedlock, shall enjoy the same social protection.

Article 26

1. Everyone has the right to education. Education shall be free, at least in the elementary and fundamental stages. Elementary education shall be compulsory. Technical and professional education shall be made generally available and higher education shall be equally accessible to all on the basis of merit.

2. Education shall be directed to the full development of the human personality and to the strengthening of respect for human rights and fundamental freedoms. It shall promote understanding, tolerance and friendship among all nations, racial or religious groups, and shall further the activities of the United Nations for the maintenance of peace.

3. Parents have a prior right to choose the kind of education that shall be given to their children.

Article 27

1. Everyone has the right freely to participate in the cultural life of the community, to enjoy the arts and to share in scientific advancement and its benefits.

2. Everyone has the right to the protection of the moral and material interests resulting from any scientific, literary or artistic production of which he is the author.

Article 28

Everyone is entitled to a social and international order in which the rights and freedoms set forth in this Declaration can be fully realized.

Article 29

1. Everyone has duties to the community in which alone the free and full development of his personality is possible.

2. In the exercise of his rights and freedoms, everyone shall be subject only to such limitations as are determined by law solely for the purpose of securing due recognition and respect for the rights and freedoms of others and of meeting the just requirements of morality, public order and the general welfare in a democratic society.

3. These rights and freedoms may in no case be exercised contrary to the purposes and principles of the United Nations.

Article 30

Nothing in this Declaration may be interpreted as implying for any State, group or person any right to engage in any activity or to perform any act aimed at the destruction of any of the rights and freedoms set forth herein.

Document 9

Economic and Social Council resolution on the problem of slavery

E/RES/238 (IX), 20 July 1949

The Economic and Social Council

Instructs the Secretary-General, after consultation with the bodies having special competence in this field, to appoint a small *ad hoc* committee of not more than five experts:

1. To survey the field of slavery and other institutions or customs resembling slavery;

2. To assess the nature and extent of these several problems at the present time;

3. To suggest methods of attacking these problems;

4. Having regard to the recognized fields of competence of the various bodies within the framework of the United Nations, to suggest an appropriate division of responsibility among these bodies; and

5. To report to the Council within twelve months of its appointment.

Document 10

Convention for the Protection of Human Rights and Fundamental Freedoms (European Convention on Human Rights), signed in Rome by the members of the Council of Europe

4 November 1950

The Governments signatory hereto, being Members of the Council of Europe,

Considering the Universal Declaration of Human Rights proclaimed by the General Assembly of the United Nations on 10th December 1948; 1/

Considering that this Declaration aims at securing the universal and effective recognition and observance of the Rights therein declared;

Considering that the aim of the Council of Europe is the achievement of greater unity between its Members and that one of the methods by which that aim is to be pursued is the maintenance and further realisation of Human Rights and Fundamental Freedoms;

Reaffirming their profound belief in those Fundamental Freedoms which are the foundation of justice and peace in the world and are best maintained on the one hand by an effective political democracy and on the other by a common understanding and observance of the Human Rights upon which they depend;

Being resolved, as the Governments of European countries which are like-minded and have a common heritage of political traditions, ideals, freedom and the rule of law, to take the first steps for the collective enforcement of certain of the Rights stated in the Universal Declaration;

Have agreed as follows:

Article 1

The High Contracting Parties shall secure to everyone within their jurisdiction the rights and freedoms defined in Section I of this Convention.

SECTION I

Article 2

1. Everyone's right to life shall be protected by law. No one shall be deprived of his life intentionally save in the execution of a sentence of a court following his conviction of a crime for which this penalty is provided by law.

2. Deprivation of life shall not be regarded as inflicted in contravention of this Article when it results from the use of force which is no more than absolutely necessary:

(a) in defence of any person from unlawful violence;

(b) in order to effect a lawful arrest or to prevent the escape of a person lawfully detained;

(c) in action lawfully taken for the purpose of quelling a riot or insurrection.

1/ United Nations, *Official Records of the Third Session of the General Assembly, Part I* (A/810), p.71.

Article 3

No one shall be subjected to torture or to inhuman or degrading treatment or punishment.

Article 4

1. No one shall be held in slavery or servitude.

2. No one shall be required to perform forced or compulsory labour.

3. For the purpose of this Article the term "forced or compulsory labour" shall not include:

(a) any work required to be done in the ordinary course of detention imposed according to the provisions of Article 5 of this Convention or during conditional release from such detention;

(b) any service of a military character or, in case of conscientious objectors in countries where they are recognized, service exacted instead of compulsory military service;

(c) any service exacted in case of an emergency or calamity threatening the life or well-being of the community;

(d) any work or service which forms part of normal civic obligations.

Article 5

1. Everyone has the right to liberty and security of person.

No one shall be deprived of his liberty save in the following cases and in accordance with a procedure prescribed by law:

(a) the lawful detention of a person after conviction by a competent court;

(b) the lawful arrest or detention of a person for non-compliance with the lawful order of a court or in order to secure the fulfilment of any obligation prescribed by law;

(c) the lawful arrest or detention of a person effected for the purpose of bringing him before the competent legal authority on reasonable suspicion of having committed an offence or when it is reasonably considered necessary to prevent his committing an offence or fleeing after having done so;

(d) the detention of a minor by lawful order for the purpose of educational supervision or his lawful detention for the purpose of bringing him before the competent legal authority;

(e) the lawful detention of persons for the prevention of the spreading of infectious diseases, of persons of unsound mind, alcoholics or drug addicts or vagrants;

(f) the lawful arrest or detention of a person to prevent his effecting an unauthorised entry into the country or of a person against whom action is being taken with a view to deportation or extradition.

2. Everyone who is arrested shall be informed promptly, in a language which he understands, of the reasons for his arrest and of any charge against him.

3. Everyone arrested or detained in accordance with the provisions of paragraph 1 (c) of this Article shall be brought promptly before a judge or other officer authorised by law to exercise judicial power and shall be entitled to trial within a reasonable time or to release pending trial. Release may be conditioned by guarantees to appear for trial.

4. Everyone who is deprived of his liberty by arrest or detention shall be entitled to take proceedings by which the lawfulness of his detention shall be decided speedily by a court and his release ordered if the detention is not lawful.

5. Everyone who has been the victim of arrest or detention in contravention of the provisions of this Article shall have an enforceable right to compensation.

Article 6

1. In the determination of his civil rights and obligations or of any criminal charge against him, everyone is entitled to a fair and public hearing within a reasonable time by an independent and impartial tribunal established by law. Judgment shall be pronounced publicly but the press and public may be excluded from all or part of the trial in the interests of morals, public order or national security in a democratic society, where the interests of juveniles or the protection of the private life of the parties so require, or to the extent strictly necessary in the opinion of the court in special circumstances where publicity would prejudice the interests of justice.

2. Everyone charged with a criminal offence shall be presumed innocent until proved guilty according to law.

3. Everyone charged with a criminal offence has the following minimum rights:

(a) to be informed promptly, in a language which he understands and in detail, of the nature and cause of the accusation against him;

(b) to have adequate time and facilities for the preparation of his defence;

(c) to defend himself in person or through legal assistance of his own choosing or, if he has not sufficient means to pay for legal assistance, to be given it free when the interests of justice so require;

(d) to examine or have examined witnesses against him and to obtain the attendance and examination of witnesses on his behalf under the same conditions as witnesses against him;

(e) to have the free assistance of an interpreter if he cannot understand or speak the language used in court.

Article 7

1. No one shall be held guilty of any criminal offence on account of any act or omission which did not constitute a criminal offence under national or international law at the time when it was committed. Nor shall a heavier penalty be imposed than the one that was applicable at the time the criminal offence was committed.

2. This Article shall not prejudice the trial and punishment of any person for any act or omission which, at the time when it was committed, was criminal according to the general principles of law recognized by civilised nations.

Article 8

1. Everyone has the right to respect for his private and family life, his home and his correspondence.

2. There shall be no interference by a public authority with the exercise of this right except such as is in accordance with the law and is necessary in a democratic society in the interests of national security, public safety or the economic well-being of the country, for the prevention of disorder or crime, for the protection of health or morals, or for the protection of the rights and freedoms of others.

Article 9

1. Everyone has the right to freedom of thought, conscience and religion; this right includes freedom to change his religion or belief and freedom, either alone or in community with others and in public or private, to manifest his religion or belief, in worship, teaching, practice and observance.

2. Freedom to manifest one's religion or beliefs shall be subject only to such limitations as are prescribed by law and are necessary in a democratic society in the interests of public safety, for the protection of public order, health or morals, or for the protection of the rights and freedoms of others.

Article 10

1. Everyone has the right to freedom of expression. This right shall include freedom to hold opinions and to receive and impart information and ideas without interference by public authority and regardless of frontiers. This Article shall not prevent States from requiring the licensing of broadcasting, television or cinema enterprises.

2. The exercise of these freedoms, since it carries with it duties and responsibilities, may be subject to such formalities, conditions, restrictions or penalties as are prescribed by law and are necessary in a democratic society, in the interests of national security, territorial integrity or public safety, for the prevention of disorder or crime, for the protection of health or morals, for the protection of the reputation or rights of others, for preventing the disclosure of information received in confidence, or for maintaining the authority and impartiality of the judiciary.

Article 11

1. Everyone has the right to freedom of peaceful assembly and to freedom of association with others, including the right to form and to join trade unions for the protection of his interests.

2. No restrictions shall be placed on the exercise of these rights other than such as are prescribed by law and are necessary in a democratic society in the interests of national security or public safety, for the prevention of disorder or crime, for the protection of health or morals or for the protection of the rights and freedoms of others. This Article shall not prevent the imposition of lawful restrictions on the exercise of these rights by members of the armed forces, of the police or of the administration of the State.

Article 12

Men and women of marriageable age have the right to marry and to found a family, according to the national laws governing the exercise of this right.

Article 13

Everyone whose rights and freedoms as set forth in this Convention are violated shall have an effective remedy before a national authority notwithstanding that the violation has been committed by persons acting in an official capacity.

Article 14

The enjoyment of the rights and freedoms set forth in this Convention shall be secured without discrimination on any ground such as sex, race, colour, language, religion, political or other opinion, national or social origin, association with a national minority, property, birth or other status.

Article 15

1. In time of war or other public emergency threatening the life of the nation any High Contracting Party may take measures derogating from its obligations under this Convention to the extent strictly required by the exigencies of the situation, provided that such measures

are not inconsistent with its other obligations under international law.

2. No derogation from Article 2, except in respect of deaths resulting from lawful acts of war, or from Articles 3, 4 (paragraph 1) and 7 shall be made under this provision.

3. Any High Contracting Party availing itself of this right of derogation shall keep the Secretary-General of the Council of Europe fully informed of the measures which it has taken and the reasons therefor. It shall also inform the Secretary-General of the Council of Europe when such measures have ceased to operate and the provisions of the Convention are again being fully executed.

Article 16

Nothing in Articles 10, 11 and 14 shall be regarded as preventing the High Contracting Parties from imposing restrictions on the political activity of aliens.

Article 17

Nothing in this Convention may be interpreted as implying for any State, group or person any right to engage in any activity or perform any act aimed at the destruction of any of the rights and freedoms set forth herein or at their limitation to a greater extent than is provided for in the Convention.

Article 18

The restrictions permitted under this Convention to the said rights and freedoms shall not be applied for any purpose other than those for which they have been prescribed.

SECTION II

Article 19

To ensure the observance of the engagements undertaken by the High Contracting Parties in the present Convention, there shall be set up:

(a) A European Commission of Human Rights hereinafter referred to as "the Commission";

(b) A European Court of Human Rights, hereinafter referred to as "the Court".

SECTION III

Article 20

The Commission shall consist of a number of members equal to that of the High Contracting Parties. No two members of the Commission may be nationals of the same State.

Article 21

1. The members of the Commission shall be elected by the Committee of Ministers by an absolute majority of votes, from a list of names drawn up by the Bureau of the Consultative Assembly; each group of the Representatives of the High Contracting Parties in the Consultative Assembly shall put forward three candidates, of whom two al least shall be its nationals.

2. As far as applicable, the same procedure shall be followed to complete the Commission in the event of other States subsequently becoming Parties to this Convention, and in filling casual vacancies.

Article 22

1. The members of the Commission shall be elected for a period of six years. They may be re-elected. However, of the members elected at the first election, the terms of seven members shall expire at the end of three years.

2. The members whose terms are to expire at the end of the initial period of three years shall be chosen by lot by the Secretary-General of the Council of Europe immediately after the first election has been completed.

3. A member of the Commission elected to replace a member whose term of office has not expired shall hold office for the remainder of his predecessor's term.

4. The members of the Commission shall hold office until replaced. After having been replaced, they shall continue to deal with such cases as they already have under consideration.

Article 23

The members of the Commission shall sit on the Commission in their individual capacity.

Article 24

Any High Contracting Party may refer to the Commission, through the Secretary-General of the Council of Europe, any alleged breach of the provisions of the Convention by another High Contracting Party.

Article 25

1. The Commission may receive petitions addressed to the Secretary-General of the Council of Europe from any person, non-governmental organisation or group of individuals claiming to be the victim of a violation by one of the High Contracting Parties of the rights set forth in this Convention, provided that the High Contracting Party against which the complaint has been lodged has declared that it recognises the cometence of the Commission to receive such petitions. Those of the High Contracting Parties who have made such a declara-

tion undertake not to hinder in any way the effective exercise of this right.

2. Such declarations may be made for a specific period.

3. The declarations shall be deposited with the Secretary-General of the Council of Europe who shall transmit copies thereof to the High Contracting Parties and publish them.

4. The Commission shall only exercise the powers provided for in this Article when at least six High Contracting Parties are bound by declarations made in accordance with the preceding paragraphs.

Article 26

The Commission may only deal with the matter after all domestic remedies have been exhausted, according to the generally recognised rules of international law, and within a period of six months from the date on which the final decision was taken.

Article 27

1. The Commission shall not deal with any petition submitted under Article 25 which

(a) is anonymous, or

(b) is substantially the same as a matter which has already been examined by the Commission or has already been submitted to another procedure of international investigation or settlement and if it contains no relevant new information.

2. The Commission shall consider inadmissible any petition submitted under Article 25 which it considers incompatible with the provisions of the present Convention, manifestly ill-founded, or an abuse of the right of petition.

3. The Commission shall reject any petition referred to it which it considers inadmissible under Article 26.

Article 28

In the event of the Commission accepting a petition referred to it:

(a) it shall, with a view to ascertaining the facts, undertake together with the representatives of the parties an examination of the petition and, if need be, an investigation, for the effective conduct of which the States concerned shall furnish all necessary facilities, after an exchange of views with the Commission;

(b) it shall place itself at the disposal of the parties concerned with a view to securing a friendly settlement of the matter on the basis of respect for Human Rights as defined in this Convention.

Article 29

1. The Commission shall perform the functions set out in Article 28 by means of a Sub-Commission consisting of seven members of the Commission.

2. Each of the parties concerned may appoint as members of this Sub-Commission a person of its choice.

3. The remaining members shall be chosen by lot in accordance with arrangements prescribed in the Rules of Procedure of the Commission.

Article 30

If the Sub-Commission succeeds in effecting a friendly settlement in accordance with Article 28, it shall draw up a Report which shall be sent to the States concerned, to the Committee of Ministers and to the Secretary-General of the Council of Europe for publication. This Report shall be confined to a brief statement of the facts and of the solution reached.

Article 31

1. If a solution is not reached, the Commission shall draw up a Report on the facts and state its opinion as to whether the facts found disclose a breach by the State concerned of its obligations under the Convention. The opinions of all the members of the Commission on this point may be stated in the Report.

2. The Report shall be transmitted to the Committee of Ministers. It shall also be transmitted to the States concerned, who shall not be at liberty to publish it.

3. In transmitting the Report to the Committee of Ministers the Commission may make such proposals as it thinks fit.

Article 32

1. If the question is not referred to the Court in accordance with Article 48 of this Convention within a period of three months from the date of the transmission of the Report to the Committee of Ministers, the Committee of Ministers shall decide by a majority of two-thirds of the members entitled to sit on the Committee whether there has been a violation of the Convention.

2. In the affirmative case the Committee of Ministers shall prescribe a period during which the High Contracting Party concerned must take the measures required by the decision of the Committee of Ministers.

3. If the High Contracting Party concerned has not taken satisfactory measures within the prescribed period, the Committee of Ministers shall decide by the majority provided for in paragraph (1) above what effect shall be given to its original decision and shall publish the Report.

4. The High Contracting Parties undertake to regard as binding on them any decision which the Commit-

tee of Ministers may take in application of the preceding paragraphs.

Article 33

The Commission shall meet in camera.

Article 34

The Commission shall take its decisions by a majority of the Members present and voting; the Sub-Commission shall take its decisions by a majority of its members.

Article 35

The Commission shall meet as the circumstances require. The meetings shall be convened by the Secretary-General of the Council of Europe.

Article 36

The Commission shall draw up its own rules of procedure.

Article 37

The secretariat of the Commission shall be provided by the Secretary-General of the Council of Europe.

SECTION IV

Article 38

The European Court of Human Rights shall consist of a number of judges equal to that of the Members of the Council of Europe. Not two judges may be nationals of the same State.

Article 39

1. The members of the Court shall be elected by the Consultative Assembly by a majority of the votes cast from a list of persons nominated by the Members of the Council of Europe; each Member shall nominate three candidates, of whom two at least shall be its nationals.

2. As for applicable, the same procedure shall be followed to complete the Court in the event of the admission of new Members of the Council of Europe, and in filling casual vacancies.

3. The candidates shall be of high moral character and must either possess the qualifications required for appointment to high judicial office or be jurisconsults of recognised competence.

Article 40

1. The members of the Court shall be elected for a period of nine years. They may be re-elected. However, of the members elected at the first election the terms of four members shall expire at the end of three years, and

the terms of four more members shall expire at the end of six years.

2. The members whose terms are to expire at the end of the initial periods of three and six years shall be chosen by lot by the Secretary-General immediately after the first election has been completed.

3. A member of the Court elected to replace a member whose term of office has not expired shall hold office for the remainder of his predecessor's term.

4. The members of the Court shall hold office until replaced. After having been replaced, they shall continue to deal with such cases as they already have under consideration.

Article 41

The Court shall elect its President and Vice-President for a period of three years. They may be re-elected.

Article 42

The members of the Court shall receive for each day of duty a compensation to be determined by the Committee of Ministers.

Article 43

For the consideration of each case brought before it the Court shall consist of a Chamber composed of seven judges. There shall sit as an *ex officio* member of the Chamber the judge who is a national of any State party concerned, or, if there is none, a person of its choice who shall sit in the capacity of judge; the names of the other judges shall be chosen by lot by the President before the opening of the case.

Article 44

Only the High Contracting Parties and the Commission shall have the right to bring a case before the Court.

Article 45

The jurisdiction of the Court shall extend to all cases concerning the interpretation and application of the present Convention which the High Contracting Parties or the Commission shall refer to it in accordance with Article 48.

Article 46

1. Any of the High Contracting Parties may at any time declare that it recognises as compulsory *ipso facto* and without special agreement the jurisdiction of the Court in all matters concerning the interpretation and application of the present Convention.

2. The declarations referred to above may be made unconditionally or on condition of reciprocity on the part

of several or certain other High Contracting Parties or for a specified period.

3. These declarations shall be deposited with the Secretary-General of the Council of Europe who shall transmit copies thereof to the High Contracting Parties.

Article 47

The Court may only deal with a case after the Commission has acknowledged the failure of efforts for a friendly settlement and within the period of three months provided for in Article 32.

Article 48

The following may bring a case before the Court, provided that the High Contracting Party concerned, if there is only one, or the High Contracting Parties concerned, if there is more than one, are subject to the compulsory jurisdiction of the Court or, failing that, with the consent of the High Contracting Party concerned, if there is only one, or of the High Contracting Parties concerned if there is more than one:

(a) the Commission;

(b) a High Contracting Party whose national is alleged to be a victim;

(c) a High Contracting Party which referred the case to the Commission;

(d) a High Contracting Party against which the complaint has been lodged.

Article 49

In the event of dispute as to whether the Court has jurisdiction, the matter shall be settled by the decision of the Court.

Article 50

If the Court finds that a decision or a measure taken by a legal authority or any other authority of a High Contracting Party is completely or partially in conflict with the obligations arising from the present Convention, and if the internal law of the said Party allows only partial reparation to be made for the consequences of this decision or measure, the decision of the Court shall, if necessary, afford just satisfaction to the injured party.

Article 51

1. Reasons shall be given for the judgment of the Court.

2. If the judgment does not represent in whole or in part the unanimous opinion of the judges, any judge shall be entitled to deliver a separate opinion.

Article 52

The judgment of the Court shall be final.

Article 53

The High Contracting Parties undertake to abide by the decision of the Court in any case to which they are parties.

Article 54

The judgment of the Court shall be transmitted to the Committee of Ministers which shall supervise its execution.

Article 55

The Court shall draw up its own rules and shall determine its own procedure.

Article 56

1. The first election of the members of the Court shall take place after the declarations by the High Contracting Parties mentioned in Article 46 have reached a total of eight.

2. No case can be brought before the Court before this election.

SECTION V

Article 57

On receipt of a request from the Secretary-General of the Council of Europe any High Contracting Party shall furnish an explanation of the manner in which its internal law ensures the effective implementation of any of the provisions of this Convention.

Article 58

The expenses of the Commission and the Court shall be borne by the Council of Europe.

Article 59

The members of the Commission and of the Court shall be entitled, during the discharge of their functions, to the privileges and immunities provided for in Article 40 of the Statute of the Council of Europe 2/ and in the agreements made thereunder.

Article 60

Nothing in this Convention shall be construed as limiting or derogating from any of the human rights and fundamental freedoms which may be ensured under the

2/ United Nations, *Treaty Series*, vol.87, p.103; vol.100, p.302, and vol.196, p.347.

laws of any High Contracting Party or under any other agreement to which it is a Party.

Article 61

Nothing in this Convention shall prejudice the powers conferred on the Committee of Ministers by the Statute of the Council of Europe.

Article 62

The High Contracting Parties agree that, except by special agreement, they will not avail themselves of treaties, conventions or declarations in force between them for the purpose of submitting, by way of petition, a dispute arising out of the interpretation or application of this Convention to a means of settlement other than those provided for in this Convention.

Article 63

1. Any State may at the time of its ratification or at any time thereafter declare by notification addressed to the Secretary-General of the Council of Europe that the present Convention shall extend to all or any of the territories for whose international relations it is responsible.

2. The Convention shall extend to the territory or territories named in the notification as from the thirtieth day after the receipt of this notification by the Secretary-General of the Council of Europe.

3. The provisions of this Convention shall be applied in such territories with dure regard, however, to local requirements.

4. Any State which has made a declaration in accordance with paragraph 1 of this Article may at any time thereafter declare on behalf of one or more of the territories to which the declaration relates that it accepts the competence of the Commission to receive petitions from individuals, non-governmental organisations or groups of individuals in accordance with Article 25 of the present Convention.

Article 64

1. Any State may, when signing this Convention or when depositing its instrument of ratification, make a reservation in respect of any particular provision of the Convention to the extent that any law then in force in its territory is not in conformity with the provision. Reservations of a general character shall not be permitted under this Article.

2. Any reservation made under this Article shall contain a brief statement of the law concerned.

Article 65

1. A High Contracting Party may denounce the present Convention only after the expiry of five years from the date on which it became a Party to it and after six months' notice contained in a notification addressed to the Secretary-General of the Council of Europe, who shall inform the other High Contracting Parties.

2. Such a denunciation shall not have the effect of releasing the High Contracting Party concerned from its obligations under this Convention in respect of any act which, being capable of constituting a violation of such obligations, may have been performed by it before the date at which the denunciation became effective.

3. Any High Contracting Party which shall cease to be a Member of the Council of Europe shall cease to be a Party to this Convention under the same conditions.

4. The Convention may be denounced in accordance with the provisions of the preceding paragraphs in respect of any territory to which it has been declared to extend under the terms of Article 63.

Article 66

1. This Convention shall be open to the signature of the Members of the Council of Europe. It shall be ratified. Ratifications shall be deposited with the Secretary-General of the Council of Europe.

2. The present Convention shall come into force after the deposit of ten instruments of ratification.

3. As regards any signatory ratifying subsequently, the Convention shall come into force at the date of the deposit of its instrument of ratification.

4. The Secretary-General of the Council of Europe shall notify all the Members of the Council of Europe of the entry into force of the Convention, the names of the High Contracting Parties who have ratified it, and the deposit of all instruments of ratification which may be effected subsequently.

DONE at Rome, this fifth day of November, one thousand nine hundred and fifty, in French and in English, the two texts being equally authentic, in a single copy which shall remain deposited in the archives of the Council of Europe. The Secretary-General shall deliver certified true copies to all signatories.

Document 11

Advisory Opinion of the International Court of Justice (Reservations to the Convention on the Prevention and Punishment of the Crime of Genocide)

28 May 1951

Advisory jurisdiction of the Court.—Objection based: on alleged existence of a dispute; on alleged exclusive right of the parties to the Genocide Convention to interpret it: on Article IX of the Convention.—Rejection of objection.

Replies limited to Genocide Convention.—Abstract questions.

Reservations.—Objections thereto.—Right of a State which has made a reservation to be a party to the Convention notwithstanding the objection made to its reservation by certain parties.—Circumstances justifying a relaxation of [the rule of integrity.—Faculty of making reservations to the Convention; intention of the General Assembly and of the contracting States; high ideals of the Convention.—Criterion of the compatibility of the reservation with object and purpose of the Convention.—Individual appraisal by States.—Absence of a rule of international law concerning the effects of reservations.—Administrative practice of the League of Nations and of the United Nations.

Effect of the reservation: between the State which makes it and the State which objects thereto.—Application of the criterion of compatibility.

Objection made: by a State which has not signed the Convention; by a signatory which has not ratified.—Provisional status of signatory State.

Advisory opinion

Present: President BASDEVANT; *Vice-President* GUERRERO; *Judges* ALVAREZ, HACKWORTH, WINIARSKI, ZORIČIČ, DE VISSCHER, Sir Arnold McNAIR, KLAESTAD, BADAWI PASHA, READ, HSU MO; *Registrar* HAMBRO.

The Court, composed as above, gives the following Advisory Opinion:

On November 16th, 1950, the General Assembly of the United Nations adopted the following resolution :

"*The General Assembly,*

"*Having examined* the report of the Secretary-General regarding reservations to multilateral conventions,

"*Considering* that certain reservations to the Convention on the Prevention and Punishment of the Crime of Genocide have been objected to by some States,

"*Considering* that the International Law Commission is studying the whole subject of the law of treaties, including the question of reservations,

"*Considering* that different views regarding reservations have been expressed during the fifth session of the General Assembly, and particularly in the Sixth Committee,

"1. *Requests* the International Court of Justice to give an Advisory Opinion on the following questions:

"In so far as concerns the Convention on the Prevention and Punishment of the Crime of Genocide in the event of a State ratifying or acceding to the Convention subject to a reservation made either on ratification or on accession, or on signature followed by ratification:

"I. Can the reserving State be regarded as being a party to the Convention while still maintaining its reservation if the reservation is objected to by one or more of the parties to the Convention but not by others ?

"II. If the answer to Question I is in the affirmative, what is the effect of the reservation as between the reserving State and:

"(a) The parties which object to the reservation?

"(b) Those which accept it ?

III. What would be the legal effect as regards the answer to Question I if an objection to a reservation is made:

"(a) By a signatory which has not yet ratified ?

"(b) By a State entitled to sign or accede but which has not yet done so?

"2. *Invites* the International Law Commission:

"(a) In the course of its work on the codification of the law of treaties, to study the question of reservations to multilateral conventions both from the point of view of codification and from that of the progressive development of international law; to give priority to this study and to report thereon, especially as regards multilateral conventions of which the Secretary-General is the depositary, this report to be considered by the General Assembly at its sixth session;

"(b) In connection with this study, to take account of all the views expressed during the fifth session of the General Assembly, and particularly in the Sixth Committee;

"3. *Instructs* the Secretary-General, pending the rendering of the Advisory Opinion by the International Court of Justice, the receipt of a report from the International Law Commission and further action by the General Assembly, to follow his prior practice with respect to the receipt of reservations to conventions and with respect to the notification and solicitation of approvals thereof, all without prejudice to the legal effect of objections to reservations to conventions as it may be recommended by the General Assembly at its sixth session."

By a letter of November 17th, 1950, filed in the Registry on November 20th, the Secretary-General of the United Nations transmitted to the Court a certified true copy of the General Assembly's resolution.

On November 25th, 1950, in accordance with Article 66, paragraph I, of the Court's Statute, the Registrar gave notice of the request to all States entitled to appear before the Court.

On December 1st 1950, the President—as the Court was not sitting—made an order by which he appointed January 20th, 1951, as the date of expiry of the time-limit for the filing of written statements and reserved the rest of the procedure for further decision. Under the terms of this order, such statements could be submitted to the Court by all States entitled to become parties to the Genocide Convention, namely, any Member of the United Nations as well as any non-member State to which an invitation to this effect had been addressed by the General Assembly. Furthermore, written statements could also be submitted by any international organization considered by the Court as likely to be able to furnish information on the questions referred to it for an Advisory Opinion, namely, the International Labour Organization and the Organization of American States.

On the same date, the Registrar addressed the special and direct communication provided for in Article 66, paragraph 2, of the Statute to all States entitled to appear before the Court, which had been invited to sign and ratify or accede to the Genocide Convention, either under Article XI of that Convention or by virtue of a resolution adopted by the General Assembly on December 3rd, 1949, which refers to Article XI; by application of the provisions of Article 63, paragraph I, and Article 68 of the Statute, the same communication was addressed to other States invited to sign and ratify or accede to the Convention, by virtue of the resolution of the General Assembly, namely, the following States: Albania, Austria, Bulgaria, Cambodia, Ceylon, Finland, Hungary, Ireland, Italy, Jordan, Korea, Laos, Monaco, Portugal, Romania, and Viet Nam. Finally, the Registrar's communication was addressed to the International Labour Organization and the Organization of American States.

Written statements were deposited within the prescribed time-limit by the following governments and international organizations: the Organization of American States, the Union of Soviet Socialist Republics, the Hashemite Kingdom of Jordan, the United States of America, the United Kingdom of Great Britain and Northern Ireland, the Secretary-General of the United Nations, Israel, the International Labour Organization, Poland, Czechoslovakia, the Netherlands, the People's Republic of Romania, the Ukrainian Soviet Socialist Republic, the People's Republic of Bulgaria, the Byelorussian Soviet Socialist Republic, the Republic of the Philippines.

By a despatch dated December 14th, 1950, and received on January 29th, 1951, the Secretary-General of the United Nations transmitted to the Registry the documents which he had been requested to furnish pursuant to Article 65 of the Court's Statute. All these documents are enumerated in the list attached to the present Opinion.

As the Federal German Republic had been invited on December 20th, 1950, to accede to the Genocide Convention, the Registrar by a telegram and a letter of January 17th, 1951, which constituted the special and direct communication provided for under Article 66, paragraph 2, of the Statute, informed the Federal German Government that the Court was prepared to receive a written statement and to hear an oral statement on its behalf; no action was taken in pursuance of this suggestion.

By a letter dated March 9th, 1951, filed in the Registry on March 15th, the Secretary-General of the United Nations announced that he had designated Dr. Ivan S. Kerno, Assistant Secretary-General in charge of the Legal Department, as his representative before the Court, and that Dr. Kerno was authorized to present any statement likely to assist the Court.

The Government of the United Kingdom, the French Government and the Government of Israel stated, in letters dated respectively January 17th, March 12th and March 19th, 1951, that they intended to present oral statements.

At public sittings held from April 10th to 14th, 1951, the Court heard oral statements presented:

on behalf of the Secretary-General of the United Nations by Dr. Ivan S. Kerno, Assistant Secretary-General in charge of the Legal Department;

on behalf of the Government of Israel by Mr. Shabtai Rosenne, Legal Adviser to the Ministry of Foreign Affairs;

on behalf of the Government of the United Kingdom of Great Britain and Northern Ireland by the Right Honourable Sir Hartley Shawcross, K.C., M.P., Attorney-General, and by Mr. G. G. Fitzmaurice, C.M.G., Second Legal Adviser to the Foreign Office;

on behalf of the Government of the French Republic by M. Charles Rousseau, Professor at the Faculty of Law in Paris, Assistant Legal Adviser of the Ministry of Foreign Affairs.

* * *

In the communications which they have addressed to the Court, certain governments have contended that the Court is not competent to exercise its advisory functions in the present case.

A first objection is founded on the argument that the making of an objection to a reservation made by a State to the Convention on the Prevention and Punishment of the Crime of Genocide constitutes a dispute and that, in order to avoid adjudicating on that dispute, the Court should refrain from replying to Questions I and II. In this connection, the Court can confine itself to recalling the principles which it laid down in its Opinion of March 30th, 1950 (I.C.J. Reports 1950, P. 71). A reply to a request for an Opinion should not, in principle, be refused. The permissive provision of Article 65 of the Statute recognizes that the Court has the power to decide whether the circumstances of a particular case are such as to lead the Court to decline to reply to the request for an Opinion. At the same time, Article 68 of the Statute recognizes that the Court has the power to decide to what extent the circumstances of each case must lead it to apply to advisory proceedings the provisions of the Statute which apply in contentious cases. The object of this request for an Opinion is to guide the United Nations in respect of its own action. It is indeed beyond dispute that the General Assembly, which I drafted and adopted the Genocide Convention, and the Secretary-General, who is the depositary of the instruments of ratification and accession, have an interest in knowing the legal effects of reservations to that Convention and more particularly the legal effects of objections to such reservations.

Following a similar line of argument, it has been contended that the request for an opinion would constitute an inadmissible interference by the General Assembly and by States hitherto strangers to the Convention in the interpretation of that Convention, as only States which are parties to the Convention are entitled to interpret it or to seek an interpretation of it. It must be pointed out in this connection that, not only did the General Assembly take the initiative in respect of the Genocide Convention, draw up its terms and open it for signature and accession by States, but that express provisions of the Convention (Articles XI and XVI) associate the General Assembly with the life of the Convention; and finally, that the General Assembly actually associated itself with it by endeavouring to secure the adoption of the Convention by as great a number of States as possible. In these circumstances, there can be no doubt that the precise determination of the conditions for participation in the Convention constitutes a permanent interest of direct concern to the United Nations which has not disappeared with the entry into force of the Convention. Moreover, the power of the General Assembly to request an Advisory Opinion from the Court in no way impairs the inherent right of States parties to the Convention in the matter of its interpretation. This right is independent of the General Assembly's power and is exercisable in a parallel direction. Furthermore, States which are parties to the Convention enjoy the faculty of referring the matter to the Court in the manner provided in Article IX of the Convention.

Another objection has been put forward to the exercise of the Court's advisory jurisdiction: it is based on Article IX of the Genocide Convention which provides that disputes relating to the interpretation, application or fulfilment of that Convention shall be submitted to the International Court of Justice at the request of any of the parties to the dispute. It has been contended that there exists no dispute in the present case and that, consequently, the effect of Article IX is to deprive the Court, not only of any contentious jurisdiction, but also of any power to give an Advisory Opinion. The Court cannot share this view. The existence of a procedure for the settlement of disputes, such as that provided by Article IX, does not in itself exclude the Court's advisory jurisdiction, for Article 96 of the Charter confers upon the General Assembly and the Security Council in general terms the right to request this Court to give an Advisory Opinion "on any legal question". Further, Article IX, before it can be applied, presupposes the status of "contracting parties"; consequently, it cannot be invoked against a request for an Opinion the very object of which is to determine, in relation to reservations and objections thereto, the conditions in which a State can become a party.

In conclusion, the Court considers that none of the above-stated objections to the exercise of its advisory function is well founded.

* * *

The Court observes that the three questions which have been referred to it for an Opinion have certain common characteristics.

All three questions are expressly limited by the terms of the Resolution of the General Assembly to the Convention on the Prevention and Punishment of the Crime of Genocide, and the same Resolution invites the International Law Commission to study the general question of reservations to multilateral conventions both from the point of view of codification and from that of the progressive development of international law. The questions thus having a clearly defined object, the replies which the Court is called upon to give to them are necessarily and strictly limited to that Convention. The Court will seek these replies in the rules of law relating to the effect to be given to the intention of the parties to multilateral conventions.

The three questions are purely abstract in character. They refer neither to the reservations which have, in fact, been made to the Convention by certain States, nor to the objections which have been made to such reservations by other States. They do not even refer to the reservations which may in future be made in respect of any particular article; nor do they refer to the objections to which these reservations might give rise.

Question I is framed in the following terms:

"Can the reserving State be regarded as being a party to the Convention while still maintaining its reservation if the reservation is objected to by one or more of the parties to the Convention but not by others ?"

The Court observes that this question refers, not to the possibility of making reservations to the Genocide Convention, but solely to the question whether a contracting State which has made a reservation can, while still maintaining it, be regarded as being a party to the Convention, when there is a divergence of views between the contracting parties concerning this reservation, some accepting the reservation, others refusing to accept it.

It is well established that in its treaty relations a State cannot be bound without its consent, and that consequently no reservation can be effective against any State without its agreement thereto. It is also a generally recognized principle that a multilateral convention is the result of an agreement freely concluded upon its clauses and that consequently none of the contracting parties is entitled to frustrate or impair, by means of unilateral

decisions or particular agreements, the purpose and *raison d'être* of the convention. To this principle was linked the notion of the integrity of the convention as adopted, a notion which in its traditional concept involved the proposition that no reservation was valid unless it was accepted by all the contracting parties without exception, as would have been the case if it had been stated during the negotiations.

This concept, which is directly inspired by the notion of contract, is of undisputed value as a principle. However, as regards the Genocide Convention, it is proper to refer to a variety of circumstances which would lead to a more flexible application of this principle. Among these circumstances may be noted the clearly universal character of the United Nations under whose auspices the Convention was concluded, and the very wide degree of participation envisaged by Article XI of the Convention. Extensive participation in conventions of this type has already given rise to greater flexibility in the international practice concerning multilateral conventions. More general resort to reservations, very great allowance made for tacit assent to reservations, the existence of practices which go so far as to admit that the author of reservations which have been rejected by certain contracting parties is nevertheless to be regarded as a party to the convention in relation to those contracting parties that have accepted the reservations—all these factors are manifestations of a new need for flexibility in the operation of multilateral conventions.

It must also be pointed out that although the Genocide Convention was finally approved unanimously, it is nevertheless the result of a series of majority votes. The majority principle, while facilitating the conclusion of multilateral conventions, may also make it necessary for certain States to make reservations. This observation is confirmed by the great number of reservations which have been made of recent years to multilateral conventions.

In this state of international practice, it could certainly not be inferred from the absence of an article providing for reservations in a multilateral convention that the contracting States are prohibited from making certain reservations. Account should also be taken of the fact that the absence of such an article or even the decision not to insert such an article can be explained by the desire not to invite a multiplicity of reservations. The character of a multilateral convention, its purpose, provisions, mode of preparation and adoption, are factors which must be considered in determining, in the absence of any express provision on the subject, the possibility of making reservations, as well as their validity and effect.

Although it was decided during the preparatory work not to insert a special article on reservations, it is none the less true that the faculty for States to make reservations was contemplated at successive stages of the drafting of the Convention. In this connection, the following passage may be quoted from the comments on the draft Convention prepared by the Secretary-General: ".... (1) It would seem that reservations of a general scope have no place in a convention of this kind which does not deal with the private interests of a State, but with the preservation of an element of international order....; (2) perhaps in the course of discussion in the General Assembly it will be possible to allow certain limited reservations."

Even more decisive in this connection is the debate on reservations in the Sixth Committee at the meetings (December 1st and 2nd, 1948) which immediately preceded the adoption of the Genocide Convention by the General Assembly. Certain delegates clearly announced that their governments could only sign or ratify the Convention subject to certain reservations.

Furthermore, the faculty to make reservations to the Convention appears to be implicitly admitted by the very terms of Question I.

The Court recognizes that an understanding was reached within the General Assembly on the faculty to make reservations to the Genocide Convention and that it is permitted to conclude therefrom that States becoming parties to the Convention gave their assent thereto. It must now determine what kind of reservations may be made and what kind of objections may be taken to them.

The solution of these problems must be found in the special characteristics of the Genocide Convention. The origins and character of that Convention, the objects pursued by the General Assembly and the contracting parties, the relations which exist between the provisions of the Convention, *inter se*, and between those provisions and these objects, furnish elements of interpretation of the will of the General Assembly and the parties.

The origins of the Convention show that it was the intention of the United Nations to condemn and punish genocide as "a crime under international law" involving a denial of the right of existence of entire human groups, a denial which shocks the conscience of mankind and results in great losses to humanity, and which is contrary to moral law and to the spirit and aims of the United Nations (Resolution 96 (I)) of the General Assembly, December 11th, 1946). The first consequence arising from this conception is that the principles underlying the Convention are principles which are recognized by civilized nations as binding on States, even without any conventional obligation.

A second consequence is the universal character both of the condemnation of genocide and of the cooperation required "in order to liberate mankind from such an odious scourge" (Preamble to the Convention). The Genocide Convention was therefore intended by the General Assembly and by the contracting parties to be definitely universal in scope. It was in fact approved on December 9th, 1948, by a resolution which was unanimously adopted by fifty-six States.

The objects of such a convention must also be considered. The Convention was manifestly adopted for a purely humanitarian and civilizing purpose. It is indeed difficult to imagine a convention that might have this dual character to a greater degree, since its object on the one hand is to safeguard the very existence of certain human groups and on the other to confirm and endorse the most elementary principles of morality. In such a convention the contracting States do not have any interests of their own; they merely have, one and all, a common interest, namely, the accomplishment of those high purposes which are the *raison d'être* of the convention. Consequently, in a convention of this type one cannot speak of individual advantages or disadvantages to States, or of the maintenance of a perfect contractual balance between rights and duties. The high ideals which inspired the Convention provide, by virtue of the common will of the parties, the foundation and measure of all its provisions.

The foregoing considerations, when applied to the question of reservations, and more particularly to the effects of objections to reservations, lead to the following conclusions.

The object and purpose of the Genocide Convention imply that it was the intention of the General Assembly and of the States which adopted it that as many States as possible should participate. The complete exclusion from the Convention of one or more States would not only restrict the scope of its application, but would detract from the authority of the moral and humanitarian principles which are its basis. It is inconceivable that the contracting parties readily contemplated that an objection to a minor reservation should produce such a result. But even less could the contracting parties have intended to sacrifice the very object of the Convention in favour of a vain desire to secure as many participants as possible. The object and purpose of the Convention thus limit both the freedom of making reservations and that of objecting to them. It follows that it is the compatibility of a reservation with the object and purpose of the Convention that must furnish the criterion for the attitude of a State in making the reservation on accession as well as for the appraisal by a State in objecting to the reservation. Such is the rule of conduct which must guide every State in the appraisal which it must make, individually and from its own standpoint, of the admissibility of any reservation.

Any other view would lead either to the acceptance of reservations which frustrate the purposes which the General Assembly and the contracting parties had in mind, or to recognition that the parties to the Convention have the power of excluding from it the author of a reservation, even a minor one, which may be quite compatible with those purposes.

It has nevertheless been argued that any State entitled to become a party to the Genocide Convention may do so while making any reservation it chooses by virtue of its sovereignty. The Court cannot share this view. It is obvious that so extreme an application of the idea of State sovereignty could lead to a complete disregard of the object and purpose of the Convention.

On the other hand, it has been argued that there exists a rule of international law subjecting the effect of a reservation to the express or tacit assent of all the contracting parties. This theory rests essentially on a contractual conception of the absolute integrity of the convention as adopted. This view, however, cannot prevail if, having regard to the character of the convention, its purpose and its mode of adoption, it can be established that the parties intended to derogate from that rule by admitting the faculty to make reservations thereto.

It does not appear, moreover, that the conception of the absolute integrity of a convention has been transformed into a rule of international law. The considerable part which tacit assent has always played in estimating the effect which is to be given to reservations scarcely permits one to state that such a rule exists, determining with sufficient precision the effect of objections made to reservations. In fact, the examples of objections made to reservations appear to be too rare in international practice to have given rise to such a rule. It cannot be recognized that the report which was adopted on the subject by the Council of the League of Nations on June 17th, 1927, has had this effect. At best, the recommendation made on that date by the Council constitutes the point of departure of an administrative practice which, after being observed by the Secretariat of the League of Nations, imposed itself, so to speak, in the ordinary course of things on the Secretary-General of the United Nations in his capacity of depositary of conventions concluded under the auspices of the League. But it cannot be concluded that the legal problem of the effect of objections to reservations has in this way been solved. The opinion of the Secretary-General of the United Nations himself is embodied in the following passage of his report of September 21st, 1950: "While it is universally recognized that the consent of the other governments concerned must be sought before they can be bound by the terms of a reservation, there has not been unanimity either as to the procedure to be followed by a depositary in obtaining the necessary consent or as to the legal effect of a State's objecting to a reservation."

It may, however, be asked whether the General Assembly of the United Nations in approving the Geno-cide Convention, had in mind the practice according to which the Secretary-General, in exercising his functions as a depositary, did not regard a reservation as definitively accepted until it had been established that none of the other contracting States objected to it. If this were the case, it might be argued that the implied intention of the contracting parties was to make the effectiveness of any reservation to the Genocide Convention conditional on the assent of all the parties.

The Court does not consider that this view corresponds to reality. It must be pointed out, first of all, that the existence of an administrative practice does not in itself constitute a decisive factor in ascertaining what views the contracting States to the Genocide Convention may have had concerning the rights and duties resulting therefrom. It must also be pointed out that there existed among the American States members both of the United Nations and of the Organization of American States, a different practice which goes so far as to permit a reserving State to become a party irrespective of the nature of the reservations or of the objections raised by other contracting States. The preparatory work of the Convention contains nothing to justify the statement that the contracting States implicitly had any definite practice in mind. Nor is there any such indication in the subsequent attitude of the contracting States: neither the reservations made by certain States nor the position adopted by other States towards those reservations permit the conclusion that assent to one or the other of these practices had been given. Finally, it is not without interest to note, in view of the preference generally said to attach to an established practice, that the debate on reservations to multilateral treaties which took place in the Sixth Committee at the fifth session of the General Assembly reveals a profound divergence of views, some delegations being attached to the idea of the absolute integrity of the Convention, others favouring a more flexible practice which would bring about the participation of as many States as possible.

It results from the foregoing considerations that Question I, on account of its abstract character, cannot be given an absolute answer. The appraisal of a reservation and the effect of objections that might be made to it depend upon the particular circumstances of each individual case.

* * *

Having replied to Question I, the Court will now examine Question II, which is framed as follows:

"If the answer to Question I is in the affirmative, what is the effect of the reservation as between the reserving State and:

"(a)   the parties which object to the reservation?

"(b)   those which accept it?"

The considerations which form the basis of the Court's reply to Question I are to a large extent equally applicable here. As has been pointed out above, each State which is a party to the Convention is entitled to appraise the validity of the reservation, and it exercises this right individually and from its own standpoint. As no State can be bound by a reservation to which it has not consented, it necessarily follows that each State objecting to it will or will not, on the basis of its individual appraisal within the limits of the criterion of the object and purpose stated above, consider the reserving State to be a party to the Convention. In the ordinary course of events, such a decision will only affect the relationship between the State making the reservation and the objecting State; on the other hand, as will be pointed out later, such a decision might aim at the complete exclusion from the Convention in a case where it was expressed by the adoption of a position on the jurisdictional plane.

The disadvantages which result from this possible divergence of views—which an article concerning the making of reservations could have obviated—are real; they are mitigated by the common duty of the contracting States to be guided in their judgement by the compatibility or incompatibility of the reservation with the object and purpose of the Convention. It must clearly be assumed that the contracting States are desirous of preserving intact at least what is essential to the object of the Convention; should this desire be absent, it is quite clear that the Convention itself would be impaired both in its principle and in its application.

It may be that the divergence of views between parties as to the admissibility of a reservation will not in fact have any consequences. On the other hand, it may be that certain parties who consider that the assent given by other parties to a reservation is incompatible with the purpose of the Convention, will decide to adopt a position on the jurisdictional plane in respect of this divergence and to settle the dispute which thus arises either by special agreement or by the procedure laid down in Article IX of the Convention.

Finally, it may be that a State, whilst not claiming that a reservation is incompatible with the object and purpose of the Convention, will nevertheless object to it, but that an understanding between that State and the reserving State will have the effect that the Convention will enter into force between them, except for the clauses affected by the reservation.

Such being the situation, the task of the Secretary-General would be simplified and would be confined to receiving reservations and objections and notifying them.

* * *

Question III is framed in the following terms:

"What would be the legal effect as regards the answer to Question I if an objection to a reservation is made:

"(a) By a signatory which has not yet ratified?

"(b) By a State entitled to sign or accede but which has not yet done so?"

The Court notes that the terms of this question link it to Question I. This link is regarded by certain States as presupposing a negative reply to Question I.

The Court considers, however, that Question III could arise in any case. Even should the reply to Question I not tend to exclude, from being a party to the Convention, a State which has made a reservation to which another State has objected, the fact remains that the Convention does not enter into force as between the reserving State and the objecting State. Even if the objection has this reduced legal effect, the question would still arise whether the States mentioned under (a) and (b) of Question III are entitled to bring about such a result by their objection.

An extreme view of the right of such States would appear to be that these two categories of States have a *right to become* parties to the Convention, and that by virtue of this right they may object to reservations in the same way as any State which is a party to the Convention with full legal effect, i.e. the exclusion from the Convention of the reserving State. By denying them this right, it is said, they would be obliged either to renounce entirely their right of participating in the Convention, or to become a party to what is, in fact, a different convention. The dilemma does not correspond to reality, as the States concerned have always a right to be parties to the Convention in their relations with other contracting States.

From the date when the Genocide Convention was opened for signature, any Member of the United Nations and any non-member State to which an invitation to sign had been addressed by the General Assembly, had the *right to be a party* to the Convention. Two courses of action were possible to this end: either signature, from December 9th, 1948, until December 31st, 1949, followed by ratification, or accession as from January 1st, 1950 (Article XI of the Convention). The Court would point out that the right to become a party to the Convention does not express any very clear notion. It is inconceivable that a State, even if it has participated in the preparation of the Convention, could, before taking one or the other of the two courses of action provided for becoming a party to the Convention, exclude another State. Possessing no rights which derive from the Convention, that State cannot claim such a right from its status as a Member of the United Nations or from the invitation to sign which has been addressed to it by the General Assembly.

The case of a signatory State is different. Without going into the question of the legal effect of signing an international convention which necessarily varies in individual cases, the Court considers that signature constitutes a first step to participation in the Convention.

It is evident that without ratification, signature does not make the signatory State a party to the Convention; nevertheless, it establishes a provisional status in favour of that State. This status may decrease in value and importance after the Convention enters into force. But, both before and after the entry into force, this status would justify more favourable treatment being meted out to signatory States in respect of objections than to States which have neither signed nor acceded.

As distinct from the latter States, signatory States have taken certain of the steps necessary for the exercise of the right of being a party. Pending ratification, the provisional status created by signature confers upon the signatory a right to formulate as a precautionary measure objections which have themselves a provisional character. These would disappear if the signature were not followed by ratification, or they would become effective on ratification.

Until this ratification is made, the objection of a signatory State can therefore not have an immediate legal effect in regard to the reserving State. It would merely express and proclaim the eventual attitude of the signatory State when it becomes a party to the convention .

The legal interest of a signatory State in objecting to a reservation would thus be amply safeguarded. The reserving State would be given notice that as soon as the constitutional or other processes, which cause the lapse of time before ratification, have been completed, it would be confronted with a valid objection which carries full legal effect and consequently, it would have to decide, when the objection is stated, whether it wishes to maintain or withdraw its reservation. In the circumstances, it is of little importance whether the ratification occurs within a more or less long time-limit. The resulting situation will always be that of a ratification accompanied by an objection to the reservation. In the event of no ratification occurring, the notice would merely have been in vain.

For these reasons,
The Court is of opinion,
In so far as concerns the Convention on the Prevention and Punishment of the Crime of Genocide, in the event of a State ratifying or acceding to the Convention subject to a reservation made either on ratification or on accession, or on signature followed by ratification,

On Question I:

by seven votes to five,

that a State which has made and maintained a reservation which has been objected to by one or more of the parties to the Convention but not by others, can be regarded as being a party to the Convention if the reservation is compatible with the object and purpose of the Convention; otherwise, that State cannot be regarded as being a party to the Convention.

On Question II:

by seven votes to five,

(a) that if a party to the Convention objects to a reservation which it considers to be incompatible with the object and purpose of the Convention, it can in fact consider that the reserving State is not a party to the Convention;

(b) that if, on the other hand, a party accepts the reservation as being compatible with the object and purpose of the Convention, It can in fact consider that the reserving State is a party to the Convention.

On Question III:

by seven votes to five,

(a) that an objection to a reservation made by a signatory State which has not yet ratified the Convention can have the legal effect indicated in the reply to Question I only upon ratification. Until that moment it merely serves as a notice to the other State of the eventual attitude of the signatory State;

(b) that an objection to a reservation made by a State which is entitled to sign or accede but which has not yet done so, is without legal effect.

Done in French and English, the French text being authoritative, at the Peace Palace, The Hague, this twenty-eighth day of May, one thousand nine hundred and fifty-one, in two copies, one of which will be placed in the archives of the Court and the other transmitted to the Secretary-General of the United Nations.

(Signed) BASDEVANT, President.

(Signed) E. HAMBRO, Registrar.

Vice-President GUERRERO, Judges Sir Arnold McNAIR, READ and HSU MO, while agreeing that the Court has competence to give an Opinion, declare that they are unable to concur in the Opinion of the Court and have availed themselves of the right conferred on them by Articles 57 and 68 of the Statute and appended to the Opinion the common statement of their dissenting opinion.

Judge ALVAREZ, declaring that he is unable to concur in the Opinion of the Court, has availed himself of the right conferred on him by Articles 57 and 68 of the Statute and has appended to the Opinion the statement of his dissenting opinion.

(Initialled) J. B.
(Initialled) E. H.

Document 12

Convention relating to the Status of Refugees, adopted by the United Nations Conference of Plenipotentiaries on the Status of Refugees and Stateless Persons convened pursuant to General Assembly resolution 429 (V) of 14 December 1950

28 July 1951

PREAMBLE

The High Contracting Parties,

Considering that the Charter of the United Nations and the Universal Declaration of Human Rights approved on 10 December 1948 by the General Assembly have affirmed the principle that human beings shall enjoy fundamental rights and freedoms without discrimination,

Considering that the United Nations has, on various occasions, manifested its profound concern for refugees and endeavoured to assure refugees the widest possible exercise of these fundamental rights and freedoms,

Considering that it is desirable to revise and consolidate previous international agreements relating to the status of refugees and to extend the scope of and the protection accorded by such instruments by means of a new agreement,

Considering that the grant of asylum may place unduly heavy burdens on certain countries, and that a satisfactory solution of a problem of which the United Nations has recognized the international scope and nature cannot therefore be achieved without international cooperation,

Expressing the wish that all States, recognizing the social and humanitarian nature of the problem of refugees, will do everything within their power to prevent this problem from becoming a cause of tension between States,

Noting that the United Nations High Commissioner for Refugees is charged with the task of supervising international conventions providing for the protection of refugees, and recognizing that the effective co-ordination of measures taken to deal with this problem will depend upon the cooperation of States with the High Commissioner,

Have agreed as follows:

CHAPTER I

GENERAL PROVISIONS

Article 1
Definition of the term "refugee"

A. For the purposes of the present Convention, the term "refugee" shall apply to any person who:

1. Has been considered a refugee under the Arrangements of 12 May 1926 and 30 June 1928 or under the Conventions of 28 October 1933 and 10 February 1938, the Protocol of 14 September 1939 or the Constitution of the International Refugee Organization;

Decisions of non-eligibility taken by the International Refugee Organization during the period of its activities shall not prevent the status of refugee being accorded to persons who fulfil the conditions of paragraph 2 of this section;

2. As a result of events occurring before 1 January 1951 and owing to well-founded fear of being persecuted for reasons of race, religion, nationality, membership of a particular social group or political opinion, is outside the country of his nationality and is unable, or owing to such fear, is unwilling to avail himself of the protection of that country; or who, not having a nationality and being outside the country of his former habitual residence as a result of such events, is unable or, owing to such fear, is unwilling to return to it;

In the case of a person who has more than one nationality, the term "the country of his nationality" shall mean each of the countries of which he is a national, and a person shall not be deemed to be lacking the protection of the country of his nationality if, without any valid reason based on well-founded fear, he has not availed himself of the protection of one of the countries of which he is a national.

B. 1. For the purposes of this Convention, the words "events occurring before 1 January 1951" in article 1, section A, shall be understood to mean either (a) "events occurring in Europe before 1 January 1951"; or (b) "events occurring in Europe or elsewhere before 1 January 1951"; and each Contracting State shall make a declaration at the time of signature, ratification or accession, specifying which of these meanings it applies for the purpose of its obligations under this Convention;

2. Any Contracting State which has adopted alternative (a) may at any time extend its obligations by adopting alternative (b) by means of a notification addressed to the Secretary-General of the United Nations.

C. This Convention shall cease to apply to any person falling under the terms of section A if:

1. He has voluntarily re-availed himself of the protection of the country of his nationality; or

2. Having lost his nationality, he has voluntarily reacquired it; or

3. He has acquired a new nationality, and enjoys the protection of the country of his new nationality; or

4. He has voluntarily re-established himself in the country which he left or outside which he remained owing to fear of persecution; or

5. He can no longer, because the circumstances in connection with which he has been recognized as a refugee have ceased to exist, continue to refuse to avail himself of the protection of the country of his nationality;

Provided that this paragraph shall not apply to a refugee falling under section A (1) of this article who is able to invoke compelling reasons arising out of previous persecution for refusing to avail himself of the protection of the country of nationality;

6. Being a person who has no nationality he is, because the circumstances in connection with which he has been recognized as a refugee have ceased to exist, able to return to the country of his former habitual residence;

Provided that this paragraph shall not apply to a refugee falling under section A (1) of this article who is able to invoke compelling reasons arising out of previous persecution for refusing to return to the country of his former habitual residence.

D. This Convention shall not apply to persons who are at present receiving from organs or agencies of the United Nations other than the United Nations High Commissioner for Refugees protection or assistance;

When such protection or assistance has ceased for any reason, without the position of such persons being definitively settled in accordance with the relevant resolutions adopted by the General Assembly of the United Nations, these persons shall *ipso facto* be entitled to the benefits of this Convention.

E. This Convention shall not apply to a person who is recognized by the competent authorities of the country in which he has taken residence as having the rights and obligations which are attached to the possession of the nationality of that country.

F. The provisions of this Convention shall not apply to any person with respect to whom there are serious reasons for considering that:

(a) He has committed a crime against peace, a war crime, or a crime against humanity, as defined in the international instruments drawn up to make provision in respect of such crimes;

(b) He has committed a serious non-political crime outside the country of refuge prior to his admission to that country as a refugee;

(c) He has been guilty of acts contrary to the purposes and principles of the United Nations.

Article 2
General obligations

Every refugee has duties to the country in which he finds himself, which require in particular that he conform to its laws and regulations as well as to measures taken for the maintenance of public order.

Article 3
Non-discrimination

The Contracting States shall apply the provisions of this Convention to refugees without discrimination as to race, religion or country of origin.

Article 4
Religion

The Contracting States shall accord to refugees within their territories treatment at least as favourable as that accorded to their nationals with respect to freedom to practise their religion and freedom as regards the religious education of their children.

Article 5
Rights granted apart from this Convention

Nothing in this Convention shall be deemed to impair any rights and benefits granted by a Contracting State to refugees apart from this Convention.

Article 6
The term "in the same circumstances"

For the purposes of this Convention, the term "in the same circumstances" implies that any requirements (including requirements as to length and conditions of sojourn or residence) which the particular individual would have to fulfil for the enjoyment of the right in question, if he were not a refugee, must be fulfilled by him, with the exception of requirements which by their nature a refugee is incapable of fulfilling.

Article 7
Exemption from reciprocity

1. Except where this Convention contains more favourable provisions, a Contracting State shall accord to refugees the same treatment as is accorded to aliens generally.

2. After a period of three years' residence, all refugees shall enjoy exemption from legislative reciprocity in the territory of the Contracting States.

3. Each Contracting State shall continue to accord to refugees the rights and benefits to which they were

already entitled, in the absence of reciprocity, at the date of entry into force of this Convention for that State.

4. The Contracting States shall consider favourably the possibility of according to refugees, in the absence of reciprocity, rights and benefits beyond those to which they are entitled according to paragraphs 2 and 3, and to extending exemption from reciprocity to refugees who do not fulfil the conditions provided for in paragraphs 2 and 3.

5. The provisions of paragraphs 2 and 3 apply both to the rights and benefits referred to in articles 13, 18, 19, 21 and 22 of this Convention and to rights and benefits for which this Convention does not provide.

Article 8
Exemption from exceptional measures

With regard to exceptional measures which may be taken against the person, property or interests of nationals of a foreign State, the Contracting States shall not apply such measures to a refugee who is formally a national of the said State solely on account of such nationality. Contracting States which, under their legislation, are prevented from applying the general principle expressed in this article, shall, in appropriate cases, grant exemptions in favour of such refugees.

Article 9
Provisional measures

Nothing in this Convention shall prevent a Contracting State, in time of war or other grave and exceptional circumstances, from taking provisionally measures which it considers to be essential to the national security in the case of a particular person, pending a determination by the Contracting State that that person is in fact a refugee and that the continuance of such measures is necessary in his case in the interests of national security.

Article 10
Continuity of residence

1. Where a refugee has been forcibly displaced during the Second World War and removed to the territory of a Contracting State, and is resident there, the period of such enforced sojourn shall be considered to have been lawful residence within that territory.

2. Where a refugee has been forcibly displaced during the Second World War from the territory of a Contracting State and has, prior to the date of entry into force of this Convention, returned there for the purpose of taking up residence, the period of residence before and after such enforced displacement shall be regarded as one uninterrupted period for any purposes for which uninterrupted residence is required.

Article 11
Refugee seamen

In the case of refugees regularly serving as crew members on board a ship flying the flag of a Contracting State, that State shall give sympathetic consideration to their establishment on its territory and the issue of travel documents to them or their temporary admission to its territory particularly with a view to facilitating their establishment in another country.

CHAPTER II

JURIDICAL STATUS

Article 12
Personal status

1. The personal status of a refugee shall be governed by the law of the country of his domicile or, if he has no domicile, by the law of the country of his residence.

2. Rights previously acquired by a refugee and dependent on personal status, more particularly rights attaching to marriage, shall be respected by a Contracting State, subject to compliance, if this be necessary, with the formalities required by the law of that State, provided that the right in question is one which would have been recognized by the law of that State had he not become a refugee.

Article 13
Movable and immovable property

The Contracting States shall accord to a refugee treatment as favourable as possible and, in any event, not less favourable than that accorded to aliens generally in the same circumstances, as regards the acquisition of movable and immovable property and other rights pertaining thereto, and to leases and other contracts relating to movable and immovable property.

Article 14
Artistic rights and industrial property

In respect of the protection of industrial property, such as inventions, designs or models, trade marks, trade names, and of rights in literary, artistic and scientific works, a refugee shall be accorded in the country in which he has his habitual residence the same protection as is accorded to nationals of that country. In the territory of any other Contracting States, he shall be accorded the same protection as is accorded in that territory to nationals of the country in which he has his habitual residence.

Article 15
Right of association

As regards non-political and non-profit-making associations and trade unions the Contracting States shall accord to refugees lawfully staying in their territory the most favourable treatment accorded to nationals of a foreign country, in the same circumstances.

Article 16
Access to courts

1. A refugee shall have free access to the courts of law on the territory of all Contracting States.

2. A refugee shall enjoy in the Contracting State in which he has his habitual residence the same treatment as a national in matters pertaining to access to the courts, including legal assistance and exemption from *cautio judicatum solvi*.

3. A refugee shall be accorded in the matters referred to in paragraph 2 in countries other than that in which he has his habitual residence the treatment granted to a national of the country of his habitual residence.

CHAPTER III

GAINFUL EMPLOYMENT

Article 17
Wage-earning employment

1. The Contracting States shall accord to refugees lawfully staying in their territory the most favourable treatment accorded to nationals of a foreign country in the same circumstances, as regards the right to engage in wage-earning employment.

2. In any case, restrictive measures imposed on aliens or the employment of aliens for the protection of the national labour market shall not be applied to a refugee who was already exempt from them at the date of entry into force of this Convention for the Contracting State concerned, or who fulfils one of the following conditions:

(a) He has completed three years' residence in the country;

(b) He has a spouse possessing the nationality of the country of residence. A refugee may not invoke the benefit of this provision if he has abandoned his spouse;

(c) He has one or more children possessing the nationality of the country of residence.

3. The Contracting States shall give sympathetic consideration to assimilating the rights of all refugees with regard to wage-earning employment to those of nationals, and in particular of those refugees who have entered their territory pursuant to programmes of labour recruitment or under immigration schemes.

Article 18
Self-employment

The Contracting States shall accord to a refugee lawfully in their territory treatment as favourable as possible and, in any event, not less favourable than that accorded to aliens generally in the same circumstances, as regards the right to engage on his own account in agriculture, industry, handicrafts and commerce and to establish commercial and industrial companies.

Article 19
Liberal professions

1. Each Contracting State shall accord to refugees lawfully staying in their territory who hold diplomas recognized by the competent authorities of that State, and who are desirous of practising a liberal profession, treatment as favourable as possible and, in any event, not less favourable than that accorded to aliens generally in the same circumstances.

2. The Contracting States shall use their best endeavours consistently with their laws and constitutions to secure the settlement of such refugees in the territories, other than the metropolitan territory, for whose international relations they are responsible.

CHAPTER IV

WELFARE

Article 20
Rationing

Where a rationing system exists, which applies to the population at large and regulates the general distribution of products in short supply, refugees shall be accorded the same treatment as nationals.

Article 21
Housing

As regards housing, the Contracting States, in so far as the matter is regulated by laws or regulations or is subject to the control of public authorities, shall accord to refugees lawfully staying in their territory treatment as favourable as possible and, in any event, not less favourable than that accorded to aliens generally in the same circumstances.

Article 22
Public education

1. The Contracting States shall accord to refugees the same treatment as is accorded to nationals with respect to elementary education.

2. The Contracting States shall accord to refugees treatment as favourable as possible, and, in any event, not

less favourable than that accorded to aliens generally in the same circumstances, with respect to education other than elementary education and, in particular, as regards access to studies, the recognition of foreign school certificates, diplomas and degrees, the remission of fees and charges and the award of scholarships.

Article 23
Public relief

The Contracting States shall accord to refugees lawfully staying in their territory the same treatment with respect to public relief and assistance as is accorded to their nationals.

Article 24
Labour legislation and social security

1. The Contracting States shall accord to refugees lawfully staying in their territory the same treatment as is accorded to nationals in respect of the following matters:

(a) In so far as such matters are governed by laws or regulations or are subject to the control of administrative authorities: remuneration, including family allowances where these form part of remuneration, hours of work, overtime arrangements, holidays with pay, restrictions on home work, minimum age of employment, apprenticeship and training, women's work and the work of young persons, and the enjoyment of the benefits of collective bargaining;

(b) Social security (legal provisions in respect of employment injury, occupational diseases, maternity, sickness, disability, old age, death, unemployment, family responsibilities and any other contingency which, according to national laws or regulations, is covered by a social security scheme), subject to the following limitations:

(i) There may be appropriate arrangements for the maintenance of acquired rights and rights in course of acquisition;

(ii) National laws or regulations of the country of residence may prescribe special arrangements concerning benefits or portions of benefits which are payable wholly out of public funds, and concerning allowances paid to persons who do not fulfil the contribution conditions prescribed for the award of a normal pension.

2. The right to compensation for the death of a refugee resulting from employment injury or from occupational disease shall not be affected by the fact that the residence of the beneficiary is outside the territory of the Contracting State.

3. The Contracting States shall extend to refugees the benefits of agreements concluded between them, or which may be concluded between them in the future, concerning the maintenance of acquired rights and rights in the process of acquisition in regard to social security, subject only to the conditions which apply to nationals of the States signatory to the agreements in question.

4. The Contracting States will give sympathetic consideration to extending to refugees so far as possible the benefits of similar agreements which may at any time be in force between such Contracting States and non-contracting States.

CHAPTER V

ADMINISTRATIVE MEASURES

Article 25
Administrative assistance

1. When the exercise of a right by a refugee would normally require the assistance of authorities of a foreign country to whom he cannot have recourse, the Contracting States in whose territory he is residing shall arrange that such assistance be afforded to him by their own authorities or by an international authority.

2. The authority or authorities mentioned in paragraph 1 shall deliver or cause to be delivered under their supervision to refugees such documents or certifications as would normally be delivered to aliens by or through their national authorities.

3. Documents or certifications so delivered shall stand in the stead of the official instruments delivered to aliens by or through their national authorities, and shall be given credence in the absence of proof to the contrary.

4. Subject to such exceptional treatment as may be granted to indigent persons, fees may be charged for the services mentioned herein, but such fees shall be moderate and commensurate with those charged to nationals for similar services.

5. The provisions of this article shall be without prejudice to articles 27 and 28.

Article 26
Freedom of movement

Each Contracting State shall accord to refugees lawfully in its territory the right to choose their place of residence and to move freely within its territory subject to any regulations applicable to aliens generally in the same circumstances.

Article 27
Identity papers

The Contracting States shall issue identity papers to any refugee in their territory who does not possess a valid travel document.

Article 28
Travel documents

1. The Contracting States shall issue to refugees lawfully staying in their territory travel documents for the purpose of travel outside their territory, unless compelling reasons of national security or public order otherwise require, and the provisions of the Schedule to this Convention shall apply with respect to such documents. The Contracting States may issue such a travel document to any other refugee in their territory; they shall in particular give sympathetic consideration to the issue of such a travel document to refugees in their territory who are unable to obtain a travel document from the country of their lawful residence.

2. Travel documents issued to refugees under previous international agreements by Parties thereto shall be recognized and treated by the Contracting States in the same way as if they had been issued pursuant to this article.

Article 29
Fiscal charges

1. The Contracting States shall not impose upon refugees duties, charges or taxes, of any description whatsoever, other or higher than those which are or may be levied on their nationals in similar situations.

2. Nothing in the above paragraph shall prevent the application to refugees of the laws and regulations concerning charges in respect of the issue to aliens of administrative documents including identity papers.

Article 30
Transfer of assets

1. A Contracting State shall, in conformity with its laws and regulations, permit refugees to transfer assets which they have brought into its territory, to another country where they have been admitted for the purposes of resettlement.

2. A Contracting State shall give sympathetic consideration to the application of refugees for permission to transfer assets wherever they may be and which are necessary for their resettlement in another country to which they have been admitted.

Article 31
Refugees unlawfully in the country of refuge

1. The Contracting States shall not impose penalties, on account of their illegal entry or presence, on refugees who, coming directly from a territory where their life or freedom was threatened in the sense of article 1, enter or are present in their territory without authorization, provided they present themselves without delay to the authorities and show good cause for their illegal entry or presence.

2. The Contracting States shall not apply to the movements of such refugees restrictions other than those which are necessary and such restrictions shall only be applied until their status in the country is regularized or they obtain admission into another country. The Contracting States shall allow such refugees a reasonable period and all the necessary facilities to obtain admission into another country.

Article 32
Expulsion

1. The Contracting States shall not expel a refugee lawfully in their territory save on grounds of national security or public order.

2. The expulsion of such a refugee shall be only in pursuance of a decision reached in accordance with due process of law. Except where compelling reasons of national security otherwise require, the refugee shall be allowed to submit evidence to clear himself, and to appeal to and be represented for the purpose before competent authority or a person or persons specially designated by the competent authority.

3. The Contracting States shall allow such a refugee a reasonable period within which to seek legal admission into another country. The Contracting States reserve the right to apply during that period such internal measures as they may deem necessary.

Article 33
Prohibition of expulsion or return ("refoulement")

1. No Contracting State shall expel or return ("refouler") a refugee in any manner whatsoever to the frontiers of territories where his life or freedom would be threatened on account of his race, religion, nationality, membership of a particular social group or political opinion.

2. The benefit of the present provision may not, however, be claimed by a refugee whom there are reasonable grounds for regarding as a danger to the security of the country in which he is, or who, having been convicted by a final judgement of a particularly serious crime, constitutes a danger to the community of that country.

Article 34
Naturalization

The Contracting States shall as far as possible facilitate the assimilation and naturalization of refugees. They shall in particular make every effort to expedite naturalization proceedings and to reduce as far as possible the charges and costs of such proceedings.

CHAPTER VI

EXECUTORY AND TRANSITORY PROVISIONS

Article 35
Cooperation of the national authorities with the United Nations

1. The Contracting States undertake to cooperate with the Office of the United Nations High Commissioner for Refugees, or any other agency of the United Nations which may succeed it, in the exercise of its functions, and shall in particular facilitate its duty of supervising the application of the provisions of this Convention.

2. In order to enable the Office of the High Commissioner or any other agency of the United Nations which may succeed it, to make reports to the competent organs of the United Nations, the Contracting States undertake to provide them in the appropriate form with information and statistical data requested concerning:

(a) The condition of refugees,

(b) The implementation of this Convention, and

(c) Laws, regulations and decrees which are, or may hereafter be, in force relating to refugees.

Article 36
Information on national legislation

The Contracting States shall communicate to the Secretary-General of the United Nations the laws and regulations which they may adopt to ensure the application of this Convention.

Article 37
Relation to previous conventions

Without prejudice to article 28, paragraph 2, of this Convention, this Convention replaces, as between Parties to it, the Arrangements of 5 July 1922, 31 May 1924, 12 May 1926, 30 June 1928 and 30 July 1935, the Conventions of 28 October 1933 and 10 February 1938, the Protocol of 14 September 1939 and the Agreement of 15 October 1946.

CHAPTER VII

FINAL CLAUSES

Article 38
Settlement of disputes

Any dispute between Parties to this Convention relating to its interpretation or application, which cannot be settled by other means, shall be referred to the International Court of Justice at the request of any one of the parties to the dispute.

Article 39
Signature, ratification and accession

1. This Convention shall be opened for signature at Geneva on 28 July 1951 and shall thereafter be deposited with the Secretary-General of the United Nations. It shall be open for signature at the European Office of the United Nations from 28 July to 31 August 1951 and shall be re-opened for signature at the Headquarters of the United Nations from 17 September 1951 to 31 December 1952.

2. This Convention shall be open for signature on behalf of all States Members of the United Nations, and also on behalf of any other State invited to attend the Conference of Plenipotentiaries on the Status of Refugees and Stateless Persons or to which an invitation to sign will have been addressed by the General Assembly. It shall be ratified and the instruments of ratification shall be deposited with the Secretary-General of the United Nations.

3. This Convention shall be open from 28 July 1951 for accession by the States referred to in paragraph 2 of this article. Accession shall be effected by the deposit of an instrument of accession with the Secretary-General of the United Nations.

Article 40
Territorial application clause

1. Any State may, at the time of signature, ratification or accession, declare that this Convention shall extend to all or any of the territories for the international relations of which it is responsible. Such a declaration shall take effect when the Convention enters into force for the State concerned.

2. At any time thereafter any such extension shall be made by notification addressed to the Secretary-General of the United Nations and shall take effect as from the ninetieth day after the day of receipt by the Secretary-General of the United Nations of this notification, or as from the date of entry into force of the Convention for the State concerned, whichever is the later.

3. With respect to those territories to which this Convention is not extended at the time of signature, ratification or accession, each State concerned shall consider the possibility of taking the necessary steps in order to extend the application of this Convention to such territories, subject, where necessary for constitutional reasons, to the consent of the Governments of such territories.

Article 41
Federal clause

In the case of a Federal or non-unitary State, the following provisions shall apply:

(a) With respect to those articles of this Convention that come within the legislative jurisdiction of the federal legislative authority, the obligations of the Federal Government shall to this extent be the same as those of parties which are not Federal States;

(b) With respect to those articles of this Convention that come within the legislative jurisdiction of constituent States, provinces or cantons which are not, under the constitutional system of the Federation, bound to take legislative action, the Federal Government shall bring such articles with a favourable recommendation to the notice of the appropriate authorities of States, provinces or cantons at the earliest possible moment;

(c) A Federal State Party to this Convention shall, at the request of any other Contracting State transmitted through the Secretary-General of the United Nations, supply a statement of the law and practice of the Federation and its constituent units in regard to any particular provision of the Convention showing the extent to which effect has been given to that provision by legislative or other action.

Article 42
Reservations

1. At the time of signature, ratification or accession, any State may make reservations to articles of the Convention other than to articles 1, 3, 4, 16 (1), 33, 36-46 inclusive.

2. Any State making a reservation in accordance with paragraph 1 of this article may at any time withdraw the reservation by a communication to that effect addressed to the Secretary-General of the United Nations.

Article 43
Entry into force

1. This Convention shall come into force on the ninetieth day following the day of deposit of the sixth instrument of ratification or accession.

2. For each State ratifying or acceding to the Convention after the deposit of the sixth instrument of ratification or accession, the Convention shall enter into force on the ninetieth day following the date of deposit by such State of its instrument of ratification or accession.

Article 44
Denunciation

1. Any Contracting State may denounce this Convention at any time by a notification addressed to the Secretary-General of the United Nations.

2. Such denunciation shall take effect for the Contracting State concerned one year from the date upon which it is received by the Secretary-General of the United Nations.

3. Any State which has made a declaration or notification under article 40 may, at any time thereafter, by a notification to the Secretary-General of the United Nations, declare that the Convention shall cease to extend to such territory one year after the date of receipt of the notification by the Secretary-General.

Article 45
Revision

1. Any Contracting State may request revision of this Convention at any time by a notification addressed to the Secretary-General of the United Nations.

2. The General Assembly of the United Nations shall recommend the steps, if any, to be taken in respect of such request.

Article 46
Notifications by the Secretary-General of the United Nations

The Secretary-General of the United Nations shall inform all Members of the United Nations and non-member States referred to in article 39:

(a) Of declarations and notifications in accordance with section B of article 1;

(b) Of signatures, ratifications and accessions in accordance with article 39;

(c) Of declarations and notifications in accordance with article 40;

(d) Of reservations and withdrawals in accordance with article 42;

(e) Of the date on which this Convention will come into force in accordance with article 43;

(f) Of denunciations and notifications in accordance with article 44;

(g) Of requests for revision in accordance with article 45.

IN FAITH WHEREOF the undersigned, duly authorized, have signed this Convention on behalf of their respective Governments.

DONE at Geneva, this twenty-eighth day of July, one thousand nine hundred and fifty-one, in a single copy, of which the English and French texts are equally authentic and which shall remain deposited in the archives of the United Nations, and certified true copies of which shall be delivered to all Members of the United Nations and to the non-member States referred to in article 39.

Document 13

Convention on the Political Rights of Women

A/RES/640 (VII), 20 December 1952

The Contracting Parties,

Desiring to implement the principle of equality of rights for men and women contained in the Charter of the United Nations,

Recognizing that everyone has the right to take part in the government of his country directly or indirectly through freely chosen representatives, and has the right to equal access to public service in his country, and desiring to equalize the status of men and women in the enjoyment and exercise of political rights, in accordance with the provisions of the Charter of the United Nations and of the Universal Declaration of Human Rights,

Having resolved to conclude a Convention for this purpose,

Hereby agree as hereinafter provided:

Article I

Women shall be entitled to vote in all elections on equal terms with men, without any discrimination.

Article II

Women shall be eligible for election to all publicly elected bodies, established by national law, on equal terms with men, without any discrimination.

Article III

Women shall be entitled to hold public office and to exercise all public functions, established by national law, on equal terms with men, without any discrimination.

Article IV

1. This Convention shall be open for signature on behalf of any Member of the United Nations and also on behalf of any other State to which an invitation has been addressed by the General Assembly.

2. This Convention shall be ratified and the instruments of ratification shall be deposited with the Secretary-General of the United Nations.

Article V

1. This Convention shall be open for accession to all States referred to in paragraph 1 of article IV.

2. Accession shall be effected by the deposit of an instrument of accession with the Secretary-General of the United Nations.

Article VI

1. This Convention shall come into force on the ninetieth day following the date of deposit of the sixth instrument of ratification or accession.

2. For each State ratifying or acceding to the Convention after the deposit of the sixth instrument of ratification or accession the Convention shall enter into force on the ninetieth day after deposit by such State of its instrument of ratification or accession.

Article VII

In the event that any State submits a reservation to any of the articles of this Convention at the time of signature, ratification or accession, the Secretary-General shall communicate the text of the reservation to all States which are or may become Parties to this Convention. Any State which objects to the reservation may, within a period of ninety days from the date of the said communication (or upon the date of its becoming a Party to the Convention), notify the Secretary-General that it does not accept it. In such case, the Convention shall not enter into force as between such State and the State making the reservation.

Article VIII

1. Any State may denounce this Convention by written notification to the Secretary-General of the United Nations. Denunciation shall take effect one year after the date of receipt of the notification by the Secretary-General.

2. This Convention shall cease to be in force as from the date when the denunciation which reduces the number of Parties to less than six becomes effective.

Article IX

Any dispute which may arise between any two or more Contracting States concerning the interpretation or application of this Convention, which is not settled by negotiation, shall at the request of any one of the parties to the dispute be referred to the International Court of Justice for decision, unless they agree to another mode of settlement.

Article X

The Secretary-General of the United Nations shall notify all Members of the United Nations and the non-member States contemplated in paragraph 1 of article IV of this Convention of the following:

(a) Signatures and instruments of ratification received in accordance with article IV;

(b) Instruments of accession received in accordance with article V;

(c) The date upon which this Convention enters into force in accordance with article VI;

(d) Communications and notifications received in accordance with article VII;

(e) Notifications of denunciation received in accordance with paragraph 1 of article VIII;

(f) Abrogation in accordance with paragraph 2 of article VIII.

Article XI

1. This Convention, of which the Chinese, English, French, Russian and Spanish texts shall be equally authentic, shall be deposited in the archives of the United Nations.

2. The Secretary-General of the United Nations shall transmit a certified copy to all Members of the United Nations and to the non-member States contemplated in paragraph 1 of article IV.

Document 14

Convention relating to the Status of Stateless Persons, adopted by a Conference of Plenipotentiaries convened pursuant to Economic and Social Council resolution 526 A (XVII) of 26 April 1954

28 September 1954

PREAMBLE

The High Contracting Parties,

Considering that the Charter of the United Nations and the Universal Declaration of Human Rights approved on 10 December 1948 by the General Assembly of the United Nations have affirmed the principle that human beings shall enjoy fundamental rights and freedoms without discrimination,

Considering that the United Nations has, on various occasions, manifested its profound concern for stateless persons and endeavoured to assure stateless persons the widest possible exercise of these fundamental rights and freedoms,

Considering that only those stateless persons who are also refugees are covered by the Convention relating to the Status of Refugees of 28 July 1951, and that there are many stateless persons who are not covered by that Convention,

Considering that it is desirable to regulate and improve the status of stateless persons by an international agreement,

Have agreed as follows:

CHAPTER I

GENERAL PROVISIONS

Article 1
Definition of the term "stateless person"

1. For the purpose of this Convention, the term "stateless person" means a person who is not considered as a national by any State under the operation of its law.

2. This Convention shall not apply:

(i) To persons who are at present receiving from organs or agencies of the United Nations other than the United Nations High Commissioner for Refugees protection or assistance so long as they are receiving such protection or assistance;

(ii) To persons who are recognized by the competent authorities of the country in which they have taken residence as having the rights and obligations which are attached to the possession of the nationality of that country;

(iii) To persons with respect to whom there are serious reasons for considering that:

(a) They have committed a crime against peace, a war crime, or a crime against humanity, as defined in the international instruments drawn up to make provisions in respect of such crimes;

(b) They have committed a serious non-political crime outside the country of their residence prior to their admission to that country;

(c) They have been guilty of acts contrary to the purposes and principles of the United Nations.

Article 2
General obligations

Every stateless person has duties to the country in which he finds himself, which require in particular that he conform to its laws and regulations as well as to measures taken for the maintenance of public order.

Article 3
Non-discrimination

The Contracting States shall apply the provisions of this Convention to stateless persons without discrimination as to race, religion or country of origin.

Article 4
Religion

The Contracting States shall accord to stateless persons within their territories treatment at least as favourable as that accorded to their nationals with respect to freedom to practise their religion and freedom as regards the religious education of their children.

Article 5
Rights granted apart from this Convention

Nothing in this Convention shall be deemed to impair any rights and benefits granted by a Contracting State to stateless persons apart from this Convention.

Article 6
The term "in the same circumstances"

For the purpose of this Convention, the term " in the same circumstances" implies that any requirements (including requirements as to length and conditions of sojourn or residence) which the particular individual would have to fulfil for the enjoyment of the right in question, if he were not a stateless person, must be fulfilled by him, with the exception of requirements which by their nature a stateless person is incapable of fulfilling.

Article 7
Exemption from reciprocity

1. Except where this Convention contains more favourable provisions, a Contracting State shall accord to stateless persons the same treatment as is accorded to aliens generally.

2. After a period of three years' residence, all stateless persons shall enjoy exemption from legislative reciprocity in the territory of the Contracting States.

3. Each Contracting State shall continue to accord to stateless persons the rights and benefits to which they were already entitled, in the absence of reciprocity, at the date of entry into force of this Convention for that State.

4. The Contracting States shall consider favourably the possibility of according to stateless persons, in the absence of reciprocity, rights and benefits beyond those to which they are entitled according to paragraphs 2 and 3, and to extending exemption from reciprocity to state-less persons who do not fulfil the conditions provided for in paragraphs 2 and 3.

5. The provisions of paragraphs 2 and 3 apply both to the rights and benefits referred to in articles 13, 18, 19, 21 and 22 of this Convention and to rights and benefits for which this Convention does not provide.

Article 8
Exemption from exceptional measures

With regard to exceptional measures which may be taken against the person, property or interests of nationals or former nationals of a foreign State, the Contracting States shall not apply such measures to a stateless person solely on account of his having previously possessed the nationality of the foreign State in question. Contracting States which, under their legislation, are prevented from applying the general principle expressed in this article shall, in appropriate cases, grant exemptions in favour of such stateless persons.

Article 9
Provisional measures

Nothing in this Convention shall prevent a Contracting State, in time of war or other grave and exceptional circumstances, from taking provisionally measures which it considers to be essential to the national security in the case of a particular person, pending a determination by the Contracting State that that person is in fact a stateless person and that the continuance of such measures is necessary in his case in the interests of national security.

Article 10
Continuity of residence

1. Where a stateless person has been forcibly displaced during the Second World War and removed to the territory of a Contracting State, and is resident there, the period of such enforced sojourn shall be considered to have been lawful residence within that territory.

2. Where a stateless person has been forcibly displaced during the Second World War from the territory of a Contracting State and has, prior to the date of entry into force of this Convention, returned there for the purpose of taking up residence, the period of residence before and after such enforced displacement shall be regarded as one uninterrupted period for any purposes for which uninterrupted residence is required.

Article 11
Stateless seamen

In the case of stateless persons regularly serving as crew members on board a ship flying the flag of a Contracting State, that State shall give sympathetic consideration to their establishment on its territory and the issue of travel documents to them or their temporary admission to its territory particularly with a view to facilitating their establishment in another country.

CHAPTER II

JURIDICAL STATUS

Article 12
Personal status

1. The personal status of a stateless person shall be governed by the law of the country of his domicile or, if he has no domicile, by the law of the country of his residence.

2. Rights previously acquired by a stateless person and dependent on personal status, more particularly rights attaching to marriage, shall be respected by a Contracting State, subject to compliance, if this be necessary, with the formalities required by the law of that State, provided that the right in question is one which would have been recognized by the law of that State had he not become stateless.

Article 13
Movable and immovable property

The Contracting States shall accord to a stateless person treatment as favourable as possible and, in any event, not less favourable than that accorded to aliens generally in the same circumstances, as regards the acquisition of movable and immovable property and other rights pertaining thereto, and to leases and other contracts relating to movable and immovable property.

Article 14
Artistic rights and industrial property

In respect of the protection of industrial property, such as inventions, designs or models, trade marks, trade names, and of rights in literary, artistic and scientific works, a stateless person shall be accorded in the country in which he has his habitual residence the same protection as is accorded to nationals of that country. In the territory of any other Contracting State, he shall be accorded the same protection as is accorded in that territory to nationals of the country in which he has his habitual residence.

Article 15
Right of association

As regards non-political and non-profit-making associations and trade unions the Contracting States shall accord to stateless persons lawfully staying in their territory treatment as favourable as possible, and in any event, not less favourable than that accorded to aliens generally in the same circumstances.

Article 16
Access to courts

1. A stateless person shall have free access to the courts of law on the territory of all Contracting States.

2. A stateless person shall enjoy in the Contracting State in which he has his habitual residence the same treatment as a national in matters pertaining to access to the courts, including legal assistance and exemption from *cautio judicatum solvi*.

3. A stateless person shall be accorded in the matters referred to in paragraph 2 in countries other than that in which he has his habitual residence the treatment granted to a national of the country of his habitual residence.

CHAPTER III

GAINFUL EMPLOYMENT

Article 17
Wage-earning employment

1. The Contracting States shall accord to stateless persons lawfully staying in their territory treatment as favourable as possible and, in any event, not less favourable than that accorded to aliens generally in the same circumstances, as regards the right to engage in wage-earning employment.

2. The Contracting States shall give sympathetic consideration to assimilating the rights of all stateless persons with regard to wage-earning employment to those of nationals, and in particular of those stateless persons who have entered their territory pursuant to programmes of labour recruitment or under immigration schemes.

Article 18
Self-employment

The Contracting States shall accord to a stateless person lawfully in their territory treatment as favourable as possible and, in any event, not less favourable than that accorded to aliens generally in the same circumstances, as regards the right to engage on his own account in agriculture, industry, handicrafts and commerce and to establish commercial and industrial companies.

Article 19
Liberal professions

Each Contracting State shall accord to stateless persons lawfully staying in their territory who hold diplomas recognized by the competent authorities of that State, and who are desirous of practising a liberal profession, treatment as favourable as possible and, in any event, not less favourable than that accorded to aliens generally in the same circumstances.

CHAPTER IV

WELFARE

Article 20
Rationing

Where a rationing system exists, which applies to the population at large and regulates the general distribution of products in short supply, stateless persons shall be accorded the same treatment as nationals.

Article 21
Housing

As regards housing, the Contracting States, in so far as the matter is regulated by laws or regulations or is subject to the control of public authorities, shall accord to stateless persons lawfully staying in their territory treatment as favourable as possible and, in any event, not less favourable than that accorded to aliens generally in the same circumstances.

Article 22
Public education

1. The Contracting States shall accord to stateless persons the same treatment as is accorded to nationals with respect to elementary education.

2. The Contracting States shall accord to stateless persons treatment as favourable as possible and, in any event, not less favourable than that accorded to aliens generally in the same circumstances, with respect to education other than elementary education and, in particular, as regards access to studies, the recognition of foreign school certificates, diplomas and degrees, the remission of fees and charges and the award of scholarships.

Article 23
Public relief

The Contracting States shall accord to stateless persons lawfully staying in their territory the same treatment with respect to public relief and assistance as is accorded to their nationals.

Article 24
Labour legislation and social security

1. The Contracting States shall accord to stateless persons lawfully staying in their territory the same treatment as is accorded to nationals in respect of the following matters:

(a) In so far as such matters are governed by laws or regulations or are subject to the control of administrative authorities; remuneration, including family allowances where these form part of remuneration, hours of work, overtime arrangements, holidays with pay, restric-

tions on home work, minimum age of employment, apprenticeship and training, women's work and the work of young persons, and the enjoyment of the benefits of collective bargaining;

(b) Social security (legal provisions in respect of employment injury, occupational diseases, maternity, sickness, disability, old age, death, unemployment, family responsibilities and any other contingency which, according to national laws or regulations, is covered by a social security scheme), subject to the following limitations:

(i) There may be appropriate arrangements for the maintenance of acquired rights and rights in course of acquisition;

(ii) National laws or regulations of the country of residence may prescribe special arrangements concerning benefits or portions of benefits which are payable wholly out of public funds, and concerning allowances paid to persons who do not fulfil the contribution conditions prescribed for the award of a normal pension.

2. The right to compensation for the death of a stateless person resulting from employment injury or from occupational disease shall not be affected by the fact that the residence of the beneficiary is outside the territory of the Contracting State.

3. The Contracting States shall extend to stateless persons the benefits of agreements concluded between them, or which may be concluded between them in the future, concerning the maintenance of acquired rights and rights in the process of acquisition in regard to social security, subject only to the conditions which apply to nationals of the States signatory to the agreements in question.

4. The Contracting States will give sympathetic consideration to extending to stateless persons so far as possible the benefits of similar agreements which may at any time be in force between such Contracting States and non-contracting States.

CHAPTER V

ADMINISTRATIVE MEASURES

Article 25
Administrative assistance

1. When the exercise of a right by a stateless person would normally require the assistance of authorities of a foreign country to whom he cannot have recourse, the Contracting State in whose territory he is residing shall arrange that such assistance be afforded to him by their own authorities.

2. The authority or authorities mentioned in paragraph 1 shall deliver or cause to be delivered under their

supervision to stateless persons such documents or certifications as would normally be delivered to aliens by or through their national authorities.

3. Documents or certifications so delivered shall stand in the stead of the official instruments delivered to aliens by or through their national authorities and shall be given credence in the absence of proof to the contrary.

4. Subject to such exceptional treatment as may be granted to indigent persons, fees may be charged for the services mentioned herein, but such fees shall be moderate and commensurate with those charged to nationals for similar services.

5. The provisions of this article shall be without prejudice to articles 27 and 28.

Article 26
Freedom of movement

Each Contracting State shall accord to stateless persons lawfully in its territory the right to choose their place of residence and to move freely within its territory, subject to any regulations applicable to aliens generally in the same circumstances.

Article 27
Identity papers

The Contracting States shall issue identity papers to any stateless person in their territory who does not possess a valid travel document.

Article 28
Travel documents

The Contracting States shall issue to stateless persons lawfully staying in their territory travel documents for the purpose of travel outside their territory, unless compelling reasons of national security or public order otherwise require, and the provisions of the schedule to this Convention shall apply with respect to such documents. The Contracting States may issue such a travel document to any other stateless person in their territory; they shall in particular give sympathetic consideration to the issue of such a travel document to stateless persons in their territory who are unable to obtain a travel document from the country of their lawful residence.

Article 29
Fiscal charges

1. The Contracting States shall not impose upon stateless persons duties, charges or taxes, of any description whatsoever, other or higher than those which are or may be levied on their nationals in similar situations.

2. Nothing in the above paragraph shall prevent the application to stateless persons of the laws and regulations concerning charges in respect of the issue to aliens of administrative documents including identity papers.

Article 30
Transfer of assets

1. A Contracting State shall, in conformity with its laws and regulations, permit stateless persons to transfer assets which they have brought into its territory, to another country where they have been admitted for the purposes of resettlement.

2. A Contracting State shall give sympathetic consideration to the application of stateless persons for permission to transfer assets wherever they may be and which are necessary for their resettlement in another country to which they have been admitted.

Article 31
Expulsion

1. The Contracting States shall not expel a stateless person lawfully in their territory save on grounds of national security or public order.

2. The expulsion of such a stateless person shall be only in pursuance of a decision reached in accordance with due process of law. Except where compelling reasons of national security otherwise require, the stateless person shall be allowed to submit evidence to clear himself, and to appeal to and be represented for the purpose before competent authority or a person or persons specially designated by the competent authority.

3. The Contracting States shall allow such a stateless person a reasonable period within which to seek legal admission into another country. The Contracting States reserve the right to apply during that period such internal measures as they may deem necessary.

Article 32
Naturalization

The Contracting States shall as far as possible facilitate the assimilation and naturalization of stateless persons. They shall in particular make every effort to expedite naturalization proceedings and to reduce as far as possible the charges and costs of such proceedings.

CHAPTER VI

FINAL CLAUSES

Article 33
Information on national legislation

The Contracting States shall communicate to the Secretary-General of the United Nations the laws and regulations which they may adopt to ensure the application of this Convention.

Article 34
Settlement of disputes

Any dispute between Parties to this Convention relating to its interpretation or application, which cannot be settled by other means, shall be referred to the International Court of Justice at the request of any one of the parties to the dispute.

Article 35
Signature, ratification and accession

1. This Convention shall be open for signature at the Headquarters of the United Nations until 31 December 1955.

2. It shall be open for signature on behalf of:

(a) Any State Member of the United Nations;

(b) Any other State invited to attend the United Nations Conference on the Status of Stateless Persons; and

(c) Any State to which an invitation to sign or to accede may be addressed by the General Assembly of the United Nations.

3. It shall be ratified and the instruments of ratification shall be deposited with the Secretary-General of the United Nations.

4. It shall be open for accession by the States referred to in paragraph 2 of this article. Accession shall be effected by the deposit of an instrument of accession with the Secretary-General of the United Nations.

Article 36
Territorial application clause

1. Any State may, at the time of signature, ratification or accession, declare that this Convention shall extend to all or any of the territories for the international relations of which it is responsible. Such a declaration shall take effect when the Convention enters into force for the State concerned.

2. At any time thereafter any such extension shall be made by notification addressed to the Secretary-General of the United Nations and shall take effect as from the ninetieth day after the day of receipt by the Secretary-General of the United Nations of this notification, or as from the date of entry into force of the Convention for the State concerned, whichever is the later.

3. With respect to those territories to which this Convention is not extended at the time of signature, ratification or accession, each State concerned shall consider the possibility of taking the necessary steps in order to extend the application of this Convention to such territories, subject, where necessary for constitutional reasons, to the consent of the Governments of such territories.

Article 37
Federal clause

In the case of a Federal or non-unitary State, the following provisions shall apply:

(a) With respect to those articles of this Convention that come within the legislative jurisdiction of the federal legislative authority, the obligations of the Federal Government shall to this extent be the same as those of Parties which are not Federal States;

(b) With respect to those articles of this Convention that come within the legislative jurisdiction of constituent States, provinces or cantons which are not, under the constitutional system of the Federation, bound to take legislative action, the Federal Government shall bring such articles with a favourable recommendation to the notice of the appropriate authorities of States, provinces or cantons at the earliest possible moment;

(c) A Federal State Party to this Convention shall, at the request of any other Contracting State transmitted through the Secretary-General of the United Nations, supply a statement of the law and practice of the Federation and its constituent units in regard to any particular provision of the Convention showing the extent to which effect has been given to that provision by legislative or other action.

Article 38
Reservations

1. At the time of signature, ratification or accession, any State may make reservations to articles of the Convention other than to articles 1, 3, 4, 16 (1) and 33 to 42 inclusive.

2. Any State making a reservation in accordance with paragraph 1 of this article may at any time withdraw the reservation by a communication to that effect addressed to the Secretary-General of the United Nations.

Article 39
Entry into force

1. This Convention shall come into force on the ninetieth day following the day of deposit of the sixth instrument of ratification or accession.

2. For each State ratifying or acceding to the Convention after the deposit of the sixth instrument of ratification or accession, the Convention shall enter into force on the ninetieth day following the date of deposit by such State of its instrument of ratification or accession.

Article 40
Denunciation

1. Any Contracting State may denounce this Convention at any time by a notification addressed to the Secretary-General of the United Nations.

2. Such denunciation shall take effect for the Contracting State concerned one year from the date upon which it is received by the Secretary-General of the United Nations.

3. Any State which has made a declaration or notification under article 36 may, at any time thereafter, by a notification to the Secretary-General of the United Nations, declare that the Convention shall cease to extend to such territory one year after the date of receipt of the notification by the Secretary-General.

Article 41
Revision

1. Any Contracting State may request revision of this Convention at any time by a notification addressed to the Secretary-General of the United Nations.

2. The General Assembly of the United Nations shall recommend the steps, if any, to be taken in respect of such request.

Article 42
Notifications by the Secretary-General of the United Nations

The Secretary-General of the United Nations shall inform all Members of the United Nations and non-member States referred to in article 35:

(a) Of signatures, ratifications and accessions in accordance with article 35;

(b) Of declarations and notifications in accordance with article 36;

(c) Of reservations and withdrawals in accordance with article 38;

(d) Of the date on which this Convention will come into force in accordance with article 39;

(e) Of denunciations and notifications in accordance with article 40;

(f) Of request for revision in accordance with article 41.

IN FAITH WHEREOF the undersigned, duly authorized, have signed this Convention on behalf of their respective Governments.

DONE at New York, this twenty-eighth day of September, one thousand nine hundred and fifty-four, in a single copy, of which the English, French and Spanish texts are equally authentic and which shall remain deposited in the archives of the United Nations, and certified true copies of which shall be delivered to all Members of the United Nations and to the non-member States referred to in article 35.

Document 15

Standard Minimum Rules for the Treatment of Prisoners, adopted by the First United Nations Congress on the Prevention of Crime and the Treatment of Offenders, held at Geneva in 1955, and approved by Economic and Social Council resolutions 663 C (XXIV) of 31 July 1957 and 2076 (LXII) of 13 May 1977

Preliminary observations

1. The following rules are not intended to describe in detail a model system of penal institutions. They seek only, on the basis of the general consensus of contemporary thought and the essential elements of the most adequate systems of today, to set out what is generally accepted as being good principle and practice in the treatment of prisoners and the management of institutions.

2. In view of the great variety of legal, social, economic and geographical conditions of the world, it is evident that not all of the rules are capable of application in all places and at all times. They should, however, serve to stimulate a constant endeavour to overcome practical difficulties in the way of their application, in the knowledge that they represent, as a whole, the minimum conditions which are accepted as suitable by the United Nations.

3. On the other hand, the rules cover a field in which thought is constantly developing. They are not intended to preclude experiment and practices, provided these are in harmony with the principles and seek to further the purposes which derive from the text of the rules as a whole. It will always be justifiable for the central

prison administration to authorize departures from the rules in this spirit.

4. (1) Part I of the rules covers the general management of institutions, and is applicable to all categories of prisoners, criminal or civil, untried or convicted, including prisoners subject to "security measures" or corrective measures ordered by the judge.

(2) Part II contains rules applicable only to the special categories dealt with in each section. Nevertheless, the rules under section A, applicable to prisoners under sentence, shall be equally applicable to categories of prisoners dealt with in sections B, C and D, provided they do not conflict with the rules governing those categories and are for their benefit.

5. (1) The rules do not seek to regulate the management of institutions set aside for young persons such as Borstal institutions or correctional schools, but in general part I would be equally applicable in such institutions.

(2) The category of young prisoners should include at least all young persons who come within the jurisdiction of juvenile courts. As a rule, such young persons should not be sentenced to imprisonment.

PART I

RULES OF GENERAL APPLICATION

Basic principle

6. (1) The following rules shall be applied impartially. There shall be no discrimination on grounds of race, colour, sex, language, religion, political or other opinion, national or social origin, property, birth or other status.

(2) On the other hand, it is necessary to respect the religious beliefs and moral precepts of the group to which a prisoner belongs.

Register

7. (1) In every place where persons are imprisoned there shall be kept a bound registration book with numbered pages in which shall be entered in respect of each prisoner received:

(a) Information concerning his identity;

(b) The reasons for his commitment and the authority therefor;

(c) The day and hour of his admission and release.

(2) No person shall be received in an institution without a valid commitment order of which the details shall have been previously entered in the register.

Separation of categories

8. The different categories of prisoners shall be kept in separate institutions or parts of institutions taking account of their sex, age, criminal record, the legal reason for their detention and the necessities of their treatment. Thus,

(a) Men and women shall so far as possible be detained in separate institutions; in an institution which receives both men and women the whole of the premises allocated to women shall be entirely separate;

(b) Untried prisoners shall be kept separate from convicted prisoners;

(c) Persons imprisoned for debt and other civil prisoners shall be kept separate from persons imprisoned by reason of a criminal offence;

(d) Young prisoners shall be kept separate from adults.

Accommodation

9. (1) Where sleeping accommodation is in individual cells or rooms, each prisoner shall occupy by night a cell or room by himself. If for special reasons, such as temporary overcrowding, it becomes necessary for the central prison administration to make an exception to this rule, it is not desirable to have two prisoners in a cell or room.

(2) Where dormitories are used, they shall be occupied by prisoners carefully selected as being suitable to associate with one another in those conditions. There shall be regular supervision by night, in keeping with the nature of the institution.

10. All accommodation provided for the use of prisoners and in particular all sleeping accommodation shall meet all requirements of health, due regard being paid to climatic conditions and particularly to cubic content of air, minimum floor space, lighting, heating and ventilation.

11. In all places where prisoners are required to live or work,

(a) The windows shall be large enough to enable the prisoners to read or work by natural light, and shall be so constructed that they can allow the entrance of fresh air whether or not there is artificial ventilation;

(b) Artificial light shall be provided sufficient for the prisoners to read or work without injury to eyesight.

12. The sanitary installations shall be adequate to enable every prisoner to comply with the needs of nature when necessary and in a clean and decent manner.

13. Adequate bathing and shower installations shall be provided so that every prisoner may be enabled and required to have a bath or shower, at a temperature suitable to the climate, as frequently as necessary for general hygiene according to season and geographical region, but at least once a week in a temperate climate.

14. All parts of an institution regularly used by prisoners shall be properly maintained and kept scrupulously clean at all times.

Personal hygiene

15. Prisoners shall be required to keep their persons clean, and to this end they shall be provided with water and with such toilet articles as are necessary for health and cleanliness.

16. In order that prisoners may maintain a good appearance compatible with their self-respect, facilities shall be provided for the proper care of the hair and beard, and men shall be enabled to shave regularly.

Clothing and bedding

17. (1) Every prisoner who is not allowed to wear his own clothing shall be provided with an outfit of clothing suitable for the climate and adequate to keep him in good health. Such clothing shall in no manner be degrading or humiliating.

(2) All clothing shall be clean and kept in proper condition. Underclothing shall be changed and washed as often as necessary for the maintenance of hygiene.

(3) In exceptional circumstances, whenever a prisoner is removed outside the institution for an authorized purpose, he shall be allowed to wear his own clothing or other inconspicuous clothing.

18. If prisoners are allowed to wear their own clothing, arrangements shall be made on their admission to the institution to ensure that it shall be clean and fit for use.

19. Every prisoner shall, in accordance with local or national standards, be provided with a separate bed, and with separate and sufficient bedding which shall be clean when issued, kept in good order and changed often enough to ensure its cleanliness.

Food

20. (1) Every prisoner shall be provided by the administration at the usual hours with food of nutritional value adequate for health and strength, of wholesome quality and well prepared and served.

(2) Drinking water shall be available to every prisoner whenever he needs it.

Exercise and sport

21. (1) Every prisoner who is not employed in outdoor work shall have at least one hour of suitable exercise in the open air daily if the weather permits.

(2) Young prisoners, and others of suitable age and physique, shall receive physical and recreational training during the period of exercise. To this end space, installations and equipment should be provided.

Medical services

22. (1) At every institution there shall be available the services of at least one qualified medical officer who should have some knowledge of psychiatry. The medical services should be organized in close relationship to the general health administration of the community or nation. They shall include a psychiatric service for the diagnosis and, in proper cases, the treatment of states of mental abnormality.

(2) Sick prisoners who require specialist treatment shall be transferred to specialized institutions or to civil hospitals. Where hospital facilities are provided in an institution, their equipment, furnishings and pharmaceutical supplies shall be proper for the medical care and treatment of sick prisoners, and there shall be a staff of suitable trained officers.

(3) The services of a qualified dental officer shall be available to every prisoner.

23. (1) In women's institutions there shall be special accommodation for all necessary pre-natal and post-natal care and treatment. Arrangements shall be made wherever practicable for children to be born in a hospital outside the institution. If a child is born in prison, this fact shall not be mentioned in the birth certificate.

(2) Where nursing infants are allowed to remain in the institution with their mothers, provision shall be made for a nursery staffed by qualified persons, where the infants shall be placed when they are not in the care of their mothers.

24. The medical officer shall see and examine every prisoner as soon as possible after his admission and thereafter as necessary, with a view particularly to the discovery of physical or mental illness and the taking of all necessary measures; the segregation of prisoners suspected of infectious or contagious conditions; the noting of physical or mental defects which might hamper rehabilitation, and the determination of the physical capacity of every prisoner for work.

25. (1) The medical officer shall have the care of the physical and mental health of the prisoners and should daily see all sick prisoners, all who complain of illness, and any prisoner to whom his attention is specially directed.

(2) The medical officer shall report to the director whenever he considers that a prisoner's physical or mental health has been or will be injuriously affected by continued imprisonment or by any condition of imprisonment.

26. (1) The medical officer shall regularly inspect and advise the director upon:

(a) The quantity, quality, preparation and service of food;

(b) The hygiene and cleanliness of the institution and the prisoners;

(c) The sanitation, heating, lighting and ventilation of the institution;

(d) The suitability and cleanliness of the prisoners' clothing and bedding;

(e) The observance of the rules concerning physical education and sports, in cases where there is no technical personnel in charge of these activities.

(2) The director shall take into consideration the reports and advice that the medical officer submits according to rules 25 (2) and 26 and, in case he concurs with the recommendations made, shall take immediate steps to give effect to those recommendations; if they are not within his competence or if he does not concur with them, he shall immediately submit his own report and the advice of the medical officer to higher authority.

Discipline and punishment

27. Discipline and order shall be maintained with firmness, but with no more restriction than is necessary for safe custody and well-ordered community life.

28. (1) No prisoner shall be employed, in the service of the institution, in any disciplinary capacity.

(2) This rule shall not, however, impede the proper functioning of systems based on self-government, under which specified social, educational or sports activities or responsibilities are entrusted, under supervision, to prisoners who are formed into groups for the purposes of treatment.

29. The following shall always be determined by the law or by the regulation of the competent administrative authority:

(a) Conduct constituting a disciplinary offence;

(b) The types and duration of punishment which may be inflicted;

(c) The authority competent to impose such punishment.

30. (1) No prisoner shall be punished except in accordance with the terms of such law or regulation, and never twice for the same offence.

(2) No prisoner shall be punished unless he has been informed of the offence alleged against him and given a proper opportunity of presenting his defence. The competent authority shall conduct a thorough examination of the case.

(3) Where necessary and practicable the prisoner shall be allowed to make his defence through an interpreter.

31. Corporal punishment, punishment by placing in a dark cell, and all cruel, inhuman or degrading punishments shall be completely prohibited as punishments for disciplinary offences.

32. (1) Punishment by close confinement or reduction of diet shall never be inflicted unless the medical officer has examined the prisoner and certified in writing that he is fit to sustain it.

(2) The same shall apply to any other punishment that may be prejudicial to the physical or mental health of a prisoner. In no case may such punishment be contrary to or depart from the principle stated in rule 31.

(3) The medical officer shall visit daily prisoners undergoing such punishments and shall advise the director if he considers the termination or alteration of the punishment necessary on grounds of physical or mental health.

Instruments of restraint

33. Instruments of restraint, such as handcuffs, chains, irons and strait-jackets, shall never be applied as a punishment. Furthermore, chains or irons shall not be used as restraints. Other instruments of restraint shall not be used except in the following circumstances:

(a) As a precaution against escape during a transfer, provided that they shall be removed when the prisoner appears before a judicial or administrative authority;

(b) On medical grounds by direction of the medical officer;

(c) By order of the director, if other methods of control fail, in order to prevent a prisoner from injuring himself or others or from damaging property; in such instances the director shall at once consult the medical officer and report to the higher administrative authority.

34. The patterns and manner of use of instruments of restraint shall be decided by the central prison administration. Such instruments must not be applied for any longer time than is strictly necessary.

Information to and complaints by prisoners

35. (1) Every prisoner on admission shall be provided with written information about the regulations governing the treatment of prisoners of his category, the disciplinary requirements of the institution, the authorized methods of seeking information and making complaints, and all such other matters as are necessary to enable him to understand both his rights and his obligations and to adapt himself to the life of the institution.

(2) If a prisoner is illiterate, the aforesaid information shall be conveyed to him orally.

36. (1) Every prisoner shall have the opportunity each week day of making requests or complaints to the director of the institution or the officer authorized to represent him.

(2) It shall be possible to make requests or complaints to the inspector of prisons during his inspection. The prisoner shall have the opportunity to talk to the inspector or to any other inspecting officer without the director or other members of the staff being present.

(3) Every prisoner shall be allowed to make a request or complaint, without censorship as to substance but in proper form, to the central prison administration, the judicial authority or other proper authorities through approved channels.

(4) Unless it is evidently frivolous or groundless, every request or complaint shall be promptly dealt with and replied to without undue delay.

Contact with the outside world

37. Prisoners shall be allowed under necessary supervision to communicate with their family and reputable friends at regular intervals, both by correspondence and by receiving visits.

38. (1) Prisoners who are foreign nationals shall be allowed reasonable facilities to communicate with the diplomatic and consular representatives of the State to which they belong.

(2) Prisoners who are nationals of States without diplomatic or consular representation in the country and refugees or stateless persons shall be allowed similar facilities to communicate with the diplomatic representative of the State which takes charge of their interests or any national or international authority whose task it is to protect such persons.

39. Prisoners shall be kept informed regularly of the more important items of news by the reading of newspapers, periodicals or special institutional publications, by hearing wireless transmissions, by lectures or by any similar means as authorized or controlled by the administration.

Books

40. Every institution shall have a library for the use of all categories of prisoners, adequately stocked with both recreational and instructional books, and prisoners shall be encouraged to make full use of it.

Religion

41. (1) If the institution contains a sufficient number of prisoners of the same religion, a qualified representative of that religion shall be appointed or approved. If the number of prisoners justifies it and conditions permit, the arrangement should be on a full-time basis.

(2) A qualified representative appointed or approved under paragraph (1) shall be allowed to hold regular services and to pay pastoral visits in private to prisoners of his religion at proper times.

(3) Access to a qualified representative of any religion shall not be refused to any prisoner. On the other hand, if any prisoner should object to a visit of any religious representative, his attitude shall be fully respected.

42. So far as practicable, every prisoner shall be allowed to satisfy the needs of his religious life by attending the services provided in the institution and having in his possession the books of religious observance and instruction of his denomination.

Retention of prisoners' property

43. (1) All money, valuables, clothing and other effects belonging to a prisoner which under the regulations of the institution he is not allowed to retain shall on his admission to the institution be placed in safe custody. An inventory thereof shall be signed by the prisoner. Steps shall be taken to keep them in good condition.

(2) On the release of the prisoner all such articles and money shall be returned to him except in so far as he has been authorized to spend money or send any such property out of the institution, or it has been found necessary on hygienic grounds to destroy any article of clothing. The prisoner shall sign a receipt for the articles and money returned to him.

(3) Any money or effects received for a prisoner from outside shall be treated in the same way.

(4) If a prisoner brings in any drugs or medicine, the medical officer shall decide what use shall be made of them.

Notification of death, illness, transfer, etc.

44. (1) Upon the death or serious illness of, or serious injury to a prisoner, or his removal to an institution for the treatment of mental affections, the director shall at once inform the spouse, if the prisoner is married, or the nearest relative and shall in any event inform any other person previously designated by the prisoner.

(2) A prisoner shall be informed at once of the death or serious illness of any near relative. In case of the critical illness of a near relative, the prisoner should be authorized, whenever circumstances allow, to go to his bedside either under escort or alone.

(3) Every prisoner shall have the right to inform at once his family of his imprisonment or his transfer to another institution.

Removal of prisoners

45. (1) When the prisoners are being removed to or from an institution, they shall be exposed to public view as little as possible, and proper safeguards shall be adopted to protect them from insult, curiosity and publicity in any form.

(2) The transport of prisoners in conveyances with inadequate ventilation or light, or in any way which would subject them to unnecessary physical hardship, shall be prohibited.

(3) The transport of prisoners shall be carried out at the expense of the administration and equal conditions shall obtain for all of them.

Institutional personnel

46. (1) The prison administration shall provide for the careful selection of every grade of the personnel, since it is on their integrity, humanity, professional capacity and personal suitability for the work that the proper administration of the institutions depends.

(2) The prison administration shall constantly seek to awaken and maintain in the minds both of the personnel and of the public the conviction that this work is a social service of great importance, and to this end all appropriate means of informing the public should be used.

(3) To secure the foregoing ends, personnel shall be appointed on a full-time basis as professional prison officers and have civil service status with security of tenure subject only to good conduct, efficiency and physical fitness. Salaries shall be adequate to attract and retain suitable men and women; employment benefits and conditions of service shall be favourable in view of the exacting nature of the work.

47. (1) The personnel shall possess an adequate standard of education and intelligence.

(2) Before entering on duty, the personnel shall be given a course of training in their general and specific duties and be required to pass theoretical and practical tests.

(3) After entering on duty and during their career, the personnel shall maintain and improve their knowledge and professional capacity by attending courses of in-service training to be organized at suitable intervals.

48. All members of the personnel shall at all times so conduct themselves and perform their duties as to influence the prisoners for good by their example and to command their respect.

49. (1) So far as possible, the personnel shall include a sufficient number of specialists such as psychiatrists, psychologists, social workers, teachers and trade instructors.

(2) The services of social workers, teachers and trade instructors shall be secured on a permanent basis, without thereby excluding part-time or voluntary workers.

50. (1) The director of an institution should be adequately qualified for his task by character, administrative ability, suitable training and experience.

(2) He shall devote his entire time to his official duties and shall not be appointed on a part-time basis.

(3) He shall reside on the premises of the institution or in its immediate vicinity.

(4) When two or more institutions are under the authority of one director, he shall visit each of them at frequent intervals. A responsible resident official shall be in charge of each of these institutions.

51. (1) The director, his deputy, and the majority of the other personnel of the institution shall be able to speak the language of the greatest number of prisoners, or a language understood by the greatest number of them.

(2) Whenever necessary, the services of an interpreter shall be used.

52. (1) In institutions which are large enough to require the services of one or more full-time medical officers, at least one of them shall reside on the premises of the institution or in its immediate vicinity.

(2) In other institutions the medical officer shall visit daily and shall reside near enough to be able to attend without delay in cases of urgency.

53. (1) In an institution for both men and women, the part of the institution set aside for women shall be under the authority of a responsible woman officer who shall have the custody of the keys of all that part of the institution.

(2) No male member of the staff shall enter the part of the institution set aside for women unless accompanied by a woman officer.

(3) Women prisoners shall be attended and supervised only by women officers. This does not, however, preclude male members of the staff, particularly doctors and teachers, from carrying out their professional duties in institutions or parts of institutions set aside for women.

54. (1) Officers of the institutions shall not, in their relations with the prisoners, use force except in self-defence or in cases of attempted escape, or active or passive physical resistance to an order based on law or regulations. Officers who have recourse to force must use no more than is strictly necessary and must report the incident immediately to the director of the institution.

(2) Prison officers shall be given special physical training to enable them to restrain aggressive prisoners.

(3) Except in special circumstances, staff performing duties which bring them into direct contact with prisoners should not be armed. Furthermore, staff should in no circumstances be provided with arms unless they have been trained in their use.

Inspection

55. There shall be a regular inspection of penal institutions and services by qualified and experienced inspectors appointed by a competent authority. Their task shall be in particular to ensure that these institutions are administered in accordance with existing laws and regulations and with a view to bringing about the objectives of penal and correctional services.

PART II

RULES APPLICABLE TO SPECIAL CATEGORIES

A. PRISONERS UNDER SENTENCE

Guiding principles

56. The guiding principles hereafter are intended to show the spirit in which penal institutions should be administered and the purposes at which they should aim, in accordance with the declaration made under Preliminary Observation 1 of the present text.

57. Imprisonment and other measures which result in cutting off an offender from the outside world are afflictive by the very fact of taking from the person the right of self-determination by depriving him of his liberty. Therefore the prison system shall not, except as incidental to justifiable segregation or the maintenance of discipline, aggravate the suffering inherent in such a situation.

58. The purpose and justification of a sentence of imprisonment or a similar measure deprivative of liberty is ultimately to protect society against crime. This end can only be achieved if the period of imprisonment is used to ensure, so far as possible, that upon his return to society the offender is not only willing but able to lead a law-abiding and self-supporting life.

59. To this end, the institution should utilize all the remedial, educational, moral, spiritual and other forces and forms of assistance which are appropriate and available, and should seek to apply them according to the individual treatment needs of the prisoners.

60. (1) The régime of the institution should seek to minimize any differences between prison life and life at liberty which tend to lessen the responsibility of the prisoners or the respect due to their dignity as human beings.

(2) Before the completion of the sentence, it is desirable that the necessary steps be taken to ensure for the prisoner a gradual return to life in society. This aim may be achieved, depending on the case, by a pre-release régime organized in the same institution or in another appropriate institution, or by release on trial under some kind of supervision which must not be entrusted to the police but should be combined with effective social aid.

61. The treatment of prisoners should emphasize not their exclusion from the community, but their continuing part in it. Community agencies should, therefore, be enlisted wherever possible to assist the staff of the institution in the task of social rehabilitation of the prisoners. There should be in connection with every institution social workers charged with the duty of maintaining and improving all desirable relations of a prisoner with his family and with valuable social agencies. Steps should be taken to safeguard, to the maximum extent compatible with the law and the sentence, the rights relating to civil interests, social security rights and other social benefits of prisoners.

62. The medical services of the institution shall seek to detect and shall treat any physical or mental illnesses or defects which may hamper a prisoner's rehabilitation. All necessary medical, surgical and psychiatric services shall be provided to that end.

63. (1) The fulfilment of these principles requires individualization of treatment and for this purpose a flexible system of classifying prisoners in groups; it is therefore desirable that such groups should be distributed in separate institutions suitable for the treatment of each group.

(2) These institutions need not provide the same degree of security for every group. It is desirable to provide varying degrees of security according to the needs of different groups. Open institutions, by the very fact that they provide no physical security against escape but rely on the self-discipline of the inmates, provide the conditions most favourable to rehabilitation for carefully selected prisoners.

(3) It is desirable that the number of prisoners in closed institutions should not be so large that the individualization of treatment is hindered. In some countries it is considered that the population of such institutions should not exceed five hundred. In open institutions the population should be as small as possible.

(4) On the other hand, it is undesirable to maintain prisons which are so small that proper facilities cannot be provided.

64. The duty of society does not end with a prisoner's release. There should, therefore, be governmental or private agencies capable of lending the released prisoner efficient after-care directed towards the lessening of prejudice against him and towards his social rehabilitation.

Treatment

65. The treatment of persons sentenced to imprisonment or a similar measure shall have as its purpose, so far as the length of the sentence permits, to establish in them the will to lead law-abiding and self-supporting lives after their release and to fit them to do so. The treatment shall be such as will encourage their self-respect and develop their sense of responsibility.

66. (1) To these ends, all appropriate means shall be used, including religious care in the countries where this is possible, education, vocational guidance and training, social casework, employment counselling, physical development and strengthening of moral character, in accordance with the individual needs of each prisoner, taking account of his social and criminal history, his physical and mental capacities and aptitudes, his personal

temperament, the length of his sentence and his prospects after release.

(2) For every prisoner with a sentence of suitable length, the director shall receive, as soon as possible after his admission, full reports on all the matters referred to in the foregoing paragraph. Such reports shall always include a report by a medical officer, wherever possible qualified in psychiatry, on the physical and mental condition of the prisoner.

(3) The reports and other relevant documents shall be placed in an individual file. This file shall be kept up to date and classified in such a way that it can be consulted by the responsible personnel whenever the need arises.

Classification and individualization

67. The purposes of classification shall be:

(a) To separate from others those prisoners who, by reason of their criminal records or bad characters, are likely to exercise a bad influence;

(b) To divide the prisoners into classes in order to facilitate their treatment with a view to their social rehabilitation.

68. So far as possible separate institutions or separate sections of an institution shall be used for the treatment of the different classes of prisoners.

69. As soon as possible after admission and after a study of the personality of each prisoner with a sentence of suitable length, a programme of treatment shall be prepared for him in the light of the knowledge obtained about his individual needs, his capacities and dispositions.

Privileges

70. Systems of privileges appropriate for the different classes of prisoners and the different methods of treatment shall be established at every institution, in order to encourage good conduct, develop a sense of responsibility and secure the interest and cooperation of the prisoners in their treatment.

Work

71. (1) Prison labour must not be of an afflictive nature.

(2) All prisoners under sentence shall be required to work, subject to their physical and mental fitness as determined by the medical officer.

(3) Sufficient work of a useful nature shall be provided to keep prisoners actively employed for a normal working day.

(4) So far as possible the work provided shall be such as will maintain or increase the prisoners' ability to earn an honest living after release.

(5) Vocational training in useful trades shall be provided for prisoners able to profit thereby and especially for young prisoners.

(6) Within the limits compatible with proper vocational selection and with the requirements of institutional administration and discipline, the prisoners shall be able to choose the type of work they wish to perform.

72. (1) The organization and methods of work in the institutions shall resemble as closely as possible those of similar work in outside institutions, so as to prepare prisoners for the conditions of normal occupational life.

(2) The interests of the prisoners and of their vocational training, however, must not be subordinated to the purpose of making a financial profit from an industry in the institution.

73. (1) Preferably institutional industries and farms should be operated directly by the administration and not by private contractors.

(2) Where prisoners are employed in work not controlled by the administration, they shall always be under the supervision of the institution's personnel. Unless the work is for other departments of the government the full normal wages for such work shall be paid to the administration by the persons to whom the labour is supplied, account being taken of the output of the prisoners.

74. (1) The precautions laid down to protect the safety and health of free workmen shall be equally observed in institutions.

(2) Provision shall be made to indemnify prisoners against industrial injury, including occupational disease, on terms not less favourable than those extended by law to free workmen.

75. (1) The maximum daily and weekly working hours of the prisoners shall be fixed by law or by administrative regulation, taking into account local rules or custom in regard to the employment of free workmen.

(2) The hours so fixed shall leave one rest day a week and sufficient time for education and other activities required as part of the treatment and rehabilitation of the prisoners.

76. (1) There shall be a system of equitable remuneration of the work of prisoners.

(2) Under the system prisoners shall be allowed to spend at least a part of their earnings on approved articles for their own use and to send a part of their earnings to their family.

(3) The system should also provide that a part of the earnings should be set aside by the administration so as to constitute a savings fund to be handed over to the prisoner on his release.

Education and recreation

77. (1) Provision shall be made for the further education of all prisoners capable of profiting thereby, including religious instruction in the countries where this is possible. The education of illiterates and young prisoners shall be compulsory and special attention shall be paid to it by the administration.

(2) So far as practicable, the education of prisoners shall be integrated with the educational system of the country so that after their release they may continue their education without difficulty.

78. Recreational and cultural activities shall be provided in all institutions for the benefit of the mental and physical health of prisoners.

Social relations and after-care

79. Special attention shall be paid to the maintenance and improvement of such relations between a prisoner and his family as are desirable in the best interests of both.

80. From the beginning of a prisoner's sentence consideration shall be given to his future after release and he shall be encouraged and assisted to maintain or establish such relations with persons or agencies outside the institution as may promote the best interests of his family and his own social rehabilitation.

81. (1) Services and agencies, governmental or otherwise, which assist released prisoners to re-establish themselves in society shall ensure, so far as is possible and necessary, that released prisoners be provided with appropriate documents and identification papers, have suitable homes and work to go to, are suitably and adequately clothed having regard to the climate and season, and have sufficient means to reach their destination and maintain themselves in the period immediately following their release.

(2) The approved representatives of such agencies shall have all necessary access to the institution and to prisoners and shall be taken into consultation as to the future of a prisoner from the beginning of his sentence.

(3) It is desirable that the activities of such agencies shall be centralized or co-ordinated as far as possible in order to secure the best use of their efforts.

B. INSANE AND MENTALLY ABNORMAL PRISONERS

82. (1) Persons who are found to be insane shall not be detained in prisons and arrangements shall be made to remove them to mental institutions as soon as possible.

(2) Prisoners who suffer from other mental diseases or abnormalities shall be observed and treated in specialized institutions under medical management.

(3) During their stay in a prison, such prisoners shall be placed under the special supervision of a medical officer.

(4) The medical or psychiatric service of the penal institutions shall provide for the psychiatric treatment of all other prisoners who are in need of such treatment.

83. It is desirable that steps should be taken, by arrangement with the appropriate agencies, to ensure if necessary the continuation of psychiatric treatment after release and the provision of social-psychiatric after-care.

C. PRISONERS UNDER ARREST OR AWAITING TRIAL

84. (1) Persons arrested or imprisoned by reason of a criminal charge against them, who are detained either in police custody or in prison custody (jail) but have not yet been tried and sentenced, will be referred to as "untried prisoners" hereinafter in these rules.

(2) Unconvicted prisoners are presumed to be innocent and shall be treated as such.

(3) Without prejudice to legal rules for the protection of individual liberty or prescribing the procedure to be observed in respect of untried prisoners, these prisoners shall benefit by a special régime which is described in the following rules in its essential requirements only.

85. (1) Untried prisoners shall be kept separate from convicted prisoners.

(2) Young untried prisoners shall be kept separate from adults and shall in principle be detained in separate institutions.

86. Untried prisoners shall sleep singly in separate rooms, with the reservation of different local custom in respect of the climate.

87. Within the limits compatible with the good order of the institution, untried prisoners may, if they so desire, have their food procured at their own expense from the outside, either through the administration or through their family or friends. Otherwise, the administration shall provide their food.

88. (1) An untried prisoner shall be allowed to wear his own clothing if it is clean and suitable.

(2) If he wears prison dress, it shall be different from that supplied to convicted prisoners.

89. An untried prisoner shall always be offered opportunity to work, but shall not be required to work. If he chooses to work, he shall be paid for it.

90. An untried prisoner shall be allowed to procure at his own expense or at the expense of a third party such books, newspapers, writing materials and other means of occupation as are compatible with the interests of the administration of justice and the security and good order of the institution.

91. An untried prisoner shall be allowed to be visited and treated by his own doctor or dentist if there

is reasonable ground for his application and he is able to pay any expenses incurred.

92. An untried prisoner shall be allowed to inform immediately his family of his detention and shall be given all reasonable facilities for communicating with his family and friends, and for receiving visits from them, subject only to restrictions and supervision as are necessary in the interests of the administration of justice and of the security and good order of the institution.

93. For the purposes of his defence, an untried prisoner shall be allowed to apply for free legal aid where such aid is available, and to receive visits from his legal adviser with a view to his defence and to prepare and hand to him confidential instructions. For these purposes, he shall if he so desires be supplied with writing material. Interviews between the prisoner and his legal adviser may be within sight but not within the hearing of a police or institution official.

D. CIVIL PRISONERS

94. In countries where the law permits imprisonment for debt, or by order of a court under any other non-criminal process, persons so imprisoned shall not be subjected to any greater restriction or severity than is necessary to ensure safe custody and good order. Their treatment shall be not less favourable than that of untried prisoners, with the reservation, however, that they may possibly be required to work.

E. PERSONS ARRESTED OR DETAINED WITHOUT CHARGE

95. Without prejudice to the provisions of article 9 of the International Covenant on Civil and Political Rights, persons arrested or imprisoned without charge shall be accorded the same protection as that accorded under part I and part II, section C. Relevant provisions of part II, section A, shall likewise be applicable where their application may be conducive to the benefit of this special group of persons in custody, provided that no measures shall be taken implying that re-education or rehabilitation is in any way appropriate to persons not convicted of any criminal offence.

Document 16

General Assembly resolution on advisory services in the field of human rights

A/RES/926 (X), 14 December 1955

The General Assembly,

Considering that, by Articles 55 and 56 of the United Nations Charter, the States Members of the United Nations have pledged themselves to promote universal respect for, and observance of, human rights and fundamental freedoms for all without distinction as to race, sex, language or religion,

Recognizing that technical assistance, by the international interchange of technical knowledge through international cooperation, represents one of the means by which it is possible to promote the human rights objectives of the United Nations as set forth in the Charter and in the Universal Declaration of Human Rights,

Recalling General Assembly resolution 729 (VIII) of 23 October 1953 authorizing the Secretary-General to render, at the request of Member States, services which do not fall within the scope of existing technical assistance programmes, in order to assist those States in promoting and safeguarding the rights of women,

Recalling General Assembly resolution 730 (VIII) of 23 October 1953 authorizing the Secretary-General to render, at the request of any Member State, technical advice and other services which do not fall within the scope of existing technical assistance programmes, in order to assist the Government of that State within its territory in the eradication of discrimination or in the protection of minorities, or both,

Recalling General Assembly resolution 839 (IX) of 17 December 1954 authorizing the Secretary-General to render, at the request of Member States, services which do not fall within the scope and objectives of existing technical assistance programmes, in order to assist those States in promoting freedom of information, and Economic and Social Council resolution 574 A (XIX) of 26 May 1955 requesting the Secretary-General to take steps to put into operation a programme to promote freedom of information by providing such services as experts, fellowships and seminars,

Taking account of the arrangements previously established by the General Assembly concerning the regular technical assistance programme and the advisory services of the United Nations in its resolutions 200 (III) of

4 December 1948, 246 (III) of 4 December 1948, 305 (IV) of 16 November 1949, 418 (V) of 1 December 1950, 518 (VI) of 12 January 1952 and 723 (VIII) of 23 October 1953,

Considering that the specialized agencies, within their competence and by virtue of their regular programmes of technical assistance, are already rendering important services to their members with a view to ensuring the effective observance of human rights,

1. *Decides* to consolidate the technical assistance programmes already approved by the General Assembly (relating to the promotion and safeguarding of the rights of women, the eradication of discrimination and the protection of minorities as well as to the promotion of freedom of information) with the broad programme of assistance in the field of human rights proposed in the present resolution, the entire programme to be known as "advisory services in the field of human rights";

2. *Authorizes* the Secretary-General:

(a) Subject to the directions of the Economic and Social Council, to make provision at the request of Governments, and with the cooperation of the specialized agencies where appropriate and without duplication of their existing activities, for the following forms of assistance with respect to the field of human rights:

(i) Advisory services of experts;

(ii) Fellowships and scholarships;

(iii) Seminars;

(b) To take the programme authorized by the present resolution into account in preparing the budgetary estimates of the United Nations;

3. *Requests* the Secretary-General to undertake the assistance provided for in paragraph 2 (a) above, in agreement with the Governments concerned, on the basis of requests received from Governments and in accordance with the following policies;

(a) The kind of service to be rendered to each country under paragraph 2 (a) (i) shall be determined by the Government concerned;

(b) The selection of the persons under paragraph 2 (a) (ii) shall be made by the Secretary-General on the basis of proposals received from Governments;

(c) The amount of assistance and the conditions under which it is to be rendered shall be decided by the Secretary-General, with due regard to the greater needs of the under-developed areas, and in conformity with the principle that each requesting Government shall be expected to assume responsibility, as far as possible, for all or a considerable part of the expenses connected with the

assistance furnished to it, either by making a contribution in cash, or by providing supporting staff, services and payment of local costs for the purpose of carrying out the programme;

(d) The assistance shall be applicable to any subject in the field of human rights, in addition to the subjects covered by the relevant resolutions of the General Assembly, provided however that the subject shall be one for which adequate advisory assistance is not available through a specialized agency and which does not fall within the scope of existing technical assistance programmes;

4. *Requests* the Secretary-General to report regularly to the Economic and Social Council, to the Commission on Human Rights and, as appropriate, to the Commission on the Status of Women, on the measures which he takes in compliance with the terms of the present resolution;

5. *Recommends* that the specialized agencies continue to develop their technical assistance activities with a view to aiding Member States to further the effective observance of human rights;

6. *Invites* the specialized agencies to communicate to the Economic and Social Council, for transmission to the Commission on Human Rights, any observations which they may find appropriate on the above-mentioned assistance and on any new measures of assistance which they may deem necessary with a view to assisting Member States in furthering the effective observance of human rights;

7. *Expresses the hope* that international and national non-governmental organizations, universities, philanthropic foundations and other private groups will supplement this United Nations programme with similar programmes designed to further research and studies, the exchange of information and assistance in the field of human rights;

8. *Requests* the Secretary-General to inform Member States of this new programme and of the procedures to be followed in obtaining assistance;

9. *Requests* the Economic and Social Council to submit to the General Assembly at its thirteenth session a report containing:

(a) An evaluation of the projects carried out under the programme of advisory services in human rights, with particular reference to the extent to which these projects have furthered the aims and purposes of the United Nations in the field of human rights;

(b) Recommendations concerning the future of the programme.

Document 17

Economic and Social Council resolution on periodic reports on human rights and studies of specific rights or groups of rights

E/RES/624 B (XXII), 1 August 1956

I

The Economic and Social Council,

Having noted the resolutions of the Commission on Human Rights relating to annual reports on human rights 1/ and to studies of specific rights or groups of rights, 2/

Considering that the purpose of the resolutions would best be served by consolidating and reducing the frequency of the reports envisaged in the resolutions,

1. *Requests* States members of the United Nations and of the specialized agencies to transmit to the Secretary-General, every three years, a report describing developments and the progress achieved during the preceding three years in the field of human rights, and measures taken to safeguard human liberty in their metropolitan area and Non-Self-Governing and Trust Territories; the report to deal with the rights enumerated in the Universal Declaration of Human Rights and with the right of peoples to self-determination, and to supplement the information furnished for publication in the *Yearbook on Human Rights*, and to make reference to any relevant parts of reports already submitted to another organ of the United Nations or to a specialized agency;

2. *Invites* States members of the United Nations or of the specialized agencies, in preparing their reports, to include a separate section on such right or group of rights as may from time to time be selected for special study by the Commission on Human Rights, subject to the approval of the Council;

3. *Invites* the specialized agencies, in respect of rights coming within their purview, to transmit to the Secretary-General, every three years, a report on a topical basis, summarizing the information which they have received from their member States during the preceding three years and to cooperate in the full realization of the aim set forth in this resolution;

4. *Requests* the Secretary-General to prepare and forward to Governments suggestions that might serve as a guide for the preparation of the reports by governments on a topical basis, and to prepare a brief summary of the reports on the same basis for the Commission on Human Rights;

5. *Invites* the specialized agencies and the non-governmental organizations in consultative relationship with the Council to cooperate in carrying out any special study undertaken by the Commission on Human Rights, in accordance with paragraph 2 of this resolution.

II

The Economic and Social Council,

With a view to implementing without delay the provisions set forth in resolution I above and the resolution of the Commission on Human Rights on studies of specific rights and groups of rights,

1. *Requests* the Secretary-General to submit to the Commission on Human Rights at its fourteenth session a summary of reports transmitted to him by the Governments, covering the years 1954, 1955 and 1956;

2. *Approves* as the first subject for special study the right of everyone to be free from arbitrary arrest, detention and exile.

1/ *Official Records of the Economic and Social Council, Twenty-second Session, Supplement No. 3 (E/2844), para. 23.*
2/ Ibid., para. 49.

Document 18

Supplementary Convention on the Abolition of Slavery, the Slave Trade, and Institutions and Practices Similar to Slavery adopted by a Conference of Plenipotentiaries convened by Economic and Social Council resolution 608 (XXI) of 30 April 1956

7 September 1956

PREAMBLE

The States Parties to the present Convention,

Considering that freedom is the birthright of every human being,

Mindful that the peoples of the United Nations reaffirmed in the Charter their faith in the dignity and worth of the human person,

Considering that the Universal Declaration of Human Rights, proclaimed by the General Assembly of the

United Nations as a common standard of achievement for all peoples and all nations, states that no one shall be held in slavery or servitude and that slavery and the slave trade shall be prohibited in all their forms,

Recognizing that, since the conclusion of the Slavery Convention signed at Geneva on 25 September 1926, which was designed to secure the abolition of slavery and of the slave trade, further progress has been made towards this end,

Having regard to the Forced Labour Convention of 1930 and to subsequent action by the International Labour Organisation in regard to forced or compulsory labour,

Being aware, however, that slavery, the slave trade and institutions and practices similar to slavery have not yet been eliminated in all parts of the world,

Having decided, therefore, that the Convention of 1926, which remains operative, should now be augmented by the conclusion of a supplementary convention designed to intensify national as well as international efforts towards the abolition of slavery, the slave trade and institutions and practices similar to slavery,

Have agreed as follows:

SECTION I
INSTITUTIONS AND PRACTICES SIMILAR TO SLAVERY

Article 1

Each of the States Parties to this Convention shall take all practicable and necessary legislative and other measures to bring about progressively and as soon as possible the complete abolition or abandonment of the following institutions and practices, where they still exist and whether or not they are covered by the definition of slavery contained in article 1 of the Slavery Convention signed at Geneva on 25 September 1926:

(a) Debt bondage, that is to say, the status or condition arising from a pledge by a debtor of his personal services or of those of a person under his control as security for a debt, if the value of those services as reasonably assessed is not applied towards the liquidation of the debt or the length and nature of those services are not respectively limited and defined;

(b) Serfdom, that is to say, the condition or status of a tenant who is by law, custom or agreement bound to live and labour on land belonging to another person and to render some determinate service to such other person, whether for reward or not, and is not free to change his status;

(c) Any institution or practice whereby:

(i) A woman, without the right to refuse, is promised or given in marriage on payment of a consideration in money or in kind to her parents, guardian, family or any other person or group; or

(ii) The husband of a woman, his family, or his clan, has the right to transfer her to another person for value received or otherwise; or

(iii) A woman on the death of her husband is liable to be inherited by another person;

(d) Any institution or practice whereby a child or young person under the age of 18 years is delivered by either or both of his natural parents or by his guardian to another person, whether for reward or not, with a view to the exploitation of the child or young person or of his labour.

Article 2

With a view to bringing to an end the institutions and practices mentioned in article 1 (c) of this Convention, the States Parties undertake to prescribe, where appropriate, suitable minimum ages of marriage, to encourage the use of facilities whereby the consent of both parties to a marriage may be freely expressed in the presence of a competent civil or religious authority, and to encourage the registration of marriages.

SECTION II
THE SLAVE TRADE

Article 3

1. The act of conveying or attempting to convey slaves from one country to another by whatever means of transport, or of being accessory thereto, shall be a criminal offence under the laws of the States Parties to this Convention and persons convicted thereof shall be liable to very severe penalties.

2. (a) The States Parties shall take all effective measures to prevent ships and aircraft authorized to fly their flags from conveying slaves and to punish persons guilty of such acts or of using national flags for that purpose.

(b) The States Parties shall take all effective measures to ensure that their ports, airfields and coasts are not used for the conveyance of slaves.

3. The States Parties to this Convention shall exchange information in order to ensure the practical coordination of the measures taken by them in combating the slave trade and shall inform each other of every case of the slave trade, and of every attempt to commit this criminal offence, which comes to their notice.

Article 4

Any slave who takes refuge on board any vessel of a State Party to this Convention shall *ipso facto* be free.

SECTION III
SLAVERY AND INSTITUTIONS AND PRACTICES SIMILAR TO SLAVERY

Article 5

In a country where the abolition or abandonment of slavery, or of the institutions or practices mentioned in article 1 of this Convention, is not yet complete, the act of mutilating, branding or otherwise marking a slave or a person of servile status in order to indicate his status, or as a punishment, or for any other reason, or of being accessory thereto, shall be a criminal offence under the laws of the States Parties to this Convention and persons convicted thereof shall be liable to punishment.

Article 6

1. The act of enslaving another person or of inducing another person to give himself or a person dependent upon him into slavery, or of attempting these acts, or being accessory thereto, or being a party to a conspiracy to accomplish any such acts, shall be a criminal offence under the laws of the States Parties to this Convention and persons convicted thereof shall be liable to punishment.

2. Subject to the provisions of the introductory paragraph of article 1 of this Convention, the provisions of paragraph 1 of the present article shall also apply to the act of inducing another person to place himself or a person dependent upon him into the servile status resulting from any of the institutions or practices mentioned in article 1, to any attempt to perform such acts, to being accessory thereto, and to being a party to a conspiracy to accomplish any such acts.

SECTION IV
DEFINITIONS

Article 7

For the purposes of the present Convention:

(a) "Slavery" means, as defined in the Slavery Convention of 1926, the status or condition of a person over whom any or all of the powers attaching to the right of ownership are exercised, and "slave" means a person in such condition or status;

(b) "A person of servile status" means a person in the condition or status resulting from any of the institutions or practices mentioned in article 1 of this Convention;

(c) "Slave trade" means and includes all acts involved in the capture, acquisition or disposal of a person with intent to reduce him to slavery; all acts involved in the acquisition of a slave with a view to selling or exchanging him; all acts of disposal by sale or exchange of a person acquired with a view to being sold or exchanged; and, in general, every act of trade or transport in slaves by whatever means of conveyance.

SECTION V
COOPERATION BETWEEN STATES PARTIES AND COMMUNICATION OF INFORMATION

Article 8

1. The States Parties to this Convention undertake to cooperate with each other and with the United Nations to give effect to the foregoing provisions.

2. The Parties undertake to communicate to the Secretary-General of the United Nations copies of any laws, regulations and administrative measures enacted or put into effect to implement the provisions of this Convention.

3. The Secretary-General shall communicate the information received under paragraph 2 of this article to the other Parties and to the Economic and Social Council as part of the documentation for any discussion which the Council might undertake with a view to making further recommendations for the abolition of slavery, the slave trade or the institutions and practices which are the subject of this Convention.

SECTION VI
FINAL CLAUSES

Article 9

No reservations may be made to this Convention.

Article 10

Any dispute between States Parties to this Convention relating to its interpretation or application, which is not settled by negotiation, shall be referred to the International Court of Justice at the request of any one of the parties to the dispute, unless the parties concerned agree on another mode of settlement.

Article 11

1. This Convention shall be open until 1 July 1957 for signature by any State Member of the United Nations or of a specialized agency. It shall be subject to ratification by the signatory States, and the instruments of ratification shall be deposited with the Secretary-General of the United Nations, who shall inform each signatory and acceding State.

2. After 1 July 1957 this Convention shall be open for accession by any State Member of the United Nations or of a specialized agency, or by any other State to which an invitation to accede has been addressed by the General Assembly of the United Nations. Accession shall be effected by the deposit of a formal instrument with the Secretary-General of the United Nations, who shall inform each signatory and acceding State.

Article 12

1. This Convention shall apply to all non-self-governing trust, colonial and other non-metropolitan territories for the international relations of which any State Party is responsible; the Party concerned shall, subject to the provisions of paragraph 2 of this article, at the time of signature, ratification or accession declare the non-metropolitan territory or territories to which the Convention shall apply *ipso facto* as a result of such signature, ratification or accession.

2. In any case in which the previous consent of a non-metropolitan territory is required by the constitutional laws or practices of the Party or of the non-metropolitan territory, the Party concerned shall endeavour to secure the needed consent of the non-metropolitan territory within the period of twelve months from the date of signature of the Convention by the metropolitan State, and when such consent has been obtained the Party shall notify the Secretary-General. This Convention shall apply to the territory or territories named in such notification from the date of its receipt by the Secretary-General.

3. After the expiry of the twelve-month period mentioned in the preceding paragraph, the States Parties concerned shall inform the Secretary-General of the results of the consultations with those non-metropolitan territories for whose international relations they are responsible and whose consent to the application of this Convention may have been withheld.

Article 13

1. This Convention shall enter into force on the date on which two States have become Parties thereto.

2. It shall thereafter enter into force with respect to each State and territory on the date of deposit of the instrument of ratification or accession of that State or notification of application to that territory.

Article 14

1. The application of this Convention shall be divided into successive periods of three years, of which the first shall begin on the date of entry into force of the Convention in accordance with paragraph 1 of article 13.

2. Any State Party may denounce this Convention by a notice addressed by that State to the Secretary-General not less than six months before the expiration of the current three-year period. The Secretary-General shall notify all other Parties of each such notice and the date of the receipt thereof.

3. Denunciations shall take effect at the expiration of the current three-year period.

4. In cases where, in accordance with the provisions of article 12, this Convention has become applicable to a non-metropolitan territory of a Party, that Party may at any time thereafter, with the consent of the territory concerned, give notice to the Secretary-General of the United Nations denouncing this Convention separately in respect of that territory. The denunciation shall take effect one year after the date of the receipt of such notice by the Secretary-General, who shall notify all other Parties of such notice and the date of the receipt thereof.

Article 15

This Convention, of which the Chinese, English, French, Russian and Spanish texts are equally authentic, shall be deposited in the archives of the United Nations Secretariat. The Secretary-General shall prepare a certified copy thereof for communication to States Parties to this Convention, as well as to all other States Members of the United Nations and of the specialized agencies.

IN WITNESS WHEREOF the undersigned, being duly authorized thereto by their respective Governments, have signed this Convention on the date appearing opposite their respective signatures.

DONE at the European Office of the United Nations at Geneva, this seventh day of September one thousand nine hundred and fifty-six.

Document 19

Convention on the Nationality of Married Women

A/RES/1040 (XI), 29 January 1957

The Contracting States,

Recognizing that, conflicts in law in practice with reference to nationality arise as a result of provisions concerning the loss or acquisition of nationality by women as a result of marriage, of its dissolution or of the change of nationality by the husband during marriage,

Recognizing that, in article 15 of the Universal Declaration of Human Rights, the General Assembly of the United Nations has proclaimed that "everyone has the right to a nationality" and that "no one shall be arbitrarily deprived of his nationality nor denied the right to change his nationality",

Desiring to cooperate with the United Nations in promoting universal respect for, and observance of, human rights and fundamental freedoms for all without distinction as to sex,

Hereby agree as hereinafter provided:

Article 1

Each Contracting State agrees that neither the celebration nor the dissolution of a marriage between one of its nationals and an alien, nor the change of nationality by the husband during marriage, shall automatically affect the nationality of the wife.

Article 2

Each Contracting State agrees that neither the voluntary acquisition of the nationality of another State nor the renunciation of its nationality by one of its nationals shall prevent the retention of its nationality by the wife of such national.

Article 3

1. Each Contracting State agrees that the alien wife of one of its nationals may, at her request, acquire the nationality of her husband through specially privileged naturalization procedures; the grant of such nationality may be subject to such limitations as may be imposed in the interests of national security or public policy.

2. Each Contracting State agrees that the present Convention shall not be construed as affecting any legislation or judicial practice by which the alien wife of one of its nationals may, at her request, acquire her husband's nationality as a matter of right.

Article 4

1. The present Convention shall be open for signature and ratification on behalf of any State Member of the United Nations and also on behalf of any other State which is or hereafter becomes a member of any specialized agency of the United Nations, or which is or hereafter becomes a Party to the Statute of the International Court of Justice, or any other State to which an invitation has been addressed by the General Assembly of the United Nations.

2. The present Convention shall be ratified and the instruments of ratification shall be deposited with the Secretary-General of the United Nations.

Article 5

1. The present Convention shall be open for accession to all States referred to in paragraph 1 of article 4.

2. Accession shall be effected by the deposit of an instrument of accession with the Secretary-General of the United Nations.

Article 6

1. The present Convention shall come into force on the nineteeth day following the date of deposit of the sixth instrument of ratification or accession.

2. For each State ratifying or acceding to the Convention after the deposit of the sixth instrument of ratification or accession, the Convention shall enter into force on the nineteeth day after deposit by such State of its instrument of ratification or accession.

Article 7

1. The present Convention shall apply to all non-self-governing, trust, colonial and other non-metropolitan territories for the international relations of which any Contracting State is responsible; the Contracting State concerned shall, subject to the provisions of paragraph 2 of the present article, at the time of signature, ratification or accession declare the non-metropolitan territory or territories to which the Convention shall apply *ipso facto* as a result of such signature, ratification or accession.

2. In any case in which, for the purpose of nationality, a non-metropolitan territory is not treated as one

with the metropolitan territory, or in any case in which the previous consent of a non-metropolitan territory is required by the constitutional laws or practices of the Contracting State or of the non-metropolitan territory for the application of the Convention to that territory, that Contracting State shall endeavour to secure the needed consent of the non-metropolitan territory within the period of twelve months from the date of signature of the Convention by that Contracting State, and when such consent has been obtained the Contracting State shall notify the Secretary-General of the United Nations. The present Convention shall apply to the territory or territories named in such notification from the date of its receipt by the Secretary-General.

3. After the expiry of the twelve-month period mentioned in paragraph 2 of the present article, the Contracting States concerned shall inform the Secretary-General of the results of the consultations with those non-metropolitan territories for whose international relations they are responsible and whose consent to the application of the present Convention may have been withheld.

Article 8

1. At the time of signature, ratification or accession, any State may make reservations to any article of the present Convention other than articles 1 and 2.

2. If any State makes a reservation in accordance with paragraph 1 of the present article, the Convention, with the exception of those provisions to which the reservation relates, shall have effect as between the reserving State and the other Parties. The Secretary-General of the United Nations shall communicate the text of the reservation to all States which are or may become Parties to the Convention. Any State Party to the Convention or which thereafter becomes a Party may notify the Secretary-General that it does not agree to consider itself bound by the Convention with respect to the State making the reservation. This notification must be made, in the case of a State already a Party, within ninety days from the date of the communication by the Secretary-General; and, in the case of a State subsequently becoming a Party, within ninety days from the date when the instrument of ratification or accession is deposited. In the event that such a notification is made, the Convention shall not be deemed to be in effect as between the State making the notification and the State making the reservation.

3. Any State making a reservation in accordance with paragraph 1 of the present article may at any time withdraw the reservation, in whole or in part, after it has been accepted, by a notification to this effect addressed to the Secretary-General of the United Nations. Such notification shall take effect on the date on which it is received.

Article 9

1. Any Contracting State may denounce the present Convention by written notification to the Secretary-General of the United Nations. Denunciation shall take effect one year after the date of receipt of the notification by the Secretary-General.

2. The present Convention shall cease to be in force as from the date when the denunciation which reduces the number of Parties to less than six becomes effective.

Article 10

Any dispute which may arise between any two or more Contracting States concerning the interpretation or application of the present Convention which is not settled by negotiation, shall, at the request of any one of the parties to the dispute, be referred to the International Court of Justice for decision, unless the parties agree to another mode of settlement.

Article 11

The Secretary-General of the United Nations shall notify all States Members of the United Nations and the non-member States contemplated in paragraph 1 of article 4 of the present Convention of the following:

(a) Signatures and instruments of ratification received in accordance with article 4;

(b) Instruments of accession received in accordance with article 5;

(c) The date upon which the present Convention enters into force in accordance with article 6;

(d) Communications and notifications received in accordance with article 8;

(e) Notifications of denunciation received in accordance with paragraph 1 of article 9;

(f) Abrogation in accordance with paragraph 2 of article 9.

Article 12

1. The present Convention, of which the Chinese, English, French, Russian and Spanish texts shall be equally authentic, shall be deposited in the archives of the United Nations.

2. The Secretary-General of the United Nations shall transmit a certified copy of the Convention to all States Members of the United Nations and to the non-member States contemplated in paragraph 1 of article 4.

IN FAITH WHEREOF the undersigned, duly authorized, have signed this Convention on behalf of their respective Governments, which opened for signature in New York on 20 February one thousand nine hundred fifty-seven.

Document 20

Economic and Social Council resolution giving the Commission on Human Rights certain responsibilities with regard to communications concerning human rights

E/RES/728 F (XXVIII), 30 July 1959

The Economic and Social Council,

Having considered chapter V of the report of the Commission on Human Rights on its first session, 1/ concerning communications, and chapter IX of the report of the Commission on its fiftieth session, 2/

1. *Approves* the statement that the Commission on Human Rights recognizes that it has no power to take any action in regard to any complaints concerning human rights;

2. *Requests* the Secretary-General:

(a) To compile and distribute to members of the Commission on Human Rights before each session a non-confidential list containing a brief indication of the substance of each communication, however addressed, which deals with the principles involved in the promotion of universal respect for, and observance of, human rights and to divulge the identity of the authors of such communications unless they indicate that they wish their names to remain confidential;

(b) To compile before each session of the Commission a confidential list containing a brief indication of the substance of other communications concerning human rights, however addressed, and to furnish this list to members of the Commission, in private meeting, without divulging the identity of the authors of communications except in cases where the authors state that they have already divulged or intend to divulge their names or that they have no objection to their names being divulged;

(c) To enable the members of the Commission, upon request, to consult the originals of communications dealing with the principles involved in the promotion of universal respect for, and observance of, human rights;

(d) To inform the writers of all communications concerning human rights, however addressed, that their communications will be handled in accordance with this resolution, indicating that the Commission has no power to take any action in regard to any complaint concerning human rights;

(e) To furnish each Member State concerned with a copy of any communication concerning human rights which refers explicitly to that State or to territories under its jurisdiction, without divulging the identity of the author, except as provided for in sub-paragraph (b) above;

(f) To ask Governments sending replies to communications brought to their attention in accordance with sub-paragraph (e) whether they wish their replies to be presented to the Commission in summary form or in full;

3. *Resolves* to give members of the Sub-Commission on Prevention of Discrimination and Protection of Minorities, with respect to communications dealing with discrimination and minorities, the same facilities as are enjoyed by members of the Commission on Human Rights under the present resolution;

4. *Suggests* to the Commission on Human Rights that it should at each session appoint an *ad hoc* committee to meet shortly before its next session for the purpose of reviewing the list of communications prepared by the Secretary-General under paragraph 2(a) above and of recommending which of these communications, in original, should, in accordance with paragraph 2(c) above, be made available to members of the Commission on request.

1/ *Official Records of the Economic and Social Council, Fourth Session, Supplement No. 3* (E/259).
2/ Ibid., *Twenty-eighth Session, Supplement No. 8* (E/3229).

Document 21

Declaration on the Granting of Independence to Colonial Countries and Peoples

A/RES/1514 (XV), 14 December 1960

The General Assembly,

Mindful of the determination proclaimed by the peoples of the world in the Charter of the United Nations to reaffirm faith in fundamental human rights, in the dignity and worth of the human person, in the equal rights of men and women and of nations large and small and to promote social progress and better standards of life in larger freedom,

Conscious of the need for the creation of conditions of stability and well-being and peaceful and friendly relations based on respect for the principles of equal rights and self-determination of all peoples, and of universal respect for, and observance of, human rights and fundamental freedoms for all without distinction as to race, sex, language or religion,

Recognizing the passionate yearning for freedom in all dependent peoples and the decisive role of such peoples in the attainment of their independence,

Aware of the increasing conflicts resulting from the denial of or impediments in the way of the freedom of such peoples, which constitute a serious threat to world peace,

Considering the important role of the United Nations in assisting the movement for independence in Trust and Non-Self-Governing Territories,

Recognizing that the peoples of the world ardently desire the end of colonialism in all its manifestations,

Convinced that the continued existence of colonialism prevents the development of international economic cooperation, impedes the social, cultural and economic development of dependent peoples and militates against the United Nations ideal of universal peace,

Affirming that peoples may, for their own ends, freely dispose of their natural wealth and resources without prejudice to any obligations arising out of international economic cooperation, based upon the principle of mutual benefit, and international law,

Believing that the process of liberation is irresistible and irreversible and that, in order to avoid serious crises, an end must be put to colonialism and all practices of segregation and discrimination associated therewith,

Welcoming the emergence in recent years of a large number of dependent territories into freedom and independence, and recognizing the increasingly powerful trends towards freedom in such territories which have not yet attained independence,

Convinced that all peoples have an inalienable right to complete freedom, the exercise of their sovereignty and the integrity of their national territory,

Solemnly proclaims the necessity of bringing to a speedy and unconditional end colonialism in all its forms and manifestations;

And to this end

Declares that:

1. The subjection of peoples to alien subjugation, domination and exploitation constitutes a denial of fundamental human rights, is contrary to the Charter of the United Nations and is an impediment to the promotion of world peace and cooperation.

2. All peoples have the right to self-determination; by virtue of that right they freely determine their political status and freely pursue their economic, social and cultural development.

3. Inadequacy of political, economic, social or educational preparedness should never serve as a pretext for delaying independence.

4. All armed action or repressive measures of all kinds directed against dependent peoples shall cease in order to enable them to exercise peacefully and freely their right to complete independence, and the integrity of their national territory shall be respected.

5. Immediate steps shall be taken, in Trust and Non-Self-Governing Territories or all other territories which have not yet attained independence, to transfer all powers to the peoples of those territories, without any conditions or reservations, in accordance with their freely expressed will and desire, without any distinction as to race, creed or colour, in order to enable them to enjoy complete independence and freedom.

6. Any attempt aimed at the partial or total disruption of the national unity and the territorial integrity of a country is incompatible with the purposes and principles of the Charter of the United Nations.

7. All States shall observe faithfully and strictly the provisions of the Charter of the United Nations, the Universal Declaration of Human Rights and the present Declaration on the basis of equality, non-interference in the internal affairs of all States, and respect for the sovereign rights of all peoples and their territorial integrity.

Document 22

Convention on the Reduction of Statelessness, adopted by a Conference of Plenipotentiaries which met in 1959 and reconvened in 1961 in pursuance of General Assembly resolution 896 (IX) of 4 December 1954

30 August 1961

The Contracting States,

Acting in pursuance of resolution 896 (IX), adopted by the General Assembly of the United Nations on 4 December 1954,

Considering it desirable to reduce statelessness by international agreement,

Have agreed as follows:

Article 1

1. A Contracting State shall grant its nationality to a person born in its territory who would otherwise be stateless. Such nationality shall be granted:

(a) At birth, by operation of law, or

(b) Upon an application being lodged with the appropriate authority, by or on behalf of the person concerned, in the manner prescribed by the national law. Subject to the provisions of paragraph 2 of this article, no such application may be rejected.

A Contracting State which provides for the grant of its nationality in accordance with subparagraph (b) of this paragraph may also provide for the grant of its nationality by operation of law at such age and subject to such conditions as may be prescribed by the national law.

2. A Contracting State may make the grant of its nationality in accordance with subparagraph (b) of paragraph 1 of this article subject to one or more of the following conditions:

(a) That the application is lodged during a period, fixed by the Contracting State, beginning not later than at the age of eighteen years and ending not earlier than at the age of twenty-one years, so, however, that the person concerned shall be allowed at least one year during which he may himself make the application without having to obtain legal authorization to do so;

(b) That the person concerned has habitually resided in the territory of the Contracting State for such period as may be fixed by that State, not exceeding five years immediately preceding the lodging of the application nor ten years in all;

(c) That the person concerned has neither been convicted of an offence against national security nor has been sentenced to imprisonment for a term of five years or more on a criminal charge;

(d) That the person concerned has always been stateless.

3. Notwithstanding the provisions of paragraphs 1 (b) and 2 of this article, a child born in wedlock in the territory of a Contracting State, whose mother has the nationality of that State, shall acquire at birth that nationality if it otherwise would be stateless.

4. A Contracting State shall grant its nationality to a person who would otherwise be stateless and who is unable to acquire the nationality of the Contracting State in whose territory he was born because he has passed the age for lodging his application or has not fulfilled the required residence conditions, if the nationality of one of his parents at the time of the person's birth was that of the Contracting State first above-mentioned. If his parents did not possess the same nationality at the time of his birth, the question whether the nationality of the person concerned should follow that of the father or that of the mother shall be determined by the national law of such Contracting State. If application for such nationality is required, the application shall be made to the appropriate authority by or on behalf of the applicant in the manner prescribed by the national law. Subject to the provisions of paragraph 5 of this article, such application shall not be refused.

5. The Contracting State may make the grant of its nationality in accordance with the provisions of paragraph 4 of this article subject to one or more of the following conditions:

(a) That the application is lodged before the applicant reaches an age, being not less than twenty-three years, fixed by the Contracting State;

(b) That the person concerned has habitually resided in the territory of the Contracting State for such period immediately preceding the lodging of the application, not exceeding three years, as may be fixed by that State;

(c) That the person concerned has always been stateless.

Article 2

A foundling found in the territory of a Contracting State shall, in the absence of proof to the contrary, be considered to have been born within that territory of parents possessing the nationality of that State.

Article 3

For the purpose of determining the obligations of Contracting States under this Convention, birth on a ship or in an aircraft shall be deemed to have taken place in the territory of the State whose flag the ship flies or in the territory of the State in which the aircraft is registered, as the case may be.

Article 4

1. A Contracting State shall grant its nationality to a person, not born in the territory of a Contracting State, who would otherwise be stateless, if the nationality of one of his parents at the time of the person's birth was that of that State. If his parents did not possess the same nationality at the time of his birth, the question whether the nationality of the person concerned should follow that of the father or that of the mother shall be determined by the national law of such Contracting State. Nationality granted in accordance with the provisions of this paragraph shall be granted:

(a) At birth, by operation of law, or

(b) Upon an application being lodged with the appropriate authority, by or on behalf of the person concerned, in the manner prescribed by the national law. Subject to the provisions of paragraph 2 of this article, no such application may be rejected.

2. A Contracting State may make the grant of its nationality in accordance with the provisions of paragraph 1 of this article subject to one or more of the following conditions:

(a) That the application is lodged before the applicant reaches an age, being not less than twenty-three years, fixed by the Contracting State;

(b) That the person concerned has habitually resided in the territory of the Contracting State for such period immediately preceding the lodging of the application, not exceeding three years, as may be fixed by that State;

(c) That the person concerned has not been convicted of an offence against national security;

(d) That the person concerned has always been stateless.

Article 5

1. If the law of a Contracting State entails loss of nationality as a consequence of any change in the personal status of a person such as marriage, termination of marriage, legitimation, recognition or adoption, such loss shall be conditional upon possession or acquisition of another nationality.

2. If, under the law of a Contracting State, a child born out of wedlock loses the nationality of that State in consequence of a recognition of affiliation, he shall be given an opportunity to recover that nationality by written application to the appropriate authority, and the conditions governing such application shall not be more rigorous than those laid down in paragraph 2 of article 1 of this Convention.

Article 6

If the law of a Contracting State provides for loss of its nationality by a person's spouse or children as a consequence of that person losing or being deprived of that nationality, such loss shall be conditional upon their possession or acquisition of another nationality.

Article 7

1. (a) If the law of a Contracting State entails loss or renunciation of nationality, such renunciation shall not result in loss of nationality unless the person concerned possesses or acquires another nationality;

(b) The provisions of subparagraph (a) of this paragraph shall not apply where their application would be inconsistent with the principles stated in articles 13 and 14 of the Universal Declaration of Human Rights approved on 10 December 1948 by the General Assembly of the United Nations.

2. A national of a Contracting State who seeks naturalization in a foreign country shall not lose his nationality unless he acquires or has been accorded assurance of acquiring the nationality of that foreign country.

3. Subject to the provisions of paragraphs 4 and 5 of this article, a national of a Contracting State shall not lose his nationality, so as to become stateless, on the ground of departure, residence abroad, failure to register or on any similar ground.

4. A naturalized person may lose his nationality on account of residence abroad for a period, not less than seven consecutive years, specified by the law of the Contracting State concerned if he fails to declare to the appropriate authority his intention to retain his nationality.

5. In the case of a national of a Contracting State, born outside its territory, the law of that State may make the retention of its nationality after the expiry of one year from his attaining his majority conditional upon residence at that time in the territory of the State or registration with the appropriate authority.

6. Except in the circumstances mentioned in this article, a person shall not lose the nationality of a Contracting State, if such loss would render him stateless, notwithstanding that such loss is not expressly prohibited by any other provision of this Convention.

Article 8

1. A Contracting State shall not deprive a person of his nationality if such deprivation would render him stateless.

2. Notwithstanding the provisions of paragraph 1 of this article, a person may be deprived of the nationality of a Contracting State:

(a) In the circumstances in which, under paragraphs 4 and 5 of article 7, it is permissible that a person should lose his nationality;

(b) Where the nationality has been obtained by misrepresentation or fraud.

3. Notwithstanding the provisions of paragraph 1 of this article, a Contracting State may retain the right to deprive a person of his nationality, if at the time of signature, ratification or accession it specifies its retention of such right on one or more of the following grounds, being grounds existing in its national law at that time:

(a) That, inconsistently with his duty of loyalty to the Contracting State, the person:

(i) Has, in disregard of an express prohibition by the Contracting State rendered or continued to render services to, or received or continued to receive emoluments from, another State, or

(ii) Has conducted himself in a manner seriously prejudicial to the vital interests of the State;

(b) That the person has taken an oath, or made a formal declaration, of allegiance to another State, or given definite evidence of his determination to repudiate his allegiance to the Contracting State.

4. A Contracting State shall not exercise a power of deprivation permitted by paragraphs 2 or 3 of this article except in accordance with law, which shall provide for the person concerned the right to a fair hearing by a court or other independent body.

Article 9

A Contracting State may not deprive any person or group of persons of their nationality on racial, ethnic, religious or political grounds.

Article 10

1. Every treaty between Contracting States providing for the transfer of territory shall include provisions designed to secure that no person shall become stateless as a result of the transfer. A Contracting State shall use its best endeavours to secure that any such treaty made by it with a State which is not a Party to this Convention includes such provisions.

2. In the absence of such provisions a Contracting State to which territory is transferred or which otherwise acquires territory shall confer its nationality on such persons as would otherwise become stateless as a result of the transfer or acquisition.

Article 11

The Contracting States shall promote the establishment within the framework of the United Nations, as soon as may be after the deposit of the sixth instrument of ratification or accession, of a body to which a person claiming the benefit of this Convention may apply for the examination of his claim and for assistance in presenting it to the appropriate authority.

Article 12

1. In relation to a Contracting State which does not, in accordance with the provisions of paragraph 1 of article 1 or of article 4 of this Convention, grant its nationality at birth by operation of law, the provisions of paragraph 1 of article 1 or of article 4, as the case may be, shall apply to persons born before as well as to persons born after the entry into force of this Convention.

2. The provisions of paragraph 4 of article 1 of this Convention shall apply to persons born before as well as to persons born after its entry into force.

3. The provisions of article 2 of this Convention shall apply only to foundlings found in the territory of a Contracting State after the entry into force of the Convention for that State.

Article 13

This Convention shall not be construed as affecting any provisions more conducive to the reduction of statelessness which may be contained in the law of any Contracting State now or hereafter in force, or may be contained in any other convention, treaty or agreement now or hereafter in force between two or more Contracting States.

Article 14

Any dispute between Contracting States concerning the interpretation or application of this Convention which cannot be settled by other means shall be submitted to the International Court of Justice at the request of any one of the parties to the dispute.

Article 15

1. This Convention shall apply to all non-self-governing, trust, colonial and other non-metropolitan territories for the international relations of which any Contracting State is responsible; the Contracting State concerned shall, subject to the provisions of paragraph 2 of this article, at the time of signature, ratification or accession, declare the non-metropolitan territory or territories

to which the Convention shall apply *ipso facto* as a result of such signature, ratification or accession.

2. In any case in which, for the purpose of nationality, a non-metropolitan territory is not treated as one with the metropolitan territory, or in any case in which the previous consent of a non-metropolitan territory is required by the constitutional laws or practices of the Contracting State or of the non-metropolitan territory for the application of the Convention to that territory, that Contracting State shall endeavour to secure the needed consent of the non-metropolitan territory within the period of twelve months from the date of signature of the Convention by that Contracting State, and when such consent has been obtained the Contracting State shall notify the Secretary-General of the United Nations. This Convention shall apply to the territory or territories named in such notification from the date of its receipt by the Secretary-General.

3. After the expiry of the twelve-month period mentioned in paragraph 2 of this article, the Contracting States concerned shall inform the Secretary-General of the results of the consultations with those non-metropolitan territories for whose international relations they are responsible and whose consent to the application of this Convention may have been withheld.

Article 16

1. This Convention shall be open for signature at the Headquarters of the United Nations from 30 August 1961 to 31 May 1962.

2. This Convention shall be open for signature on behalf of:

(a) Any State Member of the United Nations;

(b) Any other State invited to attend the United Nations Conference on the Elimination or Reduction of Future Statelessness;

(c) Any State to which an invitation to sign or to accede may be addressed by the General Assembly of the United Nations.

3. This Convention shall be ratified and the instruments of ratification shall be deposited with the Secretary-General of the United Nations.

4. This Convention shall be open for accession by the States referred to in paragraph 2 of this article. Accession shall be effected by the deposit of an instrument of accession with the Secretary-General of the United Nations.

Article 17

1. At the time of signature, ratification or accession any State may make a reservation in respect of articles 11, 14 or 15.

2. No other reservations to this Convention shall be admissible.

Article 18

1. This Convention shall enter into force two years after the date of the deposit of the sixth instrument of ratification or accession.

2. For each State ratifying or acceding to this Convention after the deposit of the sixth instrument of ratification or accession, it shall enter into force on the ninetieth day after the deposit by such State of its instrument of ratification or accession or on the date on which this Convention enters into force in accordance with the provisions of paragraph 1 of this article, whichever is the later.

Article 19

1. Any Contracting State may denounce this Convention at any time by a written notification addressed to the Secretary-General of the United Nations. Such denunciation shall take effect for the Contracting State concerned one year after the date of its receipt by the Secretary-General.

2. In cases where, in accordance with the provisions of article 15, this Convention has become applicable to a non-metropolitan territory of a Contracting State, that State may at any time thereafter, with the consent of the territory concerned, give notice to the Secretary-General of the United Nations denouncing this Convention separately in respect to that territory. The denunciation shall take effect one year after the date of the receipt of such notice by the Secretary-General, who shall notify all other Contracting States of such notice and the date of receipt thereof.

Article 20

1. The Secretary-General of the United Nations shall notify all Members of the United Nations and the non-member States referred to in article 16 of the following particulars:

(a) Signatures, ratifications and accessions under article 16;

(b) Reservations under article 17;

(c) The date upon which this Convention enters into force in pursuance of article 18;

(d) Denunciations under article 19.

2. The Secretary-General of the United Nations shall, after the deposit of the sixth instrument of ratification or accession at the latest, bring to the attention of the General Assembly the question of the establishment, in accordance with article 11, of such a body as therein mentioned.

Article 21

This Convention shall be registered by the Secretary-General of the United Nations on the date of its entry into force.

IN WITNESS WHEREOF the undersigned Plenipotentiaries have signed this Convention.

DONE at New York, this thirtieth day of August, one thousand nine hundred and sixty-one, in a single copy, of which the Chinese, English, French, Russian and Spanish texts are equally authentic and which shall be deposited in the archives of the United Nations, and certified copies of which shall be delivered by the Secretary-General of the United Nations to all members of the United Nations and to the non-member States referred to in article 16 of this Convention.

Document 23

Convention on Consent to Marriage, Minimum Age for Marriage and Registration of Marriages

A/RES/1763 A (XVII), 7 November 1962

The Contracting States,

Desiring, in conformity with the Charter of the United Nations, to promote universal respect for, and observance of, human rights and fundamental freedoms for all, without distinction as to race, sex, language or religion,

Recalling that article 16 of the Universal Declaration of Human Rights states that:

(1) Men and women of full age, without any limitation due to race, nationality or religion, have the right to marry and to found a family. They are entitled to equal rights as to marriage, during marriage and at its dissolution.

(2) Marriage shall be entered into only with the free and full consent of the intending spouses,

Recalling further that the General Assembly of the United Nations declared, by resolution 843 (IX) of 17 December 1954, that certain customs, ancient laws and practices relating to marriage and the family were inconsistent with the principles set forth in the Charter of the United Nations and in the Universal Declaration of Human Rights,

Reaffirming that all States, including those which have or assume responsibility for the administration of Non-Self-Governing and Trust Territories until their achievement of independence, should take all appropriate measures with a view to abolishing such customs, ancient laws and practices by ensuring, *inter alia,* complete freedom in the choice of a spouse, eliminating completely child marriages and the betrothal of young girls before the age of puberty, establishing appropriate penalties where necessary and establishing a civil or other register in which all marriages will be recorded,

Hereby agree as hereinafter provided:

Article 1

1. No marriage shall be legally entered into without the full and free consent of both parties, such consent to be expressed by them in person after due publicity and in the presence of the authority competent to solemnize the marriage and of witnesses, as prescribed by law.

2. Notwithstanding anything in paragraph 1 above, it shall not be necessary for one of the parties to be present when the competent authority is satisfied that the circumstances are exceptional and that the party has, before a competent authority and in such manner as may be prescribed by law, expressed and not withdrawn consent.

Article 2

States Parties to the present Convention shall take legislative action to specify a minimum age for marriage. No marriage shall be legally entered into by any person under this age, except where a competent authority has granted a dispensation as to age, for serious reasons, in the interest of the intending spouses.

Article 3

All marriages shall be registered in an appropriate official register by the competent authority.

Article 4

1. The present Convention shall, until 31 December 1963, be open for signature on behalf of all States Members of the United Nations or members of any of the specialized agencies, and of any other State invited by the General Assembly of the United Nations to become a Party to the Convention.

2. The present Convention is subject to ratification. The instruments of ratification shall be deposited with the Secretary-General of the United Nations.

Article 5

1. The present Convention shall be open for accession to all States referred to in article 4, paragraph 1.

2. Accession shall be effected by the deposit of an instrument of accession with the Secretary-General of the United Nations.

Article 6

1. The present Convention shall come into force on the ninetieth day following the date of deposit of the eighth instrument of ratification or accession.

2. For each State ratifying or acceding to the Convention after the deposit of the eighth instrument of ratification or accession, the Convention shall enter into force on the ninetieth day after deposit by such State of its instrument of ratification or accession.

Article 7

1. Any Contracting State may denounce the present Convention by written notification to the Secretary-General of the United Nations. Denunciation shall take effect one year after the date of receipt of the notification by the Secretary-General.

2. The present Convention shall cease to be in force as from the date when the denunciation which reduces the number of Parties to less than eight becomes effective.

Article 8

Any dispute which may arise between any two or more Contracting States concerning the interpretation or application of the present Convention which is not settled by negotiation shall, at the request of all the parties to the dispute, be referred to the International Court of Justice for decision, unless the parties agree to another mode of settlement.

Article 9

The Secretary-General of the United Nations shall notify all States Members of the United Nations and the non-member States contemplated in article 4, paragraph 1, of the present Convention of the following:

(a) Signatures and instruments of ratification received in accordance with article 4;

(b) Instruments of accession received in accordance with article 5;

(c) The date upon which the Convention enters into force in accordance with article 6;

(d) Notifications of denunciation received in accordance with article 7, paragraph l;

(e) Abrogation in accordance with article 7, paragraph 2.

Article 10

1. The present Convention, of which the Chinese, English, French, Russian and Spanish texts shall be equally authentic, shall be deposited in the archives of the United Nations.

2. The Secretary-General of the United Nations shall transmit a certified copy of the Convention to all States Members of the United Nations and to the non-member States contemplated in article 4, paragraph 1.

IN FAITH WHEREOF the undersigned, duly authorized, have signed this Convention on behalf of their respective Governments, which opened for signature at the Headquarters of the United Nations, in New York, on 10 December one thousand nine hundred sixty-two.

Document 24

General Assembly resolution on permanent sovereignty over natural resources

A/RES/1803 (XVII), 14 December 1962

The General Assembly,

Recalling its resolutions 523 (VI) of 12 January 1952 and 626 (VII) of 21 December 1952,

Bearing in mind its resolution 1314(XIII) of 12 December 1958, by which it established the Commission on Permanent Sovereignty over Natural Resources and instructed it to conduct a full survey of the status of permanent sovereignty over natural wealth and resources as a basic constituent of the right to self-determination, with recommendations, where necessary, for its strengthening, and decided further that, in the conduct of the full survey of the status of the permanent sovereignty of peoples and nations over their natural wealth and resources, due regard should be paid to the rights and duties of States under international law and to the importance of encouraging international cooperation in the economic development of developing countries,

Bearing in mind its resolution 1515 (XV) of 15 December 1960, in which it recommended that the sovereign right of every State to dispose of its wealth and its natural resources should be respected,

Considering that any measure in this respect must be based on the recognition of the inalienable right of all States freely to dispose of their natural wealth and resources in accordance with their national interests, and on respect for the economic independence of States,

Considering that nothing in paragraph 4 below in any way prejudices the position of any Member State on any aspect of the question of the rights and obligations of successor States and Governments in respect of property acquired before the accession to complete sovereignty of countries formerly under colonial rule,

Noting that the subject of succession of States and Governments is being examined as a matter of priority by the International Law Commission,

Considering that it is desirable to promote international cooperation for the economic development of developing countries, and that economic and financial agreements between the developed and the developing countries must be based on the principles of equality and of the right of peoples and nations to self-determination,

Considering that the provision of economic and technical assistance, loans and increased foreign investment must not be subject to conditions which conflict with the interests of the recipient State,

Considering the benefits to be derived from exchanges of technical and scientific information likely to promote the development and use of such resources and wealth, and the important part which the United Nations and other international organizations are called upon to play in that connection,

Attaching particular importance to the question of promoting the economic development of developing countries and securing their economic independence,

Noting that the creation and strengthening of the inalienable sovereignty of States over their natural wealth and resources reinforces their economic independence,

Desiring that there should be further consideration by the United Nations of the subject of permanent sovereignty over natural resources in the spirit of international cooperation in the field of economic development, particularly that of the developing countries,

Declares that:

1. The right of peoples and nations to permanent sovereignty over their natural wealth and resources must be exercised in the interest of their national development and of the well-being of the people of the State concerned.

2. The exploration, development and disposition of such resources, as well as the import of the foreign capital required for these purposes, should be in conformity with the rules and conditions which the peoples and nations freely consider to be necessary or desirable with regard to the authorization, restriction or prohibition of such activities.

3. In cases where authorization is granted, the capital imported and the earnings on that capital shall be governed by the terms thereof, by the national legislation in force, and by international law. The profits derived must be shared in the proportions freely agreed upon, in each case, between the investors and the recipient State, due care being taken to ensure that there is no impairment, for any reason, of that State's sovereignty over its natural wealth and resources.

4. Nationalization, expropriation or requisitioning shall be based on grounds or reasons of public utility, security or the national interest which are recognized as overriding purely individual or private interests, both domestic and foreign. In such cases the owner shall be paid appropriate compensation, in accordance with the rules in force in the State taking such measures in the exercise of its sovereignty and in accordance with international law. In any case where the question of compensation gives rise to a controversy, the national jurisdiction of the State taking such measures shall be exhausted. However, upon agreement by sovereign States and other parties concerned, settlement of the dispute should be made through arbitration or international adjudication.

5. The free and beneficial exercise of the sovereignty of peoples and nations over their natural resources must be furthered by the mutual respect of States based on their sovereign equality.

6. International cooperation for the economic development of developing countries, whether in the form of public or private capital investments, exchange of goods and services, technical assistance, or exchange of scientific information, shall be such as to further their independent national development and shall be based upon respect for their sovereignty over their natural wealth and resources.

7. Violation of the rights of peoples and nations to sovereignty over their natural wealth and resources is contrary to the spirit and principles of the Charter of the United Nations and hinders the development of international cooperation and the maintenance of peace.

8. Foreign investment agreements freely entered into by or between sovereign States shall be observed in good faith; States and international organizations shall strictly and conscientiously respect the sovereignty of peoples and nations over their natural wealth and resources in accordance with the Charter and the principles set forth in the present resolution.

Document 25

Economic and Social Council resolution on periodic reports on human rights and reports on freedom of information

E/RES/1074 C (XXXIX), 28 July 1965

The Economic and Social Council,

Recalling its resolution 888 B (XXXIV) of 24 July 1962 regarding periodic reports on human rights,

Considering that in accordance with the Charter of the United Nations, the Universal Declaration of Human Rights, the Declaration on the granting of independence to colonial countries and peoples, and the Declaration on the Elimination of All Forms of Racial Discrimination, human rights and fundamental freedoms for all without distinctions as to race, nationality, sex, language or religion should be strictly observed throughout the world,

Recognizing that a comprehensive system of periodic reporting on human rights is important as a source of information for the General Assembly and other United Nations bodies as well as for the Commission on Human Rights, and that it should accordingly be as inclusive and up-to-date as possible,

Noting that in addition to the periodic reports now requested from Member States on a triennial basis, annual reports are also requested on freedom of information,

Noting further the importance for the implementation of human rights of the constitutional provisions and practical procedures which, in certain specialized agencies, govern the consideration by their competent bodies of the reports of Member States on the application of conventions and recommendations adopted by those agencies,

1. *Expresses its appreciation* to all States Members of the United Nations or members of the specialized agencies that have submitted reports;

2. *Notes* that while the situation throughout the world with regard to human rights and fundamental freedoms continues to be unsatisfactory in the fields of civil and political rights as well as social, economic, and cultural rights, and particularly in connexion with the policy of apartheid and the widespread racial, ethnic and religious discrimination throughout the world which prompted the General Assembly to adopt the Declaration on the Elimination of All Forms of Racial Discrimination, the reports contain useful information indicating that some progress was achieved in the protection of human rights during 1960-1962, including rights enumerated in the Universal Declaration of Human Rights;

3. *Notes further* that measures were taken by various countries, including the conclusion of multilateral and regional agreements among Member States: to eliminate or prohibit discrimination, particularly—but not only—discrimination based on race, or sex; to protect the rights of suspects and defendants in criminal procedures, in particular by such steps as restricting detention in custody and strengthening the right to counsel by broadening counsel's rights and providing free legal aid; to repeal provisions concerning various kinds of compulsory labour; to extend, increasingly, social insurance coverage to the agricultural population; to apply social insurance protection to workers and employees who are citizens of a foreign State; to improve the conditions of work by widening the scope of minimum wage laws, shortening working hours and lengthening statutory vacations at full pay; to make education more widely available by the extension of tuition-free instruction or by assistance to cover students' expenses by grants or loans repayable after graduation;

4. *Reiterates its belief* that the reporting system is not only a source of information, but also a valuable incentive of Governments' efforts to protect human rights and fundamental freedoms and to the implementation of the Universal Declaration of Human Rights, the Declaration on the granting of independence to colonial countries and peoples and the Declaration on the Elimination of All Forms of Racial Discrimination;

5. *Expresses concern* that, despite the terms of Council resolution 888 B (XXXIV), which calls upon Member States to submit reports on developments in the field of human rights relating, *inter alia*, to the right to self-determination and the right to independence, no information regarding implementation of these rights has yet been received from States administering dependent territories;

6. *Invites* States Members of the United Nations or members of the specialized agencies to supply information regularly on human rights and fundamental freedoms in the territories subject to their jurisdiction, within a continuing three-year cycle scheduled, without prejudice to the adoption and ratification of the Covenants on Human Rights, including the measures of implementation provided therein, as follows:

(a) In the first year, on civil and political rights, the first such reports to cover the period ending 30 June 1965;

(b) In the second year, on economic, social and cultural rights, the first such report to cover the period ending 30 June 1966;

(c) In the third year, on freedom of information, the first such reports to cover the period ending 30 June 1967; Each year Governments may submit an annex to their reports containing information of particular significance which does not pertain to the subject for the year; it is understood that for the rights falling in the field of competence of specialized agencies Governments may, if they so elect, confine themselves to reference to the reports they send to the specialized agencies concerned, which will continue to submit periodic reports on these rights to the United Nations;

7. *Urges* all Member States to submit reports on developments in human rights concerning the rights enumerated in the Universal Declaration of Human Rights and the right to self-determination and the right to independence, taking fully into account the suggestions referred to in the Council's resolutions 728 B (XXVIII) of 30 July 1959 and 888 B (XXXIV);

8. *Invites* Governments and non-governmental organizations to append to their reports a brief summary thereof;

9. *Suggests* that Governments include more information on court and other decisions and administrative practices affecting human rights and on the ratification and accession to international agreements in the field of human rights;

10. *Requests* the Secretary-General to submit to the Commission on Human Rights a document indicating the status of multilateral international agreements in the field of human rights, as mentioned in paragraph 7, concluded under the auspices of the United Nations;

11. *Invites* the specialized agencies to continue their contributions to the periodic reports on human rights in accordance with this schedule and with the provisions of Council resolution 624 B (XXII) of 1 August 1956 by submitting reports as they deem appropriate and by assisting the bodies examining the reports;

12. *Invites* the non-governmental organizations in consultative status to continue to submit objective information in accordance with the provisions of Council resolution 888 B (XXXIV) and in accordance with the subject and time schedule for submission of reports by Governments established by the resolution;

13. *Requests* the Secretary-General, in accordance with the usual practice in regard to human rights communications, to forward any material received from non-governmental organizations in accordance with paragraph 12 and mentioning any particular States Members of the United Nations or members of the specialized agencies to those Member States for any comments they may wish to make;

14. *Requests* the Secretary-General to forward the information received from Member States and specialized agencies under the terms of this resolution in full, together with a subject and country index, to the Commission on Human Rights, the Commission on the Status of Women and to the Sub-Commission on Prevention of Discrimination and Protection of Minorities; the comments received from non-governmental organizations in consultative status, as well as any comments which might be made on them by the Member State concerned, are also to be made available by the Secretary-General to the Commission on Human Rights, the Commission on the Status of Women and the Sub-Commission on the Prevention of Discrimination and the Protection of Minorities;

15. *Requests* the Sub-Commission on Prevention of Discrimination and Protection of Minorities to undertake the initial study of the materials received under the terms of this resolution, to report thereon to the Commission on Human Rights, and to submit comments and recommendations for consideration by the Commission;

16. *Invites* the Commission on the Status of Women to inform the Commission on Human Rights of its comments on the materials it received under the terms of this resolution, and of any recommendations it may wish to make;

17. *Requests* the Commission on Human Rights to plan for prompt and effective consideration of the periodic reports in the light of the comments and recommendations of the Sub-Commission on Prevention of Discrimination and Protection of Minorities and the Commission on the Status of Women;

18. *Requests* the Commission on Human Rights to establish an *ad hoc* committee composed of persons chosen from its members, having as its mandate the study and evaluation of the periodic reports and other information received under the terms of this resolution, and, in the light of the comments, observations and recommendations of the Commission on the Status of Women and of the Sub-Commission on Prevention of Discrimination and Protection of Minorities, to submit to the Commission comments, conclusions and recommendations of an objective character; the *ad hoc* committee will meet before the session of the Commission and must report its findings to the Commission no later than one week prior to the end of the Commission's session; it shall ensure all necessary co-ordination with any specialized agency in considering any question or matter dealt with in that agency's report.

Document 26

General Assembly resolution on the International Year for Human Rights

A/RES/2081 (XX), 20 December 1965

The General Assembly,

Recalling its resolution 1961 (XVIII) of 12 December 1963 designating the year 1968 as International Year for Human Rights,

Considering that the Universal Declaration of Human Rights has been an instrument of the highest importance for the protection and promotion of the rights of individuals and the furtherance of peace and stability,

Convinced that its role in the future will be of equal significance,

Considering that the further promotion and development of respect for human rights and fundamental freedoms contributes to the strengthening of peace throughout the world and to friendship between peoples,

Considering that racial discrimination, and in particular the policy of apartheid, constitutes one of the most flagrant abuses of human rights and fundamental freedoms and that persistent and intense efforts must be made to secure its abandonment,

Reaffirming the belief that the cause of human rights will be well served by an increasing awareness of the extent of the progress made, and the conviction that the year 1968 should be devoted to intensified national and international efforts and undertakings in the field of human rights and also to an international review of the achievements in this field,

Stressing the importance of further development and implementation in practice of the principles of the protection of human rights laid down in the Charter of the United Nations, the Universal Declaration of Human Rights, the Declaration on the Granting of Independence to Colonial Countries and Peoples and the Declaration on the Elimination of All Forms of Racial Discrimination,

Convinced that an intensification of efforts in the intervening years will heighten the progress that can be made by 1968,

Convinced further that the proposed international review of progress in the field of human rights can advantageously be carried out by means of an international conference,

Noting the interim programme of measures and activities to be undertaken in connexion with the International Year for Human Rights and in celebration of the twentieth anniversary of the Universal Declaration of Human Rights, recommended by the Commission on Human Rights and set out in the annex to the present resolution,

Noting further that the Commission on Human Rights is continuing the preparation of a programme of observances, measures and activities to be undertaken in 1968,

1. *Calls upon* States Members of the United Nations and members of the specialized agencies, regional intergovernmental organizations, the specialized agencies and the national and international organizations concerned to devote the year 1968 to intensified efforts and undertakings in the field of human rights, including an international review of achievements in this field;

2. *Urges* Member States to take appropriate measures in preparation for the International Year for Human Rights, and in particular to emphasize the urgent need to eliminate discrimination and other violations of human dignity, with special attention to the abolition of racial discrimination and in particular the policy of apartheid;

3. *Invites* all Member States to ratify before 1968 the Conventions already concluded in the field of human rights, and in particular the following:

- Supplementary Convention on the Abolition of Slavery, the Slave Trade and Institutions and Practices Similar to Slavery;
- International Labour Organisation Convention concerning the Abolition of Forced Labour;
- International Labour Organisation Convention concerning Discrimination in respect of Employment and Occupation;
- International Labour Organisation Convention concerning Equal Remuneration for Men and Women Workers for Work of Equal Value;
- International Labour Organisation Convention concerning Freedom of Association and Protection of the Right to Organize;
- United Nations Educational, Scientific and Cultural Organization Convention against Discrimination in Education;
- Convention on the Prevention and Punishment of the Crime of Genocide;
- Convention on the Political Rights of Women;
- International Convention on the Elimination of All Forms of Racial Discrimination;

4. *Decides* to hasten the conclusion of the following draft conventions so that they may be open for ratification and accession if possible before 1968:

- Draft Covenant on Civil and Political Rights;
- Draft Covenant on Economic, Social and Cultural Rights;
- Draft International Convention on the Elimination of All Forms of Religious Intolerance;
- Draft Convention on Freedom of Information;

5. *Decides* to complete by 1968 the consideration and preparation of the draft declarations which have been approved by the Commission on Human Rights and by the Commission on the Status of Women;

6. *Approves* the interim programme of measures and activities envisaged for the United Nations annexed to the present resolution and requests the Secretary-General to proceed with the arrangements for the measures to be undertaken by the United Nations set out in the annex;

7. *Invites* Member States to consider, in connexion with the International Year for Human Rights, the possible advantage of undertaking, on a regional basis, common studies in order to establish more effective protection of human rights;

8. *Invites* regional inter-governmental organizations with competence in the field to provide the international conference envisaged for 1968 with full information on their accomplishments, programmes and other measures to realize protection of human rights;

9. *Invites* the Commission on the Status of Women to participate and cooperate at every stage in the preparatory work for the International Year for Human Rights;

10. *Requests* the Secretary-General to transmit the present resolution and the interim programme annexed thereto to States Members of the United Nations and members of the specialized agencies, regional intergovernmental organizations, the specialized agencies and the interested international organizations;

11. *Recommends* that, in view of the historic importance of the observance of the International Year for Human Rights, the United Nations Educational, Scientific and Cultural Organization should be urged to mobilize the finest resources of culture and art in order to lend the International Year for Human Rights, through literature, music, dance, cinema, television and all other forms and media of communication, a truly universal character;

12. *Commends* to the States, regional inter-governmental organizations, agencies and organizations mentioned in paragraph 10 above the programme of measures and activities set out in the annex to the present resolution and invites their cooperation and participation in this programme with a view to making the celebrations successful and meaningful;

13. *Decides* that, to promote further the principles contained in the Universal Declaration of Human Rights, to develop and guarantee political, civil, economic, social and cultural rights and to end all discrimination and denial of human rights and fundamental freedoms on grounds of race, colour, sex, language or religion, and in particular to permit the elimination of apartheid, an International Conference on Human Rights should be convened during 1968 in order to:

(a) Review the progress which has been made in the field of human rights since the adoption of the Universal Declaration of Human Rights;

(b) Evaluate the effectiveness of the methods used by the United Nations in the field of human rights, especially with respect to the elimination of all forms of racial discrimination and the practice of the policy of apartheid;

(c) Formulate and prepare a programme of further measures to be taken subsequent to the celebrations of the International Year for Human Rights;

14. *Decides* to establish, in consultation with the Commission on Human Rights, a Preparatory Committee for the International Conference on Human Rights, consisting of seventeen members, to complete the preparation for the Conference in 1968 and, in particular, to make proposals for the consideration of the General Assembly regarding the agenda, duration and venue of the Conference, and the means of defraying the expenses of the Conference, and to organize and direct the preparation of the necessary evaluation studies and other documentation;

15. *Requests* the President of the General Assembly to appoint the members of the Preparatory Committee, eight of whom shall be States represented on the Commission on Human Rights and two of whom shall be States represented on the Commission on the Status of Women;

16. Requests the Secretary-General to appoint an Executive Secretary for the Conference from within the Secretariat and to provide the Preparatory Committee with all necessary assistance;

17. *Requests* the Preparatory Committee to report on the progress of the preparation in order that such reports might be considered by the General Assembly at its twenty-first and twenty-second sessions.

* * *

The President of the General Assembly, in pursuance of paragraph 15 of the above resolution, appointed the members of the Preparatory Committee for the International Conference on Human Rights. 1/

The Preparatory Committee will be composed of the following Member States: CANADA, FRANCE, INDIA, IRAN,

1/ See *Official Records of the General Assembly, Twentieth Session, Plenary Meetings,* 1408th meeting, para. 179.

ITALY, JAMAICA, NEW ZEALAND, NIGERIA, PHILIPPINES, POLAND, SOMALIA, TUNISIA, UNION OF SOVIET SOCIALIST REPUBLICS, UNITED KINGDOM OF GREAT BRITAIN AND NORTHERN IRELAND, UNITED STATES OF AMERICA, URUGUAY AND YUGOSLAVIA.

Annex
International Year for Human Rights: interim programme recommended by the Commission of Human Rights

I. THE THEME OF CEREMONIES, ACTIVITIES AND CELEBRATION 2/

It is recommended that the programme of measures and activities to be undertaken throughout the International Year for Human Rights should be calculated to encourage, on as wide a basis as possible, both nationally and internationally, the protection of human rights and fundamental freedoms and to bring home to all the people the breadth of the concept of human rights and fundamental freedoms in all its aspects. The theme of the ceremonies, activities and celebrations should be: "Greater recognition and full enjoyment of the fundamental freedoms of the individual and of human rights everywhere". The aim should be to dramatize universal respect for and observance of human rights and fundamental freedoms for all, without distinction as to race, sex, language or religion.

II. A YEAR OF ACTIVITIES 3/

It is agreed that all the participants in the celebrations should be invited to devote the year 1968 as a whole to activities, ceremonies and observances relating to the question of human rights. International or regional seminars, national conferences, lectures and discussions on the Universal Declaration of Human Rights, and on other declarations and instruments of the United Nations relating to human rights, may be organized throughout the year. Some countries will wish to stress the entire content of the Declaration, as further elaborated in later United Nations human rights programmes. Some participating countries may wish to emphasize, during particular periods of the International Year for Human Rights, rights and freedoms in connexion with which they have faced special problems. During each such period the Governments would review, against the standards set by the Universal Declaration of Human Rights and other declarations and instruments of the United Nations relating to human rights, the domestic legislation and the practices within their society in respect of the particular right or freedom which is the subject of that period's observances. They would assess the extent to which the right had been effectively secured, give publicity to it and make special

efforts to promote among their citizens a basic understanding of its nature and significance, so that the gains already made might not easily be lost in the future. To the extent that the right or freedom had not yet been effectively secured, every effort would be made during the period towards its achievement. In the choice of subjects, priority could of course be given to rights of a civil and political character and to those of an economic, social and cultural character.

A. *Measures to be undertaken by the United Nations in the period prior to the beginning of the International Year for Human Rights*

1. *Elimination of certain practices 4/*

Believing that certain practices which constitute some of the grosser forms of the denial of human rights still persist within the territories of some Member States, the Commission on Human Rights recommends that the United Nations should adopt and set before the Member States, as a target to be achieved by the end of 1968, the complete elimination of the following violations of human rights:

(a) Slavery, the slave trade, institutions and practices similar to slavery, and forced labour;

(b) All forms of discrimination based on race, sex, language, religion, political or other opinion, national, social or ethnic origin, property, birth or other status;

(c) Colonialism and the denial of freedom and independence.

2. *International measures for the protection and guarantee of human rights 5/*

Measures for the effective implementation of the rights and freedoms set forth in the Universal Declaration of Human Rights and other declarations and instruments of the United Nations relating to human rights have been under consideration in the United Nations for many years. The Commission on Human Rights is confident that action on the draft Covenant on Civil and Political Rights and the draft Covenant on Economic, Social and Cultural Rights, and measures of implementation, and on the other conventions or international agreements in the field of human rights listed in the draft resolution prepared by the Commission in 1964 for consideration by the General Assembly, will be completed before the beginning of the International Year for Human Rights. If, however, by the beginning of 1968, international machinery for the effective implementation of these covenants

2/ See E/CN.4/886, paras. 46-52.
3/ Ibid., paras. 53-58.
4/ Ibid., paras. 73-77; see also *Official Records of the Economic and Social Council, Thirty-ninth Session, Supplement No. 8* (E/4024), paras. 424 and 425.
5/ See E/CN.4/886, paras. 93-99.

and conventions or international agreements does not form part of the instruments adopted, international measures for the guarantee or protection of human rights should be a subject of serious study during the International Year for Human Rights.

B. Measures to be undertaken by Member States in the period prior to the beginning of the International Year for Human Rights

1. Review of national legislation 6/

Governments are invited to review their national legislation against the standards of the Universal Declaration of Human Rights and other declarations and instruments of the United Nations relating to human rights, and to consider the enactment of new, or the amending of existing, laws to bring their legislation into conformity with the principles of the Declaration and other declarations and instruments of the United Nations relating to human rights.

2. Machinery for implementation on the national level 7/

All Member States are invited, as one of the measures they will undertake in connexion with the International Year for Human Rights, to establish or refine, if necessary by the end of 1968, their national machinery for giving effect to the fundamental rights and freedoms. If, for example, within any Member States, arrangements do not exist which will enable individual persons or groups of persons to bring before independent national tribunals or authorities any complaints they may have concerning the violation of their human rights and obtain effective remedies, the Member State should be invited to undertake that such arrangements will be introduced. If such arrangements already exist, the Member States should be invited to undertake to refine and improve them. This is not a recommendation that any particular improvement in machinery should be introduced. In one set of circumstances, what may be needed is the establishment of a special court; in another, the appointment of an Ombudsman or Procurator General or similar official; and in still another, simply the setting up of offices to which individual citizens may bring their complaints. The determination as to what machinery or improvement in machinery is required for giving effect to the fundamental rights and freedoms would be within the sole discretion of the Government concerned.

3. National programme of education on human rights 8/

Believing that there are limits to the effectiveness of laws in making the enjoyment of human rights and fundamental freedoms a reality, the Commission is convinced that a concentration of efforts on legal and insti-

tutional guarantees of human rights, although it will go far towards the achievement of the objectives we seek, will not go all the way. Attention needs to be concentrated, in addition, on means of changing some old ways of thinking on these subjects, and of rooting out deep-seated prejudices in regard to race, colour, sex, religion, and so on. In short, it is necessary to embark upon a complementary programme of education, including both adult and child education, designed to produce new thinking on the part of many people in regard to human rights. Accordingly, it is recommended that an integral part of any programme of intensification of effort to be undertaken in the next three years should be a world-wide educational programme in human rights. Such an educational programme would be consistent with the objectives of the United Nations Development Decade and also with the objectives in the field of human rights of the United Nations Institute for Training and Research. This programme should aim at mobilizing some of the energies and resources of:

(a) Universities, colleges and other institutions of higher learning, both private and public, within Member States;

(b) The teaching staff of primary and secondary schools;

(c) Foundations and charitable, scientific and research institutions;

(d) Media of information and mass communication, including the Press, radio and television;

(e) Interested non-governmental organizations; towards the education of the people, adults and children, about the state of human rights in their communities and elsewhere, and about the further steps which need to be taken to secure the fullest and most effective realization of these rights. Member States with federal systems of government are called upon to encourage the activities in the field of human rights of local and state educational institutions.

The success of this educational effort would be guaranteed if the national leaders within Member States would give it every encouragement. Within this effort Governments would organize conferences of universities and other institutions of higher learning within their territories and invite them to consider how the curricula and their teaching programmes might be utilized to improve the awareness in the student population of the fundamental questions of human rights, how their research programmes might be directed to this end, and how they might cooperate with other interested organi-

6/ Ibid., paras. 116-120.
7/ Ibid., paras. 121-129.
8/ Ibid., para. 130.

zations, through extra-mural and other programmes, in furthering the aims of adult education in human rights. In this context, studies of local customs and traditions could be undertaken by national authorities with a view to examining to what extent they might be fostering and encouraging attitudes or values contrary to the principles of the Universal Declaration of Human Rights and how these customs and traditions can eventually be eliminated. Charitable and philanthropic foundations might be invited to consider making grants for programmes of research and study in this field and to make bursaries and fellowships available for research in human rights. Responsible authorities of colleges, and of elementary and secondary schools, could be invited to review their curricula and textbooks in order to eradicate bias, intentional and unintentional, towards the preservation of ideas and concepts contrary to the principles of the Universal Declaration of Human Rights, and to introduce courses of study which positively promote respect for human rights and fundamental freedoms. It has been noticed with appreciation that certain universities have already included in their curricula courses in the international protection of human rights; other universities could

be guided by such programmes and benefit by those experiences. Attention is also called to the Associated Schools Project in Education for International Understanding and Cooperation, sponsored by the United Nations Educational, Scientific and Cultural Organization.

Governments might also convene, or give encouragement to the convening of, conferences among the radio and television broadcasting services within their territories, inviting them to consider how their facilities might most usefully cooperate with other organizations within the country, and with international agencies, in advancing the effort to educate the people to have greater respect for individual rights and fundamental freedoms.

The specialized agencies of the United Nations, especially the United Nations Educational, Scientific and Cultural Organization and the International Labour Organisation, can make a particularly valuable contribution towards the intensification of the educational effort with the cooperation of United Nations regional institutes, bearing in mind Economic and Social Council resolution 958 D I (XXXVI) of 12 July 1963. It is recommended that they should be invited to do so.

Document 27

International Convention on the Elimination of All Forms of Racial Discrimination

A/RES/2106 A (XX), 21 December 1965

The States Parties to this Convention,

Considering that the Charter of the United Nations is based on the principles of the dignity and equality inherent in all human beings, and that all Member States have pledged themselves to take joint and separate action, in cooperation with the Organization, for the achievement of one of the purposes of the United Nations which is to promote and encourage universal respect for and observance of human rights and fundamental freedoms for all, without distinction as to race, sex, language or religion,

Considering that the Universal Declaration of Human Rights proclaims that all human beings are born free and equal in dignity and rights and that everyone is entitled to all the rights and freedoms set out therein, without distinction of any kind, in particular as to race, colour or national origin,

Considering that all human beings are equal before the law and are entitled to equal protection of the law against any discrimination and against any incitement to discrimination,

Considering that the United Nations has condemned colonialism and all practices of segregation and discrimination associated therewith, in whatever form and wherever they exist, and that the Declaration on the Granting of Independence to Colonial Countries and Peoples of 14 December 1960 (General Assembly resolution 1514 (XV)) has affirmed and solemnly proclaimed the necessity of bringing them to a speedy and unconditional end,

Considering that the United Nations Declaration on the Elimination of All Forms of Racial Discrimination of 20 November 1963 (General Assembly resolution 1904 (XVIII)) solemnly affirms the necessity of speedily eliminating racial discrimination throughout the world in all its forms and manifestations and of securing understanding of and respect for the dignity of the human person,

Convinced that any doctrine of superiority based on racial differentiation is scientifically false, morally condemnable, socially unjust and dangerous, and that there is no justification for racial discrimination, in theory or in practice, anywhere,

Reaffirming that discrimination between human beings on the grounds of race, colour or ethnic origin is an obstacle to friendly and peaceful relations among nations and is capable of disturbing peace and security among peoples and the harmony of persons living side by side even within one and the same State,

Convinced that the existence of racial barriers is repugnant to the ideals of any human society,

Alarmed by manifestations of racial discrimination still in evidence in some areas of the world and by governmental policies based on racial superiority or hatred, such as policies of apartheid, segregation or separation,

Resolved to adopt all necessary measures for speedily eliminating racial discrimination in all its forms and manifestations, and to prevent and combat racist doctrines and practices in order to promote understanding between races and to build an international community free from all forms of racial segregation and racial discrimination,

Bearing in mind the Convention concerning Discrimination in respect of Employment and Occupation adopted by the International Labour Organisation in 1958, and the Convention against Discrimination in Education adopted by the United Nations Educational, Scientific and Cultural Organization in 1960,

Desiring to implement the principles embodied in the United Nations Declaration on the Elimination of All Forms of Racial Discrimination and to secure the earliest adoption of practical measures to that end,

Have agreed as follows:

PART I

Article 1

1. In this Convention, the term "racial discrimination" shall mean any distinction, exclusion, restriction or preference based on race, colour, descent, or national or ethnic origin which has the purpose or effect of nullifying or impairing the recognition, enjoyment or exercise, on an equal footing, of human rights and fundamental freedoms in the political, economic, social, cultural or any other field of public life.

2. This Convention shall not apply to distinctions, exclusions, restrictions or preferences made by a State Party to this Convention between citizens and non-citizens.

3. Nothing in this Convention may be interpreted as affecting in any way the legal provisions of States Parties concerning nationality, citizenship or naturalization, provided that such provisions do not discriminate against any particular nationality.

4. Special measures taken for the sole purpose of securing adequate advancement of certain racial or ethnic groups or individuals requiring such protection as may be necessary in order to ensure such groups or individuals equal enjoyment or exercise of human rights and fundamental freedoms shall not be deemed racial discrimination, provided, however, that such measures do not, as a consequence, lead to the maintenance of separate rights for different racial groups and that they shall not be continued after the objectives for which they were taken have been achieved.

Article 2

1. States Parties condemn racial discrimination and undertake to pursue by all appropriate means and without delay a policy of eliminating racial discrimination in all its forms and promoting understanding among all races, and, to this end:

(a) Each State Party undertakes to engage in no act or practice of racial discrimination against persons, groups of persons or institutions and to ensure that all public authorities and public institutions, national and local, shall act in conformity with this obligation;

(b) Each State Party undertakes not to sponsor, defend or support racial discrimination by any persons or organizations;

(c) Each State Party shall take effective measures to review governmental, national and local policies, and to amend, rescind or nullify any laws and regulations which have the effect of creating or perpetuating racial discrimination wherever it exists;

(d) Each State Party shall prohibit and bring to an end, by all appropriate means, including legislation as required by circumstances, racial discrimination by any persons, group or organization;

(e) Each State Party undertakes to encourage, where appropriate, integrationist multiracial organizations and movements and other means of eliminating barriers between races, and to discourage anything which tends to strengthen racial division.

2. States Parties shall, when the circumstances so warrant, take, in the social, economic, cultural and other fields, special and concrete measures to ensure the adequate development and protection of certain racial groups or individuals belonging to them, for the purpose of guaranteeing them the full and equal enjoyment of human rights and fundamental freedoms. These measures shall in no case entail as a consequence the maintenance of unequal or separate rights for different racial groups after the objectives for which they were taken have been achieved.

Article 3

States Parties particularly condemn racial segregation and apartheid and undertake to prevent, prohibit and eradicate all practices of this nature in territories under their jurisdiction.

Article 4

States Parties condemn all propaganda and all organizations which are based on ideas or theories of superiority of one race or group of persons of one colour or ethnic origin, or which attempt to justify or promote racial hatred and discrimination in any form, and undertake to adopt immediate and positive measures designed to eradicate all incitement to, or acts of, such discrimination and, to this end, with due regard to the principles embodied in the Universal Declaration of Human Rights and the rights expressly set forth in article 5 of this Convention, *inter alia*:

(a) Shall declare an offence punishable by law all dissemination of ideas based on racial superiority or hatred, incitement to racial discrimination, as well as all acts of violence or incitement to such acts against any race or group of persons of another colour or ethnic origin, and also the provision of any assistance to racist activities, including the financing thereof;

(b) Shall declare illegal and prohibit organizations, and also organized and all other propaganda activities, which promote and incite racial discrimination, and shall recognize participation in such organizations or activities as an offence punishable by law;

(c) Shall not permit public authorities or public institutions, national or local, to promote or incite racial discrimination.

Article 5

In compliance with the fundamental obligations laid down in article 2 of this Convention, States Parties undertake to prohibit and to eliminate racial discrimination in all its forms and to guarantee the right of everyone, without distinction as to race, colour, or national or ethnic origin, to equality before the law, notably in the enjoyment of the following rights:

(a) The right to equal treatment before the tribunals and all other organs administering justice;

(b) The right to security of person and protection by the State against violence or bodily harm, whether inflicted by government officials or by any individual group or institution;

(c) Political rights, in particular the right to participate in elections—to vote and to stand for election—on the basis of universal and equal suffrage, to take part in the Government as well as in the conduct of public affairs at any level and to have equal access to public service;

(d) Other civil rights, in particular:

(i) The right to freedom of movement and residence within the border of the State;

(ii) The right to leave any country, including one's own, and to return to one's country;

(iii) The right to nationality;

(iv) The right to marriage and choice of spouse;

(v) The right to own property alone as well as in association with others;

(vi) The right to inherit;

(vii) The right to freedom of thought, conscience and religion;

(viii) The right to freedom of opinion and expression;

(ix) The right to freedom of peaceful assembly and association;

(e) Economic, social and cultural rights, in particular:

(i) The rights to work, to free choice of employment, to just and favourable conditions of work, to protection against unemployment, to equal pay for equal work, to just and favourable remuneration;

(ii) The right to form and join trade unions;

(iii) The right to housing;

(iv) The right to public health, medical care, social security and social services;

(v) The right to education and training;

(vi) The right to equal participation in cultural activities;

(f) The right of access to any place or service intended for use by the general public, such as transport, hotels, restaurants, cafés, theatres and parks.

Article 6

States Parties shall assure to everyone within their jurisdiction effective protection and remedies, through the competent national tribunals and other State institutions, against any acts of racial discrimination which violate his human rights and fundamental freedoms contrary to this Convention, as well as the right to seek from such tribunals just and adequate reparation or satisfaction for any damage suffered as a result of such discrimination.

Article 7

States Parties undertake to adopt immediate and effective measures, particularly in the fields of teaching, education, culture and information, with a view to combating prejudices which lead to racial discrimination and to promoting understanding, tolerance and friendship among nations and racial or ethnical groups, as well as to propagating the purposes and principles of the Charter of the United Nations, the Universal Declaration of Human Rights, the United Nations Declaration on the Elimination of All Forms of Racial Discrimination, and this Convention.

PART II

Article 8

1. There shall be established a Committee on the Elimination of Racial Discrimination (hereinafter referred to as the Committee) consisting of eighteen experts of high moral standing and acknowledged impartiality elected by States Parties from among their nationals, who shall serve in their personal capacity, consideration being given to equitable geographical distribution and to the representation of the different forms of civilization as well as of the principal legal systems.

2. The members of the Committee shall be elected by secret ballot from a list of persons nominated by the States Parties. Each State Party may nominate one person from among its own nationals.

3. The initial election shall be held six months after the date of the entry into force of this Convention. At least three months before the date of each election the Secretary-General of the United Nations shall address a letter to the States Parties inviting them to submit their nominations within two months. The Secretary-General shall prepare a list in alphabetical order of all persons thus nominated, indicating the States Parties which have nominated them, and shall submit it to the States Parties.

4. Elections of the members of the Committee shall be held at a meeting of States Parties convened by the Secretary-General at United Nations Headquarters. At that meeting, for which two thirds of the States Parties shall constitute a quorum, the persons elected to the Committee shall be nominees who obtain the largest number of votes and an absolute majority of the votes of the representatives of States Parties present and voting.

5. (a) The members of the Committee shall be elected for a term of four years. However, the terms of nine of the members elected at the first election shall expire at the end of two years; immediately after the first election the names of these nine members shall be chosen by lot by the Chairman of the Committee;

(b) For the filling of casual vacancies, the State Party whose expert has ceased to function as a member of the Committee shall appoint another expert from among its nationals, subject to the approval of the Committee.

6. States Parties shall be responsible for the expenses of the members of the Committee while they are in performance of Committee duties.

Article 9

1. States Parties undertake to submit to the Secretary-General of the United Nations, for consideration by the Committee, a report on the legislative, judicial, administrative or other measures which they have adopted and which give effect to the provisions of this Convention: (a) within one year after the entry into force of the Convention for the State concerned; and (b) thereafter every two years and whenever the Committee so requests. The Committee may request further information from the States Parties.

2. The Committee shall report annually, through the Secretary-General, to the General Assembly of the United Nations on its activities and may make suggestions and general recommendations based on the examination of the reports and information received from the States Parties. Such suggestions and general recommendations shall be reported to the General Assembly together with comments, if any, from States Parties.

Article 10

1. The Committee shall adopt its own rules of procedure.

2. The Committee shall elect its officers for a term of two years.

3. The secretariat of the Committee shall be provided by the Secretary-General of the United Nations.

4. The meetings of the Committee shall normally be held at United Nations Headquarters.

Article 11

1. If a State Party considers that another State Party is not giving effect to the provisions of this Convention, it may bring the matter to the attention of the Committee. The Committee shall then transmit the communication to the State Party concerned. Within three months, the receiving State shall submit to the Committee written explanations or statements clarifying the matter and the remedy, if any, that may have been taken by that State.

2. If the matter is not adjusted to the satisfaction of both parties, either by bilateral negotiations or by any other procedure open to them, within six months after the receipt by the receiving State of the initial communication, either State shall have the right to refer the matter again to the Committee by notifying the Committee and also the other State.

3. The Committee shall deal with a matter referred to it in accordance with paragraph 2 of this article after it has ascertained that all available domestic remedies have been invoked and exhausted in the case, in conformity with the generally recognized principles of interna-

tional law. This shall not be the rule where the application of the remedies is unreasonably prolonged.

4. In any matter referred to it, the Committee may call upon the States Parties concerned to supply any other relevant information.

5. When any matter arising out of this article is being considered by the Committee, the States Parties concerned shall be entitled to send a representative to take part in the proceedings of the Committee, without voting rights, while the matter is under consideration.

Article 12

1. (a) After the Committee has obtained and collated all the information it deems necessary, the Chairman shall appoint an *ad hoc* Conciliation Commission (hereinafter referred to as the Commission) comprising five persons who may or may not be members of the Committee. The members of the Commission shall be appointed with the unanimous consent of the parties to the dispute, and its good offices shall be made available to the States concerned with a view to an amicable solution of the matter on the basis of respect for this Convention;

(b) If the States parties to the dispute fail to reach agreement within three months on all or part of the composition of the Commission, the members of the Commission not agreed upon by the States parties to the dispute shall be elected by secret ballot by a two-thirds majority vote of the Committee from among its own members.

2. The members of the Commission shall serve in their personal capacity. They shall not be nationals of the States parties to the dispute or of a State not Party to this Convention.

3. The Commission shall elect its own Chairman and adopt its own rules of procedure.

4. The meetings of the Commission shall normally be held at United Nations Headquarters or at any other convenient place as determined by the Commission.

5. The secretariat provided in accordance with article 10, paragraph 3, of this Convention shall also service the Commission whenever a dispute among States Parties brings the Commission into being.

6. The States parties to the dispute shall share equally all the expenses of the members of the Commission in accordance with estimates to be provided by the Secretary-General of the United Nations.

7. The Secretary-General shall be empowered to pay the expenses of the members of the Commission, if necessary, before reimbursement by the States parties to the dispute in accordance with paragraph 6 of this article.

8. The information obtained and collated by the Committee shall be made available to the Commission, and the Commission may call upon the States concerned to supply any other relevant information.

Article 13

1. When the Commission has fully considered the matter, it shall prepare and submit to the Chairman of the Committee a report embodying its findings on all questions of fact relevant to the issue between the parties and containing such recommendations as it may think proper for the amicable solution of the dispute.

2. The Chairman of the Committee shall communicate the report of the Commission to each of the States parties to the dispute. These States shall, within three months, inform the Chairman of the Committee whether or not they accept the recommendations contained in the report of the Commission.

3. After the period provided for in paragraph 2 of this article, the Chairman of the Committee shall communicate the report of the Commission and the declarations of the States Parties concerned to the other States Parties to this Convention.

Article 14

1. A State Party may at any time declare that it recognizes the competence of the Committee to receive and consider communications from individuals or groups of individuals within its jurisdiction claiming to be victims of a violation by that State Party of any of the rights set forth in this Convention. No communication shall be received by the Committee if it concerns a State Party which has not made such a declaration.

2. Any State Party which makes a declaration as provided for in paragraph 1 of this article may establish or indicate a body within its national legal order which shall be competent to receive and consider petitions from individuals and groups of individuals within its jurisdiction who claim to be victims of a violation of any of the rights set forth in this Convention and who have exhausted other available local remedies.

3. A declaration made in accordance with paragraph 1 of this article and the name of any body established or indicated in accordance with paragraph 2 of this article shall be deposited by the State Party concerned with the Secretary-General of the United Nations, who shall transmit copies thereof to the other States Parties. A declaration may be withdrawn at any time by notification to the Secretary-General, but such a withdrawal shall not affect communications pending before the Committee.

4. A register of petitions shall be kept by the body established or indicated in accordance with paragraph 2 of this article, and certified copies of the register shall be filed annually through appropriate channels with the

Secretary-General on the understanding that the contents shall not be publicly disclosed.

5. In the event of failure to obtain satisfaction from the body established or indicated in accordance with paragraph 2 of this article, the petitioner shall have the right to communicate the matter to the Committee within six months.

6. (a) The Committee shall confidentially bring any communication referred to it to the attention of the State Party alleged to be violating any provision of this Convention, but the identity of the individual or groups of individuals concerned shall not be revealed without his or their express consent. The Committee shall not receive anonymous communications;

(b) Within three months, the receiving State shall submit to the Committee written explanations or statements clarifying the matter and the remedy, if any, that may have been taken by that State.

7. (a) The Committee shall consider communications in the light of all information made available to it by the State Party concerned and by the petitioner. The Committee shall not consider any communication from a petitioner unless it has ascertained that the petitioner has exhausted all available domestic remedies. However, this shall not be the rule where the application of the remedies is unreasonably prolonged;

(b) The Committee shall forward its suggestions and recommendations, if any, to the State Party concerned and to the petitioner.

8. The Committee shall include in its annual report a summary of such communications and, where appropriate, a summary of the explanations and statements of the States Parties concerned and of its own suggestions and recommendations.

9. The Committee shall be competent to exercise the functions provided for in this article only when at least ten States Parties to this Convention are bound by declarations in accordance with paragraph 1 of this article.

Article 15

1. Pending the achievement of the objectives of the Declaration on the Granting of Independence to Colonial Countries and Peoples, contained in General Assembly resolution 1514 (XV) of 14 December 1960, the provisions of this Convention shall in no way limit the right of petition granted to these peoples by other international instruments or by the United Nations and its specialized agencies.

2. (a) The Committee established under article 8, paragraph 1, of this Convention shall receive copies of the petitions from, and submit expressions of opinion and recommendations on these petitions to, the bodies of the United Nations which deal with matters directly related to the principles and objectives of this Convention in their consideration of petitions from the inhabitants of Trust and Non-Self-Governing Territories and all other territories to which General Assembly resolution 1514 (XV) applies, relating to matters covered by this Convention which are before these bodies;

(b) The Committee shall receive from the competent bodies of the United Nations copies of the reports concerning the legislative, judicial, administrative or other measures directly related to the principles and objectives of this Convention applied by the administering Powers within the Territories mentioned in subparagraph (a) of this paragraph, and shall express opinions and make recommendations to these bodies.

3. The Committee shall include in its report to the General Assembly a summary of the petitions and reports it has received from United Nations bodies, and the expressions of opinion and recommendations of the Committee relating to the said petitions and reports.

4. The Committee shall request from the Secretary-General of the United Nations all information relevant to the objectives of this Convention and available to him regarding the Territories mentioned in paragraph 2 (a) of this article.

Article 16

The provisions of this Convention concerning the settlement of disputes or complaints shall be applied without prejudice to other procedures for settling disputes or complaints in the field of discrimination laid down in the constituent instruments of, or conventions adopted by, the United Nations and its specialized agencies, and shall not prevent the States Parties from having recourse to other procedures for settling a dispute in accordance with general or special international agreements in force between them.

PART III

Article 17

1. This Convention is open for signature by any State Member of the United Nations or member of any of its specialized agencies, by any State Party to the Statute of the International Court of Justice, and by any other State which has been invited by the General Assembly of the United Nations to become a Party to this Convention.

2. This Convention is subject to ratification. Instruments of ratification shall be deposited with the Secretary-General of the United Nations.

Article 18

1. This Convention shall be open to accession by any State referred to in article 17, paragraph 1, of the Convention.

2. Accession shall be effected by the deposit of an instrument of accession with the Secretary-General of the United Nations.

Article 19

1. This Convention shall enter into force on the thirtieth day after the date of the deposit with the Secretary-General of the United Nations of the twenty-seventh instrument of ratification or instrument of accession.

2. For each State ratifying this Convention or acceding to it after the deposit of the twenty-seventh instrument of ratification or instrument of accession, the Convention shall enter into force on the thirtieth day after the date of the deposit of its own instrument of ratification or instrument of accession.

Article 20

1. The Secretary-General of the United Nations shall receive and circulate to all States which are or may become Parties to this Convention reservations made by States at the time of ratification or accession. Any State which objects to the reservation shall, within a period of ninety days from the date of the said communication, notify the Secretary-General that it does not accept it.

2. A reservation incompatible with the object and purpose of this Convention shall not be permitted, nor shall a reservation the effect of which would inhibit the operation of any of the bodies established by this Convention be allowed. A reservation shall be considered incompatible or inhibitive if at least two thirds of the States Parties to this Convention object to it.

3. Reservations may be withdrawn at any time by notification to this effect addressed to the Secretary-General. Such notification shall take effect on the date on which it is received.

Article 21

A State Party may denounce this Convention by written notification to the Secretary-General of the United Nations. Denunciation shall take effect one year after the date of receipt of the notification by the Secretary-General.

Article 22

Any dispute between two or more States Parties with respect to the interpretation or application of this Convention, which is not settled by negotiation or by the procedures expressly provided for in this Convention, shall, at the request of any of the parties to the dispute, be referred to the International Court of Justice for decision, unless the disputants agree to another mode of settlement.

Article 23

1. A request for the revision of this Convention may be made at any time by any State Party by means of a notification in writing addressed to the Secretary-General of the United Nations.

2. The General Assembly of the United Nations shall decide upon the steps, if any, to be taken in respect of such a request.

Article 24

The Secretary-General of the United Nations shall inform all States referred to in article 17, paragraph 1, of this Convention of the following particulars:

(a) Signatures, ratifications and accessions under articles 17 and 18;

(b) The date of entry into force of this Convention under article 19;

(c) Communications and declarations received under articles 14, 20 and 23;

(d) Denunciations under article 21.

Article 25

1. This Convention, of which the Chinese, English, French, Russian and Spanish texts are equally authentic, shall be deposited in the archives of the United Nations.

2. The Secretary-General of the United Nations shall transmit certified copies of this Convention to all States belonging to any of the categories mentioned in article 17, paragraph 1, of the Convention.

Document 28

Economic and Social Council resolution on measures for the speedy implementation of the United Nations Declaration on the Elimination of All Forms of Racial Discrimination

E/RES/1102 (XL), 4 March 1966

The Economic and Social Council,

Considering that, in its resolution of 18 June 1965, 1/ the Special Committee on the Situation with regard to the Implementation of the Declaration on the Granting of Independence to Colonial Countries and Peoples drew the attention of the Commission on Human Rights to the evidence submitted by petitioners concerning violations of human rights committed in Territories under Portuguese administration and also in South West Africa and Southern Rhodesia,

Considering further that, in its resolution 2022 (XX), of 5 November 1965, on the question of Southern Rhodesia, and 2074 (XX), of 17 December 1965, on the question of South West Africa, the General Assembly condemned such violations of human rights as the policies of racial discrimination and segregation and the policies of apartheid and declared that they constitute a crime against humanity,

Considering further that the problem of racial discrimination involves in the world today one of the most vicious and widespread violations of human rights,

1. *Invites* the Commission on Human Rights, at its twenty-second session, to consider as a matter of importance and urgency the question of the violation of human rights and fundamental freedoms, including policies of racial discrimination and segregation and of apartheid in all countries, with particular reference to colonial and other dependent countries and territories, and to submit to the Council at its forty-first session its recommendations on measures to halt those violations;

2. *Requests* the Secretary-General to prepare for the Council a document containing the texts of (or extracts from) decisions taken by United Nations bodies which contain any relevant provisions;

3. *Requests further* the Secretary-General to supplement this document annually with the texts of (or extracts from) new decisions and to submit the document to the Commission on Human Rights, the Commission on the Status of Women and the Sub-Commission on Prevention of Discrimination and Protection of Minorities.

1/ *Official Records of the General Assembly, Twentieth Session, Annexes*, addendum to agenda item 23 (A/6000/Rev.1), chap. II, para. 463.

Document 29

Economic and Social Council resolution on the question of the violation of human rights and fundamental freedoms, including policies of racial discrimination and segregation and of apartheid in all countries, with particular reference to colonial and other dependent countries and territories

E/RES/1164 (XLI), 5 August 1966

The Economic and Social Council,

Recalling its resolution 1102 (XL) of 4 March 1966,

Noting resolution 2 (XXII) of the Commission on Human Rights 1/ relating to the question of the violation of human rights and fundamental freedoms, including policies of racial discrimination and segregation and of apartheid in all countries, with particular reference to colonial and other dependent countries and territories,

1. *Condemns* violations of human rights and fundamental freedoms wherever they occur;

2. *Shares in particular* the Commission's profound indignation at violations of human rights committed in colonial and other dependent countries and territories;

3. *Welcomes* the Commission's decision to consider, at its twenty-third session, the question of the Commission's tasks and functions and its role in relation to violations of human rights in all countries, including the giving of appropriate assistance to the Special Com-

1/ *Official Records of the Economic and Social Council, Forty-first Session, Supplement No. 8* (E/4184), para. 222.

mittee on the Situation with Regard to the Implementation of the Declaration on the Granting of Independence to Colonial Countries and Peoples;

4. *Concurs* in the Commission's view that it will be necessary for it fully to consider the means by which it may be more fully informed of violations of human rights, with a view to devising recommendations for measures to put a stop to those violations;

5. *Recommends* to the General Assembly the adoption of the following draft resolution:

"*The General Assembly*,

"*Noting* Economic and Social Council resolution 1164 (XLI) of 5 August 1966,

"*Recalling* the obligation of all Member States under Article 56 of the Charter of the United Nations to take joint and separate action in cooperation with the Organization for the achievement of the purposes set forth in Article 55, which include the promotion of universal respect for, and observance of, human rights and fundamental freedom for all, without distinction as to race, sex, language or religion,

"*Convinced* that efforts to protect and promote human rights throughout the world are still inadequate and that gross violations of the rights and freedoms set forth in the Universal Declaration of Human Rights continue to occur in certain countries, particularly in colonies and dependent territories, with respect to discrimination on grounds of race, colour, sex, language and religion, and the suppression of freedom of expression and opinion, the right to life, liberty and security of person and the right to protection by independent and impartial judicial organs,

"*Recalling further* the Declaration on the Granting of Independence to Colonial Countries and Peoples and the Declaration on the Elimination of All Forms of Racial Discrimination,

"*Deeply concerned* by the new evidence of persistent practices of racial discrimination and apartheid in the Republic of South Africa, the Trust Territory of South West Africa and the colonies of Southern Rhodesia, Angola, Mozambique and Portuguese Guinea, Cabinda, Sao Tome and Principe, such practices constituting, according to its resolutions 2022 (XX) of 5 November 1965 and 2074 (XX) of 17 December 1965, crimes against humanity,

"1. *Condemns* violations of human rights and fundamental freedoms wherever they occur;

"2. *Calls upon* all Member States to strengthen their efforts to promote the full observance of human rights in accordance with the Charter, and to attain the standards established by the Universal Declaration of Human Rights;

"3. *Urges* all Member States to take all possible measures for the suppression of the policies of apartheid and segregation and for the elimination of racial discrimination wherever it occurs, particularly in colonial and other dependent countries and territories;

"4. *Encourages* all eligible States to become parties as soon as possible to all Conventions which aim at protecting human rights and fundamental freedoms including, in particular, the International Convention on the Elimination of All Forms of Racial Discrimination;

"5. *Urges* all States which have not yet done so to comply with the relevant General Assembly resolutions recommending the application of economic and diplomatic measures against the Republic of South Africa, as well as with the relevant Security Council resolutions calling upon all States to impose an arms embargo against the Republic of South Africa;

"6. *Invites* Member States, intergovernmental organizations and non-governmental organizations to arrange for the celebration of Human Rights Day in 1966 bearing in mind the theme of protection of victims of violations of human rights and fundamental freedoms, particularly those in colonial and dependent countries and territories;

"7. *Appeals* to public opinion and in particular to juridical associations as well as other appropriate organizations to render all possible assistance to victims of violations of human rights, in particular victims of policies of racial discrimination, segregation and apartheid;

"8. *Invites* the Economic and Social Council and the Commission on Human Rights to give urgent consideration to ways and means of improving the capacity of the United Nations to put a stop to violations of human rights wherever they may occur;

"9. *Requests* the Special Committee on the Situation with Regard to the Implementation of the Declaration on the Granting of Independence to Colonial Countries and Peoples to apprise the Commission on Human Rights of its discussions and decisions and of information coming to its attention relating to questions of human rights in colonial and dependent territories."

6. *Transmits* resolution 2(XXII) of the Commission on Human Rights as well as the present resolution to the Special Committee on the Situation with regard to the Implementation of the Declaration on the Granting of Independence to Colonial Countries and Peoples.

Document 30

General Assembly resolution on the question of the violation of human rights and fundamental freedoms, including policies of racial discrimination and segregation and of apartheid, in all countries, with particular reference to colonial and other dependent countries and territories

A/RES/2144 (XXI), 26 October 1966

A

The General Assembly,

Noting Economic and Social Council resolution 1164 (XLI) of 5 August 1966,

Confirming that the United Nations has a fundamental interest in combating policies of apartheid and that, as a matter of urgency, ways and means must be devised for their elimination,

Bearing in mind the obligation of all Member States under Article 56 of the Charter of the United Nations to take joint and separate action in cooperation with the Organization for the achievement of the purposes set forth in Article 55, which include the promotion of universal respect for, and observance of, human rights and fundamental freedoms for all without distinction as to race, sex, language or religion,

Convinced that gross violations of the rights and fundamental freedoms set forth in the Universal Declaration of Human Rights continue to occur in certain countries, especially in colonies and dependent territories, involving discrimination on grounds of race, colour, sex, language and religion, and the suppression of freedom of expression and opinion, the right to life, liberty and security of person and the right to protection by independent and impartial judicial organs, and that these violations are designed to stifle the legitimate struggle of the people for independence and human dignity,

Recalling the Declaration on the Granting of Independence to Colonial Countries and Peoples and the United Nations Declaration on the Elimination of All Forms of Racial Discrimination,

Deeply concerned by the evidence of persistent practices of apartheid in the Republic of South Africa and South West Africa and the racial discrimination practiced in the colonies of Southern Rhodesia, Angola, Mozambique, Portuguese Guinea, Cabinda, Sao Tome and Principe, brought to its attention by the Special Committee on the Situation with regard to the Implementation of the Declaration on the Granting of Independence to Colonial Countries and Peoples and the Special Committee on the Policies of Apartheid of the Government of the Republic of South Africa, such practices constituting, according to General Assembly resolutions 2022 (XX) of 5 November

1965 and 2074 (XX) of 17 December 1965, crimes against humanity,

Taking note of the conclusions and recommendations of the Seminar on Apartheid, 1/ organized under the programme of advisory services in the field of human rights and held at Brasilia in 1966,

1. *Reaffirms* its strong condemnation of the violations of human rights and fundamental freedoms wherever they occur, especially in all colonial and dependent territories, including the policies of apartheid in the Republic of South Africa and the Territory of South West Africa and racial discrimination in the colonies of Southern Rhodesia, Angola, Mozambique, Portuguese Guinea, Cabinda, Sao Tome and Principe;

2. *Regrets* the policy pursued by colonial Powers in order to circumvent the rights of peoples under their rule through the promotion of the systematic influx of foreign immigrants, and the dislocation, dispossession, deportation and eviction of the indigenous inhabitants;

3. *Further regrets* the actions of those States which, through political, trading, economic and military collaboration with the Governments of South Africa and Portugal and the illegal régime in Southern Rhodesia, are encouraging them to persist in their racial policies;

4. *Urges* all States which have not yet done so to comply with the relevant General Assembly resolutions recommending the application of economic and diplomatic measures against South Africa and with the relevant Security Council resolutions calling upon all States to impose an arms embargo against South Africa;

5. *Calls upon* all States to strengthen their efforts to promote the full observance of human rights and the right to self-determination in accordance with the Charter of the United Nations, and to attain the standards established by the Universal Declaration of Human Rights;

6. *Urges* all States to take effective measures, in accordance with the provisions of the Charter, the General Assembly resolutions pertaining to human rights, and the relevant Security Council resolutions, for the suppression of the policies of apartheid and segregation and for the elimination of racial discrimination, wherever it oc-

1/ ST/TAO/HR/27, para. 138.

curs, especially in colonial and other dependent countries and territories;

7. *Appeals* to all States, governmental and non-governmental organizations, and individuals:

(a) To support the United Nations Trust Fund for South Africa and voluntary organizations engaged in providing relief and assistance to victims of colonialism and apartheid;

(b) To encourage judicial associations and other appropriate organizations, and the public in general, to provide such relief and assistance;

8. *Urges* Member States to take all necessary measures, in accordance with their domestic laws, against the operations of propaganda organizations of the Government of South Africa and of private organizations which advocate apartheid and policies of racial discrimination and domination;

9. *Invites* States to become parties as soon as possible to all conventions which aim at protecting human rights and fundamental freedoms, including in particular the International Convention on the Elimination of All Forms of Racial Discrimination;

10. *Requests* the Special Committee on the Situation with regard to the Implementation of the Declaration on the Granting of Independence to Colonial Countries and Peoples, the Special Committee on the Policies of Apartheid of the Government of the Republic of South Africa and the Commission on Human Rights to take appropriate measures for the implementation of the present resolution as it affects the responsibilities of these organs;

11. *Requests* the Secretary-General to assist in the implementation of the present resolution and to report to the General Assembly at its twenty-second session;

12. *Invites* the Economic and Social Council and the Commission on Human Rights to give urgent consideration to ways and means of improving the capacity of the United Nations to put a stop to violations of human rights wherever they may occur;

13. *Requests* the Secretary-General to establish a unit within the Secretariat of the United Nations to deal exclusively with policies of apartheid, in consultation with the Special Committee on the Policies of Apartheid of the Government of the Republic of South Africa, in order that maximum publicity may be given to the evils of those policies;

14. *Further decides* to place this item on the provisional agenda of its twenty-second session.

B

The General Assembly,

Taking note of Economic and Social Council resolution 1164 (XLI) of 5 August 1966,

Having adopted resolution A above,

Bearing in mind the various recommendations embodied in the report of the Seminar on Apartheid, 1/ organized under the programme of advisory services in the field of human rights,

Noting that all the General Assembly recommendations on apartheid have so far been ignored by the Government of South Africa and the authorities in Southern Rhodesia,

Convinced more than ever that apartheid in South Africa constitutes a menace to international peace and security,

1. *Appeals* to the Security Council urgently to take effective measures with a view to eradicating apartheid in South Africa and other adjacent territories;

2. *Requests* the Secretary-General to provide the Security Council with all the resolutions adopted by the General Assembly on the question of apartheid, at the present session and at previous sessions, together with all the reports available on this item.

Document 31

International Covenant on Economic, Social and Cultural Rights

A/RES/2200 A (XXI), 16 December 1966

Preamble

The States Parties to the present Covenant,

Considering that, in accordance with the principles proclaimed in the Charter of the United Nations, recognition of the inherent dignity and of the equal and inalienable rights of all members of the human family is the foundation of freedom, justice and peace in the world,

Recognizing that these rights derive from the inherent dignity of the human person,

Recognizing that, in accordance with the Universal Declaration of Human Rights, the ideal of free human beings enjoying freedom from fear and want can only be achieved if conditions are created whereby everyone may enjoy his economic, social and cultural rights, as well as his civil and political rights,

Considering the obligation of States under the Charter of the United Nations to promote universal respect for, and observance of, human rights and freedoms,

Realizing that the individual, having duties to other individuals and to the community to which he belongs, is under a responsibility to strive for the promotion and observance of the rights recognized in the present Covenant,

Agree upon the following articles:

PART I

Article 1

1. All peoples have the right of self-determination. By virtue of that right they freely determine their political status and freely pursue their economic, social and cultural development.

2. All peoples may, for their own ends, freely dispose of their natural wealth and resources without prejudice to any obligations arising out of international economic cooperation, based upon the principle of mutual benefit, and international law. In no case may a people be deprived of its own means of subsistence.

3. The States Parties to the present Covenant, including those having responsibility for the administration of Non-Self-Governing and Trust Territories, shall promote the realization of the right of self-determination, and shall respect that right, in conformity with the provisions of the Charter of the United Nations.

PART II

Article 2

1. Each State Party to the present Covenant undertakes to take steps, individually and through international assistance and cooperation, especially economic and technical, to the maximum of its available resources, with a view to achieving progressively the full realization of the rights recognized in the present Covenant by all appropriate means, including particularly the adoption of legislative measures.

2. The States Parties to the present Covenant undertake to guarantee that the rights enunciated in the present Covenant will be exercised without discrimination of any kind as to race, colour, sex, language, religion, political or other opinion, national or social origin, property, birth or other status.

3. Developing countries, with due regard to human rights and their national economy, may determine to what extent they would guarantee the economic rights recognized in the present Covenant to non-nationals.

Article 3

The States Parties to the present Covenant undertake to ensure the equal right of men and women to the enjoyment of all economic, social and cultural rights set forth in the present Covenant.

Article 4

The States Parties to the present Covenant recognize that, in the enjoyment of those rights provided by the State in conformity with the present Covenant, the State may subject such rights only to such limitations as are determined by law only in so far as this may be compatible with the nature of these rights and solely for the purpose of promoting the general welfare in a democratic society.

Article 5

1. Nothing in the present Covenant may be interpreted as implying for any State, group or person any right to engage in any activity or to perform any act aimed at the destruction of any of the rights or freedoms recognized herein, or at their limitation to a greater extent than is provided for in the present Covenant.

2. No restriction upon or derogation from any of the fundamental human rights recognized or existing in any country in virtue of law, conventions, regulations or custom shall be admitted on the pretext that the present Covenant does not recognize such rights or that it recognizes them to a lesser extent.

PART III

Article 6

1. The States Parties to the present Covenant recognize the right to work, which includes the right of everyone to the opportunity to gain his living by work which he freely chooses or accepts, and will take appropriate steps to safeguard this right.

2. The steps to be taken by a State Party to the present Covenant to achieve the full realization of this right shall include technical and vocational guidance and training programmes, policies and techniques to achieve steady economic, social and cultural development and full and productive employment under conditions safeguarding fundamental political and economic freedoms to the individual.

Article 7

The States Parties to the present Covenant recognize the right of everyone to the enjoyment of just and favourable conditions of work which ensure, in particular:

(a) Remuneration which provides all workers, as a minimum, with:

(i) Fair wages and equal remuneration for work of equal value without distinction of any kind, in particular women being guaranteed conditions of work not inferior to those enjoyed by men, with equal pay for equal work;

(ii) A decent living for themselves and their families in accordance with the provisions of the present Covenant;

(b) Safe and healthy working conditions;

(c) Equal opportunity for everyone to be promoted in his employment to an appropriate higher level, subject to no considerations other than those of seniority and competence;

(d) Rest, leisure and reasonable limitation of working hours and periodic holidays with pay, as well as remuneration for public holidays

Article 8

1. The States Parties to the present Covenant undertake to ensure:

(a) The right of everyone to form trade unions and join the trade union of his choice, subject only to the rules of the organization concerned, for the promotion and protection of his economic and social interests. No restrictions may be placed on the exercise of this right other than those prescribed by law and which are necessary in a democratic society in the interests of national security or public order or for the protection of the rights and freedoms of others;

(b) The right of trade unions to establish national federations or confederations and the right of the latter to form or join international trade-union organizations;

(c) The right of trade unions to function freely subject to no limitations other than those prescribed by law and which are necessary in a democratic society in the interests of national security or public order or for the protection of the rights and freedoms of others;

(d) The right to strike, provided that it is exercised in conformity with the laws of the particular country.

2. This article shall not prevent the imposition of lawful restrictions on the exercise of these rights by members of the armed forces or of the police or of the administration of the State.

3. Nothing in this article shall authorize States Parties to the International Labour Organisation Convention of 1948 concerning Freedom of Association and Protection of the Right to Organize to take legislative measures which would prejudice, or apply the law in such a manner as would prejudice, the guarantees provided for in that Convention.

Article 9

The States Parties to the present Covenant recognize the right of everyone to social security, including social insurance.

Article 10

The States Parties to the present Covenant recognize that:

1. The widest possible protection and assistance should be accorded to the family, which is the natural and fundamental group unit of society, particularly for its establishment and while it is responsible for the care and education of dependent children. Marriage must be entered into with the free consent of the intending spouses.

2. Special protection should be accorded to mothers during a reasonable period before and after childbirth. During such period working mothers should be accorded paid leave or leave with adequate social security benefits.

3. Special measures of protection and assistance should be taken on behalf of all children and young persons without any discrimination for reasons of parentage or other conditions. Children and young persons should be protected from economic and social exploitation. Their employment in work harmful to their morals or health or dangerous to life or likely to hamper their normal development should be punishable by law. States should also set age limits below which the paid employment of child labour should be prohibited and punishable by law.

Article 11

1. The States Parties to the present Covenant recognize the right of everyone to an adequate standard of living for himself and his family, including adequate food, clothing and housing, and to the continuous improvement of living conditions. The States Parties will take appropriate steps to ensure the realization of this right, recognizing to this effect the essential importance of international cooperation based on free consent.

2. The States Parties to the present Covenant, recognizing the fundamental right of everyone to be free from hunger, shall take, individually and through international cooperation, the measures, including specific programmes, which are needed:

(a) To improve methods of production, conservation and distribution of food by making full use of technical and scientific knowledge, by disseminating knowledge of the principles of nutrition and by developing or reforming agrarian systems in such a way as to achieve the most efficient development and utilization of natural resources;

(b) Taking into account the problems of both food-importing and food-exporting countries, to ensure an equitable distribution of world food supplies in relation to need.

Article 12

1. The States Parties to the present Covenant recognize the right of everyone to the enjoyment of the highest attainable standard of physical and mental health.

2. The steps to be taken by the States Parties to the present Covenant to achieve the full realization of this right shall include those necessary for:

(a) The provision for the reduction of the stillbirth-rate and of infant mortality and for the healthy development of the child;

(b) The improvement of all aspects of environmental and industrial hygiene;

(c) The prevention, treatment and control of epidemic, endemic, occupational and other diseases;

(d) The creation of conditions which would assure to all medical service and medical attention in the event of sickness.

Article 13

1. The States Parties to the present Covenant recognize the right of everyone to education. They agree that education shall be directed to the full development of the human personality and the sense of its dignity, and shall strengthen the respect for human rights and fundamental freedoms. They further agree that education shall enable all persons to participate effectively in a free society, promote understanding, tolerance and friendship among all nations and all racial, ethnic or religious groups, and further the activities of the United Nations for the maintenance of peace.

2. The States Parties to the present Covenant recognize that, with a view to achieving the full realization of this right:

(a) Primary education shall be compulsory and available free to all;

(b) Secondary education in its different forms, including technical and vocational secondary education, shall be made generally available and accessible to all by every appropriate means, and in particular by the progressive introduction of free education;

(c) Higher education shall be made equally accessible to all, on the basis of capacity, by every appropriate means, and in particular by the progressive introduction of free education;

(d) Fundamental education shall be encouraged or intensified as far as possible for those persons who have not received or completed the whole period of their primary education;

(e) The development of a system of schools at all levels shall be actively pursued, an adequate fellowship system shall be established, and the material conditions of teaching staff shall be continuously improved.

3. The States Parties to the present Covenant undertake to have respect for the liberty of parents and, when applicable, legal guardians to choose for their children schools, other than those established by the public authorities, which conform to such minimum educational standards as may be laid down or approved by the State and to ensure the religious and moral education of their children in conformity with their own convictions.

4. No part of this article shall be construed so as to interfere with the liberty of individuals and bodies to establish and direct educational institutions, subject always to the observance of the principles set forth in paragraph 1 of this article and to the requirement that the education given in such institutions shall conform to such minimum standards as may be laid down by the State.

Article 14

Each State Party to the present Covenant which, at the time of becoming a Party, has not been able to secure in its metropolitan territory or other territories under its jurisdiction compulsory primary education, free of charge, undertakes, within two years, to work out and adopt a detailed plan of action for the progressive implementation, within a reasonable number of years, to be fixed in the plan, of the principle of compulsory education free of charge for all.

Article 15

1. The States Parties to the present Covenant recognize the right of everyone:

(a) To take part in cultural life;

(b) To enjoy the benefits of scientific progress and its applications;

(c) To benefit from the protection of the moral and material interests resulting from any scientific, literary or artistic production of which he is the author.

2. The steps to be taken by the States Parties to the present Covenant to achieve the full realization of this right shall include those necessary for the conservation, the development and the diffusion of science and culture.

3. The States Parties to the present Covenant undertake to respect the freedom indispensable for scientific research and creative activity.

4. The States Parties to the present Covenant recognize the benefits to be derived from the encouragement and development of international contacts and cooperation in the scientific and cultural fields.

PART IV

Article 16

1. The States Parties to the present Covenant undertake to submit in conformity with this part of the Covenant reports on the measures which they have adopted and the progress made in achieving the observance of the rights recognized herein.

2. (a) All reports shall be submitted to the Secretary-General of the United Nations, who shall transmit copies to the Economic and Social Council for consideration in accordance with the provisions of the present Covenant;

(b) The Secretary-General of the United Nations shall also transmit to the specialized agencies copies of the reports, or any relevant parts therefrom, from States Parties to the present Covenant which are also members of these specialized agencies in so far as these reports, or parts therefrom, relate to any matters which fall within the responsibilities of the said agencies in accordance with their constitutional instruments.

Article 17

1. The States Parties to the present Covenant shall furnish their reports in stages, in accordance with a programme to be established by the Economic and Social Council within one year of the entry into force of the present Covenant after consultation with the States Parties and the specialized agencies concerned.

2. Reports may indicate factors and difficulties affecting the degree of fulfilment of obligations under the present Covenant.

3. Where relevant information has previously been furnished to the United Nations or to any specialized agency by any State Party to the present Covenant, it will not be necessary to reproduce that information, but a precise reference to the information so furnished will suffice.

Article 18

Pursuant to its responsibilities under the Charter of the United Nations in the field of human rights and fundamental freedoms, the Economic and Social Council may make arrangements with the specialized agencies in respect of their reporting to it on the progress made in achieving the observance of the provisions of the present Covenant falling within the scope of their activities. These reports may include particulars of decisions and recommendations on such implementation adopted by their competent organs.

Article 19

The Economic and Social Council may transmit to the Commission on Human Rights for study and general recommendation or, as appropriate, for information the reports concerning human rights submitted by States in accordance with articles 16 and 17, and those concerning human rights submitted by the specialized agencies in accordance with article 18.

Article 20

The States Parties to the present Covenant and the specialized agencies concerned may submit comments to the Economic and Social Council on any general recommendation under article 19 or reference to such general recommendation in any report of the Commission on Human Rights or any documentation referred to therein.

Article 21

The Economic and Social Council may submit from time to time to the General Assembly reports with recommendations of a general nature and a summary of the information received from the States Parties to the present Covenant and the specialized agencies on the measures taken and the progress made in achieving general observance of the rights recognized in the present Covenant.

Article 22

The Economic and Social Council may bring to the attention of other organs of the United Nations, their subsidiary organs and specialized agencies concerned with furnishing technical assistance any matters arising out of the reports referred to in this part of the present Covenant which may assist such bodies in deciding, each within its field of competence, on the advisability of international measures likely to contribute to the effective progressive implementation of the present Covenant.

Article 23

The States Parties to the present Covenant agree that international action for the achievement of the rights recognized in the present Covenant includes such methods as the conclusion of conventions, the adoption of recommendations, the furnishing of technical assistance and the holding of regional meetings and technical meetings for the purpose of consultation and study organized in conjunction with the Governments concerned.

Article 24

Nothing in the present Covenant shall be interpreted as impairing the provisions of the Charter of the United Nations and of the constitutions of the specialized agencies which define the respective responsibilities of the various organs of the United Nations and of the specialized agencies in regard to the matters dealt with in the present Covenant.

Article 25

Nothing in the present Covenant shall be interpreted as impairing the inherent right of all peoples to enjoy and utilize fully and freely their natural wealth and resources.

PART V

Article 26

1. The present Covenant is open for signature by any State Member of the United Nations or member of any of its specialized agencies, by any State Party to the Statute of the International Court of Justice, and by any other State which has been invited by the General Assembly of the United Nations to become a party to the present Covenant.

2. The present Covenant is subject to ratification. Instruments of ratification shall be deposited with the Secretary-General of the United Nations.

3. The present Covenant shall be open to accession by any State referred to in paragraph 1 of this article.

4. Accession shall be effected by the deposit of an instrument of accession with the Secretary-General of the United Nations.

5. The Secretary-General of the United Nations shall inform all States which have signed the present Covenant or acceded to it of the deposit of each instrument of ratification or accession.

Article 27

1. The present Covenant shall enter into force three months after the date of the deposit with the Secretary-General of the United Nations of the thirty-fifth instrument of ratification or instrument of accession.

2. For each State ratifying the present Covenant or acceding to it after the deposit of the thirty-fifth instrument of ratification or instrument of accession, the present Covenant shall enter into force three months after the date of the deposit of its own instrument of ratification or instrument of accession.

Article 28

The provisions of the present Covenant shall extend to all parts of federal States without any limitations or exceptions.

Article 29

1. Any State Party to the present Covenant may propose an amendment and file it with the Secretary-General of the United Nations. The Secretary-General shall thereupon communicate any proposed amendments to the States Parties to the present Covenant with a request that they notify him whether they favour a conference of States Parties for the purpose of considering and voting upon the proposals. In the event that at least one third of the States Parties favours such a conference, the Secretary-General shall convene the conference under the auspices of the United Nations. Any amendment adopted by a majority of the States Parties present and voting at the conference shall be submitted to the General Assembly of the United Nations for approval.

2. Amendments shall come into force when they have been approved by the General Assembly of the United Nations and accepted by a two-thirds majority of the States Parties to the present Covenant in accordance with their respective constitutional processes.

3. When amendments come into force they shall be binding on those States Parties which have accepted them, other States Parties still being bound by the provisions of the present Covenant and any earlier amendment which they have accepted.

Article 30

Irrespective of the notifications made under article 26, paragraph 5, the Secretary-General of the United Nations shall inform all States referred to in paragraph 1 of the same article of the following particulars:

(a) Signatures, ratifications and accessions under article 26;

(b) The date of the entry into force of the present Covenant under article 27 and the date of the entry into force of any amendments under article 29.

Article 31

1. The present Covenant, of which the Chinese, English, French, Russian and Spanish texts are equally authentic, shall be deposited in the archives of the United Nations.

2. The Secretary-General of the United Nations shall transmit certified copies of the present Covenant to all States referred to in article 26.

Document 32

International Covenant on Civil and Political Rights

A/RES/2200 A (XXI), 16 December 1966

PREAMBLE

The States Parties to the present Covenant,

Considering that, in accordance with the principles proclaimed in the Charter of the United Nations, recognition of the inherent dignity and of the equal and inalienable rights of all members of the human family is the foundation of freedom, justice and peace in the world,

Recognizing that these rights derive from the inherent dignity of the human person,

Recognizing that, in accordance with the Universal Declaration of Human Rights, the ideal of free human beings enjoying civil and political freedom and freedom from fear and want can only be achieved if conditions are created whereby everyone may enjoy his civil and political rights, as well as his economic, social and cultural rights,

Considering the obligation of States under the Charter of the United Nations to promote universal respect for, and observance of, human rights and freedoms,

Realizing that the individual, having duties to other individuals and to the community to which he belongs, is under a responsibility to strive for the promotion and observance of the rights recognized in the present Covenant,

Agree upon the following articles:

PART I

Article 1

1. All peoples have the right of self-determination. By virtue of that right they freely determine their political status and freely pursue their economic, social and cultural development.

2. All peoples may, for their own ends, freely dispose of their natural wealth and resources without prejudice to any obligations arising out of international economic cooperation, based upon the principle of mutual benefit, and international law. In no case may a people be deprived of its own means of subsistence.

3. The States Parties to the present Covenant, including those having responsibility for the administration of Non-Self-Governing and Trust Territories, shall promote the realization of the right of self-determination, and shall respect that right, in conformity with the provisions of the Charter of the United Nations.

PART II

Article 2

1. Each State Party to the present Covenant undertakes to respect and to ensure to all individuals within its territory and subject to its jurisdiction the rights recognized in the present Covenant, without distinction of any kind, such as race, colour, sex, language, religion, political or other opinion, national or social origin, property, birth or other status.

2. Where not already provided for by existing legislative or other measures, each State Party to the present Covenant undertakes to take the necessary steps, in accordance with its constitutional processes and with the provisions of the present Covenant, to adopt such legislative or other measures as may be necessary to give effect to the rights recognized in the present Covenant.

3. Each State Party to the present Covenant undertakes:

(a) To ensure that any person whose rights or freedoms as herein recognized are violated shall have an effective remedy, notwithstanding that the violation has been committed by persons acting in an official capacity;

(b) To ensure that any person claiming such a remedy shall have his right thereto determined by competent judicial, administrative or legislative authorities, or by any other competent authority provided for by the legal system of the State, and to develop the possibilities of judicial remedy;

(c) To ensure that the competent authorities shall enforce such remedies when granted.

Article 3

The States Parties to the present Covenant undertake to ensure the equal right of men and women to the enjoyment of all civil and political rights set forth in the present Covenant.

Article 4

1. In time of public emergency which threatens the life of the nation and the existence of which is officially proclaimed, the States Parties to the present Covenant may take measures derogating from their obligations under the present Covenant to the extent strictly required by the exigencies of the situation, provided that such measures are not inconsistent with their other obligations under international law and do not involve discrimina-

tion solely on the ground of race, colour, sex, language, religion or social origin.

2. No derogation from articles 6, 7, 8 (paragraphs 1 and 2), 11, 15, 16 and 18 may be made under this provision.

3. Any State Party to the present Covenant availing itself of the right of derogation shall immediately inform the other States Parties to the present Covenant, through the intermediary of the Secretary-General of the United Nations, of the provisions from which it has derogated and of the reasons by which it was actuated. A further communication shall be made, through the same intermediary, on the date on which it terminates such derogation.

Article 5

1. Nothing in the present Covenant may be interpreted as implying for any State, group or person any right to engage in any activity or perform any act aimed at the destruction of any of the rights and freedoms recognized herein or at their limitation to a greater extent than is provided for in the present Covenant.

2. There shall be no restriction upon or derogation from any of the fundamental human rights recognized or existing in any State Party to the present Covenant pursuant to law, conventions, regulations or custom on the pretext that the present Covenant does not recognize such rights or that it recognizes them to a lesser extent.

PART III

Article 6

1. Every human being has the inherent right to life. This right shall be protected by law. No one shall be arbitrarily deprived of his life.

2. In countries which have not abolished the death penalty, sentence of death may be imposed only for the most serious crimes in accordance with the law in force at the time of the commission of the crime and not contrary to the provisions of the present Covenant and to the Convention on the Prevention and Punishment of the Crime of Genocide. This penalty can only be carried out pursuant to a final judgement rendered by a competent court.

3. When deprivation of life constitutes the crime of genocide, it is understood that nothing in this article shall authorize any State Party to the present Covenant to derogate in any way from any obligation assumed under the provisions of the Convention on the Prevention and Punishment of the Crime of Genocide.

4. Anyone sentenced to death shall have the right to seek pardon or commutation of the sentence. Amnesty, pardon or commutation of the sentence of death may be granted in all cases.

5. Sentence of death shall not be imposed for crimes committed by persons below eighteen years of age and shall not be carried out on pregnant women.

6. Nothing in this article shall be invoked to delay or to prevent the abolition of capital punishment by any State Party to the present Covenant.

Article 7

No one shall be subjected to torture or to cruel, inhuman or degrading treatment or punishment. In particular, no one shall be subjected without his free consent to medical or scientific experimentation.

Article 8

1. No one shall be held in slavery; slavery and the slave-trade in all their forms shall be prohibited.

2. No one shall be held in servitude.

3. (a) No one shall be required to perform forced or compulsory labour;

(b) Paragraph 3 (a) shall not be held to preclude, in countries where imprisonment with hard labour may be imposed as a punishment for a crime, the performance of hard labour in pursuance of a sentence to such punishment by a competent court;

(c) For the purpose of this paragraph the term "forced or compulsory labour" shall not include:

(i) Any work or service, not referred to in subparagraph (b), normally required of a person who is under detention in consequence of a lawful order of a court, or of a person during conditional release from such detention;

(ii) Any service of a military character and, in countries where conscientious objection is recognized, any national service required by law of conscientious objectors;

(iii) Any service exacted in cases of emergency or calamity threatening the life or well-being of the community;

(iv) Any work or service which forms part of normal civil obligations.

Article 9

1. Everyone has the right to liberty and security of person. No one shall be subjected to arbitrary arrest or detention. No one shall be deprived of his liberty except on such grounds and in accordance with such procedure as are established by law.

2. Anyone who is arrested shall be informed, at the time of arrest, of the reasons for his arrest and shall be promptly informed of any charges against him.

3. Anyone arrested or detained on a criminal charge shall be brought promptly before a judge or other

officer authorized by law to exercise judicial power and shall be entitled to trial within a reasonable time or to release. It shall not be the general rule that persons awaiting trial shall be detained in custody, but release may be subject to guarantees to appear for trial, at any other stage of the judicial proceedings, and, should occasion arise, for execution of the judgement.

4. Anyone who is deprived of his liberty by arrest or detention shall be entitled to take proceedings before a court, in order that that court may decide without delay on the lawfulness of his detention and order his release if the detention is not lawful.

5. Anyone who has been the victim of unlawful arrest or detention shall have an enforceable right to compensation.

Article 10

1. All persons deprived of their liberty shall be treated with humanity and with respect for the inherent dignity of the human person.

2. (a) Accused persons shall, save in exceptional circumstances, be segregated from convicted persons and shall be subject to separate treatment appropriate to their status as unconvicted persons;

(b) Accused juvenile persons shall be separated from adults and brought as speedily as possible for adjudication.

3. The penitentiary system shall comprise treatment of prisoners the essential aim of which shall be their reformation and social rehabilitation. Juvenile offenders shall be segregated from adults and be accorded treatment appropriate to their age and legal status.

Article 11

No one shall be imprisoned merely on the ground of inability to fulfil a contractual obligation.

Article 12

1. Everyone lawfully within the territory of a State shall, within that territory, have the right to liberty of movement and freedom to choose his residence.

2. Everyone shall be free to leave any country, including his own.

3. The above-mentioned rights shall not be subject to any restrictions except those which are provided by law, are necessary to protect national security, public order (*ordre public*), public health or morals or the rights and freedoms of others, and are consistent with the other rights recognized in the present Covenant.

4. No one shall be arbitrarily deprived of the right to enter his own country.

Article 13

An alien lawfully in the territory of a State Party to the present Covenant may be expelled therefrom only in pursuance of a decision reached in accordance with law and shall, except where compelling reasons of national security otherwise require, be allowed to submit the reasons against his expulsion and to have his case reviewed by, and be represented for the purpose before, the competent authority or a person or persons especially designated by the competent authority.

Article 14

1. All persons shall be equal before the courts and tribunals. In the determination of any criminal charge against him, or of his rights and obligations in a suit at law, everyone shall be entitled to a fair and public hearing by a competent, independent and impartial tribunal established by law. The press and the public may be excluded from all or part of a trial for reasons of morals, public order (*ordre public*) or national security in a democratic society, or when the interest of the private lives of the parties so requires, or to the extent strictly necessary in the opinion of the court in special circumstances where publicity would prejudice the interests of justice; but any judgement rendered in a criminal case or in a suit at law shall be made public except where the interest of juvenile persons otherwise requires or the proceedings concern matrimonial disputes or the guardianship of children.

2. Everyone charged with a criminal offence shall have the right to be presumed innocent until proved guilty according to law.

3. In the determination of any criminal charge against him, everyone shall be entitled to the following minimum guarantees, in full equality:

(a) To be informed promptly and in detail in a language which he understands of the nature and cause of the charge against him;

(b) To have adequate time and facilities for the preparation of his defence and to communicate with counsel of his own choosing;

(c) To be tried without undue delay;

(d) To be tried in his presence, and to defend himself in person or through legal assistance of his own choosing; to be informed, if he does not have legal assistance, of this right; and to have legal assistance assigned to him, in any case where the interests of justice so require, and without payment by him in any such case if he does not have sufficient means to pay for it;

(e) To examine, or have examined, the witnesses against him and to obtain the attendance and examination of witnesses on his behalf under the same conditions as witnesses against him;

(f) To have the free assistance of an interpreter if he cannot understand or speak the language used in court;

(g) Not to be compelled to testify against himself or to confess guilt.

4. In the case of juvenile persons, the procedure shall be such as will take account of their age and the desirability of promoting their rehabilitation.

5. Everyone convicted of a crime shall have the right to his conviction and sentence being reviewed by a higher tribunal according to law.

6. When a person has by a final decision been convicted of a criminal offence and when subsequently his conviction has been reversed or he has been pardoned on the ground that a new or newly discovered fact shows conclusively that there has been a miscarriage of justice, the person who has suffered punishment as a result of such conviction shall be compensated according to law, unless it is proved that the non-disclosure of the unknown fact in time is wholly or partly attributable to him.

7. No one shall be liable to be tried or punished again for an offence for which he has already been finally convicted or acquitted in accordance with the law and penal procedure of each country.

Article 15

1. No one shall be held guilty of any criminal offence on account of any act or omission which did not constitute a criminal offence, under national or international law, at the time when it was committed. Nor shall a heavier penalty be imposed than the one that was applicable at the time when the criminal offence was committed. If, subsequent to the commission of the offence, provision is made by law for the imposition of the lighter penalty, the offender shall benefit thereby.

2. Nothing in this article shall prejudice the trial and punishment of any person for any act or omission which, at the time when it was committed, was criminal according to the general principles of law recognized by the community of nations.

Article 16

Everyone shall have the right to recognition everywhere as a person before the law.

Article 17

1. No one shall be subjected to arbitrary or unlawful interference with his privacy, family, home or correspondence, nor to unlawful attacks on his honour and reputation.

2. Everyone has the right to the protection of the law against such interference or attacks.

Article 18

1. Everyone shall have the right to freedom of thought, conscience and religion. This right shall include freedom to have or to adopt a religion or belief of his choice, and freedom, either individually or in community with others and in public or private, to manifest his religion or belief in worship, observance, practice and teaching.

2. No one shall be subject to coercion which would impair his freedom to have or to adopt a religion or belief of his choice.

3. Freedom to manifest one's religion or beliefs may be subject only to such limitations as are prescribed by law and are necessary to protect public safety, order, health, or morals or the fundamental rights and freedoms of others.

4. The States Parties to the present Covenant undertake to have respect for the liberty of parents and, when applicable, legal guardians to ensure the religious and moral education of their children in conformity with their own convictions.

Article 19

1. Everyone shall have the right to hold opinions without interference.

2. Everyone shall have the right to freedom of expression; this right shall include freedom to seek, receive and impart information and ideas of all kinds, regardless of frontiers, either orally, in writing or in print, in the form of art, or through any other media of his choice.

3. The exercise of the rights provided for in paragraph 2 of this article carries with it special duties and responsibilities. It may therefore be subject to certain restrictions, but these shall only be such as are provided by law and are necessary:

(a) For respect of the rights or reputations of others;

(b) For the protection of national security or of public order (*ordre public*), or of public health or morals.

Article 20

1. Any propaganda for war shall be prohibited by law.

2. Any advocacy of national, racial or religious hatred that constitutes incitement to discrimination, hostility or violence shall be prohibited by law.

Article 21

The right of peaceful assembly shall be recognized. No restrictions may be placed on the exercise of this right other than those imposed in conformity with the law and which are necessary in a democratic society in the interests of national security or public safety, public order (*ordre public*), the protection of public health or morals or the protection of the rights and freedoms of others.

Article 22

1. Everyone shall have the right to freedom of association with others, including the right to form and join trade unions for the protection of his interests.

2. No restrictions may be placed on the exercise of this right other than those which are prescribed by law and which are necessary in a democratic society in the interests of national security or public safety, public order (*ordre public*), the protection of public health or morals or the protection of the rights and freedoms of others. This article shall not prevent the imposition of lawful restrictions on members of the armed forces and of the police in their exercise of this right.

3. Nothing in this article shall authorize States Parties to the International Labour Organisation Convention of 1948 concerning Freedom of Association and Protection of the Right to Organize to take legislative measures which would prejudice, or to apply the law in such a manner as to prejudice, the guarantees provided for in that Convention.

Article 23

1. The family is the natural and fundamental group unit of society and is entitled to protection by society and the State.

2. The right of men and women of marriageable age to marry and to found a family shall be recognized.

3. No marriage shall be entered into without the free and full consent of the intending spouses.

4. States Parties to the present Covenant shall take appropriate steps to ensure equality of rights and responsibilities of spouses as to marriage, during marriage and at its dissolution. In the case of dissolution, provision shall be made for the necessary protection of any children.

Article 24

1. Every child shall have, without any discrimination as to race, colour, sex, language, religion, national or social origin, property or birth, the right to such measures of protection as are required by his status as a minor, on the part of his family, society and the State.

2. Every child shall be registered immediately after birth and shall have a name.

3. Every child has the right to acquire a nationality.

Article 25

Every citizen shall have the right and the opportunity, without any of the distinctions mentioned in article 2 and without unreasonable restrictions:

(a) To take part in the conduct of public affairs, directly or through freely chosen representatives;

(b) To vote and to be elected at genuine periodic elections which shall be by universal and equal suffrage and shall be held by secret ballot, guaranteeing the free expression of the will of the electors;

(c) To have access, on general terms of equality, to public service in his country.

Article 26

All persons are equal before the law and are entitled without any discrimination to the equal protection of the law. In this respect, the law shall prohibit any discrimination and guarantee to all persons equal and effective protection against discrimination on any ground such as race, colour, sex, language, religion, political or other opinion, national or social origin, property, birth or other status.

Article 27

In those States in which ethnic, religious or linguistic minorities exist, persons belonging to such minorities shall not be denied the right, in community with the other members of their group, to enjoy their own culture, to profess and practise their own religion, or to use their own language.

PART IV

Article 28

1. There shall be established a Human Rights Committee (hereafter referred to in the present Covenant as the Committee). It shall consist of eighteen members and shall carry out the functions hereinafter provided.

2. The Committee shall be composed of nationals of the States Parties to the present Covenant who shall be persons of high moral character and recognized competence in the field of human rights, consideration being given to the usefulness of the participation of some persons having legal experience.

3. The members of the Committee shall be elected and shall serve in their personal capacity.

Article 29

1. The members of the Committee shall be elected by secret ballot from a list of persons possessing the qualifications prescribed in article 28 and nominated for the purpose by the States Parties to the present Covenant.

2. Each State Party to the present Covenant may nominate not more than two persons. These persons shall be nationals of the nominating State.

3. A person shall be eligible for renomination.

Article 30

1. The initial election shall be held no later than six months after the date of the entry into force of the present Covenant.

2. At least four months before the date of each election to the Committee, other than an election to fill a vacancy declared in accordance with article 34, the Secretary-General of the United Nations shall address a written invitation to the States Parties to the present Covenant to submit their nominations for membership of the Committee within three months.

3. The Secretary-General of the United Nations shall prepare a list in alphabetical order of all the persons thus nominated, with an indication of the States Parties which have nominated them, and shall submit it to the States Parties to the present Covenant no later than one month before the date of each election.

4. Elections of the members of the Committee shall be held at a meeting of the States Parties to the present Covenant convened by the Secretary-General of the United Nations at the Headquarters of the United Nations. At that meeting, for which two thirds of the States Parties to the present Covenant shall constitute a quorum, the persons elected to the Committee shall be those nominees who obtain the largest number of votes and an absolute majority of the votes of the representatives of States Parties present and voting.

Article 31

1. The Committee may not include more than one national of the same State.

2. In the election of the Committee, consideration shall be given to equitable geographical distribution of membership and to the representation of the different forms of civilization and of the principal legal systems.

Article 32

1. The members of the Committee shall be elected for a term of four years. They shall be eligible for re-election if renominated. However, the terms of nine of the members elected at the first election shall expire at the end of two years; immediately after the first election, the names of these nine members shall be chosen by lot by the Chairman of the meeting referred to in article 30, paragraph 4.

2. Elections at the expiry of office shall be held in accordance with the preceding articles of this part of the present Covenant.

Article 33

1. If, in the unanimous opinion of the other members, a member of the Committee has ceased to carry out his functions for any cause other than absence of a temporary character, the Chairman of the Committee shall notify the Secretary-General of the United Nations, who shall then declare the seat of that member to be vacant.

2. In the event of the death or the resignation of a member of the Committee, the Chairman shall immediately notify the Secretary-General of the United Nations, who shall declare the seat vacant from the date of death or the date on which the resignation takes effect.

Article 34

1. When a vacancy is declared in accordance with article 33 and if the term of office of the member to be replaced does not expire within six months of the declaration of the vacancy, the Secretary-General of the United Nations shall notify each of the States Parties to the present Covenant, which may within two months submit nominations in accordance with article 29 for the purpose of filling the vacancy.

2. The Secretary-General of the United Nations shall prepare a list in alphabetical order of the persons thus nominated and shall submit it to the States Parties to the present Covenant. The election to fill the vacancy shall then take place in accordance with the relevant provisions of this part of the present Covenant.

3. A member of the Committee elected to fill a vacancy declared in accordance with article 33 shall hold office for the remainder of the term of the member who vacated the seat on the Committee under the provisions of that article.

Article 35

The members of the Committee shall, with the approval of the General Assembly of the United Nations, receive emoluments from United Nations resources on such terms and conditions as the General Assembly may decide, having regard to the importance of the Committee's responsibilities.

Article 36

The Secretary-General of the United Nations shall provide the necessary staff and facilities for the effective performance of the functions of the Committee under the present Covenant.

Article 37

1. The Secretary-General of the United Nations shall convene the initial meeting of the Committee at the Headquarters of the United Nations.

2. After its initial meeting, the Committee shall meet at such times as shall be provided in its rules of procedure.

3. The Committee shall normally meet at the Headquarters of the United Nations or at the United Nations Office at Geneva.

Article 38

Every member of the Committee shall, before taking up his duties, make a solemn declaration in open committee that he will perform his functions impartially and conscientiously.

Article 39

1. The Committee shall elect its officers for a term of two years. They may be re-elected.

2. The Committee shall establish its own rules of procedure, but these rules shall provide, *inter alia*, that:

(a) Twelve members shall constitute a quorum;

(b) Decisions of the Committee shall be made by a majority vote of the members present.

Article 40

1. The States Parties to the present Covenant undertake to submit reports on the measures they have adopted which give effect to the rights recognized herein and on the progress made in the enjoyment of those rights:

(a) Within one year of the entry into force of the present Covenant for the States Parties concerned;

(b) Thereafter whenever the Committee so requests.

2. All reports shall be submitted to the Secretary-General of the United Nations, who shall transmit them to the Committee for consideration. Reports shall indicate the factors and difficulties, if any, affecting the implementation of the present Covenant.

3. The Secretary-General of the United Nations may, after consultation with the Committee, transmit to the specialized agencies concerned copies of such parts of the reports as may fall within their field of competence.

4. The Committee shall study the reports submitted by the States Parties to the present Covenant. It shall transmit its reports, and such general comments as it may consider appropriate, to the States Parties. The Committee may also transmit to the Economic and Social Council these comments along with the copies of the reports it has received from States Parties to the present Covenant.

5. The States Parties to the present Covenant may submit to the Committee observations on any comments that may be made in accordance with paragraph 4 of this article.

Article 41

1. A State Party to the present Covenant may at any time declare under this article that it recognizes the competence of the Committee to receive and consider communications to the effect that a State Party claims that another State Party is not fulfilling its obligations under the present Covenant. Communications under this article may be received and considered only if submitted by a State Party which has made a declaration recognizing in regard to itself the competence of the Committee. No communication shall be received by the Committee if it concerns a State Party which has not made such a declaration. Communications received under this article shall be dealt with in accordance with the following procedure:

(a) If a State Party to the present Covenant considers that another State Party is not giving effect to the provisions of the present Covenant, it may, by written communication, bring the matter to the attention of that State Party. Within three months after the receipt of the communication the receiving State shall afford the State which sent the communication an explanation, or any other statement in writing clarifying the matter which should include, to the extent possible and pertinent, reference to domestic procedures and remedies taken, pending, or available in the matter;

(b) If the matter is not adjusted to the satisfaction of both States Parties concerned within six months after the receipt by the receiving State of the initial communication, either State shall have the right to refer the matter to the Committee, by notice given to the Committee and to the other State;

(c) The Committee shall deal with a matter referred to it only after it has ascertained that all available domestic remedies have been invoked and exhausted in the matter, in conformity with the generally recognized principles of international law. This shall not be the rule where the application of the remedies is unreasonably prolonged;

(d) The Committee shall hold closed meetings when examining communications under this article;

(e) Subject to the provisions of subparagraph (c), the Committee shall make available its good offices to the States Parties concerned with a view to a friendly solution of the matter on the basis of respect for human rights and fundamental freedoms as recognized in the present Covenant;

(f) In any matter referred to it, the Committee may call upon the States Parties concerned, referred to in subparagraph (b), to supply any relevant information;

(g) The States Parties concerned, referred to in subparagraph (b), shall have the right to be represented when the matter is being considered in the Committee and to make submissions orally and/or in writing;

(h) The Committee shall, within twelve months after the date of receipt of notice under subparagraph (b), submit a report:

(i) If a solution within the terms of subparagraph (e) is reached, the Committee shall confine its report to a brief statement of the facts and of the solution reached;

(ii) If a solution within the terms of subparagraph (e) is not reached, the Committee shall confine its report to a brief statement of the facts; the written submissions and record of the oral submissions made by the States Parties concerned shall be attached to the report.

In every matter, the report shall be communicated to the States Parties concerned.

2. The provisions of this article shall come into force when ten States Parties to the present Covenant have made declarations under paragraph 1 of this article. Such declarations shall be deposited by the States Parties with the Secretary-General of the United Nations, who shall transmit copies thereof to the other States Parties. A declaration may be withdrawn at any time by notification to the Secretary-General. Such a withdrawal shall not prejudice the consideration of any matter which is the subject of a communication already transmitted under this article; no further communication by any State Party shall be received after the notification of withdrawal of the declaration has been received by the Secretary-General, unless the State Party concerned has made a new declaration.

Article 42

1. (a) If a matter referred to the Committee in accordance with article 41 is not resolved to the satisfaction of the States Parties concerned, the Committee may, with the prior consent of the States Parties concerned, appoint an *ad hoc* Conciliation Commission (hereinafter referred to as the Commission). The good offices of the Commission shall be made available to the States Parties concerned with a view to an amicable solution of the matter on the basis of respect for the present Covenant;

(b) The Commission shall consist of five persons acceptable to the States Parties concerned. If the States Parties concerned fail to reach agreement within three months on all or part of the composition of the Commission, the members of the Commission concerning whom no agreement has been reached shall be elected by secret ballot by a two-thirds majority vote of the Committee from among its members.

2. The members of the Commission shall serve in their personal capacity. They shall not be nationals of the States Parties concerned, or of a State not Party to the present Covenant, or of a State Party which has not made a declaration under article 41.

3. The Commission shall elect its own Chairman and adopt its own rules of procedure.

4. The meetings of the Commission shall normally be held at the Headquarters of the United Nations or at the United Nations Office at Geneva. However, they may be held at such other convenient places as the Commission may determine in consultation with the Secretary-General of the United Nations and the States Parties concerned.

5. The secretariat provided in accordance with article 36 shall also service the commissions appointed under this article.

6. The information received and collated by the Committee shall be made available to the Commission and the Commission may call upon the States Parties concerned to supply any other relevant information.

7. When the Commission has fully considered the matter, but in any event not later than twelve months after having been seized of the matter, it shall submit to the Chairman of the Committee a report for communication to the States Parties concerned:

(a) If the Commission is unable to complete its consideration of the matter within twelve months, it shall confine its report to a brief statement of the status of its consideration of the matter;

(b) If an amicable solution to the matter on the basis of respect for human rights as recognized in the present Covenant is reached, the Commission shall confine its report to a brief statement of the facts and of the solution reached;

(c) If a solution within the terms of subparagraph (b) is not reached, the Commission's report shall embody its findings on all questions of fact relevant to the issues between the States Parties concerned, and its views on the possibilities of an amicable solution of the matter. This report shall also contain the written submissions and a record of the oral submissions made by the States Parties concerned;

(d) If the Commission's report is submitted under subparagraph (c), the States Parties concerned shall, within three months of the receipt of the report, notify the Chairman of the Committee whether or not they accept the contents of the report of the Commission.

8. The provisions of this article are without prejudice to the responsibilities of the Committee under article 41.

9. The States Parties concerned shall share equally all the expenses of the members of the Commission in accordance with estimates to be provided by the Secretary-General of the United Nations.

10. The Secretary-General of the United Nations shall be empowered to pay the expenses of the members of the Commission, if necessary, before reimbursement by the States Parties concerned, in accordance with paragraph 9 of this article.

Article 43

The members of the Committee, and of the *ad hoc* conciliation commissions which may be appointed under article 42, shall be entitled to the facilities, privileges and immunities of experts on mission for the United Nations as laid down in the relevant sections of the Convention on the Privileges and Immunities of the United Nations.

Article 44

The provisions for the implementation of the present Covenant shall apply without prejudice to the procedures prescribed in the field of human rights by or under the constituent instruments and the conventions of the United Nations and of the specialized agencies and shall not prevent the States Parties to the present Covenant from having recourse to other procedures for settling a dispute in accordance with general or special international agreements in force between them.

Article 45

The Committee shall submit to the General Assembly of the United Nations, through the Economic and Social Council, an annual report on its activities.

PART V

Article 46

Nothing in the present Covenant shall be interpreted as impairing the provisions of the Charter of the United Nations and of the constitutions of the specialized agencies which define the respective responsibilities of the various organs of the United Nations and of the specialized agencies in regard to the matters dealt with in the present Covenant.

Article 47

Nothing in the present Covenant shall be interpreted as impairing the inherent right of all peoples to enjoy and utilize fully and freely their natural wealth and resources.

PART VI

Article 48

1. The present Covenant is open for signature by any State Member of the United Nations or member of any of its specialized agencies, by any State Party to the Statute of the International Court of Justice, and by any other State which has been invited by the General Assembly of the United Nations to become a Party to the present Covenant.

2. The present Covenant is subject to ratification. Instruments of ratification shall be deposited with the Secretary-General of the United Nations.

3. The present Covenant shall be open to accession by any State referred to in paragraph 1 of this article.

4. Accession shall be effected by the deposit of an instrument of accession with the Secretary-General of the United Nations.

5. The Secretary-General of the United Nations shall inform all States which have signed this Covenant or acceded to it of the deposit of each instrument of ratification or accession.

Article 49

1. The present Covenant shall enter into force three months after the date of the deposit with the Secretary-General of the United Nations of the thirty-fifth instrument of ratification or instrument of accession.

2. For each State ratifying the present Covenant or acceding to it after the deposit of the thirty-fifth instrument of ratification or instrument of accession, the present Covenant shall enter into force three months after the date of the deposit of its own instrument of ratification or instrument of accession.

Article 50

The provisions of the present Covenant shall extend to all parts of federal States without any limitations or exceptions.

Article 51

1. Any State Party to the present Covenant may propose an amendment and file it with the Secretary-General of the United Nations. The Secretary-General of the United Nations shall thereupon communicate any proposed amendments to the States Parties to the present Covenant with a request that they notify him whether they favour a conference of States Parties for the purpose of considering and voting upon the proposals. In the event that at least one third of the States Parties favours such a conference, the Secretary-General shall convene the conference under the auspices of the United Nations. Any amendment adopted by a majority of the States Parties present and voting at the conference shall be submitted to the General Assembly of the United Nations for approval.

2. Amendments shall come into force when they have been approved by the General Assembly of the United Nations and accepted by a two-thirds majority of the States Parties to the present Covenant in accordance with their respective constitutional processes.

3. When amendments come into force, they shall be binding on those States Parties which have accepted them, other States Parties still being bound by the provisions of the present Covenant and any earlier amendment which they have accepted.

Article 52

Irrespective of the notifications made under article 48, paragraph 5, the Secretary-General of the United Nations shall inform all States referred to in paragraph 1 of the same article of the following particulars:

(a) Signatures, ratifications and accessions under article 48;

(b) The date of the entry into force of the present Covenant under article 49 and the date of the entry into force of any amendments under article 51.

Article 53

1. The present Covenant, of which the Chinese, English, French, Russian and Spanish texts are equally authentic, shall be deposited in the archives of the United Nations.

2. The Secretary-General of the United Nations shall transmit certified copies of the present Covenant to all States referred to in article 48.

Document 33

Optional Protocol to the International Covenant on Civil and Political Rights

A/RES/2200 A (XXI), 16 December 1966

The States Parties to the present Protocol,

Considering that in order further to achieve the purposes of the International Covenant on Civil and Political Rights (hereinafter referred to as the Covenant) and the implemention of its provisions it would be appropriate to enable the Human Rights Committee set up in part IV of the Covenant (hereinafter referred to as the Committee) to receive and consider, as provided in the present Protocol, communications from individuals claiming to be victims of violations of any of the rights set forth in the Covenant,

Have agreed as follows:

Article 1

A State Party to the Covenant that becomes a Party to the present Protocol recognizes the competence of the Committee to receive and consider communications from individuals subject to its jurisdiction who claim to be victims of a violation by that State Party of any of the rights set forth in the Covenant. No communication shall be received by the Committee if it concerns a State Party to the Covenant which is not a Party to the present Protocol.

Article 2

Subject to the provisions of article 1, individuals who claim that any of their rights enumerated in the Covenant have been violated and who have exhausted all available domestic remedies may submit a written communication to the Committee for consideration.

Article 3

The Committee shall consider inadmissible any communication under the present Protocol which is anonymous, or which it considers to be an abuse of the right of submission of such communications or to be incompatible with the provisions of the Covenant.

Article 4

1. Subject to the provisions of article 3, the Committee shall bring any communications submitted to it under the present Protocol to the attention of the State Party to the present Protocol alleged to be violating any provision of the Covenant.

2. Within six months, the receiving State shall submit to the Committee written explanations or statements clarifying the matter and the remedy, if any, that may have been taken by that State.

Article 5

1. The Committee shall consider communications received under the present Protocol in the light of all written information made available to it by the individual and by the State Party concerned.

2. The Committee shall not consider any communication from an individual unless it has ascertained that:

(a) The same matter is not being examined under another procedure of international investigation or settlement;

(b) The individual has exhausted all available domestic remedies. This shall not be the rule where the application of the remedies is unreasonably prolonged.

3. The Committee shall hold closed meetings when examining communications under the present Protocol.

4. The Committee shall forward its views to the State Party concerned and to the individual.

Article 6

The Committee shall include in its annual report under article 45 of the Covenant a summary of its activities under the present Protocol.

Article 7

Pending the achievement of the objectives of resolution 1514 (XV) adopted by the General Assembly of the United Nations on 14 December 1960 concerning the Declaration on the Granting of Independence to Colonial Countries and Peoples, the provisions of the present Protocol shall in no way limit the right of petition granted to these peoples by the Charter of the United Nations and other international conventions and instruments under the United Nations and its specialized agencies.

Article 8

1. The present Protocol is open for signature by any State which has signed the Covenant.

2. The present Protocol is subject to ratification by any State which has ratified or acceded to the Covenant. Instruments of ratification shall be deposited with the Secretary-General of the United Nations.

3. The present Protocol shall be open to accession by any State which has ratified or acceded to the Covenant.

4. Accession shall be effected by the deposit of an instrument of accession with the Secretary-General of the United Nations.

5. The Secretary-General of the United Nations shall inform all States which have signed the present Protocol or acceded to it of the deposit of each instrument of ratification or accession.

Article 9

1. Subject to the entry into force of the Covenant, the present Protocol shall enter into force three months after the date of the deposit with the Secretary-General of the United Nations of the tenth instrument of ratification or instrument of accession.

2. For each State ratifying the present Protocol or acceding to it after the deposit of the tenth instrument of ratification or instrument of accession, the present Protocol shall enter into force three months after the date of the deposit of its own instrument of ratification or instrument of accession.

Article 10

The provisions of the present Protocol shall extend to all parts of federal States without any limitations or exceptions.

Article 11

1. Any State Party to the present Protocol may propose an amendment and file it with the Secretary-General of the United Nations. The Secretary-General shall thereupon communicate any proposed amendments to the States Parties to the present Protocol with a request that they notify him whether they favour a conference of States Parties for the purpose of considering and voting upon the proposal. In the event that at least one third of the States Parties favours such a conference, the Secretary-General shall convene the conference under the auspices of the United Nations. Any amendment adopted by a majority of the States Parties present and voting at the conference shall be submitted to the General Assembly of the United Nations for approval.

2. Amendments shall come into force when they have been approved by the General Assembly of the United Nations and accepted by a two-thirds majority of the States Parties to the present Protocol in accordance with their respective constitutional processes.

3. When amendments come into force, they shall be binding on those States Parties which have accepted them, other States Parties still being bound by the provisions of the present Protocol and any earlier amendment which they have accepted.

Article 12

1. Any State Party may denounce the present Protocol at any time by written notification addressed to the Secretary-General of the United Nations. Denunciation shall take effect three months after the date of receipt of the notification by the Secretary-General.

2. Denunciation shall be without prejudice to the continued application of the provisions of the present Protocol to any communication submitted under article 2 before the effective date of denunciation.

Article 13

Irrespective of the notifications made under article 8, paragraph 5, of the present Protocol, the Secretary-General of the United Nations shall inform all States referred to in article 48, paragraph 1, of the Covenant of the following particulars:

(a) Signatures, ratifications and accessions under article 8;

(b) The date of the entry into force of the present Protocol under article 9 and the date of the entry into force of any amendments under article 11;

(c) Denunciations under article 12.

Article 14

1. The present Protocol, of which the Chinese, English, French, Russian and Spanish texts are equally authentic, shall be deposited in the archives of the United Nations.

2. The Secretary-General of the United Nations shall transmit certified copies of the present Protocol to all States referred to in article 48 of the Covenant.

Document 34

Economic and Social Council resolution authorizing the Commission on Human Rights and the Subcommission on Prevention of Discrimination and Protection of Minorities to examine information relevant to gross violations of human rights and fundamental freedoms

E/RES/1235 (XLII), 6 June 1967

The Economic and Social Council,

Noting resolutions 8 (XXIII) and 9 (XXIII) of the Commission on Human Rights, 1/

1. *Welcomes* the decision of the Commission on Human Rights to give annual consideration to the item entitled "Question of the violation of human rights and fundamental freedoms, including policies of racial discrimination and segregation and of apartheid, in all countries, with particular reference to colonial and other dependent countries and territories", without prejudice to the functions and powers of organs already in existence or which may be established within the framework of measures of implementation included in international covenants and conventions on the protection of human rights and fundamental freedoms; and concurs with the requests for assistance addressed to the Sub-Commission on Prevention of Discrimination and Protection of Minorities and to the Secretary-General;

2. *Authorizes* the Commission on Human Rights and the Sub-Commission on Prevention of Discrimination and Protection of Minorities, in conformity with the provisions of paragraph 1 of the Commission's resolution 8 (XXIII), to examine information relevant to gross violations of human rights and fundamental freedoms, as exemplified by the policy of apartheid as practised in the Republic of South Africa and in the Territory of South West Africa under the direct responsibility of the United Nations and now illegally occupied by the Government of the Republic of South Africa, and to racial discrimination as practised notably in Southern Rhodesia, contained in the communications listed by the Secretary-General pursuant to Economic and Social Council resolution 728 F (XXVIII) of 30 July 1959;

3. *Decides* that the Commission on Human Rights may, in appropriate cases, and after careful consideration of the information thus made available to it, in conformity with the provisions of paragraph 1 above, make a thorough study of situations which reveal a consistent pattern of violations of human rights, as exemplified by the policy of apartheid as practised in the Republic of South Africa and in the Territory of South West Africa under the direct responsibility of the United Nations and now illegally occupied by the Government of the Republic of South Africa, and racial discrimination as practised notably in Southern Rhodesia, and report, with recommendations thereon, to the Economic and Social Council;

4. *Decides* to review the provisions of paragraphs 2 and 3 of the present resolution after the entry into force of the International Covenants on Human Rights;

5. *Takes note* of the fact that the Commission on Human Rights, in its resolution 6 (XXIII), 2/ has instructed an *ad hoc* study group to study in all its aspects the question of the ways and means by which the Commission might be enabled or assisted to discharge functions in relation to violations of human rights and fundamental freedoms, whilst maintaining and fulfilling its other functions;

6. *Requests* the Commission on Human Rights to report to it on the result of this study after having given consideration to the conclusions of the *ad hoc* study group referred to in paragraph 5 above.

1/ See *Official Records of the Economic and Social Council, Forty-second Session*, paras. 394 and 404.
2/ Ibid., para. 368.

Document 35

Proclamation of Teheran, proclaimed by the International Conference on Human Rights held in Teheran

13 May 1968

The International Conference on Human Rights,

Having met at Teheran from April 22 to May 13, 1968 to review the progress made in the twenty years since the adoption of the Universal Declaration of Human Rights and to formulate a programme for the future,

Having considered the problems relating to the activities of the United Nations for the promotion and encouragement of respect for human rights and fundamental freedoms,

Bearing in mind the resolutions adopted by the Conference,

Noting that the observance of the International Year for Human Rights takes place at a time when the world is undergoing a process of unprecedented change,

Having regard to the new opportunities made available by the rapid progress of science and technology,

Believing that, in an age when conflict and violence prevail in many parts of the world, the fact of human interdependence and the need for human solidarity are more evident than ever before,

Recognizing that peace is the universal aspiration of mankind and that peace and justice are indispensable to the full realization of human rights and fundamental freedoms,

Solemnly proclaims that:

1. It is imperative that the members of the international community fulfil their solemn obligations to promote and encourage respect for human rights and fundamental freedoms for all without distinctions of any kind such as race, colour, sex, language, religion, political or other opinions;

2. The Universal Declaration of Human Rights states a common understanding of the peoples of the world concerning the inalienable and inviolable rights of all members of the human family and constitutes an obligation for the members of the international community;

3. The International Covenant on Civil and Political Rights, the International Covenant on Economic, Social and Cultural Rights, the Declaration on the Granting of Independence to Colonial Countries and Peoples, the International Convention on the Elimination of All Forms of Racial Discrimination as well as other conventions and declarations in the field of human rights adopted under the auspices of the United Nations, the specialized agencies and the regional intergovernmental organizations, have created new standards and obligations to which States should conform;

4. Since the adoption of the Universal Declaration of Human Rights the United Nations has made substantial progress in defining standards for the enjoyment and protection of human rights and fundamental freedoms. During this period many important international instruments were adopted but much remains to be done in regard to the implementation of those rights and freedoms;

5. The primary aim of the United Nations in the sphere of human rights is the achievement by each individual of the maximum freedom and dignity. For the realization of this objective, the laws of every country should grant each individual, irrespective of race, language, religion or political belief, freedom of expression, of information, of conscience and of religion, as well as the right to participate in the political, economic, cultural and social life of his country;

6. States should reaffirm their determination effectively to enforce the principles enshrined in the Charter of the United Nations and in other international instruments that concern human rights and fundamental freedoms;

7. Gross denials of human rights under the repugnant policy of *apartheid* is a matter of the gravest concern to the international community. This policy of *apartheid*, condemned as a crime against humanity, continues seriously to disturb international peace and security. It is therefore imperative for the international community to use every possible means to eradicate this evil. The struggle against *apartheid* is recognized as legitimate;

8. The peoples of the world must be made fully aware of the evils of racial discrimination and must join in combating them. The implementation of this principle of non-discrimination, embodied in the Charter of the United Nations, the Universal Declaration of Human Rights, and other international instruments in the field of human rights, constitutes a most urgent task of mankind at the international as well as at the national level. All ideologies based on racial superiority and intolerance must be condemned and resisted;

9. Eight years after the General Assembly's Declaration on the Granting of Independence to Colonial Countries and Peoples the problems of colonialism continue to preoccupy the international community. It is a matter of urgency that all Member States should cooperate with the appropriate organs of the United Nations so that effective measures can be taken to ensure that the Declaration is fully implemented;

10. Massive denials of human rights, arising out of aggression or any armed conflict with their tragic consequences, and resulting in untold human misery, engender reactions which could engulf the world in ever growing hostilities. It is the obligation of the international community to cooperate in eradicating such scourges;

11. Gross denials of human rights arising from discrimination on grounds of race, religion, belief or expressions of opinion outrage the conscience of mankind and endanger the foundations of freedom, justice and peace in the world;

12. The widening gap between the economically developed and developing countries impedes the realization of human rights in the international community. The failure of the Development Decade to reach its modest objectives makes it all the more imperative for every nation, according to its capacities, to make the maximum possible effort to close this gap;

13. Since human rights and fundamental freedoms are indivisible, the full realization of civil and political rights without the enjoyment of economic, social and cultural rights is impossible. The achievement of lasting progress in the implementation of human rights is dependent upon sound and effective national and international policies of economic and social development;

14. The existence of over seven hundred million illiterates throughout the world is an enormous obstacle to all efforts at realizing the aims and purposes of the Charter of the United Nations and the provisions of the Universal Declaration of Human Rights. International action aimed at eradicating illiteracy from the face of the earth and promoting education at all levels requires urgent attention;

15. The discrimination of which women are still victims in various regions of the world must be eliminated. An inferior status for women is contrary to the Charter of the United Nations as well as the provisions of the Universal Declaration of Human Rights. The full implementation of the Declaration on the Elimination of Discrimination against Women is a necessity for the progress of mankind;

16. The protection of the family and of the child remains the concern of the international community. Parents have a basic human right to determine freely and responsibly the number and the spacing of their children;

17. The aspirations of the younger generation for a better world, in which human rights and fundamental freedoms are fully implemented, must be given the highest encouragement. It is imperative that youth participate in shaping the future of mankind;

18. While recent scientific discoveries and technological advances have opened vast prospects for economic, social and cultural progress, such developments may nevertheless endanger the rights and freedoms of individuals and will require continuing attention;

19. Disarmament would release immense human and material resources now devoted to military purposes. These resources should be used for the promotion of human rights and fundamental freedoms. General and complete disarmament is one of the highest aspirations of all peoples;

Therefore,

The International Conference on Human Rights,

1. *Affirming* its faith in the principles of the Universal Declaration of Human Rights and other international instruments in this field,

2. *Urges* all peoples and governments to dedicate themselves to the principles enshrined in the Universal Declaration of Human Rights and to redouble their efforts to provide for all human beings a life consonant with freedom and dignity and conducive to physical, mental, social and spiritual welfare.

Document 36

American Convention on Human Rights (Pact of San José), signed at San José, Costa Rica

22 November 1969

PREAMBLE

The American states signatory to the present Convention,

Reaffirming their intention to consolidate in this hemisphere, within the framework of democratic institutions, a system of personal liberty and social justice based on respect for the essential rights of man,

Recognizing that the essential rights of man are not derived from one's being a national of a certain state, but are based upon attributes of the human personality, and that they therefore justify international protection in the form of a convention reinforcing or complementing the protection provided by the domestic law of the American states,

Considering that these principles have been set forth in the Charter of the Organization of American States, in the American Declaration of the Rights and Duties of Man, and in the Universal Declaration of Human Rights, and that they have been reaffirmed and refined in other international instruments, worldwide as well as regional in scope,

Reiterating that, in accordance with the Universal Declaration of Human Rights, the ideal of free men enjoying freedom from fear and want can be achieved only if conditions are created whereby everyone may enjoy his economic, social, and cultural rights, as well as his civil and political rights, and

Considering that the Third Special Inter-American Conference (Buenos Aires, 1967) approved the incorporation into the Charter of the Organization 1/ itself of broader standards with respect to economic, social, and educational rights and resolved that an inter-American convention on human rights should determine the structure, competence, and procedure of the organs responsible for these matters,

Have agreed upon the following:

PART I. STATE OBLIGATIONS AND RIGHTS PROTECTED

CHAPTER I. GENERAL OBLIGATIONS

Article 1
Obligation to respect rights

1. The States Parties to this Convention undertake to respect the rights and freedoms recognized herein and to ensure to all persons subject to their jurisdiction the free and full exercise of those rights and freedoms, without any discrimination for reasons of race, color, sex, language, religion, political or other opinion, national or social origin, economic status, birth, or any other social condition.

2. For the purposes of this Convention, "person" means every human being.

Article 2
Domestic legal effects

Where the exercise of any of the rights or freedoms referred to in Article I is not already ensured by legislative or other provisions, the States Parties undertake to adopt, in accordance with their constitutional processes and the provisions of this Convention, such legislative or other measures as may be necessary to give effect to those rights or freedoms.

CHAPTER II. CIVIL AND POLITICAL RIGHTS

Article 3
Right to juridical personality

Every person has the right to recognition as a person before the law.

Article 4
Right to life

1. Every person has the right to have his life respected. This right shall be protected by law and, in general, from the moment of conception. No one shall be arbitrarily deprived of his life.

2. In countries that have not abolished the death penalty, it may be imposed only for the most serious crimes and pursuant to a final judgment rendered by a competent court and in accordance with a law establishing such punishment, enacted prior to the commission of the crime. The application of such punishment shall not be extended to crimes to which it does not presently apply.

3. The death penalty shall not be reestablished in states that have abolished it.

4. In no case shall capital punishment be inflicted for political offenses or related common crimes.

5. Capital punishment shall not be imposed upon persons who, at the time the crime was committed, were under 18 years of age or over 70 years of age; nor shall it be applied to pregnant women.

6. Every person condemned to death shall have the right to apply for amnesty, pardon, or commutation of sentence, which may be granted in all cases. Capital punishment shall not be imposed while such a petition is pending decision by the competent authority.

Article 5
Right to humane treatment

1. Every person has the right to have his physical, mental, and moral integrity respected.

2. No one shall be subjected to torture or to cruel, inhuman, or degrading punishment or treatment. All persons deprived of their liberty shall be treated with respect for the inherent dignity of the human person.

3. Punishment shall not be extended to any person other than the criminal.

4. Accused persons shall, save in exceptional circumstances, be segregated from convicted persons, and shall be subject to separate treatment appropriate to their status as unconvicted persons.

1/ United Nations, *Treaty Series*, vol. 119, p.3.

5. Minors while subject to criminal proceedings shall be separated from adults and brought before specialized tribunals, as speedily as possible, so that they may be treated in accordance with their status as minors.

6. Punishments consisting of deprivation of liberty shall have as an essential aim the reform and social readaptation of the prisoners.

Article 6
Freedom from slavery

1. No one shall be subject to slavery or to involuntary servitude, which are prohibited in all their forms, as are the slave trade and traffic in women.

2. No one shall be required to perform forced or compulsory labor. This provision shall not be interpreted to mean that, in those countries in which the penalty established for certain crimes is deprivation of liberty at forced labor, the carrying out of such a sentence imposed by a competent court is prohibited. Forced labor shall not adversely affect the dignity or the physical or intellectual capacity of the prisoner.

3. For the purposes of this article, the following do not constitute forced or compulsory labor:

a. Work or service normally required of a person imprisoned in execution of a sentence or formal decision passed by the competent judicial authority; such work or service shall be carried out under the supervision and control of public authorities, and any persons performing such work or service shall not be placed at the disposal of any private party, company, or juridical person;

b. Military service and, in countries in which conscientious objectors are recognized, national service that the law may provide for in lieu of military service;

c. Service exacted in time of danger or calamity that threatens the existence or the well-being of the community; or

d. Work or service that forms part of normal civic obligations.

Article 7
Right to personal liberty

1. Every person has the right to personal liberty and security.

2. No one shall be deprived of his physical liberty except for the reasons and under the conditions established beforehand by the constitution of the State Party concerned or by a law established pursuant thereto.

3. No one shall be subject to arbitrary arrest or imprisonment.

4. Anyone who is detained shall be informed of the reasons for his detention and shall be promptly notified of the charge or charges against him.

5. Any person detained shall be brought promptly before a judge or other officer authorized by law to exercise judicial power and shall be entitled to trial within a reasonable time or to be released without prejudice to the continuation of the proceedings. His release may be subject to guarantees to assure his appearance for trial.

6. Anyone who is deprived of his liberty shall be entitled to recourse to a competent court, in order that the court may decide without delay on the lawfulness of his arrest or detention and order his release if the arrest or detention is unlawful. In States Parties whose laws provide that anyone who believes himself to be threatened with deprivation of his liberty is entitled to recourse to a competent court in order that it may decide on the lawfulness of such threat, this remedy may not be restricted or abolished. The interested party or another person in his behalf is entitled to seek these remedies.

7. No one shall be detained for debt. This principle shall not limit the orders of a competent judicial authority issued for nonfulfillment of duties of support.

Article 8
Right to a fair trial

1. Every person has the right to a hearing, with due guarantees and within a reasonable time, by a competent, independent, and impartial tribunal, previously established by law, in the substantiation of any accusation of a criminal nature made against him or for the determination of his rights and obligations of a civil, labor, fiscal, or any other nature.

2. Every person accused of a criminal offense has the right to be presumed innocent so long as his guilt has not been proven according to law. During the proceedings, every person is entitled, with full equality, to the following minimum guarantees:

a. The right of the accused to be assisted without charge by a translator or interpreter, if he does not understand or does not speak the language of the tribunal or court;

b. Prior notification in detail to the accused of the charges against him;

c. Adequate time and means for the preparation of his defense;

d. The right of the accused to defend himself personally or to be assisted by legal counsel of his own choosing, and to communicate freely and privately with his counsel;

e. The inalienable right to be assisted by counsel provided by the State, paid or not as the domestic law provides, if the accused does not defend himself personally or engage his own counsel within the time period established by law;

f. The right of the defense to examine witnesses present in the court and to obtain the appearance, as witnesses, of experts or other persons who may throw light on the facts;

g. The right not to be compelled to be a witness against himself or to plead guilty; and

h. The right to appeal the judgment to a higher court.

3. A confession of guilt by the accused shall be valid only if it is made without coercion of any kind.

4. An accused person acquitted by a nonappealable judgment shall not be subjected to a new trial for the same cause.

5. Criminal proceedings shall be public, except insofar as may be necessary to protect the interests of justice.

Article 9
Freedom from "ex post facto" laws

No one shall be convicted of any act or omission that did not constitute a criminal offense, under the applicable law, at the time it was committed. A heavier penalty shall not be imposed than the one that was applicable at the time the criminal offense was committed. If subsequent to the commission of the offense the law provides for the imposition of a lighter punishment, the guilty person shall benefit therefrom.

Article 10
Right to compensation

Every person has the right to be compensated in accordance with the law in the event he has been sentenced by a final judgment through a miscarriage of justice.

Article 11
Right to privacy

1. Everyone has the right to have his honor respected and his dignity recognized.

2. No one may be the object of arbitrary or abusive interference with his private life, his family, his home, or his correspondence, or of unlawful attacks on his honor or reputation.

3. Everyone has the right to the protection of the law against such interference or attacks.

Article 12
Freedom of conscience and religion

1. Everyone has the right to freedom of conscience and of religion. This right includes freedom to maintain or to change one's religion or beliefs, and freedom to profess or disseminate one's religion or beliefs, either individually or together with others, in public or in private.

2. No one shall be subject to restrictions that might impair his freedom to maintain or to change his religion or beliefs.

3. Freedom to manifest one's religion and beliefs may be subject only to the limitations prescribed by law that are necessary to protect public safety, order, health, or morals, or the rights or freedoms of others.

4. Parents or guardians, as the case may be, have the right to provide for the religious and moral education of their children or wards that is in accord with their own convictions.

Article 13
Freedom of thought and expression

1. Everyone has the right to freedom of thought and expression. This right includes freedom to seek, receive, and impart information and ideas of all kinds, regardless of frontiers, either orally, in writing, in print, in the form of art, or through any other medium of one's choice.

2. The exercise of the right provided for in the foregoing paragraph shall not be subject to prior censorship but shall be subject to subsequent imposition of liability, which shall be expressly established by law to the extent necessary to ensure:

a. Respect for the rights or reputations of others; or

b. The protection of national security, public order, or public health or morals.

3. The right of expression may not be restricted by indirect methods or means, such as the abuse of government or private controls over newsprint, radio broadcasting frequencies, or equipment used in the dissemination of information, or by any other means tending to impede the communication and circulation of ideas and opinions.

4. Notwithstanding the provisions of paragraph 2 above, public entertainments may be subject by law to prior censorship for the sole purpose of regulating access to them for the moral protection of childhood and adolescence.

5. Any propaganda for war and any advocacy of national, racial, or religious hatred that constitute incitements to lawless violence or to any other similar illegal action against any person or group of persons on any grounds including those of race, color, religion, language, or national origin shall be considered as offenses punishable by law.

Article 14
Right of reply

1. Anyone injured by inaccurate or offensive statements or ideas disseminated to the public in general by a

legally regulated medium of communication has the right to reply or to make a correction using the same communications outlet, under such conditions as the law may establish.

2. The correction or reply shall not in any case remit other legal liabilities that may have been incurred.

3. For the effective protection of honor and reputation, every publisher, and every newspaper, motion picture, radio, and television company, shall have a person responsible who is not protected by immunities or special privileges.

Article 15
Right of assembly

The right of peaceful assembly, without arms, is recognized. No restrictions may be placed on the exercise of this right other than those imposed in conformity with the law and necessary in a democratic society in the interest of national security, public safety or public order, or to protect public health or morals or the rights or freedoms of others.

Article 16
Freedom of association

1. Everyone has the right to associate freely for ideological, religious, political, economic, labor, social, cultural, sports, or other purposes.

2. The exercise of this right shall be subject only to such restrictions established by law as may be necessary in a democratic society, in the interest of national security, public safety or public order, or to protect public health or morals or the rights and freedoms of others.

3. The provisions of this article do not bar the imposition of legal restrictions, including even deprivation of the exercise of the right of association, on members of the armed forces and the police.

Article 17
Rights of the family

1. The family is the natural and fundamental group unit of society and is entitled to protection by society and the state.

2. The right of men and women of marriageable age to marry and to raise a family shall be recognized, if they meet the conditions required by domestic laws, insofar as such conditions do not affect the principle of nondiscrimination established in this Convention.

3. No marriage shall be entered into without the free and full consent of the intending spouses.

4. The States Parties shall take appropriate steps to ensure the equality of rights and the adequate balancing of responsibilities of the spouses as to marriage, during marriage, and in the event of its dissolution. In case of dissolution, provision shall be made for the necessary protection of any children solely on the basis of their own best interests.

5. The law shall recognize equal rights for children born out of wedlock and those born in wedlock.

Article 18
Right to a name

Every person has the right to a given name and to the surnames of his parents or that of one of them. The law shall regulate the manner in which this right shall be ensured for all, by the use of assumed names if necessary.

Article 19
Rights of the child

Every minor child has the right to the measures of protection required by his condition as a minor on the part of his family, society, and the state.

Article 20
Right to nationality

1. Every person has the right to a nationality.

2. Every person has the right to the nationality of the state in whose territory he was born if he does not have the right to any other nationality.

3. No one shall be arbitrarily deprived of his nationality or of the right to change it.

Article 21
Right to property

1. Everyone has the right to the use and enjoyment of his property. The law may subordinate such use and enjoyment to the interest of society.

2. No one shall be deprived of his property except upon payment of just compensation, for reasons of public utility or social interest, and in the cases and according to the forms established by law.

3. Usury and any other form of exploitation of man by man shall be prohibited by law.

Article 22
Freedom of movement and residence

1. Every person lawfully in the territory of a State Party has the right to move about in it, and to reside in it subject to the provisions of the law.

2. Every person has the right to leave any country freely, including his own.

3. The exercise of the foregoing rights may be restricted only pursuant to a law to the extent necessary in a democratic society to prevent crime or to protect national security, public safety, public order, public morals, public health, or the rights or freedoms of others.

4. The exercise of the rights recognized in paragraph 1 may also be restricted by law in designated zones for reasons of public interest.

5. No one can be expelled from the territory of the state of which he is a national or be deprived of the right to enter it.

6. An alien lawfully in the territory of a State Party to this Convention may be expelled from it only pursuant to a decision reached in accordance with law.

7. Every person has the right to seek and be granted asylum in a foreign territory, in accordance with the legislation of the state and international conventions, in the event he is being pursued for political offenses or related common crimes.

8. In no case may an alien be deported or returned to a country, regardless of whether or not it is his country of origin, if in that country his right to life or personal freedom is in danger of being violated because of his race, nationality, religion, social status, or political opinions.

9. The collective expulsion of aliens is prohibited.

Article 23
Right to participate in Government

1. Every citizen shall enjoy the following rights and opportunities:

a. To take part in the conduct of public affairs, directly or through freely chosen representatives;

b. To vote and to be elected in genuine periodic elections, which shall be by universal and equal suffrage and by secret ballot that guarantees the free expression of the will of the voters; and

c. To have access, under general conditions of equality, to the public service of his country.

2. The law may regulate the exercise of the rights and opportunities referred to in the preceding paragraph only on the basis of age, nationality, residence, language, education, civil and mental capacity, or sentencing by a competent court in criminal proceedings.

Article 24
Right to equal protection

All persons are equal before the law. Consequently, they are entitled, without discrimination, to equal protection of the law.

Article 25
Right to judicial protection

1. Everyone has the right to simple and prompt recourse, or any other effective recourse, to a competent court or tribunal for protection against acts that violate his fundamental rights recognized by the constitution or laws of the state concerned or by this Convention, even though such violation may have been committed by persons acting in the course of their official duties.

2. The States Parties undertake:

a. To ensure that any person claiming such remedy shall have his rights determined by the competent authority provided for by the legal system of the state;

b. To develop the possibilities of judicial remedy; and

c. To ensure that the competent authorities shall enforce such remedies when granted.

CHAPTER III. ECONOMIC, SOCIAL, AND CULTURAL RIGHTS

Article 26
Progressive development

The States Parties undertake to adopt measures, both internally and through international cooperation, especially those of an economic and technical nature, with a view to achieving progressively, by legislation or other appropriate means, the full realization of the rights implicit in the economic, social, educational, scientific, and cultural standards set forth in the Charter of the Organization of American States as amended by the Protocol of Buenos Aires. 2/

CHAPTER IV. SUSPENSION OF GUARANTEES, INTERPRETATION, AND APPLICATION

Article 27
Suspension of guarantees

1. In time of war, public danger, or other emergency that threatens the independence or security of a State Party, it may take measures derogating from its obligations under the present Convention to the extent and for the period of time strictly required by the exigencies of the situation, provided that such measures are not inconsistent with its other obligations under international law and do not involve discrimination on the ground of race, color, sex, language, religion, or social origin.

2. The foregoing provision does not authorize any suspension of the following articles: Article 3 (Right to juridical personality), Article 4 (Right to life), Article 5 (Right to humane treatment), Article 6 (Freedom from slavery), Article 9 (Freedom from *ex post facto* laws), Article 12 (Freedom of conscience and religion), Article 17 (Rights of the family), Article 18 (Right to a name), Article 19 (Rights of the child), Article 20 (Right to nationality), and Article 23 (Right to participate in Gov-

2/ United Nations, *Treaty Series*, vol. 721, p. 324.

ernment), or of the judicial guarantees essential for the protection of such rights.

3. Any State Party availing itself of the right of suspension shall immediately inform the other States Parties, through the Secretary General of the Organization of American States, of the provisions the application of which it has suspended, the reasons that gave rise to the suspension, and the date set for the termination of such suspension.

Article 28
Federal clause

1. Where a State Party is constituted as a federal state, the national government of such State Party shall implement all the provisions of the Convention over whose subject matter it exercises legislative and judicial jurisdiction.

2. With respect to the provisions over whose subject matter the constituent units of the federal state have jurisdiction, the national government shall immediately take suitable measures, in accordance with its constitution and its laws, to the end that the competent authorities of the constituent units may adopt appropriate provisions for the fulfillment of this Convention.

3. Whenever two or more States Parties agree to form a federation or other type of association, they shall take care that the resulting federal or other compact contains the provisions necessary for continuing and rendering effective the standards of this Convention in the new state that is organized.

Article 29
Restrictions regarding interpretation

No provision of this Convention shall be interpreted as:

a. Permitting any State Party, group, or person to suppress the enjoyment or exercise of the rights and freedoms recognized in this Convention or to restrict them to a greater extent than is provided for herein;

b. Restricting the enjoyment or exercise of any right or freedom recognized by virtue of the laws of any State Party or by virtue of another convention to which one of the said states is a party;

c. Precluding other rights or guarantees that are inherent in the human personality or derived from representative democracy as a form of government; or

d. Excluding or limiting the effect that the American Declaration of the Rights and Duties of Man and other international acts of the same nature may have.

Article 30
Scope of restrictions

The restrictions that, pursuant to this Convention, may be placed on the enjoyment or exercise of the rights or freedoms recognized herein may not be applied except in accordance with laws enacted for reasons of general interest and in accordance with the purpose for which such restrictions have been established.

Article 31
Recognition of other rights

Other rights and freedoms recognized in accordance with the procedures established in Articles 76 and 77 may be included in the system of protection of this Convention.

CHAPTER V. PERSONAL RESPONSIBILITIES

Article 32
Relationship between duties and rights

1. Every person has responsibilities to his family, his community, and mankind.

2. The rights of each person are limited by the rights of others, by the security of all, and by the just demands of the general welfare, in a democratic society.

PART II. MEANS OF PROTECTION

CHAPTER VI. COMPETENT ORGANS

Article 33

The following organs shall have competence with respect to matters relating to the fulfillment of the commitments made by the States Parties to this Convention:

a. The Inter-American Commission on Human Rights, referred to as "The Commission"; and

b. The Inter-American Court of Human Rights, referred to as "The Court."

CHAPTER VII. INTER-AMERICAN COMMISSION ON HUMAN RIGHTS

Section 1. Organization

Article 34

The Inter-American Commission on Human Rights shall be composed of seven members, who shall be persons of high moral character and recognized competence in the field of human rights.

Article 35

The Commission shall represent all the member countries of the Organization of American States.

Article 36

1. The members of the Commission shall be elected in a personal capacity by the General Assembly of the Organization from a list of candidates proposed by the governments of the member states.

2. Each of those governments may propose up to three candidates, who may be nationals of the states proposing them or of any other member state of the Organization of American States. When a slate of three is proposed, at least one of the candidates shall be a national of a state other than the one proposing the slate.

Article 37

1. The members of the Commission shall be elected for a term of four years and may be reelected only once, but the terms of three of the members chosen in the first election shall expire at the end of two years. Immediately following that election the General Assembly shall determine the names of those three members by lot.

2. No two nationals of the same state may be members of the Commission.

Article 38

Vacancies that may occur on the Commission for reasons other than the normal expiration of a term shall be filled by the Permanent Council of the Organization in accordance with the provisions of the Statute of the Commission.

Article 39

The Commission shall prepare its Statute, which it shall submit to the General Assembly for approval. It shall establish its own Regulations.

Article 40

Secretariat services for the Commission shall be furnished by the appropriate specialized unit of the General Secretariat of the Organization. This unit shall be provided with the resources required to accomplish the tasks assigned to it by the Commission.

Section 2. Functions

Article 41

The main function of the Commission shall be to promote respect for and defense of human rights. In the exercise of its mandate, it shall have the following functions and powers:

a. To develop an awareness of human rights among the peoples of America;

b. To make recommendations to the governments of the member states, when it considers such action advisable, for the adoption of progressive measures in favor of human rights within the framework of their domestic law and constitutional provisions as well as appropriate measures to further the observance of those rights;

c. To prepare such studies or reports as it considers advisable in the performance of its duties;

d. To request the governments of the member states to supply it with information on the measures adopted by them in matters of human rights;

e. To respond, through the General Secretariat of the Organization of American States, to inquiries made by the member states on matters related to human rights and, within the limits of its possibilities, to provide those states with the advisory services they request;

f. To take action on petitions and other communications pursuant to its authority under the provisions of Articles 44 through 51 of this Convention; and

g. To submit an annual report to the General Assembly of the Organization of American States.

Article 42

The States Parties shall transmit to the Commission a copy of each of the reports and studies that they submit annually to the Executive Committees of the Inter-American Economic and Social Council and the Inter-American Council for Education, Science, and Culture, in their respective fields, so that the Commission may watch over the promotion of the rights implicit in the economic, social, educational, scientific, and cultural standards set forth in the Charter of the Organization of American States as amended by the Protocol of Buenos Aires.

Article 43

The States Parties undertake to provide the Commission with such information as it may request of them as to the manner in which their domestic law ensures the effective application of any provisions of this Convention.

Section 3. Competence

Article 44

Any person or group of persons, or any nongovernmental entity legally recognized in one or more member states of the Organization, may lodge petitions with the Commission containing denunciations or complaints of violation of this Convention by a State Party.

Article 45

1. Any State Party may, when it deposits its instrument of ratification of or adherence to this Convention, or at any later time, declare that it recognizes the competence of the Commission to receive and examine communications in which a State Party alleges that another State Party has committed a violation of a human right set forth in this Convention.

2. Communications presented by virtue of this article may be admitted and examined only if they are presented by a State Party that has made a declaration recognizing the aforementioned competence of the Commission. The Commission shall not admit any communication against a State Party that has not made such a declaration.

3. A declaration concerning recognition of competence may be made to be valid for an indefinite time, for a specified period, or for a specific case.

4. Declarations shall be deposited with the General Secretariat of the Organization of American States, which shall transmit copies thereof to the member states of that Organization.

Article 46

1. Admission by the Commission of a petition or communication lodged in accordance with Articles 44 or 45 shall be subject to the following requirements:

a. That the remedies under domestic law have been pursued and exhausted in accordance with generally recognized principles of international law;

b. That the petition or communication is lodged within a period of six months from the date on which the party alleging violation of his rights was notified of the final judgment;

c. That the subject of the petition or communication is not pending in another international proceeding for settlement; and

d. That, in the case of Article 44, the petition contains the name, nationality, profession, domicile, and signature of the person or persons or of the legal representative of the entity lodging the petition.

2. The provisions of paragraphs 1a and 1b of this article shall not be applicable when:

a. The domestic legislation of the state concerned does not afford due process of law for the protection of the right or rights that have allegedly been violated;

b. The party alleging violation of his rights has been denied access to the remedies under domestic law or has been prevented from exhausting them; or

c. There has been unwarranted delay in rendering a final judgment under the aforementioned remedies.

Article 47

The Commission shall consider inadmissible any petition or communication submitted under Articles 44 or 45 if:

a. Any of the requirements indicated in Article 46 has not been met;

b. The petition or communication does not state facts that tend to establish a violation of the rights guaranteed by this Convention;

c. The statements of the petitioner or of the state indicate that the petition or communication is manifestly groundless or obviously out of order; or

d. The petition or communication is substantially the same as one previously studied by the Commission or by another international organization.

Section 4. Procedure

Article 48

1. When the Commission receives a petition or communication alleging violation of any of the rights protected by this Convention, it shall proceed as follows:

a. If it considers the petition or communication admissible, it shall request information from the government of the state indicated as being responsible for the alleged violations and shall furnish that government a transcript of the pertinent portions of the petition or communication. This information shall be submitted within a reasonable period to be determined by the Commission in accordance with the circumstances of each case.

b. After the information has been received, or after the period established has elapsed and the information has not been received, the Commission shall ascertain whether the grounds for the petition or communication still exist. If they do not, the Commission shall order the record to be closed.

c. The Commission may also declare the petition or communication inadmissible or out of order on the basis of information or evidence subsequently received.

d. If the record has not been closed, the Commission shall, with the knowledge of the parties, examine the matter set forth in the petition or communication in order to verify the facts. If necessary and advisable, the Commission shall carry out an investigation, for the effective conduct of which it shall request, and the states concerned shall furnish to it, all necessary facilities.

e. The Commission may request the states concerned to furnish any pertinent information and, if so requested, shall hear oral statements or receive written statements from the parties concerned.

f. The Commission shall place itself at the disposal of the parties concerned with a view to reaching a friendly settlement of the matter on the basis of respect for the human rights recognized in this Convention.

2. However, in serious and urgent cases, only the presentation of a petition or communication that fulfills all the formal requirements of admissibility shall be necessary in order for the Commission to conduct an investigation with the prior consent of the state in whose territory a violation has allegedly been committed.

Article 49

If a friendly settlement has been reached in accordance with paragraph 1f of Article 48, the Commission shall draw up a report, which shall be transmitted to the petitioner and to the States Parties to this Convention, and shall then be communicated to the Secretary General of the Organization of American States for publication. This report shall contain a brief statement of the facts and of the solution reached. If any party in the case so requests, the fullest possible information shall be provided to it.

Article 50

1. If a settlement is not reached, the Commission shall, within the time limit established by its Statute, draw up a report setting forth the facts and stating its conclusions. If the report, in whole or in part, does not represent the unanimous agreement of the members of the Commission, any member may attach to it a separate opinion. The written and oral statements made by the parties in accordance with paragraph 1e of Article 48 shall also be attached to the report.

2. The report shall be transmitted to the states concerned, which shall not be at liberty to publish it.

3. In transmitting the report, the Committee may make such proposals and recommendations as it sees fit.

Article 51

1. If, within a period of three months from the date of the transmittal of the report of the Commission to the states concerned, the matter has not either been settled or submitted by the Commission or by the state concerned to the Court and its jurisdiction accepted, the Commission may, by the vote of an absolute majority of its members, set forth its opinion and conclusions concerning the question submitted for its consideration.

2. Where appropriate, the Commission shall make pertinent recommendations and shall prescribe a period within which the state is to take the measures that are incumbent upon it to remedy the situation examined.

3. When the prescribed period has expired, the Commission shall decide by the vote of an absolute majority of its members whether the state has taken adequate measures and whether to publish its report.

CHAPTER VIII. INTER-AMERICAN COURT OF HUMAN RIGHTS

Section 1. Organization

Article 52

1. The Court shall consist of seven judges, nationals of the member states of the Organization, elected in an individual capacity from among jurists of the highest moral authority and of recognized competence in the field of human rights, who possess the qualifications required for the exercise of the highest judicial functions in conformity with the law of the state of which they are nationals or of the state that proposes them as candidates.

2. No two judges may be nationals of the same state.

Article 53

1. The judges of the Court shall be elected by secret ballot by an absolute majority vote of the States Parties to the Convention, in the General Assembly of the Organization, from a panel of candidates proposed by those states.

2. Each of the States Parties may propose up to three candidates, nationals of the state that proposes them or of any other member state of the Organization of American States. When a slate of three is proposed, at least one of the candidates shall be a national of a state other than the one proposing the slate.

Article 54

1. The judges of the Court shall be elected for a term of six years and may be reelected only once. The term of three of the judges chosen in the first election shall expire at the end of three years. Immediately after the election, the names of the three judges shall be determined by lot in the General Assembly.

2. A judge elected to replace a judge whose term has not expired shall complete the term of the latter.

3. The judges shall continue in office until the expiration of their term. However, they shall continue to serve with regard to cases that they have begun to hear and that are still pending, for which purposes they shall not be replaced by the newly elected judges.

Article 55

1. If a judge is a national of any of the States Parties to a case submitted to the Court, he shall retain his right to hear that case.

2. If one of the judges called upon to hear a case should be a national of one [of] the States Parties to the

case, any other State Party in the case may appoint a person of its choice to serve on the Court as an *ad hoc* judge.

3. If among the judges called upon to hear a case none is a national of any of the States Parties to the case, each of the latter may appoint an *ad hoc* judge.

4. An *ad hoc* judge shall possess the qualifications indicated in Article 52.

5. If several States Parties to the Convention should have the same interest in a case, they shall be considered as a single party for purposes of the above provisions. In case of doubt, the Court shall decide.

Article 56

Five judges shall constitute a quorum for the transaction of business by the Court.

Article 57

The Commission shall appear in all cases before the Court.

Article 58

1. The Court shall have its seat at the place determined by the States Parties to the Convention in the General Assembly of the Organization; however, it may convene in the territory of any member state of the Organization of American States when a majority of the Court consider it desirable, and with the prior consent of the state concerned. The seat of the Court may be changed by the States Parties to the Convention in the General Assembly by a two-thirds vote.

2. The Court shall appoint its own Secretary.

3. The Secretary shall have his office at the place where the Court has its seat and shall attend the meetings that the Court may hold away from its seat.

Article 59

The Court shall establish its Secretariat, which shall function under the direction of the Secretary of the Court, in accordance with the administrative standards of the General Secretariat of the Organization in all respect[s] not incompatible with the independence of the Court. The staff of the Court's Secretariat shall be appointed by the Secretary General of the Organization, in consultation with the Secretary of the Court.

Article 60

The Court shall draw up its Statute which it shall submit to the General Assembly for approval. It shall adopt its own Rules of Procedure.

Section 2. *Jurisdiction and functions*

Article 61

1. Only the States Parties and the Commission shall have the right to submit a case to the Court.

2. In order for the Court to hear a case, it is necessary that the procedures set forth in Articles 48 to 50 shall have been completed.

Article 62

1. A State Party may, upon depositing its instrument of ratification or adherence to this Convention, or at any subsequent time, declare that it recognizes as binding, *ipso facto*, and not requiring special agreement, the jurisdiction of the Court on all matters relating to the interpretation or application of this Convention.

2. Such declaration may be made unconditionally, on the condition of reciprocity, for a specified period, or for specific cases. It shall be presented to the Secretary General of the Organization, who shall transmit copies thereof to the other member states of the Organization and to the Secretary of the Court.

3. The jurisdiction of the Court shall comprise all cases concerning the interpretation and application of the provisions of this Convention that are submitted to it, provided that the States Parties to the case recognize or have recognized such jurisdiction, whether by special declaration pursuant to the preceding paragraphs, or by a special agreement.

Article 63

1. If the Court finds that there has been a violation of a right or freedom protected by this Convention, the Court shall rule that the injured party be ensured the enjoyment of his right or freedom that was violated. It shall also rule, if appropriate, that the consequences of the measure or situation that constituted the breach of such right or freedom be remedied and that fair compensation be paid to the injured party.

2. In cases of extreme gravity and urgency, and when necessary to avoid irreparable damage to persons, the Court shall adopt such provisional measures as it deems pertinent in matters it has under consideration. With respect to a case not yet submitted to the Court, it may act at the request of the Commission.

Article 64

1. The member states of the Organization may consult the Court regarding the interpretation of this Convention or of other treaties concerning the protection of human rights in the American states. Within their spheres of competence, the organs listed in Chapter X of the Charter of the Organization of American States, as

amended by the Protocol of Buenos Aires, may in like manner consult the Court.

2. The Court, at the request of a member state of the Organization, may provide that state with opinions regarding the compatibility of any of its domestic laws with the aforesaid international instruments.

Article 65

To each regular session of the General Assembly of the Organization of American States the Court shall submit, for the Assembly's consideration, a report on its work during the previous year. It shall specify, in particular, the cases in which a state has not complied with its judgments, making any pertinent recommendations.

Section 3. Procedure

Article 66

1. Reasons shall be given for the judgment of the Court.

2. If the judgment does not represent in whole or in part the unanimous opinion of the judges, any judge shall be entitled to have his dissenting or separate opinion attached to the judgment.

Article 67

The judgment of the Court shall be final and not subject to appeal. In case of disagreement as to the meaning or scope of the judgment, the Court shall interpret it at the request of any of the parties, provided the request is made within ninety days from the date of notification of the judgment.

Article 68

1. The States Parties to the Convention undertake to comply with the judgment of the Court in any case to which they are parties.

2. That part of a judgment that stipulates compensatory damages may be executed in the country concerned in accordance with domestic procedure governing the execution of judgments against the state.

Article 69

The parties to the case shall be notified of the judgment of the Court and it shall be transmitted to the States Parties to the Convention.

CHAPTER IX. COMMON PROVISIONS

Article 70

1. The judges of the Court and the members of the Commission shall enjoy, from the moment of their election and throughout their term of office, the immunities extended to diplomatic agents in accordance with international law. During the exercise of their official function they shall, in addition, enjoy the diplomatic privileges necessary for the performance of their duties.

2. At no time shall the judges of the Court or the members of the Commission be held liable for any decisions or opinions issued in the exercise of their functions.

Article 71

The position of judge of the Court or member of the Commission is incompatible with any other activity that might affect the independence or impartiality of such judge or member, as determined in the respective statutes.

Article 72

The judges of the Court and the members of the Commission shall receive emoluments and travel allowances in the form and under the conditions set forth in their statutes, with due regard for the importance and independence of their office. Such emoluments and travel allowances shall be determined in the budget of the Organization of American States, which shall also include the expenses of the Court and its Secretariat. To this end, the Court shall draw up its own budget and submit it for approval to the General Assembly through the General Secretariat. The latter may not introduce any changes in it.

Article 73

The General Assembly may, only at the request of the Commission or the Court, as the case may be, determine sanctions to be applied against members of the Commission or judges of the Court when there are justifiable grounds for such action as set forth in the respective statutes. A vote of a two-thirds majority of the member states of the Organization shall be required for a decision in the case of members of the Commission and, in the case of judges of the Court, a two-thirds majority vote of the States Parties to the Convention shall also be required.

PART III. GENERAL AND TRANSITORY PROVISIONS

CHAPTER X. SIGNATURE, RATIFICATION, RESERVATIONS, AMENDMENTS, PROTOCOLS, AND DENUNCIATION

Article 74

1. This Convention shall be open for signature and ratification by or adherence of any member state of the Organization of American States.

2. Ratification of or adherence to this Convention shall be made by the deposit of an instrument of ratification or adherence with the General Secretariat of the Organization of American States. As soon as eleven states

have deposited their instruments of ratification or adherence, the Convention shall enter into force. With respect to any state that ratifies or adheres thereafter, the Convention shall enter into force on the date of the deposit of its instrument of ratification or adherence.

3. The Secretary General shall inform all member states of the Organization of the entry into force of the Convention.

Article 75

This Convention shall be subject to reservations only in conformity with the provisions of the Vienna Convention on the Law of Treaties signed on May 23, 1969. 3/

Article 76

1. Proposals to amend this Convention may be submitted to the General Assembly for the action it deems appropriate by any State Party directly, and by the Commission or the Court through the Secretary General.

2. Amendments shall enter into force for the states ratifying them on the date when two-thirds of the States Parties to this Convention have deposited their respective instruments of ratification. With respect to the other States Parties, the amendments shall enter into force on the dates on which they deposit their respective instruments of ratification.

Article 77

1. In accordance with Article 31, any State Party and the Commission may submit proposed protocols to this Convention for consideration by the States Parties at the General Assembly with a view to gradually including other rights and freedoms within its system of protection.

2. Each protocol shall determine the manner of its entry into force and shall be applied only among the States Parties to it.

Article 78

1. The States Parties may denounce this Convention at the expiration of a five-year period starting from the date of its entry into force and by means of notice given one year in advance. Notice of the denunciation shall be addressed to the Secretary General of the Organization, who shall inform the other States Parties.

2. Such a denunciation shall not have the effect of releasing the State Party concerned from the obligations contained in this Convention with respect to any act that may constitute a violation of those obligations and that has been taken by that state prior to the effective date of denunciation.

CHAPTER XI.   TRANSITORY PROVISIONS

Section 1.   Inter-American Commission on Human Rights

Article 79

Upon the entry into force of this Convention, the Secretary General shall, in writing, request each member state of the Organization to present, within ninety days, its candidates for membership on the Inter-American Commission on Human Rights. The Secretary General shall prepare a list in alphabetical order of the candidates presented, and transmit it to the member states of the Organization at least thirty days prior to the next session of the General Assembly.

Article 80

The members of the Commission shall be elected by secret ballot of the General Assembly from the list of candidates referred to in Article 79. The candidates who obtain the largest number of votes and an absolute majority of the votes of the representatives of the member states shall be declared elected. Should it become necessary to have several ballots in order to elect all the members of the Commission, the candidates who receive the smallest number of votes shall be eliminated successively, in the manner determined by the General Assembly.

Section 2.   Inter-American Court of Human Rights

Article 81

Upon the entry into force of this Convention, the Secretary General shall, in writing, request each State Party to present, within ninety days, its candidates for membership on the Inter-American Court of Human Rights. The Secretary General shall prepare a list in alphabetical order of the candidates presented and transmit it to the States Parties at least thirty days prior to the next session of the General Assembly.

Article 82

The judges of the Court shall be elected from the list of candidates referred to in Article 81, by secret ballot of the States Parties to the Convention in the General Assembly. The candidates who obtain the largest number of votes and an absolute majority of the votes of the representatives of the States Parties shall be declared elected. Should it become necessary to have several ballots in order to elect all the judges of the Court, the candidates who receive the smallest number of votes shall be eliminated successively, in the manner determined by the States Parties.

3/ United Nations, *Treaty Series*, vol. 1155, No. I-18232.

STATEMENTS AND RESERVATIONS

Statement of Chile

The Delegation of Chile signs this Convention, subject to its subsequent parliamentary approval and ratification, in accordance with the constitutional rules in force.

Statement of Ecuador

The Delegation of Ecuador has the honor of signing the American Convention on Human Rights. It does not believe that it is necessary to make any specific reservation at this time, without prejudice to the general power set forth in the Convention itself that leaves the governments free to ratify it or not.

Reservation of Uruguay

Article 80.2 of the Constitution of Uruguay provides that citizenship is suspended "for a person indicted according to law in a criminal prosecution that may result in a sentence of imprisonment in a penitentiary". This restriction on the exercise of the rights recognized in Article 23 of the Convention is not envisaged among the circumstances provided for in this respect by paragraph 2 of Article 23, for which reason the Delegation of Uruguay expresses a reservation on this matter.

IN WITNESS WHEREOF, the undersigned Plenipotentiaries, whose full powers were found in good and due form, sign this Convention, which shall be called "Pact of San José, Costa Rica" (in the city of San José, Costa Rica, this twenty-second day of November, nineteen hundred and sixty-nine).

Document 37

General Assembly resolution on the United Nations Relief and Works Agency for Palestine Refugees in the Near East

A/RES/2535 B (XXIV), 10 December 1969

B

The General Assembly,

Recognizing that the problem of the Palestine Arab refugees has arisen from the denial of their inalienable rights under the Charter of the United Nations and the Universal Declaration of Human Rights,

Gravely concerned that the denial of their rights has been aggravated by the reported acts of collective punishment, arbitrary detention, curfews, destruction of homes and property, deportation and other repressive acts against the refugees and other inhabitants of the occupied territories,

Recalling Security Council resolution 237 (1967) of 14 June 1967,

Recalling also its resolution 2252 (ES-V) of 4 July 1967 and its resolution 2452 A (XXIII) of 19 December 1968 calling upon the Government of Israel to take effective and immediate steps for the return without delay of those inhabitants who had fled the areas since the outbreak of hostilities,

Desirous of giving effect to its resolutions for relieving the plight of the displaced persons and the refugees,

1. *Reaffirms* the inalienable rights of the people of Palestine;

2. *Draws the attention* of the Security Council to the grave situation resulting from Israeli policies and practices in the occupied territories and Israel's refusal to implement the above resolutions;

3. *Requests* the Security Council to take effective measures in accordance with the relevant provisions of the Charter of the United Nations to ensure the implementation of these resolutions.

Document 38

Economic and Social Council resolution instituting procedures to enable the Commission on Human Rights and the Subcommission on Prevention of Discrimination and Protection of Minorities to deal with communications relating to violations of human rights and fundamental freedoms in private meetings

E/RES/1503 (XLVIII), 27 May 1970

The Economic and Social Council,

Noting resolutions 7 (XXVI) 1/ and 17 (XXV) 2/ of the Commission on Human Rights and resolution 2 (XXI) 3/ of the Sub-Commission on Prevention of Discrimination and Protection of Minorities,

1. *Authorizes* the Sub-Commission on Prevention of Discrimination and Protection of Minorities to appoint a working group consisting of not more than five of its members, with due regard to geographical distribution, to meet once a year in private meetings for a period not exceeding ten days immediately before the sessions of the Sub-Commission to consider all communications, including replies of Governments thereon, received by the Secretary-General under Council resolution 728 F (XXVIII) of 30 July 1959 with a view to bringing to the attention of the Sub-Commission those communications, together with replies of Governments, if any, which appear to reveal a consistent pattern of gross and reliably attested violations of human rights and fundamental freedoms within the terms of reference of the Sub-Commission;

2. *Decides* that the Sub-Commission on Prevention of Discrimination and Protection of Minorities should, as the first stage in the implementation of the present resolution, devise at its twenty-third session appropriate procedures for dealing with the question of admissibility of communications received by the Secretary-General under Council resolution 728 F (XXVIII) and in accordance with Council resolution 1235 (XLII) of 6 June 1967;

3. *Requests* the Secretary-General to prepare a document on the question of admissibility of communications for the Sub-Commission's consideration at its twenty-third session;

4. *Further requests* the Secretary-General:

(a) To furnish to the members of the Sub-Commission every month a list of communications prepared by him in accordance with Council resolution 728 F (XXVIII) and a brief description of them, together with the text of any replies received from Governments;

(b) To make available to the members of the working group at their meetings the originals of such communications listed as they may request, having due regard to the provisions of paragraph 2 (b) of Council resolution 728 F (XXVIII) concerning the divulging of the identity of the authors of communications;

(c) To circulate to the members of the Sub-Commission, in the working languages, the originals of such communications as are referred to the Sub-Commission by the working group;

5. *Requests* the Sub-Commission on Prevention of Discrimination and Protection of Minorities to consider in private meetings, in accordance with paragraph 1 above, the communications brought before it in accordance with the decision of a majority of the members of the working group and any replies of Governments relating thereto and other relevant information, with a view to determining whether to refer to the Commission on Human Rights particular situations which appear to reveal a consistent pattern of gross and reliably attested violations of human rights requiring consideration by the Commission;

6. *Requests* the Commission on Human Rights after it has examined any situation referred to it by the Sub-Commission to determine:

(a) Whether it requires a thorough study by the Commission and a report and recommendations thereon to the Council in accordance with paragraph 3 of Council resolution 1235 (XLII);

(b) Whether it may be a subject of any investigation by an *ad hoc* committee to be appointed by the Commission which shall be undertaken only with the express consent of the State concerned and shall be conducted in constant cooperation with that State and under conditions determined by agreement with it. In any event, the investigation may be undertaken only if:

(i) All available means at the national level have been resorted to and exhausted;

(ii) The situation does not relate to a matter which is being dealt with under other procedures prescribed in the constituent instruments of, or conventions adopted by, the United Nations and the specialized agencies, or in regional conventions, or which the

---

1/ See *Official Records of the Economic and Social Council, Forty-eighth Session, Supplement No. 5* (E/4816), chap. XXIII.
2/ Ibid., *Forty-sixth Session,* document E/4621, chap. XVIII.
3/ E/CN.4/976, chap. VI.

State concerned wishes to submit to other procedures in accordance with general or special international agreements to which it is a party.

7. *Decides* that if the Commission on Human Rights appoints an *ad hoc* committee to carry on an investigation with the consent of the State concerned:

(a) The composition of the committee shall be determined by the Commission. The members of the committee shall be independent persons whose competence and impartiality is beyond question. Their appointment shall be subject to the consent of the Government concerned;

(b) The committee shall establish its own rules of procedure. It shall be subject to the quorum rule. It shall have authority to receive communications and hear witnesses, as necessary. The investigation shall be conducted in cooperation with the Government concerned;

(c) The committee's procedure shall be confidential, its proceedings shall be conducted in private meetings and its communications shall not be publicized in any way;

(d) The committee shall strive for friendly solutions before, during and even after the investigation;

(e) The committee shall report to the Commission on Human Rights with such observations and suggestions as it may deem appropriate;

8. *Decides* that all actions envisaged in the implementation of the present resolution by the Sub-Commission on Prevention of Discrimination and Protection of Minorities or the Commission on Human Rights shall remain confidential until such time as the Commission may decide to make recommendations to the Economic and Social Council;

9. *Decides* to authorize the Secretary-General to provide all facilities which may be required to carry out the present resolution, making use of the existing staff of the Division of Human Rights of the United Nations Secretariat;

10. *Decides* that the procedure set out in the present resolution for dealing with communications relating to violations of human rights and fundamental freedoms should be reviewed if any new organ entitled to deal with such communications should be established within the United Nations or by international agreement.

Document 39

Resolution 1 (XXIV) of the Subcommission on Prevention of Discrimination and Protection of Minorities concerning procedures for the implementation of Economic and Social Council resolution 1503 (XLVIII)

13 August 1971

1 (XXIV). QUESTION OF THE VIOLATION OF HUMAN RIGHTS AND FUNDAMENTAL FREEDOMS, INCLUDING POLICIES OF RACIAL DISCRIMINATION AND SEGREGATION AND OF *APARTHEID* IN ALL COUNTRIES, WITH PARTICULAR REFERENCE TO COLONIAL AND OTHER DEPENDENT COUNTRIES AND TERRITORIES 1/

The Sub-Commission on Prevention of Discrimination and Protection of Minorities,

Considering that the Economic and Social Council, by its resolution 1503 (XLVIII), decided that the Sub-Commission should devise appropriate procedures for dealing with the question of admissibility of communications received by the Secretary-General under Council resolution 728 F (XXVIII) of 30 July 1959 and in accordance with Council resolution 1235 (XLII) of 6 June 1967,

Adopts the following provisional procedures for dealing with the question of admissibility of communications referred to above:

(1) *Standards and criteria*

(a) The object of the communication must not be inconsistent with the relevant principles of the Charter, of the Universal Declaration of Human Rights and of the other applicable instruments in the field of human rights.

(b) Communications shall be admissible only if, after consideration thereof, together with the replies of any of the Governments concerned, there are reasonable grounds to believe that they may reveal a consistent pattern of gross and reliably attested violations of human rights and fundamental freedoms, including policies of racial discrimination and segregation and of *apartheid* in any country, including colonial and other dependent countries and peoples.

(2) *Source of communications*

(a) Admissible communications may originate from a person or group of persons who, it can be reason-

1/ Adopted at the 627th meeting, on 13 August 1971.

ably presumed, are victims of the violations referred to in subparagraph (1) (b) above, any person or group of persons who have direct and reliable knowledge of those violations, or non-governmental organizations acting in good faith in accordance with recognized principles of human rights, not resorting to politically motivated stands contrary to the provisions of the Charter of the United Nations and having direct and reliable knowledge of such violations.

(b) Anonymous communications shall be inadmissible; subject to the requirements of subparagraph 2 (b) of resolution 728 F (XXVIII) of the Economic and Social Council, the author of a communication, whether an individual, a group of individuals or an organization, must be clearly identified.

(c) Communications shall not be inadmissible solely because the knowledge of the individual authors is second-hand, provided that they are accompanied by clear evidence.

(3) Contents of communications and nature of allegations

(a) The communication must contain a description of the facts and must indicate the purpose of the petition and the rights that have been violated.

(b) Communications shall be inadmissible if their language is essentially abusive and in particular if they contain insulting references to the State against which the complaint is directed. Such communications may be con-

sidered if they meet the other criteria for admissibility after deletion of the abusive language.

(c) A communication shall be inadmissible if it has manifestly political motivations and its subject is contrary to the provisions of the Charter of the United Nations.

(d) A communication shall be inadmissible if it appears that it is based exclusively on reports disseminated by mass media.

(4) Existence of other remedies

(a) Communications shall be inadmissible if their admission would prejudice the functions of the specialized agencies of the United Nations system.

(b) Communications shall be inadmissible if domestic remedies have not been exhausted, unless it appears that such remedies would be ineffective or unreasonably prolonged. Any failure to exhaust remedies should be satisfactorily established.

(c) Communications relating to cases which have been settled by the State concerned in accordance with the principles set forth in the Universal Declaration of Human Rights and other applicable documents in the field of human rights will not be considered.

(5) Timeliness

A communication shall be inadmissible if it is not submitted to the United Nations within a reasonable time after the exhaustion of the domestic remedies as provided above.

Document 40

International Convention on the Suppression and Punishment of the Crime of Apartheid

A/RES/3068 (XXVIII), 30 November 1973

The States Parties to the present Convention,

Recalling the provisions of the Charter of the United Nations, in which all Members pledged themselves to take joint and separate action in cooperation with the Organization for the achievement of universal respect for, and observance of, human rights and fundamental freedoms for all without distinction as to race, sex, language or religion,

Considering the Universal Declaration of Human Rights, which states that all human beings are born free and equal in dignity and rights and that everyone is entitled to all the rights and freedoms set forth in the

Declaration, without distinction of any kind, such as race, colour or national origin,

Considering the Declaration on the Granting of Independence to Colonial Countries and Peoples, in which the General Assembly stated that the process of liberation is irresistible and irreversible and that, in the interests of human dignity, progress and justice, an end must be put to colonialism and all practices of segregation and discrimination associated therewith,

Observing that, in accordance with the International Convention on the Elimination of All Forms of Racial Discrimination, States particularly condemn racial segregation and apartheid and undertake to prevent, prohibit and eradicate all practices of this nature in territories under their jurisdiction,

Observing that, in the Convention on the Prevention and Punishment of the Crime of Genocide, certain acts which may also be qualified as acts of apartheid constitute a crime under international law,

Observing that, in the Convention on the Non-Applicability of Statutory Limitations to War Crimes and Crimes against Humanity, "inhuman acts resulting from the policy of apartheid" are qualified as crimes against humanity,

Observing that the General Assembly of the United Nations has adopted a number of resolutions in which the policies and practices of apartheid are condemned as a crime against humanity,

Observing that the Security Council has emphasized that apartheid and its continued intensification and expansion seriously disturb and threaten international peace and security,

Convinced that an International Convention on the Suppression and Punishment of the Crime of Apartheid would make it possible to take more effective measures at the international and national levels with a view to the suppression and punishment of the crime of apartheid,

Have agreed as follows:

Article I

1. The States Parties to the present Convention declare that apartheid is a crime against humanity and that inhuman acts resulting from the policies and practices of apartheid and similar policies and practices of racial segregation and discrimination, as defined in article II of the Convention, are crimes violating the principles of international law, in particular the purposes and principles of the Charter of the United Nations, and constituting a serious threat to international peace and security.

2. The States Parties to the present Convention declare criminal those organizations, institutions and individuals committing the crime of apartheid.

Article II

For the purpose of the present Convention, the term "the crime of apartheid", which shall include similar policies and practices of racial segregation and discrimination as practised in southern Africa, shall apply to the following inhuman acts committed for the purpose of establishing and maintaining domination by one racial group of persons over any other racial group of persons and systematically oppressing them:

(a) Denial to a member or members of a racial group or groups of the right to life and liberty of person:

(i) By murder of members of a racial group or groups;

(ii) By the infliction upon the members of a racial group or groups of serious bodily or mental harm, by the infringement of their freedom or dignity, or by subjecting them to torture or to cruel, inhuman or degrading treatment or punishment;

(iii) By arbitrary arrest and illegal imprisonment of the members of a racial group or groups;

(b) Deliberate imposition on a racial group or groups of living conditions calculated to cause its or their physical destruction in whole or in part;

(c) Any legislative measures and other measures calculated to prevent a racial group or groups from participation in the political, social, economic and cultural life of the country and the deliberate creation of conditions preventing the full development of such a group or groups, in particular by denying to members of a racial group or groups basic human rights and freedoms, including the right to work, the right to form recognized trade unions, the right to education, the right to leave and to return to their country, the right to a nationality, the right to freedom of movement and residence, the right to freedom of opinion and expression, and the right to freedom of peaceful assembly and association;

(d) Any measures, including legislative measures, designed to divide the population along racial lines by the creation of separate reserves and ghettos for the members of a racial group or groups, the prohibition of mixed marriages among members of various racial groups, the expropriation of landed property belonging to a racial group or groups or to members thereof;

(e) Exploitation of the labour of the members of a racial group or groups, in particular by submitting them to forced labour;

(f) Persecution of organizations and persons, by depriving them of fundamental rights and freedoms, because they oppose apartheid.

Article III

International criminal responsibility shall apply, irrespective of the motive involved, to individuals, members of organizations and institutions and representatives of the State, whether residing in the territory of the State in which the acts are perpetrated or in some other State, whenever they:

(a) Commit, participate in, directly incite or conspire in the commission of the acts mentioned in article II of the present Convention;

(b) Directly abet, encourage or cooperate in the commission of the crime of apartheid.

Article IV

The States Parties to the present Convention undertake:

(a) To adopt any legislative or other measures necessary to suppress as well as to prevent any encouragement of the crime of apartheid and similar segregationist policies or their manifestations and to punish persons guilty of that crime;

(b) To adopt legislative, judicial and administrative measures to prosecute, bring to trial and punish in accordance with their jurisdiction persons responsible for, or accused of, the acts defined in article II of the present Convention, whether or not such persons reside in the territory of the State in which the acts are committed or are nationals of that State or of some other State or are stateless persons.

Article V

Persons charged with the acts enumerated in article II of the present Convention may be tried by a competent tribunal of any State Party to the Convention which may acquire jurisdiction over the person of the accused or by an international penal tribunal having jurisdiction with respect to those States Parties which shall have accepted its jurisdiction.

Article VI

The States Parties to the present Convention undertake to accept and carry out in accordance with the Charter of the United Nations the decisions taken by the Security Council aimed at the prevention, suppression and punishment of the crime of apartheid, and to cooperate in the implementation of decisions adopted by other competent organs of the United Nations with a view to achieving the purposes of the Convention.

Article VII

1. The States Parties to the present Convention undertake to submit periodic reports to the group established under article IX on the legislative, judicial, administrative or other measures that they have adopted and that give effect to the provisions of the Convention.

2. Copies of the reports shall be transmitted through the Secretary-General of the United Nations to the Special Committee on Apartheid.

Article VIII

Any State Party to the present Convention may call upon any competent organ of the United Nations to take such action under the Charter of the United Nations as it considers appropriate for the prevention and suppression of the crime of apartheid.

Article IX

1. The Chairman of the Commission on Human Rights shall appoint a group consisting of three members of the Commission on Human Rights, who are also representatives of States Parties to the present Convention, to consider reports submitted by States Parties in accordance with article VII.

2. If, among the members of the Commission on Human Rights, there are no representatives of States Parties to the present Convention or if there are fewer than three such representatives, the Secretary-General of the United Nations shall, after consulting all States Parties to the Convention, designate a representative of the State Party or representatives of the States Parties which are not members of the Commission on Human Rights to take part in the work of the group established in accordance with paragraph 1 of this article, until such time as representatives of the States Parties to the Convention are elected to the Commission on Human Rights.

3. The group may meet for a period of not more than five days, either before the opening or after the closing of the session of the Commission on Human Rights, to consider the reports submitted in accordance with article VII.

Article X

1. The States Parties to the present Convention empower the Commission on Human Rights:

(a) To request United Nations organs, when transmitting copies of petitions under article 15 of the International Convention on the Elimination of All Forms of Racial Discrimination, to draw its attention to complaints concerning acts which are enumerated in article II of the present Convention;

(b) To prepare, on the basis of reports from competent organs of the United Nations and periodic reports from States Parties to the present Convention, a list of individuals, organizations, institutions and representatives of States which are alleged to be responsible for the crimes enumerated in article II of the Convention, as well as those against whom legal proceedings have been undertaken by States Parties to the Convention;

(c) To request information from the competent United Nations organs concerning measures taken by the authorities responsible for the administration of Trust and Non-Self-Governing Territories, and all other Territories to which General Assembly resolution 1514 (XV) of 14 December 1960 applies, with regard to such individuals alleged to be responsible for crimes under article

II of the Convention who are believed to be under their territorial and administrative jurisdiction.

2. Pending the achievement of the objectives of the Declaration on the Granting of Independence to Colonial Countries and Peoples, contained in General Assembly resolution 1514 (XV), the provisions of the present Convention shall in no way limit the right of petition granted to those peoples by other international instruments or by the United Nations and its specialized agencies.

Article XI

1. Acts enumerated in article II of the present Convention shall not be considered political crimes for the purpose of extradition.

2. The States Parties to the present Convention undertake in such cases to grant extradition in accordance with their legislation and with the treaties in force.

Article XII

Disputes between States Parties arising out of the interpretation, application or implementation of the present Convention which have not been settled by negotiation shall, at the request of the States parties to the dispute, be brought before the International Court of Justice, save where the parties to the dispute have agreed on some other form of settlement.

Article XIII

The present Convention is open for signature by all States. Any State which does not sign the Convention before its entry into force may accede to it.

Article XIV

1. The present Convention is subject to ratification. Instruments of ratification shall be deposited with the Secretary-General of the United Nations.

2. Accession shall be effected by the deposit of an instrument of accession with the Secretary-General of the United Nations.

Article XV

1. The present Convention shall enter into force on the thirtieth day after the date of the deposit with the Secretary-General of the United Nations of the twentieth instrument of ratification or accession.

2. For each State ratifying the present Convention or acceding to it after the deposit of the twentieth instrument of ratification or instrument of accession, the Convention shall enter into force on the thirtieth day after the date of the deposit of its own instrument of ratification or instrument of accession.

Article XVI

A State Party may denounce the present Convention by written notification to the Secretary-General of the United Nations. Denunciation shall take effect one year after the date of receipt of the notification by the Secretary-General.

Article XVII

1. A request for the revision of the present Convention may be made at any time by any State Party by means of a notification in writing addressed to the Secretary-General of the United Nations.

2. The General Assembly of the United Nations shall decide upon the steps, if any, to be taken in respect of such request.

Article XVIII

The Secretary-General of the United Nations shall inform all States of the following particulars:

(a) Signatures, ratifications and accessions under articles XIII and XIV;

(b) The date of entry into force of the present Convention under article XV;

(c) Denunciations under article XVI;

(d) Notifications under article XVII.

Article XIX

1. The present Convention, of which the Chinese, English, French, Russian and Spanish texts are equally authentic, shall be deposited in the archives of the United Nations.

2. The Secretary-General of the United Nations shall transmit certified copies of the present Convention to all States.

Document 41

General Assembly resolution on the question of Palestine

A/RES/3236 (XXIX), 22 November 1974

The General Assembly,

Having considered the question of Palestine,

Having heard the statement of the Palestine Liberation Organization, the representative of the Palestinian people, 1/

Having also heard other statements made during the debate,

Deeply concerned that no just solution to the problem of Palestine has yet been achieved and recognizing that the problem of Palestine continues to endanger international peace and security,

Recognizing that the Palestinian people is entitled to self-determination in accordance with the Charter of the United Nations.

Expressing its grave concern that the Palestinian people has been prevented from enjoying its inalienable rights, in particular its right to self-determination,

Guided by the purposed and principles of the Charter,

Recalling its relevant resolutions which affirm the right of the Palestinian people to self-determination,

1. *Reaffirms* the inalienable rights of the Palestinian people in Palestine, including:

(a) The right to self-determination without external interference;

(b) The right to national independence and sovereignty;

2. *Reaffirms also* the inalienable right of the Palestinians to return to their homes and property from which they have been displaced and uprooted, and calls for their return;

3. *Emphasizes* that full respect for and the realization of these inalienable rights of the Palestinian people are indispensable for the solution of the question of Palestine;

4. *Recognizes* that the Palestinian people is a principal party in the establishment of a just and lasting peace in the Middle East;

5. *Further recognizes* the right of the Palestinian people to regain its rights by all means in accordance with the purposes and principles of the Charter of the United Nations;

6. *Appeals* to all States and international organizations to extend their support to the Palestinian people in its struggle to restore its rights, in accordance with the Charter;

7. *Requests* the Secretary-General to establish contacts with the Palestine Liberation Organization on all matters concerning the question of Palestine;

8. *Requests* the Secretary-General to report to the General Assembly at its thirtieth session on the implementation of the present resolution;

9. *Decides* to include the item entitled "Question of Palestine" in the provisional agenda of its thirtieth session.

1/ *Official Records of the General Assembly, Twenty-ninth Session, Plenary Meetings,* 2282nd meeting, paras. 3-83.

Document 42

General Assembly resolution on the question of Palestine

A/RES/3376 (XXX), 10 November 1975

The General Assembly,

Recalling its resolution 3236 (XXIX) of 22 November 1974,

Taking note of the report of the Secretary-General on the implementation of that resolution, 1/

Deeply concerned that no just solution to the problem of Palestine has yet been achieved,

Recognizing that the problem of Palestine continues to endanger international peace and security,

1. *Reaffirms* its resolution 3236 (XXIX);

2. *Expresses its grave concern* that no progress has been achieved towards:

1/ A/10265.

(a) The exercise by the Palestinian people of its inalienable rights in Palestine, including the right to self-determination without external interference and the right to national independence and sovereignty;

(b) The exercise by Palestinians of their inalienable right to return to their homes and property from which they have been displaced and uprooted;

3. *Decides* to establish a Committee on the Exercise of the Inalienable Rights of the Palestinian People composed of twenty Member States to be appointed by the General Assembly at the current session;

4. *Requests* the Committee to consider and recommend to the General Assembly a programme of implementation, designed to enable the Palestinian people to exercise the rights recognized in paragraphs 1 and 2 of Assembly resolution 3236 (XXIX), and to take into account, in the formulation of its recommendations for the implementation of that programme, all the powers conferred by the Charter upon the principal organs of the United Nations;

5. *Authorizes* the Committee, in the fulfilment of its mandate, to establish contact with, and to receive and consider suggestions and proposals from, any State and intergovernmental regional organization and the Palestine Liberation Organization;

6. *Requests* the Secretary-General to provide the Committee with all the necessary facilities for the performance of its tasks;

7. *Requests* the Committee to submit its report and recommendations to the Secretary-General no later than 1 June 1976 and requests the Secretary-General to transmit the report to the Security Council;

8. *Requests* the Security Council to consider, as soon as possible after 1 June 1976, the question of the exercise by the Palestinian people of the inalienable rights recognized in paragraphs 1 and 2 of resolution 3236 (XXIX);

9. *Requests* the Secretary-General to inform the Committee of the action taken by the Security Council in accordance with paragraph 8 above;

10. *Authorizes* the Committee, taking into consideration the action taken by the Security Council, to submit to the General Assembly, at its thirty-first session, a report containing its observations and recommendations;

11. *Decides* to include the item entitled "Question of Palestine" in the provisional agenda of its thirty-first session.

Document 43

Protocol Additional to the Geneva Conventions of 12 August 1949, and relating to the Protection of Victims of Non-International Armed Conflicts (Protocol II), adopted by the Diplomatic Conference on the Reaffirmation and Development of International Humanitarian Law applicable in Armed Conflicts

8 June 1977

PREAMBLE

The High Contracting Parties,

Recalling that the humanitarian principles enshrined in Article 3 common to the Geneva Conventions of 12 August 1949 constitute the foundation of respect for the human person in cases of armed conflict not of an international character,

Recalling furthermore that international instruments relating to human rights offer a basic protection to the human person,

Emphasizing the need to ensure a better protection for the victims of those armed conflicts,

Recalling that, in cases not covered by the law in force, the human person remains under the protection of the principles of humanity and the dictates of the public conscience,

Have agreed on the following:

PART I

SCOPE OF THIS PROTOCOL

Article 1
Material field of application

1. This Protocol, which develops and supplements Article 3 common to the Geneva Conventions of 12 August 1949 without modifying its existing conditions of application, shall apply to all armed conflicts which are not covered by Article 1 of the Protocol Additional to the Geneva Conventions of 12 August 1949, and relating to

the Protection of Victims of International Armed Conflicts (Protocol I) and which take place in the territory of a High Contracting Party between its armed forces and dissident armed forces or other organized armed groups which, under responsible command, exercise such control over a part of its territory as to enable them to carry out sustained and concerted military operations and to implement this Protocol.

2. This Protocol shall not apply to situations of internal disturbances and tensions, such as riots, isolated and sporadic acts of violence and other acts of a similar nature, as not being armed conflicts.

Article 2
Personal field of application

1. This Protocol shall be applied without any adverse distinction founded on race, colour, sex, language, religion or belief, political or other opinion, national or social origin, wealth, birth or other status, or on any other similar criteria (hereinafter referred to as "adverse distinction") to all persons affected by an armed conflict as defined in Article 1.

2. At the end of the armed conflict, all the persons who have been deprived of their liberty or whose liberty has been restricted for reasons related to such conflict, as well as those deprived of their liberty or whose liberty is restricted after the conflict for the same reasons, shall enjoy the protection of Articles 5 and 6 until the end of such deprivation or restriction of liberty.

Article 3
Non-intervention

1. Nothing in this Protocol shall be invoked for the purpose of affecting the sovereignty of a State or the responsibility of the government, by all legitimate means, to maintain or re-establish law and order in the State or to defend the national unity and territorial integrity of the State.

2. Nothing in this Protocol shall be invoked as a justification for intervening, directly or indirectly, for any reason whatever, in the armed conflict or in the internal or external affairs of the High Contracting Party in the territory of which that conflict occurs.

PART II

HUMANE TREATMENT

Article 4
Fundamental guarantees

1. All persons who do not take a direct part or who have ceased to take part in hostilities, whether or not their liberty has been restricted, are entitled to respect for their person, honour and convictions and religious practices. They shall in all circumstances be treated humanely, without any adverse distinction. It is prohibited to order that there shall be no survivors.

2. Without prejudice to the generality of the foregoing, the following acts against the persons referred to in paragraph 1 are and shall remain prohibited at any time and in any place whatsoever:

(a) Violence to the life, health and physical or mental well-being of persons, in particular murder as well as cruel treatment such as torture, mutilation or any form of corporal punishment;

(b) Collective punishments;

(c) Taking of hostages;

(d) Acts of terrorism;

(e) Outrages upon personal dignity, in particular humiliating and degrading treatment, rape, enforced prostitution and any form of indecent assault;

(f) Slavery and the slave trade in all their forms;

(g) Pillage;

(h) Threats to commit any of the foregoing acts.

3. Children shall be provided with the care and aid they require, and in particular:

(a) They shall receive an education, including religious and moral education, in keeping with the wishes of their parents, or in the absence of parents, of those responsible for their care;

(b) All appropriate steps shall be taken to facilitate the reunion of families temporarily separated;

(c) Children who have not attained the age of fifteen years shall neither be recruited in the armed forces or groups nor allowed to take part in hostilities;

(d) The special protection provided by this Article to children who have not attained the age of fifteen years shall remain applicable to them if they take a direct part in hostilities despite the provisions of sub-paragraph (c) and are captured;

(e) Measures shall be taken, if necessary, and whenever possible with the consent of their parents or persons who by law or custom are primarily responsible for their care, to remove children temporarily from the area in which hostilities are taking place to a safer area within the country and ensure that they are accompanied by persons responsible for their safety and well-being.

Article 5
Persons whose liberty has been restricted

1. In addition to the provisions of Article 4, the following provisions shall be respected as a minimum with regard to persons deprived of their liberty for reasons related to the armed conflict, whether they are interned or detained:

(a) The wounded and the sick shall be treated in accordance with Article 7;

(b) The persons referred to in this paragraph shall, to the same extent as the local civilian population, be provided with food and drinking water and be afforded safeguards as regards health and hygiene and protection against the rigours of the climate and the dangers of the armed conflict;

(c) They shall be allowed to receive individual or collective relief;

(d) They shall be allowed to practise their religion and, if requested and appropriate, to receive spiritual assistance from persons, such as chaplains, performing religious functions;

(e) They shall, if made to work, have the benefit of working conditions and safeguards similar to those enjoyed by the local civilian population.

2. Those who are responsible for the internment or detention of the persons referred to in paragraph 1 shall also, within the limits of their capabilities, respect the following provisions relating to such persons:

(a) Except when men and women of a family are accommodated together, women shall be held in quarters separated from those of men and shall be under the immediate supervision of women;

(b) They shall be allowed to send and receive letters and cards, the number of which may be limited by the competent authority if it deems necessary;

(c) Places of internment and detention shall not be located close to the combat zone. The persons referred to in paragraph 1 shall be evacuated when the places where they are interned or detained become particularly exposed to danger arising out of the armed conflict, if their evacuation can be carried out under adequate conditions of safety;

(d) They shall have the benefit of medical examinations;

(e) Their physical or mental health and integrity shall not be endangered by an unjustified act or omission. Accordingly, it is prohibited to subject the persons described in this Article to any medical procedure which is not indicated by the state of health of the person concerned, and which is not consistent with the generally accepted medical standards applied to free persons under similar medical circumstances.

3. Persons who are not covered by paragraph 1 but whose liberty has been restricted in any way whatsoever for reasons related to the armed conflict shall be treated humanely in accordance with Article 4 and with paragraphs 1 (a), (c) and (d), and 2 (b) of this Article.

4. If it is decided to release persons deprived of their liberty, necessary measures to ensure their safety shall be taken by those so deciding.

Article 6
Penal prosecutions

1. This Article applies to the prosecution and punishment of criminal offences related to the armed conflict.

2. No sentence shall be passed and no penalty shall be executed on a person found guilty of an offence except pursuant to a conviction pronounced by a court offering the essential guarantees of independence and impartiality. In particular:

(a) The procedure shall provide for an accused to be informed without delay of the particulars of the offence alleged against him and shall afford the accused before and during his trial all necessary rights and means of defence;

(b) No one shall be convicted of an offence except on the basis of individual penal responsibility;

(c) No one shall be held guilty of any criminal offence on account of any act or omission which did not constitute a criminal offence, under the law, at the time when it was committed; nor shall a heavier penalty be imposed than that which was applicable at the time when the criminal offence was committed; if, after the commission of the offence, provision is made by law for the imposition of a lighter penalty, the offender shall benefit thereby;

(d) Anyone charged with an offence is presumed innocent until proved guilty according to law;

(e) Anyone charged with an offence shall have the right to be tried in his presence;

(f) No one shall be compelled to testify against himself or to confess guilt.

3. A convicted person shall be advised on conviction of his judicial and other remedies and of the time-limits within which they may be exercised.

4. The death penalty shall not be pronounced on persons who were under the age of eighteen years at the time of the offence and shall not be carried out on pregnant women or mothers of young children.

5. At the end of hostilities, the authorities in power shall endeavour to grant the broadest possible amnesty to persons who have participated in the armed conflict, or those deprived of their liberty for reasons related to the armed conflict, whether they are interned or detained.

PART III

WOUNDED, SICK AND SHIPWRECKED

Article 7
Protection and care

1. All the wounded, sick and shipwrecked, whether or not they have taken part in the armed conflict, shall be respected and protected.

2. In all circumstances they shall be treated humanely and shall receive, to the fullest extent practicable and with the least possible delay, the medical care and attention required by their condition. There shall be no distinction among them founded on any grounds other than medical ones.

Article 8
Search

Whenever circumstances permit, and particularly after an engagement, all possible measures shall be taken, without delay, to search for and collect the wounded, sick and shipwrecked, to protect them against pillage and ill-treatment, to ensure their adequate care, and to search for the dead, prevent their being despoiled, and decently dispose of them.

Article 9
Protection of medical and religious personnel

1. Medical and religious personnel shall be respected and protected and shall be granted all available help for the performance of their duties. They shall not be compelled to carry out tasks which are not compatible with their humanitarian mission.

2. In the performance of their duties medical personnel may not be required to give priority to any person except on medical grounds.

Article 10
General protection of medical duties

1. Under no circumstances shall any person be punished for having carried out medical activities compatible with medical ethics, regardless of the person benefiting therefrom.

2. Persons engaged in medical activities shall neither be compelled to perform acts or to carry out work contrary to, nor be compelled to refrain from acts required by, the rules of medical ethics or other rules designed for the benefit of the wounded and sick, or this Protocol.

3. The professional obligations of persons engaged in medical activities regarding information which they may acquire concerning the wounded and sick under their care shall, subject to national law, be respected.

4. Subject to national law, no person engaged in medical activities may be penalized in any way for refusing or failing to give information concerning the wounded and sick who are, or who have been, under his care.

Article 11
Protection of medical units and transports

1. Medical units and transports shall be respected and protected at all times and shall not be the object of attack.

2. The protection to which medical units and transports are entitled shall not cease unless they are used to commit hostile acts, outside their humanitarian function. Protection may, however, cease only after a warning has been given setting, whenever appropriate, a reasonable time-limit, and after such warning has remained unheeded.

Article 12
The distinctive emblem

Under the direction of the competent authority concerned, the distinctive emblem of the red cross, red crescent or red lion and sun on a white ground shall be displayed by medical and religious personnel and medical units, and on medical transports. It shall be respected in all circumstances. It shall not be used improperly.

PART IV

CIVILIAN POPULATION

Article 13
Protection of the civilian population

1. The civilian population and individual civilians shall enjoy general protection against the dangers arising from military operations. To give effect to this protection, the following rules shall be observed in all circumstances.

2. The civilian population as such, as well as individual civilians, shall not be the object of attack. Acts or threats of violence the primary purpose of which is to spread terror among the civilian population are prohibited.

3. Civilians shall enjoy the protection afforded by this Part, unless and for such time as they take a direct part in hostilities.

Article 14
Protection of objects indispensable to the survival of the civilian population

Starvation of civilians as a method of combat is prohibited. It is therefore prohibited to attack, destroy, remove or render useless, for that purpose, objects indispensable to the survival of the civilian population, such as foodstuffs, agricultural areas for the production of foodstuffs, crops, livestock, drinking water installations and supplies and irrigation works.

Article 15
Protection of works and installations containing dangerous forces

Works or installations containing dangerous forces, namely dams, dykes and nuclear electrical generating stations, shall not be made the object of attack, even where these objects are military objectives, if such attack may cause the release of dangerous forces and consequent severe losses among the civilian population.

Article 16
Protection of cultural objects and of places of worship

Without prejudice to the provisions of The Hague Convention for the Protection of Cultural Property in the Event of Armed Conflict of 14 May 1954, it is prohibited to commit any acts of hostility directed against historic monuments, works of art or places of worship which constitute the cultural or spiritual heritage of peoples, and to use them in support of the military effort.

Article 17
Prohibition of forced movement of civilians

1. The displacement of the civilian population shall not be ordered for reasons related to the conflict unless the security of the civilians involved or imperative military reasons so demand. Should such displacements have to be carried out, all possible measures shall be taken in order that the civilian population may be received under satisfactory conditions of shelter, hygiene, health, safety and nutrition.

2. Civilians shall not be compelled to leave their own territory for reasons connected with the conflict.

Article 18
Relief societies and relief actions

1. Relief societies located in the territory of the High Contracting Party, such as Red Cross (Red Crescent, Red Lion and Sun) organizations, may offer their services for the performance of their traditional functions in relation to the victims of the armed conflict. The civilian population may, even on its own initiative, offer to collect and care for the wounded, sick and shipwrecked.

2. If the civilian population is suffering undue hardship owing to a lack of the supplies essential for its survival, such as foodstuffs and medical supplies, relief actions for the civilian population which are of an exclusively humanitarian and impartial nature and which are conducted without any adverse distinction shall be undertaken subject to the consent of the High Contracting Party concerned.

PART V

FINAL PROVISIONS

Article 19
Dissemination

This Protocol shall be disseminated as widely as possible.

Article 20
Signature

This Protocol shall be open for signature by the Parties to the Conventions six months after the signing of the Final Act and will remain open for a period of twelve months.

Article 21
Ratification

This Protocol shall be ratified as soon as possible. The instruments of ratification shall be deposited with the Swiss Federal Council, depositary of the Conventions.

Article 22
Accession

This Protocol shall be open for accession by any Party to the Conventions which has not signed it. The instruments of accession shall be deposited with the depositary.

Article 23
Entry into force

1. This Protocol shall enter into force six months after two instruments of ratification or accession have been deposited.

2. For each Party to the Conventions thereafter ratifying or acceding to this Protocol, it shall enter into force six months after the deposit by such Party of its instrument of ratification or accession.

Article 24
Amendment

1. Any High Contracting Party may propose amendments to this Protocol. The text of any proposed amendment shall be communicated to the depositary which shall decide, after consultation with all the High Contracting Parties and the International Committee of the Red Cross, whether a conference should be convened to consider the proposed amendment.

2. The depositary shall invite to that conference all the High Contracting Parties as well as the Parties to the Conventions, whether or not they are signatories of this Protocol.

Article 25
Denunciation

1. In case a High Contracting Party should denounce this Protocol, the denunciation shall only take effect six months after receipt of the instrument of denunciation. If, however, on the expiry of six months, the denouncing Party is engaged in the situation referred to in Article l, the denunciation shall not take effect before the end of the armed conflict. Persons who have been deprived of liberty, or whose liberty has been restricted,

for reasons related to the conflict shall nevertheless continue to benefit from the provisions of this Protocol until their final release.

2. The denunciation shall be notified in writing to the depositary, which shall transmit it to all the High Contracting Parties.

Article 26
Notifications

The depositary shall inform the High Contracting Parties as well as the Parties to the Conventions, whether or not they are signatories of this Protocol, of:

(a) Signatures affixed to this Protocol and the deposit of instruments of ratification and accession under Articles 21 and 22;

(b) The date of entry into force of this Protocol under Article 23; and

(c) Communications and declarations received under Article 24.

Article 27
Registration

1. After its entry into force, this Protocol shall be transmitted by the depositary to the Secretariat of the United Nations for registration and publication, in accordance with Article 102 of the Charter of the United Nations.

2. The depositary shall also inform the Secretariat of the United Nations of all ratifications and accessions received by it with respect to this Protocol.

Article 28
Authentic texts

The original of this Protocol, of which the Arabic, Chinese, English, French, Russian and Spanish texts are equally authentic shall be deposited with the depositary, which shall transmit certified true copies thereof to all the Parties to the Conventions.

Document 44

Code of Conduct for Law Enforcement Officials

A/RES/34/169, 17 December 1979

Article 1

Law enforcement officials shall at all times fulfil the duty imposed upon them by law, by serving the community and by protecting all persons against illegal acts, consistent with the high degree of responsibility required by their profession.

Commentary:

(a) The term "law enforcement officials" includes all officers of the law, whether appointed or elected, who exercise police powers, especially the powers of arrest or detention.

(b) In countries where police powers are exercised by military authorities, whether uniformed or not, or by State security forces, the definition of law enforcement officials shall be regarded as including officers of such services.

(c) Service to the community is intended to include particularly the rendition of services of assistance to those members of the community who by reason of personal, economic, social or other emergencies are in need of immediate aid.

(d) This provision is intended to cover not only all violent, predatory and harmful acts, but extends to the full range of prohibitions under penal statutes. It extends to conduct by persons not capable of incurring criminal liability.

Article 2

In the performance of their duty, law enforcement officials shall respect and protect human dignity and maintain and uphold the human rights of all persons.

Commentary:

(a) The human rights in question are identified and protected by national and international law. Among the relevant international instruments are the Universal Declaration of Human Rights, the International Covenant on Civil and Political Rights, the Declaration on the Protection of All Persons from Being Subjected to Torture and Other Cruel, Inhuman or Degrading Treatment or Punishment, the United Nations Declaration on the Elimination of All Forms of Racial Discrimination, the International Convention on the Elimination of All Forms of Racial Discrimination, the International Convention on the Suppression and Punishment of the Crime of Apartheid, the Convention on the Prevention and Punishment of the Crime of Genocide, the Standard

Minimum Rules for the Treatment of Prisoners and the Vienna Convention on Consular Relations.

(b) National commentaries to this provision should indicate regional or national provisions identifying and protecting these rights.

Article 3

Law enforcement officials may use force only when strictly necessary and to the extent required for the performance of their duty.

Commentary:

(a) This provision emphasizes that the use of force by law enforcement officials should be exceptional; while it implies that law enforcement officials may be authorized to use force as is reasonably necessary under the circumstances for the prevention of crime or in effecting or assisting in the lawful arrest of offenders or suspected offenders, no force going beyond that may be used.

(b) National law ordinarily restricts the use of force by law enforcement officials in accordance with a principle of proportionality. It is to be understood that such national principles of proportionality are to be respected in the interpretation of this provision. In no case should this provision be interpreted to authorize the use of force which is disproportionate to the legitimate objective to be achieved.

(c) The use of firearms is considered an extreme measure. Every effort should be made to exclude the use of firearms, especially against children. In general, firearms should not be used except when a suspected offender offers armed resistance or otherwise jeopardizes the lives of others and less extreme measures are not sufficient to restrain or apprehend the suspected offender. In every instance in which a firearm is discharged, a report should be made promptly to the competent authorities.

Article 4

Matters of a confidential nature in the possession of law enforcement officials shall be kept confidential, unless the performance of duty or the needs of justice strictly require otherwise.

Commentary:

By the nature of their duties, law enforcement officials obtain information which may relate to private lives or be potentially harmful to the interests, and especially the reputation, of others. Great care should be exercised in safeguarding and using such information, which should be disclosed only in the performance of duty or to serve the needs of justice. Any disclosure of such information for other purposes is wholly improper.

Article 5

No law enforcement official may inflict, instigate or tolerate any act of torture or other cruel, inhuman or degrading treatment or punishment, nor may any law enforcement official invoke superior orders or exceptional circumstances such as a state of war or a threat of war, a threat to national security, internal political instability or any other public emergency as a justification of torture or other cruel, inhuman or degrading treatment or punishment.

Commentary:

(a) This prohibition derives from the Declaration on the Protection of All Persons from Being Subjected to Torture and Other Cruel, Inhuman or Degrading Treatment or Punishment, adopted by the General Assembly, according to which:

"[Such an act is] an offence to human dignity and shall be condemned as a denial of the purposes of the Charter of the United Nations and as a violation of the human rights and fundamental freedoms proclaimed in the Universal Declaration of Human Rights [and other international human rights instruments]."

(b) The Declaration defines torture as follows:

". . . torture means any act by which severe pain or suffering, whether physical or mental, is intentionally inflicted by or at the instigation of a public official on a person for such purposes as obtaining from him or a third person information or confession, punishing him for an act he has committed or is suspected of having committed, or intimidating him or other persons. It does not include pain or suffering arising only from, inherent in or incidental to, lawful sanctions to the extent consistent with the Standard Minimum Rules for the Treatment of Prisoners."

(c) The term "cruel, inhuman or degrading treatment or punishment" has not been defined by the General Assembly but should be interpreted so as to extend the widest possible protection against abuses, whether physical or mental.

Article 6

Law enforcement officials shall ensure the full protection of the health of persons in their custody and, in particular, shall take immediate action to secure medical attention whenever required.

Commentary:

(a) "Medical attention", which refers to services rendered by any medical personnel, including certified medical practitioners and paramedics, shall be secured when needed or requested.

(b) While the medical personnel are likely to be attached to the law enforcement operation, law enforcement officials must take into account the judgement of such personnel when they recommend providing the person in custody with appropriate treatment through, or in consultation with, medical personnel from outside the law enforcement operation.

(c) It is understood that law enforcement officials shall also secure medical attention for victims of violations of law or of accidents occurring in the course of violations of law.

Article 7

Law enforcement officials shall not commit any act of corruption. They shall also rigorously oppose and combat all such acts.

Commentary:

(a) Any act of corruption, in the same way as any other abuse of authority, is incompatible with the profession of law enforcement officials. The law must be enforced fully with respect to any law enforcement official who commits an act of corruption, as Governments cannot expect to enforce the law among their citizens if they cannot, or will not, enforce the law against their own agents and within their agencies.

(b) While the definition of corruption must be subject to national law, it should be understood to encompass the commission or omission of an act in the performance of or in connection with one's duties, in response to gifts, promises or incentives demanded or accepted, or the wrongful receipt of these once the act has been committed or omitted.

(c) The expression "act of corruption" referred to above should be understood to encompass attempted corruption.

Article 8

Law enforcement officials shall respect the law and the present Code. They shall also, to the best of their capability, prevent and rigorously oppose any violations of them.

Law enforcement officials who have reason to believe that a violation of the present Code has occurred or is about to occur shall report the matter to their superior authorities and, where necessary, to other appropriate authorities or organs vested with reviewing or remedial power.

Commentary:

(a) This Code shall be observed whenever it has been incorporated into national legislation or practice. If legislation or practice contains stricter provisions than those of the present Code, those stricter provisions shall be observed.

(b) The article seeks to preserve the balance between the need for internal discipline of the agency on which public safety is largely dependent, on the one hand, and the need for dealing with violations of basic human rights, on the other. Law enforcement officials shall report violations within the chain of command and take other lawful action outside the chain of command only when no other remedies are available or effective. It is understood that law enforcement officials shall not suffer administrative or other penalties because they have reported that a violation of this Code has occurred or is about to occur.

(c) The term "appropriate authorities or organs vested with reviewing or remedial power" refers to any authority or organ existing under national law, whether internal to the law enforcement agency or independent thereof, with statutory, customary or other power to review grievances and complaints arising out of violations within the purview of this Code.

(d) In some countries, the mass media may be regarded as performing complaint review functions similar to those described in subparagraph (c) above. Law enforcement officials may, therefore, be justified if, as a last resort and in accordance with the laws and customs of their own countries and with the provisions of article 4 of the present Code, they bring violations to the attention of public opinion through the mass media.

(e) Law enforcement officials who comply with the provisions of this Code deserve the respect, the full support and the cooperation of the community and of the law enforcement agency in which they serve, as well as the law enforcement profession.

Document 45

Convention on the Elimination of All Forms of Discrimination against Women

A/RES/34/180, 18 December 1979

The States Parties to the present Convention,

Noting that the Charter of the United Nations reaffirms faith in fundamental human rights, in the dignity and worth of the human person and in the equal rights of men and women,

Noting that the Universal Declaration of Human Rights affirms the principle of the inadmissibility of discrimination and proclaims that all human beings are born free and equal in dignity and rights and that everyone is entitled to all the rights and freedoms set forth therein, without distinction of any kind, including distinction based on sex,

Noting that the States Parties to the International Covenants on Human Rights have the obligation to ensure the equal rights of men and women to enjoy all economic, social, cultural, civil and political rights,

Considering the international conventions concluded under the auspices of the United Nations and the specialized agencies promoting equality of rights of men and women,

Noting also the resolutions, declarations and recommendations adopted by the United Nations and the specialized agencies promoting equality of rights of men and women,

Concerned, however, that despite these various instruments extensive discrimination against women continues to exist,

Recalling that discrimination against women violates the principles of equality of rights and respect for human dignity, is an obstacle to the participation of women, on equal terms with men, in the political, social, economic and cultural life of their countries, hampers the growth of the prosperity of society and the family and makes more difficult the full development of the potentialities of women in the service of their countries and of humanity,

Concerned that in situations of poverty women have the least access to food, health, education, training and opportunities for employment and other needs,

Convinced that the establishment of the new international economic order based on equity and justice will contribute significantly towards the promotion of equality between men and women,

Emphasizing that the eradication of apartheid, all forms of racism, racial discrimination, colonialism, neo-colonialism, aggression, foreign occupation and domination and interference in the internal affairs of States is essential to the full enjoyment of the rights of men and women,

Affirming that the strengthening of international peace and security, the relaxation of international tension, mutual cooperation among all States irrespective of their social and economic systems, general and complete disarmament, in particular nuclear disarmament under strict and effective international control, the affirmation of the principles of justice, equality and mutual benefit in relations among countries and the realization of the right of peoples under alien and colonial domination and foreign occupation to self-determination and independence, as well as respect for national sovereignty and territorial integrity, will promote social progress and development and as a consequence will contribute to the attainment of full equality between men and women,

Convinced that the full and complete development of a country, the welfare of the world and the cause of peace require the maximum participation of women on equal terms with men in all fields,

Bearing in mind the great contribution of women to the welfare of the family and to the development of society, so far not fully recognized, the social significance of maternity and the role of both parents in the family and in the upbringing of children, and aware that the role of women in procreation should not be a basis for discrimination but that the upbringing of children requires a sharing of responsibility between men and women and society as a whole,

Aware that a change in the traditional role of men as well as the role of women in society and in the family is needed to achieve full equality between men and women,

Determined to implement the principles set forth in the Declaration on the Elimination of Discrimination against Women and, for that purpose, to adopt the measures required for the elimination of such discrimination in all its forms and manifestations,

Have agreed on the following:

PART I

Article 1

For the purposes of the present Convention, the term "discrimination against women" shall mean any distinction, exclusion or restriction made on the basis of sex which has the effect or purpose of impairing or nullifying the recognition, enjoyment or exercise by women, irrespective of their marital status, on a basis of equality of men and women, of human rights and fundamental freedoms in the political, economic, social, cultural, civil or any other field.

Article 2

States Parties condemn discrimination against women in all its forms, agree to pursue by all appropriate means and without delay a policy of eliminating discrimination against women and, to this end, undertake:

(a) To embody the principle of the equality of men and women in their national constitutions or other appropriate legislation if not yet incorporated therein and to ensure, through law and other appropriate means, the practical realization of this principle;

(b) To adopt appropriate legislative and other measures, including sanctions where appropriate, prohibiting all discrimination against women;

(c) To establish legal protection of the rights of women on an equal basis with men and to ensure through competent national tribunals and other public institutions the effective protection of women against any act of discrimination;

(d) To refrain from engaging in any act or practice of discrimination against women and to ensure that public authorities and institutions shall act in conformity with this obligation;

(e) To take all appropriate measures to eliminate discrimination against women by any person, organization or enterprise;

(f) To take all appropriate measures, including legislation, to modify or abolish existing laws, regulations, customs and practices which constitute discrimination against women;

(g) To repeal all national penal provisions which constitute discrimination against women.

Article 3

States Parties shall take in all fields, in particular in the political, social, economic and cultural fields, all appropriate measures, including legislation, to ensure the full development and advancement of women, for the purpose of guaranteeing them the exercise and enjoyment of human rights and fundamental freedoms on a basis of equality with men.

Article 4

1. Adoption by States Parties of temporary special measures aimed at accelerating de facto equality between men and women shall not be considered discrimination

as defined in the present Convention, but shall in no way entail as a consequence the maintenance of unequal or separate standards; these measures shall be discontinued when the objectives of equality of opportunity and treatment have been achieved.

2. Adoption by States Parties of special measures, including those measures contained in the present Convention, aimed at protecting maternity shall not be considered discriminatory.

Article 5

States Parties shall take all appropriate measures:

(a) To modify the social and cultural patterns of conduct of men and women, with a view to achieving the elimination of prejudices and customary and all other practices which are based on the idea of the inferiority or the superiority of either of the sexes or on stereotyped roles for men and women;

(b) To ensure that family education includes a proper understanding of maternity as a social function and the recognition of the common responsibility of men and women in the upbringing and development of their children, it being understood that the interest of the children is the primordial consideration in all cases.

Article 6

States Parties shall take all appropriate measures, including legislation, to suppress all forms of traffic in women and exploitation of prostitution of women.

PART II

Article 7

States Parties shall take all appropriate measures to eliminate discrimination against women in the political and public life of the country and, in particular, shall ensure to women, on equal terms with men, the right:

(a) To vote in all elections and public referenda and to be eligible for election to all publicly elected bodies;

(b) To participate in the formulation of government policy and the implementation thereof and to hold public office and perform all public functions at all levels of government;

(c) To participate in non-governmental organizations and associations concerned with the public and political life of the country.

Article 8

States Parties shall take all appropriate measures to ensure to women, on equal terms with men and without any discrimination, the opportunity to represent their Governments at the international level and to participate in the work of international organizations.

Article 9

1. States Parties shall grant women equal rights with men to acquire, change or retain their nationality. They shall ensure in particular that neither marriage to an alien nor change of nationality by the husband during marriage shall automatically change the nationality of the wife, render her stateless or force upon her the nationality of the husband.

2. States Parties shall grant women equal rights with men with respect to the nationality of their children.

PART III

Article 10

States Parties shall take all appropriate measures to eliminate discrimination against women in order to ensure to them equal rights with men in the field of education and in particular to ensure, on a basis of equality of men and women:

(a) The same conditions for career and vocational guidance, for access to studies and for the achievement of diplomas in educational establishments of all categories in rural as well as in urban areas; this equality shall be ensured in pre-school, general, technical, professional and higher technical education, as well as in all types of vocational training;

(b) Access to the same curricula, the same examinations, teaching staff with qualifications of the same standard and school premises and equipment of the same quality;

(c) The elimination of any stereotyped concept of the roles of men and women at all levels and in all forms of education by encouraging coeducation and other types of education which will help to achieve this aim and, in particular, by the revision of textbooks and school programmes and the adaptation of teaching methods;

(d) The same opportunities to benefit from scholarships and other study grants;

(e) The same opportunities for access to programmes of continuing education, including adult and functional literacy programmes, particularly those aimed at reducing, at the earliest possible time, any gap in education existing between men and women;

(f) The reduction of female student drop-out rates and the organization of programmes for girls and women who have left school prematurely;

(g) The same opportunities to participate actively in sports and physical education;

(h) Access to specific educational information to help to ensure the health and well-being of families, including information and advice on family planning.

Article 11

1. States Parties shall take all appropriate measures to eliminate discrimination against women in the field of employment in order to ensure, on a basis of equality of men and women, the same rights, in particular:

(a) The right to work as an inalienable right of all human beings;

(b) The right to the same employment opportunities, including the application of the same criteria for selection in matters of employment;

(c) The right to free choice of profession and employment, the right to promotion, job security and all benefits and conditions of service and the right to receive vocational training and retraining, including apprenticeships, advanced vocational training and recurrent training;

(d) The right to equal remuneration, including benefits, and to equal treatment in respect of work of equal value, as well as equality of treatment in the evaluation of the quality of work;

(e) The right to social security, particularly in cases of retirement, unemployment, sickness, invalidity and old age and other incapacity to work, as well as the right to paid leave;

(f) The right to protection of health and to safety in working conditions, including the safeguarding of the function of reproduction.

2. In order to prevent discrimination against women on the grounds of marriage or maternity and to ensure their effective right to work, States Parties shall take appropriate measures:

(a) To prohibit, subject to the imposition of sanctions, dismissal on the grounds of pregnancy or of maternity leave and discrimination in dismissals on the basis of marital status;

(b) To introduce maternity leave with pay or with comparable social benefits without loss of former employment, seniority or social allowances;

(c) To encourage the provision of the necessary supporting social services to enable parents to combine family obligations with work responsibilities and participation in public life, in particular through promoting the establishment and development of a network of childcare facilities;

(d) To provide special protection to women during pregnancy in types of work proved to be harmful to them.

3. Protective legislation relating to matters covered in this article shall be reviewed periodically in the light of scientific and technological knowledge and shall be revised, repealed or extended as necessary.

Article 12

1. States Parties shall take all appropriate measures to eliminate discrimination against women in the field of

health care in order to ensure, on a basis of equality of men and women, access to health care services, including those related to family planning.

2. Notwithstanding the provisions of paragraph 1 of this article, States Parties shall ensure to women appropriate services in connection with pregnancy, confinement and the post-natal period, granting free services where necessary, as well as adequate nutrition during pregnancy and lactation.

Article 13

States Parties shall take all appropriate measures to eliminate discrimination against women in other areas of economic and social life in order to ensure, on a basis of equality of men and women, the same rights, in particular:

(a) The right to family benefits;

(b) The right to bank loans, mortgages and other forms of financial credit;

(c) The right to participate in recreational activities, sports and all aspects of cultural life.

Article 14

1. States Parties shall take into account the particular problems faced by rural women and the significant roles which rural women play in the economic survival of their families, including their work in the non-monetized sectors of the economy, and shall take all appropriate measures to ensure the application of the provisions of the present Convention to women in rural areas.

2. States Parties shall take all appropriate measures to eliminate discrimination against women in rural areas in order to ensure, on a basis of equality of men and women, that they participate in and benefit from rural development and, in particular, shall ensure to such women the right:

(a) To participate in the elaboration and implementation of development planning at all levels;

(b) To have access to adequate health care facilities, including information, counselling and services in family planning;

(c) To benefit directly from social security programmes;

(d) To obtain all types of training and education, formal and non-formal, including that relating to functional literacy, as well as, *inter alia*, the benefit of all community and extension services, in order to increase their technical proficiency;

(e) To organize self-help groups and co-operatives in order to obtain equal access to economic opportunities through employment or self-employment;

(f) To participate in all community activities;

(g) To have access to agricultural credit and loans, marketing facilities, appropriate technology and equal treatment in land and agrarian reform as well as in land resettlement schemes;

(h) To enjoy adequate living conditions, particularly in relation to housing, sanitation, electricity and water supply, transport and communications.

PART IV

Article 15

1. States Parties shall accord to women equality with men before the law.

2. States Parties shall accord to women, in civil matters, a legal capacity identical to that of men and the same opportunities to exercise that capacity. In particular, they shall give women equal rights to conclude contracts and to administer property and shall treat them equally in all stages of procedure in courts and tribunals.

3. States Parties agree that all contracts and all other private instruments of any kind with a legal effect which is directed at restricting the legal capacity of women shall be deemed null and void.

4. States Parties shall accord to men and women the same rights with regard to the law relating to the movement of persons and the freedom to choose their residence and domicile.

Article 16

1. States Parties shall take all appropriate measures to eliminate discrimination against women in all matters relating to marriage and family relations and in particular shall ensure, on a basis of equality of men and women:

(a) The same right to enter into marriage;

(b) The same right freely to choose a spouse and to enter into marriage only with their free and full consent;

(c) The same rights and responsibilities during marriage and at its dissolution;

(d) The same rights and responsibilities as parents, irrespective of their marital status, in matters relating to their children; in all cases the interests of the children shall be paramount;

(e) The same rights to decide freely and responsibly on the number and spacing of their children and to have access to the information, education and means to enable them to exercise these rights;

(f) The same rights and responsibilities with regard to guardianship, wardship, trusteeship and adoption of children, or similar institutions where these concepts exist in national legislation; in all cases the interests of the children shall be paramount;

(g) The same personal rights as husband and wife, including the right to choose a family name, a profession and an occupation;

(h) The same rights for both spouses in respect of the ownership, acquisition, management, administration, enjoyment and disposition of property, whether free of charge or for a valuable consideration.

2. The betrothal and the marriage of a child shall have no legal effect, and all necessary action, including legislation, shall be taken to specify a minimum age for marriage and to make the registration of marriages in an official registry compulsory.

PART V

Article 17

1. For the purpose of considering the progress made in the implementation of the present Convention, there shall be established a Committee on the Elimination of Discrimination against Women (hereinafter referred to as the Committee) consisting, at the time of entry into force of the Convention, of eighteen and, after ratification of or accession to the Convention by the thirty-fifth State Party, of twenty-three experts of high moral standing and competence in the field covered by the Convention. The experts shall be elected by States Parties from among their nationals and shall serve in their personal capacity, consideration being given to equitable geographical distribution and to the representation of the different forms of civilization as well as the principal legal systems.

2. The members of the Committee shall be elected by secret ballot from a list of persons nominated by States Parties. Each State Party may nominate one person from among its own nationals.

3. The initial election shall be held six months after the date of the entry into force of the present Convention. At least three months before the date of each election the Secretary-General of the United Nations shall address a letter to the States Parties inviting them to submit their nominations within two months. The Secretary-General shall prepare a list in alphabetical order of all persons thus nominated, indicating the States Parties which have nominated them, and shall submit it to the States Parties.

4. Elections of the members of the Committee shall be held at a meeting of States Parties convened by the Secretary-General at United Nations Headquarters. At that meeting, for which two thirds of the States Parties shall constitute a quorum, the persons elected to the Committee shall be those nominees who obtain the largest number of votes and an absolute majority of the votes of the representatives of States Parties present and voting.

5. The members of the Committee shall be elected for a term of four years. However, the terms of nine of the members elected at the first election shall expire at the end of two years; immediately after the first election the names of these nine members shall be chosen by lot by the Chairman of the Committee.

6. The election of the five additional members of the Committee shall be held in accordance with the provisions of paragraphs 2, 3 and 4 of this article, following the thirty-fifth ratification or accession. The terms of two of the additional members elected on this occasion shall expire at the end of two years, the names of these two members having been chosen by lot by the Chairman of the Committee.

7. For the filling of casual vacancies, the State Party whose expert has ceased to function as a member of the Committee shall appoint another expert from among its nationals, subject to the approval of the Committee.

8. The members of the Committee shall, with the approval of the General Assembly, receive emoluments from United Nations resources on such terms and conditions as the Assembly may decide, having regard to the importance of the Committee's responsibilities.

9. The Secretary-General of the United Nations shall provide the necessary staff and facilities for the effective performance of the functions of the Committee under the present Convention.

Article 18

1. States Parties undertake to submit to the Secretary-General of the United Nations, for consideration by the Committee, a report on the legislative, judicial, administrative or other measures which they have adopted to give effect to the provisions of the present Convention and on the progress made in this respect:

(a) Within one year after the entry into force for the State concerned;

(b) Thereafter at least every four years and further whenever the Committee so requests.

2. Reports may indicate factors and difficulties affecting the degree of fulfilment of obligations under the present Convention.

Article 19

1. The Committee shall adopt its own rules of procedure.

2. The Committee shall elect its officers for a term of two years.

Article 20

1. The Committee shall normally meet for a period of not more than two weeks annually in order to consider the reports submitted in accordance with article 18 of the present Convention.

2. The meetings of the Committee shall normally be held at United Nations Headquarters or at any other convenient place as determined by the Committee.

Article 21

1. The Committee shall, through the Economic and Social Council, report annually to the General Assembly of the United Nations on its activities and may make suggestions and general recommendations based on the examination of reports and information received from the States Parties. Such suggestions and general recommendations shall be included in the report of the Committee together with comments, if any, from States Parties.

2. The Secretary-General of the United Nations shall transmit the reports of the Committee to the Commission on the Status of Women for its information.

Article 22

The specialized agencies shall be entitled to be represented at the consideration of the implementation of such provisions of the present Convention as fall within the scope of their activities. The Committee may invite the specialized agencies to submit reports on the implementation of the Convention in areas falling within the scope of their activities.

PART VI

Article 23

Nothing in the present Convention shall affect any provisions that are more conducive to the achievement of equality between men and women which may be contained:

(a) In the legislation of a State Party; or

(b) In any other international convention, treaty or agreement in force for that State.

Article 24

States Parties undertake to adopt all necessary measures at the national level aimed at achieving the full realization of the rights recognized in the present Convention.

Article 25

1. The present Convention shall be open for signature by all States.

2. The Secretary-General of the United Nations is designated as the depositary of the present Convention.

3. The present Convention is subject to ratification. Instruments of ratification shall be deposited with the Secretary-General of the United Nations.

4. The present Convention shall be open to accession by all States. Accession shall be effected by the deposit of an instrument of accession with the Secretary-General of the United Nations.

Article 26

1. A request for the revision of the present Convention may be made at any time by any State Party by means of a notification in writing addressed to the Secretary-General of the United Nations.

2. The General Assembly of the United Nations shall decide upon the steps, if any, to be taken in respect of such a request.

Article 27

1. The present Convention shall enter into force on the thirtieth day after the date of deposit with the Secretary-General of the United Nations of the twentieth instrument of ratification or accession.

2. For each State ratifying the present Convention or acceding to it after the deposit of the twentieth instrument of ratification or accession, the Convention shall enter into force on the thirtieth day after the date of the deposit of its own instrument of ratification or accession.

Article 28

1. The Secretary-General of the United Nations shall receive and circulate to all States the text of reservations made by States at the time of ratification or accession.

2. A reservation incompatible with the object and purpose of the present Convention shall not be permitted.

3. Reservations may be withdrawn at any time by notification to this effect addressed to the Secretary-General of the United Nations, who shall then inform all States thereof. Such notification shall take effect on the date on which it is received.

Article 29

1. Any dispute between two or more States Parties concerning the interpretation or application of the present Convention which is not settled by negotiation shall, at the request of one of them, be submitted to arbitration. If within six months from the date of the request for arbitration the parties are unable to agree on the organization of the arbitration, any one of those parties may refer the dispute to the International Court of Justice by request in conformity with the Statute of the Court.

2. Each State Party may at the time of signature or ratification of the present Convention or accession thereto declare that it does not consider itself bound by

paragraph 1 of this article. The other States Parties shall not be bound by that paragraph with respect to any State Party which has made such a reservation.

3. Any State Party which has made a reservation in accordance with paragraph 2 of this article may at any time withdraw that reservation by notification to the Secretary-General of the United Nations.

Article 30

The present Convention, the Arabic, Chinese, English, French, Russian and Spanish texts of which are equally authentic, shall be deposited with the Secretary-General of the United Nations.

IN WITNESS WHEREOF the undersigned, duly authorized, have signed the present Convention.

Document 46

General Assembly resolution on identification of activities that have been completed or are obsolete, of marginal usefulness or ineffective

A/RES/35/209, 17 December 1980

The General Assembly,

Recalling its resolutions 3534 (XXX) of 17 December 1975, 31/93 of 14 December 1976, 32/201 of 21 December 1977, 33/204 of 29 January 1979 and 34/225 of 20 December 1979,

Reaffirming the importance of identifying activities that have been completed or are obsolete, of marginal usefulness or ineffective in order to redeploy resources to finance new United Nations activities,

1. *Takes note* of the report of the Secretary-General 1/ submitted to the General Assembly at the request of the Economic and Social Council, and the related report of the Advisory Committee on Administrative and Budgetary Questions; 2/

2. *Decides* to terminate the activities identified in the Secretary-General's report as obsolete, ineffective or of marginal usefulness, taking into consideration the opinions of competent bodies;

3. *Approves* the proposals of the Secretary-General that an integrated and comprehensive procedure for the identification of completed, obsolete, ineffective and marginally useful activities should be established within the framework of the planning, programming and budgeting cycles of the United Nations;

4. *Requests*, to this end, the Committee for Programme and Co-ordination at its twenty-first session to undertake, in the context of its consideration of programme priority setting, a comprehensive study of this subject and to submit its conclusions to the Economic and Social Council at its second regular session of 1981 and to the General Assembly at its thirty-sixth session;

5. *Transmits* the report of the Secretary-General to the Committee for Programme and Co-ordination for further consideration at its twenty-first session;

6. *Requests* the Secretary-General in the meantime to identify obsolete, marginally useful and ineffective activities, in the preparation of the programme budget for the biennium 1982-1983, for the consideration of the Committee for Programme and Co-ordination and the Advisory Committee on Administrative and Budgetary Questions in their examinations of the programme budget proposals;

7. *Endorses* the recommendation of the Advisory Committee on Administrative and Budgetary Questions that the submission of a full and comprehensive report on the implementation of General Assembly resolution 3534 (XXX) and subsequent resolutions affirming it, requested by the Assembly in its resolution 34/225, be deferred until the thirty-seventh session.

1/ A/C.5/35/40 and Add.1.
2/ A/35/709.

Document 47

African Charter on Human and Peoples' Rights, adopted by the Eighteenth Conference of Heads of State and Government at Nairobi, Kenya

June 1981

PREAMBLE

The African States members of the Organization of African Unity, parties to the present convention entitled "African Charter on Human and Peoples' Rights";

Recalling Decision 115 (XVI) of the Assembly of Heads of State and Government at its Sixteenth Ordinary Session held in Monrovia, Liberia, from 17 to 20 July 1979 on the preparation of "a preliminary draft on an African Charter on Human and Peoples' Rights providing *inter alia* for the establishment of bodies to promote and protect human and peoples' rights";

Considering the Charter of the Organization of African Unity, which stipulates that "freedom, equality, justice and dignity are essential objectives for the achievement of the legitimate aspirations of the African peoples";

Reaffirming the pledge they solemnly made in Article 2 of the said Charter to eradicate all forms of colonialism from Africa, to coordinate and intensify their cooperation and efforts to achieve a better life for the peoples of Africa and to promote international cooperation having due regard to the Charter of the United Nations and the Universal Declaration of Human Rights;

Taking into consideration the virtues of their historical tradition and the values of African civilization which should inspire and characterize their reflection on the concept of human and peoples rights;

Recognizing on the one hand, that fundamental human rights stem from the attributes of human beings, which justifies their international protection and on the other hand, that the reality and respect of peoples' rights should necessarily guarantee human rights;

Considering that the enjoyment of rights and freedoms also implies the performance of duties on the part of everyone;

Convinced that it is henceforth essential to pay particular attention to the right to development and that civil and political rights cannot be dissociated from economic, social and cultural rights in their conception as well as universality and that the satisfaction of economic, social and cultural rights is a guarantee for the enjoyment of civil and political rights;

Conscious of their duty to achieve the total liberation of Africa, the peoples of which are still struggling for their dignity and genuine independence, and undertaking to eliminate colonialism, neo-colonialism, apartheid, zionism and to dismantle aggressive foreign military bases and all forms of discrimination, particularly those based on race, ethnic group, color, sex, language, religion or political opinions;

Reaffirming their adherence to the principles of human and peoples' rights and freedoms contained in the declarations, conventions and other instruments adopted by the Organization of African Unity, the Movement of Non-Aligned Countries and the United Nations;

Firmly convinced of their duty to promote and protect human and peoples' rights and freedoms taking into account the importance traditionally attached to these rights and freedoms in Africa;

Have agreed as follows:

PART I. RIGHTS AND DUTIES

CHAPTER I. HUMAN AND PEOPLES' RIGHTS

Article 1

The Member States of the Organization of African Unity parties to the present Charter shall recognize the rights, duties and freedoms enshrined in this Charter and shall undertake to adopt legislative or other measures to give effect to them.

Article 2

Every individual shall be entitled to the enjoyment of the rights and freedoms recognized and guaranteed in the present Charter without distinction of any kind such as race, ethnic group, colour, sex, language, religion, political or any other opinion, national and social origin, fortune, birth or other status.

Article 3

1. Every individual shall be equal before the law.
2. Every individual shall be entitled to equal protection of the law.

Article 4

Human beings are inviolable. Every human being shall be entitled to respect for his life and the integrity of his person. No one may be arbitrarily deprived of this right.

Article 5

Every individual shall have the right to the respect of the dignity inherent in a human being and to the recognition of his legal status. All forms of exploitation and degradation of man particularly slavery, slave trade, torture, cruel, inhuman or degrading punishment and treatment shall be prohibited.

Article 6

Every individual shall have the right to liberty and to the security of his person. No one may be deprived of his freedom except for reasons and conditions previously laid down by law. In particular, no one may be arbitrarily arrested or detained.

Article 7

1. Every individual shall have the right to have his cause heard. This comprises:

(a) The right to an appeal to competent national organs against acts of violating his fundamental rights as recognized and guaranteed by conventions, laws, regulations and customs in force;

(b) the right to be presumed innocent until proved guilty by a competent court or tribunal;

(c) the right to defence, including the right to be defended by counsel of his choice;

(d) the right to be tried within a reasonable time by an impartial court or tribunal.

2. No one may be condemned for an act or omission which did not constitute a legally punishable offence at the time it was committed. No penalty may be inflicted for an offence for which no provision was made at the time it was committed. Punishment is personal and can be imposed only on the offender.

Article 8

Freedom of conscience, the profession and free practice of religion shall be guaranteed. No one may, subject to law and order, be submitted to measures restricting the exercise of these freedoms.

Article 9

1. Every individual shall have the right to receive information.

2. Every individual shall have the right to express and disseminate his opinions within the law.

Article 10

1. Every individual shall have the right to free association provided that he abides by the law.

2. Subject to the obligation of solidarity provided for in Article 29 no one may be compelled to join an association.

Article 11

Every individual shall have the right to assemble freely with others. The exercise of this right shall be subject only to necessary restrictions provided for by law in particular those enacted in the interest of national security, the safety, health, ethics, rights and freedoms of others.

Article 12

1. Every individual shall have the right to freedom of movement and residence within the borders of a State provided he abides by the law.

2. Every individual shall have the right to leave any country including his own, and to return to his country. This right may only be subject to restrictions, provided for by law for the protection of national security, law and order, public health or morality.

3. Every individual shall have the right, when persecuted, to seek and obtain asylum in other countries in accordance with the law of those countries and international conventions.

4. A non-national legally admitted in a territory of a State Party to the present Charter, may only be expelled from it by virtue of a decision taken in accordance with the law.

5. The mass expulsion of non-nationals shall be prohibited. Mass expulsion shall be that which is aimed at national, racial, ethnic or religious groups.

Article 13

1. Every citizen shall have the right to participate freely in the government of his country, either directly or through freely chosen representatives in accordance with the provisions of the law.

2. Every citizen shall have the right of equal access to the public service of his country.

3. Every individual shall have the right of access to public property and services in strict equality of all persons before the law.

Article 14

The right to property shall be guaranteed. It may only be encroached upon in the interest of public need or in the general interest of the community and in accordance with the provisions of appropriate laws.

Article 15

Every individual shall have the right to work under equitable and satisfactory conditions, and shall receive equal pay for equal work.

Article 16

1. Every individual shall have the right to enjoy the best attainable state of physical and mental health.

2. States Parties to the present Charter shall take the necessary measures to protect the health of their people and to ensure that they receive medical attention when they are sick.

Article 17

1. Every individual shall have the right to education.

2. Every individual may freely take part in the cultural life of his community.

3. The promotion and protection of morals and traditional values recognized by the community shall be the duty of the State.

Article 18

1. The family shall be the natural unit and basis of society. It shall be protected by the State which shall take care of its physical and moral health.

2. The State shall have the duty to assist the family which is the custodian of morals and traditional values recognized by the community.

3. The State shall ensure the elimination of every discrimination against women and also ensure the protection of the rights of the woman and the child as stipulated in international declarations and conventions.

4. The aged and the disabled shall also have the right to special measures of protection in keeping with their physical or moral needs.

Article 19

All peoples shall be equal; they shall enjoy the same respect and shall have the same rights. Nothing shall justify the domination of a people by another.

Article 20

1. All peoples shall have right to existence. They shall have the unquestionable and inalienable right to self-determination. They shall freely determine their political status and shall pursue their economic and social development according to the policy they have freely chosen.

2. Colonized or oppressed peoples shall have the right to free themselves from the bonds of domination by resorting to any means recognized by the international community.

3. All peoples shall have the right to the assistance of the States Parties to the present Charter in their liberation struggle against foreign domination, be it political, economic or cultural.

Article 21

1. All peoples shall freely dispose of their wealth and natural resources. This right shall be exercised in the exclusive interest of the people. In no case shall a people be deprived of it.

2. In case of spoliation the dispossessed people shall have the right to the lawful recovery of its property as well as to an adequate compensation.

3. The free disposal of wealth and natural resources shall be exercised without prejudice to the obligation of promoting international economic cooperation based on mutual respect, equitable exchange and the principles of international law.

4. States parties to the present Charter shall individually and collectively exercise the right to free disposal of their wealth and natural resources with a view to strengthening African unity and solidarity.

5. States Parties to the present Charter shall undertake to eliminate all forms of foreign economic exploitation particularly that practised by international monopolies so as to enable their peoples to fully benefit from the advantages derived from their national resources.

Article 22

1. All peoples shall have the right to their economic, social and cultural development with due regard to their freedom and identity and in the equal enjoyment of the common heritage of mankind.

2. States shall have the duty, individually or collectively, to ensure the exercise of the right to development.

Article 23

1. All peoples shall have the right to national and international peace and security. The principles of solidarity and friendly relations implicitly affirmed by the Charter of the United Nations and reaffirmed by that of the Organization of African Unity shall govern relations between States.

2. For the purpose of strengthening peace, solidarity and friendly relations, States parties to the present Charter shall ensure that:

(a) Any individual enjoying the right of asylum under Article 12 of the present Charter shall not engage in subversive activities against his country of origin or any other State party to the present Charter;

(b) Their territories shall not be used as bases for subversive or terrorist activities against the people of any other State party to the present Charter.

Article 24

All peoples shall have the right to a general satisfactory environment favourable to their development.

Article 25

States parties to the present Charter shall have the duty to promote and ensure through teaching, education and publication, the respect of the rights and freedoms contained in the present Charter and to see to it that these freedoms and rights as well as corresponding obligations and duties are understood.

Article 26

States parties to the present Charter shall have the duty to guarantee the independence of the Courts and shall allow the establishment and improvement of appropriate national institutions entrusted with the promotion and protection of the rights and freedoms guaranteed by the present Charter.

CHAPTER II. DUTIES

Article 27

1. Every individual shall have duties towards his family and society, the State and other legally recognized communities and the international community.

2. The rights and freedoms of each individual shall be exercised with due regard to the rights of others, collective security, morality and common interest.

Article 28

Every individual shall have the duty to respect and consider his fellow beings without discrimination, and to maintain relations aimed at promoting, safeguarding and reinforcing mutual respect and tolerance.

Article 29

The individual shall also have the duty:

1. To preserve the harmonious development of the family and to work for the cohesion and respect of the family; to respect, his parents at all times, to maintain them in case of need;

2. To serve his national community by placing his physical and intellectual abilities at its service;

3. Not to compromise the security of the State whose national or resident he is;

4. To preserve and strengthen social and national solidarity, particularly when the latter is threatened;

5. To preserve and strengthen the national independence and the territorial integrity of his country and to contribute to its defence in accordance with the law;

6. To work to the best of his abilities and competence, and to pay taxes imposed by law in the interest of the society;

7. To preserve and strengthen positive African cultural values in his relations with other members of the society, in the spirit of tolerance, dialogue and consultation and, in general, to contribute to the promotion of the moral well-being of society;

8. To contribute to the best of his abilities, at all times and at all levels, to the promotion and achievement of African unity.

PART II. MEASURES OF SAFEGUARD

CHAPTER I. ESTABLISHMENT AND ORGANIZATION OF THE AFRICAN COMMISSION ON HUMAN AND PEOPLES' RIGHTS

Article 30

An African Commission on Human and Peoples' Rights, hereinafter called "the Commission", shall be established within the Organization of African Unity to promote human and peoples' rights and ensure their protection in Africa.

Article 31

1. The Commission shall consist of eleven members chosen from amongst African personalities of the highest reputation, known for their high morality, integrity, impartiality and competence in matters of human and peoples' rights; particular consideration being given to persons having legal experience.

2. The members of the Commission shall serve in their personal capacity.

Article 32

The Commission shall not include more than one national of the same State.

Article 33

The members of the Commission shall be elected by secret ballot by the Assembly of Heads of State and Government, from a list of persons nominated by the States parties to the present Charter.

Article 34

Each State party to the present Charter may not nominate more than two candidates. The candidates must have the nationality of one of the States parties to the present Charter. When two candidates are nominated by a State, one of them may not be a national of that State.

Article 35

1. The Secretary-General of the Organization of African Unity shall invite States parties to the present Charter at least four months before the elections to nominate candidates;

2. The Secretary-General of the Organization of African Unity shall make an alphabetical list of the persons thus nominated and communicate it to the Heads of State and Government at least one month before the elections.

Article 36

The members of the Commission shall be elected for a six-year period and shall be eligible for re-election. However, the term of office of four of the members elected at the first election shall terminate after two years and the term of office of three others, at the end of four years.

Article 37

Immediately after the first election, the Chairman of the Assembly of Heads of State and Government of the Organization of African Unity shall draw lots to decide the names of those members referred to in Article 36.

Article 38

After their election, the members of the Commission shall make a solemn declaration to discharge their duties impartially and faithfully.

Article 39

1. In case of death or resignation of a member of the Commission, the Chairman of the Commission shall immediately inform the Secretary-General of the Organization of African Unity, who shall declare the seat vacant from the date of death or from the date on which the resignation takes effect.

2. If, in the unanimous opinion of other members of the Commission, a member has stopped discharging his duties for any reason other than a temporary absence, the Chairman of the Commission shall inform the Secretary-General of the Organization of African Unity, who shall then declare the seat vacant.

3. In each of the cases anticipated above, the Assembly of Heads of State and Government shall replace the member whose seat became vacant for the remaining period of his term unless the period is less than six months.

Article 40

Every member of the Commission shall be in office until the date his successor assumes office.

Article 41

The Secretary-General of the Organization of African Unity shall appoint the Secretary of the Commission. He shall provide the staff and services necessary for the effective discharge of the duties of the Commission. The Organization of African Unity shall bear cost of the staff and services.

Article 42

1. The Commission shall elect its Chairman and Vice-Chairman for a two-year period. They shall be eligible for re-election.

2. The Commission shall lay down its rules of procedure.

3. Seven members shall form the quorum.

4. In case of an equality of votes, the Chairman shall have a casting vote.

5. The Secretary-General may attend the meetings of the Commission. He shall neither participate in deliberations nor shall he be entitled to vote. The Chairman of the Commission may, however, invite him to speak.

Article 43

In discharging their duties, members of the Commission shall enjoy diplomatic privileges and immunities provided for in the General Convention on the Privileges and Immunities of the Organization of African Unity.

Article 44

Provision shall be made for the emoluments and allowances of the members of the Commission in the Regular Budget of the Organization of African Unity.

CHAPTER II. MANDATE OF THE COMMISSION

Article 45

The functions of the Commission shall be:

1. To promote Human and Peoples' Rights and in particular:

(a) To collect documents, undertake studies and researches on African problems in the field of human and peoples' rights, organize seminars, symposia and conferences, disseminate information, encourage national and local institutions concerned with human and peoples' rights and, should the case arise, give its views or make recommendations to Governments.

(b) To formulate and lay down, principles and rules aimed at solving legal problems relating to human and peoples' rights and fundamental freedoms upon which African Governments may base their legislation.

(c) Cooperate with other African and international institutions concerned with the promotion and protection of human and peoples' rights.

2. Ensure the protection of human and peoples' rights under conditions laid down by the present Charter.

3. Interpret all the provisions of the present Charter at the request of a State party, an institution of the Organization of African Unity or an African organization recognized by the Organization of African Unity.

4. Perform any other tasks which may be entrusted to it by the the Assembly of Heads of State and Government.

CHAPTER III. PROCEDURE OF THE COMMISSION

Article 46

The Commission may resort to any appropriate method of investigation; it may hear from the Secretary General of the Organization of African Unity or any other person capable of enlightening it.

Communication from States

Article 47

If a State party to the present Charter has good reasons to believe that another State party to this Charter has violated the provisions of the Charter, it may draw, by written communication, the attention of that State to the matter. This communication shall also be addressed to the Secretary-General of the Organization of African Unity and to the Chairman of the Commission. Within three months of the receipt of the communication the State to which the communication is addressed shall give the enquiring State, written explanation or statement elucidating the matter. This should include as much as possible relevant information relating to the laws and rules of procedure applied and applicable and the redress already given or course of action available.

Article 48

If within three months from the date on which the original communication is received by the State to which it is addressed, the issue is not settled to the satisfaction of the two States involved through bilateral negotiation or by any other peaceful procedure, either State shall have the right to submit the matter to the Commission through the Chairman and shall notify the other States involved.

Article 49

Notwithstanding the provisions of Article 47, if a State party to the present Charter considers that another State party has violated the provisions of the Charter, it may refer the matter directly to the Commission by addressing a communication to the Chairman, to the Secretary-General of the Organization of African Unity and the State concerned.

Article 50

The Commission can only deal with a matter submitted to it after making sure that all local remedies, if they exist, have been exhausted, unless it is obvious to the Commission that the procedure of achieving these remedies would be unduly prolonged.

Article 51

1. The Commission may ask the States concerned to provide it with all relevant information.

2. When the Commission is considering the matter, States concerned may be represented before it and submit written or oral representations.

Article 52

After having obtained from the States concerned and from other sources all the information it deems necessary and after having tried all appropriate means to reach an amicable solution based on the respect of human and peoples' rights, the Commission shall prepare, within a reasonable period of time from the notification referred to in Article 48, a report stating the facts and its findings. This report shall be sent to the States concerned and communicated to the Assembly of Heads of State and Government.

Article 53

While transmitting its report, the Commission may make to the Assembly of Heads of State and Government such recommendations as it deems useful.

Article 54

The Commission shall submit to each Ordinary Session of the Assembly of Heads of State and Government a report on its activities.

Other communications

Article 55

1. Before each session, the Secretary of the Commission shall make a list of the communications other than those of States parties to the present Charter and transmit them to the members of the Commission, who shall indicate which communications should be considered by the Commission.

2. A communication shall be considered by the Commission if a simple majority of its members so decide.

Article 56

Communications relating to human and peoples' rights referred to in Article 55 received by the commission, shall be considered if they:

1. Indicate their authors even if the latter request anonymity;

2. Are compatible with the Charter of the Organization of African Unity or with the present Charter;

3. Are not written in disparaging or insulting language directed against the State concerned and its institutions or to the Organization of African Unity;

4. Are not based exclusively on news disseminated through the mass media;

5. Are sent after exhausting local remedies, if any, unless it is obvious that this procedure is unduly prolonged;

6. Are submitted within a reasonable period from the time local remedies are exhausted or from the date the Commission is seized with the matter; and

7. Do not deal with cases which have been settled by these States involved in accordance with the principles of the Charter of the United Nations, or the Charter of the Organization of African Unity or the provisions of the present Charter.

Article 57

Prior to any substantive consideration, all communications shall be brought to the knowledge of the State concerned by the Chairman of the Commission.

Article 58

1. When it appears after deliberations of the Commission that one or more communications apparently relate to special cases which reveal the existence of a series of serious or massive violations of human and peoples' rights, the Commission shall draw the attention of the Assembly of Heads of State and Government to these special cases.

2. The Assembly of Heads of State and Government may then request the Commission to undertake an in-depth study of these cases and make a factual report, accompanied by its finding and recommendations.

3. A case of emergency duly noticed by the Commission shall be submitted by the latter to the Chairman of the Assembly of Heads of State and Government who may request an in-depth study.

Article 59

1. All measures taken within the provisions of the present Charter shall remain confidential until such a time as the Assembly of Heads of State and Government shall otherwise decide.

2. However, the report shall be published by the Chairman of the Commission upon the decision of the Assembly of Heads of State and Government.

3. The report on the activities of the Commission shall be published by its Chairman after it has been considered by the Assembly of Heads of State and Government.

CHAPTER IV. APPLICABLE PRINCIPLES

Article 60

The Commission shall draw inspiration from international law on human and peoples' rights, particularly from the provisions of various African instruments on human and peoples' rights, the Charter of the United Nations, the Charter of the Organization of African Unity, the Universal Declaration of Human Rights, other instruments adopted by the United Nations and by African countries in the field of human and peoples' rights as well as from the provisions of various instruments adopted within the Specialised Agencies of the United Nations of which the parties to the present Charter are members.

Article 61

The Commission shall also take into consideration, as subsidiary measures to determine the principles of law, other general or special international conventions, laying down rules expressly recognized by Member States of the Organization of African Unity, African practices consistent with international norms on human and peoples' rights, customs generally accepted as law, general principles of law recognized by African states as well as legal precedents and doctrine.

Article 62

Each State party shall undertake to submit every two years, from the date the present Charter comes into force, a report on the legislative or other measures taken with a view to giving effect to the rights and freedoms recognized and guaranteed by the present Charter.

Article 63

1. The present Charter shall be open to signature, ratification or adherence of the Member States of the Organization of African Unity.

2. The instruments of ratification or adherence to the present Charter shall be deposited with the Secretary-General of the Organization of African Unity.

3. The present Charter shall come into force three months after the reception by the Secretary-General of the instruments of ratification or adherence of a simple

majority of the Member States of the Organization of African Unity.

PART III. GENERAL PROVISIONS

Article 64

1. After the coming into force of the present Charter, members of the Commission shall be elected in accordance with the relevant Articles of the present Charter.

2. The Secretary-General of the Organization of African Unity shall convene the first meeting of the Commission at the Headquarters of the Organization within three months of the constitution of the Commission. Thereafter, the Commission shall be convened by its Chairman whenever necessary but at least once a year.

Article 65

For each of the States that will ratify or adhere to the present Charter after its coming into force, the Charter shall take effect three months after the date of the deposit by that State of its instrument of ratification or adherence.

Article 66

Special protocols or agreements may, if necessary, supplement the provisions of the present Charter.

Article 67

The Secretary-General of the Organization of African Unity shall inform Member States of the Organization of the deposit of each instrument of ratification or adherence.

Article 68

The present Charter may be amended if a State party makes a written request to that effect to the Secretary-General of the Organization of African Unity. The Assembly of Heads of State and Government may only consider the draft amendment after all the States parties have been duly informed of it and the Commission has given its opinion on it at the request of the sponsoring State. The amendment shall be approved by a simple majority of the States parties. It shall come into force for each State which has accepted it in accordance with its constitutional procedure three months after the Secretary-General has received notice of the acceptance.

Adopted by the eighteenth Conference of Heads of State and Government of the Organization of African Unity, June 1981—Nairobi, Kenya.

Document 48

Declaration on the Elimination of All Forms of Intolerance and of Discrimination Based on Religion or Belief

A/RES/36/55, 25 November 1981

The General Assembly,

Considering that one of the basic principles of the Charter of the United Nations is that of the dignity and equality inherent in all human beings, and that all Member States have pledged themselves to take joint and separate action in cooperation with the Organization to promote and encourage universal respect for and observance of human rights and fundamental freedoms for all, without distinction as to race, sex, language or religion,

Considering that the Universal Declaration of Human Rights and the International Covenants on Human Rights proclaim the principles of non-discrimination and equality before the law and the right to freedom of thought, conscience, religion and belief,

Considering that the disregard and infringement of human rights and fundamental freedoms, in particular of the right to freedom of thought, conscience, religion or whatever belief, have brought, directly or indirectly, wars and great suffering to mankind, especially where they serve as a means of foreign interference in the internal affairs of other States and amount to kindling hatred between peoples and nations,

Considering that religion or belief, for anyone who professes either, is one of the fundamental elements in his conception of life and that freedom of religion or belief should be fully respected and guaranteed,

Considering that it is essential to promote understanding, tolerance and respect in matters relating to freedom of religion and belief and to ensure that the use of religion or belief for ends inconsistent with the Charter of the United Nations, other relevant instruments of the United Nations and the purposes and principles of the present Declaration is inadmissible,

Convinced that freedom of religion and belief should also contribute to the attainment of the goals of world peace, social justice and friendship among peoples and to the elimination of ideologies or practices of colonialism and racial discrimination,

Noting with satisfaction the adoption of several, and the coming into force of some, conventions, under the aegis of the United Nations and of the specialized agencies, for the elimination of various forms of discrimination,

Concerned by manifestations of intolerance and by the existence of discrimination in matters of religion or belief still in evidence in some areas of the world,

Resolved to adopt all necessary measures for the speedy elimination of such intolerance in all its forms and manifestations and to prevent and combat discrimination on the ground of religion or belief,

Proclaims this Declaration on the Elimination of All Forms of Intolerance and of Discrimination Based on Religion or Belief:

Article 1

1. Everyone shall have the right to freedom of thought, conscience and religion. This right shall include freedom to have a religion or whatever belief of his choice, and freedom, either individually or in community with others and in public or private, to manifest his religion or belief in worship, observance, practice and teaching.

2. No one shall be subject to coercion which would impair his freedom to have a religion or belief of his choice.

3. Freedom to manifest one's religion or belief may be subject only to such limitations as are prescribed by law and are necessary to protect public safety, order, health or morals or the fundamental rights and freedoms of others.

Article 2

1. No one shall be subject to discrimination by any State, institution, group of persons, or person on the grounds of religion or other belief.

2. For the purposes of the present Declaration, the expression "intolerance and discrimination based on religion or belief" means any distinction, exclusion, restriction or preference based on religion or belief and having as its purpose or as its effect nullification or impairment of the recognition, enjoyment or exercise of human rights and fundamental freedoms on an equal basis.

Article 3

Discrimination between human beings on the grounds of religion or belief constitutes an affront to human dignity and a disavowal of the principles of the Charter of the United Nations, and shall be condemned as a violation of the human rights and fundamental freedoms proclaimed in the Universal Declaration of Human Rights and enunciated in detail in the International Covenants on Human Rights, and as an obstacle to friendly and peaceful relations between nations.

Article 4

1. All States shall take effective measures to prevent and eliminate discrimination on the grounds of religion or belief in the recognition, exercise and enjoyment of human rights and fundamental freedoms in all fields of civil, economic, political, social and cultural life.

2. All States shall make all efforts to enact or rescind legislation where necessary to prohibit any such discrimination, and to take all appropriate measures to combat intolerance on the grounds of religion or other beliefs in this matter.

Article 5

1. The parents or, as the case may be, the legal guardians of the child have the right to organize the life within the family in accordance with their religion or belief and bearing in mind the moral education in which they believe the child should be brought up.

2. Every child shall enjoy the right to have access to education in the matter of religion or belief in accordance with the wishes of his parents or, as the case may be, legal guardians, and shall not be compelled to receive teaching on religion or belief against the wishes of his parents or legal guardians, the best interests of the child being the guiding principle.

3. The child shall be protected from any form of discrimination on the ground of religion or belief. He shall be brought up in a spirit of understanding, tolerance, friendship among peoples, peace and universal brotherhood, respect for freedom of religion or belief of others, and in full consciousness that his energy and talents should be devoted to the service of his fellow men.

4. In the case of a child who is not under the care either of his parents or of legal guardians, due account shall be taken of their expressed wishes or of any other proof of their wishes in the matter of religion or belief, the best interests of the child being the guiding principle.

5. Practices of a religion or belief in which a child is brought up must not be injurious to his physical or mental health or to his full development, taking into account article 1, paragraph 3, of the present Declaration.

Article 6

In accordance with article 1 of the present Declaration, and subject to the provisions of article 1, paragraph

3, the right to freedom of thought, conscience, religion or belief shall include, *inter alia*, the following freedoms:

(a) To worship or assemble in connection with a religion or belief, and to establish and maintain places for these purposes;

(b) To establish and maintain appropriate charitable or humanitarian institutions;

(c) To make, acquire and use to an adequate extent the necessary articles and materials related to the rites or customs of a religion or belief;

(d) To write, issue and disseminate relevant publications in these areas;

(e) To teach a religion or belief in places suitable for these purposes;

(f) To solicit and receive voluntary financial and other contributions from individuals and institutions;

(g) To train, appoint, elect or designate by succession appropriate leaders called for by the requirements and standards of any religion or belief;

(h) To observe days of rest and to celebrate holidays and ceremonies in accordance with the precepts of one's religion or belief;

(i) To establish and maintain communications with individuals and communities in matters of religion and belief at the national and international levels.

Article 7

The rights and freedoms set forth in the present Declaration shall be accorded in national legislation in such a manner that everyone shall be able to avail himself of such rights and freedoms in practice.

Article 8

Nothing in the present Declaration shall be construed as restricting or derogating from any right defined in the Universal Declaration of Human Rights and the International Covenants on Human Rights.

Document 49

Safeguards guaranteeing protection of the rights of those facing the death penalty, approved by the Economic and Social Council

E/RES/1984/50, 25 May 1984

1. In countries which have not abolished the death penalty, capital punishment may be imposed only for the most serious crimes, it being understood that their scope should not go beyond intentional crimes with lethal or other extremely grave consequences.

2. Capital punishment may be imposed only for a crime for which the death penalty is prescribed by law at the time of its commission, it being understood that if, subsequent to the commission of the crime, provision is made by law for the imposition of a lighter penalty, the offender shall benefit thereby.

3. Persons below 18 years of age at the time of the commission of the crime shall not be sentenced to death, nor shall the death sentence be carried out on pregnant women, or on new mothers, or on persons who have become insane.

4. Capital punishment may be imposed only when the guilt of the person charged is based upon clear and convincing evidence leaving no room for an alternative explanation of the facts.

5. Capital punishment may only be carried out pursuant to a final judgement rendered by a competent court after legal process which gives all possible safeguards to ensure a fair trial, at least equal to those contained in article 14 of the International Covenant on Civil and Political Rights, including the right of anyone suspected of or charged with a crime for which capital punishment may be imposed to adequate legal assistance at all stages of the proceedings.

6. Anyone sentenced to death shall have the right to appeal to a court of higher jurisdiction, and steps should be taken to ensure that such appeals shall become mandatory.

7. Anyone sentenced to death shall have the right to seek pardon, or commutation of sentence; pardon or commutation of sentence may be granted in all cases of capital punishment.

8. Capital punishment shall not be carried out pending any appeal or other recourse procedure or other proceeding relating to pardon or commutation of the sentence.

9. Where capital punishment occurs, it shall be carried out so as to inflict the minimum possible suffering.

Document 50

Convention against Torture and Other Cruel, Inhuman or Degrading Treatment or Punishment

A/RES/39/46, 10 December 1984

The States Parties to this Convention,

Considering that, in accordance with the principles proclaimed in the Charter of the United Nations, recognition of the equal and inalienable rights of all members of the human family is the foundation of freedom, justice and peace in the world,

Recognizing that those rights derive from the inherent dignity of the human person,

Considering the obligation of States under the Charter, in particular Article 55, to promote universal respect for, and observance of, human rights and fundamental freedoms,

Having regard to article 5 of the Universal Declaration of Human Rights and article 7 of the International Covenant on Civil and Political Rights, both of which provide that no one shall be subjected to torture or to cruel, inhuman or degrading treatment or punishment,

Having regard also to the Declaration on the Protection of All Persons from Being Subjected to Torture and Other Cruel, Inhuman or Degrading Treatment or Punishment, adopted by the General Assembly on 9 December 1975,

Desiring to make more effective the struggle against torture and other cruel, inhuman or degrading treatment or punishment throughout the world,

Have agreed as follows:

PART I

Article 1

1. For the purposes of this Convention, the term "torture" means any act by which severe pain or suffering, whether physical or mental, is intentionally inflicted on a person for such purposes as obtaining from him or a third person information or a confession, punishing him for an act he or a third person has committed or is suspected of having committed, or intimidating or coercing him or a third person, or for any reason based on discrimination of any kind, when such pain or suffering is inflicted by or at the instigation of or with the consent or acquiescence of a public official or other person acting in an official capacity. It does not include pain or suffering arising only from, inherent in or incidental to lawful sanctions.

2. This article is without prejudice to any international instrument or national legislation which does or may contain provisions of wider application.

Article 2

1. Each State Party shall take effective legislative, administrative, judicial or other measures to prevent acts of torture in any territory under its jurisdiction.

2. No exceptional circumstances whatsoever, whether a state of war or a threat of war, internal political instability or any other public emergency, may be invoked as a justification of torture.

3. An order from a superior officer or a public authority may not be invoked as a justification of torture.

Article 3

1. No State Party shall expel, return ("*refouler*") or extradite a person to another State where there are substantial grounds for believing that he would be in danger of being subjected to torture.

2. For the purpose of determining whether there are such grounds, the competent authorities shall take into account all relevant considerations including, where applicable, the existence in the State concerned of a consistent pattern of gross, flagrant or mass violations of human rights.

Article 4

1. Each State Party shall ensure that all acts of torture are offences under its criminal law. The same shall apply to an attempt to commit torture and to an act by any person which constitutes complicity or participation in torture.

2. Each State Party shall make these offences punishable by appropriate penalties which take into account their grave nature.

Article 5

1. Each State Party shall take such measures as may be necessary to establish its jurisdiction over the offences referred to in article 4 in the following cases:

(a) When the offences are committed in any territory under its jurisdiction or on board a ship or aircraft registered in that State;

(b) When the alleged offender is a national of that State;

(c) When the victim is a national of that State if that State considers it appropriate.

2. Each State Party shall likewise take such measures as may be necessary to establish its jurisdiction over such offences in cases where the alleged offender is present in any territory under its jurisdiction and it does not extradite him pursuant to article 8 to any of the States mentioned in paragraph 1 of this article.

3. This Convention does not exclude any criminal jurisdiction exercised in accordance with internal law.

Article 6

1. Upon being satisfied, after an examination of information available to it, that the circumstances so warrant, any State Party in whose territory a person alleged to have committed any offence referred to in article 4 is present shall take him into custody or take other legal measures to ensure his presence. The custody and other legal measures shall be as provided in the law of that State but may be continued only for such time as is necessary to enable any criminal or extradition proceedings to be instituted.

2. Such State shall immediately make a preliminary inquiry into the facts.

3. Any person in custody pursuant to paragraph 1 of this article shall be assisted in communicating immediately with the nearest appropriate representative of the State of which he is a national, or, if he is a stateless person, with the representative of the State where he usually resides.

4. When a State, pursuant to this article, has taken a person into custody, it shall immediately notify the States referred to in article 5, paragraph 1, of the fact that such person is in custody and of the circumstances which warrant his detention. The State which makes the preliminary inquiry contemplated in paragraph 2 of this article shall promptly report its findings to the said States and shall indicate whether it intends to exercise jurisdiction.

Article 7

1. The State Party in the territory under whose jurisdiction a person alleged to have committed any offence referred to in article 4 is found shall in the cases contemplated in article 5, if it does not extradite him, submit the case to its competent authorities for the purpose of prosecution.

2. These authorities shall take their decision in the same manner as in the case of any ordinary offence of a serious nature under the law of that State. In the cases referred to in article 5, paragraph 2, the standards of evidence required for prosecution and conviction shall in no way be less stringent than those which apply in the cases referred to in article 5, paragraph 1.

3. Any person regarding whom proceedings are brought in connection with any of the offences referred to in article 4 shall be guaranteed fair treatment at all stages of the proceedings.

Article 8

1. The offences referred to in article 4 shall be deemed to be included as extraditable offences in any extradition treaty existing between States Parties. States Parties undertake to include such offences as extraditable offences in every extradition treaty to be concluded between them.

2. If a State Party which makes extradition conditional on the existence of a treaty receives a request for extradition from another State Party with which it has no extradition treaty, it may consider this Convention as the legal basis for extradition in respect of such offences. Extradition shall be subject to the other conditions provided by the law of the requested State.

3. States Parties which do not make extradition conditional on the existence of a treaty shall recognize such offences as extraditable offences between themselves subject to the conditions provided by the law of the requested State.

4. Such offences shall be treated, for the purpose of extradition between States Parties, as if they had been committed not only in the place in which they occurred but also in the territories of the States required to establish their jurisdiction in accordance with article 5, paragraph 1.

Article 9

1. States Parties shall afford one another the greatest measure of assistance in connection with criminal proceedings brought in respect of any of the offences referred to in article 4, including the supply of all evidence at their disposal necessary for the proceedings.

2. States Parties shall carry out their obligations under paragraph 1 of this article in conformity with any treaties on mutual judicial assistance that may exist between them.

Article 10

1. Each State Party shall ensure that education and information regarding the prohibition against torture are fully included in the training of law enforcement personnel, civil or military, medical personnel, public officials and other persons who may be involved in the custody, interrogation or treatment of any individual subjected to any form of arrest, detention or imprisonment.

2. Each State Party shall include this prohibition in the rules or instructions issued in regard to the duties and functions of any such person.

Article 11

Each State Party shall keep under systematic review interrogation rules, instructions, methods and practices as well as arrangements for the custody and treatment of persons subjected to any form of arrest, detention or imprisonment in any territory under its jurisdiction, with a view to preventing any cases of torture.

Article 12

Each State Party shall ensure that its competent authorities proceed to a prompt and impartial investigation, wherever there is reasonable ground to believe that an act of torture has been committed in any territory under its jurisdiction.

Article 13

Each State Party shall ensure that any individual who alleges he has been subjected to torture in any territory under its jurisdiction has the right to complain to, and to have his case promptly and impartially examined by, its competent authorities. Steps shall be taken to ensure that the complainant and witnesses are protected against all ill-treatment or intimidation as a consequence of his complaint or any evidence given.

Article 14

1. Each State Party shall ensure in its legal system that the victim of an act of torture obtains redress and has an enforceable right to fair and adequate compensation, including the means for as full rehabilitation as possible. In the event of the death of the victim as a result of an act of torture, his dependants shall be entitled to compensation.

2. Nothing in this article shall affect any right of the victim or other persons to compensation which may exist under national law.

Article 15

Each State Party shall ensure that any statement which is established to have been made as a result of torture shall not be invoked as evidence in any proceedings, except against a person accused of torture as evidence that the statement was made.

Article 16

1. Each State Party shall undertake to prevent in any territory under its jurisdiction other acts of cruel, inhuman or degrading treatment or punishment which do not amount to torture as defined in article 1, when such acts are committed by or at the instigation of or with the consent or acquiescence of a public official or other person acting in an official capacity. In particular, the obligations contained in articles 10, 11, 12 and 13 shall apply with the substitution for references to torture of references to other forms of cruel, inhuman or degrading treatment or punishment.

2. The provisions of this Convention are without prejudice to the provisions of any other international instrument or national law which prohibits cruel, inhuman or degrading treatment or punishment or which relates to extradition or expulsion.

PART II

Article 17

1. There shall be established a Committee against Torture (hereinafter referred to as the Committee) which shall carry out the functions hereinafter provided. The Committee shall consist of ten experts of high moral standing and recognized competence in the field of human rights, who shall serve in their personal capacity. The experts shall be elected by the States Parties, consideration being given to equitable geographical distribution and to the usefulness of the participation of some persons having legal experience.

2. The members of the Committee shall be elected by secret ballot from a list of persons nominated by States Parties. Each State Party may nominate one person from among its own nationals. States Parties shall bear in mind the usefulness of nominating persons who are also members of the Human Rights Committee established under the International Covenant on Civil and Political Rights and who are willing to serve on the Committee against Torture.

3. Elections of the members of the Committee shall be held at biennial meetings of States Parties convened by the Secretary-General of the United Nations. At those meetings, for which two thirds of the States Parties shall constitute a quorum, the persons elected to the Committee shall be those who obtain the largest number of votes and an absolute majority of the votes of the representatives of States Parties present and voting.

4. The initial election shall be held no later than six months after the date of the entry into force of this Convention. At least four months before the date of each election, the Secretary-General of the United Nations shall address a letter to the States Parties inviting them to submit their nominations within three months. The Secretary-General shall prepare a list in alphabetical order of all persons thus nominated, indicating the States Parties which have nominated them, and shall submit it to the States Parties.

5. The members of the Committee shall be elected for a term of four years. They shall be eligible for re-election if renominated. However, the term of five of the members elected at the first election shall expire at the end of two years; immediately after the first election the names of these five members shall be chosen by lot by the chairman of the meeting referred to in paragraph 3 of this article.

6. If a member of the Committee dies or resigns or for any other cause can no longer perform his Committee duties, the State Party which nominated him shall appoint another expert from among its nationals to serve for the remainder of his term, subject to the approval of the majority of the States Parties. The approval shall be considered given unless half or more of the States Parties respond negatively within six weeks after having been informed by the Secretary-General of the United Nations of the proposed appointment.

7. States Parties shall be responsible for the expenses of the members of the Committee while they are in performance of Committee duties.

Article 18

1. The Committee shall elect its officers for a term of two years. They may be re-elected.

2. The Committee shall establish its own rules of procedure, but these rules shall provide, *inter alia*, that:

(a) Six members shall constitute a quorum;

(b) Decisions of the Committee shall be made by a majority vote of the members present.

3. The Secretary-General of the United Nations shall provide the necessary staff and facilities for the effective performance of the functions of the Committee under this Convention.

4. The Secretary-General of the United Nations shall convene the initial meeting of the Committee. After its initial meeting, the Committee shall meet at such times as shall be provided in its rules of procedure.

5. The States Parties shall be responsible for expenses incurred in connection with the holding of meetings of the States Parties and of the Committee, including reimbursement to the United Nations for any expenses, such as the cost of staff and facilities, incurred by the United Nations pursuant to paragraph 3 of this article.

Article 19

1. The States Parties shall submit to the Committee, through the Secretary-General of the United Nations, reports on the measures they have taken to give effect to their undertakings under this Convention, within one year after the entry into force of the Convention for the State Party concerned. Thereafter the States Parties shall submit supplementary reports every four years on any new measures taken and such other reports as the Committee may request.

2. The Secretary-General of the United Nations shall transmit the reports to all States Parties.

3. Each report shall be considered by the Committee which may make such general comments on the report as it may consider appropriate and shall forward these to the State Party concerned. That State Party may respond with any observations it chooses to the Committee.

4. The Committee may, at its discretion, decide to include any comments made by it in accordance with paragraph 3 of this article, together with the observations thereon received from the State Party concerned, in its annual report made in accordance with article 24. If so requested by the State Party concerned, the Committee may also include a copy of the report submitted under paragraph 1 of this article.

Article 20

1. If the Committee receives reliable information which appears to it to contain well-founded indications that torture is being systematically practised in the territory of a State Party, the Committee shall invite that State Party to cooperate in the examination of the information and to this end to submit observations with regard to the information concerned.

2. Taking into account any observations which may have been submitted by the State Party concerned, as well as any other relevant information available to it, the Committee may, if it decides that this is warranted, designate one or more of its members to make a confidential inquiry and to report to the Committee urgently.

3. If an inquiry is made in accordance with paragraph 2 of this article, the Committee shall seek the cooperation of the State Party concerned. In agreement with that State Party, such an inquiry may include a visit to its territory.

4. After examining the findings of its member or members submitted in accordance with paragraph 2 of this article, the Commission shall transmit these findings to the State Party concerned together with any comments or suggestions which seem appropriate in view of the situation.

5. All the proceedings of the Committee referred to in paragraphs 1 to 4 of this article shall be confidential, and at all stages of the proceedings the cooperation of the State Party shall be sought. After such proceedings have been completed with regard to an inquiry made in accordance with paragraph 2, the Committee may, after consultations with the State Party concerned, decide to include a summary account of the results of the proceedings in its annual report made in accordance with article 24.

Article 21

1. A State Party to this Convention may at any time declare under this article that it recognizes the competence of the Committee to receive and consider communications to the effect that a State Party claims that another State Party is not fulfilling its obligations under this Convention. Such communications may be received and considered according to the procedures laid down in this article only if submitted by a State Party which has made a declaration recognizing in regard to itself the competence of the Committee. No communication shall be dealt with by the Committee under this article if it concerns a State Party which has not made such a declaration. Communications received under this article shall be dealt with in accordance with the following procedure:

(a) If a State Party considers that another State Party is not giving effect to the provisions of this Convention, it may, by written communication, bring the matter to the attention of that State Party. Within three months after the receipt of the communication the receiving State shall afford the State which sent the communication an explanation or any other statement in writing clarifying the matter, which should include, to the extent possible and pertinent, reference to domestic procedures and remedies taken, pending or available in the matter;

(b) If the matter is not adjusted to the satisfaction of both States Parties concerned within six months after the receipt by the receiving State of the initial communication, either State shall have the right to refer the matter to the Committee, by notice given to the Committee and to the other State;

(c) The Committee shall deal with a matter referred to it under this article only after it has ascertained that all domestic remedies have been invoked and exhausted in the matter, in conformity with the generally recognized principles of international law. This shall not be the rule where the application of the remedies is unreasonably prolonged or is unlikely to bring effective relief to the person who is the victim of the violation of this Convention;

(d) The Committee shall hold closed meetings when examining communications under this article;

(e) Subject to the provisions of subparagraph (c), the Committee shall make available its good offices to the States Parties concerned with a view to a friendly solution of the matter on the basis of respect for the obligations provided for in this Convention. For this purpose, the Committee may, when appropriate, set up an *ad hoc* conciliation commission;

(f) In any matter referred to it under this article, the Committee may call upon the States Parties concerned, referred to in subparagraph (b), to supply any relevant information;

(g) The States Parties concerned, referred to in subparagraph (b), shall have the right to be represented when the matter is being considered by the Committee and to make submissions orally and/or in writing;

(h) The Committee shall, within twelve months after the date of receipt of notice under subparagraph (b), submit a report:

(i) If a solution within the terms of subparagraph (e) is reached, the Committee shall confine its report to a brief statement of the facts and of the solution reached;

(ii) If a solution within the terms of subparagraph (e) is not reached, the Committee shall confine its report to a brief statement of the facts; the written submissions and record of the oral submissions made by the States Parties concerned shall be attached to the report. In every matter, the report shall be communicated to the States Parties concerned.

2. The provisions of this article shall come into force when five States Parties to this Convention have made declarations under paragraph 1 of this article. Such declarations shall be deposited by the States Parties with the Secretary-General of the United Nations, who shall transmit copies thereof to the other States Parties. A declaration may be withdrawn at any time by notification to the Secretary-General. Such a withdrawal shall not prejudice the consideration of any matter which is the subject of a communication already transmitted under this article; no further communication by any State Party shall be received under this article after the notification of withdrawal of the declaration has been received by the Secretary-General, unless the State Party concerned has made a new declaration.

Article 22

1. A State Party to this Convention may at any time declare under this article that it recognizes the competence of the Committee to receive and consider communications from or on behalf of individuals subject to its jurisdiction who claim to be victims of a violation by a State Party of the provisions of the Convention. No communication shall be received by the Committee if it concerns a State Party which has not made such a declaration.

2. The Committee shall consider inadmissible any communication under this article which is anonymous or which it considers to be an abuse of the right of submission of such communications or to be incompatible with the provisions of this Convention.

3. Subject to the provisions of paragraph 2, the Committee shall bring any communications submitted to it under this article to the attention of the State Party to this Convention which has made a declaration under

paragraph 1 and is alleged to be violating any provisions of the Convention. Within six months, the receiving State shall submit to the Committee written explanations or statements clarifying the matter and the remedy, if any, that may have been taken by that State.

4. The Committee shall consider communications received under this article in the light of all information made available to it by or on behalf of the individual and by the State Party concerned.

5. The Committee shall not consider any communications from an individual under this article unless it has ascertained that:

(a) The same matter has not been, and is not being, examined under another procedure of international investigation or settlement;

(b) The individual has exhausted all available domestic remedies; this shall not be the rule where the application of the remedies is unreasonably prolonged or is unlikely to bring effective relief to the person who is the victim of the violation of this Convention.

6. The Committee shall hold closed meetings when examining communications under this article.

7. The Committee shall forward its views to the State Party concerned and to the individual.

8. The provisions of this article shall come into force when five States Parties to this Convention have made declarations under paragraph 1 of this article. Such declarations shall be deposited by the States Parties with the Secretary-General of the United Nations, who shall transmit copies thereof to the other States Parties. A declaration may be withdrawn at any time by notification to the Secretary-General. Such a withdrawal shall not prejudice the consideration of any matter which is the subject of a communication already transmitted under this article; no further communication by or on behalf of an individual shall be received under this article after the notification of withdrawal of the declaration has been received by the Secretary-General, unless the State Party has made a new declaration.

Article 23

The members of the Committee and of the *ad hoc* conciliation commissions which may be appointed under article 21, paragraph 1 (e), shall be entitled to the facilities, privileges and immunities of experts on mission for the United Nations as laid down in the relevant sections of the Convention on the Privileges and Immunities of the United Nations.

Article 24

The Committee shall submit an annual report on its activities under this Convention to the States Parties and to the General Assembly of the United Nations.

PART III

Article 25

1. This Convention is open for signature by all States.

2. This Convention is subject to ratification. Instruments of ratification shall be deposited with the Secretary-General of the United Nations.

Article 26

This Convention is open to accession by all States. Accession shall be effected by the deposit of an instrument of accession with the Secretary-General of the United Nations.

Article 27

1. This Convention shall enter into force on the thirtieth day after the date of the deposit with the Secretary-General of the United Nations of the twentieth instrument of ratification or accession.

2. For each State ratifying this Convention or acceding to it after the deposit of the twentieth instrument of ratification or accession, the Convention shall enter into force on the thirtieth day after the date of the deposit of its own instrument of ratification or accession.

Article 28

1. Each State may, at the time of signature or ratification of this Convention or accession thereto, declare that it does not recognize the competence of the Committee provided for in article 20.

2. Any State Party having made a reservation in accordance with paragraph 1 of this article may, at any time, withdraw this reservation by notification to the Secretary-General of the United Nations.

Article 29

1. Any State Party to this Convention may propose an amendment and file it with the Secretary-General of the United Nations. The Secretary-General shall thereupon communicate the proposed amendment to the States Parties with a request that they notify him whether they favour a conference of States Parties for the purpose of considering and voting upon the proposal. In the event that within four months from the date of such communication at least one third of the States Parties favours such a conference, the Secretary-General shall convene the conference under the auspices of the United Nations. Any amendment adopted by a majority of the States Parties present and voting at the conference shall be submitted by the Secretary-General to all the States Parties for acceptance.

2. An amendment adopted in accordance with paragraph 1 of this article shall enter into force when two thirds of the States Parties to this Convention have notified the Secretary-General of the United Nations that they have accepted it in accordance with their respective constitutional processes.

3. When amendments enter into force, they shall be binding on those States Parties which have accepted them, other States Parties still being bound by the provisions of this Convention and any earlier amendments which they have accepted.

Article 30

1. Any dispute between two or more States Parties concerning the interpretation or application of this Convention which cannot be settled through negotiation shall, at the request of one of them, be submitted to arbitration. If within six months from the date of the request for arbitration the Parties are unable to agree on the organization of the arbitration, any one of those Parties may refer the dispute to the International Court of Justice by request in conformity with the Statute of the Court.

2. Each State may, at the time of signature or ratification of this Convention or accession thereto, declare that it does not consider itself bound by paragraph 1 of this article. The other States Parties shall not be bound by paragraph 1 of this article with respect to any State Party having made such a reservation.

3. Any State Party having made a reservation in accordance with paragraph 2 of this article may at any time withdraw this reservation by notification to the Secretary-General of the United Nations.

Article 31

1. A State Party may denounce this Convention by written notification to the Secretary-General of the United Nations. Denunciation becomes effective one year after the date of receipt of the notification by the Secretary-General.

2. Such a denunciation shall not have the effect of releasing the State Party from its obligations under this Convention in regard to any act or omission which occurs prior to the date at which the denunciation becomes effective, nor shall denunciation prejudice in any way the continued consideration of any matter which is already under consideration by the Committee prior to the date at which the denunciation becomes effective.

3. Following the date at which the denunciation of a State Party becomes effective, the Committee shall not commence consideration of any new matter regarding that State.

Article 32

The Secretary-General of the United Nations shall inform all States Members of the United Nations and all States which have signed this Convention or acceded to it of the following:

(a) Signatures, ratifications and accessions under articles 25 and 26;

(b) The date of entry into force of this Convention under article 27 and the date of the entry into force of any amendments under article 29;

(c) Denunciations under article 31.

Article 33

1. This Convention, of which the Arabic, Chinese, English, French, Russian and Spanish texts are equally authentic, shall be deposited with the Secretary-General of the United Nations.

2. The Secretary-General of the United Nations shall transmit certified copies of this Convention to all States.

Document 51

United Nations Standard Minimum Rules for the Administration of Juvenile Justice (The Beijing Rules)

A/RES/40/33, 29 November 1985

PART ONE

GENERAL PRINCIPLES

1. *Fundamental perspectives*

1.1 Member States shall seek, in conformity with their respective general interests, to further the well-being of the juvenile and her or his family.

1.2 Member States shall endeavour to develop conditions that will ensure for the juvenile a meaningful life in the community, which, during that period in life when she or he is most susceptible to deviant behaviour, will foster a process of personal development and education that is as free from crime and delinquency as possible.

1.3 Sufficient attention shall be given to positive measures that involve the full mobilization of all possible resources, including the family, volunteers and other community groups, as well as schools and other community institutions, for the purpose of promoting the well-being of the juvenile, with a view to reducing the need for intervention under the law, and of effectively, fairly and humanely dealing with the juvenile in conflict with the law.

1.4 Juvenile justice shall be conceived as an integral part of the national development process of each country, within a comprehensive framework of social justice for all juveniles, thus, at the same time, contributing to the protection of the young and the maintenance of a peaceful order in society.

1.5 These Rules shall be implemented in the context of the economic, social and cultural conditions prevailing in each Member State.

1.6 Juvenile justice services shall be systematically developed and coordinated with a view to improving and sustaining the competence of personnel involved in the services, including their methods, approaches and attitudes.

Commentary

These broad fundamental perspectives refer to comprehensive social policy in general and aim at promoting juvenile welfare to the greatest possible extent, which will minimize the necessity of intervention by the juvenile justice system, and in turn, will reduce the harm that may be caused by any intervention. Such care measures for the young, before the onset of delinquency, are basic policy requisites designed to obviate the need for the application of the Rules.

Rules 1.1 to 1.3 point to the important role that a constructive social policy for juveniles will play, *inter alia*, in the prevention of juvenile crime and delinquency. Rule 1.4 defines juvenile justice as an integral part of social justice for juveniles, while rule 1.6 refers to the necessity of constantly improving juvenile justice, without falling behind the development of progressive social policy for juveniles in general and bearing in mind the need for consistent improvement of staff services.

Rule 1.5 seeks to take account of existing conditions in Member States which would cause the manner of implementation of particular rules necessarily to be different from the manner adopted in other States.

2. *Scope of the Rules and definitions used*

2.1 The following Standard Minimum Rules shall be applied to juvenile offenders impartially, without distinction of any kind, for example as to race, colour, sex, language, religion, political or other opinions, national or social origin, property, birth or other status.

2.2 For purposes of these Rules, the following definitions shall be applied by Member States in a manner which is compatible with their respective legal systems and concepts:

(a) A *juvenile* is a child or young person who, under the respective legal systems, may be dealt with for an offence in a manner which is different from an adult;

(b) An *offence* is any behaviour (act or omission) that is punishable by law under the respective legal systems;

(c) A *juvenile offender* is a child or young person who is alleged to have committed or who has been found to have committed an offence.

2.3 Efforts shall be made to establish, in each national jurisdiction, a set of laws, rules and provisions specifically applicable to juvenile offenders and institutions and bodies entrusted with the functions of the administration of juvenile justice and designed:

(a) To meet the varying needs of juvenile offenders, while protecting their basic rights;

(b) To meet the needs of society;

(c) To implement the following rules thoroughly and fairly.

Commentary

The Standard Minimum Rules are deliberately formulated so as to be applicable within different legal systems and, at the same time, to set some minimum standards for the handling of juvenile offenders under any definition of a juvenile and under any system of dealing with juvenile offenders. The Rules are always to be applied impartially and without distinction of any kind.

Rule 2.1 therefore stresses the importance of the Rules always being applied impartially and without distinction of any kind. The rule follows the formulation of principle 2 of the Declaration of the Rights of the Child.

Rule 2.2 defines "juvenile" and "offence" as the components of the notion of the "juvenile offender", who is the main subject of these Standard Minimum Rules (see, however, also rules 3 and 4). It should be noted that age limits will depend on, and are explicitly made dependent on, each respective legal system, thus fully respecting the economic, social, political, cultural and legal systems of Member States. This makes for a wide variety of ages coming under the definition of "juvenile", ranging from 7 years to 18 years or above. Such a variety seems inevitable in view of the different national legal systems and does not diminish the impact of these Standard Minimum Rules.

Rule 2.3 is addressed to the necessity of specific national legislation for the optimal implementation of these Standard Minimum Rules, both legally and practically.

3. Extension of the Rules

3.1 The relevant provisions of the Rules shall be applied not only to juvenile offenders but also to juveniles who may be proceeded against for any specific behaviour that would not be punishable if committed by an adult.

3.2 Efforts shall be made to extend the principles embodied in the Rules to all juveniles who are dealt with in welfare and care proceedings.

3.3 Efforts shall also be made to extend the principles embodied in the Rules to young adult offenders.

Commentary

Rule 3 extends the protection afforded by the Standard Minimum Rules for the Administration of Juvenile Justice to cover:

(a) The so-called "status offences" prescribed in various national legal systems where the range of behaviour considered to be an offence is wider for juveniles than it is for adults (for example, truancy, school and family disobedience, public drunkenness, etc.) (rule 3.1);

(b) Juvenile welfare and care proceedings (rule 3.2);

(c) Proceedings dealing with young adult offenders, depending of course on each given age limit (rule 3.3).

The extension of the Rules to cover these three areas seems to be justified. Rule 3.1 provides minimum guarantees in those fields, and rule 3.2 is considered a desirable step in the direction of more fair, equitable and humane justice for all juveniles in conflict with the law.

4. Age of criminal responsibility

4.1 In those legal systems recognizing the concept of the age of criminal responsibility for juveniles, the beginning of that age shall not be fixed at too low an age level, bearing in mind the facts of emotional, mental and intellectual maturity.

Commentary

The minimum age of criminal responsibility differs widely owing to history and culture. The modern approach would be to consider whether a child can live up to the moral and psychological components of criminal responsibility; that is, whether a child, by virtue of her or his individual discernment and understanding, can be held responsible for essentially antisocial behaviour. If the age of criminal responsibility is fixed too low or if there is no lower age limit at all, the notion of responsibility would become meaningless. In general, there is a close relationship between the notion of responsibility for delinquent or criminal behaviour and other social rights and responsibilities (such as marital status, civil majority, etc.).

Efforts should therefore be made to agree on a reasonable lowest age limit that is applicable internationally.

5. Aims of juvenile justice

5.1 The juvenile justice system shall emphasize the well-being of the juvenile and shall ensure that any reaction to juvenile offenders shall always be in proportion to the circumstances of both the offenders and the offence.

Commentary

Rule 5 refers to two of the most important objectives of juvenile justice. The first objective is the promotion of the well-being of the juvenile. This is the main focus of those legal systems in which juvenile offenders are dealt with by family courts or administrative authorities, but the well-being of the juvenile should also be emphasized in legal systems that follow the criminal court model, thus contributing to the avoidance of merely punitive sanctions. (See also rule 14.)

The second objective is "the principle of proportionality". This principle is well-known as an instrument for curbing punitive sanctions, mostly expressed in terms of just deserts in relation to the gravity of the offence. The response to young offenders should be based on the consideration not only of the gravity of the offence but also of personal circumstances. The individual circumstances of the offender (for example social status, family situation, the harm caused by the offence or other factors affecting personal circumstances) should influence the proportionality of the reactions (for example by having regard to the offender's endeavour to indemnify the victim or to her or his willingness to turn to wholesome and useful life).

By the same token, reactions aiming to ensure the welfare of the young offender may go beyond necessity and therefore infringe upon the fundamental rights of the young individual, as has been observed in some juvenile justice systems. Here, too, the proportionality of the reaction to the circumstances of both the offender and the offence, including the victim, should be safeguarded.

In essence, rule 5 calls for no less and no more than a fair reaction in any given cases of juvenile delinquency and crime. The issues combined in the rule may help to stimulate development in both regards: new and innovative types of reactions are as desirable as precautions against any undue widening of the net of formal social control over juveniles.

6. Scope of discretion

6.1 In view of the varying special needs of juveniles as well as the variety of measures available, appropriate scope for discretion shall be allowed at all stages of proceedings and at the different levels of juvenile justice administration, including investigation, prosecution, adjudication and the follow-up of dispositions.

6.2 Efforts shall be made, however, to ensure sufficient accountability at all stages and levels in the exercise of any such discretion.

6.3 Those who exercise discretion shall be specially qualified or trained to exercise it judiciously and in accordance with their functions and mandates.

Commentary

Rules 6.1, 6.2 and 6.3 combine several important features of effective, fair and humane juvenile justice administration: the need to permit the exercise of discretionary power at all significant levels of processing so that those who make determinations can take the actions deemed to be most appropriate in each individual case; and the need to provide checks and balances in order to curb any abuses of discretionary power and to safeguard the rights of the young offender. Accountability and professionalism are instruments best apt to curb broad discretion. Thus, professional qualifications and expert training are emphasized here as a valuable means of ensuring the judicious exercise of discretion in matters of juvenile offenders. (See also rules 1.6 and 2.2.) The formulation of specific guidelines on the exercise of discretion and the provision of systems of review, appeal and the like in order to permit scrutiny of decisions and accountability are emphasized in this context. Such mechanisms are not specified here, as they do not easily lend themselves to incorporation into international standard minimum rules, which cannot possibly cover all differences in justice systems.

7. *Rights of juveniles*

7.1 Basic procedural safeguards such as the presumption of innocence, the right to be notified of the charges, the right to remain silent, the right to counsel, the right to the presence of a parent or guardian, the right to confront and cross-examine witnesses and the right to appeal to a higher authority shall be guaranteed at all stages of proceedings.

Commentary

Rule 7.1 emphasizes some important points that represent essential elements for a fair and just trial and that are internationally recognized in existing human rights instruments. (See also rule 14.) The presumption of innocence, for instance, is also to be found in article 11 of the Universal Declaration of Human Rights and in article 14, paragraph 2, of the International Covenant on Civil and Political Rights.

Rules 14 *seq.* of these Standard Minimum Rules specify issues that are important for proceedings in juvenile cases, in particular, while rule 7.1 affirms the most basic procedural safeguards in a general way.

8. *Protection of privacy*

8.1 The juvenile's right to privacy shall be respected at all stages in order to avoid harm being caused to her or him by undue publicity or by the process of labelling.

8.2 In principle, no information that may lead to the identification of a juvenile offender shall be published.

Commentary

Rule 8 stresses the importance of the protection of the juvenile's right to privacy. Young persons are particularly susceptible to stigmatization. Criminological research into labelling processes has provided evidence of the detrimental effects (of different kinds) resulting from the permanent identification of young persons as "delinquent" or "criminal".

Rule 8 stresses the importance of protecting the juvenile from the adverse effects that may result from the publication in the mass media of information about the case (for example the names of young offenders, alleged or convicted). The interest of the individual should be protected and upheld, at least in principle. (The general contents of rule 8 are further specified in rule 21.)

9. *Saving clause*

9.1 Nothing in these Rules shall be interpreted as precluding the application of the Standard Minimum Rules for the Treatment of Prisoners adopted by the United Nations and other human rights instruments and standards recognized by the international community that relate to the care and protection of the young.

Commentary

Rule 9 is meant to avoid any misunderstanding in interpreting and implementing the present Rules in conformity with principles contained in relevant existing or emerging international human rights instruments and standards—such as the Universal Declaration of Human Rights, the International Covenant on Economic, Social and Cultural Rights and the International Covenant on Civil and Political Rights, and the Declaration of the Rights of the Child and the draft convention on the rights ·of the child. It should be understood that the application of the present Rules is without prejudice to any such international instruments which may contain provisions of wider application. (See also rule 27.)

PART TWO

INVESTIGATION AND PROSECUTION

10. *Initial contact*

10.1 Upon the apprehension of a juvenile, her or his parents or guardian shall be immediately notified of such apprehension, and, where such immediate notification is not possible, the parents or guardian shall be notified within the shortest possible time thereafter.

10.2 A judge or other competent official or body shall, without delay, consider the issue of release.

10.3 Contacts between the law enforcement agencies and a juvenile offender shall be managed in such a way as to respect the legal status of the juvenile, promote the well-being of the juvenile and avoid harm to her or him, with due regard to the circumstances of the case.

Commentary

Rule 10.1 is in principle contained in rule 92 of the Standard Minimum Rules for the Treatment of Prisoners.

The question of release (rule 10.2) shall be considered without delay by a judge or other competent official. The latter refers to any person or institution in the broadest sense of the term, including community boards or police authorities having power to release an arrested person. (See also the International Covenant on Civil and Political Rights, article 9, paragraph 3.)

Rule 10.3 deals with some fundamental aspects of the procedures and behaviour on the part of the police and other law enforcement officials in cases of juvenile crime. To "avoid harm" admittedly is flexible wording and covers many features of possible interaction (for example the use of harsh language, physical violence or exposure to the environment). Involvement in juvenile justice processes in itself can be "harmful" to juveniles; the term "avoid harm" should be broadly interpreted, therefore, as doing the least harm possible to the juvenile in the first instance, as well as any additional or undue harm. This is especially important in the initial contact with law enforcement agencies, which might profoundly influence the juvenile's attitude towards the State and society. Moreover, the success of any further intervention is largely dependent on such initial contacts. Compassion and kind firmness are important in these situations.

11. *Diversion*

11.1 Consideration shall be given, wherever appropriate, to dealing with juvenile offenders without resorting to formal trial by the competent authority, referred to in rule 14.1 below.

11.2 The police, the prosecution or other agencies dealing with juvenile cases shall be empowered to dispose of such cases, at their discretion, without recourse to formal hearings, in accordance with the criteria laid down for that purpose in the respective legal system and also in accordance with the principles contained in these Rules.

11.3 Any diversion involving referral to appropriate community or other services shall require the consent of the juvenile, or her or his parents or guardian, provided that such decision to refer a case shall be subject to review by a competent authority, upon application.

11.4 In order to facilitate the discretionary disposition of juvenile cases, efforts shall be made to provide for community programmes, such as temporary supervision and guidance, restitution, and compensation of victims.

Commentary

Diversion, involving removal from criminal justice processing and, frequently, redirection to community support services, is commonly practised on a formal and informal basis in many legal systems. This practice serves to hinder the negative effects of subsequent proceedings in juvenile justice administration (for example the stigma of conviction and sentence). In many cases, non-intervention would be the best response. Thus, diversion at the outset and without referral to alternative (social) services may be the optimal response. This is especially the case where the offence is of a non-serious nature and where the family, the school or other informal social control institutions have already reacted, or are likely to react, in an appropriate and constructive manner.

As stated in rule 11.2, diversion may be used at any point of decision-making—by the police, the prosecution or other agencies such as the courts, tribunals, boards or councils. It may be exercised by one authority or several or all authorities, according to the rules and policies of the respective systems and in line with the present Rules. It need not necessarily be limited to petty cases, thus rendering diversion an important instrument.

Rule 11.3 stresses the important requirement of securing the consent of the young offender (or the parent or guardian) to the recommended diversionary measure(s). (Diversion to community service without such consent would contradict the Abolition of Forced Labour Convention.) However, this consent should not be left unchallengeable, since it might sometimes be given out of sheer desperation on the part of the juvenile. The rule underlines that care should be taken to minimize the potential for coercion and intimidation at all levels in the diversion process. Juveniles should not feel pressured (for example in order to avoid court appearance) or be pressured into consenting to diversion programmes. Thus, it is advocated that provision should be made for an objective appraisal of the appropriateness of dispositions involving young offenders by a "competent authority upon application". (The "competent authority" may be different from that referred to in rule 14.)

Rule 11.4 recommends the provision of viable alternatives to juvenile justice processing in the form of community-based diversion. Programmes that involve settlement by victim restitution and those that seek to avoid future conflict with the law through temporary supervision and guidance are especially commended. The merits of individual cases would make diversion appropriate, even when more serious offences have been committed (for example first offence, the act having been committed under peer pressure, etc.).

12. *Specialization within the police*

12.1 In order to best fulfil their functions, police officers who frequently or exclusively deal with juveniles or who are primarily engaged in the prevention of juvenile crime shall be specially instructed and trained. In large cities, special police units should be established for that purpose.

Commentary

Rule 12 draws attention to the need for specialized training for all law enforcement officials who are involved in the administration of juvenile justice. As police are the first point of contact with the juvenile justice system, it is most important that they act in an informed and appropriate manner.

While the relationship between urbanization and crime is clearly complex, an increase in juvenile crime has been associated with the growth of large cities, particularly with rapid and unplanned growth. Specialized police units would therefore be indispensable, not only in the interest of implementing specific principles contained in the present instrument (such as rule 1.6) but more generally for improving the prevention and control of juvenile crime and the handling of juvenile offenders.

13. *Detention pending trial*

13.1 Detention pending trial shall be used only as a measure of last resort and for the shortest possible period of time.

13.2 Whenever possible, detention pending trial shall be replaced by alternative measures, such as close supervision, intensive care or placement with a family or in an educational setting or home.

13.3 Juveniles under detention pending trial shall be entitled to all rights and guarantees of the Standard Minimum Rules for the Treatment of Prisoners adopted by the United Nations.

13.4 Juveniles under detention pending trial shall be kept separate from adults and shall be detained in a separate institution or in a separate part of an institution also holding adults.

13.5 While in custody, juveniles shall receive care, protection and all necessary individual assistance—social, educational, vocational, psychological, medical and physical—that they may require in view of their age, sex and personality.

Commentary

The danger to juveniles of "criminal contamination" while in detention pending trial must not be underestimated. It is therefore important to stress the need for alternative measures. By doing so, rule 13.1 encourages the devising of new and innovative measures to avoid such detention in the interest of the well-being of the juvenile.

Juveniles under detention pending trial are entitled to all the rights and guarantees of the Standard Minimum Rules for the Treatment of Prisoners as well as the International Covenant on Civil and Political Rights, especially article 9 and article 10, paragraphs 2 (b) and 3.

Rule 13.4 does not prevent States from taking other measures against the negative influences of adult offenders which are at least as effective as the measures mentioned in the rule.

Different forms of assistance that may become necessary have been enumerated to draw attention to the broad range of particular needs of young detainees to be addressed (for example females or males, drug addicts, alcoholics, mentally ill juveniles, young persons suffering from the trauma, for example, of arrest, etc.).

Varying physical and psychological characteristics of young detainees may warrant classification measures by which some are kept separate while in detention pending trial, thus contributing to the avoidance of victimization and rendering more appropriate assistance.

The Sixth United Nations Congress on the Prevention of Crime and the Treatment of Offenders, in its resolution 4 on juvenile justice standards, specified that the Rules, *inter alia*, should reflect the basic principle that pre-trial detention should be used only as a last resort, that no minors should be held in a facility where they are vulnerable to the negative influences of adult detainees and that account should always be taken of the needs particular to their stage of development.

PART THREE

ADJUDICATION AND DISPOSITION

14. *Competent authority to adjudicate*

14.1 Where the case of a juvenile offender has not been diverted (under rule 11), she or he shall be dealt with by the competent authority (court, tribunal, board, council, etc.) according to the principles of a fair and just trial.

14.2 The proceedings shall be conducive to the best interests of the juvenile and shall be conducted in an atmosphere of understanding, which shall allow the juvenile to participate therein and to express herself or himself freely.

Commentary

It is difficult to formulate a definition of the competent body or person that would universally describe an adjudicating authority. "Competent authority" is meant to include those who preside over courts or tribunals (composed of a single judge or of several members), including professional and lay magistrates as well as administrative boards (for example the Scottish and Scandinavian systems) or other more informal community and conflict resolution agencies of an adjudicatory nature.

The procedure for dealing with juvenile offenders shall in any case follow the minimum standards that are applied almost universally for any criminal defendant under the procedure known as "due process of law". In accordance with due process, a "fair and just trial" includes such basic safeguards as the presumption of innocence, the presentation and examination of witnesses, the common legal defences, the right to remain silent, the right to have the last word in a hearing, the right to appeal, etc. (See also rule 7.1.)

15. *Legal counsel, parents and guardians*

15.1 Throughout the proceedings the juvenile shall have the right to be represented by a legal adviser or to apply for free legal aid where there is provision for such aid in the country.

15.2 The parents or the guardian shall be entitled to participate in the proceedings and may be required by the competent authority to attend them in the interest of the juvenile. They may, however, be denied participation by the competent authority if there are reasons to assume that such exclusion is necessary in the interest of the juvenile.

Commentary

Rule 15.1 uses terminology similar to that found in rule 93 of the Standard Minimum Rules for the Treatment of Prisoners. Whereas legal counsel and free legal aid are needed to assure the juvenile legal assistance, the right of the parents or guardian to participate as stated in rule 15.2 should be viewed as general psychological and emotional assistance to the juvenile—a function extending throughout the procedure.

The competent authority's search for an adequate disposition of the case may profit, in particular, from the cooperation of the legal representatives of the juvenile (or, for that matter, some other personal assistant who the juvenile can and does really trust). Such concern can be thwarted if the presence of parents or guardians at the hearings plays a negative role, for instance, if they display a hostile attitude towards the juvenile, hence, the possibility of their exclusion must be provided for.

16. *Social inquiry reports*

16.1 In all cases except those involving minor offences, before the competent authority renders a final disposition prior to sentencing, the background and circumstances in which the juvenile is living or the conditions under which the offence has been committed shall be properly investigated so as to facilitate judicious adjudication of the case by the competent authority.

Commentary

Social inquiry reports (social reports or pre-sentence reports) are an indispensable aid in most legal proceedings involving juveniles. The competent authority should be informed of relevant facts about the juvenile, such as social and family background, school career, educational experiences, etc. For this purpose, some jurisdictions use special social services or personnel attached to the court or board. Other personnel, including probation officers, may serve the same function. The rule therefore requires that adequate social services should be available to deliver social inquiry reports of a qualified nature.

17. *Guiding principles in adjudication and disposition*

17.1 The disposition of the competent authority shall be guided by the following principles:

(a) The reaction taken shall always be in proportion not only to the circumstances and the gravity of the offence but also to the circumstances and the needs of the juvenile as well as to the needs of the society;

(b) Restrictions on the personal liberty of the juvenile shall be imposed only after careful consideration and shall be limited to the possible minimum;

(c) Deprivation of personal liberty shall not be imposed unless the juvenile is adjudicated of a serious act involving violence against another person or of persistence in committing other serious offences and unless there is no other appropriate response;

(d) The well-being of the juvenile shall be the guiding factor in the consideration of her or his case.

17.2 Capital punishment shall not be imposed for any crime committed by juveniles.

17.3 Juveniles shall not be subject to corporal punishment.

17.4 The competent authority shall have the power to discontinue the proceedings at any time.

Commentary

The main difficulty in formulating guidelines for the adjudication of young persons stems from the fact that there are unresolved conflicts of a philosophical nature, such as the following:

(a) Rehabilitation versus just desert;

(b) Assistance versus repression and punishment;

(c) Reaction according to the singular merits of an individual case versus reaction according to the protection of society in general;

(d) General deterrence versus individual incapacitation.

The conflict between these approaches is more pronounced in juvenile cases than in adult cases. With the variety of causes and reactions characterizing juvenile cases, these alternatives become intricately interwoven.

It is not the function of the Standard Minimum Rules for the Administration of Juvenile Justice to prescribe which approach is to be followed but rather to identify one that is most closely in consonance with internationally accepted principles. Therefore the essential elements as laid down in rule 17.1, in particular in subparagraphs (a) and (c), are mainly to be understood as practical guidelines that should ensure a common starting point; if heeded by the concerned authorities (see also rule 5), they could contribute considerably to ensuring that the fundamental rights of juvenile offenders are protected, especially the fundamental rights of personal development and education.

Rule 17.1 (b) implies that strictly punitive approaches are not appropriate. Whereas in adult cases, and possibly also in cases of severe offences by juveniles, just desert and retributive sanctions might be considered to have some merit, in juvenile cases such considerations should always be outweighed by the interest of safeguarding the well-being and the future of the young person.

In line with resolution 8 of the Sixth United Nations Congress, rule 17.1 (b) encourages the use of alternatives to institutionalization to the maximum extent possible, bearing in mind the need to respond to the specific requirements of the young. Thus, full use should be made of the range of existing alternative sanctions and new alternative sanctions should be developed, bearing the public safety in mind. Probation should be granted to the greatest possible extent via suspended sentences, conditional sentences, board orders and other dispositions.

Rule 17.1 (c) corresponds to one of the guiding principles in resolution 4 of the Sixth Congress which aims at avoiding incarceration in the case of juveniles unless there is no other appropriate response that will protect the public safety.

The provision prohibiting capital punishment in rule 17.2 is in accordance with article 6, paragraph 5, of the International Covenant on Civil and Political Rights.

The provision against corporal punishment is in line with article 7 of the International Covenant on Civil and Political Rights and the Declaration on the Protection of All Persons from Being Subjected to Torture and Other Cruel, Inhuman or Degrading Treatment or Punishment, as well as the Convention against Torture and Other Cruel, Inhuman or Degrading Treatment or Punishment and the draft convention on the rights of the child.

The power to discontinue the proceedings at any time (rule 17.4) is a characteristic inherent in the handling of juvenile offenders as opposed to adults. At any time, circumstances may become known to the competent authority which would make a complete cessation of the intervention appear to be the best disposition of the case.

18. *Various disposition measures*

18.1 A large variety of disposition measures shall be made available to the competent authority, allowing for flexibility so as to avoid institutionalization to the greatest extent possible. Such measures, some of which may be combined, include:

(a) Care, guidance and supervision orders;

(b) Probation;

(c) Community service orders;

(d) Financial penalties, compensation and restitution;

(e) Intermediate treatment and other treatment orders;

(f) Orders to participate in group counselling and similar activities;

(g) Orders concerning foster care, living communities or other educational settings;

(h) Other relevant orders.

18.2 No juvenile shall be removed from parental supervision, whether partly or entirely, unless the circumstances of her or his case make this necessary.

Commentary

Rule 18.1 attempts to enumerate some of the important reactions and sanctions that have been practised and proved successful thus far, in different legal systems. On the whole they represent promising opinions that deserve replication and further development. The rule does not enumerate staffing requirements because of possible shortages of adequate staff in some regions; in those regions measures requiring less staff may be tried or developed.

The examples given in rule 18.1 have in common, above all, a reliance on and an appeal to the community for the effective implementation of alternative dispositions. Community-based correction is a traditional measure that has taken on many aspects. On that basis, relevant authorities should be encouraged to offer community-based services.

Rule 18.2 points to the importance of the family which, according to article 10, paragraph 1, of the International Covenant on Economic, Social and Cultural Rights, is "the natural and fundamental group unit of society". Within the family, the parents have not only the right but also the responsibility to care for and supervise their children. Rule 18.2, therefore, requires that the separation of children from their parents is a measure of last resort. It may be resorted to only when the facts of the case clearly warrant this grave step (for example child abuse).

19. Least possible use of institutionalization

19.1 The placement of a juvenile in an institution shall always be a disposition of last resort and for the minimum necessary period.

Commentary

Progressive criminology advocates the use of non-institutional over institutional treatment. Little or no difference has been found in terms of the success of institutionalization as compared to non-institutionalization. The many adverse influences on an individual that seem unavoidable within any institutional setting evidently cannot be outbalanced by treatment efforts. This is especially the case for juveniles, who are vulnerable to negative influences. Moreover, the negative effects, not only of loss of liberty but also of separation from the usual social environment, are certainly more acute for juveniles than for adults because of their early stage of development.

Rule 19 aims at restricting institutionalization in two regards: in quantity ("last resort") and in time ("minimum necessary period"). Rule 19 reflects one of the basic guiding principles of resolution 4 of the Sixth United Nations Congress: a juvenile offender should not be incarcerated unless there is no other appropriate response. The rule, therefore, makes the appeal that if a juvenile must be institutionalized, the loss of liberty should be restricted to the least possible degree, with special institutional arrangements for confinement and bearing in mind the differences in kinds of offenders, offences and institutions. In fact, priority should be given to "open" over "closed" institutions. Furthermore, any facility should be of a correctional or educational rather than of a prison type.

20. Avoidance of unnecessary delay

20.1 Each case shall from the outset be handled expeditiously, without any unnecessary delay.

Commentary

The speedy conduct of formal procedures in juvenile cases is a paramount concern. Otherwise whatever good may be achieved by the procedure and the disposition is at risk. As time passes, the juvenile will find it increasingly difficult, if not impossible, to relate the procedure and disposition to the offence, both intellectually and psychologically.

21. Records

21.1 Records of juvenile offenders shall be kept strictly confidential and closed to third parties. Access to such records shall be limited to persons directly concerned with the disposition of the case at hand or other duly authorized persons.

21.2 Records of juvenile offenders shall not be used in adult proceedings in subsequent cases involving the same offender.

Commentary

The rule attempts to achieve a balance between conflicting interests connected with records or files: those of the police, prosecution and other authorities in improving control versus the interests of the juvenile offender. (See also rule 8.) "Other duly authorized persons" would generally include among others, researchers.

22. Need for professionalism and training

22.1 Professional education, in-service training, refresher courses and other appropriate modes of instruction shall be utilized to establish and maintain the necessary professional competence of all personnel dealing with juvenile cases.

22.2 Juvenile justice personnel shall reflect the diversity of juveniles who come into contact with the juvenile justice system. Efforts shall be made to ensure the fair representation of women and minorities in juvenile justice agencies.

Commentary

The authorities competent for disposition may be persons with very different backgrounds (magistrates in the United Kingdom of Great Britain and Northern Ireland and in regions influenced by the common law system; legally trained judges in countries using Roman law and in regions influenced by them; and elsewhere elected or appointed laymen or jurists, members of community-based boards, etc.). For all these authorities, a minimum training in law, sociology, psychology, criminology and behavioural sciences would be required. This is considered as important as the organizational specialization and independence of the competent authority.

For social workers and probation officers, it might not be feasible to require professional specialization as a prerequisite for taking over any function dealing with juvenile offenders. Thus, professional on-the-job instruction would be minimum qualifications.

Professional qualifications are an essential element in ensuring the impartial and effective administration of juvenile justice. Accordingly, it is necessary to improve the recruitment, advancement and professional training of personnel and to provide them with the necessary means to enable them to properly fulfil their functions.

All political, social, sexual, racial, religious, cultural or any other kind of discrimination in the selection, appointment and advancement of juvenile justice personnel should be avoided in order to achieve impartiality in the administration of juvenile justice. This was recommended by the Sixth Congress. Furthermore, the Sixth Congress called on Member States to ensure the fair and equal treatment of women as criminal justice personnel and recommended that special measures should be taken to recruit, train and facilitate the advancement of female personnel in juvenile justice administration.

PART FOUR

NON-INSTITUTIONAL TREATMENT

23. *Effective implementation of disposition*

23.1 Appropriate provisions shall be made for the implementation of orders of the competent authority, as referred to in rule 14.1 above, by that authority itself or by some other authority as circumstances may require.

23.2 Such provisions shall include the power to modify the orders as the competent authority may deem necessary from time to time, provided that such modification shall be determined in accordance with the principles contained in these Rules.

Commentary

Disposition in juvenile cases, more so than in adult cases, tends to influence the offender's life for a long period of time. Thus, it is important that the competent authority or an independent body (parole board, probation office, youth welfare institutions or others) with qualifications equal to those of the competent authority that originally disposed of the case should monitor the implementation of the disposition. In some countries, a *juge de l'exécution des peines* has been installed for this purpose.

The composition, powers and functions of the authority must be flexible; they are described in general terms in rule 23 in order to ensure wide acceptability.

24. *Provision of needed assistance*

24.1 Efforts shall be made to provide juveniles, at all stages of the proceedings, with necessary assistance such as lodging, education or vocational training, employment or any other assistance, helpful and practical, in order to facilitate the rehabilitative process.

Commentary

The promotion of the well-being of the juvenile is of paramount consideration. Thus, rule 24 emphasizes the importance of providing requisite facilities, services and other necessary assistance as may further the best interests of the juvenile throughout the rehabilitative process.

25. *Mobilization of volunteers and other community services*

25.1 Volunteers, voluntary organizations, local institutions and other community resources shall be called upon to contribute effectively to the rehabilitation of the juvenile in a community setting and, as far as possible, within the family unit.

Commentary

This rule reflects the need for a rehabilitative orientation of all work with juvenile offenders. Cooperation with the community is indispensable if the directives of the competent authority are to be carried out effectively. Volunteers and voluntary services, in particular, have proved to be valuable resources but are at present under-utilized. In some instances, the cooperation of ex-offenders (including ex-addicts) can be of considerable assistance.

Rule 25 emanates from the principles laid down in rules 1.1 to 1.6 and follows the relevant provisions of the International Covenant on Civil and Political Rights.

PART FIVE

INSTITUTIONAL TREATMENT

26. *Objectives of institutional treatment*

26.1 The objective of training and treatment of juveniles placed in institutions is to provide care, protection, education and vocational skills, with a view to assisting them to assume socially constructive and productive roles in society.

26.2 Juveniles in institutions shall receive care, protection and all necessary assistance—social, educational, vocational, psychological, medical and physical—that they may require because of their age, sex, and personality and in the interest of their wholesome development.

26.3 Juveniles in institutions shall be kept separate from adults and shall be detained in a separate institution or in a separate part of an institution also holding adults.

26.4 Young female offenders placed in an institution deserve special attention as to their personal needs and problems. They shall by no means receive less care, protection, assistance, treatment and training than young male offenders. Their fair treatment shall be ensured.

26.5 In the interest and well-being of the institutionalized juvenile, the parents or guardians shall have a right of access.

26.6 Inter-ministerial and inter-departmental co-operation shall be fostered for the purpose of providing adequate academic or, as appropriate, vocational training to institutionalized juveniles, with a view to ensuring that they do not leave the institution at an educational disadvantage.

Commentary

The objectives of institutional treatment as stipulated in rules 26.1 and 26.2 would be acceptable to any system and culture. However, they have not yet been attained everywhere, and much more has to be done in this respect.

Medical and psychological assistance, in particular, are extremely important for institutionalized drug addicts, violent and mentally ill young persons.

The avoidance of negative influences through adult offenders and the safeguarding of the well-being of juveniles in an institutional setting, as stipulated in rule 26.3, are in line with one of the basic guiding principles of the Rules, as set out by the Sixth Congress in its resolution 4. The rule does not prevent States from taking other measures against the negative influences of adult offenders, which are at least as effective as the measures mentioned in the rule. (See also rule 13.4.)

Rule 26.4 addresses the fact that female offenders normally receive less attention than their male counterparts, as pointed out by the Sixth Congress. In particular, resolution 9 of the Sixth Congress calls for the fair treatment of female offenders at every stage of criminal justice processes and for special attention to their particular problems and needs while in custody. Moreover, this rule should also be considered in the light of the Caracas Declaration of the Sixth Congress, which, *inter alia*, calls for equal treatment in criminal justice administration, and against the background of the Declaration on the Elimination of Discrimination against Women and the Convention on the Elimination of All Forms of Discrimination against Women.

The right of access (rule 26.5) follows from the provisions of rules 7.1, 10.1, 15.2 and 18.2. Inter-ministerial and inter-departmental cooperation (rule 26.6) are of particular importance in the interest of generally enhancing the quality of institutional treatment and training.

27. *Application of the Standard Minimum Rules for the Treatment of Prisoners adopted by the United Nations*

27.1 The Standard Minimum Rules for the Treatment of Prisoners and related recommendations shall be applicable as far as relevant to the treatment of juvenile offenders in institutions, including those in detention pending adjudication.

27.2 Efforts shall be made to implement the relevant principles laid down in the Standard Minimum Rules for the Treatment of Prisoners to the largest possible extent so as to meet the varying needs of juveniles specific to their age, sex and personality.

Commentary

The Standard Minimum Rules for the Treatment of Prisoners were among the first instruments of this kind to be promulgated by the United Nations. It is generally agreed that they have had a world-wide impact. Although there are still countries where implementation is more an aspiration than a fact, those Standard Minimum Rules continue to be an important influence in the humane and equitable administration of correctional institutions.

Some essential protections covering juvenile offenders in institutions are contained in the Standard Minimum Rules for the Treatment of Prisoners (accommodation, architecture, bedding, clothing, complaints and requests, contact with the outside world, food, medical care, religious service, separation of ages, staffing, work, etc.) as are provisions concerning punishment and discipline, and restraint for dangerous offenders. It would not be appropriate to modify those Standard Minimum Rules according to the particular characteristics of institutions for juvenile offenders within the scope of the Standard Minimum Rules for the Administration of Juvenile Justice.

Rule 27 focuses on the necessary requirements for juveniles in institutions (rule 27.1) as well as on the varying needs specific to their age, sex and personality (rule 27.2). Thus, the objectives and content of the rule interrelate to the relevant provisions of the Standard Minimum Rules for the Treatment of Prisoners.

28. *Frequent and early recourse to conditional release*

28.1 Conditional release from an institution shall be used by the appropriate authority to the greatest possible extent, and shall be granted at the earliest possible time.

28.2 Juveniles released conditionally from an institution shall be assisted and supervised by an appropriate authority and shall receive full support by the community.

Commentary

The power to order conditional release may rest with the competent authority, as mentioned in rule 14.1 or with some other authority. In view of this, it is adequate to refer here to the "appropriate" rather than to the "competent" authority.

Circumstances permitting, conditional release shall be preferred to serving a full sentence. Upon evidence of satisfactory progress towards rehabilitation, even offenders who had been deemed dangerous at the time of their institutionalization can be conditionally released whenever feasible. Like probation, such release may be conditional on the satisfactory fulfilment of the requirements specified by the relevant authorities for a period of time established in the decision, for example relating to "good behaviour" of the offender, attendance in community programmes, residence in half-way houses, etc.

In the case of offenders conditionally released from an institution, assistance and supervision by a probation or other officer (particularly where probation has not yet been adopted) should be provided and community support should be encouraged.

29. *Semi-institutional arrangements*

29.1 Efforts shall be made to provide semi-institutional arrangements, such as half-way houses, educational homes, day-time training centres and other such appropriate arrangements that may assist juveniles in their proper reintegration into society.

Commentary

The importance of care following a period of institutionalization should not be underestimated. This rule emphasizes the necessity of forming a net of semi-institutional arrangements.

This rule also emphasizes the need for a diverse range of facilities and services designed to meet the different needs of young offenders re-entering the community and to provide guidance and structural support as an important step towards successful reintegration into society.

PART SIX

RESEARCH, PLANNING, POLICY FORMULATION AND EVALUATION

30. *Research as a basis for planning, policy formulation and evaluation*

30.1 Efforts shall be made to organize and promote necessary research as a basis for effective planning and policy formulation.

30.2 Efforts shall be made to review and appraise periodically the trends, problems and causes of juvenile delinquency and crime as well as the varying particular needs of juveniles in custody.

30.3 Efforts shall be made to establish a regular evaluative research mechanism built into the system of juvenile justice administration and to collect and analyse relevant data and information for appropriate assessment and future improvement and reform of the administration.

30.4 The delivery of services in juvenile justice administration shall be systematically planned and implemented as an integral part of national development efforts.

Commentary

The utilization of research as a basis for an informed juvenile justice policy is widely acknowledged as an important mechanism for keeping practices abreast of advances in knowledge and the continuing development and improvement of the juvenile justice system. The mutual feedback between research and policy is especially important in juvenile justice. With rapid and often drastic changes in the life-styles of the young and in the forms and dimensions of juvenile crime, the societal and justice responses to juvenile crime and delinquency quickly become outmoded and inadequate.

Rule 30 thus establishes standards for integrating research into the process of policy formulation and application in juvenile justice administration. The rule draws particular attention to the need for regular review and evaluation of existing programmes and measures and for planning within the broader context of overall development objectives.

A constant appraisal of the needs of juveniles, as well as the trends and problems of delinquency, is a prerequisite for improving the methods of formulating appropriate policies and establishing adequate interventions, at both formal and informal levels. In this context, research by independent persons and bodies should be facilitated by responsible agencies, and it may be valuable to obtain and to take into account the views of juveniles themselves, not only those who come into contact with the system.

The process of planning must particularly emphasize a more effective and equitable system for the delivery of necessary services. Towards that end, there should be a comprehensive and regular assessment of the wide-ranging, particular needs and problems of juveniles and an identification of clear-cut priorities. In that connection, there should also be a co-ordination in the use of existing resources, including alternatives and community support that would be suitable in setting up specific procedures designed to implement and monitor established programmes.

Document 52

Declaration of the Basic Principles of Justice for Victims of Crime and Abuse of Power

A/RES/40/34, 29 November 1985

A. *Victims of crime*

1. "Victims" means persons who, individually or collectively, have suffered harm, including physical or mental injury, emotional suffering, economic loss or substantial impairment of their fundamental rights, through acts or omissions that are in violation of criminal laws operative within Member States, including those laws proscribing criminal abuse of power.

2. A person may be considered a victim, under this Declaration, regardless of whether the perpetrator is identified, apprehended, prosecuted or convicted and regardless of the familial relationship between the perpetrator and the victim. The term "victim" also includes, where appropriate, the immediate family or dependants of the direct victim and persons who have suffered harm in intervening to assist victims in distress or to prevent victimization.

3. The provisions contained herein shall be applicable to all, without distinction of any kind, such as race, colour, sex, age, language, religion, nationality, political or other opinion, cultural beliefs or practices, property, birth or family status, ethnic or social origin, and disability.

Access to justice and fair treatment

4. Victims should be treated with compassion and respect for their dignity. They are entitled to access to the mechanisms of justice and to prompt redress, as provided for by national legislation, for the harm that they have suffered.

5. Judicial and administrative mechanisms should be established and strengthened where necessary to enable victims to obtain redress through formal or informal procedures that are expeditious, fair, inexpensive and accessible. Victims should be informed of their rights in seeking redress through such mechanisms.

6. The responsiveness of judicial and administrative processes to the needs of victims should be facilitated by:

(a) Informing victims of their role and the scope, timing and progress of the proceedings and of the disposition of their cases, especially where serious crimes are involved and where they have requested such information;

(b) Allowing the views and concerns of victims to be presented and considered at appropriate stages of the proceedings where their personal interests are affected, without prejudice to the accused and consistent with the relevant national criminal justice system;

(c) Providing proper assistance to victims throughout the legal process;

(d) Taking measures to minimize inconvenience to victims, protect their privacy, when necessary, and ensure their safety, as well as that of their families and witnesses on their behalf, from intimidation and retaliation;

(e) Avoiding unnecessary delay in the disposition of cases and the execution of orders or decrees granting awards to victims.

7. Informal mechanisms for the resolution of disputes, including mediation, arbitration and customary justice or indigenous practices, should be utilized where appropriate to facilitate conciliation and redress for victims.

Restitution

8. Offenders or third parties responsible for their behaviour should, where appropriate, make fair restitution to victims, their families or dependants. Such restitution should include the return of property or payment for the harm or loss suffered, reimbursement of expenses incurred as a result of the victimization, the provision of services and the restoration of rights.

9. Governments should review their practices, regulations and laws to consider restitution as an available sentencing option in criminal cases, in addition to other criminal sanctions.

10. In cases of substantial harm to the environment, restitution, if ordered, should include, as far as possible, restoration of the environment, reconstruction of the infrastructure, replacement of community facilities and reimbursement of the expenses of relocation, whenever such harm results in the dislocation of a community.

11. Where public officials or other agents acting in an official or quasi-official capacity have violated national criminal laws, the victims should receive restitution from the State whose officials or agents were responsible for the harm inflicted. In cases where the Government under whose authority the victimizing act or omission occurred is no longer in existence, the State or Government successor in title should provide restitution to the victims.

12. When compensation is not fully available from the offender or other sources, States should endeavour to provide financial compensation to:

(a) Victims who have sustained significant bodily injury or impairment of physical or mental health as a result of serious crimes;

(b) The family, in particular dependants of persons who have died or become physically or mentally incapacitated as a result of such victimization.

13. The establishment, strengthening and expansion of national funds for compensation to victims should be encouraged. Where appropriate, other funds may also be established for this purpose, including in those cases where the State of which the victim is a national is not in a position to compensate the victim for the harm.

Assistance

14. Victims should receive the necessary material, medical, psychological and social assistance through governmental, voluntary, community-based and indigenous means.

15. Victims should be informed of the availability of health and social services and other relevant assistance and be readily afforded access to them.

16. Police, justice, health, social service and other personnel concerned should receive training to sensitize them to the needs of victims, and guidelines to ensure proper and prompt aid.

17. In providing services and assistance to victims, attention should be given to those who have special needs because of the nature of the harm inflicted or because of factors such as those mentioned in paragraph 3 above.

B. *Victims of abuse of power*

18. "Victims" means persons who, individually or collectively, have suffered harm, including physical or mental injury, emotional suffering, economic loss or substantial impairment of their fundamental rights, through acts or omissions that do not yet constitute violations of national criminal laws but of internationally recognized norms relating to human rights.

19. States should consider incorporating into the national law norms proscribing abuses of power and providing remedies to victims of such abuses. In particular, such remedies should include restitution and/or compensation, and necessary material, medical, psychological and social assistance and support.

20. States should consider negotiating multilateral international treaties relating to victims, as defined in paragraph 18.

21. States should periodically review existing legislation and practices to ensure their responsiveness to changing circumstances, should enact and enforce, if necessary, legislation proscribing acts that constitute serious abuses of political or economic power, as well as promoting policies and mechanisms for the prevention of such acts, and should develop and make readily available appropriate rights and remedies for victims of such acts.

Document 53

Basic Principles on the Independence of the Judiciary, adopted by the Seventh United Nations Congress on the Prevention of Crime and the Treatment of Offenders held at Milan from 26 August to 6 September 1985 and endorsed by General Assembly resolutions 40/32 of 29 November 1985 and 40/146 of 13 December 1985

Whereas in the Charter of the United Nations the peoples of the world affirm, *inter alia*, their determination to establish conditions under which justice can be maintained to achieve international cooperation in promoting and encouraging respect for human rights and fundamental freedoms without any discrimination,

Whereas the Universal Declaration of Human Rights enshrines in particular the principles of equality before the law, of the presumption of innocence and of the right to a fair and public hearing by a competent, independent and impartial tribunal established by law,

Whereas the International Covenants on Economic, Social and Cultural Rights and on Civil and Political Rights both guarantee the exercise of those rights, and in addition, the Covenant on Civil and Political Rights further guarantees the right to be tried without undue delay,

Whereas frequently there still exists a gap between the vision underlying those principles and the actual situation,

Whereas the organization and administration of justice in every country should be inspired by those principles, and efforts should be undertaken to translate them fully into reality,

Whereas rules concerning the exercise of judicial office should aim at enabling judges to act in accordance with those principles,

Whereas judges are charged with the ultimate decision over life, freedoms, rights, duties and property of citizens,

Whereas the Sixth United Nations Congress on the Prevention of Crime and the Treatment of Offenders, by its resolution 16, called upon the Committee on Crime Prevention and Control to include among its priorities the elaboration of guidelines relating to the independence of judges and the selection, professional training and status of judges and prosecutors,

Whereas it is, therefore, appropriate that consideration be first given to the role of judges in relation to the system of justice and to the importance of their selection, training and conduct,

The following basic principles, formulated to assist Member States in their task of securing and promoting the independence of the judiciary should be taken into account and respected by Governments within the framework of their national legislation and practice and be brought to the attention of judges, lawyers, members of the executive and the legislature and the public in general. The principles have been formulated principally with professional judges in mind, but they apply equally, as appropriate, to lay judges, where they exist.

Independence of the judiciary

1. The independence of the judiciary shall be guaranteed by the State and enshrined in the Constitution or the law of the country. It is the duty of all governmental and other institutions to respect and observe the independence of the judiciary.

2. The judiciary shall decide matters before them impartially, on the basis of facts and in accordance with the law, without any restrictions, improper influences, inducements, pressures, threats or interferences, direct or indirect, from any quarter or for any reason.

3. The judiciary shall have jurisdiction over all issues of a judicial nature and shall have exclusive authority to decide whether an issue submitted for its decision is within its competence as defined by law.

4. There shall not be any inappropriate or unwarranted interference with the judicial process, nor shall judicial decisions by the courts be subject to revision. This principle is without prejudice to judicial review or to mitigation or commutation by competent authorities of sentences imposed by the judiciary, in accordance with the law.

5. Everyone shall have the right to be tried by ordinary courts or tribunals using established legal procedures. Tribunals that do not use the duly established procedures of the legal process shall not be created to displace the jurisdiction belonging to the ordinary courts or judicial tribunals.

6. The principle of the independence of the judiciary entitles and requires the judiciary to ensure that judicial proceedings are conducted fairly and that the rights of the parties are respected.

7. It is the duty of each Member State to provide adequate resources to enable the judiciary to properly perform its functions.

Freedom of expression and association

8. In accordance with the Universal Declaration of Human Rights, members of the judiciary are like other citizens entitled to freedom of expression, belief, association and assembly; provided, however, that in exercising such rights, judges shall always conduct themselves in such a manner as to preserve the dignity of their office and the impartiality and independence of the judiciary.

9. Judges shall be free to form and join associations of judges or other organizations to represent their interests, to promote their professional training and to protect their judicial independence.

Qualifications, selection and training

10. Persons selected for judicial office shall be individuals of integrity and ability with appropriate training or qualifications in law. Any method of judicial selection shall safeguard against judicial appointments for improper motives. In the selection of judges, there shall be no discrimination against a person on the grounds of race, colour, sex, religion, political or other opinion, national or social origin, property, birth or status, except that a requirement, that a candidate for judicial office must be a national of the country concerned, shall not be considered discriminatory.

Conditions of service and tenure

11. The term of office of judges, their independence, security, adequate remuneration, conditions of service, pensions and the age of retirement shall be adequately secured by law.

12. Judges, whether appointed or elected, shall have guaranteed tenure until a mandatory retirement age or the expiry of their term of office, where such exists.

13. Promotion of judges, wherever such a system exists, should be based on objective factors, in particular ability, integrity and experience.

14. The assignment of cases to judges within the court to which they belong is an internal matter of judicial administration.

Professional secrecy and immunity

15. The judiciary shall be bound by professional secrecy with regard to their deliberations and to confidential information acquired in the course of their duties other than in public proceedings, and shall not be compelled to testify on such matters.

16. Without prejudice to any disciplinary procedure or to any right of appeal or to compensation from the State, in accordance with national law, judges should enjoy personal immunity from civil suits for monetary damages for improper acts or omissions in the exercise of their judicial functions.

Discipline, suspension and removal

17. A charge or complaint made against a judge in his/her judicial and professional capacity shall be processed expeditiously and fairly under an appropriate procedure. The judge shall have the right to a fair hearing. The examination of the matter at its initial stage shall be kept confidential, unless otherwise requested by the judge.

18. Judges shall be subject to suspension or removal only for reasons of incapacity or behaviour that renders them unfit to discharge their duties.

19. All disciplinary, suspension or removal proceedings shall be determined in accordance with established standards of judicial conduct.

20. Decisions in disciplinary, suspension or removal proceedings should be subject to an independent review. This principle may not apply to the decisions of the highest court and those of the legislature in impeachment or similar proceedings.

Document 54

International Convention against Apartheid in Sports

A/RES/40/64 G, 10 December 1985

The States Parties to the present Convention,

Recalling the provisions of the Charter of the United Nations, in which all Members pledged themselves to take joint and separate action, in cooperation with the Organization, for the achievement of universal respect for, and observance of, human rights and fundamental freedoms for all without distinction as to race, sex, language or religion,

Considering that the Universal Declaration of Human Rights proclaims that all human beings are born free and equal in dignity and rights and that everyone is entitled to all the rights and freedoms set forth in the Declaration without distinction of any kind, particularly in regard to race, colour or national origin,

Observing that, in accordance with the International Convention on the Elimination of All Forms of Racial Discrimination, States Parties to that Convention particularly condemn racial segregation and apartheid and undertake to prevent, prohibit and eradicate all practices of this nature in all fields,

Observing that the General Assembly of the United Nations has adopted a number of resolutions condemning the practice of apartheid in sports and has affirmed its unqualified support for the Olympic principle that no discrimination be allowed on the grounds of race, religion or political affiliation and that merit should be the sole criterion for participation in sports activities,

Considering that the International Declaration against Apartheid in Sports, which was adopted by the General Assembly on 14 December 1977, solemnly affirms the necessity for the speedy elimination of apartheid in sports,

Recalling the provisions of the International Convention on the Suppression and Punishment of the Crime of Apartheid and recognizing, in particular, that participation in sports exchanges with teams selected on the basis of apartheid directly abets and encourages the commission of the crime of apartheid, as defined in that Convention,

Resolved to adopt all necessary measures to eradicate the practice of apartheid in sports and to promote international sports contacts based on the Olympic principle,

Recognizing that sports contact with any country practising apartheid in sports condones and strengthens apartheid in violation of the Olympic principle and thereby becomes the legitimate concern of all Governments,

Desiring to implement the principles embodied in the International Declaration against Apartheid in Sports and to secure the earliest adoption of practical measures to that end,

Convinced that the adoption of an International Convention against Apartheid in Sports would result in more effective measures at the international and national levels, with a view to eliminating apartheid in sports,

Have agreed as follows:

Article 1

For the purposes of the present Convention:

(a) The expression "apartheid" shall mean a system of institutionalized racial segregation and discrimination for the purpose of establishing and maintaining domination by one racial group of persons over another racial group of persons and systematically oppressing them, such as that pursued by South Africa, and "apartheid in sports" shall mean the application of the policies and practices of such a system in sports activities, whether organized on a professional or an amateur basis;

(b) The expression "national sports facilities" shall mean any sports facility operated within the framework of a sports programme conducted under the auspices of a national government;

(c) The expression "Olympic principle" shall mean the principle that no discrimination be allowed on the grounds of race, religion or political affiliation;

(d) The expression "sports contracts" shall mean any contract concluded for the organization, promotion, performance or derivative rights, including servicing, of any sports activity;

(e) The expression "sports bodies" shall mean any organization constituted to organize sports activities at the national level, including national Olympic committees, national sports federations or national governing sports committees;

(f) The expression "team" shall mean a group of sportsmen organized for the purpose of participating in sports activities in competition with other such organized groups;

(g) The expression "sportsmen" shall mean men and women who participate in sports activities on an individual or team basis, as well as managers, coaches, trainers and other officials whose functions are essential for the operation of a team.

Article 2

States Parties strongly condemn apartheid and undertake to pursue immediately by all appropriate means the policy of eliminating the practice of apartheid in all its forms from sports.

Article 3

States Parties shall not permit sports contact with a country practising apartheid and shall take appropriate action to ensure that their sports bodies, teams, and individual sportsmen do not have such contact.

Article 4

States Parties shall take all possible measures to prevent sports contact with a country practising apartheid and shall ensure that effective means exist for bringing about compliance with such measures.

Article 5

States Parties shall refuse to provide financial or other assistance to enable their sports bodies, teams and individual sportsmen to participate in sports activities in a country practising apartheid or with teams or individual sportsmen selected on the basis of apartheid.

Article 6

Each State Party shall take appropriate action against its sports bodies, teams and individual sportsmen that participate in sports activities in a country practising apartheid or with teams representing a country practising apartheid, which in particular shall include:

(a) Refusal to provide financial or other assistance for any purpose to such sports bodies, teams and individual sportsmen;

(b) Restriction of access to national sports facilities by such sports bodies, teams and individual sportsmen;

(c) Non-enforceability of all sports contracts which involve sports activities in a country practising apartheid or with teams or individual sportsmen selected on the basis of apartheid;

(d) Denial and withdrawal of national honours or awards in sports to such teams and individual sportsmen;

(e) Denial of official receptions in honour of such teams or sportsmen.

Article 7

States Parties shall deny visas and/or entry to representatives of sports bodies, teams and individual sportsmen representing a country practising apartheid.

Article 8

States Parties shall take all appropriate action to secure the expulsion of a country practising apartheid from international and regional sports bodies.

Article 9

States Parties shall take all appropriate measures to prevent international sports bodies from imposing financial or other penalties on affiliated bodies which, in accordance with United Nations resolutions, the provisions of the present Convention and the spirit of the Olympic principle, refuse to participate in sports with a country practising apartheid.

Article 10

1. States Parties shall use their best endeavours to ensure universal compliance with the Olympic principles of non-discrimination and the provisions of the present Convention.

2. Towards this end, States Parties shall prohibit entry into their countries of members of teams and individual sportsmen participating or who have participated in sports competitions in South Africa and shall prohibit entry into their countries of representatives of sports bodies, members of teams and individual sportsmen who invite on their own initiative sports bodies, teams and sportsmen officially representing a country practising apartheid and participating under its flag. States Parties may also prohibit entry of representatives of sports bodies, members of teams or individual sportsmen who maintain sports contacts with sports bodies, teams or sportsmen representing a country practising apartheid and participating under its flag. Prohibition of entry should not violate the regulations of the relevant sports federations which support the elimination of apartheid in sports and shall apply only to participation in sports activities.

3. States Parties shall advise their national representatives to international sports federations to take all possible and practical steps to prevent the participation of the sports bodies, teams and sportsmen referred to in paragraph 2 above in international sports competitions and shall, through their representatives in international sports organizations, take every possible measure:

(a) To ensure the expulsion of South Africa from all federations in which it still holds membership as well as to deny South Africa reinstatement to membership in any federation from which it has been expelled;

(b) In case of national federations condoning sports exchanges with a country practising apartheid, to impose sanctions against such national federations including, if necessary, expulsion from the relevant international sports organization and exclusion of their representatives from participation in international sports competitions.

4. In cases of flagrant violations of the provisions of the present Convention, States Parties shall take appropriate action as they deem fit, including, where necessary, steps aimed at the exclusion of the responsible national sports governing bodies, national sports federations or sportsmen of the countries concerned from international sports competition.

5. The provisions of the present article relating specifically to South Africa shall cease to apply when the system of apartheid is abolished in that country.

Article 11

1. There shall be established a Commission against Apartheid in Sports (hereinafter referred to as "the Commission") consisting of fifteen members of high moral character and committed to the struggle against apartheid, particular attention being paid to participation of persons having experience in sports administration, elected by the States Parties from among their nationals, having regard to the most equitable geographical distribution and the representation of the principal legal systems.

2. The members of the Commission shall be elected by secret ballot from a list of persons nominated by the States Parties. Each State Party may nominate one person from among its own nationals.

3. The initial election shall be held six months after the date of the entry into force of the present Convention. At least three months before the date of each election, the Secretary-General of the United Nations shall address a letter to the States Parties inviting them to submit their nominations within two months. The Secretary-General shall prepare a list in alphabetical order of all persons thus nominated, indicating the States Parties which have nominated them, and shall submit it to the States Parties.

4. Elections of the members of the Commission shall be held at a meeting of States Parties convened by the Secretary-General at United Nations Headquarters. At that meeting, for which two thirds of the States Parties shall constitute a quorum, the persons elected to the Commission shall be those nominees who obtain the largest number of votes and an absolute majority of the votes of the representatives of States Parties present and voting.

5. The members of the Commission shall be elected for a term of four years. However, the terms of nine of the members elected at the first election shall expire at the end of two years; immediately after the first election, the names of these nine members shall be chosen by lot by the Chairman of the Commission.

6. For the filling of casual vacancies, the State Party whose national has ceased to function as a member of the Commission shall appoint another person from among its nationals, subject to the approval of the Commission.

7. States Parties shall be responsible for the expenses of the members of the Commission while they are in performance of Commission duties.

Article 12

1. States Parties undertake to submit to the Secretary-General of the United Nations, for consideration by the

Commission, a report on the legislative, judicial, administrative or other measures which they have adopted to give effect to the provisions of the present Convention within one year of its entry into force and thereafter every two years. The Commission may request further information from the States Parties.

2. The Commission shall report annually through the Secretary-General to the General Assembly of the United Nations on its activities and may make suggestions and general recommendations based on the examination of the reports and information received from the States Parties. Such suggestions and recommendations shall be reported to the General Assembly together with comments, if any, from States Parties concerned.

3. The Commission shall examine, in particular, the implementation of the provisions of article 10 of the present Convention and make recommendations on action to be undertaken.

4. A meeting of States Parties shall be convened by the Secretary-General at the request of a majority of the States Parties to consider further action with respect to the implementation of the provisions of article 10 of the present Convention. In cases of flagrant violation of the provisions of the present Convention, a meeting of States Parties shall be convened by the Secretary-General at the request of the Commission.

Article 13

1. Any State Party may at any time declare that it recognizes the competence of the Commission to receive and examine complaints concerning breaches of the provisions of the present Convention submitted by States Parties which have also made such a declaration. The Commission may decide on the appropriate measures to be taken in respect of breaches.

2. States Parties against which a complaint has been made, in accordance with paragraph 1 of the present article, shall be entitled to be represented and take part in the proceedings of the Commission.

Article 14

1. The Commission shall meet at least once a year.

2. The Commission shall adopt its own rules of procedure.

3. The secretariat of the Commission shall be provided by the Secretary-General of the United Nations.

4. The meetings of the Commission shall normally be held at United Nations Headquarters.

5. The Secretary-General shall convene the initial meeting of the Commission.

Article 15

The Secretary-General of the United Nations shall be the depositary of the present Convention.

Article 16

1. The present Convention shall be open for signature at United Nations Headquarters by all States until its entry into force.

2. The present Convention shall be subject to ratification, acceptance or approval by the signatory States.

Article 17

The present Convention shall be open for accession by all States.

Article 18

1. The present Convention shall enter into force on the thirtieth day after the date of deposit with the Secretary-General of the United Nations of the twenty-seventh instrument of ratification, acceptance, approval or accession.

2. For each State ratifying, accepting, approving or acceding to the present Convention after its entry into force, the Convention shall enter into force on the thirtieth day after the date of deposit of the relevant instrument.

Article 19

Any dispute between States Parties arising out of the interpretation, application or implementation of the present Convention which is not settled by negotiation shall be brought before the International Court of Justice at the request and with the mutual consent of the States Parties to the dispute, save where the Parties to the dispute have agreed on some other form of settlement.

Article 20

1. Any State Party may propose an amendment or revision to the present Convention and file it with the depositary. The Secretary-General of the United Nations shall thereupon communicate the proposed amendment or revision to the States Parties with a request that they notify him whether they favour a conference of States Parties for the purpose of considering and voting upon the proposal. In the event that at least one third of the States Parties favour such a conference, the Secretary-General shall convene the conference under the auspices of the United Nations. Any amendment or revision adopted by the majority of the States Parties present and voting at the conference shall be submitted to the General Assembly of the United Nations for approval.

2. Amendments or revisions shall come into force when they have been approved by the General Assembly and accepted by a two-thirds majority of the States Parties, in accordance with their respective constitutional processes.

3. When amendments or revisions come into force, they shall be binding on those States Parties which have accepted them, other States Parties still being bound by the provisions of the present Convention and any earlier amendment or revision which they have accepted.

Article 21

A State Party may withdraw from the present Convention by written notification to the depositary. Such withdrawal shall take effect one year after the date of receipt of the notification by the depositary.

Article 22

The present Convention has been concluded in Arabic, Chinese, English, French, Russian and Spanish, all texts being equally authentic.

Document 55

General Assembly resolution on implementation of the Nairobi Forward-looking Strategies for the Advancement of Women

A/RES/40/108, 13 December 1985

The General Assembly,

Recalling its resolution 3520 (XXX) of 15 December 1975, in which it proclaimed the period from 1976 to 1985 the United Nations Decade for Women: Equality, Development and Peace,

Bearing in mind the Convention on the Elimination of All Forms of Discrimination against Women, 1/ which was adopted on 18 December 1979 and which came into force on 3 September 1981,

Recalling also the principles and objectives set forth in the Declaration of Mexico on the Equality of Women and Their Contribution to Development and Peace, 1975, 2/ the World Plan of Action for the Implementation of the Objectives of the International Women's Year 3/ and the Programme of Action for the Second Half of the United Nations Decade for Women, 4/

Bearing in mind also its resolutions 3201 (S-VI) and 3202 (S-VI) of 1 May 1974, containing the Declaration and Programme of Action on the Establishment of a New International Economic Order, 3281 (XXIX) of 12 December 1974, containing the Charter of Economic Rights and Duties of States, 3362 (S-VII) of 16 September 1975 on development and international economic cooperation and 2542 (XXIV) of 11 December 1969 proclaiming the Declaration on Social Progress and Development,

Bearing in mind further the consensus achieved in the text of the International Development Strategy for the Third United Nations Development Decade, contained in the annex to its resolution 35/56 of 5 December 1980, in particular regarding the implementation of the objectives of the United Nations Decade for Women within the framework of the Strategy,

Recalling also its resolution 37/63 of 3 December 1982, by which it proclaimed the Declaration on the Participation of Women in Promoting International Peace and Cooperation,

Recalling further its resolution 39/29 of 3 December 1984 on the critical economic situation in Africa,

Recalling its resolution 35/136 of 11 December 1980, in which it decided to convene in 1985, at the conclusion of the Decade, a World Conference to Review and Appraise the Achievements of the United Nations Decade for Women,

Conscious of the considerable and constructive contribution made by the Commission on the Status of Women acting as preparatory body for the Conference, the specialized agencies, the regional commissions and other organizations of the United Nations system, Member States and non-governmental organizations in the preparations for the Conference,

Aware of the continued contribution made by the Non-Governmental Organizations Forum to the advancement of women,

Convinced that the full integration of women in all aspects of political, economic and social life, at the international, regional and national levels, is essential if the

1/ Resolution 34/180, annex.
2/ *Report of the World Conference of the International Women's Year, Mexico City, 19 June-2 July 1975* (United Nations publication, Sales No. E.76.IV.1), chap. I.
3/ Ibid., chap. II, sect. A.
4/ *Report of the World Conference on the United Nations Decade for Women: Equality, Development and Peace, Copenhagen, 14-30 July 1980* (United Nations publication, Sales No. E.80.IV.3 and corrigendum), chap. I, sect. A.

obstacles to the achievement of the goals and objectives of the Decade are to be overcome,

Having considered the report of the World Conference to Review and Appraise the Achievements of the United Nations Decade for Women: Equality, Development and Peace, 5/

Convinced that the Conference, by adopting the Nairobi Forward-looking Strategies for the Advancement of Women, 6/ has made an important and positive contribution to the attainment of the objectives of the Decade and provided a policy framework for advancing the status of women to the year 2000,

Further convinced that the Conference has made an important and constructive contribution by appraising the progress achieved and obstacles encountered in the implementation of the objectives of the Decade and by preparing and adopting strategies to advance the status of women for the next fifteen years,

Stressing that during the period 1986-2000 the primary responsibility for implementing the Forward-looking Strategies rests with individual countries, as they are intended to serve as guidelines for a process of continuous adaptation to diverse and changing situations at speeds and in modes determined by overall national priorities, within which the integration of women in development should rank high,

Reaffirming that the realization of equal rights for women at all levels and in all areas of life will contribute to the achievement of a just and lasting peace, to social progress and to respect for human rights and fundamental freedoms, and that the integration of women in the mainstream of the development process requires not only commitment at the national, regional and international levels, but also continuing financial and technical support, and also requires the establishment of the new international economic order,

Considering that the Forward-looking Strategies should immediately be translated into concrete action by Governments, as determined by overall national priorities, by organizations of the United Nations system, specialized agencies and intergovernmental and non-governmental organizations, including women's organizations,

Persuaded of the importance of taking measures to ensure system-wide co-ordination within the United Nations in order to develop a comprehensive and integrated approach to the issues which are crucial to the advancement of women,

1. *Takes note with satisfaction* of the report of the World Conference to Review and Appraise the Achievement of the United Nations Decade for Women: Equality, Development and Peace; 5/

2. *Endorses* the Nairobi Forward-looking Strategies for the Advancement of Women; 6/

3. *Affirms* that the implementation of the Forward-looking Strategies should result in the elimination of all forms of inequality between women and men and in the complete integration of women into the development process and that that should guarantee broad participation by women in efforts to strengthen peace and security in the world;

4. *Declares* that the objectives of the United Nations Decade for Women: Equality, Development and Peace, with the subtheme "Employment, Health and Education", remain valid;

5. *Calls upon* Governments to allocate adequate resources and to take effective appropriate measures to implement the Forward-looking Strategies as a matter of high priority, including the establishment or reinforcement, as appropriate, of national machineries to promote the advancement of women, and to monitor the implementation of these strategies with a view to ensuring the full integration of women in the political, economic, social and cultural life of their countries;

6. *Calls upon* all Governments of Member States to appoint women to decision-making positions, bearing in mind their contribution to national development;

7. *Invites* Governments, when preparing and evaluating national plans and programmes of action, to incorporate measurable targets for overcoming obstacles to the advancement of women and to include measures for the involvement of women in development, both as agents and beneficiaries, on an equal basis with men, and to review the impact of development policies and programmes on women;

8. *Invites* governmental, intergovernmental and non-governmental organizations to give high priority to the implementation of the Forward-looking Strategies and, in particular, to ensure that sectoral policies and programmes for development include strategies to promote the participation of women as agents and beneficiaries on an equal basis with men;

9. *Urges* all Governments to contribute to the strengthening of institutional co-ordination in their regions and subregions in order to establish collaborative arrangements and to develop approaches for the implementation of the Forward-looking Strategies at those levels;

10. *Urges* all organizations of the United Nations system, including the regional commissions and all specialized agencies, to take the necessary measures to ensure

5/ *Report of the World Conference to Review and Appraise the Achievements of the United Nations Decade for Women: Equality, Development and Peace, Nairobi, 15-26 July 1985* (United Nations publication, Sales No. E.85.IV.10).
6/ Ibid., chap. I, sect. A.

a concerted and sustained effort for the implementation of the provisions of the Forward-looking Strategies with a view to achieving a substantial improvement in the status of women by the year 2000 and to ensure that all projects and programmes take into account the need for the complete integration of women and women's concerns;

11. *Requests* the Secretary-General and the specialized agencies and bodies of the United Nations system to establish, where they do not already exist, focal points on women's issues in all sectors of the work of the organizations of the United Nations system;

12. *Urges* the Administrative Committee on Co-ordination to review periodically the system-wide implementation of the Forward-looking Strategies and to hold regular inter-agency meetings on women within the framework of the Administrative Committee on Co-ordination;

13. *Emphasizes* the central role of the Commission on the Status of Women in matters related to the advancement of the status of women and calls upon it to promote the implementation of the Forward-looking Strategies to the year 2000 based on the goals of the United Nations Decade for Women: Equality, Development and Peace, and the subtheme "Employment, Health and Education", and urges all organizations of the United Nations system to cooperate with the Commission in this task;

14. *Requests* the Secretary-General to ensure that the Commission on the Status of Women receives the support services it requires to fulfil its central role effectively;

15. *Also requests* the Secretary-General to invite Governments, organizations of the United Nations system, including regional commissions and specialized agencies, intergovernmental and non-governmental organizations to report periodically through the Commission on the Status of Women to the Economic and Social Council on the activities undertaken at all levels to implement the Forward-looking Strategies;

16. *Further requests* the Secretary-General, in preparing the note on the integrated reporting system for periodic review and appraisal of progress in the advancement of women for submission to the Commission on the Status of Women at its thirty-first session, as called for in Economic and Social Council decision 1984/123 of 24 May 1984, to include proposals for a reporting system to facilitate the monitoring of the implementation of the Forward-looking Strategies as set out in paragraph 15 above, taking into account the experience gained during the Decade, the views of Governments and the need not to duplicate existing reporting obligations, bearing in mind the need to carry out periodical in-depth sectoral reviews of progress achieved and obstacles encountered in implementing the Forward-looking Strategies to the year 2000;

17. *Recommends* that the Secretary-General prepare and submit to the Commission on the Status of Women at its thirty-first session, bearing in mind the remarks and concrete recommendations made during the debate at the fortieth session, in particular the proposals about increasing the number of members and the frequency of meetings of the Commission, a report on alternative measures to strengthen the Commission in the discharge of its functions following the United Nations Decade for Women, and also recommends that the recommendations of the Commission on the matter be reported to the General Assembly at its forty-first session through the Economic and Social Council;

18. *Reaffirms* the role of the Centre for Social Development and Humanitarian Affairs of the Department of International Economic and Social Affairs of the Secretariat, in particular the Branch for the Advancement of Women, as the substantive secretariat of the Commission and as a focal point for matters on women, and requests the Secretariat to collect and disseminate information on system-wide activities related to the implementation of the Forward-looking Strategies;

19. *Takes note with satisfaction* of the appointment of the Co-ordinator for the Improvement of the Status of Women in the Secretariat of the United Nations, in accordance with General Assembly resolution 39/245 of 18 December 1984, and, in this context, of the fact that the Secretary-General should continue to plan and implement positive actions and programmes to improve the status of women in the Secretariat and to monitor the progress achieved;

20. *Calls upon* the Secretary-General and the heads of the specialized agencies and other United Nations bodies to establish new five-year targets at each level for the percentage of women in Professional and decision-making positions, in accordance with the criteria established by the General Assembly, in particular that of equitable geographical distribution, in order that a definite upward trend in the application of Assembly resolution 33/143 of 20 December 1978 be registered in the number of Professional and decision-making positions held by women by 1990 and to set additional targets every five years;

21. *Welcomes* Economic and Social Council resolution 1985/46 of 31 May 1985 regarding women and development and, noting the particular importance of paragraph 4 of that resolution, recommends that immediate measures be taken to ensure that future medium-term plans of the United Nations and the specialized agencies should contain intersectoral presentations of the various programmes dealing with issues of concern to

women and that revisions of current plans should be considered in the light of the results of the World Conference to Review and Appraise the Achievements of the United Nations Decade for Women: Equality, Development and Peace; 5/

22. *Requests* the Secretary-General to take into account the requirements of the Forward-looking Strategies in preparing the programme budget and programme of work for the biennium 1988-1989;

23. *Urges* all financial institutions and all international regional and subregional organizations, institutions, development banks and general funding agencies to ensure that their policies and programmes promote the full participation of women as agents and beneficiaries in the development process;

24. *Invites* the Secretary-General to circulate the report of the Conference among Member States, all organizations of the United Nations system and specialized agencies, intergovernmental and non-governmental organizations in order to ensure that the Forward-looking Strategies are publicized and disseminated as widely as possible, and encourages Governments to translate the Strategies into their national languages;

25. *Requests* the Secretary-General and the heads of all organizations within the United Nations system and of the specialized agencies to continue to give high priority in their public information programmes to disseminating information concerning women and, in particular, the Forward-looking Strategies and, in the light of the recommendations contained in the Strategies, further requests the Secretary-General to provide in the regular budget for the continuation of the existing weekly radio programmes on women, with adequate provision for distributing them in different languages;

26. *Also requests* the Secretary-General to report to the General Assembly at its forty-first session on measures taken to implement the present resolution;

27. *Decides* to consider these questions further at its forty-first session under an item entitled "Forward-looking strategies for the advancement of women to the year 2000".

Document 56

Declaration on the Right to Development

A/RES/41/128, 4 December 1986

The General Assembly,

Bearing in mind the purposes and principles of the Charter of the United Nations relating to the achievement of international cooperation in solving international problems of an economic, social, cultural or humanitarian nature, and in promoting and encouraging respect for human rights and fundamental freedoms for all without distinction as to race, sex, language or religion,

Recognizing that development is a comprehensive economic, social, cultural and political process, which aims at the constant improvement of the well-being of the entire population and of all individuals on the basis of their active, free and meaningful participation in development and in the fair distribution of benefits resulting therefrom,

Considering that under the provisions of the Universal Declaration of Human Rights everyone is entitled to a social and international order in which the rights and freedoms set forth in that Declaration can be fully realized,

Recalling the provisions of the International Covenant on Economic, Social and Cultural Rights and of the International Covenant on Civil and Political Rights,

Recalling further the relevant agreements, conventions, resolutions, recommendations and other instruments of the United Nations and its specialized agencies concerning the integral development of the human being, economic and social progress and development of all peoples, including those instruments concerning decolonization, the prevention of discrimination, respect for and observance of, human rights and fundamental freedoms, the maintenance of international peace and security and the further promotion of friendly relations and cooperation among States in accordance with the Charter,

Recalling the right of peoples to self-determination, by virtue of which they have the right freely to determine their political status and to pursue their economic, social and cultural development,

Recalling also the right of peoples to exercise, subject to the relevant provisions of both International Covenants on Human Rights, full and complete sovereignty over all their natural wealth and resources,

Mindful of the obligation of States under the Charter to promote universal respect for and observance of human rights and fundamental freedoms for all without distinction of any kind such as race, colour, sex, language, religion, political or other opinion, national or social origin, property, birth or other status,

Considering that the elimination of the massive and flagrant violations of the human rights of the peoples and individuals affected by situations such as those resulting from colonialism, neo-colonialism, apartheid, all forms of racism and racial discrimination, foreign domination and occupation, aggression and threats against national sovereignty, national unity and territorial integrity and threats of war would contribute to the establishment of circumstances propitious to the development of a great part of mankind,

Concerned at the existence of serious obstacles to development, as well as to the complete fulfilment of human beings and of peoples, constituted, *inter alia*, by the denial of civil, political, economic, social and cultural rights, and considering that all human rights and fundamental freedoms are indivisible and interdependent and that, in order to promote development, equal attention and urgent consideration should be given to the implementation, promotion and protection of civil, political, economic, social and cultural rights and that, accordingly, the promotion of, respect for and enjoyment of certain human rights and fundamental freedoms cannot justify the denial of other human rights and fundamental freedoms,

Considering that international peace and security are essential elements for the realization of the right to development,

Reaffirming that there is a close relationship between disarmament and development and that progress in the field of disarmament would considerably promote progress in the field of development and that resources released through disarmament measures should be devoted to the economic and social development and well-being of all peoples and, in particular, those of the developing countries,

Recognizing that the human person is the central subject of the development process and that development policy should therefore make the human being the main participant and beneficiary of development,

Recognizing that the creation of conditions favourable to the development of peoples and individuals is the primary responsibility of their States,

Aware that efforts at the international level to promote and protect human rights should be accompanied by efforts to establish a new international economic order,

Confirming that the right to development is an inalienable human right and that equality of opportunity for development is a prerogative both of nations and of individuals who make up nations,

Proclaims the following Declaration on the Right to Development:

Article 1

1. The right to development is an inalienable human right by virtue of which every human person and all peoples are entitled to participate in, contribute to, and enjoy economic, social, cultural and political development, in which all human rights and fundamental freedoms can be fully realized.

2. The human right to development also implies the full realization of the right of peoples to self-determination, which includes, subject to the relevant provisions of both International Covenants on Human Rights, the exercise of their inalienable right to full sovereignty over all their natural wealth and resources.

Article 2

1. The human person is the central subject of development and should be the active participant and beneficiary of the right to development.

2. All human beings have a responsibility for development, individually and collectively, taking into account the need for full respect for their human rights and fundamental freedoms as well as their duties to the community, which alone can ensure the free and complete fulfilment of the human being, and they should therefore promote and protect an appropriate political, social and economic order for development.

3. States have the right and the duty to formulate appropriate national development policies that aim at the constant improvement of the well-being of the entire population and of all individuals, on the basis of their active, free and meaningful participation in development and in the fair distribution of the benefits resulting therefrom.

Article 3

1. States have the primary responsibility for the creation of national and international conditions favourable to the realization of the right to development.

2. The realization of the right to development requires full respect for the principles of international law concerning friendly relations and cooperation among States in accordance with the Charter of the United Nations.

3. States have the duty to cooperate with each other in ensuring development and eliminating obstacles to development. States should realize their rights and fulfil their duties in such a manner as to promote a new international economic order based on sovereign equality, interdependence, mutual interest and cooperation

among all States, as well as to encourage the observance and realization of human rights.

Article 4

1. States have the duty to take steps, individually and collectively, to formulate international development policies with a view to facilitating the full realization of the right to development.

2. Sustained action is required to promote more rapid development of developing countries. As a complement to the efforts of developing countries, effective international cooperation is essential in providing these countries with appropriate means and facilities to foster their comprehensive development.

Article 5

States shall take resolute steps to eliminate the massive and flagrant violations of the human rights of peoples and human beings affected by situations such as those resulting from apartheid, all forms of racism and racial discrimination, colonialism, foreign domination and occupation, aggression, foreign interference and threats against national sovereignty, national unity and territorial integrity, threats of war and refusal to recognize the fundamental right of peoples to self-determination.

Article 6

1. All States should cooperate with a view to promoting, encouraging and strengthening universal respect for and observance of all human rights and fundamental freedoms for all without any distinction as to race, sex, language or religion.

2. All human rights and fundamental freedoms are indivisible and interdependent; equal attention and urgent consideration should be given to the implementation, promotion and protection of civil, political, economic, social and cultural rights.

3. States should take steps to eliminate obstacles to development resulting from failure to observe civil and political rights, as well as economic, social and cultural rights.

Article 7

All States should promote the establishment, maintenance and strengthening of international peace and security and, to that end, should do their utmost to achieve general and complete disarmament under effective international control, as well as to ensure that the resources released by effective disarmament measures are used for comprehensive development, in particular that of the developing countries.

Article 8

1. States should undertake, at the national level, all necessary measures for the realization of the right to development and shall ensure, *inter alia*, equality of opportunity for all in their access to basic resources, education, health services, food, housing, employment and the fair distribution of income. Effective measures should be undertaken to ensure that women have an active role in the development process. Appropriate economic and social reforms should be carried out with a view to eradicating all social injustices.

2. States should encourage popular participation in all spheres as an important factor in development and in the full realization of all human rights.

Article 9

1. All the aspects of the right to development set forth in the present Declaration are indivisible and interdependent and each of them should be considered in the context of the whole.

2. Nothing in the present Declaration shall be construed as being contrary to the purposes and principles of the United Nations, or as implying that any State, group or person has a right to engage in any activity or to perform any act aimed at the violation of the rights set forth in the Universal Declaration of Human Rights and in the International Covenants on Human Rights.

Article 10

Steps should be taken to ensure the full exercise and progressive enhancement of the right to development, including the formulation, adoption and implementation of policy, legislative and other measures at the national and international levels.

Document 57

Economic and Social Council resolution on the establishment of a comprehensive reporting system to monitor, review and appraise the implementation of the Nairobi Forward-looking Strategies for the Advancement of Women

E/RES/1988/22, 26 May 1988

The Economic and Social Council,

Reaffirming the importance attached by the World Conference to Review and Appraise the Achievements of the United Nations Decade for Women: Equality, Development and Peace to monitoring, review and appraisal as outlined in the Nairobi Forward-looking Strategies for the Advancement of Women, 1/

Bearing in mind the guidelines set out in its resolution 1987/18 of 26 May 1987, which the Secretary-General was requested to take into account in further developing and implementing the reporting system to monitor, review and appraise progress in the advancement of women,

Recalling its resolution 1987/22 of 26 May 1987, in which it decided to expand the terms of reference of the Commission on the Status of Women to include the functions of promoting the objectives of equality, development and peace, monitoring the implementation of measures for the advancement of women, and reviewing and appraising progress made at the national, sub-regional, regional, sectoral and global levels,

Reaffirming the request made by the General Assembly, in its resolution 42/62 of 30 November 1987, that the Secretary-General invite Governments, organizations of the United Nations system, including the regional commissions and the specialized agencies, and intergovernmental and non-governmental organizations to report periodically to the Economic and Social Council, through the Commission, on activities undertaken at all levels to implement the Nairobi Forward-looking Strategies,

Reaffirming the appropriateness of a two-year cycle of system-wide monitoring of progress made in implementing the Nairobi Forward-looking Strategies and a five-year cycle of longer-term review and appraisal to continue the cycle established by the World Conference,

Recognizing that effective monitoring, review and appraisal should be conducted at the national, regional, sectoral and international levels to achieve optimal results,

Mindful of the need to avoid duplication of reporting obligations, in view of the burden that coexisting reporting systems place on Member States, especially those with limited resources, and in view of the financial stringencies facing the United Nations system,

1. *Endorses* the comprehensive reporting system to monitor, review and appraise the implementation of the Nairobi Forward-looking Strategies for the Advancement of Women, set out in the annex to the present resolution;

2. *Decides* that its intergovernmental subsidiary bodies, including the regional commissions, should monitor, as necessary, the follow-up to their recommendations relating to the advancement of women;

3. *Requests* the Secretary-General to include the resolutions of those bodies in the report requested by the General Assembly in resolution 42/178 of 11 December 1987 and the results of their monitoring activities in his biennial report to the Commission on the Status of Women on monitoring the Nairobi Forward-looking Strategies;

4. *Also requests* the Secretary-General to invite Governments and intergovernmental and non-governmental organizations to report to the Economic and Social Council, through the Commission, on monitoring, review and appraisal of progress at all levels in the implementation of the Nairobi Forward-looking Strategies, in the manner set out in the annex to the present resolution;

5. *Decides* that the biennial reports of the Secretary-General on monitoring of progress made by the organizations of the United Nations system in the implementation of the Nairobi Forward-looking Strategies should be considered by the Commission in even-numbered years, beginning in 1990;

6. *Also decides* that, for the purpose of monitoring progress at the national level, the Secretary-General should, within existing resources, make available a summary compilation of available statistical indicators relating to the implementation of the Nairobi Forward-looking Strategies and submit a progress report on national reporting of statistics and indicators on women to the Commission in odd-numbered years, beginning in 1989;

7. *Urges* the organizations of the United Nations system to incorporate in their regular work programmes, as necessary, monitoring, review and appraisal of the im-

1/ *Report of the World Conference to Review and Appraise the Achievements of the United Nations Decade for Women: Equality, Development and Peace, Nairobi, 15-26 July 1985* (United Nations publication, Sales No. E.85.IV.10), chap. I, sect. A, paras. 317-321.

plementation of the Nairobi Forward-looking Strategies and to submit reports thereon to their governing bodies;

8. *Decides* that the first quinquennial report on review and appraisal of the implementation of the Nairobi Forward-looking Strategies will be considered by the Commission at its thirty-fourth session, in 1990, and that subsequent reports will be considered in 1995 and 2000, so as to continue the five-year cycle of reporting established during the United Nations Decade for Women;

9. *Encourages* Member States to make use of the reports prepared for the Committee on the Elimination of Discrimination against Women and other relevant international bodies in the preparation of the quinquennial review and appraisal reports, in order to minimize duplication of effort;

10. *Encourages* the provision of technical assistance to national machinery for the advancement of women and the sharing of support and expertise among such machineries, particularly those in developing countries, to facilitate the preparation of the national reports for the quinquennial review and appraisal;

11. *Requests* the Commission to make action-oriented recommendations for the further implementation of the Nairobi Forward-looking Strategies following the quinquennial review and appraisal;

12. *Decides* that, after consideration by the Commission, the monitoring, review and appraisal reports should be made available to the General Assembly so that the Assembly may be kept informed of progress in the implementation of the Nairobi Forward-looking Strategies.

Annex

Comprehensive reporting system to monitor, review and appraise the implementation of the Nairobi Forward-looking Strategies for the Advancement of Women

I. *Biennial monitoring of progress made by the organizations of the United Nations system*

1. The Secretary-General should prepare biennial reports on monitoring of the implementation of the Nairobi Forward-looking Strategies for the Advancement of Women by the organizations of the United Nations system, including monitoring at the regional level. The reports should address the three interrelated and mutually reinforcing objectives of the Nairobi Forward-looking Strategies; equality, development and peace. Each objective should be reported on separately, as appropriate.

2. An introductory commentary should be included covering the basic strategies, relevant institutions, mandates and programmes of action employed to advance each objective.

3. An account of measures taken for the implementation of the basic strategies for international and regional cooperation set out in chapter V of the Nairobi Forward-looking Strategies should be included under each objective.

4. The reports should contain specific information on:

(a) Measures to ensure the integration of the Nairobi Forward-looking Strategies in the programmes of the organization of the United Nations system, including measures to strengthen institutional co-ordination and focal points on the status of women;

(b) Progress made by each organization in establishing and meeting five-year targets at each level for the percentage of women in professional and decision-making positions, as called for by the General Assembly.

5. Reports should be prepared according to a standardized format.

6. In order to minimize duplication of effort, the biennial monitoring reports should make use of reports prepared to meet other reporting requirements, *inter alia,* any other reports required under subprogramme 5A of the proposed revisions to the medium-term plan for 1984-1989 2/ to cover the period 1990-1991, the biennial reports requested by the General Assembly in resolution 42/178 of 11 December 1987 and reports on the improvement of the status of women in the United Nations Secretariat, as requested by the General Assembly.

II. *Quinquennial review and appraisal*

7. The quinquennial review and appraisal will be based on responses from Member States to a questionnaire on the progress achieved in the implementation of the Nairobi Forward-looking Strategies, including an assessment of the effectiveness of methods and programmes introduced and an account of new programmes planned as a result of the national review and appraisal.

8. The national reports should address the three interrelated and mutually reinforcing objectives of the Nairobi Forward-looking Strategies: equality, development and peace. Each objective should be monitored and reported on separately.

9. Each national report should include an introductory commentary covering the basic strategies and programmes of action employed to advance each objective and a review and appraisal of their effectiveness.

10. The national reports should include, under each of the three objectives, an account of measures taken to implement the basic strategies for international and regional cooperation set out in paragraphs 356 to 365 of the Nairobi Forward-looking Strategies.

2/ A/43/6 and Corr. 1, chap. 21.

11. The questionnaire should be simple and direct and structured according to the Nairobi Forward-looking Strategies.

12. The national reports should include an account of the measures taken to meet relevant international standards, such as the Convention on the Elimination of All Forms of Discrimination against Women, 3/ the International Convention on the Elimination of All Forms of Racial Discrimination 4/ and the conventions of the International Labour Organisation.

13. Non-governmental bodies should be invited to submit reports for the quinquennial review and appraisal.

14. The biennial statistical reports provided by the Secretary-General to the Commission on the Status of women for monitoring progress at the national level should be consolidated and made available to the Commission for the quinquennial review and appraisal.

15. Every five years, the Commission should review its conclusions on priority themes on the basis of a compilation of relevant resolutions and should select priority themes for the following five-year period.

16. Reports of Member States to relevant international supervisory bodies, such as the Committee on the Elimination of Discrimination against Women, the Committee on the Elimination of Racial Discrimination, the International Labour Organisation and the United Nations Educational, Scientific and Cultural Organization, and the World Survey on the Role of Women in Development should be made available in a consolidated form to the Commission on the Status of Women for consideration in the quinquennial review and appraisal.

17. Reports prepared by the regional commissions on changes in the situation of women within their region, as requested by the General Assembly in resolution 42/178, should be made available to the Commission every five years for the review and appraisal.

3/ General Assembly resolution 34/180, annex.
4/ General Assembly resolution 2106 A(XX), annex.

Document 58

Body of Principles for the Protection of All Persons under Any Form of Detention or Imprisonment

A/RES/43/173, 9 December 1988

Scope of the body of principles

These principles apply for the protection of all persons under any form of detention or imprisonment.

Use of terms

For the purposes of the Body of Principles:

(a) "Arrest" means the act of apprehending a person for the alleged commission of an offence or by the action of an authority;

(b) "Detained person" means any person deprived of personal liberty except as a result of conviction for an offence;

(c) "Imprisoned person" means any person deprived of personal liberty as a result of conviction for an offence;

(d) "Detention" means the condition of detained persons as defined above;

(e) "Imprisonment" means the condition of imprisoned persons as defined above;

(f) The words "a judicial or other authority" means a judicial or other authority under the law whose status and tenure should afford the strongest possible guarantees of competence, impartiality and independence.

Principle 1

All persons under any form of detention or imprisonment shall be treated in a humane manner and with respect for the inherent dignity of the human person.

Principle 2

Arrest, detention or imprisonment shall only be carried out strictly in accordance with the provisions of the law and by competent officials or persons authorized for that purpose.

Principle 3

There shall be no restriction upon or derogation from any of the human rights of persons under any form of detention or imprisonment recognized or existing in any State pursuant to law, conventions, regulations or custom on the pretext that this Body of Principles does not recognize such rights or that it recognizes them to a lesser extent.

Principle 4

Any form of detention or imprisonment and all measures affecting the human rights of a person under any form of detention or imprisonment shall be ordered by, or be subject to the effective control of, a judicial or other authority.

Principle 5

1. These principles shall be applied to all persons within the territory of any given State, without distinction of any kind, such as race, colour, sex, language, religion or religious belief, political or other opinion, national, ethnic or social origin, property, birth or other status.

2. Measures applied under the law and designed solely to protect the rights and special status of women, especially pregnant women and nursing mothers, children and juveniles, aged, sick or handicapped persons shall not be deemed to be discriminatory. The need for, and the application of, such measures shall always be subject to review by a judicial or other authority.

Principle 6

No person under any form of detention or imprisonment shall be subjected to torture or to cruel, inhuman or degrading treatment or punishment.* No circumstance whatever may be invoked as a justification for torture or other cruel, inhuman or degrading treatment or punishment.

Principle 7

1. States should prohibit by law any act contrary to the rights and duties contained in these principles, make any such act subject to appropriate sanctions and conduct impartial investigations upon complaints.

2. Officials who have reason to believe that a violation of this Body of Principles has occurred or is about to occur shall report the matter to their superior authorities and, where necessary, to other appropriate authorities or organs vested with reviewing or remedial powers.

3. Any other person who has ground to believe that a violation of this Body of Principles has occurred or is about to occur shall have the right to report the matter to the superiors of the officials involved as well as to other appropriate authorities or organs vested with reviewing or remedial powers.

Principle 8

Persons in detention shall be subject to treatment appropriate to their unconvicted status. Accordingly, they shall, whenever possible, be kept separate from imprisoned persons.

Principle 9

The authorities which arrest a person, keep him under detention or investigate the case shall exercise only the powers granted to them under the law and the exercise of these powers shall be subject to recourse to a judicial or other authority.

Principle 10

Anyone who is arrested shall be informed at the time of his arrest of the reason for his arrest and shall be promptly informed of any charges against him.

Principle 11

1. A person shall not be kept in detention without being given an effective opportunity to be heard promptly by a judicial or other authority. A detained person shall have the right to defend himself or to be assisted by counsel as prescribed by law.

2. A detained person and his counsel, if any, shall receive prompt and full communication of any order of detention, together with the reasons therefor.

3. A judicial or other authority shall be empowered to review as appropriate the continuance of detention.

Principle 12

1. There shall be duly recorded:

(a) The reasons for the arrest;

(b) The time of the arrest and the taking of the arrested person to a place of custody as well as that of his first appearance before a judicial or other authority;

(c) The identity of the law enforcement officials concerned;

(d) Precise information concerning the place of custody.

2. Such records shall be communicated to the detained person, or his counsel, if any, in the form prescribed by law.

Principle 13

Any person shall, at the moment of arrest and at the commencement of detention or imprisonment, or promptly thereafter, be provided by the authority responsible for his arrest, detention or imprisonment, respectively with information on and an explanation of his rights and how to avail himself of such rights.

Principle 14

A person who does not adequately understand or speak the language used by the authorities responsible for

---

*The term "cruel, inhuman or degrading treatment or punishment" should be interpreted so as to extend the widest possible protection against abuses, whether physical or mental, including the holding of a detained or imprisoned person in conditions which deprive him, temporarily or permanently. of the use of any of his natural senses, such as sight or hearing, or of his awareness of place and the passing of time.

his arrest, detention or imprisonment is entitled to receive promptly in a language which he understands the information referred to in principle 10, principle 11, paragraph 2, principle 12, paragraph 1, and principle 13 and to have the assistance, free of charge, if necessary, of an interpreter in connection with legal proceedings subsequent to his arrest.

Principle 15

Notwithstanding the exceptions contained in principle 16, paragraph 4, and principle 18, paragraph 3, communication of the detained or imprisoned person with the outside world, and in particular his family or counsel, shall not be denied for more than a matter of days.

Principle 16

1. Promptly after arrest and after each transfer from one place of detention or imprisonment to another, a detained or imprisoned person shall be entitled to notify or to require the competent authority to notify members of his family or other appropriate persons of his choice of his arrest, detention or imprisonment or of the transfer and of the place where he is kept in custody.

2. If a detained or imprisoned person is a foreigner, he shall also be promptly informed of his right to communicate by appropriate means with a consular post or the diplomatic mission of the State of which he is a national or which is otherwise entitled to receive such communication in accordance with international law or with the representative of the competent international organization, if he is a refugee or is otherwise under the protection of an intergovernmental organization.

3. If a detained or imprisoned person is a juvenile or is incapable of understanding his entitlement, the competent authority shall on its own initiative undertake the notification referred to in the present principle. Special attention shall be given to notifying parents or guardians.

4. Any notification referred to in the present principle shall be made or permitted to be made without delay. The competent authority may however delay a notification for a reasonable period where exceptional needs of the investigation so require.

Principle 17

1. A detained person shall be entitled to have the assistance of a legal counsel. He shall be informed of his right by the competent authority promptly after arrest and shall be provided with reasonable facilities for exercising it.

2. If a detained person does not have a legal counsel of his own choice, he shall be entitled to have a legal counsel assigned to him by a judicial or other authority in all cases where the interests of justice so require and without payment by him if he does not have sufficient means to pay.

Principle 18

1. A detained or imprisoned person shall be entitled to communicate and consult with his legal counsel.

2. A detained or imprisoned person shall be allowed adequate time and facilities for consultation with his legal counsel.

3. The right of a detained or imprisoned person to be visited by and to consult and communicate, without delay or censorship and in full confidentiality, with his legal counsel may not be suspended or restricted save in exceptional circumstances, to be specified by law or lawful regulations, when it is considered indispensable by a judicial or other authority in order to maintain security and good order.

4. Interviews between a detained or imprisoned person and his legal counsel may be within sight, but not within the hearing, of a law enforcement official.

5. Communications between a detained or imprisoned person and his legal counsel mentioned in the present principle shall be inadmissible as evidence against the detained or imprisoned person unless they are connected with a continuing or contemplated crime.

Principle 19

A detained or imprisoned person shall have the right to be visited by and to correspond with, in particular, members of his family and shall be given adequate opportunity to communicate with the outside world, subject to reasonable conditions and restrictions as specified by law or lawful regulations.

Principle 20

If a detained or imprisoned person so requests, he shall if possible be kept in a place of detention or imprisonment reasonably near his usual place of residence.

Principle 21

1. It shall be prohibited to take undue advantage of the situation of a detained or imprisoned person for the purpose of compelling him to confess, to incriminate himself otherwise or to testify against any other person.

2. No detained person while being interrogated shall be subject to violence, threats or methods of interrogation which impair his capacity of decision or his judgement.

Principle 22

No detained or imprisoned person shall, even with his consent, be subjected to any medical or scientific experimentation which may be detrimental to his health.

Principle 23

1. The duration of any interrogation of a detained or imprisoned person and of the intervals between interrogations as well as the identity of the officials who conducted the interrogations and other persons present shall be recorded and certified in such form as may be prescribed by law.

2. A detained or imprisoned person, or his counsel when provided by law, shall have access to the information described in paragraph 1 of the present principle.

Principle 24

A proper medical examination shall be offered to a detained or imprisoned person as promptly as possible after his admission to the place of detention or imprisonment, and thereafter medical care and treatment shall be provided whenever necessary. This care and treatment shall be provided free of charge.

Principle 25

A detained or imprisoned person or his counsel shall, subject only to reasonable conditions to ensure security and good order in the place of detention or imprisonment, have the right to request or petition a judicial or other authority for a second medical examination or opinion.

Principle 26

The fact that a detained or imprisoned person underwent a medical examination, the name of the physician and the results of such an examination shall be duly recorded. Access to such records shall be ensured. Modalities therefore shall be in accordance with relevant rules of domestic law.

Principle 27

Non-compliance with these principles in obtaining evidence shall be taken into account in determining the admissibility of such evidence against a detained or imprisoned person.

Principle 28

A detained or imprisoned person shall have the right to obtain within the limits of available resources, if from public sources, reasonable quantities of educational, cultural and informational material, subject to reasonable conditions to ensure security and good order in the place of detention or imprisonment.

Principle 29

1. In order to supervise the strict observance of relevant laws and regulations, places of detention shall be visited regularly by qualified and experienced persons appointed by, and responsible to, a competent authority distinct from the authority directly in charge of the administration of the place of detention or imprisonment.

2. A detained or imprisoned person shall have the right to communicate freely and in full confidentiality with the persons who visit the places of detention or imprisonment in accordance with paragraph 1 of the present principle, subject to reasonable conditions to ensure security and good order in such places.

Principle 30

1. The types of conduct of the detained or imprisoned person that constitute disciplinary offences during detention or imprisonment, the description and duration of disciplinary punishment that may be inflicted and the authorities competent to impose such punishment shall be specified by law or lawful regulations and duly published.

2. A detained or imprisoned person shall have the right to be heard before disciplinary action is taken. He shall have the right to bring such action to higher authorities for review.

Principle 31

The appropriate authorities shall endeavour to ensure, according to domestic law, assistance when needed to dependent and, in particular, minor members of the families of detained or imprisoned persons and shall devote a particular measure of care to the appropriate custody of children left without supervision.

Principle 32

1. A detained person or his counsel shall be entitled at any time to take proceedings according to domestic law before a judicial or other authority to challenge the lawfulness of his detention in order to obtain his release without delay, if it is unlawful.

2. The proceedings referred to in paragraph 1 of the present principle shall be simple and expeditious and at no cost for detained persons without adequate means. The detaining authority shall produce without unreasonable delay the detained person before the reviewing authority.

Principle 33

1. A detained or imprisoned person or his counsel shall have the right to make a request or complaint regarding his treatment, in particular in case of torture or

other cruel, inhuman or degrading treatment, to the authorities responsible for the administration of the place of detention and to higher authorities and, when necessary, to appropriate authorities vested with reviewing or remedial powers.

2. In those cases where neither the detained or imprisoned person nor his counsel has the possibility to exercise his rights under paragraph 1 of the present principle, a member of the family of the detained or imprisoned person or any other person who has knowledge of the case may exercise such rights.

3. Confidentiality concerning the request or complaint shall be maintained if so requested by the complainant.

4. Every request or complaint shall be promptly dealt with and replied to without undue delay. If the request or complaint is rejected or, in case of inordinate delay, the complainant shall be entitled to bring it before a judicial or other authority. Neither the detained or imprisoned person nor any complainant under paragraph 1 of the present principle shall suffer prejudice for making a request or complaint.

Principle 34

Whenever the death or disappearance of a detained or imprisoned person occurs during his detention or imprisonment, an inquiry into the cause of death or disappearance shall be held by a judicial or other authority, either on its own motion or at the instance of a member of the family of such a person or any person who has knowledge of the case. When circumstances so warrant, such an inquiry shall be held on the same procedural basis whenever the death or disappearance occurs shortly after the termination of the detention or imprisonment. The findings of such inquiry or a report thereon shall be made available upon request, unless doing so would jeopardize an ongoing criminal investigation.

Principle 35

1. Damage incurred because of acts or omissions by a public official contrary to the rights contained in these principles shall be compensated according to the applicable rules or liability provided by domestic law.

2. Information required to be recorded under these principles shall be available in accordance with procedures provided by domestic law for use in claiming compensation under the present principle.

Principle 36

1. A detained person suspected of or charged with a criminal offence shall be presumed innocent and shall be treated as such until proved guilty according to law in a public trial at which he has had all the guarantees necessary for his defence.

2. The arrest or detention of such a person pending investigation and trial shall be carried out only for the purposes of the administration of justice on grounds and under conditions and procedures specified by law. The imposition of restrictions upon such a person which are not strictly required for the purpose of the detention or to prevent hindrance to the process of investigation or the administration of justice, or for the maintenance of security and good order in the place of detention shall be forbidden.

Principle 37

A person detained on a criminal charge shall be brought before a judicial or other authority provided by law promptly after his arrest. Such authority shall decide without delay upon the lawfulness and necessity of detention. No person may be kept under detention pending investigation or trial except upon the written order of such an authority. A detained person shall, when brought before such an authority, have the right to make a statement on the treatment received by him while in custody.

Principle 38

A person detained on a criminal charge shall be entitled to trial within a reasonable time or to release pending trial.

Principle 39

Except in special cases provided for by law, a person detained on a criminal charge shall be entitled, unless a judicial or other authority decides otherwise in the interest of the administration of justice, to release pending trial subject to the conditions that may be imposed in accordance with the law. Such authority shall keep the necessity of detention under review.

General clause

Nothing in this Body of Principles shall be construed as restricting or derogating from any right defined in the International Covenant on Civil and Political Rights.

Document 59

Principles on the Effective Prevention and Investigation of Extra-legal, Arbitrary and Summary Executions, recommended by the Economic and Social Council

E/RES/1989/65, 24 May 1989*

Prevention

1. Governments shall prohibit by law all extra-legal, arbitrary and summary executions and shall ensure that any such executions are recognized as offences under their criminal laws, and are punishable by appropriate penalties which take into account the seriousness of such offences. Exceptional circumstances including a state of war or threat of war, internal political instability or any other public emergency may not be invoked as a justification of such executions. Such executions shall not be carried out under any circumstances including, but not limited to, situations of internal armed conflict, excessive or illegal use of force by a public official or other person acting in an official capacity or by a person acting at the instigation, or with the consent or acquiescence of such person, and situations in which deaths occur in custody. This prohibition shall prevail over decrees issued by governmental authority.

2. In order to prevent extra-legal, arbitrary and summary executions, Governments shall ensure strict control, including a clear chain of command over all officials responsible for apprehension, arrest, detention, custody and imprisonment, as well as those officials authorized by law to use force and firearms.

3. Governments shall prohibit orders from superior officers or public authorities authorizing or inciting other persons to carry out any such extralegal, arbitrary or summary executions. All persons shall have the right and the duty to defy such orders. Training of law enforcement officials shall emphasize the above provisions.

4. Effective protection through judicial or other means shall be guaranteed to individuals and groups who are in danger of extra-legal, arbitrary or summary executions, including those who receive death threats.

5. No one shall be involuntarily returned or extradited to a country where there are substantial grounds for believing that he or she may become a victim of extra-legal, arbitrary or summary execution in that country.

6. Governments shall ensure that persons deprived of their liberty are held in officially recognized places of custody, and that accurate information on their custody and whereabouts, including transfers, is made promptly available to their relatives and lawyer or other persons of confidence.

7. Qualified inspectors, including medical personnel, or an equivalent independent authority, shall conduct inspections in places of custody on a regular basis, and be empowered to undertake unannounced inspections on their own initiative, with full guarantees of independence in the exercise of this function. The inspectors shall have unrestricted access to all persons in such places of custody, as well as to all their records.

8. Governments shall make every effort to prevent extra-legal, arbitrary and summary executions through measures such as diplomatic intercession, improved access of complainants to intergovernmental and judicial bodies, and public denunciation. Intergovernmental mechanisms shall be used to investigate reports of any such executions and to take effective action against such practices. Governments, including those of countries where extra-legal, arbitrary and summary executions are reasonably suspected to occur, shall cooperate fully in international investigations on the subject.

Investigation

9. There shall be thorough, prompt and impartial investigation of all suspected cases of extra-legal, arbitrary and summary executions, including cases where complaints by relatives or other reliable reports suggest unnatural death in the above circumstances. Governments shall maintain investigative offices and procedures to undertake such inquiries. The purpose of the investigation shall be to determine the cause, manner and time of death, the person responsible, and any pattern or practice which may have brought about that death. It shall include an adequate autopsy, collection and analysis of all physical and documentary evidence and statements from witnesses. The investigation shall distinguish between natural death, accidental death, suicide and homicide.

10. The investigative authority shall have the power to obtain all the information necessary to the inquiry. Those persons conducting the investigation shall have at their disposal all the necessary budgetary and technical resources for effective investigation. They shall

*In resolution 1989/65, paragraph 1, the Economic and Social Council recommended that the Principles on the Effective Prevention and Investigation of Extra-legal, Arbitrary and Summary Executions should be taken into account and respected by Governments within the framework of their national legislation and practices.

also have the authority to oblige officials allegedly involved in any such executions to appear and testify. The same shall apply to any witness. To this end, they shall be entitled to issue summonses to witnesses, including the officials allegedly involved and to demand the production of evidence.

11. In cases in which the established investigative procedures are inadequate because of lack of expertise or impartiality, because of the importance of the matter or because of the apparent existence of a pattern of abuse, and in cases where there are complaints from the family of the victim about these inadequacies or other substantial reasons, Governments shall pursue investigations through an independent commission of inquiry or similar procedure. Members of such a commission shall be chosen for their recognized impartiality, competence and independence as individuals. In particular, they shall be independent of any institution, agency or person that may be the subject of the inquiry. The commission shall have the authority to obtain all information necessary to the inquiry and shall conduct the inquiry as provided for under these Principles.

12. The body of the deceased person shall not be disposed of until an adequate autopsy is conducted by a physician, who shall, if possible, be an expert in forensic pathology. Those conducting the autopsy shall have the right of access to all investigative data, to the place where the body was discovered, and to the place where the death is thought to have occurred. If the body has been buried and it later appears that an investigation is required, the body shall be promptly and competently exhumed for an autopsy. If skeletal remains are discovered, they should be carefully exhumed and studied according to systematic anthropological techniques.

13. The body of the deceased shall be available to those conducting the autopsy for a sufficient amount of time to enable a thorough investigation to be carried out. The autopsy shall, at a minimum, attempt to establish the identity of the deceased and the cause and manner of death. The time and place of death shall also be determined to the extent possible. Detailed colour photographs of the deceased shall be included in the autopsy report in order to document and support the findings of the investigation. The autopsy report must describe any and all injuries to the deceased including any evidence of torture.

14. In order to ensure objective results, those conducting the autopsy must be able to function impartially and independently of any potentially implicated persons or organizations or entities.

15. Complainants, witnesses, those conducting the investigation and their families shall be protected from violence, threats of violence or any other form of intimidation. Those potentially implicated in extra-legal, arbitrary or summary executions shall be removed from any position of control or power, whether direct or indirect, over complainants, witnesses and their families, as well as over those conducting investigations.

16. Families of the deceased and their legal representatives shall be informed of, and have access to. any hearing as well as to all information relevant to the investigation, and shall be entitled to present other evidence. The family of the deceased shall have the right to insist that a medical or other qualified representative be present at the autopsy. When the identity of a deceased person has been determined, a notification of death shall be posted, and the family or relatives of the deceased shall be informed immediately. The body of the deceased shall be returned to them upon completion of the investigation.

17. A written report shall be made within a reasonable period of time on the methods and findings of such investigations. The report shall be made public immediately and shall include the scope of the inquiry, procedures and methods used to evaluate evidence as well as conclusions and recommendations based on findings of fact and on applicable law. The report shall also describe in detail specific events that were found to have occurred and the evidence upon which such findings were based, and list the names of witnesses who testified, with the exception of those whose identities have been withheld for their own protection. The Government shall, within a reasonable period of time, either reply to the report of the investigation, or indicate the steps to be taken in response to it.

Legal proceedings

18. Governments shall ensure that persons identified by the investigation as having participated in extra-legal, arbitrary or summary executions in any territory under their jurisdiction are brought to justice. Governments shall either bring such persons to justice or cooperate to extradite any such persons to other countries wishing to exercise jurisdiction. This principle shall apply irrespective of who and where the perpetrators or the victims are, their nationalities or where the offence was committed.

19. Without prejudice to principle 3 above, an order from a superior officer or a public authority may not be invoked as a justification for extra-legal, arbitrary or summary executions. Superiors, officers or other public officials may be held responsible for acts committed by officials under their authority if they had a reasonable opportunity to prevent such acts. In no circumstances, including a state of war, siege or other public emergency, shall blanket immunity from prosecution be granted to any person allegedly involved in extra-legal, arbitrary or summary executions.

20. The families and dependents of victims of extra-legal, arbitrary or summary executions shall be entitled to fair and adequate compensation within a reasonable period of time.

Document 60

Convention on the Rights of the Child

A/RES/44/25, 20 November 1989

PREAMBLE

The States Parties to the present Convention,

Considering that, in accordance with the principles proclaimed in the Charter of the United Nations, recognition of the inherent dignity and of the equal and inalienable rights of all members of the human family is the foundation of freedom, justice and peace in the world,

Bearing in mind that the peoples of the United Nations have, in the Charter, reaffirmed their faith in fundamental human rights and in the dignity and worth of the human person, and have determined to promote social progress and better standards of life in larger freedom,

Recognizing that the United Nations has, in the Universal Declaration of Human Rights and in the International Covenants on Human Rights, proclaimed and agreed that everyone is entitled to all the rights and freedoms set forth therein, without distinction of any kind, such as race, colour, sex, language, religion, political or other opinion, national or social origin, property, birth or other status,

Recalling that, in the Universal Declaration of Human Rights, the United Nations has proclaimed that childhood is entitled to special care and assistance,

Convinced that the family, as the fundamental group of society and the natural environment for the growth and well-being of all its members and particularly children, should be afforded the necessary protection and assistance so that it can fully assume its responsibilities within the community,

Recognizing that the child, for the full and harmonious development of his or her personality, should grow up in a family environment, in an atmosphere of happiness, love and understanding,

Considering that the child should be fully prepared to live an individual life in society, and brought up in the spirit of the ideals proclaimed in the Charter of the United Nations, and in particular in the spirit of peace, dignity, tolerance, freedom, equality and solidarity,

Bearing in mind that the need to extend particular care to the child has been stated in the Geneva Declaration of the Rights of the Child of 1924 and in the Declaration of the Rights of the Child adopted by the General Assembly on 20 November 1959 and recognized in the Universal Declaration of Human Rights, in the International Covenant on Civil and Political Rights (in particular in articles 23 and 24), in the International Covenant on Economic, Social and Cultural Rights (in particular in article 10) and in the statutes and relevant instruments of specialized agencies and international organizations concerned with the welfare of children,

Bearing in mind that, as indicated in the Declaration of the Rights of the Child, "the child, by reason of his physical and mental immaturity, needs special safeguards and care, including appropriate legal protection, before as well as after birth",

Recalling the provisions of the Declaration on Social and Legal Principles relating to the Protection and Welfare of Children, with Special Reference to Foster Placement and Adoption Nationally and Internationally; the United Nations Standard Minimum Rules for the Administration of Juvenile Justice (The Beijing Rules); and the Declaration on the Protection of Women and Children in Emergency and Armed Conflict,

Recognizing that, in all countries in the world, there are children living in exceptionally difficult conditions, and that such children need special consideration,

Taking due account of the importance of the traditions and cultural values of each people for the protection and harmonious development of the child,

Recognizing the importance of international cooperation for improving the living conditions of children in every country, in particular in the developing countries,

Have agreed as follows:

PART I

Article 1

For the purposes of the present Convention, a child means every human being below the age of eighteen years unless under the law applicable to the child, majority is attained earlier.

Article 2

1. States Parties shall respect and ensure the rights set forth in the present Convention to each child within their jurisdiction without discrimination of any kind, irrespective of the child's or his or her parent's or legal guardian's race, colour, sex, language, religion, political or other opinion, national, ethnic or social origin, property, disability, birth or other status.

2. States Parties shall take all appropriate measures to ensure that the child is protected against all forms of discrimination or punishment on the basis of the status, activities, expressed opinions, or beliefs of the child's parents, legal guardians, or family members.

Article 3

1. In all actions concerning children, whether undertaken by public or private social welfare institutions, courts of law, administrative authorities or legislative bodies, the best interests of the child shall be a primary consideration.

2. States Parties undertake to ensure the child such protection and care as is necessary for his or her wellbeing, taking into account the rights and duties of his or her parents, legal guardians, or other individuals legally responsible for him or her, and, to this end, shall take all appropriate legislative and administrative measures.

3. States Parties shall ensure that the institutions, services and facilities responsible for the care or protection of children shall conform with the standards established by competent authorities, particularly in the areas of safety, health, in the number and suitability of their staff, as well as competent supervision.

Article 4

States Parties shall undertake all appropriate legislative, administrative, and other measures for the implementation of the rights recognized in the present Convention. With regard to economic, social and cultural rights, States Parties shall undertake such measures to the maximum extent of their available resources and, where needed, within the framework of international cooperation.

Article 5

States Parties shall respect the responsibilities, rights and duties of parents or, where applicable, the members of the extended family or community as provided for by local custom, legal guardians or other persons legally responsible for the child, to provide, in a manner consistent with the evolving capacities of the child, appropriate direction and guidance in the exercise by the child of the rights recognized in the present Convention.

Article 6

1. States Parties recognize that every child has the inherent right to life.

2. States Parties shall ensure to the maximum extent possible the survival and development of the child.

Article 7

1. The child shall be registered immediately after birth and shall have the right from birth to a name, the right to acquire a nationality and, as far as possible, the right to know and be cared for by his or her parents.

2. States Parties shall ensure the implementation of these rights in accordance with their national law and their obligations under the relevant international instruments in this field, in particular where the child would otherwise be stateless.

Article 8

1. States Parties undertake to respect the right of the child to preserve his or her identity, including nationality, name and family relations as recognized by law without unlawful interference.

2. Where a child is illegally deprived of some or all of the elements of his or her identity, States Parties shall provide appropriate assistance and protection, with a view to re-establishing speedily his or her identity.

Article 9

1. States Parties shall ensure that a child shall not be separated from his or her parents against their will, except when competent authorities subject to judicial review determine, in accordance with applicable law and procedures, that such separation is necessary for the best interests of the child. Such determination may be necessary in a particular case such as one involving abuse or neglect of the child by the parents, or one where the parents are living separately and a decision must be made as to the child's place of residence.

2. In any proceedings pursuant to paragraph 1 of the present article, all interested parties shall be given an opportunity to participate in the proceedings and make their views known.

3. States Parties shall respect the right of the child who is separated from one or both parents to maintain personal relations and direct contact with both parents on a regular basis, except if it is contrary to the child's best interests.

4. Where such separation results from any action initiated by a State Party, such as the detention, imprisonment, exile, deportation or death (including death arising from any cause while the person is in the custody of the State) of one or both parents or of the child, that

State Party shall, upon request, provide the parents, the child or, if appropriate, another member of the family with the essential information concerning the whereabouts of the absent member(s) of the family unless the provision of the information would be detrimental to the well-being of the child. States Parties shall further ensure that the submission of such a request shall of itself entail no adverse consequences for the person(s) concerned.

Article 10

1. In accordance with the obligation of States Parties under article 9, paragraph 1, applications by a child or his or her parents to enter or leave a State Party for the purpose of family reunification shall be dealt with by States Parties in a positive, humane and expeditious manner. States Parties shall further ensure that the submission of such a request shall entail no adverse consequences for the applicants and for the members of their family.

2. A child whose parents reside in different States shall have the right to maintain on a regular basis, save in exceptional circumstances, personal relations and direct contacts with both parents. Towards that end and in accordance with the obligation of States Parties under article 9, paragraph 1, States Parties shall respect the right of the child and his or her parents to leave any country, including their own, and to enter their own country. The right to leave any country shall be subject only to such restrictions as are prescribed by law and which are necessary to protect the national security, public order (*ordre public*), public health or morals or the rights and freedoms of others and are consistent with the other rights recognized in the present Convention.

Article 11

1. States Parties shall take measures to combat the illicit transfer and non-return of children abroad.

2. To this end, States Parties shall promote the conclusion of bilateral or multilateral agreements or accession to existing agreements.

Article 12

1. States Parties shall assure to the child who is capable of forming his or her own views the right to express those views freely in all matters affecting the child, the views of the child being given due weight in accordance with the age and maturity of the child.

2. For this purpose, the child shall in particular be provided the opportunity to be heard in any judicial and administrative proceedings affecting the child, either directly, or through a representative or an appropriate body, in a manner consistent with the procedural rules of national law.

Article 13

1. The child shall have the right to freedom of expression; this right shall include freedom to seek, receive and impart information and ideas of all kinds, regardless of frontiers, either orally, in writing or in print, in the form of art, or through any other media of the child's choice.

2. The exercise of this right may be subject to certain restrictions, but these shall only be such as are provided by law and are necessary:

(a) For respect of the rights or reputations of others; or

(b) For the protection of national security or of public order (*ordre public*), or of public health or morals.

Article 14

1. States Parties shall respect the right of the child to freedom of thought, conscience and religion.

2. States Parties shall respect the rights and duties of the parents and, when applicable, legal guardians, to provide direction to the child in the exercise of his or her right in a manner consistent with the evolving capacities of the child.

3. Freedom to manifest one's religion or beliefs may be subject only to such limitations as are prescribed by law and are necessary to protect public safety, order, health or morals, or the fundamental rights and freedoms of others.

Article 15

1. States Parties recognize the rights of the child to freedom of association and to freedom of peaceful assembly.

2. No restrictions may be placed on the exercise of these rights other than those imposed in conformity with the law and which are necessary in a democratic society in the interests of national security or public safety, public order (*ordre public*), the protection of public health or morals or the protection of the rights and freedoms of others.

Article 16

1. No child shall be subjected to arbitrary or unlawful interference with his or her privacy, family, home or correspondence, nor to unlawful attacks on his or her honour and reputation.

2. The child has the right to the protection of the law against such interference or attacks.

Article 17

States Parties recognize the important function performed by the mass media and shall ensure that the child has access to information and material from a diversity of national and international sources, especially those aimed at the promotion of his or her social, spiritual and moral well-being and physical and mental health. To this end, States Parties shall:

(a) Encourage the mass media to disseminate information and material of social and cultural benefit to the child and in accordance with the spirit of article 29;

(b) Encourage international cooperation in the production, exchange and dissemination of such information and material from a diversity of cultural, national and international sources;

(c) Encourage the production and dissemination of children's books;

(d) Encourage the mass media to have particular regard to the linguistic needs of the child who belongs to a minority group or who is indigenous;

(e) Encourage the development of appropriate guidelines for the protection of the child from information and material injurious to his or her well-being, bearing in mind the provisions of articles 13 and 18.

Article 18

1. States Parties shall use their best efforts to ensure recognition of the principle that both parents have common responsibilities for the upbringing and development of the child. Parents or, as the case may be, legal guardians, have the primary responsibility for the upbringing and development of the child. The best interests of the child will be their basic concern.

2. For the purpose of guaranteeing and promoting the rights set forth in the present Convention, States Parties shall render appropriate assistance to parents and legal guardians in the performance of their child-rearing responsibilities and shall ensure the development of institutions, facilities and services for the care of children.

3. States Parties shall take all appropriate measures to ensure that children of working parents have the right to benefit from child-care services and facilities for which they are eligible.

Article 19

1. States Parties shall take all appropriate legislative, administrative, social and educational measures to protect the child from all forms of physical or mental violence, injury or abuse, neglect or negligent treatment, maltreatment or exploitation, including sexual abuse, while in the care of parent(s), legal guardian(s) or any other person who has the care of the child.

2. Such protective measures should, as appropriate, include effective procedures for the establishment of social programmes to provide necessary support for the child and for those who have the care of the child, as well as for other forms of prevention and for identification, reporting, referral, investigation, treatment and follow-up of instances of child maltreatment described heretofore, and, as appropriate, for judicial involvement.

Article 20

1. A child temporarily or permanently deprived of his or her family environment, or in whose own best interests cannot be allowed to remain in that environment, shall be entitled to special protection and assistance provided by the State.

2. States Parties shall in accordance with their national laws ensure alternative care for such a child.

3. Such care could include, *inter alia*, foster placement, *kafalah* of Islamic law, adoption or if necessary placement in suitable institutions for the care of children. When considering solutions, due regard shall be paid to the desirability of continuity in a child's upbringing and to the child's ethnic, religious, cultural and linguistic background.

Article 21

States Parties that recognize and/or permit the system of adoption shall ensure that the best interests of the child shall be the paramount consideration and they shall:

(a) Ensure that the adoption of a child is authorized only by competent authorities who determine, in accordance with applicable law and procedures and on the basis of all pertinent and reliable information, that the adoption is permissible in view of the child's status concerning parents, relatives and legal guardians and that, if required, the persons concerned have given their informed consent to the adoption on the basis of such counselling as may be necessary;

(b) Recognize that inter-country adoption may be considered as an alternative means of child's care, if the child cannot be placed in a foster or an adoptive family or cannot in any suitable manner be cared for in the child's country of origin;

(c) Ensure that the child concerned by inter-country adoption enjoys safeguards and standards equivalent to those existing in the case of national adoption;

(d) Take all appropriate measures to ensure that, in inter-country adoption, the placement does not result in improper financial gain for those involved in it;

(e) Promote, where appropriate, the objectives of the present article by concluding bilateral or multilateral arrangements or agreements, and endeavour, within this framework, to ensure that the placement of the child in another country is carried out by competent authorities or organs.

Article 22

1. States Parties shall take appropriate measures to ensure that a child who is seeking refugee status or who is considered a refugee in accordance with applicable international or domestic law and procedures shall, whether unaccompanied or accompanied by his or her parents or by any other person, receive appropriate protection and humanitarian assistance in the enjoyment of applicable rights set forth in the present Convention and in other international human rights or humanitarian instruments to which the said States are Parties.

2. For this purpose, States Parties shall provide, as they consider appropriate, cooperation in any efforts by the United Nations and other competent intergovernmental organizations or non-governmental organizations cooperating with the United Nations to protect and assist such a child and to trace the parents or other members of the family of any refugee child in order to obtain information necessary for reunification with his or her family. In cases where no parents or other members of the family can be found, the child shall be accorded the same protection as any other child permanently or temporarily deprived of his or her family environment for any reason, as set forth in the present Convention.

Article 23

1. States Parties recognize that a mentally or physically disabled child should enjoy a full and decent life, in conditions which ensure dignity, promote self-reliance and facilitate the child's active participation in the community.

2. States Parties recognize the right of the disabled child to special care and shall encourage and ensure the extension, subject to available resources, to the eligible child and those responsible for his or her care, of assistance for which application is made and which is appropriate to the child's condition and to the circumstances of the parents or others caring for the child.

3. Recognizing the special needs of a disabled child, assistance extended in accordance with paragraph 2 of the present article shall be provided free of charge, whenever possible, taking into account the financial resources of the parents or others caring for the child, and shall be designed to ensure that the disabled child has effective access to and receives education, training, health care services, rehabilitation services, preparation for employment and recreation opportunities in a manner conducive to the child's achieving the fullest possible social integration and individual development, including his or her cultural and spiritual development.

4. States Parties shall promote, in the spirit of international cooperation, the exchange of appropriate information in the field of preventive health care and of medical, psychological and functional treatment of disabled children, including dissemination of and access to information concerning methods of rehabilitation, education and vocational services, with the aim of enabling States Parties to improve their capabilities and skills and to widen their experience in these areas. In this regard, particular account shall be taken of the needs of developing countries.

Article 24

1. States Parties recognize the right of the child to the enjoyment of the highest attainable standard of health and to facilities for the treatment of illness and rehabilitation of health. States Parties shall strive to ensure that no child is deprived of his or her right of access to such health care services.

2. States Parties shall pursue full implementation of this right and, in particular, shall take appropriate measures:

(a) To diminish infant and child mortality;

(b) To ensure the provision of necessary medical assistance and health care to all children with emphasis on the development of primary health care;

(c) To combat disease and malnutrition, including within the framework of primary health care, through, *inter alia*, the application of readily available technology and through the provision of adequate nutritious foods and clean drinking-water, taking into consideration the dangers and risks of environmental pollution;

(d) To ensure appropriate pre-natal and post-natal health care for mothers;

(e) To ensure that all segments of society, in particular parents and children, are informed, have access to education and are supported in the use of basic knowledge of child health and nutrition, the advantages of breast-feeding, hygiene and environmental sanitation and the prevention of accidents;

(f) To develop preventive health care, guidance for parents and family planning education and services.

3. States Parties shall take all effective and appropriate measures with a view to abolishing traditional practices prejudicial to the health of children.

4. States Parties undertake to promote and encourage international cooperation with a view to achieving progressively the full realization of the right recognized in the present article. In this regard, particular account shall be taken of the needs of developing countries.

Article 25

States Parties recognize the right of a child who has been placed by the competent authorities for the purposes of care, protection or treatment of his or her physical or mental health, to a periodic review of the treatment provided to the child and all other circumstances relevant to his or her placement.

Article 26

1. States Parties shall recognize for every child the right to benefit from social security, including social insurance, and shall take the necessary measures to achieve the full realization of this right in accordance with their national law.

2. The benefits should, where appropriate, be granted, taking into account the resources and the circumstances of the child and persons having responsibility for the maintenance of the child, as well as any other consideration relevant to an application for benefits made by or on behalf of the child.

Article 27

1. States Parties recognize the right of every child to a standard of living adequate for the child's physical, mental, spiritual, moral and social development.

2. The parent(s) or others responsible for the child have the primary responsibility to secure, within their abilities and financial capacities, the conditions of living necessary for the child's development.

3. States Parties, in accordance with national conditions and within their means, shall take appropriate measures to assist parents and others responsible for the child to implement this right and shall in case of need provide material assistance and support programmes, particularly with regard to nutrition, clothing and housing.

4. States Parties shall take all appropriate measures to secure the recovery of maintenance for the child from the parents or other persons having financial responsibility for the child, both within the State Party and from abroad. In particular, where the person having financial responsibility for the child lives in a State different from that of the child, States Parties shall promote the accession to international agreements or the conclusion of such agreements, as well as the making of other appropriate arrangements.

Article 28

1. States Parties recognize the right of the child to education, and with a view to achieving this right progressively and on the basis of equal opportunity, they shall, in particular:

(a) Make primary education compulsory and available free to all;

(b) Encourage the development of different forms of secondary education, including general and vocational education, make them available and accessible to every child, and take appropriate measures such as the intro-

duction of free education and offering financial assistance in case of need;

(c) Make higher education accessible to all on the basis of capacity by every appropriate means;

(d) Make educational and vocational information and guidance available and accessible to all children;

(e) Take measures to encourage regular attendance at schools and the reduction of drop-out rates.

2. States Parties shall take all appropriate measures to ensure that school discipline is administered in a manner consistent with the child's human dignity and in conformity with the present Convention.

3. States Parties shall promote and encourage international cooperation in matters relating to education, in particular with a view to contributing to the elimination of ignorance and illiteracy throughout the world and facilitating access to scientific and technical knowledge and modern teaching methods. In this regard, particular account shall be taken of the needs of developing countries.

Article 29

1. States Parties agree that the education of the child shall be directed to:

(a) The development of the child's personality, talents and mental and physical abilities to their fullest potential;

(b) The development of respect for human rights and fundamental freedoms, and for the principles enshrined in the Charter of the United Nations;

(c) The development of respect for the child's parents, his or her own cultural identity, language and values, for the national values of the country in which the child is living, the country from which he or she may originate, and for civilizations different from his or her own;

(d) The preparation of the child for responsible life in a free society, in the spirit of understanding, peace, tolerance, equality of sexes, and friendship among all peoples, ethnic, national and religious groups and persons of indigenous origin;

(e) The development of respect for the natural environment.

2. No part of the present article or article 28 shall be construed so as to interfere with the liberty of individuals and bodies to establish and direct educational institutions, subject always to the observance of the principle set forth in paragraph 1 of the present article and to the requirements that the education given in such institutions shall conform to such minimum standards as may be laid down by the State.

Article 30

In those States in which ethnic, religious or linguistic minorities or persons of indigenous origin exist, a child belonging to such a minority or who is indigenous shall not be denied the right, in community with other members of his or her group, to enjoy his or her own culture, to profess and practise his or her own religion, or to use his or her own language.

Article 31

1. States Parties recognize the right of the child to rest and leisure, to engage in play and recreational activities appropriate to the age of the child and to participate freely in cultural life and the arts.

2. States Parties shall respect and promote the right of the child to participate fully in cultural and artistic life and shall encourage the provision of appropriate and equal opportunities for cultural, artistic, recreational and leisure activity.

Article 32

1. States Parties recognize the right of the child to be protected from economic exploitation and from performing any work that is likely to be hazardous or to interfere with the child's education, or to be harmful to the child's health or physical, mental, spiritual, moral or social development.

2. States Parties shall take legislative, administrative, social and educational measures to ensure the implementation of the present article. To this end, and having regard to the relevant provisions of other international instruments, States Parties shall in particular:

(a) Provide for a minimum age or minimum ages for admission to employment;

(b) Provide for appropriate regulation of the hours and conditions of employment;

(c) Provide for appropriate penalties or other sanctions to ensure the effective enforcement of the present article.

Article 33

States Parties shall take all appropriate measures, including legislative, administrative, social and educational measures, to protect children from the illicit use of narcotic drugs and psychotropic substances as defined in the relevant international treaties, and to prevent the use of children in the illicit production and trafficking of such substances.

Article 34

States Parties undertake to protect the child from all forms of sexual exploitation and sexual abuse. For these purposes, States Parties shall in particular take all appropriate national, bilateral and multilateral measures to prevent:

(a) The inducement or coercion of a child to engage in any unlawful sexual activity;

(b) The exploitative use of children in prostitution or other unlawful sexual practices;

(c) The exploitative use of children in pornographic performances and materials.

Article 35

States Parties shall take all appropriate national, bilateral and multilateral measures to prevent the abduction of, the sale of or traffic in children for any purpose or in any form.

Article 36

States Parties shall protect the child against all other forms of exploitation prejudicial to any aspects of the child's welfare.

Article 37

States Parties shall ensure that:

(a) No child shall be subjected to torture or other cruel, inhuman or degrading treatment or punishment. Neither capital punishment nor life imprisonment without possibility of release shall be imposed for offences committed by persons below eighteen years of age;

(b) No child shall be deprived of his or her liberty unlawfully or arbitrarily. The arrest, detention or imprisonment of a child shall be in conformity with the law and shall be used only as a measure of last resort and for the shortest appropriate period of time;

(c) Every child deprived of liberty shall be treated with humanity and respect for the inherent dignity of the human person, and in a manner which takes into account the needs of persons of his or her age. In particular, every child deprived of liberty shall be separated from adults unless it is considered in the child's best interest not to do so and shall have the right to maintain contact with his or her family through correspondence and visits, save in exceptional circumstances;

(d) Every child deprived of his or her liberty shall have the right to prompt access to legal and other appropriate assistance, as well as the right to challenge the legality of the deprivation of his or her liberty before a court or other competent, independent and impartial authority, and to a prompt decision on any such action.

Article 38

1. States Parties undertake to respect and to ensure respect for rules of international humanitarian law appli-

cable to them in armed conflicts which are relevant to the child.

2. States Parties shall take all feasible measures to ensure that persons who have not attained the age of fifteen years do not take a direct part in hostilities.

3. States Parties shall refrain from recruiting any person who has not attained the age of fifteen years into their armed forces. In recruiting among those persons who have attained the age of fifteen years but who have not attained the age of eighteen years, States Parties shall endeavour to give priority to those who are oldest.

4. In accordance with their obligations under international humanitarian law to protect the civilian population in armed conflicts, States Parties shall take all feasible measures to ensure protection and care of children who are affected by an armed conflict.

Article 39

States Parties shall take all appropriate measures to promote physical and psychological recovery and social reintegration of a child victim of: any form of neglect, exploitation, or abuse; torture or any other form of cruel, inhuman or degrading treatment or punishment; or armed conflicts. Such recovery and reintegration shall take place in an environment which fosters the health, self-respect and dignity of the child.

Article 40

1. States Parties recognize the right of every child alleged as, accused of, or recognized as having infringed the penal law to be treated in a manner consistent with the promotion of the child's sense of dignity and worth, which reinforces the child's respect for the human rights and fundamental freedoms of others and which takes into account the child's age and the desirability of promoting the child's reintegration and the child's assuming a constructive role in society.

2. To this end, and having regard to the relevant provisions of international instruments, States Parties shall, in particular, ensure that:

(a) No child shall be alleged as, be accused of, or recognized as having infringed the penal law by reason of acts or omissions that were not prohibited by national or international law at the time they were committed;

(b) Every child alleged as or accused of having infringed the penal law has at least the following guarantees:

(i) To be presumed innocent until proven guilty according to law;

(ii) To be informed promptly and directly of the charges against him or her, and, if appropriate, through his or her parents or legal guardians, and

to have legal or other appropriate assistance in the preparation and presentation of his or her defence;

(iii) To have the matter determined without delay by a competent, independent and impartial authority or judicial body in a fair hearing according to law, in the presence of legal or other appropriate assistance and, unless it is considered not to be in the best interest of the child, in particular, taking into account his or her age or situation, his or her parents or legal guardians;

(iv) Not to be compelled to give testimony or to confess guilt; to examine or have examined adverse witnesses and to obtain the participation and examination of witnesses on his or her behalf under conditions of equality;

(v) If considered to have infringed the penal law, to have this decision and any measures imposed in consequence thereof reviewed by a higher competent, independent and impartial authority or judicial body according to law;

(vi) To have the free assistance of an interpreter if the child cannot understand or speak the language used;

(vii) To have his or her privacy fully respected at all stages of the proceedings.

3. States Parties shall seek to promote the establishment of laws, procedures, authorities and institutions specifically applicable to children alleged as, accused of, or recognized as having infringed the penal law, and, in particular:

(a) The establishment of a minimum age below which children shall be presumed not to have the capacity to infringe the penal law;

(b) Whenever appropriate and desirable, measures for dealing with such children without resorting to judicial proceedings, providing that human rights and legal safeguards are fully respected.

4. A variety of dispositions, such as care, guidance and supervision orders; counselling; probation; foster care; education and vocational training programmes and other alternatives to institutional care shall be available to ensure that children are dealt with in a manner appropriate to their well-being and proportionate both to their circumstances and the offence.

Article 41

Nothing in the present Convention shall affect any provisions which are more conducive to the realization of the rights of the child and which may be contained in:

(a) The law of a State party; or

(b) International law in force for that State.

PART II

Article 42

States Parties undertake to make the principles and provisions of the Convention widely known, by appropriate and active means, to adults and children alike.

Article 43

1. For the purpose of examining the progress made by States Parties in achieving the realization of the obligations undertaken in the present Convention, there shall be established a Committee on the Rights of the Child, which shall carry out the functions hereinafter provided.

2. The Committee shall consist of ten experts of high moral standing and recognized competence in the field covered by this Convention. The members of the Committee shall be elected by States Parties from among their nationals and shall serve in their personal capacity, consideration being given to equitable geographical distribution, as well as to the principal legal systems.

3. The members of the Committee shall be elected by secret ballot from a list of persons nominated by States Parties. Each State Party may nominate one person from among its own nationals.

4. The initial election to the Committee shall be held no later than six months after the date of the entry into force of the present Convention and thereafter every second year. At least four months before the date of each election, the Secretary-General of the United Nations shall address a letter to States Parties inviting them to submit their nominations within two months. The Secretary-General shall subsequently prepare a list in alphabetical order of all persons thus nominated, indicating States Parties which have nominated them, and shall submit it to the States Parties to the present Convention.

5. The elections shall be held at meetings of States Parties convened by the Secretary-General at United Nations Headquarters. At those meetings, for which two thirds of States Parties shall constitute a quorum, the persons elected to the Committee shall be those who obtain the largest number of votes and an absolute majority of the votes of the representatives of States Parties present and voting.

6. The members of the Committee shall be elected for a term of four years. They shall be eligible for re-election if renominated. The term of five of the members elected at the first election shall expire at the end of two years; immediately after the first election, the names of these five members shall be chosen by lot by the Chairman of the meeting.

7. If a member of the Committee dies or resigns or declares that for any other cause he or she can no longer perform the duties of the Committee, the State Party which nominated the member shall appoint another expert from among its nationals to serve for the remainder of the term, subject to the approval of the Committee.

8. The Committee shall establish its own rules of procedure.

9. The Committee shall elect its officers for a period of two years.

10. The meetings of the Committee shall normally be held at United Nations Headquarters or at any other convenient place as determined by the Committee. The Committee shall normally meet annually. The duration of the meetings of the Committee shall be determined, and reviewed, if necessary, by a meeting of the States Parties to the present Convention, subject to the approval of the General Assembly.

11. The Secretary-General of the United Nations shall provide the necessary staff and facilities for the effective performance of the functions of the Committee under the present Convention.

12. With the approval of the General Assembly, the members of the Committee established under the present Convention shall receive emoluments from United Nations resources on such terms and conditions as the Assembly may decide.

Article 44

1. States Parties undertake to submit to the Committee, through the Secretary-General of the United Nations, reports on the measures they have adopted which give effect to the rights recognized herein and on the progress made on the enjoyment of those rights:

(a) Within two years of the entry into force of the Convention for the State Party concerned;

(b) Thereafter every five years.

2. Reports made under the present article shall indicate factors and difficulties, if any, affecting the degree of fulfilment of the obligations under the present Convention. Reports shall also contain sufficient information to provide the Committee with a comprehensive understanding of the implementation of the Convention in the country concerned.

3. A State Party which has submitted a comprehensive initial report to the Committee need not, in its subsequent reports submitted in accordance with paragraph 1 (b) of the present article, repeat basic information previously provided.

4. The Committee may request from States Parties further information relevant to the implementation of the Convention.

5. The Committee shall submit to the General Assembly, through the Economic and Social Council, every two years, reports on its activities.

6. States Parties shall make their reports widely available to the public in their own countries.

Article 45

In order to foster the effective implementation of the Convention and to encourage international cooperation in the field covered by the Convention:

(a) The specialized agencies, the United Nations Children's Fund, and other United Nations organs shall be entitled to be represented at the consideration of the implementation of such provisions of the present Convention as fall within the scope of their mandate. The Committee may invite the specialized agencies, the United Nations Children's Fund and other competent bodies as it may consider appropriate to provide expert advice on the implementation of the Convention in areas falling within the scope of their respective mandates. The Committee may invite the specialized agencies, the United Nations Children's Fund, and other United Nations organs to submit reports on the implementation of the Convention in areas falling within the scope of their activities;

(b) The Committee shall transmit, as it may consider appropriate, to the specialized agencies, the United Nations Children's Fund and other competent bodies, any reports from States Parties that contain a request, or indicate a need, for technical advice or assistance, along with the Committee's observations and suggestions, if any, on these requests or indications;

(c) The Committee may recommend to the General Assembly to request the Secretary-General to undertake on its behalf studies on specific issues relating to the rights of the child;

(d) The Committee may make suggestions and general recommendations based on information received pursuant to articles 44 and 45 of the present Convention. Such suggestions and general recommendations shall be transmitted to any State Party concerned and reported to the General Assembly, together with comments, if any, from States Parties.

PART III

Article 46

The present Convention shall be open for signature by all States.

Article 47

The present Convention is subject to ratification. Instruments of ratification shall be deposited with the Secretary-General of the United Nations.

Article 48

The present Convention shall remain open for accession by any State. The instruments of accession shall be deposited with the Secretary-General of the United Nations.

Article 49

1. The present Convention shall enter into force on the thirtieth day following the date of deposit with the Secretary-General of the United Nations of the twentieth instrument of ratification or accession.

2. For each State ratifying or acceding to the Convention after the deposit of the twentieth instrument of ratification or accession, the Convention shall enter into force on the thirtieth day after the deposit by such State of its instrument of ratification or accession.

Article 50

1. Any State Party may propose an amendment and file it with the Secretary-General of the United Nations. The Secretary-General shall thereupon communicate the proposed amendment to States Parties, with a request that they indicate whether they favour a conference of States Parties for the purpose of considering and voting upon the proposals. In the event that, within four months from the date of such communication, at least one third of the States Parties favour such a conference, the Secretary-General shall convene the conference under the auspices of the United Nations. Any amendment adopted by a majority of States Parties present and voting at the conference shall be submitted to the General Assembly for approval.

2. An amendment adopted in accordance with paragraph 1 of the present article shall enter into force when it has been approved by the General Assembly of the United Nations and accepted by a two-thirds majority of States Parties.

3. When an amendment enters into force, it shall be binding on those States Parties which have accepted it, other States Parties still being bound by the provisions of the present Convention and any earlier amendments which they have accepted.

Article 51

1. The Secretary-General of the United Nations shall receive and circulate to all States the text of reservations made by States at the time of ratification or accession.

2. A reservation incompatible with the object and purpose of the present Convention shall not be permitted.

3. Reservations may be withdrawn at any time by notification to that effect addressed to the Secretary-General of the United Nations, who shall then inform all States. Such notification shall take effect on the date on which it is received by the Secretary-General.

Article 52

A State Party may denounce the present Convention by written notification to the Secretary-General of the United Nations. Denunciation becomes effective one year after the date of receipt of the notification by the Secretary-General.

Article 53

The Secretary-General of the United Nations is designated as the depositary of the present Convention.

Article 54

The original of the present Convention, of which the Arabic, Chinese, English, French, Russian and Spanish texts are equally authentic, shall be deposited with the Secretary-General of the United Nations.

IN WITNESS THEREOF the undersigned plenipotentiaries, being duly authorized thereto by their respective Governments, have signed the present Convention.

Document 61

Second Optional Protocol to the International Covenant on Civil and Political Rights, aiming at the abolition of the death penalty

A/RES/44/128, 15 December 1989

The States Parties to the present Protocol,

Believing that abolition of the death penalty contributes to enhancement of human dignity and progressive development of human rights,

Recalling article 3 of the Universal Declaration of Human Rights, adopted on 10 December 1948, and article 6 of the International Covenant on Civil and Political Rights, adopted on 16 December 1966,

Noting that article 6 of the International Covenant on Civil and Political Rights refers to abolition of the death penalty in terms that strongly suggest that abolition is desirable,

Convinced that all measures of abolition of the death penalty should be considered as progress in the enjoyment of the right to life,

Desirous to undertake hereby an international commitment to abolish the death penalty,

Have agreed as follows:

Article 1

1. No one within the jurisdiction of a State Party to the present Protocol shall be executed.

2. Each State Party shall take all necessary measures to abolish the death penalty within its jurisdiction.

Article 2

1. No reservation is admissible to the present Protocol, except for a reservation made at the time of ratification or accession that provides for the application of the death penalty in time of war pursuant to a conviction for a most serious crime of a military nature committed during wartime.

2. The State Party making such a reservation shall at the time of ratification or accession communicate to the Secretary-General of the United Nations the relevant provisions of its national legislation applicable during wartime.

3. The State Party having made such a reservation shall notify the Secretary-General of the United Nations of any beginning or ending of a state of war applicable to its territory.

Article 3

The States Parties to the present Protocol shall include in the reports they submit to the Human Rights Committee, in accordance with article 40 of the Covenant, information on the measures that they have adopted to give effect to the present Protocol.

Article 4

With respect to the States Parties to the Covenant that have made a declaration under article 41, the competence of the Human Rights Committee to receive and consider communications when a State Party claims that another State Party is not fulfilling its obligations shall extend to the provisions of the present Protocol, unless the State Party concerned has made a statement to the contrary at the moment of ratification or accession.

Article 5

With respect to the States Parties to the first Optional Protocol to the International Covenant on Civil and Political Rights adopted on 16 December 1966, the competence of the Human Rights Committee to receive and consider communications from individuals subject to its jurisdiction shall extend to the provisions of the present Protocol, unless the State Party concerned has made a statement to the contrary at the moment of ratification or accession.

Article 6

1. The provisions of the present Protocol shall apply as additional provisions to the Covenant.

2. Without prejudice to the possibility of a reservation under article 2 of the present Protocol, the right guaranteed in article 1, paragraph 1, of the present Protocol shall not be subject to any derogation under article 4 of the Covenant.

Article 7

1. The present Protocol is open for signature by any State that has signed the Covenant.

2. The present Protocol is subject to ratification by any State that has ratified the Covenant or acceded to it. Instruments of ratification shall be deposited with the Secretary-General of the United Nations.

3. The present Protocol shall be open to accession by any State that has ratified the Covenant or acceded to it.

4. Accession shall be effected by the deposit of an instrument of accession with the Secretary-General of the United Nations.

5. The Secretary-General of the United Nations shall inform all States that have signed the present Protocol or acceded to it of the deposit of each instrument of ratification or accession.

Article 8

1. The present Protocol shall enter into force three months after the date of the deposit with the Secretary-General of the United Nations of the tenth instrument of ratification or accession.

2. For each State ratifying the present Protocol or acceding to it after the deposit of the tenth instrument of ratification or accession, the present Protocol shall enter into force three months after the date of the deposit of its own instrument of ratification or accession.

Article 9

The provisions of the present Protocol shall extend to all parts of federal States without any limitations or exceptions.

Article 10

The Secretary-General of the United Nations shall inform all States referred to in article 48, paragraph 1, of the Covenant of the following particulars:

(a) Reservations, communications and notifications under article 2 of the present Protocol;

(b) Statements made under articles 4 or 5 of the present Protocol;

(c) Signatures, ratifications and accessions under article 7 of the present Protocol;

(d) The date of the entry into force of the present Protocol under article 8 thereof.

Article 11

1. The present Protocol, of which the Arabic, Chinese, English, French, Russian and Spanish texts are equally authentic, shall be deposited in the archives of the United Nations.

2. The Secretary-General of the United Nations shall transmit certified copies of the present Protocol to all States referred to in article 48 of the Covenant.

Document 62

Basic Principles on the Use of Force and Firearms by Law Enforcement Officials, adopted by the Eighth United Nations Congress on the Prevention of Crime and the Treatment of Offenders, Havana, Cuba, 27 August to 7 September 1990

Whereas the work of law enforcement officials* is a social service of great importance and there is, therefore, a need to maintain and, whenever necessary, to improve the working conditions and status of these officials,

Whereas a threat to the life and safety of law enforcement officials must be seen as a threat to the stability of society as a whole,

Whereas law enforcement officials have a vital role in the protection of the right to life, liberty and security of the person, as guaranteed in the Universal Declaration of Human Rights and reaffirmed in the International Covenant on Civil and Political Rights,

Whereas the Standard Minimum Rules for the Treatment of Prisoners provide for the circumstances in which prison officials may use force in the course of their duties,

Whereas article 3 of the Code of Conduct for Law Enforcement Officials provides that law enforcement officials may use force only when strictly necessary and to the extent required for the performance of their duty,

Whereas the preparatory meeting for the Seventh United Nations Congress on the Prevention of Crime and the Treatment of Offenders, held at Varenna, Italy, agreed on elements to be considered in the course of further work on restraints on the use of force and firearms by law enforcement officials,

Whereas the Seventh Congress, in its resolution 14, *inter alia*, emphasizes that the use of force and firearms by law enforcement officials should be commensurate with due respect for human rights,

Whereas the Economic and Social Council, in its resolution 1986/10, section IX, of 21 May 1986, invited Member States to pay particular attention in the implementation of the Code to the use of force and firearms by law enforcement officials, and the General Assembly, in its resolution 41/149 of 4 December 1986, *inter alia*, welcomed this recommendation made by the Council,

Whereas it is appropriate that, with due regard to their personal safety, consideration be given to the role of law enforcement officials in relation to the administration of justice, to the protection of the right to life, liberty and security of the person, to their responsibility to maintain public safety and social peace and to the importance of their qualifications, training and conduct,

The basic principles set forth below, which have been formulated to assist Member States in their task of ensuring and promoting the proper role of law enforcement officials, should be taken into account and respected by Governments within the framework of their national legislation and practice, and be brought to the attention of law enforcement officials as well as other persons, such as judges, prosecutors, lawyers, members of the executive branch and the legislature, and the public.

General provisions

1. Governments and law enforcement agencies shall adopt and implement rules and regulations on the use of force and firearms against persons by law enforcement officials. In developing such rules and regulations, Governments and law enforcement agencies shall keep the ethical issues associated with the use of force and firearms constantly under review.

2. Governments and law enforcement agencies should develop a range of means as broad as possible and equip law enforcement officials with various types of weapons and ammunition that would allow for a differentiated use of force and firearms. These should include the development of non-lethal incapacitating weapons for use in appropriate situations, with a view to increasingly restraining the application of means capable of causing death or injury to persons. For the same purpose, it should also be possible for law enforcement officials to be equipped with self-defensive equipment such as shields, helmets, bullet-proof vests and bullet-proof means of transportation, in order to decrease the need to use weapons of any kind.

3. The development and deployment of non-lethal incapacitating weapons should be carefully evaluated in order to minimize the risk of endangering uninvolved persons, and the use of such weapons should be carefully controlled.

4. Law enforcement officials, in carrying out their duty, shall, as far as possible, apply non-violent means before resorting to the use of force and firearms. They may use force and firearms only if other means remain

*In accordance with the commentary to article 1 of the Code of Conduct for Law Enforcement Officials, the term "law enforcement officials" includes all officers of the law, whether appointed or elected, who exercise police powers, especially the powers of arrest or detention. In countries where police powers are exercised by military authorities, whether uniformed or not, or by State security forces, the definition of law enforcement officials shall be regarded as including officers of such services.

ineffective or without any promise of achieving the intended result.

5. Whenever the lawful use of force and firearms is unavoidable, law enforcement officials shall:

(a) Exercise restraint in such use and act in proportion to the seriousness of the offence and the legitimate objective to be achieved;

(b) Minimize damage and injury, and respect and preserve human life;

(c) Ensure that assistance and medical aid are rendered to any injured or affected persons at the earliest possible moment;

(d) Ensure that relatives or close friends of the injured or affected person are notified at the earliest possible moment.

6. Where injury or death is caused by the use of force and firearms by law enforcement officials, they shall report the incident promptly to their superiors, in accordance with principle 22.

7. Governments shall ensure that arbitrary or abusive use of force and firearms by law enforcement officials is punished as a criminal offence under their law.

8. Exceptional circumstances such as internal political instability or any other public emergency may not be invoked to justify any departure from these basic principles.

Special provisions

9. Law enforcement officials shall not use firearms against persons except in self-defence or defence of others against the imminent threat of death or serious injury, to prevent the perpetration of a particularly serious crime involving grave threat to life, to arrest a person presenting such a danger and resisting their authority, or to prevent his or her escape, and only when less extreme means are insufficient to achieve these objectives. In any event, intentional lethal use of firearms may only be made when strictly unavoidable in order to protect life.

10. In the circumstances provided for under principle 9, law enforcement officials shall identify themselves as such and give a clear warning of their intent to use firearms, with sufficient time for the warning to be observed, unless to do so would unduly place the law enforcement officials at risk or would create a risk of death or serious harm to other persons, or would be clearly inappropriate or pointless in the circumstances of the incident.

11. Rules and regulations on the use of firearms by law enforcement officials should include guidelines that:

(a) Specify the circumstances under which law enforcement officials are authorized to carry firearms and prescribe the types of firearms and ammunition permitted;

(b) Ensure that firearms are used only in appropriate circumstances and in a manner likely to decrease the risk of unnecessary harm;

(c) Prohibit the use of those firearms and ammunition that cause unwarranted injury or present an unwarranted risk;

(d) Regulate the control, storage and issuing of firearms, including procedures for ensuring that law enforcement officials are accountable for the firearms and ammunition issued to them;

(e) Provide for warnings to be given, if appropriate, when firearms are to be discharged;

(f) Provide for a system of reporting whenever law enforcement officials use firearms in the performance of their duty.

Policing unlawful assemblies

12. As everyone is allowed to participate in lawful and peaceful assemblies, in accordance with the principles embodied in the Universal Declaration of Human Rights and the International Covenant on Civil and Political Rights, Governments and law enforcement agencies and officials shall recognize that force and firearms may be used only in accordance with principles 13 and 14.

13. In the dispersal of assemblies that are unlawful but non-violent, law enforcement officials shall avoid the use of force or, where that is not practicable, shall restrict such force to the minimum extent necessary.

14. In the dispersal of violent assemblies, law enforcement officials may use firearms only when less dangerous means are not practicable and only to the minimum extent necessary. Law enforcement officials shall not use firearms in such cases, except under the conditions stipulated in principle 9.

Policing persons in custody or detention

15. Law enforcement officials, in their relations with persons in custody or detention, shall not use force, except when strictly necessary for the maintenance of security and order within the institution, or when personal safety is threatened.

16. Law enforcement officials, in their relations with persons in custody or detention, shall not use firearms, except in self-defence or in the defence of others against the immediate threat of death or serious injury, or when strictly necessary to prevent the escape of a person in custody or detention presenting the danger referred to in principle 9.

17. The preceding principles are without prejudice to the rights, duties and responsibilities of prison officials, as set out in the Standard Minimum Rules for the Treatment of Prisoners, particularly rules 33, 34 and 54.

18. Governments and law enforcement agencies shall ensure that all law enforcement officials are selected by proper screening procedures, have appropriate moral, psychological and physical qualities for the effective exercise of their functions and receive continuous and thorough professional training. Their continued fitness to perform these functions should be subject to periodic review.

19. Governments and law enforcement agencies shall ensure that all law enforcement officials are provided with training and are tested in accordance with appropriate proficiency standards in the use of force. Those law enforcement officials who are required to carry firearms should be authorized to do so only upon completion of special training in their use.

20. In the training of law enforcement officials, Governments and law enforcement agencies shall give special attention to issues of police ethics and human rights, especially in the investigative process, to alternatives to the use of force and firearms, including the peaceful settlement of conflicts, the understanding of crowd behaviour, and the methods of persuasion, negotiation and mediation, as well as to technical means, with a view to limiting the use of force and firearms. Law enforcement agencies should review their training programmes and operational procedures in the light of particular incidents.

21. Governments and law enforcement agencies shall make stress counselling available to law enforcement officials who are involved in situations where force and firearms are used.

Reporting and review procedures

22. Governments and law enforcement agencies shall establish effective reporting and review procedures for all incidents referred to in principles 6 and 11 (f). For incidents reported pursuant to these principles, Governments and law enforcement agencies shall ensure that an effective review process is available and that independent administrative or prosecutorial authorities are in a position to exercise jurisdiction in appropriate circumstances. In cases of death and serious injury or other grave consequences, a detailed report shall be sent promptly to the competent authorities responsible for administrative review and judicial control.

23. Persons affected by the use of force and firearms or their legal representatives shall have access to an independent process, including a judicial process. In the event of the death of such persons, this provision shall apply to their dependants accordingly.

24. Governments and law enforcement agencies shall ensure that superior officers are held responsible if they know, or should have known, that law enforcement officials under their command are resorting, or have resorted, to the unlawful use of force and firearms, and they did not take all measures in their power to prevent, suppress or report such use.

25. Governments and law enforcement agencies shall ensure that no criminal or disciplinary sanction is imposed on law enforcement officials who, in compliance with the Code of Conduct for Law Enforcement Officials and these basic principles, refuse to carry out an order to use force and firearms, or who report such use by other officials.

26. Obedience to superior orders shall be no defence if law enforcement officials knew that an order to use force and firearms resulting in the death or serious injury of a person was manifestly unlawful and had a reasonable opportunity to refuse to follow it. In any case, responsibility also rests on the superiors who gave the unlawful orders.

Document 63

Basic Principles on the Role of Lawyers, adopted by the Eighth United Nations Congress on the Prevention of Crime and the Treatment of Offenders, Havana, Cuba, 27 August to 7 September 1990

Whereas in the Charter of the United Nations the peoples of the world affirm, *inter alia*, their determination to establish conditions under which justice can be maintained, and proclaim as one of their purposes the achievement of international cooperation in promoting and encouraging respect for human rights and fundamental freedoms without distinction as to race, sex, language or religion,

Whereas the Universal Declaration of Human Rights enshrines the principles of equality before the law, the presumption of innocence, the right to a fair and public hearing by an independent and impartial tribunal, and all the guarantees necessary for the defence of everyone charged with a penal offence,

Whereas the International Covenant on Civil and Political Rights proclaims, in addition, the right to be tried without undue delay and the right to a fair and public hearing by a competent, independent and impartial tribunal established by law,

Whereas the International Covenant on Economic, Social and Cultural Rights recalls the obligation of States under the Charter to promote universal respect for, and observance of, human rights and freedoms,

Whereas the Body of Principles for the Protection of All Persons under Any Form of Detention or Imprisonment provides that a detained person shall be entitled to have the assistance of, and to communicate and consult with, legal counsel,

Whereas the Standard Minimum Rules for the Treatment of Prisoners recommend, in particular, that legal assistance and confidential communication with counsel should be ensured to untried prisoners,

Whereas the Safeguards guaranteeing protection of those facing the death penalty reaffirm the right of everyone suspected or charged with a crime for which capital punishment may be imposed to adequate legal assistance at all stages of the proceedings, in accordance with article 14 of the International Covenant on Civil and Political Rights,

Whereas the Declaration of Basic Principles of Justice for Victims of Crime and Abuse of Power recommends measures to be taken at the international and national levels to improve access to justice and fair treatment, restitution, compensation and assistance for victims of crime,

Whereas adequate protection of the human rights and fundamental freedoms to which all persons are entitled, be they economic, social and cultural, or civil and political, requires that all persons have effective access to legal services provided by an independent legal profession,

Whereas professional associations of lawyers have a vital role to play in upholding professional standards and ethics, protecting their members from persecution and improper restrictions and infringements, providing legal services to all in need of them, and cooperating with governmental and other institutions in furthering the ends of justice and public interest,

The Basic Principles on the Role of Lawyers, set forth below, which have been formulated to assist Member States in their task of promoting and ensuring the proper role of lawyers, should be respected and taken into account by Governments within the framework of their national legislation and practice and should be brought to the attention of lawyers as well as other persons, such as judges, prosecutors, members of the executive and the legislature, and the public in general. These principles shall also apply, as appropriate, to persons who exercise the functions of lawyers without having the formal status of lawyers.

Access to lawyers and legal services

1. All persons are entitled to call upon the assistance of a lawyer of their choice to protect and establish their rights and to defend them in all stages of criminal proceedings.

2. Governments shall ensure that efficient procedures and responsive mechanisms for effective and equal access to lawyers are provided for all persons within their territory and subject to their jurisdiction, without distinction of any kind, such as discrimination based on race, colour, ethnic origin, sex, language, religion, political or other opinion, national or social origin, property, birth, economic or other status.

3. Governments shall ensure the provision of sufficient funding and other resources for legal services to the poor and, as necessary, to other disadvantaged persons. Professional associations of lawyers shall cooperate in the organization and provision of services, facilities and other resources.

4. Governments and professional associations of lawyers shall promote programmes to inform the public about their rights and duties under the law and the important role of lawyers in protecting their fundamental freedoms. Special attention should be given to assisting the poor and other disadvantaged persons so as to enable them to assert their rights and where necessary call upon the assistance of lawyers.

Special safeguards in criminal justice matters

5. Governments shall ensure that all persons are immediately informed by the competent authority of their right to be assisted by a lawyer of their own choice upon arrest or detention or when charged with a criminal offence.

6. Any such persons who do not have a lawyer shall, in all cases in which the interests of justice so require, be entitled to have a lawyer of experience and competence commensurate with the nature of the offence assigned to them in order to provide effective legal assistance, without payment by them if they lack sufficient means to pay for such services.

7. Governments shall further ensure that all persons arrested or detained, with or without criminal charge, shall have prompt access to a lawyer, and in any case not later than forty-eight hours from the time of arrest or detention.

8. All arrested, detained or imprisoned persons shall be provided with adequate opportunities, time and facilities to be visited by and to communicate and consult with a lawyer, without delay, interception or censorship and in full confidentiality. Such consultations may be within sight, but not within the hearing, of law enforcement officials.

9. Governments, professional associations of lawyers and educational institutions shall ensure that lawyers have appropriate education and training and be made aware of the ideals and ethical duties of the lawyer and of human rights and fundamental freedoms recognized by national and international law.

10. Governments, professional associations of lawyers and educational institutions shall ensure that there is no discrimination against a person with respect to entry into or continued practice within the legal profession on the grounds of race, colour, sex, ethnic origin, religion, political or other opinion, national or social origin, property, birth, economic or other status, except that a requirement, that a lawyer must be a national of the country concerned, shall not be considered discriminatory.

11. In countries where there exist groups, communities or regions whose needs for legal services are not met, particularly where such groups have distinct cultures, traditions or languages or have been the victims of past discrimination, Governments, professional associations of lawyers and educational institutions should take special measures to provide opportunities for candidates from these groups to enter the legal profession and should ensure that they receive training appropriate to the needs of their groups.

Duties and responsibilities

12. Lawyers shall at all times maintain the honour and dignity of their profession as essential agents of the administration of justice.

13. The duties of lawyers towards their clients shall include:

(a) Advising clients as to their legal rights and obligations, and as to the working of the legal system in so far as it is relevant to the legal rights and obligations of the clients;

(b) Assisting clients in every appropriate way, and taking legal action to protect their interests;

(c) Assisting clients before courts, tribunals or administrative authorities, where appropriate.

14. Lawyers, in protecting the rights of their clients and in promoting the cause of justice, shall seek to uphold human rights and fundamental freedoms recognized by national and international law and shall at all times act freely and diligently in accordance with the law and recognized standards and ethics of the legal profession.

15. Lawyers shall always loyally respect the interests of their clients.

16. Governments shall ensure that lawyers (a) are able to perform all of their professional functions without intimidation, hindrance, harassment or improper interference; (b) are able to travel and to consult with their clients freely both within their own country and abroad; and (c) shall not suffer, or be threatened with, prosecution or administrative, economic or other sanctions for any action taken in accordance with recognized professional duties, standards and ethics.

17. Where the security of lawyers is threatened as a result of discharging their functions, they shall be adequately safeguarded by the authorities.

18. Lawyers shall not be identified with their clients or their clients' causes as a result of discharging their functions.

19. No court or administrative authority before whom the right to counsel is recognized shall refuse to recognize the right of a lawyer to appear before it for his or her client unless that lawyer has been disqualified in accordance with national law and practice and in conformity with these principles.

20. Lawyers shall enjoy civil and penal immunity for relevant statements made in good faith in written or oral pleadings or in their professional appearances before a court, tribunal or other legal or administrative authority.

21. It is the duty of the competent authorities to ensure lawyers access to appropriate information, files and documents in their possession or control in sufficient time to enable lawyers to provide effective legal assistance to their clients. Such access should be provided at the earliest appropriate time.

22. Governments shall recognize and respect that all communications and consultations between lawyers and their clients within their professional relationship are confidential.

Freedom of expression and association

23. Lawyers like other citizens are entitled to freedom of expression, belief, association and assembly. In particular, they shall have the right to take part in public discussion of matters concerning the law, the administration of justice and the promotion and protection of human rights and to join or form local, national or international organizations and attend their meetings, without suffering professional restrictions by reason of their lawful action or their membership in a lawful organization. In exercising these rights, lawyers shall always conduct themselves in accordance with the law and the recognized standards and ethics of the legal profession.

24. Lawyers shall be entitled to form and join self-governing professional associations to represent their interests, promote their continuing education and training and protect their professional integrity. The executive body of the professional associations shall be elected by its members and shall exercise its functions without external interference.

25. Professional associations of lawyers shall co-operate with Governments to ensure that everyone has effective and equal access to legal services and that lawyers are able, without improper interference, to counsel and assist their clients in accordance with the law and recognized professional standards and ethics.

Disciplinary proceedings

26. Codes of professional conduct for lawyers shall be established by the legal profession through its appro-priate organs, or by legislation, in accordance with national law and custom and recognized international standards and norms.

27. Charges or complaints made against lawyers in their professional capacity shall be processed expeditiously and fairly under appropriate procedures. Lawyers shall have the right to a fair hearing, including the right to be assisted by a lawyer of their choice.

28. Disciplinary proceedings against lawyers shall be brought before an impartial disciplinary committee established by the legal profession, before an independent statutory authority, or before a court, and shall be subject to an independent judicial review.

29. All disciplinary proceedings shall be determined in accordance with the code of professional conduct and other recognized standards and ethics of the legal profession and in the light of these principles.

Document 64

Guidelines on the Role of Prosecutors, adopted by the Eighth United Nations Congress on the Prevention of Crime and the Treatment of Offenders, Havana, Cuba, 27 August to 7 September 1990

Whereas in the Charter of the United Nations the peoples of the world affirm, *inter alia*, their determination to establish conditions under which justice can be maintained, and proclaim as one of their purposes the achievement of international cooperation in promoting and encouraging respect for human rights and fundamental freedoms without distinction as to race, sex, language or religion,

Whereas the Universal Declaration of Human Rights enshrines the principles of equality before the law, the presumption of innocence and the right to a fair and public hearing by an independent and impartial tribunal,

Whereas frequently there still exists a gap between the vision underlying those principles and the actual situation,

Whereas the organization and administration of justice in every country should be inspired by those principles, and efforts undertaken to translate them fully into reality,

Whereas prosecutors play a crucial role in the administration of justice, and rules concerning the performance of their important responsibilities should promote their respect for and compliance with the above-mentioned principles, thus contributing to fair and equitable criminal justice and the effective protection of citizens against crime,

Whereas it is essential to ensure that prosecutors possess the professional qualifications required for the accomplishment of their functions, through improved methods of recruitment and legal and professional training, and through the provision of all necessary means for the proper performance of their role in combating criminality, particularly in its new forms and dimensions,

Whereas the General Assembly, by its resolution 34/169 of 17 December 1979, adopted the Code of Conduct for Law Enforcement Officials, on the recommendation of the Fifth United Nations Congress on the Prevention of Crime and the Treatment of Offenders,

Whereas in resolution 16 of the Sixth United Nations Congress on the Prevention of Crime and the Treatment of Offenders, the Committee on Crime Prevention and Control was called upon to include among its priorities the elaboration of guidelines relating to the independence of judges and the selection, professional training and status of judges and prosecutors,

Whereas the Seventh United Nations Congress on the Prevention of Crime and the Treatment of Offenders adopted the Basic Principles on the Independence of the Judiciary, subsequently endorsed by the General Assembly in its resolutions 40/32 of 29 November 1985 and 40/146 of 13 December 1985,

Whereas the Declaration of Basic Principles of Justice for Victims of Crime and Abuse of Power recommends measures to be taken at the international and national levels to improve access to justice and fair treatment, restitution, compensation and assistance for victims of crime,

Whereas, in resolution 7 of the Seventh Congress, the Committee was called upon to consider the need for guidelines relating, *inter alia*, to the selection, professional training and status of prosecutors, their expected tasks and conduct, means to enhance their contribution to the smooth functioning of the criminal justice system and their cooperation with the police, the scope of their discretionary powers, and their role in criminal proceedings, and to report thereon to future United Nations congresses,

The Guidelines set forth below, which have been formulated to assist Member States in their tasks of securing and promoting the effectiveness, impartiality and fairness of prosecutors in criminal proceedings, should be respected and taken into account by Governments within the framework of their national legislation and practice, and should be brought to the attention of prosecutors, as well as other persons, such as judges, lawyers, members of the executive and the legislature and the public in general. The present Guidelines have been formulated principally with public prosecutors in mind, but they apply equally, as appropriate, to prosecutors appointed on an *ad hoc* basis.

Qualifications, selection and training

1. Persons selected as prosecutors shall be individuals of integrity and ability, with appropriate training and qualifications.

2. States shall ensure that:

(a) Selection criteria for prosecutors embody safeguards against appointments based on partiality or prejudice, excluding any discrimination against a person on the grounds of race, colour, sex, language, religion, political or other opinion, national, social or ethnic origin, property, birth, economic or other status, except that it shall not be considered discriminatory to require a candidate for prosecutorial office to be a national of the country concerned;

(b) Prosecutors have appropriate education and training and should be made aware of the ideals and ethical duties of their office, of the constitutional and statutory protections for the rights of the suspect and the victim, and of human rights and fundamental freedoms recognized by national and international law.

Status and conditions of service

3. Prosecutors, as essential agents of the administration of justice, shall at all times maintain the honour and dignity of their profession.

4. States shall ensure that prosecutors are able to perform their professional functions without intimidation, hindrance, harassment, improper interference or unjustified exposure to civil, penal or other liability.

5. Prosecutors and their families shall be physically protected by the authorities when their personal safety is threatened as a result of the discharge of prosecutorial functions.

6. Reasonable conditions of service of prosecutors, adequate remuneration and, where applicable, tenure, pension and age of retirement shall be set out by law or published rules or regulations.

7. Promotion of prosecutors, wherever such a system exists, shall be based on objective factors, in particular professional qualifications, ability, integrity and experience, and decided upon in accordance with fair and impartial procedures.

Freedom of expression and association

8. Prosecutors like other citizens are entitled to freedom of expression, belief, association and assembly. In particular, they shall have the right to take part in public discussion of matters concerning the law, the administration of justice and the promotion and protection of human rights and to join or form local, national or international organizations and attend their meetings, without suffering professional disadvantage by reason of their lawful action or their membership in a lawful organization. In exercising these rights, prosecutors shall always conduct themselves in accordance with the law and the recognized standards and ethics of their profession.

9. Prosecutors shall be free to form and join professional associations or other organizations to represent their interests, to promote their professional training and to protect their status.

Role in criminal proceedings

10. The office of prosecutors shall be strictly separated from judicial functions.

11. Prosecutors shall perform an active role in criminal proceedings, including institution of prosecution and, where authorized by law or consistent with local practice, in the investigation of crime, supervision over the legality of these investigations, supervision of the execution of court decisions and the exercise of other functions as representatives of the public interest.

12. Prosecutors shall, in accordance with the law, perform their duties fairly, consistently and expeditiously, and respect and protect human dignity and uphold human rights, thus contributing to ensuring due process and the smooth functioning of the criminal justice system.

13. In the performance of their duties, prosecutors shall:

(a) Carry out their functions impartially and avoid all political, social, religious, racial, cultural, sexual or any other kind of discrimination;

(b) Protect the public interest, act with objectivity, take proper account of the position of the suspect and the victim, and pay attention to all relevant circumstances, irrespective of whether they are to the advantage or disadvantage of the suspect;

(c) Keep matters in their possession confidential, unless the performance of duty or the needs of justice require otherwise;

(d) Consider the views and concerns of victims when their personal interests are affected and ensure that victims are informed of their rights in accordance with the Declaration of Basic Principles of Justice for Victims of Crime and Abuse of Power.

14. Prosecutors shall not initiate or continue prosecution, or shall make every effort to stay proceedings, when an impartial investigation shows the charge to be unfounded.

15. Prosecutors shall give due attention to the prosecution of crimes committed by public officials, particularly corruption, abuse of power, grave violations of human rights and other crimes recognized by international law and, where authorized by law or consistent with local practice, the investigation of such offences.

16. When prosecutors come into possession of evidence against suspects that they know or believe on reasonable grounds was obtained through recourse to unlawful methods, which constitute a grave violation of the suspect's human rights, especially involving torture or cruel, inhuman or degrading treatment or punishment, or other abuses of human rights, they shall refuse to use such evidence against anyone other than those who used such methods, or inform the Court accordingly, and shall take all necessary steps to ensure that those responsible for using such methods are brought to justice.

Discretionary functions

17. In countries where prosecutors are vested with discretionary functions, the law or published rules or regulations shall provide guidelines to enhance fairness and consistency of approach in taking decisions in the prosecution process, including institution or waiver of prosecution.

Alternatives to prosecution

18. In accordance with national law, prosecutors shall give due consideration to waiving prosecution, discontinuing proceedings conditionally or unconditionally, or diverting criminal cases from the formal justice system, with full respect for the rights of suspect(s) and the victim(s). For this purpose, States should fully explore the possibility of adopting diversion schemes not only to alleviate excessive court loads, but also to avoid the stigmatization of pre-trial detention, indictment and conviction, as well as the possible adverse effects of imprisonment.

19. In countries where prosecutors are vested with discretionary functions as to the decision whether or not to prosecute a juvenile, special considerations shall be given to the nature and gravity of the offence, protection of society and the personality and background of the juvenile. In making that decision, prosecutors shall particularly consider available alternatives to prosecution under the relevant juvenile justice laws and procedures. Prosecutors shall use their best efforts to take prosecutory action against juveniles only to the extent strictly necessary.

Relations with other government agencies or institutions

20. In order to ensure the fairness and effectiveness of prosecution, prosecutors shall strive to cooperate with the police, the courts, the legal profession, public defenders and other government agencies or institutions.

Disciplinary proceedings

21. Disciplinary offences of prosecutors shall be based on law or lawful regulations. Complaints against prosecutors which allege that they acted in a manner clearly out of the range of professional standards shall be processed expeditiously and fairly under appropriate procedures. Prosecutors shall have the right to a fair hearing. The decision shall be subject to independent review.

22. Disciplinary proceedings against prosecutors shall guarantee an objective evaluation and decision. They shall be determined in accordance with the law, the code of professional conduct and other established standards and ethics and in the light of the present Guidelines.

Observance of the Guidelines

23. Prosecutors shall respect the present Guidelines. They shall also, to the best of their capability, prevent and actively oppose any violations thereof.

24. Prosecutors who have reason to believe that a violation of the present Guidelines has occurred or is about to occur shall report the matter to their superior authorities and, where necessary, to other appropriate authorities or organs vested with reviewing or remedial power.

Document 65

World Declaration on the Survival, Protection and Development of Children and Plan of Action for Implementing the World Declaration, adopted by the World Summit for Children in New York

30 September 1990

World Declaration on the Survival, Protection and Development of Children

1. We have gathered at the World Summit for Children to undertake a joint commitment and to make an urgent universal appeal—to give every child a better future.

2. The children of the world are innocent, vulnerable and dependent. They are also curious, active and full of hope. Their time should be one of joy and peace, of playing, learning and growing. Their future should be shaped in harmony and cooperation. Their lives should mature, as they broaden their perspectives and gain new experiences.

3. But for many children, the reality of childhood is altogether different.

The challenge

4. Each day, countless children around the world are exposed to dangers that hamper their growth and development. They suffer immensely as casualties of war and violence; as victims of racial discrimination, apartheid, aggression, foreign occupation and annexation; as refugees and displaced children, forced to abandon their homes and their roots; as disabled; or as victims of neglect, cruelty and exploitation.

5. Each day, millions of children suffer from the scourges of poverty and economic crisis—from hunger and homelessness, from epidemics and illiteracy, from degradation of the environment. They suffer from the grave effects of the problems of external indebtedness and also from the lack of sustained and sustainable growth in many developing countries, particularly the least developed ones.

6. Each day, 40,000 children die from malnutrition and disease, including acquired immunodeficiency syndrome (AIDS), from the lack of clean water and inadequate sanitation and from the effects of the drug problem.

7. These are challenges that we, as political leaders, must meet.

The opportunity

8. Together, our nations have the means and the knowledge to protect the lives and to diminish enormously the suffering of children, to promote the full development of their human potential and to make them aware of their needs, rights and opportunities. The Convention on the Rights of the Child provides a new opportunity to make respect for children's rights and welfare truly universal.

9. Recent improvements in the international political climate can facilitate this task. Through international cooperation and solidarity it should now be possible to achieve concrete results in many fields—to revitalize economic growth and development, to protect the environment, to prevent the spread of fatal and crippling diseases and to achieve greater social and economic justice. The current moves towards disarmament also mean that significant resources could be released for purposes other than military ones. Improving the well-being of children must be a very high priority when these resources are reallocated.

The task

10. Enhancement of children's health and nutrition is a first duty, and also a task for which solutions are now within reach. The lives of tens of thousands of boys and girls can be saved every day, because the causes of their death are readily preventable. Child and infant mortality is unacceptably high in many parts of the world, but can be lowered dramatically with means that are already known and easily accessible.

11. Further attention, care and support should be accorded to disabled children, as well as to other children in very difficult circumstances.

12. Strengthening the role of women in general and ensuring their equal rights will be to the advantage of the world's children. Girls must be given equal treatment and opportunities from the very beginning.

13. At present, over 100 million children are without basic schooling, and two-thirds of them are girls. The provision of basic education and literacy for all are among the most important contributions that can be made to the development of the world's children.

14. Half a million mothers die each year from causes related to childbirth. Safe motherhood must be promoted in all possible ways. Emphasis must be placed on responsible planning of family size and on child spacing. The family, as a fundamental group and natural

environment for the growth and well-being of children, should be given all necessary protection and assistance.

15. All children must be given the chance to find their identity and realize their worth in a safe and supportive environment, through families and other care-givers committed to their welfare. They must be prepared for responsible life in a free society. They should, from their early years, be encouraged to participate in the cultural life of their societies.

16. Economic conditions will continue to influence greatly the fate of children, especially in developing nations. For the sake of the future of all children, it is urgently necessary to ensure or reactivate sustained and sustainable economic growth and development in all countries and also to continue to give urgent attention to an early, broad and durable solution to the external debt problems facing developing debtor countries.

17. These tasks require a continued and concerted effort by all nations, through national action and international cooperation.

The commitment

18. The well-being of children requires political action at the highest level. We are determined to take that action.

19. We ourselves hereby make a solemn commitment to give high priority to the rights of children, to their survival and to their protection and development. This will also ensure the well-being of all societies.

20. We have agreed that we will act together, in international cooperation, as well as in our respective countries. We now commit ourselves to the following 10-point programme to protect the rights of children and to improve their lives:

(1) We will work to promote earliest possible ratification and implementation of the Convention on the Rights of the Child. Programmes to encourage information about children's rights should be launched worldwide, taking into account the distinct cultural and social values in different countries.

(2) We will work for a solid effort of national and international action to enhance children's health, to promote prenatal care and to lower infant and child mortality in all countries and among all peoples. We will promote the provision of clean water in all communities for all their children, as well as universal access to sanitation.

(3) We will work for optimal growth and development in childhood, through measures to eradicate hunger, malnutrition and famine, and thus to relieve millions of children of tragic sufferings in a world that has the means to feed all its citizens.

(4) We will work to strengthen the role and status of women. We will promote responsible planning of family size, child spacing, breastfeeding and safe motherhood.

(5) We will work for respect for the role of the family in providing for children and will support the efforts of parents, other care-givers and communities to nurture and care for children, from the earliest stages of childhood through adolescence. We also recognize the special needs of children who are separated from their families.

(6) We will work for programmes that reduce illiteracy and provide educational opportunities for all children, irrespective of their background and gender; that prepare children for productive employment and lifelong learning opportunities, i.e., through vocational training; and that enable children to grow to adulthood within a supportive and nurturing cultural and social context.

(7) We will work to ameliorate the plight of millions of children who live under especially difficult circumstances—as victims of apartheid and foreign occupation; orphans and street children and children of migrant workers; the displaced children and victims of natural and man-made disasters; the disabled and the abused, the socially disadvantaged and the exploited. Refugee children must be helped to find new roots in life. We will work for special protection of the working child and for the abolition of illegal child labour. We will do our best to ensure that children are not drawn into becoming victims of the scourge of illicit drugs.

(8) We will work carefully to protect children from the scourge of war and to take measures to prevent further armed conflicts, in order to give children everywhere a peaceful and secure future. We will promote the values of peace, understanding and dialogue in the education of children. The essential needs of children and families must be protected even in times of war and in violence-ridden areas. We ask that periods of tranquillity and special relief corridors be observed for the benefit of children, where war and violence are still taking place.

(9) We will work for common measures for the protection of the environment, at all levels, so that all children can enjoy a safer and healthier future.

(10) We will work for a global attack on poverty, which would have immediate benefits for children's welfare. The vulnerability and special needs of the children of the developing countries, and in particu-

lar the least developed ones, deserve priority. But growth and development need promotion in all States, through national action and international cooperation. That calls for transfers of appropriate additional resources to developing countries as well as improved terms of trade, further trade liberalization and measures for debt relief. It also implies structural adjustments that promote world economic growth, particularly in developing countries, while ensuring the well-being of the most vulnerable sectors of the populations, in particular the children.

The next steps

21. The World Summit for Children has presented us with a challenge to take action. We have agreed to take up that challenge.

22. Among the partnerships we seek, we turn especially to children themselves. We appeal to them to participate in this effort.

23. We also seek the support of the United Nations system, as well as other international and regional organizations, in the universal effort to promote the well-being of children. We ask for greater involvement on the part of non-governmental organizations, in complementing national efforts and joint international action in this field.

24. We have decided to adopt and implement a Plan of Action, as a framework for more specific national and international undertakings. We appeal to all our colleagues to endorse that Plan. We are prepared to make available the resources to meet these commitments, as part of the priorities of our national plans.

25. We do this not only for the present generation, but for all generations to come. There can be no task nobler than giving every child a better future.

New York, 30 September 1990

Plan of action for implementing the World Declaration on the Survival, Protection and Development of Children in the 1990s

I. Introduction

1. This Plan of Action is intended as a guide for national Governments, international organizations, bilateral aid agencies, non-governmental organizations (NGOs) and all other sectors of society in formulating their own programmes of action for ensuring the implementation of the Declaration of the World Summit for Children.

2. The needs and problems of children vary from country to country, and indeed from community to community. Individual countries and groups of countries, as well as international, regional, national and local organizations, may use this Plan of Action to develop their own

specific programmes in line with their needs, capacity and mandates. However, parents, elders and leaders at all levels throughout the world have certain common aspirations for the well-being of their children. This Plan of Action deals with these common aspirations, suggesting a set of goals and targets for children in the 1990s, strategies for reaching those goals and commitments for action and follow-up measures at various levels.

3. Progress for children should be a key goal of overall national development. It should also form an integral part of the broader international development strategy for the Fourth United Nations Development Decade. As today's children are the citizens of tomorrow's world, their survival, protection and development is the prerequisite for the future development of humanity. Empowerment of the younger generation with knowledge and resources to meet their basic human needs and to grow to their full potential should be a primary goal of national development. As their individual development and social contribution will shape the future of the world, investment in children's health, nutrition and education is the foundation for national development.

4. The aspirations of the international community for the well-being of children are best reflected in the Convention on the Rights of the Child unanimously adopted by the General Assembly of the United Nations in 1989. This Convention sets universal legal standards for the protection of children against neglect, abuse and exploitation, as well as guaranteeing to them their basic human rights, including survival, development and full participation in social, cultural, educational and other endeavours necessary for their individual growth and well-being. The Declaration of the World Summit calls on all Governments to promote earliest possible ratification and implementation of the Convention.

5. In the past two years, a set of goals for children and development in the 1990s has been formulated in several international forums attended by virtually all Governments, relevant United Nations agencies and major NGOs. In support of these goals and in line with the growing international consensus in favour of greater attention to the human dimension of development in the 1990s, this Plan of Action calls for concerted national action and international cooperation to strive for the achievement, in all countries, of the following major goals for the survival, protection and development of children by the year 2000:

(a) Reduction of 1990 under-5 child mortality rates by one third or to a level of 70 per 1,000 live births, whichever is the greater reduction;

(b) Reduction of maternal mortality rates by half of 1990 levels;

(c) Reduction of severe and moderate malnutrition among under-5 children by one half of 1990 levels;

(d) Universal access to safe drinking-water and to sanitary means of excreta disposal;

(e) Universal access to basic education and completion of primary education by at least 80 per cent of primary school-age children;

(f) Reduction of the adult illiteracy rate to at least half its 1990 level (the appropriate age group to be determined in each country), with emphasis on female literacy;

(g) Protection of children in especially difficult circumstances, particularly in situations of armed conflicts.

6. A list of more detailed sectoral goals and specific actions which would enable the attainment of the above major goals can be found in the appendix to this Plan of Action. These goals will first need to be adapted to the specific realities of each country in terms of phasing, priorities, standards and availability of resources. The strategies for the achievement of the goals may also vary from country to country. Some countries may wish to add other development goals that are uniquely important and relevant for their specific country situation. Such adaptation of the goals is of crucial importance to ensure their technical validity, logistical feasibility, financial affordability and to secure political commitment and broad public support for their achievement.

II. Specific actions for child survival, protection and development

7. Within the context of these overall goals, there are promising opportunities for eradicating or virtually eliminating age-old diseases that have afflicted tens of millions of children for centuries and for improving the quality of life of generations to come. Achievement of these goals would also contribute to lowering population growth, as sustained decline in child death rates towards the level at which parents become confident that their first children will survive is, with some time-lag, followed by even greater reduction in child births. To seize these opportunities, the Declaration of the World Summit for Children calls for specific actions in the following areas:

The Convention on the Rights of the Child

8. The Convention on the Rights of the Child, unanimously adopted by the United Nations General Assembly, contains a comprehensive set of international legal norms for the protection and well-being of children. All Governments are urged to promote earliest possible ratification of the Convention, where it has not already been ratified. Every possible effort should be made in all countries to disseminate the Convention and, wherever it has already been ratified, to promote its implementation and monitoring.

Child health

9. Preventable childhood diseases—such as measles, polio, tetanus, tuberculosis, whooping cough and diphtheria, against which there are effective vaccines, and diarrhoeal diseases, pneumonia and other acute respiratory infections that can be prevented or effectively treated through relatively low-cost remedies—are currently responsible for the great majority of the world's 14 million deaths of children under 5 years and disability of millions more every year. Effective action can and must be taken to combat these diseases by strengthening primary health care and basic health services in all countries.

10. Besides these readily preventable or treatable diseases and some others, such as malaria, which have proved more difficult to combat, children today are faced with the new spectre of the acquired immunodeficiency syndrome (AIDS) pandemic. In the most seriously affected countries HIV/AIDS threatens to offset the gains of child survival programmes. It is already a major drain on limited public health resources needed to support other priority health services. The consequences of HIV/AIDS go well beyond the suffering and death of the infected child and include risks and stigmas that affect parents and siblings and the tragedy of "AIDS orphans". There is an urgent need to ensure that programmes for the prevention and treatment of AIDS, including research on possible vaccines and cures that can be applicable in all countries and situations, and massive information and education campaigns, receive a high priority for both national action and international cooperation.

11. A major factor affecting the health of children as well as adults is the availability of clean water and safe sanitation. These are not only essential for human health and well-being, but also contribute greatly to the emancipation of women from the drudgery that has a pernicious impact on children, especially girls. Progress in child health is unlikely to be sustained if one third of the developing world's children remain without access to clean drinking-water and half of them without adequate sanitary facilities.

12. Based on the experience of the past decade, including the many innovations in simple, low-cost techniques and technologies to provide clean water and safe sanitary facilities in rural areas and urban shanty towns, it is now desirable as well as feasible, through concerted national action and international cooperation, to aim at providing all the world's children with universal access to safe drinking-water and sanitary means of excreta disposal by the year 2000. An important related benefit of universal access to water and sanitation combined with

health education will be the control of many water-borne diseases, among them elimination of guinea-worm disease (dracunculiasis), which currently afflicts some 10 million children in parts of Africa and Asia.

Food and nutrition

13. Hunger and malnutrition in their different forms contribute to about half of the deaths of young children. More than 20 million children suffer from severe malnutrition, 150 million are underweight and 350 million women suffer from nutritional anaemia. Improved nutrition requires (a) adequate household food security, (b) healthy environment and control of infections and (c) adequate maternal and child care. With the right policies, appropriate institutional arrangements and political priority, the world is now in a position to feed all the world's children and to overcome the worst forms of malnutrition, i.e., drastically to reduce diseases that contribute to malnutrition, to halve protein-energy malnutrition, virtually to eliminate vitamin A deficiency and iodine deficiency disorders and to reduce nutritional anaemia significantly.

14. For the young child and the pregnant woman, provision of adequate food during pregnancy and lactation; promotion, protection and support of breast-feeding and complementary feeding practices, including frequent feeding; growth monitoring with appropriate follow-up actions; and nutritional surveillance are the most essential needs. As the child grows older, and for the adult population as a whole, an adequate diet is an obvious human priority. Meeting this need requires employment and income-generating opportunities, dissemination of knowledge and supporting services to increase food production and distribution. These are key actions within broader national strategies to combat hunger and malnutrition.

Role of women, maternal health and family planning

15. Women in their various roles play a critical part in the well-being of children. The enhancement of the status of women and their equal access to education, training, credit and other extension services constitute a valuable contribution to a nation's social and economic development. Efforts for the enhancement of women's status and their role in development must begin with the girl child. Equal opportunity should be provided for the girl child to benefit from the health, nutrition, education and other basic services to enable her to grow to her full potential.

16. Maternal health, nutrition and education are important for the survival and well-being of women in their own right and are key determinants of the health and well-being of the child in early infancy. The causes of the high rates of infant mortality, especially neonatal mortality, are linked to untimely pregnancies, low birth weight and pre-term births, unsafe delivery, neonatal tetanus, high fertility rates, etc. These are also major risk factors for maternal mortality claiming the lives of 500,000 young women each year and resulting in ill-health and suffering for many millions more. To redress this tragedy, special attention should be given to health, nutrition and education of women.

17. All couples should have access to information on the importance of responsible planning of family size and the many advantages of child spacing to avoid pregnancies that are too early, too late, too many or too frequent. Prenatal care, clean delivery, access to referral facilities in complicated cases, tetanus toxoid vaccination and prevention of anaemia and other nutritional deficiencies during pregnancy are other important interventions to ensure safe motherhood and a healthy start in life for the newborn. There is an added benefit of promoting maternal and child health programmes and family planning together in that, acting synergistically, these activities help accelerate the reduction of both mortality and fertility rates, and contribute more to lowering rates of population growth than either type of activity alone.

Role of the family

18. The family has the primary responsibility for the nurturing and protection of children from infancy to adolescence. Introduction of children to the culture, values and norms of their society begins in the family. For the full and harmonious development of their personality, children should grow up in a family environment, in an atmosphere of happiness, love and understanding. Accordingly, all institutions of society should respect and support the efforts of parents and other care-givers to nurture and care for children in a family environment.

19. Every effort should be made to prevent the separation of children from their families. Whenever children are separated from their family owing to *force majeure* or in their own best interest, arrangements should be made for appropriate alternative family care or institutional placement, due regard being paid to the desirability of continuity in a child's upbringing in his or her own cultural milieu. Extended families, relatives and community institutions should be given support to help to meet the special needs of orphaned, displaced and abandoned children. Efforts must be made to ensure that no child is treated as an outcast from society.

Basic education and literacy

20. The international community, including virtually all the Governments of the world, have undertaken a commitment at the World Conference on Education for

All at Jomtien, Thailand, to increase significantly educational opportunity for over 100 million children and nearly 1 billion adults, two thirds of them girls and women, who at present have no access to basic education and literacy. In fulfilment of that commitment, specific measures must be adopted for (a) the expansion of early childhood development activities, (b) universal access to basic education, including completion of primary education or equivalent learning achievement by at least 80 per cent of the relevant school-age children with emphasis on reducing the current disparities between boys and girls, (c) the reduction of adult illiteracy by half, with emphasis on female literacy, (d) vocational training and preparation for employment and (e) increased acquisition of knowledge, skills and values through all educational channels, including modern and traditional communication media, to improve the quality of life of children and families.

21. Besides its intrinsic value for human development and improving the quality of life, progress in education and literacy can contribute significantly to improvement in maternal and child health, in protection of the environment and in sustainable development. As such, investment in basic education must be accorded a high priority in national action as well as international cooperation.

Children in especially difficult circumstances

22. Millions of children around the world live under especially difficult circumstances—as orphans and street children, as refugees or displaced persons, as victims of war and natural and man-made disasters, including such perils as exposure to radiation and dangerous chemicals, as children of migrant workers and other socially disadvantaged groups, as child workers or youth trapped in the bondage of prostitution, sexual abuse and other forms of exploitation, as disabled children and juvenile delinquents and as victims of apartheid and foreign occupation. Such children deserve special attention, protection and assistance from their families and communities and as part of national efforts and international cooperation.

23. More than 100 million children are engaged in employment, often heavy and hazardous and in contravention of international conventions which provide for their protection from economic exploitation and from performing work that interferes with their education and is harmful to their health and full development. With this in mind, all States should work to end such child-labour practices and see how the conditions and circumstances of children in legitimate employment can be protected to provide adequate opportunity for their healthy upbringing and development.

24. Drug abuse has emerged as a global menace to very large numbers of young people and, increasingly, children—including permanent damage incurred in the prenatal stages of life. Concerted action is needed by Governments and intergovernmental agencies to combat illicit production, supply, demand, trafficking and distribution of narcotic drugs and psychotropic substances to counter this tragedy. Equally important is community action and education, which are vitally needed to curb both the supply of and the demand for illicit drugs. Tobacco and alcohol abuse are also problems requiring action, especially preventive measures and education among young people.

Protection of children during armed conflicts

25. Children need special protection in situations of armed conflict. Recent examples in which countries and opposing factions have agreed to suspend hostilities and adopt special measures such as "corridors of peace" to allow relief supplies to reach women and children and "days of tranquillity" to vaccinate and to provide other health services for children and their families in areas of conflict need to be applied in all such situations. Resolution of a conflict need not be a prerequisite for measures explicitly to protect children and their families to ensure their continuing access to food, medical care and basic services, to deal with trauma resulting from violence and to exempt them from other direct consequences of violence and hostilities. To build the foundation for a peaceful world where violence and war will cease to be acceptable means for settling disputes and conflicts, children's education should inculcate the values of peace, tolerance, understanding and dialogue.

Children and the environment

26. Children have the greatest stake in the preservation of the environment and its judicious management for sustainable development as their survival and development depend on it. The child survival and development goals proposed for the 1990s in this Plan of Action seek to improve the environment by combating disease and malnutrition and promoting education. These contribute to lowering death rates as well as birth rates, improved social services, better use of natural resources and, ultimately, to the breaking of the vicious cycle of poverty and environmental degradation.

27. With their relatively low use of capital resources and high reliance on social mobilization, community participation and appropriate technology, the programmes designed to reach the child-related goals of the 1990s are highly compatible with and supportive of environmental protection. The goals for the survival, protection and development of children as enunciated in

this Plan of Action should therefore be seen as helping to protect and preserve the environment. Still more action is needed, of course, to prevent the degradation of the environment in both the industrialized and the developing countries, through changes in the wasteful consumption patterns of the affluent and by helping to meet the necessities of survival and development of the poor. Programmes for children that not only help to meet their basic needs but which inculcate in them respect for the natural environment with the diversity of life that it sustains and its beauty and resourcefulness that enhance the quality of human life must figure prominently in the world's environmental agenda.

Alleviation of poverty and revitalization of economic growth

28. Achievement of child-related goals in the areas of health, nutrition, education, etc., will contribute much to alleviating the worst manifestations of poverty. But much more will need to be done to ensure that a solid economic base is established to meet and sustain the goals for long-term child survival, protection and development.

29. As affirmed by the international community at the eighteenth special session of the United Nations General Assembly (April 1990), a most important challenge for the 1990s is the need for revitalization of economic growth and social development in the developing countries and to address together the problems of abject poverty and hunger that continue to afflict far too many people in the world. As the most vulnerable segment of human society, children have a particular stake in sustained economic growth and alleviation of poverty, without which their well-being cannot be secured.

30. To foster a favourable international economic environment, it is essential to continue to give urgent attention to an early, broad and durable solution to the external debt problems facing developing debtor countries; to mobilize external and domestic resources to meet the increasing needs for development finance of developing countries; to take steps to ensure that the problem of the net transfer of resources from developing to developed countries does not continue in the 1990s and that its impact is effectively addressed; to create a more open and equitable trading system to facilitate the diversification and modernization of the economies of developing countries, particularly those that are commodity-dependent; and to make available substantial concessional resources, particularly for the least developed countries.

31. In all of these efforts the fulfilment of the basic needs of children must receive a high priority. Every possible opportunity should be explored to ensure that programmes benefiting children, women and other vulnerable groups are protected in times of structural adjustments and other economic restructuring. For example, as countries reduce military expenditures, part of the resources released should be channelled to programmes for social and economic development, including those benefiting children. Debt-relief schemes could be formulated in ways that the budget reallocations and renewed economic growth made possible through such schemes would benefit programmes for children. Debt relief for children, including debt swaps for investment in social development programmes, should be considered by debtors and creditors. The international community, including private-sector creditors, are urged to work with developing countries and relevant agencies to support debt relief for children. To match increased efforts by developing countries themselves, the donor countries and international institutions should consider targetting more development assistance to primary health care, basic education, low-cost water and sanitation programmes and other interventions specifically endorsed in the Summit Declaration and this Plan of Action.

32. The international community has recognized the need to stop and reverse the increasing marginalization of the least developed countries, including most countries of sub-Saharan Africa and many land-locked and island countries that face special development problems. These countries will require additional long-term international support to complement their own national efforts to meet the pressing needs of children over the 1990s.

III. Follow-up actions and monitoring

33. Effective implementation of this Plan of Action will require concerted national action and international cooperation. As affirmed in the Declaration, such action and cooperation must be guided by the principle of a "first call for children"—a principle that the essential needs of children should be given high priority in the allocation of resources, in bad times as well as in good times, at national and international as well as at family levels.

34. It is particularly important that the child-specific actions proposed must be pursued as part of strengthening broader national development programmes combining revitalized economic growth, poverty reduction, human resource development and environmental protection. Such programmes must also strengthen community organizations, inculcate civic responsibility and be sensitive to the cultural heritage and social values which support progress without alienation of the younger generation. With these broad objectives in mind, we commit ourselves and our Governments to the following actions:

Action at the national level

(i) All Governments are urged to prepare, before the end of 1991, national programmes of action to implement the commitments undertaken in the World Summit Declaration and this Plan of Action. National Governments should encourage and assist provincial and local governments as well as NGOs, the private sector and civic groups to prepare their own programmes of action to help to implement the goals and objectives included in the Declaration and this Plan of Action;

(ii) Each country is encouraged to re-examine, in the context of its national plans, programmes and policies, how it might accord higher priority to programmes for the well-being of children in general, and for meeting over the 1990s the major goals for child survival, development and protection as enumerated in the World Summit Declaration and this Plan of Action;

(iii) Each country is urged to re-examine, in the context of its particular national situation, its current national budget, and in the case of donor countries, their development assistance budgets, to ensure that programmes aimed at the achievement of goals for the survival, protection and development of children will have a priority when resources are allocated. Every effort should be made to ensure that such programmes are protected in times of economic austerity and structural adjustments;

(iv) Families, communities, local governments, NGOs, social, cultural, religious, business and other institutions, including the mass media, are encouraged to play an active role in support of the goals enunciated in this Plan of Action. The experience of the 1980s shows that it is only through the mobilization of all sectors of society, including those that traditionally did not consider child survival, protection and development as their major focus, that significant progress can be achieved in these areas. All forms of social mobilization, including the effective use of the great potential of the new information and communication capacity of the world, should be marshalled to convey to all families the knowledge and skills required for dramatically improving the situation of children;

(v) Each country should establish appropriate mechanisms for the regular and timely collection, analysis and publication of data required to monitor relevant social indicators relating to the well-being of children—such as neonatal, infant and under-5 mortality rates, maternal mortality and fertility rates, nutritional levels, immunization coverage, morbidity rates of diseases of public health importance, school enrolment and achievement and literacy rates—which record the progress being made towards the goals set forth in this Plan of Action and corresponding national plans of action. Statistics should be disaggregated by gender to ensure that any inequitable impact of programmes on girls and women can be monitored and corrected. It is particularly important that mechanisms be established to alert policy makers quickly to any adverse trends to enable timely corrective action. Indicators of human development should be periodically reviewed by national leaders and decision makers, as is currently done with indicators of economic development;

(vi) Each country is urged to re-examine its current arrangements for responding to natural disasters and man-made calamities which often afflict women and children the hardest. Countries that do not have adequate contingency planning for disaster preparedness are urged to establish such plans, seeking support from appropriate international institutions where necessary;

(vii) Progress towards the goals endorsed in the Summit Declaration and this Plan of Action could be further accelerated, and solutions to many other major problems confronting children and families greatly facilitated, through further research and development. Governments, industry and academic institutions are requested to increase their efforts in both basic and operational research, aimed at new technical and technological breakthroughs, more effective social mobilization and better delivery of existing social services. Prime examples of the areas in which research is urgently needed include, in the field of health, improved vaccination technologies, malaria, AIDS, respiratory infections, diarrhoeal diseases, nutritional deficiencies, tuberculosis, family planning and care of the newborn. Similarly there are important research needs in the area of early child development, basic education, hygiene and sanitation, and in coping with the trauma facing children who are uprooted from their families and face other particularly difficult circumstances. Such research should involve collaboration among institutions in both the developing and the industrialized countries of the world.

Action at the international level

35. Action at the community and national levels is, of course, of critical importance in meeting the goals and aspirations for children and development. However, many developing countries, particularly the least developed and the most indebted ones, will need substantial international cooperation to enable them to participate effectively in the worldwide effort for child survival, protection and development. Accordingly, the following specific actions are proposed to create an enabling international environment for the implementation of this Plan of Action:

(i) All international development agencies—multilateral, bilateral and non-governmental—are urged to examine how they can contribute to the achievement of the goals and strategies enunciated in the Declaration and this Plan of Action as part of more general attention to human development in the 1990s. They are requested to report their plans and programmes to their respective governing bodies before the end of 1991 and periodically thereafter;

(ii) All regional institutions, including regional political and economic organizations, are requested to include consideration of the Declaration and this Plan of Action on the agenda of their meetings, including at the highest political level, with a view to developing agreements for mutual collaboration for implementation and ongoing monitoring;

(iii) Full cooperation and collaboration of all relevant United Nations agencies and organs as well as other international institutions are requested in ensuring the achievement of the goals and objectives of the national plans envisaged in the World Summit Declaration and Plan of Action. The governing bodies of all concerned agencies are requested to ensure that within their mandates the fullest possible support is given by these agencies for the achievement of these goals;

(iv) The assistance of the United Nations is requested to institute appropriate mechanisms for monitoring the implementation of this Plan of Action, using existing expertise of the relevant United Nations statistical offices, the specialized agencies, UNICEF and other United Nations organs. Furthermore, the Secretary-General of the United Nations is requested to arrange for a mid-decade review, at all appropriate levels, of the progress being made towards implementing the commitments of the Declaration and Plan of Action;

(v) As the world's lead agency for children, the United Nations Children's Fund is requested to prepare, in close collaboration with the relevant specialized agencies and other United Nations organs, a consolidated analysis of the plans and actions undertaken by individual countries and the international community in support of the child-related development goals for the 1990s. The governing bodies of the relevant specialized agencies and United Nations organs are requested to include a periodic review of the implementation of the Declaration and this Plan of Action at their regular sessions and to keep the General Assembly of the United Nations, through the Economic and Social Council, fully informed of progress to date and additional action required during the decade ahead.

36. The goals enunciated in the Declaration and this Plan of Action are ambitious and the commitments required to implement them will demand consistent and extraordinary effort on the part of all concerned. Fortunately, the necessary knowledge and techniques for reaching most of the goals already exist. The financial resources required are modest in relation to the great achievements that beckon. And the most essential factor—the provision to families of the information and services necessary to protect their children—is now within reach in every country and for virtually every community. There is no cause which merits a higher priority than the protection and development of children, on whom the survival, stability and advancement of all nations—and, indeed, of human civilization—depend. Full implementation of the Declaration and this Plan of Action must therefore be accorded a high priority for national action and international cooperation.

Appendix

Goals for children and development in the 1990s

The following goals have been formulated through extensive consultation in various international forums attended by virtually all Governments, the relevant United Nations agencies including the World Health Organization (WHO), UNICEF, the United Nations Population Fund (UNFPA), the United Nations Educational, Scientific and Cultural Organization (UNESCO), the United Nations Development Programme (UNDP) and the International Bank for Reconstruction and Development (IBRD) and a large number of NGOs. These goals are recommended for implementation by all countries where they are applicable, with appropriate adaptation to the specific situation of each country in terms of phasing, standards, priorities and availability of resources, with respect for cultural, religious and social traditions. Additional goals that are particularly relevant to a country's specific situation should be added in its national plan of action.

I. *Major goals for child survival, development and protection*

(a) Between 1990 and the year 2000, reduction of infant and under-5 child mortality rate by one third or to 50 and 70 per 1,000 live births respectively, whichever is less;

(b) Between 1990 and the year 2000, reduction of maternal mortality rate by half;

(c) Between 1990 and the year 2000, reduction of severe and moderate malnutrition among under-5 children by half;

(d) Universal access to safe drinking-water and to sanitary means of excreta disposal;

(e) By the year 2000, universal access to basic education and completion of primary education by at least 80 per cent of primary school-age children;

(f) Reduction of the adult illiteracy rate (the appropriate age group to be determined in each country) to at least half its 1990 level with emphasis on female literacy;

(g) Improved protection of children in especially difficult circumstances.

II. *Supporting/sectoral goals*

A. *Women's health and education*

(i) Special attention to the health and nutrition of the female child and to pregnant and lactating women;

(ii) Access by all couples to information and services to prevent pregnancies that are too early, too closely spaced, too late or too many;

(iii) Access by all pregnant women to prenatal care, trained attendants during childbirth and referral facilities for high-risk pregnancies and obstetric emergencies;

(iv) Universal access to primary education with special emphasis for girls and accelerated literacy programmes for women.

B. *Nutrition*

(i) Reduction in severe, as well as moderate, malnutrition among under-5 children by half of 1990 levels;

(ii) Reduction of the rate of low birth weight (2.5 kg or less) to less than 10 per cent;

(iii) Reduction of iron deficiency anaemia in women by one third of the 1990 levels;

(iv) Virtual elimination of iodine deficiency disorders;

(v) Virtual elimination of vitamin A deficiency and its consequences, including blindness;

(vi) Empowerment of all women to breast-feed their children exclusively for four to six months and to continue breast-feeding, with complementary food, well into the second year;

(vii) Growth promotion and its regular monitoring to be institutionalized in all countries by the end of the 1990s;

(viii) Dissemination of knowledge and supporting services to increase food production to ensure household food security.

C. *Child health*

(i) Global eradication of poliomyelitis by the year 2000;

(ii) Elimination of neonatal tetanus by 1995;

(iii) Reduction by 95 per cent in measles deaths and reduction by 90 per cent of measles cases compared to pre-immunization levels by 1995, as a major step to the global eradication of measles in the longer run;

(iv) Maintenance of a high level of immunization coverage (at least 90 per cent of children under one year of age by the year 2000) against diphtheria, pertussis, tetanus, measles, poliomyelitis, tuberculosis and against tetanus for women of child-bearing age;

(v) Reduction by 50 per cent in the deaths due to diarrhoea in children under the age of five years and 25 per cent reduction in the diarrhoea incidence rate;

(vi) Reduction by one third in the deaths due to acute respiratory infections in children under five years.

D. *Water and sanitation*

(i) Universal access to safe drinking-water;

(ii) Universal access to sanitary means of excreta disposal;

(iii) Elimination of guinea-worm disease (dracunculiasis) by the year 2000.

(i) Expansion of early childhood development activities, including appropriate low-cost family- and community-based interventions;

(ii) Universal access to basic education, and achievement of primary education by at least 80 per cent of primary school-age children through formal schooling or non-formal education of comparable learning standard, with emphasis on reducing the current disparities between boys and girls;

(iii) Reduction of the adult illiteracy rate (the appropriate age group to be determined in each country) to at least half its 1990 level, with emphasis on female literacy;

(iv) Increased acquisition by individuals and families of the knowledge, skills and values required for better living, made available through all educational channels, including the mass media, other forms of modern and traditional communication and social action, with effectiveness measured in terms of behavioural change.

F. *Children in difficult circumstances*

Provide improved protection of children in especially difficult circumstances and tackle the root causes leading to such situations.

Document 66

United Nations Standard Minimum Rules for Non-custodial Measures (The Tokyo Rules)

A/RES/45/110, 14 December 1990

I. General principles

1. *Fundamental aims*

1.1 The present Standard Minimum Rules provide a set of basic principles to promote the use of non-custodial measures, as well as minimum safeguards for persons subject to alternatives to imprisonment.

1.2 The Rules are intended to promote greater community involvement in the management of criminal justice, specifically in the treatment of offenders, as well as to promote among offenders a sense of responsibility towards society.

1.3 The Rules shall be implemented taking into account the political, economic, social and cultural conditions of each country and the aims and objectives of its criminal justice system.

1.4 When implementing the Rules, Member States shall endeavour to ensure a proper balance between the rights of individual offenders, the rights of victims, and the concern of society for public safety and crime prevention.

1.5 Member States shall develop non-custodial measures within their legal systems to provide other options, thus reducing the use of imprisonment, and to rationalize criminal justice policies, taking into account the observance of human rights, the requirements of social justice and the rehabilitation needs of the offender.

2. *The scope of non-custodial measures*

2.1 The relevant provisions of the present Rules shall be applied to all persons subject to prosecution, trial or the execution of a sentence, at all stages of the administration of criminal justice. For the purposes of the Rules, these persons are referred to as "offenders", irrespective of whether they are suspected, accused or sentenced.

2.2 The Rules shall be applied without any discrimination on the grounds of race, colour, sex, age, language, religion, political or other opinion, national or social origin, property, birth or other status.

2.3 In order to provide greater flexibility consistent with the nature and gravity of the offence, with the personality and background of the offender and with the protection of society and to avoid unnecessary use of imprisonment, the criminal justice system should provide a wide range of non-custodial measures, from pre-trial to post-sentencing dispositions. The number and types of non-custodial measures available should be determined in such a way so that consistent sentencing remains possible.

2.4 The development of new non-custodial measures should be encouraged and closely monitored and their use systematically evaluated.

2.5 Consideration shall be given to dealing with offenders in the community avoiding as far as possible resort to formal proceedings or trial by a court, in accordance with legal safeguards and the rule of law.

2.6 Non-custodial measures should be used in accordance with the principle of minimum intervention.

2.7 The use of non-custodial measures should be part of the movement towards depenalization and decriminalization instead of interfering with or delaying efforts in that direction.

3. *Legal safeguards*

3.1 The introduction, definition and application of non-custodial measures shall be prescribed by law.

3.2 The selection of a non-custodial measure shall be based on an assessment of established criteria in respect of both the nature and gravity of the offence and the personality, background of the offender, the purposes of sentencing and the rights of victims.

3.3 Discretion by the judicial or other competent independent authority shall be exercised at all stages of the proceedings by ensuring full accountability and only in accordance with the rule of law.

3.4 Non-custodial measures imposing an obligation on the offender, applied before or instead of formal proceedings or trial, shall require the offender's consent.

3.5 Decisions on the imposition of non-custodial measures shall be subject to review by a judicial or other competent independent authority, upon application by the offender.

3.6 The offender shall be entitled to make a request or complaint to a judicial or other competent independent authority on matters affecting his or her individual rights in the implementation of non-custodial measures.

3.7 Appropriate machinery shall be provided for the recourse and, if possible, redress of any grievance related to non-compliance with internationally recognized human rights.

3.8 Non-custodial measures shall not involve medical or psychological experimentation on, or undue risk of physical or mental injury to, the offender.

3.9 The dignity of the offender subject to non-custodial measures shall be protected at all times.

3.10 In the implementation of non-custodial measures, the offender's rights shall not be restricted further than was authorized by the competent authority that rendered the original decision.

3.11 In the application of non-custodial measures, the offender's right to privacy shall be respected, as shall be the right to privacy of the offender's family.

3.12 The offender's personal records shall be kept strictly confidential and closed to third parties. Access to such records shall be limited to persons directly concerned with the disposition of the offender's case or to other duly authorized persons.

4. *Saving clause*

4.1 Nothing in these Rules shall be interpreted as precluding the application of the Standard Minimum Rules for the Treatment of Prisoners, the United Nations Standard Minimum Rules for the Administration of Juvenile Justice, the Body of Principles for the Protection of All Persons under Any Form of Detention or Imprisonment or any other human rights instruments and standards recognized by the international community and relating to the treatment of offenders and the protection of their basic human rights.

II. Pre-trial stage

5. *Pre-trial dispositions*

5.1 Where appropriate and compatible with the legal system, the police, the prosecution service or other agencies dealing with criminal cases should be empowered to discharge the offender if they consider that it is not necessary to proceed with the case for the protection of society, crime prevention or the promotion of respect for the law and the rights of victims. For the purpose of deciding upon the appropriateness of discharge or determination of proceedings, a set of established criteria shall be developed within each legal system. For minor cases the prosecutor may impose suitable non-custodial measures, as appropriate.

6. *Avoidance of pre-trial detention*

6.1 Pre-trial detention shall be used as a means of last resort in criminal proceedings, with due regard for the investigation of the alleged offence and for the protection of society and the victim.

6.2 Alternatives to pre-trial detention shall be employed at as early a stage as possible. Pre-trial detention shall last no longer than necessary to achieve the objectives stated under rule 5.1 and shall be administered humanely and with respect for the inherent dignity of human beings.

6.3 The offender shall have the right to appeal to a judicial or other competent independent authority in cases where pre-trial detention is employed.

III. Trial and sentencing stage

7. *Social inquiry reports*

7.1 If the possibility of social inquiry reports exists, the judicial authority may avail itself of a report prepared by a competent, authorized official or agency. The report should contain social information on the offender that is relevant to the person's pattern of offending and current offences. It should also contain information and recommendations that are relevant to the sentencing procedure. The report shall be factual, objective and unbiased, with any expression of opinion clearly identified.

8. *Sentencing dispositions*

8.1 The judicial authority, having at its disposal a range of non-custodial measures, should take into consideration in making its decision the rehabilitative needs of the offender, the protection of society and the interests of the victim, who should be consulted whenever appropriate.

8.2 Sentencing authorities may dispose of cases in the following ways:

(a) Verbal sanctions, such as admonition, reprimand and warning;

(b) Conditional discharge;

(c) Status penalties;

(d) Economic sanctions and monetary penalties, such as fines and day-fines;

(e) Confiscation or an expropriation order;

(f) Restitution to the victim or a compensation order;

(g) Suspended or deferred sentence;

(h) Probation and judicial supervision;

(i) A community service order;

(j) Referral to an attendance centre;

(k) House arrest;

(l) Any other mode of non-institutional treatment;

(m) Some combination of the measures listed above.

IV. Post-sentencing stage

9. *Post-sentencing dispositions*

9.1 The competent authority shall have at its disposal a wide range of post-sentencing alternatives in order to avoid institutionalization and to assist offenders in their early reintegration into society.

9.2 Post-sentencing dispositions may include:

(a) Furlough and halfway houses;

(b) Work or education release;

(c) Various forms of parole;

(d) Remission;

(e) Pardon.

9.3 The decision on post-sentencing dispositions, except in the case of pardon, shall be subject to review by a judicial or other competent independent authority, upon application of the offender.

9.4 Any form of release from an institution to a non-custodial programme shall be considered at the earliest possible stage.

V. Implementation of non-custodial measures

10. *Supervision*

10.1 The purpose of supervision is to reduce reoffending and to assist the offender's integration into society in a way which minimizes the likelihood of a return to crime.

10.2 If a non-custodial measure entails supervision, the latter shall be carried out by a competent authority under the specific conditions prescribed by law.

10.3 Within the framework of a given non-custodial measure, the most suitable type of supervision and treatment should be determined for each individual case aimed at assisting the offender to work on his or her offending. Supervision and treatment should be periodically reviewed and adjusted as necessary.

10.4 Offenders should, when needed, be provided with psychological, social and material assistance and with opportunities to strengthen links with the community and facilitate their reintegration into society.

11. *Duration*

11.1 The duration of a non-custodial measure shall not exceed the period established by the competent authority in accordance with the law.

11.2 Provision may be made for early termination of the measure if the offender has responded favourably to it.

12. *Conditions*

12.1 If the competent authority shall determine the conditions to be observed by the offender, it should take into account both the needs of society and the needs and rights of the offender and the victim.

12.2 The conditions to be observed shall be practical, precise and as few as possible, and be aimed at reducing the likelihood of an offender relapsing into criminal behaviour and of increasing the offender's chances of social integration, taking into account the needs of the victim.

12.3 At the beginning of the application of a non-custodial measure, the offender shall receive an explanation, orally and in writing, of the conditions governing the application of the measure, including the offender's obligations and rights.

12.4 The conditions may be modified by the competent authority under the established statutory provisions, in accordance with the progress made by the offender.

13. *Treatment process*

13.1 Within the framework of a given non-custodial measure, in appropriate cases, various schemes, such as casework, group therapy, residential programmes and the specialized treatment of various categories of offenders, should be developed to meet the needs of offenders more effectively.

13.2 Treatment should be conducted by professionals who have suitable training and practical experience.

13.3 When it is decided that treatment is necessary, efforts should be made to understand the offender's background, personality, aptitude, intelligence, values and, especially, the circumstances leading to the commission of the offence.

13.4 The competent authority may involve the community and social support systems in the application of non-custodial measures.

13.5 Case-load assignments shall be maintained as far as practicable at a manageable level to ensure the effective implementation of treatment programmes.

13.6 For each offender, a case record shall be established and maintained by the competent authority.

14. *Discipline and breach of conditions*

14.1 A breach of the conditions to be observed by the offender may result in a modification or revocation of the non-custodial measure.

14.2 The modification or revocation of the non-custodial measure shall be made by the competent authority; this shall be done only after a careful examination of the facts adduced by both the supervising officer and the offender.

14.3 The failure of a non-custodial measure should not automatically lead to the imposition of a custodial measure.

14.4 In the event of a modification or revocation of the non-custodial measure, the competent authority shall attempt to establish a suitable alternative non-custodial measure. A sentence of imprisonment may be imposed only in the absence of other suitable alternatives.

14.5 The power to arrest and detain the offender under supervision in cases where there is a breach of the conditions shall be prescribed by law.

14.6 Upon modification or revocation of the non-custodial measure, the offender shall have the right to appeal to a judicial or other competent independent authority.

VI. Staff

15. *Recruitment*

15.1 There shall be no discrimination in the recruitment of staff on the grounds of race, colour, sex, age, language, religion, political or other opinion, national or social origin, property, birth or other status. The policy regarding staff recruitment should take into consideration national policies of affirmative action and reflect the diversity of the offenders to be supervised.

15.2 Persons appointed to apply non-custodial measures should be personally suitable and, whenever possible, have appropriate professional training and practical experience. Such qualifications shall be clearly specified.

15.3 To secure and retain qualified professional staff, appropriate service status, adequate salary and benefits commensurate with the nature of the work should be ensured and ample opportunities should be provided for professional growth and career development.

16. *Staff training*

16.1 The objective of training shall be to make clear to staff their responsibilities with regard to rehabilitating the offender, ensuring the offender's rights and protecting society. Training should also give staff an understanding of the need to cooperate in and coordinate activities with the agencies concerned.

16.2 Before entering duty, staff shall be given training that includes instruction on the nature of non-custodial measures, the purposes of supervision and the various modalities of the application of non-custodial measures.

16.3 After entering duty, staff shall maintain and improve their knowledge and professional capacity by attending in-service training and refresher courses. Adequate facilities shall be made available for that purpose.

VII. Volunteers and other community resources

17. *Public participation*

17.1 Public participation should be encouraged as it is a major resource and one of the most important factors in improving ties between offenders undergoing non-custodial measures and the family and community. It should complement the efforts of the criminal justice administration.

17.2 Public participation should be regarded as an opportunity for members of the community to contribute to the protection of their society.

18. *Public understanding and cooperation*

18.1 Government agencies, the private sector and the general public should be encouraged to support voluntary organizations that promote non-custodial measures.

18.2 Conferences, seminars, symposia and other activities should be regularly organized to stimulate awareness of the need for public participation in the application of non-custodial measures.

18.3 All forms of the mass media should be utilized to help to create a constructive public attitude, leading to activities conducive to a broader application of non-custodial treatment and the social integration of offenders.

18.4 Every effort should be made to inform the public of the importance of its role in the implementation of non-custodial measures.

19. *Volunteers*

19.1 Volunteers shall be carefully screened and recruited on the basis of their aptitude for and interest in the work involved. They shall be properly trained for the specific responsibilities to be discharged by them and shall have access to support and counselling from, and the opportunity to consult with, the competent authority.

19.2 Volunteers should encourage offenders and their families to develop meaningful ties with the community and a broader sphere of contact by providing counselling and other appropriate forms of assistance according to their capacity and the offenders' needs.

19.3 Volunteers shall be insured against accident, injury and public liability when carrying out their duties. They shall be reimbursed for authorized expenditures incurred in the course of their work. Public recognition should be extended to them for the services they render for the well-being of the community.

VIII. Research, planning, policy formulation and evaluation

20. *Research and planning*

20.1 As an essential aspect of the planning process, efforts should be made to involve both public and private bodies in the organization and promotion of research on the non-custodial treatment of offenders.

20.2 Research on the problems that confront clients, practitioners, the community and policy-makers should be carried out on a regular basis.

20.3 Research and information mechanisms should be built into the criminal justice system for the collection and analysis of data and statistics on the implementation of non-custodial treatment for offenders.

21. *Policy formulation and programme development*

21.1 Programmes for non-custodial measures should be systematically planned and implemented as an integral part of the criminal justice system within the national development process.

21.2 Regular evaluations should be carried out with a view to implementing non-custodial measures more effectively.

21.3 Periodic reviews should be concluded to assess the objectives, functioning and effectiveness of non-custodial measures.

22. *Linkages with relevant agencies and activities*

22.1 Suitable mechanisms should be evolved at various levels to facilitate the establishment of linkages between services responsible for non-custodial measures, other branches of the criminal justice system, social development and welfare agencies, both governmental and non-governmental, in such fields as health, housing, education and labour, and the mass media.

23. *International cooperation*

23.1 Efforts shall be made to promote scientific cooperation between countries in the field of non-institutional treatment. Research, training, technical assistance and the exchange of information among Member States on non-custodial measures should be strengthened, through the United Nations institutes for the prevention of crime and the treatment of offenders, in close collaboration with the Crime Prevention and Criminal Justice Branch of the Centre for Social Development and Humanitarian Affairs of the United Nations Secretariat.

23.2 Comparative studies and the harmonization of legislative provisions should be furthered to expand the range of non-institutional options and facilitate their application across national frontiers, in accordance with the Model Treaty on the Transfer of Supervision of Offenders Conditionally Sentenced or Conditionally Released.

Document 67

Basic Principles for the Treatment of Prisoners

A/RES/45/111, 14 December 1990

1. All prisoners shall be treated with the respect due to their inherent dignity and value as human beings.

2. There shall be no discrimination on the grounds of race, colour, sex, language, religion, political or other opinion, national or social origin, property, birth or other status.

3. It is, however, desirable to respect the religious beliefs and cultural precepts of the group to which prisoners belong, whenever local conditions so require.

4. The responsibility of prisons for the custody of prisoners and for the protection of society against crime shall be discharged in keeping with a State's other social objectives and its fundamental responsibilities for promoting the well-being and development of all members of society.

5. Except for those limitations that are demonstrably necessitated by the fact of incarceration, all prisoners shall retain the human rights and fundamental freedoms set out in the Universal Declaration of Human Rights, and, where the State concerned is a party, the International Covenant on Economic, Social and Cultural Rights, and the International Covenant on Civil and Political Rights and the Optional Protocol thereto, as well as such other rights as are set out in other United Nations covenants.

6. All prisoners shall have the right to take part in cultural activities and education aimed at the full development of the human personality.

7. Efforts addressed to the abolition of solitary confinement as a punishment, or to the restriction of its use, should be undertaken and encouraged.

8. Conditions shall be created enabling prisoners to undertake meaningful remunerated employment which will facilitate their reintegration into the country's labour market and permit them to contribute to their own financial support and to that of their families.

9. Prisoners shall have access to the health services available in the country without discrimination on the grounds of their legal situation.

10. With the participation and help of the community and social institutions, and with due regard to the interests of victims, favourable conditions shall be created for the reintegration of the ex-prisoner into society under the best possible conditions.

11. The above Principles shall be applied impartially.

Document 68

United Nations Guidelines for the Prevention of Juvenile Delinquency (The Riyadh Guidelines)

A/RES/45/112, 14 December 1990

I. Fundamental principles

1. The prevention of juvenile delinquency is an essential part of crime prevention in society. By engaging in lawful, socially useful activities and adopting a humanistic orientation towards society and outlook on life, young persons can develop non-criminogenic attitudes.

2. The successful prevention of juvenile delinquency requires efforts on the part of the entire society to ensure the harmonious development of adolescents, with respect for and promotion of their personality from early childhood.

3. For the purposes of the interpretation of the present Guidelines, a child-centred orientation should be pursued. Young persons should have an active role and partnership within society and should not be considered as mere objects of socialization or control.

4. In the implementation of the present Guidelines, in accordance with national legal systems, the well-being of young persons from their early childhood should be the focus of any preventive programme.

5. The need for and importance of progressive delinquency prevention policies and the systematic study and the elaboration of measures should be recognized. These should avoid criminalizing and penalizing a child for behaviour that does not cause serious damage to the development of the child or harm to others. Such policies and measures should involve:

(a) The provision of opportunities, in particular educational opportunities, to meet the varying needs of young persons and to serve as a supportive framework for safeguarding the personal development of all young persons, particularly those who are demonstrably endangered or at social risk and are in need of special care and protection;

(b) Specialized philosophies and approaches for delinquency prevention, on the basis of laws, processes, institutions, facilities and a service delivery network aimed at reducing the motivation, need and opportunity for, or conditions giving rise to, the commission of infractions;

(c) Official intervention to be pursued primarily in the overall interest of the young person and guided by fairness and equity;

(d) Safeguarding the well-being, development, rights and interests of all young persons;

(e) Consideration that youthful behaviour or conduct that does not conform to overall social norms and values is often part of the maturation and growth process and tends to disappear spontaneously in most individuals with the transition to adulthood;

(f) Awareness that, in the predominant opinion of experts, labelling a young person as "deviant", "delinquent" or "pre-delinquent" often contributes to the development of a consistent pattern of undesirable behaviour by young persons.

6. Community-based services and programmes should be developed for the prevention of juvenile delinquency, particularly where no agencies have yet been established. Formal agencies of social control should only be utilized as a means of last resort.

II. Scope of the guidelines

7. The present Guidelines should be interpreted and implemented within the broad framework of the Universal Declaration of Human Rights, the International Covenant on Economic, Social and Cultural Rights, the International Covenant on Civil and Political Rights, the Declaration of the Rights of the Child and the Convention on the Rights of the Child, and in the context of the United Nations Standard Minimum Rules for the Administration of Juvenile Justice (The Beijing Rules), as well as other instruments and norms relating to the rights, interests and well-being of all children and young persons.

8. The present Guidelines should also be implemented in the context of the economic, social and cultural conditions prevailing in each Member State.

III. General prevention

9. Comprehensive prevention plans should be instituted at every level of Government and include the following:

(a) In-depth analyses of the problem and inventories of programmes, services, facilities and resources available;

(b) Well-defined responsibilities for the qualified agencies, institutions and personnel involved in preventive efforts;

(c) Mechanisms for the appropriate co-ordination of prevention efforts between governmental and non-governmental agencies;

(d) Policies, programmes and strategies based on prognostic studies to be continuously monitored and carefully evaluated in the course of implementation;

(e) Methods for effectively reducing the opportunity to commit delinquent acts;

(f) Community involvement through a wide range of services and programmes;

(g) Close interdisciplinary cooperation between national, State, provincial and local governments, with the involvement of the private sector, representative citizens of the community to be served, and labour, childcare, health education, social, law enforcement and judicial agencies in taking concerted action to prevent juvenile delinquency and youth crime;

(h) Youth participation in delinquency prevention policies and processes, including recourse to community resources, youth self-help, and victim compensation and assistance programmes;

(i) Specialized personnel at all levels.

IV. Socialization processes

10. Emphasis should be placed on preventive policies facilitating the successful socialization and integration of all children and young persons, in particular through the family, the community, peer groups, schools, vocational training and the world of work, as well as through voluntary organizations. Due respect should be given to the proper personal development of children and young persons, and they should be accepted as full and equal partners in socialization and integration processes.

A. Family

11. Every society should place a high priority on the needs and well-being of the family and of all its members.

12. Since the family is the central unit responsible for the primary socialization of children, governmental and social efforts to preserve the integrity of the family, including the extended family, should be pursued. The society has a responsibility to assist the family in providing care and protection and in ensuring the physical and mental well-being of children. Adequate arrangements including daycare should be provided.

13. Governments should establish policies that are conducive to the bringing up of children in stable and settled family environments. Families in need of assistance in the resolution of conditions of instability or conflict should be provided with requisite services.

14. Where a stable and settled family environment is lacking and when community efforts to assist parents in this regard have failed and the extended family cannot fulfil this role, alternative placements, including foster care and adoption, should be considered. Such placements should replicate, to the extent possible, a stable and settled family environment, while, at the same time, establishing a sense of permanency for children, thus avoiding problems associated with "foster drift".

15. Special attention should be given to children of families affected by problems brought about by rapid and uneven economic, social and cultural change, in particular the children of indigenous, migrant and refugee families. As such changes may disrupt the social capacity of the family to secure the traditional rearing and nurturing of children, often as a result of role and culture conflict,

innovative and socially constructive modalities for the socialization of children have to be designed.

16. Measures should be taken and programmes developed to provide families with the opportunity to learn about parental roles and obligations as regards child development and child care, promoting positive parent-child relationships, sensitizing parents to the problems of children and young persons and encouraging their involvement in family and community-based activities.

17. Governments should take measures to promote family cohesion and harmony and to discourage the separation of children from their parents, unless circumstances affecting the welfare and future of the child leave no viable alternative.

18. It is important to emphasize the socialization function of the family and extended family; it is also equally important to recognize the future role, responsibilities, participation and partnership of young persons in society.

19. In ensuring the right of the child to proper socialization, Governments and other agencies should rely on existing social and legal agencies, but, whenever traditional institutions and customs are no longer effective, they should also provide and allow for innovative measures.

B. *Education*

20. Governments are under an obligation to make public education accessible to all young persons.

21. Education systems should, in addition to their academic and vocational training activities, devote particular attention to the following:

(a) Teaching of basic values and developing respect for the child's own cultural identity and patterns, for the social values of the country in which the child is living, for civilizations different from the child's own and for human rights and fundamental freedoms;

(b) Promotion and development of the personality, talents and mental and physical abilities of young people to their fullest potential;

(c) Involvement of young persons as active and effective participants in, rather than mere objects of, the educational process;

(d) Undertaking activities that foster a sense of identity with and of belonging to the school and the community;

(e) Encouragement of young persons to understand and respect diverse views and opinions, as well as cultural and other differences;

(f) Provision of information and guidance regarding vocational training, employment opportunities and career development;

(g) Provision of positive emotional support to young persons and the avoidance of psychological maltreatment;

(h) Avoidance of harsh disciplinary measures, particularly corporal punishment.

22. Educational systems should seek to work together with parents, community organizations and agencies concerned with the activities of young persons.

23. Young persons and their families should be informed about the law and their rights and responsibilities under the law, as well as the universal value system, including United Nations instruments.

24. Educational systems should extend particular care and attention to young persons who are at social risk. Specialized prevention programmes and educational materials, curricula, approaches and tools should be developed and fully utilized.

25. Special attention should be given to comprehensive policies and strategies for the prevention of alcohol, drug and other substance abuse by young persons. Teachers and other professionals should be equipped and trained to prevent and deal with these problems. Information on the use and abuse of drugs, including alcohol, should be made available to the student body.

26. Schools should serve as resource and referral centres for the provision of medical, counselling and other services to young persons, particularly those with special needs and suffering from abuse, neglect, victimization and exploitation.

27. Through a variety of educational programmes, teachers and other adults and the student body should be sensitized to the problems, needs and perceptions of young persons, particularly those belonging to underprivileged, disadvantaged, ethnic or other minority and low-income groups.

28. School systems should attempt to meet and promote the highest professional and educational standards with respect to curricula, teaching and learning methods and approaches, and the recruitment and training of qualified teachers. Regular monitoring and assessment of performance by the appropriate professional organizations and authorities should be ensured.

29. School systems should plan, develop and implement extracurricular activities of interest to young persons, in cooperation with community groups.

30. Special assistance should be given to children and young persons who find it difficult to comply with attendance codes, and to "drop-outs".

31. Schools should promote policies and rules that are fair and just; students should be represented in bodies formulating policy, including policy on discipline, and decision-making.

C. *Community*

32. Community-based services and programmes which respond to the special needs, problems, interests and concerns of young persons and which offer appropriate counselling and guidance to young persons and their families should be developed, or strengthened where they exist.

33. Communities should provide, or strengthen where they exist, a wide range of community-based support measures for young persons, including community development centres, recreational facilities and services to respond to the special problems of children who are at social risk. In providing these helping measures, respect for individual rights should be ensured.

34. Special facilities should be set up to provide adequate shelter for young persons who are no longer able to live at home or who do not have homes to live in.

35. A range of services and helping measures should be provided to deal with the difficulties experienced by young persons in the transition to adulthood. Such services should include special programmes for young drug abusers which emphasize care, counselling, assistance and therapy-oriented interventions.

36. Voluntary organizations providing services for young persons should be given financial and other support by Governments and other institutions.

37. Youth organizations should be created or strengthened at the local level and given full participatory status in the management of community affairs. These organizations should encourage youth to organize collective and voluntary projects, particularly projects aimed at helping young persons in need of assistance.

38. Government agencies should take special responsibility and provide necessary services for homeless or street children; information about local facilities, accommodation, employment and other forms and sources of help should be made readily available to young persons.

39. A wide range of recreational facilities and services of particular interest to young persons should be established and made easily accessible to them.

D. *Mass media*

40. The mass media should be encouraged to ensure that young persons have access to information and material from a diversity of national and international sources.

41. The mass media should be encouraged to portray the positive contribution of young persons to society.

42. The mass media should be encouraged to disseminate information on the existence of services, facilities and opportunities for young persons in society.

43. The mass media generally, and the television and film media in particular, should be encouraged to minimize the level of pornography, drugs and violence portrayed and to display violence and exploitation disfavourably, as well as to avoid demeaning and degrading presentations, especially of children, women and interpersonal relations, and to promote egalitarian principles and roles.

44. The mass media should be aware of its extensive social role and responsibility, as well as its influence, in communications relating to youthful drug and alcohol abuse. It should use its power for drug abuse prevention by relaying consistent messages through a balanced approach. Effective drug awareness campaigns at all levels should be promoted.

V. Social policy

45. Government agencies should give high priority to plans and programmes for young persons and should provide sufficient funds and other resources for the effective delivery of services, facilities and staff for adequate medical and mental health care, nutrition, housing and other relevant services, including drug and alcohol abuse prevention and treatment, ensuring that such resources reach and actually benefit young persons.

46. The institutionalization of young persons should be a measure of last resort and for the minimum necessary period, and the best interests of the young person should be of paramount importance. Criteria authorizing formal intervention of this type should be strictly defined and limited to the following situations: (a) where the child or young person has suffered harm that has been inflicted by the parents or guardians; (b) where the child or young person has been sexually, physically or emotionally abused by the parents or guardians; (c) where the child or young person has been neglected, abandoned or exploited by the parents or guardians; (d) where the child or young person is threatened by physical or moral danger due to the behaviour of the parents or guardians; and (e) where a serious physical or psychological danger to the child or young person has manifested itself in his or her own behaviour and neither the parents, the guardians, the juvenile himself or herself nor non-residential community services can meet the danger by means other than institutionalization.

47. Government agencies should provide young persons with the opportunity of continuing in full-time education, funded by the State where parents or guardians are unable to support the young persons, and of receiving work experience.

48. Programmes to prevent delinquency should be planned and developed on the basis of reliable, scientific

research findings, and periodically monitored, evaluated and adjusted accordingly.

49. Scientific information should be disseminated to the professional community and to the public at large about the sort of behaviour or situation which indicates or may result in physical and psychological victimization, harm and abuse, as well as exploitation, of young persons.

50. Generally, participation in plans and programmes should be voluntary. Young persons themselves should be involved in their formulation, development and implementation.

51. Government should begin or continue to explore, develop and implement policies, measures and strategies within and outside the criminal justice system to prevent domestic violence against and affecting young persons and to ensure fair treatment to these victims of domestic violence.

VI. Legislation and juvenile justice administration

52. Governments should enact and enforce specific laws and procedures to promote and protect the rights and well-being of all young persons.

53. Legislation preventing the victimization, abuse, exploitation and the use for criminal activities of children and young persons should be enacted and enforced.

54. No child or young person should be subjected to harsh or degrading correction or punishment measures at home, in schools or in any other institutions.

55. Legislation and enforcement aimed at restricting and controlling accessibility of weapons of any sort to children and young persons should be pursued.

56. In order to prevent further stigmatization, victimization and criminalization of young persons, legislation should be enacted to ensure that any conduct not considered an offence or not penalized if committed by an adult is not considered an offence and not penalized if committed by a young person.

57. Consideration should be given to the establishment of an office of ombudsman or similar independent organ, which would ensure that the status, rights and interests of young persons are upheld and that proper referral to available services is made. The ombudsman or other organ designated would also supervise the implementation of the Riyadh Guidelines, the Beijing Rules and the Rules for the Protection of Juveniles Deprived of their Liberty. The ombudsman or other organ would, at regular intervals, publish a report on the progress made and on the difficulties encountered in the implementation of the instrument. Child advocacy services should also be established.

58. Law enforcement and other relevant personnel, of both sexes, should be trained to respond to the special needs of young persons and should be familiar with and use, to the maximum extent possible, programmes and referral possibilities for the diversion of young persons from the justice system.

59. Legislation should be enacted and strictly enforced to protect children and young persons from drug abuse and drug traffickers.

VII. Research, policy development and co-ordination

60. Efforts should be made and appropriate mechanisms established to promote, on both a multidisciplinary and an intradisciplinary basis, interaction and co-ordination between economic, social, education and health agencies and services, the justice system, youth, community and development agencies and other relevant institutions.

61. The exchange of information, experience and expertise gained through projects, programmes, practices and initiatives relating to youth crime, delinquency prevention and juvenile justice should be intensified at the national, regional and international levels.

62. Regional and international cooperation on matters of youth crime, delinquency prevention and juvenile justice involving practitioners, experts and decision makers should be further developed and strengthened.

63. Technical and scientific cooperation on practical and policy-related matters, particularly in training, pilot and demonstration projects, and on specific issues concerning the prevention of youth crime and juvenile delinquency should be strongly supported by all Governments, the United Nations system and other concerned organizations.

64. Collaboration should be encouraged in undertaking scientific research with respect to effective modalities for youth crime and juvenile delinquency prevention, and the findings of such research should be widely disseminated and evaluated.

65. Appropriate United Nations bodies, institutes, agencies and offices should pursue close collaboration and co-ordination on various questions related to children, juvenile justice and youth crime and juvenile delinquency prevention.

66. On the basis of the present Guidelines, the United Nations Secretariat, in cooperation with interested institutions, should play an active role in the conduct of research, scientific collaboration, the formulation of policy options and the review and monitoring of their implementation, and should serve as a source of reliable information on effective modalities for delinquency prevention.

Document 69

United Nations Rules for the Protection of Juveniles Deprived of their Liberty

A/RES/45/113, 14 December 1990

I. Fundamental perspectives

1. The juvenile justice system should uphold the rights and safety and promote the physical and mental well-being of juveniles. Imprisonment should be used as a last resort.

2. Juveniles should only be deprived of their liberty in accordance with the principles and procedures set forth in these Rules and in the United Nations Standard Minimum Rules for the Administration of Juvenile Justice (The Beijing Rules). Deprivation of the liberty of a juvenile should be a disposition of last resort and for the minimum necessary period and should be limited to exceptional cases. The length of the sanction should be determined by the judicial authority, without precluding the possibility of his or her early release.

3. The Rules are intended to establish minimum standards accepted by the United Nations for the protection of juveniles deprived of their liberty in all forms, consistent with human rights and fundamental freedoms, and with a view to counteracting the detrimental effects of all types of detention and to fostering integration in society.

4. The Rules should be applied impartially, without discrimination of any kind as to race, colour, sex, age, language, religion, nationality, political or other opinion, cultural beliefs or practices, property, birth or family status, ethnic or social origin, and disability. The religious and cultural beliefs, practices and moral concepts of the juvenile should be respected.

5. The Rules are designed to serve as convenient standards of reference and to provide encouragement and guidance to professionals involved in the management of the juvenile justice system.

6. The Rules should be made readily available to juvenile justice personnel in their national languages. Juveniles who are not fluent in the language spoken by the personnel of the detention facility should have the right to the services of an interpreter free of charge whenever necessary, in particular during medical examinations and disciplinary proceedings.

7. Where appropriate, States should incorporate the Rules into their legislation or amend it accordingly and provide effective remedies for their breach, including compensation when injuries are inflicted on juveniles. States should also monitor the application of the Rules.

8. The competent authorities should constantly seek to increase the awareness of the public that the care of detained juveniles and preparation for their return to society is a social service of great importance, and to this end active steps should be taken to foster open contacts between the juveniles and the local community.

9. Nothing in the Rules should be interpreted as precluding the application of the relevant United Nations and human rights instruments and standards, recognized by the international community, that are more conducive to ensuring the rights, care and protection of juveniles, children and all young persons.

10. In the event that the practical application of particular Rules contained in sections II to V, inclusive, presents any conflict with the Rules contained in the present section, compliance with the latter shall be regarded as the predominant requirement.

II. Scope and application of the rules

11. For the purposes of the Rules, the following definitions should apply:

(a) A juvenile is every person under the age of 18. The age limit below which it should not be permitted to deprive a child of his or her liberty should be determined by law;

(b) The deprivation of liberty means any form of detention or imprisonment or the placement of a person in a public or private custodial setting, from which this person is not permitted to leave at will, by order of any judicial, administrative or other public authority.

12. The deprivation of liberty should be effected in conditions and circumstances which ensure respect for the human rights of juveniles. Juveniles detained in facilities should be guaranteed the benefit of meaningful activities and programmes which would serve to promote and sustain their health and self-respect, to foster their sense of responsibility and encourage those attitudes and skills that will assist them in developing their potential as members of society.

13. Juveniles deprived of their liberty shall not for any reason related to their status be denied the civil, economic, political, social or cultural rights to which they are entitled under national or international law, and which are compatible with the deprivation of liberty.

14. The protection of the individual rights of juveniles with special regard to the legality of the execution

of the detention measures shall be ensured by the competent authority, while the objectives of social integration should be secured by regular inspections and other means of control carried out, according to international standards, national laws and regulations, by a duly constituted body authorized to visit the juveniles and not belonging to the detention facility.

15. The Rules apply to all types and forms of detention facilities in which juveniles are deprived of their liberty. Sections I, II, IV and V of the Rules apply to all detention facilities and institutional settings in which juveniles are detained, and section III applies specifically to juveniles under arrest or awaiting trial.

16. The Rules shall be implemented in the context of the economic, social and cultural conditions prevailing in each Member State.

III. Juveniles under arrest or awaiting trial

17. Juveniles who are detained under arrest or awaiting trial ("untried") are presumed innocent and shall be treated as such. Detention before trial shall be avoided to the extent possible and limited to exceptional circumstances. Therefore, all efforts shall be made to apply alternative measures. When preventive detention is nevertheless used, juvenile courts and investigative bodies shall give the highest priority to the most expeditious processing of such cases to ensure the shortest possible duration of detention. Untried detainees should be separated from convicted juveniles.

18. The conditions under which an untried juvenile is detained should be consistent with the rules set out below, with additional specific provisions as are necessary and appropriate, given the requirements of the presumption of innocence, the duration of the detention and the legal status and circumstances of the juvenile. These provisions would include, but not necessarily be restricted to, the following:

(a) Juveniles should have the right of legal counsel and be enabled to apply for free legal aid, where such aid is available, and to communicate regularly with their legal advisers. Privacy and confidentiality shall be ensured for such communications;

(b) Juveniles should be provided, where possible, with opportunities to pursue work, with remuneration, and continue education or training, but should not be required to do so. Work, education or training should not cause the continuation of the detention;

(c) Juveniles should receive and retain materials for their leisure and recreation as are compatible with the interests of the administration of justice.

IV. The management of juvenile facilities

A. *Records*

19. All reports, including legal records, medical records and records of disciplinary proceedings, and all other documents relating to the form, content and details of treatment, should be placed in a confidential individual file, which should be kept up to date, accessible only to authorized persons and classified in such a way as to be easily understood. Where possible, every juvenile should have the right to contest any fact or opinion contained in his or her file so as to permit rectification of inaccurate, unfounded or unfair statements. In order to exercise this right, there should be procedures that allow an appropriate third party to have access to and to consult the file on request. Upon release, the records of juveniles shall be sealed, and, at an appropriate time, expunged.

20. No juvenile should be received in any detention facility without a valid commitment order of a judicial, administrative or other public authority. The details of this order should be immediately entered in the register. No juvenile should be detained in any facility where there is no such register.

B. *Admission, registration, movement and transfer*

21. In every place where juveniles are detained, a complete and secure record of the following information should be kept concerning each juvenile received:

(a) Information on the identity of the juvenile;

(b) The fact of and reasons for commitment and the authority therefor;

(c) The day and hour of admission, transfer and release;

(d) Details of the notifications to parents and guardians on every admission, transfer or release of the juvenile in their care at the time of commitment;

(e) Details of known physical and mental health problems, including drug and alcohol abuse.

22. The information on admission, place, transfer and release should be provided without delay to the parents and guardians or closest relative of the juvenile concerned.

23. As soon as possible after reception, full reports and relevant information on the personal situation and circumstances of each juvenile should be drawn up and submitted to the administration.

24. On admission, all juveniles shall be given a copy of the rules governing the detention facility and a written description of their rights and obligations in a language they can understand, together with the address of the authorities competent to receive complaints, as well as the address of public or private agencies and organizations which provide legal assistance. For those juveniles

who are illiterate or who cannot understand the language in the written form, the information should be conveyed in a manner enabling full comprehension.

25. All juveniles should be helped to understand the regulations governing the internal organization of the facility, the goals and methodology of the care provided, the disciplinary requirements and procedures, other authorized methods of seeking information and of making complaints, and all such other matters as are necessary to enable them to understand fully their rights and obligations during detention.

26. The transport of juveniles should be carried out at the expense of the administration in conveyances with adequate ventilation and light, in conditions that should in no way subject them to hardship or indignity. Juveniles should not be transferred from one facility to another arbitrarily.

C. *Classification and placement*

27. As soon as possible after the moment of admission, each juvenile should be interviewed, and a psychological and social report identifying any factors relevant to the specific type and level of care and programme required by the juvenile should be prepared. This report, together with the report prepared by a medical officer who has examined the juvenile upon admission, should be forwarded to the director for purposes of determining the most appropriate placement for the juvenile within the facility and the specific type and level of care and programme required and to be pursued. When special rehabilitative treatment is required, and the length of stay in the facility permits, trained personnel of the facility should prepare a written, individualized treatment plan specifying treatment objectives and time-frame and the means, stages and delays with which the objectives should be approached.

28. The detention of juveniles should only take place under conditions that take full account of their particular needs, status and special requirements according to their age, personality, sex and type of offence, as well as mental and physical health, and which ensure their protection from harmful influences and risk situations. The principal criterion for the separation of different categories of juveniles deprived of their liberty should be the provision of the type of care best suited to the particular needs of the individuals concerned and the protection of their physical, mental and moral integrity and well-being.

29. In all detention facilities juveniles should be separated from adults, unless they are members of the same family. Under controlled conditions, juveniles may be brought together with carefully selected adults as part of a special programme that has been shown to be beneficial for the juveniles concerned.

30. Open detention facilities for juveniles should be established. Open detention facilities are those with no or minimal security measures. The population in such detention facilities should be as small as possible. The number of juveniles detained in closed facilities should be small enough to enable individualized treatment. Detention facilities for juveniles should be decentralized and of such size as to facilitate access and contact between the juveniles and their families. Small-scale detention facilities should be established and integrated into the social, economic and cultural environment of the community.

D. *Physical environment and accommodation*

31. Juveniles deprived of their liberty have the right to facilities and services that meet all the requirements of health and human dignity.

32. The design of detention facilities for juveniles and the physical environment should be in keeping with the rehabilitative aim of residential treatment, with due regard to the need of the juvenile for privacy, sensory stimuli, opportunities for association with peers and participation in sports, physical exercise and leisure-time activities. The design and structure of juvenile detention facilities should be such as to minimize the risk of fire and to ensure safe evacuation from the premises. There should be an effective alarm system in case of fire, as well as formal and drilled procedures to ensure the safety of the juveniles. Detention facilities should not be located in areas where there are known health or other hazards or risks.

33. Sleeping accommodation should normally consist of small group dormitories or individual bedrooms, while bearing in mind local standards. During sleeping hours there should be regular, unobtrusive supervision of all sleeping areas, including individual rooms and group dormitories, in order to ensure the protection of each juvenile. Every juvenile should, in accordance with local or national standards, be provided with separate and sufficient bedding, which should be clean when issued, kept in good order and changed often enough to ensure cleanliness.

34. Sanitary installations should be so located and of a sufficient standard to enable every juvenile to comply, as required, with their physical needs in privacy and in a clean and decent manner.

35. The possession of personal effects is a basic element of the right to privacy and essential to the psychological well-being of the juvenile. The right of every juvenile to possess personal effects and to have adequate storage facilities for them should be fully recognized and respected. Personal effects that the juvenile does not choose to retain or that are confiscated should be placed

in safe custody. An inventory thereof should be signed by the juvenile. Steps should be taken to keep them in good condition. All such articles and money should be returned to the juvenile on release, except in so far as he or she has been authorized to spend money or send such property out of the facility. If a juvenile receives or is found in possession of any medicine, the medical officer should decide what use should be made of it.

36. To the extent possible juveniles should have the right to use their own clothing. Detention facilities should ensure that each juvenile has personal clothing suitable for the climate and adequate to ensure good health, and which should in no manner be degrading or humiliating. Juveniles removed from or leaving a facility for any purpose should be allowed to wear their own clothing.

37. Every detention facility shall ensure that every juvenile receives food that is suitably prepared and presented at normal mealtimes and of a quality and quantity to satisfy the standards of dietetics, hygiene and health and, as far as possible, religious and cultural requirements. Clean drinking-water should be available to every juvenile at any time.

E. *Education, vocational training and work*

38. Every juvenile of compulsory school age has the right to education suited to his or her needs and abilities and designed to prepare him or her for return to society. Such education should be provided outside the detention facility in community schools wherever possible and, in any case, by qualified teachers through programmes integrated with the education system of the country so that, after release, juveniles may continue their education without difficulty. Special attention should be given by the administration of the detention facilities to the education of juveniles of foreign origin or with particular cultural or ethnic needs. Juveniles who are illiterate or have cognitive or learning difficulties should have the right to special education.

39. Juveniles above compulsory school age who wish to continue their education should be permitted and encouraged to do so, and every effort should be made to provide them with access to appropriate educational programmes.

40. Diplomas or educational certificates awarded to juveniles while in detention should not indicate in any way that the juvenile has been institutionalized.

41. Every detention facility should provide access to a library that is adequately stocked with both instructional and recreational books and periodicals suitable for the juveniles, who should be encouraged and enabled to make full use of it.

42. Every juvenile should have the right to receive vocational training in occupations likely to prepare him or her for future employment.

43. With due regard to proper vocational selection and to the requirements of institutional administration, juveniles should be able to choose the type of work they wish to perform.

44. All protective national and international standards applicable to child labour and young workers should apply to juveniles deprived of their liberty.

45. Wherever possible, juveniles should be provided with the opportunity to perform remunerated labour, if possible within the local community, as a complement to the vocational training provided in order to enhance the possibility of finding suitable employment when they return to their communities. The type of work should be such as to provide appropriate training that will be of benefit to the juveniles following release. The organization and methods of work offered in detention facilities should resemble as closely as possible those of similar work in the community, so as to prepare juveniles for the conditions of normal occupational life.

46. Every juvenile who performs work should have the right to an equitable remuneration. The interests of the juveniles and of their vocational training should not be subordinated to the purpose of making a profit for the detention facility or a third party. Part of the earnings of a juvenile should normally be set aside to constitute a savings fund to be handed over to the juvenile on release. The juvenile should have the right to use the remainder of those earnings to purchase articles for his or her own use or to indemnify the victim injured by his or her offence or to send it to his or her family or other persons outside the detention facility.

F. *Recreation*

47. Every juvenile should have the right to a suitable amount of time for daily free exercise, in the open air whenever weather permits, during which time appropriate recreational and physical training should normally be provided. Adequate space, installations and equipment should be provided for these activities. Every juvenile should have additional time for daily leisure activities, part of which should be devoted, if the juvenile so wishes, to arts and crafts skill development. The detention facility should ensure that each juvenile is physically able to participate in the available programmes of physical education. Remedial physical education and therapy should be offered, under medical supervision, to juveniles needing it.

G. Religion

48. Every juvenile should be allowed to satisfy the needs of his or her religious and spiritual life, in particular by attending the services or meetings provided in the detention facility or by conducting his or her own services and having possession of the necessary books or items of religious observance and instruction of his or her denomination. If a detention facility contains a sufficient number of juveniles of a given religion, one or more qualified representatives of that religion should be appointed or approved and allowed to hold regular services and to pay pastoral visits in private to juveniles at their request. Every juvenile should have the right to receive visits from a qualified representative of any religion of his or her choice, as well as the right not to participate in religious services and freely to decline religious education, counselling or indoctrination.

H. Medical care

49. Every juvenile shall receive adequate medical care, both preventive and remedial, including dental, ophthalmological and mental health care, as well as pharmaceutical products and special diets as medically indicated. All such medical care should, where possible, be provided to detained juveniles through the appropriate health facilities and services of the community in which the detention facility is located, in order to prevent stigmatization of the juvenile and promote self-respect and integration into the community.

50. Every juvenile has a right to be examined by a physician immediately upon admission to a detention facility, for the purpose of recording any evidence of prior ill-treatment and identifying any physical or mental condition requiring medical attention.

51. The medical services provided to juveniles should seek to detect and should treat any physical or mental illness, substance abuse or other condition that may hinder the integration of the juvenile into society. Every detention facility for juveniles should have immediate access to adequate medical facilities and equipment appropriate to the number and requirements of its residents and staff trained in preventive health care and the handling of medical emergencies. Every juvenile who is ill, who complains of illness or who demonstrates symptoms of physical or mental difficulties, should be examined promptly by a medical officer.

52. Any medical officer who has reason to believe that the physical or mental health of a juvenile has been or will be injuriously affected by continued detention, a hunger strike or any condition of detention should report this fact immediately to the director of the detention facility in question and to the independent authority responsible for safeguarding the well-being of the juvenile.

53. A juvenile who is suffering from mental illness should be treated in a specialized institution under independent medical management. Steps should be taken, by arrangement with appropriate agencies, to ensure any necessary continuation of mental health care after release.

54. Juvenile detention facilities should adopt specialized drug abuse prevention and rehabilitation programmes administered by qualified personnel. These programmes should be adapted to the age, sex and other requirements of the juveniles concerned, and detoxification facilities and services staffed by trained personnel should be available to drug- or alcohol-dependent juveniles.

55. Medicines should be administered only for necessary treatment on medical grounds and, when possible, after having obtained the informed consent of the juvenile concerned. In particular, they must not be administered with a view to eliciting information or a confession, as a punishment or as a means of restraint. Juveniles shall never be testees in the experimental use of drugs and treatment. The administration of any drug should always be authorized and carried out by qualified medical personnel.

I. Notification of illness, injury and death

56. The family or guardian of a juvenile and any other person designated by the juvenile have the right to be informed of the state of health of the juvenile on request and in the event of any important changes in the health of the juvenile. The director of the detention facility should notify immediately the family or guardian of the juvenile concerned, or other designated person, in case of death, illness requiring transfer of the juvenile to an outside medical facility, or a condition requiring clinical care within the detention facility for more than 48 hours. Notification should also be given to the consular authorities of the State of which a foreign juvenile is a citizen.

57. Upon the death of a juvenile during the period of deprivation of liberty, the nearest relative should have the right to inspect the death certificate, see the body and determine the method of disposal of the body. Upon the death of a juvenile in detention, there should be an independent inquiry into the causes of death, the report of which should be made accessible to the nearest relative. This inquiry should also be made when the death of a juvenile occurs within six months from the date of his or her release from the detention facility and there is reason to believe that the death is related to the period of detention.

58. A juvenile should be informed at the earliest possible time of the death, serious illness or injury of any immediate family member and should be provided with the opportunity to attend the funeral of the deceased or go to the bedside of a critically ill relative.

J. Contacts with the wider community

59. Every means should be provided to ensure that juveniles have adequate communication with the outside world, which is an integral part of the right to fair and humane treatment and is essential to the preparation of juveniles for their return to society. Juveniles should be allowed to communicate with their families, friends and other persons or representatives of reputable outside organizations, to leave detention facilities for a visit to their home and family and to receive special permission to leave the detention facility for educational, vocational or other important reasons. Should the juvenile be serving a sentence, the time spent outside a detention facility should be counted as part of the period of sentence.

60. Every juvenile should have the right to receive regular and frequent visits, in principle once a week and not less than once a month, in circumstances that respect the need of the juvenile for privacy, contact and unrestricted communication with the family and the defence counsel.

61. Every juvenile should have the right to communicate in writing or by telephone at least twice a week with the person of his or her choice, unless legally restricted, and should be assisted as necessary in order effectively to enjoy this right. Every juvenile should have the right to receive correspondence.

62. Juveniles should have the opportunity to keep themselves informed regularly of the news by reading newspapers, periodicals and other publications, through access to radio and television programmes and motion pictures, and through the visits of the representatives of any lawful club or organization in which the juvenile is interested.

K. Limitations of physical restraint and the use of force

63. Recourse to instruments of restraint and to force for any purpose should be prohibited, except as set forth in rule 64 below.

64. Instruments of restraint and force can only be used in exceptional cases, where all other control methods have been exhausted and failed, and only as explicitly authorized and specified by law and regulation. They should not cause humiliation or degradation, and should be used restrictively and only for the shortest possible period of time. By order of the director of the administration, such instruments might be resorted to in order to prevent the juvenile from inflicting self-injury, injuries to others or serious destruction of property. In such instances, the director should at once consult medical and other relevant personnel and report to the higher administrative authority.

65. The carrying and use of weapons by personnel should be prohibited in any facility where juveniles are detained.

L. Disciplinary procedures

66. Any disciplinary measures and procedures should maintain the interest of safety and an ordered community life and should be consistent with the upholding of the inherent dignity of the juvenile and the fundamental objective of institutional care, namely, instilling a sense of justice, self-respect and respect for the basic rights of every person.

67. All disciplinary measures constituting cruel, inhuman or degrading treatment shall be strictly prohibited, including corporal punishment, placement in a dark cell, closed or solitary confinement or any other punishment that may compromise the physical or mental health of the juvenile concerned. The reduction of diet and the restriction or denial of contact with family members should be prohibited for any purpose. Labour should always be viewed as an educational tool and a means of promoting the self-respect of the juvenile in preparing him or her for return to the community and should not be imposed as a disciplinary sanction. No juvenile should be sanctioned more than once for the same disciplinary infraction. Collective sanctions should be prohibited.

68. Legislation or regulations adopted by the competent administrative authority should establish norms concerning the following, taking full account of the fundamental characteristics, needs and rights of juveniles:

(a) Conduct constituting a disciplinary offence;

(b) Type and duration of disciplinary sanctions that may be inflicted;

(c) The authority competent to impose such sanctions;

(d) The authority competent to consider appeals.

69. A report of misconduct should be presented promptly to the competent authority, which should decide on it without undue delay. The competent authority should conduct a thorough examination of the case.

70. No juvenile should be disciplinarily sanctioned except in strict accordance with the terms of the law and regulations in force. No juvenile should be sanctioned unless he or she has been informed of the alleged infraction in a manner appropriate to the full understanding of the juvenile, and given a proper opportunity of presenting his or her defence, including the right of appeal to a

competent impartial authority. Complete records should be kept of all disciplinary proceedings.

71. No juveniles should be responsible for disciplinary functions except in the supervision of specified social, educational or sports activities or in self-government programmes.

M. *Inspection and complaints*

72. Qualified inspectors or an equivalent duly constituted authority not belonging to the administration of the facility should be empowered to conduct inspections on a regular basis and to undertake unannounced inspections on their own initiative, and should enjoy full guarantees of independence in the exercise of this function. Inspectors should have unrestricted access to all persons employed by or working in any facility where juveniles are or may be deprived of their liberty, to all juveniles and to all records of such facilities.

73. Qualified medical officers attached to the inspecting authority or the public health service should participate in the inspections, evaluating compliance with the rules concerning the physical environment, hygiene, accommodation, food, exercise and medical services, as well as any other aspect or conditions of institutional life that affect the physical and mental health of juveniles. Every juvenile should have the right to talk in confidence to any inspecting officer.

74. After completing the inspection, the inspector should be required to submit a report on the findings. The report should include an evaluation of the compliance of the detention facilities with the present rules and relevant provisions of national law, and recommendations regarding any steps considered necessary to ensure compliance with them. Any facts discovered by an inspector that appear to indicate that a violation of legal provisions concerning the rights of juveniles or the operation of a juvenile detention facility has occurred should be communicated to the competent authorities for investigation and prosecution.

75. Every juvenile should have the opportunity of making requests or complaints to the director of the detention facility and to his or her authorized representative.

76. Every juvenile should have the right to make a request or complaint, without censorship as to substance, to the central administration, the judicial authority or other proper authorities through approved channels, and to be informed of the response without delay.

77. Efforts should be made to establish an independent office (ombudsman) to receive and investigate complaints made by juveniles deprived of their liberty and to assist in the achievement of equitable settlements.

78. Every juvenile should have the right to request assistance from family members, legal counsellors, humanitarian groups or others where possible, in order to make a complaint. Illiterate juveniles should be provided with assistance should they need to use the services of public or private agencies and organizations which provide legal counsel or which are competent to receive complaints.

N. *Return to the community*

79. All juveniles should benefit from arrangements designed to assist them in returning to society, family life, education or employment after release. Procedures, including early release, and special courses should be devised to this end.

80. Competent authorities should provide or ensure services to assist juveniles in re-establishing themselves in society and to lessen prejudice against such juveniles. These services should ensure, to the extent possible, that the juvenile is provided with suitable residence, employment, clothing, and sufficient means to maintain himself or herself upon release in order to facilitate successful reintegration. The representatives of agencies providing such services should be consulted and should have access to juveniles while detained, with a view to assisting them in their return to the community.

V. Personnel

81. Personnel should be qualified and include a sufficient number of specialists such as educators, vocational instructors, counsellors, social workers, psychiatrists and psychologists. These and other specialist staff should normally be employed on a permanent basis. This should not preclude part-time or volunteer workers when the level of support and training they can provide is appropriate and beneficial. Detention facilities should make use of all remedial, educational, moral, spiritual, and other resources and forms of assistance that are appropriate and available in the community, according to the individual needs and problems of detained juveniles.

82. The administration should provide for the careful selection and recruitment of every grade and type of personnel, since the proper management of detention facilities depends on their integrity, humanity, ability and professional capacity to deal with juveniles, as well as personal suitability for the work.

83. To secure the foregoing ends, personnel should be appointed as professional officers with adequate remuneration to attract and retain suitable women and men. The personnel of juvenile detention facilities should be continually encouraged to fulfil their duties and obligations in a humane, committed, professional, fair and efficient manner, to conduct themselves at all times in

such a way as to deserve and gain the respect of the juveniles, and to provide juveniles with a positive role model and perspective.

84. The administration should introduce forms of organization and management that facilitate communications between different categories of staff in each detention facility so as to enhance cooperation between the various services engaged in the care of juveniles, as well as between staff and the administration, with a view to ensuring that staff directly in contact with juveniles are able to function in conditions favourable to the efficient fulfilment of their duties.

85. The personnel should receive such training as will enable them to carry out their responsibilities effectively, in particular training in child psychology, child welfare and international standards and norms of human rights and the rights of the child, including the present Rules. The personnel should maintain and improve their knowledge and professional capacity by attending courses of in-service training, to be organized at suitable intervals throughout their career.

86. The director of a facility should be adequately qualified for his or her task, with administrative ability and suitable training and experience, and should carry out his or her duties on a full-time basis.

87. In the performance of their duties, personnel of detention facilities should respect and protect the human dignity and fundamental human rights of all juveniles, in particular, as follows:

(a) No member of the detention facility or institutional personnel may inflict, instigate or tolerate any act of torture or any form of harsh, cruel, inhuman or degrading treatment, punishment, correction or discipline under any pretext or circumstance whatsoever;

(b) All personnel should rigorously oppose and combat any act of corruption, reporting it without delay to the competent authorities;

(c) All personnel should respect the present Rules. Personnel who have reason to believe that a serious violation of the present Rules has occurred or is about to occur should report the matter to their superior authorities or organs vested with reviewing or remedial power;

(d) All personnel should ensure the full protection of the physical and mental health of juveniles, including protection from physical, sexual and emotional abuse and exploitation, and should take immediate action to secure medical attention whenever required;

(e) All personnel should respect the right of the juvenile to privacy, and, in particular, should safeguard all confidential matters concerning juveniles or their families learned as a result of their professional capacity;

(f) All personnel should seek to minimize any differences between life inside and outside the detention facility which tend to lessen due respect for the dignity of juveniles as human beings.

Document 70

General Assembly resolution on the convening of a World Conference on Human Rights in 1993

A/RES/45/155, 18 December 1990

The General Assembly,

Mindful of the goal of the United Nations to promote and encourage respect for human rights and fundamental freedoms for all without distinction as to race, sex, language or religion, as set out in the Charter of the United Nations and the Universal Declaration of Human Rights, 1/

Recognizing that all human rights and fundamental freedoms are indivisible and interrelated and that the promotion and protection of one category of rights should never exempt or excuse States from the promotion and protection of another,

Bearing in mind that all Member States have pledged themselves to achieve the promotion of universal respect for and observance of human rights and fundamental freedoms in conformity with relevant articles of the Charter,

Noting the progress made by the United Nations towards this goal and the fact that there are areas in which further progress should be made,

Noting also that violations of human rights and fundamental freedoms continue to occur,

Considering that, in view of the progress made, the problems that remain and the new challenges that lie ahead, it would be appropriate to conduct a review of what has been accomplished through the human rights programme and what remains to be done,

1/ Resolution 217 A (III).

Recalling its resolution 44/156 of 15 December 1989, in which it requested the Secretary-General to seek the views of Governments, specialized agencies, non-governmental organizations and United Nations bodies concerned with human rights on the desirability of convening a world conference on human rights for the purpose of dealing at the highest level with the crucial questions facing the United Nations in connection with the promotion and protection of human rights,

Taking note of the report of the Secretary-General containing those views, 2/

Noting the expressions of support for the convening of a world conference on human rights from many Governments, specialized agencies and United Nations bodies concerned with human rights and from non-governmental organizations,

Noting also the many views concerning the importance of thorough advance preparation for the success of the conference,

Convinced that the holding of a world conference on human rights could make a significant contribution to the effectiveness of the actions of the United Nations and its Member States in the promotion and protection of human rights,

1. *Decides* to convene at a high level a World Conference on Human Rights in 1993 with the following objectives:

(a) To review and assess the progress that has been made in the field of human rights since the adoption of the Universal Declaration of Human Rights and to identify obstacles to further progress in this area, and ways in which they can be overcome;

(b) To examine the relation between development and the enjoyment by everyone of economic, social and cultural rights as well as civil and political rights, recognizing the importance of creating the conditions whereby everyone may enjoy these rights as set out in the International Covenants on Human Rights; 3/

(c) To examine ways and means to improve the implementation of existing human rights standards and instruments;

(d) To evaluate the effectiveness of the methods and mechanisms used by the United Nations in the field of human rights;

(e) To formulate concrete recommendations for improving the effectiveness of United Nations activities and mechanisms in the field of human rights through programmes aimed at promoting, encouraging and monitoring respect for human rights and fundamental freedoms;

(f) To make recommendations for ensuring the necessary financial and other resources for United Nations activities in the promotion and protection of human rights and fundamental freedoms;

2. *Decides* to establish a Preparatory Committee for the World Conference on Human Rights, which shall be open to all States Members of the United Nations or members of the specialized agencies, with the participation of observers, in accordance with the established practice of the General Assembly;

3. *Also decides* that the Preparatory Committee should have the mandate to make proposals for the consideration of the General Assembly regarding the agenda, date, duration, venue of and participation in the Conference, preparatory meetings and activities at the international, regional and national levels, which should take place in 1992, and on desirable studies and other documentation;

4. *Further decides* that the Preparatory Committee, at its first session, shall elect a five-member bureau composed of a chairman, three vice-chairmen and a rapporteur, with due regard to equitable geographic representation;

5. *Instructs* the Preparatory Committee to deal with the substantive preparations for the Conference in accordance with the goals and objectives set out in paragraph 1 above and bearing in mind the recommendations of the Commission on Human Rights at its forty-seventh session;

6. *Decides* that the Preparatory Committee shall hold a five-day session at Geneva in September 1991;

7. *Also decides*, in accordance with its resolution 42/211 of 21 December 1987 and without prejudice to the overall level of resources adopted by the General Assembly for the biennium 1990-1991 and the proposed programme budget outline for the biennium 1992-1993, that the preparatory process and the Conference itself should be funded through the regular budget of the United Nations, without any implications for the programmes provided for under section 23 of the programme budget, and invites contributions of extrabudgetary resources to meet, *inter alia*, the cost of participation of representatives of least developed countries in the preparatory meetings and the Conference itself;

8. *Requests* the Commission on Human Rights to make recommendations to the Preparatory Committee on the above issues during those sessions that will take place prior to the Conference;

9. *Encourages* the Chairman of the Commission on Human Rights, the chairmen or other designated members of human rights expert bodies as well as special rapporteurs and chairmen or designated members of working groups to take part in the work of the Preparatory Committee;

2/ A/45/564 and Add.1.
3/ See resolution 2200 A (XXI), annex.

10. *Requests* Governments, the specialized agencies, other international organizations, concerned United Nations bodies, regional organizations and non-governmental organizations concerned with human rights to assist the Preparatory Committee and to undertake reviews and submit recommendations concerning the Conference and the preparations therefor to the Preparatory Committee through the Secretary-General and to participate actively in the Conference;

11. *Requests* the Secretary-General to submit to the Preparatory Committee a report on the contributions made pursuant to paragraphs 9 and 10 above;

12. *Also requests* the Secretary-General to appoint a Secretary-General for the Conference from within the Secretariat and to provide the Preparatory Committee with all necessary assistance;

13. *Requests* the Preparatory Committee to report to the General Assembly at its forty-sixth and forty-seventh sessions on the progress of its work.

Document 71

International Convention on the Protection of the Rights of All Migrant Workers and Members of Their Families

A/RES/45/158, 18 December 1990

PREAMBLE

The States Parties to the present Convention,

Taking into account the principles embodied in the basic instruments of the United Nations concerning human rights, in particular the Universal Declaration of Human Rights, the International Covenant on Economic, Social and Cultural Rights, the International Covenant on Civil and Political Rights, the International Convention on the Elimination of All Forms of Racial Discrimination, the Convention on the Elimination of All Forms of Discrimination against Women and the Convention on the Rights of the Child,

Taking into account also the principles and standards set forth in the relevant instruments elaborated within the framework of the International Labour Organisation, especially the Convention concerning Migration for Employment (No. 97), the Convention concerning Migrations in Abusive Conditions and the Promotion of Equality of Opportunity and Treatment of Migrant Workers (No. 143), the Recommendation concerning Migration for Employment (No. 86), the Recommendation concerning Migrant Workers (No. 151), the Convention concerning Forced or Compulsory Labour (No. 29) and the Convention concerning Abolition of Forced Labour (No. 105),

Reaffirming the importance of the principles contained in the Convention against Discrimination in Education of the United Nations Educational, Scientific and Cultural Organization,

Recalling the Convention against Torture and Other Cruel, Inhuman or Degrading Treatment or Punishment, the Declaration of the Fourth United Nations Congress on the Prevention of Crime and the Treatment of Offenders, the Code of Conduct for Law Enforcement Officials, and the Slavery Conventions,

Recalling that one of the objectives of the International Labour Organisation, as stated in its Constitution, is the protection of the interests of workers when employed in countries other than their own, and bearing in mind the expertise and experience of that organization in matters related to migrant workers and members of their families,

Recognizing the importance of the work done in connection with migrant workers and members of their families in various organs of the United Nations, in particular in the Commission on Human Rights and the Commission for Social Development, and in the Food and Agriculture Organization of the United Nations, the United Nations Educational, Scientific and Cultural Organization and the World Health Organization, as well as in other international organizations,

Recognizing also the progress made by certain States on a regional or bilateral basis towards the protection of the rights of migrant workers and members of their families, as well as the importance and usefulness of bilateral and multilateral agreements in this field,

Realizing the importance and extent of the migration phenomenon, which involves millions of people and affects a large number of States in the international community,

Aware of the impact of the flows of migrant workers on States and people concerned, and desiring to establish norms which may contribute to the harmonization of the attitudes of States through the acceptance of basic principles concerning the treatment of migrant workers and members of their families,

Considering the situation of vulnerability in which migrant workers and members of their families frequently find themselves owing, among other things, to their absence from their State of origin and to the difficulties they may encounter arising from their presence in the State of employment,

Convinced that the rights of migrant workers and members of their families have not been sufficiently recognized everywhere and therefore require appropriate international protection,

Taking into account the fact that migration is often the cause of serious problems for the members of the families of migrant workers as well as for the workers themselves, in particular because of the scattering of the family,

Bearing in mind that the human problems involved in migration are even more serious in the case of irregular migration and convinced therefore that appropriate action should be encouraged in order to prevent and eliminate clandestine movements and trafficking in migrant workers, while at the same time assuring the protection of their fundamental human rights,

Considering that workers who are non-documented or in an irregular situation are frequently employed under less favourable conditions of work than other workers and that certain employers find this an inducement to seek such labour in order to reap the benefits of unfair competition,

Considering also that recourse to the employment of migrant workers who are in an irregular situation will be discouraged if the fundamental human rights of all migrant workers are more widely recognized and, moreover, that granting certain additional rights to migrant workers and members of their families in a regular situation will encourage all migrants and employers to respect and comply with the laws and procedures established by the States concerned,

Convinced, therefore, of the need to bring about the international protection of the rights of all migrant workers and members of their families, reaffirming and establishing basic norms in a comprehensive convention which could be applied universally,

Have agreed as follows:

PART I

SCOPE AND DEFINITIONS

Article 1

1. The present Convention is applicable, except as otherwise provided hereafter, to all migrant workers and members of their families without distinction of any kind such as sex, race, colour, language, religion or conviction, political or other opinion, national, ethnic or social ori-

gin, nationality, age, economic position, property, marital status, birth or other status.

2. The present Convention shall apply during the entire migration process of migrant workers and members of their families, which comprises preparation for migration, departure, transit and the entire period of stay and remunerated activity in the State of employment as well as return to the State of origin or the State of habitual residence.

Article 2

For the purposes of the present Convention:

1. The term "migrant worker" refers to a person who is to be engaged, is engaged or has been engaged in a remunerated activity in a State of which he or she is not a national.

2. (a) The term "frontier worker" refers to a migrant worker who retains his or her habitual residence in a neighbouring State to which he or she normally returns every day or at least once a week;

(b) The term "seasonal worker" refers to a migrant worker whose work by its character is dependent on seasonal conditions and is performed only during part of the year;

(c) The term "seafarer", which includes a fisherman, refers to a migrant worker employed on board a vessel registered in a State of which he or she is not a national;

(d) The term "worker on an offshore installation" refers to a migrant worker employed on an offshore installation that is under the jurisdiction of a State of which he or she is not a national;

(e) The term "itinerant worker" refers to a migrant worker who, having his or her habitual residence in one State, has to travel to another State or States for short periods, owing to the nature of his or her occupation;

(f) The term "project-tied worker" refers to a migrant worker admitted to a State of employment for a defined period to work solely on a specific project being carried out in that State by his or her employer;

(g) The term "specified-employment worker" refers to a migrant worker:

(i) Who has been sent by his or her employer for a restricted and defined period of time to a State of employment to undertake a specific assignment or duty; or

(ii) Who engages for a restricted and defined period of time in work that requires professional, commercial, technical or other highly specialized skill; or

(iii) Who, upon the request of his or her employer in the State of employment, engages for a restricted and defined period of time in work whose nature is transitory or brief;

and who is required to depart from the State of employment either at the expiration of his or her authorized period of stay, or earlier if he or she no longer undertakes that specific assignment or duty or engages in that work;

(h) The term "self-employed worker" refers to a migrant worker who is engaged in a remunerated activity otherwise than under a contract of employment and who earns his or her living through this activity normally working alone or together with members of his or her family, and to any other migrant worker recognized as self-employed by applicable legislation of the State of employment or bilateral or multilateral agreements.

Article 3

The present Convention shall not apply to:

(a) Persons sent or employed by international organizations and agencies or persons sent or employed by a State outside its territory to perform official functions, whose admission and status are regulated by general international law or by specific international agreements or conventions;

(b) Persons sent or employed by a State or on its behalf outside its territory who participate in development programmes and other co-operation programmes, whose admission and status are regulated by agreement with the State of employment and who, in accordance with that agreement, are not considered migrant workers;

(c) Persons taking up residence in a State different from their State of origin as investors;

(d) Refugees and stateless persons, unless such application is provided for in the relevant national legislation of, or international instruments in force for, the State Party concerned;

(e) Students and trainees;

(f) Seafarers and workers on an offshore installation who have not been admitted to take up residence and engage in a remunerated activity in the State of employment.

Article 4

For the purposes of the present Convention the term "members of the family" refers to persons married to migrant workers or having with them a relationship that, according to applicable law, produces effects equivalent to marriage, as well as their dependent children and other dependent persons who are recognized as members of the family by applicable legislation or applicable bilateral or multilateral agreements between the States concerned.

Article 5

For the purposes of the present Convention, migrant workers and members of their families:

(a) Are considered as documented or in a regular situation if they are authorized to enter, to stay and to engage in a remunerated activity in the State of employment pursuant to the law of that State and to international agreements to which that State is a party;

(b) Are considered as non-documented or in an irregular situation if they do not comply with the conditions provided for in subparagraph (a) of the present article.

Article 6

For the purposes of the present Convention:

(a) The term "State of origin" means the State of which the person concerned is a national;

(b) The term "State of employment" means a State where the migrant worker is to be engaged, is engaged or has been engaged in a remunerated activity, as the case may be;

(c) The term "State of transit" means any State through which the person concerned passes on any journey to the State of employment or from the State of employment to the State of origin or the State of habitual residence.

PART II

NON-DISCRIMINATION WITH RESPECT TO RIGHTS

Article 7

States Parties undertake, in accordance with the international instruments concerning human rights, to respect and to ensure to all migrant workers and members of their families within their territory or subject to their jurisdiction the rights provided for in the present Convention without distinction of any kind such as to sex, race, colour, language, religion or conviction, political or other opinion, national, ethnic or social origin, nationality, age, economic position, property, marital status, birth or other status.

PART III

HUMAN RIGHTS OF ALL MIGRANT WORKERS AND MEMBERS OF THEIR FAMILIES

Article 8

1. Migrant workers and members of their families shall be free to leave any State, including their State of origin. This right shall not be subject to any restrictions except those that are provided by law, are necessary to

protect national security, public order (*ordre public*), public health or morals or the rights and freedoms of others and are consistent with the other rights recognized in the present part of the Convention.

2. Migrant workers and members of their families shall have the right at any time to enter and remain in their State of origin.

Article 9

The right to life of migrant workers and members of their families shall be protected by law.

Article 10

No migrant worker or member of his or her family shall be subjected to torture or to cruel, inhuman or degrading treatment or punishment.

Article 11

1. No migrant worker or member of his or her family shall be held in slavery or servitude.

2. No migrant worker or member of his or her family shall be required to perform forced or compulsory labour.

3. Paragraph 2 of the present article shall not be held to preclude, in States where imprisonment with hard labour may be imposed as a punishment for a crime, the performance of hard labour in pursuance of a sentence to such punishment by a competent court.

4. For the purpose of the present article the term "forced or compulsory labour" shall not include:

(a) Any work or service not referred to in paragraph 3 of the present article normally required of a person who is under detention in consequence of a lawful order of a court or of a person during conditional release from such detention;

(b) Any service exacted in cases of emergency or calamity threatening the life or well-being of the community;

(c) Any work or service that forms part of normal civil obligations so far as it is imposed also on citizens of the State concerned.

Article 12

1. Migrant workers and members of their families shall have the right to freedom of thought, conscience and religion. This right shall include freedom to have or to adopt a religion or belief of their choice and freedom either individually or in community with others and in public or private to manifest their religion or belief in worship, observance, practice and teaching.

2. Migrant workers and members of their families shall not be subject to coercion that would impair their freedom to have or to adopt a religion or belief of their choice.

3. Freedom to manifest one's religion or belief may be subject only to such limitations as are prescribed by law and are necessary to protect public safety, order, health or morals or the fundamental rights and freedoms of others.

4. States Parties to the present Convention undertake to have respect for the liberty of parents, at least one of whom is a migrant worker, and, when applicable, legal guardians to ensure the religious and moral education of their children in conformity with their own convictions.

Article 13

1. Migrant workers and members of their families shall have the right to hold opinions without interference.

2. Migrant workers and members of their families shall have the right to freedom of expression; this right shall include freedom to seek, receive and impart information and ideas of all kinds, regardless of frontiers, either orally, in writing or in print, in the form of art or through any other media of their choice.

3. The exercise of the right provided for in paragraph 2 of the present article carries with it special duties and responsibilities. It may therefore be subject to certain restrictions, but these shall only be such as are provided by law and are necessary:

(a) For respect of the rights or reputation of others;

(b) For the protection of the national security of the States concerned or of public order (*ordre public*) or of public health or morals;

(c) For the purpose of preventing any propaganda for war;

(d) For the purpose of preventing any advocacy of national, racial or religious hatred that constitutes incitement to discrimination, hostility or violence.

Article 14

No migrant worker or member of his or her family shall be subjected to arbitrary or unlawful interference with his or her privacy, family, home, correspondence or other communications, or to unlawful attacks on his or her honour and reputation. Each migrant worker and member of his or her family shall have the right to the protection of the law against such interference or attacks.

Article 15

No migrant worker or member of his or her family shall be arbitrarily deprived of property, whether owned individually or in association with others. Where, under the legislation in force in the State of employment, the assets of a migrant worker or a member of his or her family are expropriated in whole or in part, the person concerned shall have the right to fair and adequate compensation.

Article 16

1. Migrant workers and members of their families shall have the right to liberty and security of person.

2. Migrant workers and members of their families shall be entitled to effective protection by the State against violence, physical injury, threats and intimidation, whether by public officials or by private individuals, groups or institutions.

3. Any verification by law enforcement officials of the identity of migrant workers or members of their families shall be carried out in accordance with procedure established by law.

4. Migrant workers and members of their families shall not be subjected individually or collectively to arbitrary arrest or detention; they shall not be deprived of their liberty except on such grounds and in accordance with such procedures as are established by law.

5. Migrant workers and members of their families who are arrested shall be informed at the time of arrest as far as possible in a language they understand of the reasons for their arrest and they shall be promptly informed in a language they understand of any charges against them.

6. Migrant workers and members of their families who are arrested or detained on a criminal charge shall be brought promptly before a judge or other officer authorized by law to exercise judicial power and shall be entitled to trial within a reasonable time or to release. It shall not be the general rule that while awaiting trial they shall be detained in custody, but release may be subject to guarantees to appear for trial, at any other stage of the judicial proceedings and, should the occasion arise, for the execution of the judgement.

7. When a migrant worker or a member of his or her family is arrested or committed to prison or custody pending trial or is detained in any other manner:

(a) The consular or diplomatic authorities of his or her State of origin or of a State representing the interests of that State shall, if he or she so requests, be informed without delay of his or her arrest or detention and of the reasons therefor;

(b) The person concerned shall have the right to communicate with the said authorities. Any communication by the person concerned to the said authorities shall be forwarded without delay, and he or she shall also have the right to receive communications sent by the said authorities without delay;

(c) The person concerned shall be informed without delay of this right and of rights deriving from relevant treaties, if any, applicable between the States concerned, to correspond and to meet with representatives of the said authorities and to make arrangements with them for his or her legal representation.

8. Migrant workers and members of their families who are deprived of their liberty by arrest or detention shall be entitled to take proceedings before a court, in order that that court may decide without delay on the lawfulness of their detention and order their release if the detention is not lawful. When they attend such proceedings, they shall have the assistance, if necessary without cost to them, of an interpreter, if they cannot understand or speak the language used.

9. Migrant workers and members of their families who have been victims of unlawful arrest or detention shall have an enforceable right to compensation.

Article 17

1. Migrant workers and members of their families who are deprived of their liberty shall be treated with humanity and with respect for the inherent dignity of the human person and for their cultural identity.

2. Accused migrant workers and members of their families shall, save in exceptional circumstances, be separated from convicted persons and shall be subject to separate treatment appropriate to their status as unconvicted persons. Accused juvenile persons shall be separated from adults and brought as speedily as possible for adjudication.

3. Any migrant worker or member of his or her family who is detained in a State of transit or in a State of employment for violation of provisions relating to migration shall be held, in so far as practicable, separately from convicted persons or persons detained pending trial.

4. During any period of imprisonment in pursuance of a sentence imposed by a court of law, the essential aim of the treatment of a migrant worker or a member of his or her family shall be his or her reformation and social rehabilitation. Juvenile offenders shall be separated from adults and be accorded treatment appropriate to their age and legal status.

5. During detention or imprisonment, migrant workers and members of their families shall enjoy the same rights as nationals to visits by members of their families.

6. Whenever a migrant worker is deprived of his or her liberty, the competent authorities of the State concerned shall pay attention to the problems that may be posed for members of his or her family, in particular for spouses and minor children.

7. Migrant workers and members of their families who are subjected to any form of detention or imprisonment in accordance with the law in force in the State of employment or in the State of transit shall enjoy the same rights as nationals of those States who are in the same situation.

8. If a migrant worker or a member of his or her family is detained for the purpose of verifying any infraction of provisions related to migration, he or she shall not bear any costs arising therefrom.

Article 18

1. Migrant workers and members of their families shall have the right to equality with nationals of the State concerned before the courts and tribunals. In the determination of any criminal charge against them or of their rights and obligations in a suit of law, they shall be entitled to a fair and public hearing by a competent, independent and impartial tribunal established by law.

2. Migrant workers and members of their families who are charged with a criminal offence shall have the right to be presumed innocent until proven guilty according to law.

3. In the determination of any criminal charge against them, migrant workers and members of their families shall be entitled to the following minimum guarantees:

(a) To be informed promptly and in detail in a language they understand of the nature and cause of the charge against them;

(b) To have adequate time and facilities for the preparation of their defence and to communicate with counsel of their own choosing;

(c) To be tried without undue delay;

(d) To be tried in their presence and to defend themselves in person or through legal assistance of their own choosing; to be informed, if they do not have legal assistance, of this right; and to have legal assistance assigned to them, in any case where the interests of justice so require and without payment by them in any such case if they do not have sufficient means to pay;

(e) To examine or have examined the witnesses against them and to obtain the attendance and examination of witnesses on their behalf under the same conditions as witnesses against them;

(f) To have the free assistance of an interpreter if they cannot understand or speak the language used in court;

(g) Not to be compelled to testify against themselves or to confess guilt.

4. In the case of juvenile persons, the procedure shall be such as will take account of their age and the desirability of promoting their rehabilitation.

5. Migrant workers and members of their families convicted of a crime shall have the right to their conviction and sentence being reviewed by a higher tribunal according to law.

6. When a migrant worker or a member of his or her family has, by a final decision, been convicted of a criminal offence and when subsequently his or her con-viction has been reversed or he or she has been pardoned on the ground that a new or newly discovered fact shows conclusively that there has been a miscarriage of justice, the person who has suffered punishment as a result of such conviction shall be compensated according to law, unless it is proved that the non-disclosure of the unknown fact in time is wholly or partly attributable to that person.

7. No migrant worker or member of his or her family shall be liable to be tried or punished again for an offence for which he or she has already been finally convicted or acquitted in accordance with the law and penal procedure of the State concerned.

Article 19

1. No migrant worker or member of his or her family shall be held guilty of any criminal offence on account of any act or omission that did not constitute a criminal offence under national or international law at the time when the criminal offence was committed, nor shall a heavier penalty be imposed than the one that was applicable at the time when it was committed. If, subsequent to the commission of the offence, provision is made by law for the imposition of a lighter penalty, he or she shall benefit thereby.

2. Humanitarian considerations related to the status of a migrant worker, in particular with respect to his or her right of residence or work, should be taken into account in imposing a sentence for a criminal offence committed by a migrant worker or a member of his or her family.

Article 20

1. No migrant worker or member of his or her family shall be imprisoned merely on the ground of failure to fulfil a contractual obligation.

2. No migrant worker or member of his or her family shall be deprived of his or her authorization of residence or work permit or expelled merely on the ground of failure to fulfil an obligation arising out of a work contract unless fulfilment of that obligation constitutes a condition for such authorization or permit.

Article 21

It shall be unlawful for anyone, other than a public official duly authorized by law, to confiscate, destroy or attempt to destroy identity documents, documents authorizing entry to or stay, residence or establishment in the national territory or work permits. No authorized confiscation of such documents shall take place without delivery of a detailed receipt. In no case shall it be permitted to destroy the passport or equivalent document of a migrant worker or a member of his or her family.

Article 22

1. Migrant workers and members of their families shall not be subject to measures of collective expulsion. Each case of expulsion shall be examined and decided individually.

2. Migrant workers and members of their families may be expelled from the territory of a State Party only in pursuance of a decision taken by the competent authority in accordance with law.

3. The decision shall be communicated to them in a language they understand. Upon their request where not otherwise mandatory, the decision shall be communicated to them in writing and, save in exceptional circumstances on account of national security, the reasons for the decision likewise stated. The persons concerned shall be informed of these rights before or at the latest at the time the decision is rendered.

4. Except where a final decision is pronounced by a judicial authority, the person concerned shall have the right to submit the reason he or she should not be expelled and to have his or her case reviewed by the competent authority, unless compelling reasons of national security require otherwise. Pending such review, the person concerned shall have the right to seek a stay of the decision of expulsion.

5. If a decision of expulsion that has already been executed is subsequently annulled, the person concerned shall have the right to seek compensation according to law and the earlier decision shall not be used to prevent him or her from re-entering the State concerned.

6. In case of expulsion, the person concerned shall have a reasonable opportunity before or after departure to settle any claims for wages and other entitlements due to him or her and any pending liabilities.

7. Without prejudice to the execution of a decision of expulsion, a migrant worker or a member of his or her family who is subject to such a decision may seek entry into a State other than his or her State of origin.

8. In case of expulsion of a migrant worker or a member of his or her family the costs of expulsion shall not be borne by him or her. The person concerned may be required to pay his or her own travel costs.

9. Expulsion from the State of employment shall not in itself prejudice any rights of a migrant worker or a member of his or her family acquired in accordance with the law of that State, including the right to receive wages and other entitlements due to him or her.

Article 23

Migrant workers and members of their families shall have the right to have recourse to the protection and assistance of the consular or diplomatic authorities of their State of origin or of a State representing the interests of that State whenever the rights recognized in the present Convention are impaired. In particular, in case of expulsion, the person concerned shall be informed of this right without delay and the authorities of the expelling State shall facilitate the exercise of such right.

Article 24

Every migrant worker and every member of his or her family shall have the right to recognition everywhere as a person before the law.

Article 25

1. Migrant workers shall enjoy treatment not less favourable than that which applies to nationals of the State of employment in respect of remuneration and:

(a) Other conditions of work, that is to say, overtime, hours of work, weekly rest, holidays with pay, safety, health, termination of the employment relationship and any other conditions of work which, according to national law and practice, are covered by these terms;

(b) Other terms of employment, that is to say, minimum age of employment, restriction on home work and any other matters which, according to national law and practice, are considered a term of employment.

2. It shall not be lawful to derogate in private contracts of employment from the principle of equality of treatment referred to in paragraph 1 of the present article.

3. States Parties shall take all appropriate measures to ensure that migrant workers are not deprived of any rights derived from this principle by reason of any irregularity in their stay or employment. In particular, employers shall not be relieved of any legal or contractual obligations, nor shall their obligations be limited in any manner by reason of such irregularity.

Article 26

1. States Parties recognize the right of migrant workers and members of their families:

(a) To take part in meetings and activities of trade unions and of any other associations established in accordance with law, with a view to protecting their economic, social, cultural and other interests, subject only to the rules of the organization concerned;

(b) To join freely any trade union and any such association as aforesaid, subject only to the rules of the organization concerned;

(c) To seek the aid and assistance of any trade union and of any such association as aforesaid.

2. No restrictions may be placed on the exercise of these rights other than those that are prescribed by law and which are necessary in a democratic society in the

interests of national security, public order (*ordre public*) or the protection of the rights and freedoms of others.

Article 27

1. With respect to social security, migrant workers and members of their families shall enjoy in the State of employment the same treatment granted to nationals in so far as they fulfil the requirements provided for by the applicable legislation of that State and the applicable bilateral and multilateral treaties. The competent authorities of the State of origin and the State of employment can at any time establish the necessary arrangements to determine the modalities of application of this norm.

2. Where the applicable legislation does not allow migrant workers and members of their families a benefit, the States concerned shall examine the possibility of reimbursing interested persons the amount of contributions made by them with respect to that benefit on the basis of the treatment granted to nationals who are in similar circumstances.

Article 28

Migrant workers and members of their families shall have the right to receive any medical care that is urgently required for the preservation of their life or the avoidance of irreparable harm to their health on the basis of equality of treatment with nationals of the State concerned. Such emergency medical care shall not be refused them by reason of any irregularity with regard to stay or employment.

Article 29

Each child of a migrant worker shall have the right to a name, to registration of birth and to a nationality.

Article 30

Each child of a migrant worker shall have the basic right of access to education on the basis of equality of treatment with nationals of the State concerned. Access to public pre-school educational institutions or schools shall not be refused or limited by reason of the irregular situation with respect to stay or employment of either parent or by reason of the irregularity of the child's stay in the State of employment.

Article 31

1. States Parties shall ensure respect for the cultural identity of migrant workers and members of their families and shall not prevent them from maintaining their cultural links with their State of origin.

2. States Parties may take appropriate measures to assist and encourage efforts in this respect.

Article 32

Upon the termination of their stay in the State of employment, migrant workers and members of their families shall have the right to transfer their earnings and savings and, in accordance with the applicable legislation of the States concerned, their personal effects and belongings.

Article 33

1. Migrant workers and members of their families shall have the right to be informed by the State of origin, the State of employment or the State of transit as the case may be concerning:

(a) Their rights arising out of the present Convention;

(b) The conditions of their admission, their rights and obligations under the law and practice of the State concerned and such other matters as will enable them to comply with administrative or other formalities in that State.

2. States Parties shall take all measures they deem appropriate to disseminate the said information or to ensure that it is provided by employers, trade unions or other appropriate bodies or institutions. As appropriate, they shall co-operate with other States concerned.

3. Such adequate information shall be provided upon request to migrant workers and members of their families, free of charge, and, as far as possible, in a language they are able to understand.

Article 34

Nothing in the present part of the Convention shall have the effect of relieving migrant workers and the members of their families from either the obligation to comply with the laws and regulations of any State of transit and the State of employment or the obligation to respect the cultural identity of the inhabitants of such States.

Article 35

Nothing in the present part of the Convention shall be interpreted as implying the regularization of the situation of migrant workers or members of their families who are non-documented or in an irregular situation or any right to such regularization of their situation, nor shall it prejudice the measures intended to ensure sound and equitable conditions for international migration as provided in part VI of the present Convention.

PART IV

OTHER RIGHTS OF MIGRANT WORKERS AND MEMBERS OF THEIR FAMILIES WHO ARE DOCUMENTED OR IN A REGULAR SITUATION

Article 36

Migrant workers and members of their families who are documented or in a regular situation in the State of employment shall enjoy the rights set forth in the present part of the Convention in addition to those set forth in part III.

Article 37

Before their departure, or at the latest at the time of their admission to the State of employment, migrant workers and members of their families shall have the right to be fully informed by the State of origin or the State of employment, as appropriate, of all conditions applicable to their admission and particularly those concerning their stay and the remunerated activities in which they may engage as well as of the requirements they must satisfy in the State of employment and the authority to which they must address themselves for any modification of those conditions.

Article 38

1. States of employment shall make every effort to authorize migrant workers and members of their families to be temporarily absent without effect upon their authorization to stay or to work, as the case may be. In doing so, States of employment shall take into account the special needs and obligations of migrant workers and members of their families, in particular in their States of origin.

2. Migrant workers and members of their families shall have the right to be fully informed of the terms on which such temporary absences are authorized.

Article 39

1. Migrant workers and members of their families shall have the right to liberty of movement in the territory of the State of employment and freedom to choose their residence there.

2. The rights mentioned in paragraph 1 of the present article shall not be subject to any restrictions except those that are provided by law, are necessary to protect national security, public order (*ordre public*), public health or morals, or the rights and freedoms of others and are consistent with the other rights recognized in the present Convention.

Article 40

1. Migrant workers and members of their families shall have the right to form associations and trade unions in the State of employment for the promotion and protection of their economic, social, cultural and other interests.

2. No restrictions may be placed on the exercise of this right other than those that are prescribed by law and are necessary in a democratic society in the interests of national security, public order (*ordre public*) or the protection of the rights and freedoms of others.

Article 41

1. Migrant workers and members of their families shall have the right to participate in public affairs of their State of origin and to vote and to be elected at elections of that State, in accordance with its legislation.

2. The States concerned shall, as appropriate and in accordance with their legislation, facilitate the exercise of these rights.

Article 42

1. States Parties shall consider the establishment of procedures or institutions through which account may be taken, both in States of origin and in States of employment, of special needs, aspirations and obligations of migrant workers and members of their families and shall envisage, as appropriate, the possibility for migrant workers and members of their families to have their freely chosen representatives in those institutions.

2. States of employment shall facilitate, in accordance with their national legislation, the consultation or participation of migrant workers and members of their families in decisions concerning the life and administration of local communities.

3. Migrant workers may enjoy political rights in the State of employment if that State, in the exercise of its sovereignty, grants them such rights.

Article 43

1. Migrant workers shall enjoy equality of treatment with nationals of the State of employment in relation to:

(a) Access to educational institutions and services subject to the admission requirements and other regulations of the institutions and services concerned;

(b) Access to vocational guidance and placement services;

(c) Access to vocational training and retraining facilities and institutions;

(d) Access to housing, including social housing schemes, and protection against exploitation in respect of rents;

(e) Access to social and health services, provided that the requirements for participation in the respective schemes are met;

(f) Access to co-operatives and self-managed enterprises, which shall not imply a change of their migration status and shall be subject to the rules and regulations of the bodies concerned;

(g) Access to and participation in cultural life.

2. States Parties shall promote conditions to ensure effective equality of treatment to enable migrant workers to enjoy the rights mentioned in paragraph 1 of the present article whenever the terms of their stay, as authorized by the State of employment, meet the appropriate requirements.

3. States of employment shall not prevent an employer of migrant workers from establishing housing or social or cultural facilities for them. Subject to article 70 of the present Convention, a State of employment may make the establishment of such facilities subject to the requirements generally applied in that State concerning their installation.

Article 44

1. States Parties, recognizing that the family is the natural and fundamental group unit of society and is entitled to protection by society and the State, shall take appropriate measures to ensure the protection of the unity of the families of migrant workers.

2. States Parties shall take measures that they deem appropriate and that fall within their competence to facilitate the reunification of migrant workers with their spouses or persons who have with the migrant worker a relationship that, according to applicable law, produces effects equivalent to marriage, as well as with their minor dependent unmarried children.

3. States of employment, on humanitarian grounds, shall favourably consider granting equal treatment, as set forth in paragraph 2 of the present article, to other family members of migrant workers.

Article 45

1. Members of the families of migrant workers shall, in the State of employment, enjoy equality of treatment with nationals of that State in relation to:

(a) Access to educational institutions and services, subject to the admission requirements and other regulations of the institutions and services concerned;

(b) Access to vocational guidance and training institutions and services, provided that requirements for participation are met;

(c) Access to social and health services, provided that requirements for participation in the respective schemes are met;

(d) Access to and participation in cultural life.

2. States of employment shall pursue a policy, where appropriate in collaboration with the States of origin, aimed at facilitating the integration of children of migrant workers in the local school system, particularly in respect of teaching them the local language.

3. States of employment shall endeavour to facilitate for the children of migrant workers the teaching of their mother tongue and culture and, in this regard, States of origin shall collaborate whenever appropriate.

4. States of employment may provide special schemes of education in the mother tongue of children of migrant workers, if necessary in collaboration with the States of origin.

Article 46

Migrant workers and members of their families shall, subject to the applicable legislation of the States concerned, as well as relevant international agreements and the obligations of the States concerned arising out of their participation in customs unions, enjoy exemption from import and export duties and taxes in respect of their personal and household effects as well as the equipment necessary to engage in the remunerated activity for which they were admitted to the State of employment:

(a) Upon departure from the State of origin or State of habitual residence;

(b) Upon initial admission to the State of employment;

(c) Upon final departure from the State of employment;

(d) Upon final return to the State of origin or State of habitual residence.

Article 47

1. Migrant workers shall have the right to transfer their earnings and savings, in particular those funds necessary for the support of their families, from the State of employment to their State of origin or any other State. Such transfers shall be made in conformity with procedures established by applicable legislation of the State concerned and in conformity with applicable international agreements.

2. States concerned shall take appropriate measures to facilitate such transfers.

Article 48

1. Without prejudice to applicable double taxation agreements, migrant workers and members of their families shall, in the matter of earnings in the State of employment:

(a) Not be liable to taxes, duties or charges of any description higher or more onerous than those imposed on nationals in similar circumstances;

(b) Be entitled to deductions or exemptions from taxes of any description and to any tax allowances applicable to nationals in similar circumstances, including tax allowances for dependent members of their families.

2. States Parties shall endeavour to adopt appropriate measures to avoid double taxation of the earnings and savings of migrant workers and members of their families.

Article 49

1. Where separate authorizations to reside and to engage in employment are required by national legislation, the States of employment shall issue to migrant workers authorization of residence for at least the same period of time as their authorization to engage in remunerated activity.

2. Migrant workers who in the State of employment are allowed freely to choose their remunerated activity shall neither be regarded as in an irregular situation nor shall they lose their authorization of residence by the mere fact of the termination of their remunerated activity prior to the expiration of their work permits or similar authorizations.

3. In order to allow migrant workers referred to in paragraph 2 of the present article sufficient time to find alternative remunerated activities, the authorization of residence shall not be withdrawn at least for a period corresponding to that during which they may be entitled to unemployment benefits.

Article 50

1. In the case of death of a migrant worker or dissolution of marriage, the State of employment shall favourably consider granting family members of that migrant worker residing in that State on the basis of family reunion an authorization to stay; the State of employment shall take into account the length of time they have already resided in that State.

2. Members of the family to whom such authorization is not granted shall be allowed before departure a reasonable period of time in order to enable them to settle their affairs in the State of employment.

3. The provisions of paragraphs 1 and 2 of the present article may not be interpreted as adversely affecting any right to stay and work otherwise granted to such family members by the legislation of the State of employment or by bilateral and multilateral treaties applicable to that State.

Article 51

Migrant workers who in the State of employment are not permitted freely to choose their remunerated activity shall neither be regarded as in an irregular situation nor shall they lose their authorization of residence by the mere fact of the termination of their remunerated activity prior to the expiration of their work permit, except where the authorization of residence is expressly dependent upon the specific remunerated activity for which they were admitted. Such migrant workers shall have the right to seek alternative employment, participation in public work schemes and retraining during the remaining period of their authorization to work, subject to such conditions and limitations as are specified in the authorization to work.

Article 52

1. Migrant workers in the State of employment shall have the right freely to choose their remunerated activity, subject to the following restrictions or conditions.

2. For any migrant worker a State of employment may:

(a) Restrict access to limited categories of employment, functions, services or activities where this is necessary in the interests of this State and provided for by national legislation;

(b) Restrict free choice of remunerated activity in accordance with its legislation concerning recognition of occupational qualifications acquired outside its territory. However, States Parties concerned shall endeavour to provide for recognition of such qualifications.

3. For migrant workers whose permission to work is limited in time, a State of employment may also:

(a) Make the right freely to choose their remunerated activities subject to the condition that the migrant worker has resided lawfully in its territory for the purpose of remunerated activity for a period of time prescribed in its national legislation that should not exceed two years;

(b) Limit access by a migrant worker to remunerated activities in pursuance of a policy of granting priority to its nationals or to persons who are assimilated to them for these purposes by virtue of legislation or bilateral or multilateral agreements. Any such limitation shall cease to apply to a migrant worker who has resided lawfully in its territory for the purpose of remunerated activity for a period of time prescribed in its national legislation that should not exceed five years.

4. States of employment shall prescribe the conditions under which a migrant worker who has been admitted to take up employment may be authorized to engage in work on his or her own account. Account shall be taken

of the period during which the worker has already been lawfully in the State of employment.

Article 53

1. Members of a migrant worker's family who have themselves an authorization of residence or admission that is without limit of time or is automatically renewable shall be permitted freely to choose their remunerated activity under the same conditions as are applicable to the said migrant worker in accordance with article 52 of the present Convention.

2. With respect to members of a migrant worker's family who are not permitted freely to choose their remunerated activity, States Parties shall consider favourably granting them priority in obtaining permission to engage in a remunerated activity over other workers who seek admission to the State of employment, subject to applicable bilateral and multilateral agreements.

Article 54

1. Without prejudice to the terms of their authorization of residence or their permission to work and the rights provided for in articles 25 and 27 of the present Convention, migrant workers shall enjoy equality of treatment with nationals of the State of employment in respect of:

(a) Protection against dismissal;

(b) Unemployment benefits;

(c) Access to public work schemes intended to combat unemployment;

(d) Access to alternative employment in the event of loss of work or termination of other remunerated activity, subject to article 52 of the present Convention.

2. If a migrant worker claims that the terms of his or her work contract have been violated by his or her employer, he or she shall have the right to address his or her case to the competent authorities of the State of employment, on terms provided for in article 18, paragraph 1, of the present Convention.

Article 55

Migrant workers who have been granted permission to engage in a remunerated activity, subject to the conditions attached to such permission, shall be entitled to equality of treatment with nationals of the State of employment in the exercise of that remunerated activity.

Article 56

1. Migrant workers and members of their families referred to in the present part of the Convention may not be expelled from a State of employment, except for reasons defined in the national legislation of that State, and subject to the safeguards established in part III.

2. Expulsion shall not be resorted to for the purpose of depriving a migrant worker or a member of his or her family of the rights arising out of the authorization of residence and the work permit.

3. In considering whether to expel a migrant worker or a member of his or her family, account should be taken of humanitarian considerations and of the length of time that the person concerned has already resided in the State of employment.

PART V

PROVISIONS APPLICABLE TO PARTICULAR CATEGORIES OF MIGRANT WORKERS AND MEMBERS OF THEIR FAMILIES

Article 57

The particular categories of migrant workers and members of their families specified in the present part of the Convention who are documented or in a regular situation shall enjoy the rights set forth in part III and, except as modified below, the rights set forth in part IV.

Article 58

1. Frontier workers, as defined in article 2, paragraph 2 (a), of the present Convention, shall be entitled to the rights provided for in part IV that can be applied to them by reason of their presence and work in the territory of the State of employment, taking into account that they do not have their habitual residence in that State.

2. States of employment shall consider favourably granting frontier workers the right freely to choose their remunerated activity after a specified period of time. The granting of that right shall not affect their status as frontier workers.

Article 59

1. Seasonal workers, as defined in article 2, paragraph 2 (b), of the present Convention, shall be entitled to the rights provided for in part IV that can be applied to them by reason of their presence and work in the territory of the State of employment and that are compatible with their status in that State as seasonal workers, taking into account the fact that they are present in that State for only part of the year.

2. The State of employment shall, subject to paragraph 1 of the present article, consider granting seasonal workers who have been employed in its territory for a significant period of time the possibility of taking up other remunerated activities and giving them priority over other workers who seek admission to that State, subject to applicable bilateral and multilateral agreements.

Article 60

Itinerant workers, as defined in article 2, paragraph 2 (e), of the present Convention, shall be entitled to the rights provided for in part IV that can be granted to them by reason of their presence and work in the territory of the State of employment and that are compatible with their status as itinerant workers in that State.

Article 61

1. Project-tied workers, as defined in article 2, paragraph 2 (f),of the present Convention, and members of their families shall be entitled to the rights provided for in part IV except the provisions of article 43, paragraph 1 (b) and (c), article 43, paragraph 1 (d), as it pertains to social housing schemes, article 45, paragraph 1 (b), and articles 52 to 55.

2. If a project-tied worker claims that the terms of his or her work contract have been violated by his or her employer, he or she shall have the right to address his or her case to the competent authorities of the State which has jurisdiction over that employer, on terms provided for in article 18, paragraph 1, of the present Convention.

3. Subject to bilateral or multilateral agreements in force for them, the States Parties concerned shall endeavour to enable project-tied workers to remain adequately protected by the social security systems of their States of origin or habitual residence during their engagement in the project. States Parties concerned shall take appropriate measures with the aim of avoiding any denial of rights or duplication of payments in this respect.

4. Without prejudice to the provisions of article 47 of the present Convention and to relevant bilateral or multilateral agreements, States Parties concerned shall permit payment of the earnings of project-tied workers in their State of origin or habitual residence.

Article 62

1. Specified-employment workers as defined in article 2, paragraph 2 (g), of the present Convention, shall be entitled to the rights provided for in part IV, except the provisions of article 43, paragraphs 1 (b) and (c), article 43, paragraph 1 (d), as it pertains to social housing schemes, article 52, and article 54, paragraph 1 (d).

2. Members of the families of specified-employment workers shall be entitled to the rights relating to family members of migrant workers provided for in part IV of the present Convention, except the provisions of article 53.

Article 63

1. Self-employed workers, as defined in article 2, paragraph 2 (h), of the present Convention, shall be entitled to the rights provided for in part IV with the exception of those rights which are exclusively applicable to workers having a contract of employment.

2. Without prejudice to articles 52 and 79 of the present Convention, the termination of the economic activity of the self-employed workers shall not in itself imply the withdrawal of the authorization for them or for the members of their families to stay or to engage in a remunerated activity in the State of employment except where the authorization of residence is expressly dependent upon the specific remunerated activity for which they were admitted.

PART VI

PROMOTION OF SOUND, EQUITABLE, HUMANE AND LAWFUL CONDITIONS IN CONNECTION WITH INTERNATIONAL MIGRATION OF WORKERS AND MEMBERS OF THEIR FAMILIES

Article 64

1. Without prejudice to article 79 of the present Convention, the States Parties concerned shall as appropriate consult and co-operate with a view to promoting sound, equitable and humane conditions in connection with international migration of workers and members of their families.

2. In this respect, due regard shall be paid not only to labour needs and resources, but also to the social, economic, cultural and other needs of migrant workers and members of their families involved, as well as to the consequences of such migration for the communities concerned.

Article 65

1. States Parties shall maintain appropriate services to deal with questions concerning international migration of workers and members of their families. Their functions shall include, *inter alia*:

(a) The formulation and implementation of policies regarding such migration;

(b) An exchange of information, consultation and co-operation with the competent authorities of other States Parties involved in such migration;

(c) The provision of appropriate information, particularly to employers, workers and their organizations on policies, laws and regulations relating to migration and employment, on agreements concluded with other States concerning migration and on other relevant matters;

(d) The provision of information and appropriate assistance to migrant workers and members of their families regarding requisite authorizations and formalities and arrangements for departure, travel, arrival, stay, remunerated activities, exit and return, as well as on conditions of work and life in the State of employment and on customs, currency, tax and other relevant laws and regulations.

2. States Parties shall facilitate as appropriate the provision of adequate consular and other services that are necessary to meet the social, cultural and other needs of migrant workers and members of their families.

Article 66

1. Subject to paragraph 2 of the present article, the right to undertake operations with a view to the recruitment of workers for employment in another State shall be restricted to:

(a) Public services or bodies of the State in which such operations take place;

(b) Public services or bodies of the State of employment on the basis of agreement between the States concerned;

(c) A body established by virtue of a bilateral or multilateral agreement.

2. Subject to any authorization, approval and supervision by the public authorities of the States Parties concerned as may be established pursuant to the legislation and practice of those States, agencies, prospective employers or persons acting on their behalf may also be permitted to undertake the said operations.

Article 67

1. States Parties concerned shall co-operate as appropriate in the adoption of measures regarding the orderly return of migrant workers and members of their families to the State of origin when they decide to return or their authorization of residence or employment expires or when they are in the State of employment in an irregular situation.

2. Concerning migrant workers and members of their families in a regular situation, States Parties concerned shall co-operate as appropriate, on terms agreed upon by those States, with a view to promoting adequate economic conditions for their resettlement and to facilitating their durable social and cultural reintegration in the State of origin.

Article 68

1. States Parties, including States of transit, shall collaborate with a view to preventing and eliminating illegal or clandestine movements and employment of migrant workers in an irregular situation. The measures to be taken to this end within the jurisdiction of each State concerned shall include:

(a) Appropriate measures against the dissemination of misleading information relating to emigration and immigration;

(b) Measures to detect and eradicate illegal or clandestine movements of migrant workers and members of their families and to impose effective sanctions on persons, groups or entities which organize, operate or assist in organizing or operating such movements;

(c) Measures to impose effective sanctions on persons, groups or entities which use violence, threats or intimidation against migrant workers or members of their families in an irregular situation.

2. States of employment shall take all adequate and effective measures to eliminate employment in their territory of migrant workers in an irregular situation, including, whenever appropriate, sanctions on employers of such workers. The rights of migrant workers *vis-à-vis* their employer arising from employment shall not be impaired by these measures.

Article 69

1. States Parties shall, when there are migrant workers and members of their families within their territory in an irregular situation, take appropriate measures to ensure that such a situation does not persist.

2. Whenever States Parties concerned consider the possibility of regularizing the situation of such persons in accordance with applicable national legislation and bilateral or multilateral agreements, appropriate account shall be taken of the circumstances of their entry, the duration of their stay in the States of employment and other relevant considerations, in particular those relating to their family situation.

Article 70

States Parties shall take measures not less favourable than those applied to nationals to ensure that working and living conditions of migrant workers and members of their families in a regular situation are in keeping with the standards of fitness, safety, health and principles of human dignity.

Article 71

1. States Parties shall facilitate, whenever necessary, the repatriation to the State of origin of the bodies of deceased migrant workers or members of their families.

2. As regards compensation matters relating to the death of a migrant worker or a member of his or her family, States Parties shall, as appropriate, provide assistance to the persons concerned with a view to the prompt settlement of such matters. Settlement of these matters shall be carried out on the basis of applicable national law in accordance with the provisions of the present Convention and any relevant bilateral or multilateral agreements.

PART VII

APPLICATION OF THE CONVENTION

Article 72

1. (a) For the purpose of reviewing the application of the present Convention, there shall be established a Committee on the Protection of the Rights of All Migrant Workers and Members of Their Families (hereinafter referred to as "the Committee");

(b) The Committee shall consist, at the time of entry into force of the present Convention, of ten and, after the entry into force of the Convention for the forty-first State Party, of fourteen experts of high moral standing, impartiality and recognized competence in the field covered by the Convention.

2. (a) Members of the Committee shall be elected by secret ballot by the States Parties from a list of persons nominated by the States Parties, due consideration being given to equitable geographical distribution, including both States of origin and States of employment, and to the representation of the principal legal systems. Each State Party may nominate one person from among its own nationals;

(b) Members shall be elected and shall serve in their personal capacity.

3. The initial election shall be held no later than six months after the date of the entry into force of the present Convention and subsequent elections every second year. At least four months before the date of each election, the Secretary-General of the United Nations shall address a letter to all States Parties inviting them to submit their nominations within two months. The Secretary-General shall prepare a list in alphabetical order of all persons thus nominated, indicating the States Parties that have nominated them, and shall submit it to the States Parties not later than one month before the date of the corresponding election, together with the curricula vitae of the persons thus nominated.

4. Elections of members of the Committee shall be held at a meeting of States Parties convened by the Secretary-General at United Nations Headquarters. At that meeting, for which two thirds of the States Parties shall constitute a quorum, the persons elected to the Committee shall be those nominees who obtain the largest number of votes and an absolute majority of the votes of the States Parties present and voting.

5. (a) The members of the Committee shall serve for a term of four years. However, the terms of five of the members elected in the first election shall expire at the end of two years; immediately after the first election, the names of these five members shall be chosen by lot by the Chairman of the meeting of States Parties;

(b) The election of the four additional members of the Committee shall be held in accordance with the provisions of paragraphs 2, 3 and 4 of the present article, following the entry into force of the Convention for the forty-first State Party. The term of two of the additional members elected on this occasion shall expire at the end of two years; the names of these members shall be chosen by lot by the Chairman of the meeting of States Parties;

(c) The members of the Committee shall be eligible for re-election if renominated.

6. If a member of the Committee dies or resigns or declares that for any other cause he or she can no longer perform the duties of the Committee, the State Party that nominated the expert shall appoint another expert from among its own nationals for the remaining part of the term. The new appointment is subject to the approval of the Committee.

7. The Secretary-General of the United Nations shall provide the necessary staff and facilities for the effective performance of the functions of the Committee.

8. The members of the Committee shall receive emoluments from United Nations resources on such terms and conditions as the General Assembly may decide.

9. The members of the Committee shall be entitled to the facilities, privileges and immunities of experts on mission for the United Nations as laid down in the relevant sections of the Convention on the Privileges and Immunities of the United Nations.

Article 73

1. States Parties undertake to submit to the Secretary-General of the United Nations for consideration by the Committee a report on the legislative, judicial, administrative and other measures they have taken to give effect to the provisions of the present Convention:

(a) Within one year after the entry into force of the Convention for the State Party concerned;

(b) Thereafter every five years and whenever the Committee so requests.

2. Reports prepared under the present article shall also indicate factors and difficulties, if any, affecting the implementation of the Convention and shall include information on the characteristics of migration flows in which the State Party concerned is involved.

3. The Committee shall decide any further guidelines applicable to the content of the reports.

4. States Parties shall make their reports widely available to the public in their own countries.

Article 74

1. The Committee shall examine the reports submitted by each State Party and shall transmit such com-

ments as it may consider appropriate to the State Party concerned. This State Party may submit to the Committee observations on any comment made by the Committee in accordance with the present article. The Committee may request supplementary information from States Parties when considering these reports.

2. The Secretary-General of the United Nations shall, in due time before the opening of each regular session of the Committee, transmit to the Director-General of the International Labour Office copies of the reports submitted by States Parties concerned and information relevant to the consideration of these reports, in order to enable the Office to assist the Committee with the expertise the Office may provide regarding those matters dealt with by the present Convention that fall within the sphere of competence of the International Labour Organisation. The Committee shall consider in its deliberations such comments and materials as the Office may provide.

3. The Secretary-General of the United Nations may also, after consultation with the Committee, transmit to other specialized agencies as well as to intergovernmental organizations, copies of such parts of these reports as may fall within their competence.

4. The Committee may invite the specialized agencies and organs of the United Nations, as well as intergovernmental organizations and other concerned bodies to submit, for consideration by the Committee, written information on such matters dealt with in the present Convention as fall within the scope of their activities.

5. The International Labour Office shall be invited by the Committee to appoint representatives to participate, in a consultative capacity, in the meetings of the Committee.

6. The Committee may invite representatives of other specialized agencies and organs of the United Nations, as well as of intergovernmental organizations, to be present and to be heard in its meetings whenever matters falling within their field of competence are considered.

7. The Committee shall present an annual report to the General Assembly of the United Nations on the implementation of the present Convention, containing its own considerations and recommendations, based, in particular, on the examination of the reports and any observations presented by States Parties.

8. The Secretary-General of the United Nations shall transmit the annual reports of the Committee to the States Parties to the present Convention, the Economic and Social Council, the Commission on Human Rights of the United Nations, the Director-General of the International Labour Office and other relevant organizations.

Article 75

1. The Committee shall adopt its own rules of procedure.

2. The Committee shall elect its officers for a term of two years.

3. The Committee shall normally meet annually.

4. The meetings of the Committee shall normally be held at United Nations Headquarters.

Article 76

1. A State Party to the present Convention may at any time declare under this article that it recognizes the competence of the Committee to receive and consider communications to the effect that a State Party claims that another State Party is not fulfilling its obligations under the present Convention. Communications under this article may be received and considered only if submitted by a State Party that has made a declaration recognizing in regard to itself the competence of the Committee. No communication shall be received by the Committee if it concerns a State Party which has not made such a declaration. Communications received under this article shall be dealt with in accordance with the following procedure:

(a) If a State Party to the present Convention considers that another State Party is not fulfilling its obligations under the present Convention, it may, by written communication, bring the matter to the attention of that State Party. The State Party may also inform the Committee of the matter. Within three months after the receipt of the communication the receiving State shall afford the State that sent the communication an explanation, or any other statement in writing clarifying the matter which should include, to the extent possible and pertinent, reference to domestic procedures and remedies taken, pending or available in the matter;

(b) If the matter is not adjusted to the satisfaction of both States Parties concerned within six months after the receipt by the receiving State of the initial communication, either State shall have the right to refer the matter to the Committee, by notice given to the Committee and to the other State;

(c) The Committee shall deal with a matter referred to it only after it has ascertained that all available domestic remedies have been invoked and exhausted in the matter, in conformity with the generally recognized principles of international law. This shall not be the rule where, in the view of the Committee, the application of the remedies is unreasonably prolonged;

(d) Subject to the provisions of subparagraph (c) of the present paragraph, the Committee shall make available its good offices to the States Parties concerned with a view to a friendly solution of the matter on the basis of the respect for the obligations set forth in the present Convention;

(e) The Committee shall hold closed meetings when examining communications under the present article;

(f) In any matter referred to it in accordance with subparagraph (b) of the present paragraph, the Committee may call upon the States Parties concerned, referred to in subparagraph (b), to supply any relevant information;

(g) The States Parties concerned, referred to in subparagraph (b) of the present paragraph, shall have the right to be represented when the matter is being considered by the Committee and to make submissions orally and/or in writing;

(h) The Committee shall, within twelve months after the date of receipt of notice under subparagraph (b) of the present paragraph, submit a report, as follows:

(i) If a solution within the terms of subparagraph (d) of the present paragraph is reached, the Committee shall confine its report to a brief statement of the facts and of the solution reached;

(ii) If a solution within the terms of subparagraph (d) is not reached, the Committee shall, in its report, set forth the relevant facts concerning the issue between the States Parties concerned. The written submissions and record of the oral submissions made by the States Parties concerned shall be attached to the report. The Committee may also communicate only to the States Parties concerned any views that it may consider relevant to the issue between them.

In every matter, the report shall be communicated to the States Parties concerned.

2. The provisions of the present article shall come into force when ten States Parties to the present Convention have made a declaration under paragraph 1 of the present article. Such declarations shall be deposited by the States Parties with the Secretary-General of the United Nations, who shall transmit copies thereof to the other States Parties. A declaration may be withdrawn at any time by notification to the Secretary-General. Such a withdrawal shall not prejudice the consideration of any matter that is the subject of a communication already transmitted under the present article; no further communication by any State Party shall be received under the present article after the notification of withdrawal of the declaration has been received by the Secretary-General, unless the State Party concerned has made a new declaration.

Article 77

1. A State Party to the present Convention may at any time declare under the present article that it recognizes the competence of the Committee to receive and consider communications from or on behalf of individuals subject to its jurisdiction who claim that their individual rights as established by the present Convention have been violated by that State Party. No communication shall be received by the Committee if it concerns a State Party that has not made such a declaration.

2. The Committee shall consider inadmissible any communication under the present article which is anonymous or which it considers to be an abuse of the right of submission of such communications or to be incompatible with the provisions of the present Convention.

3. The Committee shall not consider any communication from an individual under the present article unless it has ascertained that:

(a) The same matter has not been, and is not being, examined under another procedure of international investigation or settlement;

(b) The individual has exhausted all available domestic remedies; this shall not be the rule where, in the view of the Committee, the application of the remedies is unreasonably prolonged or is unlikely to bring effective relief to that individual.

4. Subject to the provisions of paragraph 2 of the present article, the Committee shall bring any communications submitted to it under this article to the attention of the State Party to the present Convention that has made a declaration under paragraph 1 and is alleged to be violating any provisions of the Convention. Within six months, the receiving State shall submit to the Committee written explanations or statements clarifying the matter and the remedy, if any, that may have been taken by that State.

5. The Committee shall consider communications received under the present article in the light of all information made available to it by or on behalf of the individual and by the State Party concerned.

6. The Committee shall hold closed meetings when examining communications under the present article.

7. The Committee shall forward its views to the State Party concerned and to the individual.

8. The provisions of the present article shall come into force when ten States Parties to the present Convention have made declarations under paragraph 1 of the present article. Such declarations shall be deposited by the States Parties with the Secretary-General of the United Nations, who shall transmit copies thereof to the other States Parties. A declaration may be withdrawn at any time by notification to the Secretary-General. Such a withdrawal shall not prejudice the consideration of any

matter that is the subject of a communication already transmitted under the present article; no further communication by or on behalf of an individual shall be received under the present article after the notification of withdrawal of the declaration has been received by the Secretary-General, unless the State Party has made a new declaration.

Article 78

The provisions of article 76 of the present Convention shall be applied without prejudice to any procedures for settling disputes or complaints in the field covered by the present Convention laid down in the constituent instruments of, or in conventions adopted by, the United Nations and the specialized agencies and shall not prevent the States Parties from having recourse to any procedures for settling a dispute in accordance with international agreements in force between them.

PART VIII

GENERAL PROVISIONS

Article 79

Nothing in the present Convention shall affect the right of each State Party to establish the criteria governing admission of migrant workers and members of their families. Concerning other matters related to their legal situation and treatment as migrant workers and members of their families, States Parties shall be subject to the limitations set forth in the present Convention.

Article 80

Nothing in the present Convention shall be interpreted as impairing the provisions of the Charter of the United Nations and of the constitutions of the specialized agencies which define the respective responsibilities of the various organs of the United Nations and of the specialized agencies in regard to the matters dealt with in the present Convention.

Article 81

1. Nothing in the present Convention shall affect more favourable rights or freedoms granted to migrant workers and members of their families by virtue of:

(a) The law or practice of a State Party; or

(b) Any bilateral or multilateral treaty in force for the State Party concerned.

2. Nothing in the present Convention may be interpreted as implying for any State, group or person any right to engage in any activity or perform any act that would impair any of the rights and freedoms as set forth in the present Convention.

Article 82

The rights of migrant workers and members of their families provided for in the present Convention may not be renounced. It shall not be permissible to exert any form of pressure upon migrant workers and members of their families with a view to their relinquishing or foregoing any of the said rights. It shall not be possible to derogate by contract from rights recognized in the present Convention. States Parties shall take appropriate measures to ensure that these principles are respected.

Article 83

Each State Party to the present Convention undertakes:

(a) To ensure that any person whose rights or freedoms as herein recognized are violated shall have an effective remedy, notwithstanding that the violation has been committed by persons acting in an official capacity;

(b) To ensure that any person seeking such a remedy shall have his or her claim reviewed and decided by competent judicial, administrative or legislative authorities, or by any other competent authority provided for by the legal system of the State, and to develop the possibilities of judicial remedy;

(c) To ensure that the competent authorities shall enforce such remedies when granted.

Article 84

Each State Party undertakes to adopt the legislative and other measures that are necessary to implement the provisions of the present Convention.

PART IX

FINAL PROVISIONS

Article 85

The Secretary-General of the United Nations is designated as the depositary of the present Convention.

Article 86

1. The present Convention shall be open for signature by all States. It is subject to ratification.

2. The present Convention shall be open to accession by any State.

3. Instruments of ratification or accession shall be deposited with the Secretary-General of the United Nations.

Article 87

1. The present Convention shall enter into force on the first day of the month following a period of three

months after the date of the deposit of the twentieth instrument of ratification or accession.

2. For each State ratifying or acceding to the present Convention after its entry into force, the Convention shall enter into force on the first day of the month following a period of three months after the date of the deposit of its own instrument of ratification or accession.

Article 88

A State ratifying or acceding to the present Convention may not exclude the application of any part of it, or, without prejudice to article 3, exclude any particular category of migrant workers from its application.

Article 89

1. Any State Party may denounce the present Convention, not earlier than five years after the Convention has entered into force for the State concerned, by means of a notification in writing addressed to the Secretary-General of the United Nations.

2. Such denunciation shall become effective on the first day of the month following the expiration of a period of twelve months after the date of the receipt of the notification by the Secretary-General of the United Nations.

3. Such a denunciation shall not have the effect of releasing the State Party from its obligations under the present Convention in regard to any act or omission which occurs prior to the date at which the denunciation becomes effective, nor shall denunciation prejudice in any way the continued consideration of any matter which is already under consideration by the Committee prior to the date at which the denunciation becomes effective.

4. Following the date at which the denunciation of a State Party becomes effective, the Committee shall not commence consideration of any new matter regarding that State.

Article 90

1. After five years from the entry into force of the Convention a request for the revision of the Convention may be made at any time by any State Party by means of a notification in writing addressed to the Secretary-General of the United Nations. The Secretary-General shall thereupon communicate any proposed amendments to the States Parties with a request that they notify him whether they favour a conference of States Parties for the purpose of considering and voting upon the proposals. In the event that within four months from the date of such communication at least one third of the States Parties favours such a conference, the Secretary-General shall convene the conference under the auspices of the United Nations. Any amendment adopted by a majority of the States Parties present and voting shall be submitted to the General Assembly for approval.

2. Amendments shall come into force when they have been approved by the General Assembly of the United Nations and accepted by a two-thirds majority of the States Parties in accordance with their respective constitutional processes.

3. When amendments come into force, they shall be binding on those States Parties that have accepted them, other States Parties still being bound by the provisions of the present Convention and any earlier amendment that they have accepted.

Article 91

1. The Secretary-General of the United Nations shall receive and circulate to all States the text of reservations made by States at the time of signature, ratification or accession.

2. A reservation incompatible with the object and purpose of the present Convention shall not be permitted.

3. Reservations may be withdrawn at any time by notification to this effect addressed to the Secretary-General of the United Nations, who shall then inform all States thereof. Such notification shall take effect on the date on which it is received.

Article 92

1. Any dispute between two or more States Parties concerning the interpretation or application of the present Convention that is not settled by negotiation shall, at the request of one of them, be submitted to arbitration. If within six months from the date of the request for arbitration the Parties are unable to agree on the organization of the arbitration, any one of those Parties may refer the dispute to the International Court of Justice by request in conformity with the Statute of the Court.

2. Each State Party may at the time of signature or ratification of the present Convention or accession thereto declare that it does not consider itself bound by paragraph 1 of the present article. The other States Parties shall not be bound by that paragraph with respect to any State Party that has made such a declaration.

3. Any State Party that has made a declaration in accordance with paragraph 2 of the present article may at any time withdraw that declaration by notification to the Secretary-General of the United Nations.

Article 93

1. The present Convention, of which the Arabic, Chinese, English, French, Russian and Spanish texts are equally authentic, shall be deposited with the Secretary-General of the United Nations.

2. The Secretary-General of the United Nations shall transmit certified copies of the present Convention to all States.

IN WITNESS WHEREOF the undersigned plenipotentiaries, being duly authorized thereto by their respective Governments, have signed the present Convention.

Document 72

Security Council resolution establishing the United Nations Observer Mission in El Salvador (ONUSAL)

S/RES/693 (1991), 20 May 1991

The Security Council,

Recalling its resolution 637 (1989) of 27 July 1989, in which it lent its full support to the Secretary-General for the continuation of his mission of good offices in Central America,

Recalling also the Geneva Agreement of 4 April 1990 1/ and the Caracas Agenda of 21 May 1990 2/ concluded between the Government of El Salvador and the Frente Farabundo Martí para la Liberación Nacional,

Deeply concerned at the persistence of and the increase in the climate of violence in El Salvador, which seriously affects the civilian population, and thus stressing the importance of the full implementation of the Agreement on Human Rights signed by the two parties at San José on 26 July 1990, 3/

Welcoming the Mexico Agreements between the two parties of 27 April 1991, 4/

Having considered the reports of the Secretary-General of 21 December 1990 5/ and 16 April and 20 May 1991, 6/

Commending the Secretary-General and his Personal Representative for Central America for their efforts at good offices, and expressing its full support for their continuing efforts to facilitate a peaceful settlement to the conflict in El Salvador,

Underlining the great importance that it attaches to the exercise of moderation and restraint by both sides to ensure the security of all United Nations-employed personnel as well as to the adoption by them of all other appropriate and necessary measures to facilitate the negotiations leading to the achievement of the objectives set forth in the Geneva and other above-mentioned agreements as soon as possible, including their full cooperation with the Secretary-General and his Personal Representative to this end,

Recognizing the right of the parties to determine their own negotiating process,

Calling upon both parties to pursue the current negotiations urgently and with flexibility, in a concentrated format on the items agreed upon in the Caracas Agenda, in order to reach, as a matter of priority, a political agreement on the armed forces and the accords necessary for the cessation of the armed confrontation and to achieve as soon as possible thereafter a process which will lead to the establishment of the necessary guarantees and conditions for reintegrating the members of the Frente Farabundo Martí para la Liberación Nacional within a framework of full legality into the civil, institutional and political life of the country,

Expressing its conviction that a peaceful settlement in El Salvador will contribute to a successful outcome in the Central American peace process,

1. *Approves* the report of the Secretary-General of 16 April and 20 May 1991; 6/

2. *Decides* to establish, under its authority and based on the Secretary-General's report referred to in paragraph 1, a United Nations Observer Mission in El Salvador to monitor all agreements concluded between the two parties, whose initial mandate in its first phase as an integrated peace-keeping operation will be to verify the compliance by the parties with the Agreement on Human Rights signed at San José on 26 July 1990, 3/ and also decides that the subsequent tasks or phases of the Mission will be subject to approval by the Council;

3. *Also decides* that the United Nations Observer Mission in El Salvador will be established for an initial period of twelve months;

1/ *Official Records of the Security Council, Forty-sixth Year, Supplement for April, May and June 1990*, document S/21931, annex I.
2/ Ibid., annex II.

3/ *Official Records of the Security Council, Forty-fifth Year, Supplement for July, August and September 1990*, document S/21541, annex.

4/ Ibid., *Forty-sixth Year, Supplement for April, May and June 1991*, document S/23130.

5/ Ibid., *Forty-fifth Year, Supplement for October, November and December 1990*, document S/22031.

6/ Ibid., *Forty-sixth Year, Supplement for April, May and June 1991*, document S/22494 and Corr.1 and Add.1.

4. *Requests* the Secretary-General to take the necessary measures to establish the first phase of the Mission as described in paragraphs 2 and 3;

5. *Calls upon* both parties, as agreed by them, to pursue a continuous process of negotiations in order to reach at the earliest possible date the objectives set forth in the Mexico Agreements of 27 April 1991 4/ and all other objectives contained in the Geneva Agreement of 4 April 1990, 1/ and to this end to cooperate fully with the Secretary-General and his Personal Representative in their efforts;

6. *Requests* the Secretary-General to keep the Security Council fully informed on the implementation of the present resolution.

Document 73

Security Council resolution on the deployment of the United Nations Protection Force (UNPROFOR)

S/RES/749 (1992), 7 April 1992

The Security Council,

Reaffirming its resolutions 713 (1991) of 25 September 1991, 721 (1991) of 27 November 1991, 724 (1991) of 15 December 1991, 727 (1992) of 8 January 1992, 740 (1992) of 7 February 1992 and 743 (1992) of 21 February 1992,

Taking note of the report of the Secretary-General of 2 April 1992 1/ submitted pursuant to Security Council resolution 743 (1992),

Recalling its primary responsibility under the Charter of the United Nations for the maintenance of international peace and security,

Welcoming the progress made towards the establishment of the United Nations Protection Force and the continuing contacts by the Secretary-General with all parties and others concerned to stabilize the cease-fire,

Expressing its concern about reports on the daily violations of the cease-fire and the continuing tension in a number of regions even after the arrival of advance elements of the Force,

1. *Approves* the report of the Secretary-General of 2 April 1992 1/ submitted pursuant to Security Council resolution 743 (1992);

2. *Decides* to authorize the earliest possible full deployment of the United Nations Protection Force;

3. *Urges* all parties and others concerned to make further efforts to maximize their contributions towards offsetting the costs of the Force, in order to help secure the most efficient and cost-effective operation possible;

4. *Also urges* all parties and others concerned to take all action necessary to ensure complete freedom of aerial movement for the Force;

5. *Calls upon* all parties and others concerned not to resort to violence, particularly in any area where the Force is to be based or deployed;

6. *Appeals* to all parties and others concerned in Bosnia and Herzegovina to cooperate with the efforts of the European Community to bring about a cease-fire and a negotiated political solution.

1/ See *Official Records of the Security Council, Forty-seventh Year, Supplement for April, May and June* 1992, document S/23777.

Document 74

Security Council resolution demanding that the parties to the conflict create the conditions for unimpeded delivery of humanitarian supplies to Bosnia and Herzegovina

S/RES/757 (1992), 30 May 1992

The Security Council,

Reaffirming its resolutions 713 (1991) of 25 September 1991, 721 (1991) of 27 November 1991, 724 (1991) of 15 December 1991, 727 (1992) of 8 January 1992, 740 (1992) of 7 February 1992, 743 (1992) of 21 February 1992, 749 (1992) of 7 April 1992 and 752 (1992) of 15 May 1992,

Noting that in the very complex context of events in

the former Socialist Federal Republic of Yugoslavia all parties bear some responsibility for the situation,

Reaffirming its support for the Conference on Yugoslavia, including the efforts undertaken by the European Community in the framework of the discussions on constitutional arrangements for Bosnia and Herzegovina, and recalling that no territorial gains or changes brought about by violence are acceptable and that the borders of Bosnia and Herzegovina are inviolable,

Deploring the fact that the demands in resolution 752 (1992) have not been complied with, including its demands that:

- All parties and others concerned in Bosnia and Herzegovina stop the fighting immediately,
- All forms of interference from outside Bosnia and Herzegovina cease immediately,
- Bosnia and Herzegovina's neighbours take swift action to end all interference and respect the territorial integrity of Bosnia and Herzegovina,
- Action be taken as regards units of the Yugoslav People's Army in Bosnia and Herzegovina, including the disbanding and disarming with weapons placed under effective international monitoring of any units that are neither withdrawn nor placed under the authority of the Government of Bosnia and Herzegovina,
- All irregular forces in Bosnia and Herzegovina be disbanded and disarmed,

Deploring also that its call for the immediate cessation of forcible expulsions and attempts to change the ethnic composition of the population has not been heeded, and reaffirming in this context the need for the effective protection of human rights and fundamental freedoms, including those of ethnic minorities,

Dismayed that conditions have not yet been established for the effective and unhindered delivery of humanitarian assistance, including safe and secure access to and from Sarajevo and other airports in Bosnia and Herzegovina,

Deeply concerned that those United Nations Protection Force personnel remaining in Sarajevo have been subjected to deliberate mortar and small-arms fire, and that the United Nations Military Observers deployed in the Mostar region have had to be withdrawn,

Deeply concerned also at developments in Croatia, including persistent cease-fire violations and the continued expulsion of non-Serb civilians, and at the obstruction of and lack of cooperation with the Force in other parts of Croatia,

Deploring the tragic incident on 18 May 1992 which caused the death of a member of the International Committee of the Red Cross team in Bosnia and Herzegovina,

Noting that the claim by the Federal Republic of Yugoslavia (Serbia and Montenegro) to continue automatically the membership of the former Socialist Federal Republic of Yugoslavia in the United Nations has not been generally accepted,

Expressing its appreciation for the report of the Secretary-General of 26 May 1992 1/ submitted pursuant to Security Council resolution 752 (1992),

Recalling its primary responsibility under the Charter of the United Nations for the maintenance of international peace and security,

Recalling also the provisions of Chapter VIII of the Charter, and the continuing role that the European Community is playing in working for a peaceful solution in Bosnia and Herzegovina, as well as in other republics of the former Socialist Federal Republic of Yugoslavia,

Recalling further its decision in resolution 752 (1992) to consider further steps to achieve a peaceful solution in conformity with its relevant resolutions, and affirming its determination to take measures against any party or parties which fail to fulfil the requirements of resolution 752 (1992) and its other relevant resolutions,

Determined in this context to adopt certain measures with the sole objective of achieving a peaceful solution and encouraging the efforts undertaken by the European Community and its member States,

Recalling the right of States, under Article 50 of the Charter, to consult the Council where they find themselves confronted with special economic problems arising from the carrying out of preventive or enforcement measures,

Determining that the situation in Bosnia and Herzegovina and in other parts of the former Socialist Federal Republic of Yugoslavia constitutes a threat to international peace and security,

Acting under Chapter VII of the Charter,

1. *Condemns* the failure of the authorities in the Federal Republic of Yugoslavia (Serbia and Montenegro), including the Yugoslav People's Army, to take effective measures to fulfil the requirements of resolution 752 (1992);

2. *Demands* that any elements of the Croatian Army still present in Bosnia and Herzegovina act in accordance with paragraph 4 of resolution 752 (1992) without further delay;

3. *Decides* that all States shall adopt the measures set out below, which shall apply until the Council decides that the authorities in the Federal Republic of Yugoslavia (Serbia and Montenegro), including the Yugoslav People's Army, have taken effective measures to fulfil the requirements of resolution 752 (1992);

1/ *Official Records of the Security Council, Forty-seventh Year, Supplement for April, May and June 1992*, document S/24000.

4. *Decides also* that all States shall prevent:

(*a*) The import into their territories of all commodities and products originating in the Federal Republic of Yugoslavia (Serbia and Montenegro) exported therefrom after the date of the present resolution;

(*b*) Any activities by their nationals or in their territories which would promote or are calculated to promote the export or trans-shipment of any commodities or products originating in the Federal Republic of Yugoslavia (Serbia and Montenegro); and any dealings by their nationals or their flag vessels or aircraft or in their territories in any commodities or products originating in the Federal Republic of Yugoslavia (Serbia and Montenegro) and exported therefrom after the date of the present resolution, including in particular any transfer of funds to the Federal Republic of Yugoslavia (Serbia and Montenegro) for the purposes of such activities or dealings;

(*c*) The sale or supply by their nationals or from their territories or using their flag vessels or aircraft of any commodities or products, whether or not originating in their territories—but not including supplies intended strictly for medical purposes and foodstuffs notified to the Security Council Committee established pursuant to resolution 724 (1991) on Yugoslavia—to any person or body in the Federal Republic of Yugoslavia (Serbia and Montenegro) or to any person or body for the purposes of any business carried on in or operated from the Federal Republic of Yugoslavia (Serbia and Montenegro), and any activities by their nationals or in their territories which promote or are calculated to promote such sale or supply of such commodities or products;

5. *Decides further* that no State shall make available to the authorities in the Federal Republic of Yugoslavia (Serbia and Montenegro) or to any commercial, industrial or public utility undertaking in the Federal Republic of Yugoslavia (Serbia and Montenegro), any funds or any other financial or economic resources and shall prevent their nationals and any persons within their territories from removing from their territories or otherwise making available to those authorities or to any such undertaking any such funds or resources and from remitting any other funds to persons or bodies within the Federal Republic of Yugoslavia (Serbia and Montenegro), except payments exclusively for strictly medical or humanitarian purposes and foodstuffs;

6. *Decides* that the prohibitions in paragraphs 4 and 5 shall not apply to the trans-shipment through the Federal Republic of Yugoslavia (Serbia and Montenegro) of commodities and products originating outside the Federal Republic of Yugoslavia (Serbia and Montenegro) and temporarily present in the territory of the Federal Republic of Yugoslavia (Serbia and Montenegro) only for the purpose of such trans-shipment, in accordance with guidelines approved by the Security Council Committee established by resolution 724 (1991);

7. *Decides* that all States shall:

(*a*) Deny permission to any aircraft to take off from, land in or overfly their territory if it is destined to land in or has taken off from the territory of the Federal Republic of Yugoslavia (Serbia and Montenegro), unless the particular flight has been approved, for humanitarian or other purposes consistent with the relevant resolutions of the Council, by the Security Council Committee established by resolution 724 (1991);

(*b*) Prohibit, by their nationals or from their territory, the provision of engineering and maintenance servicing of aircraft registered in the Federal Republic of Yugoslavia (Serbia and Montenegro) or operated by or on behalf of entities in the Federal Republic of Yugoslavia (Serbia and Montenegro) or components for such aircraft, the certification of airworthiness for such aircraft, and the payment of new claims against existing insurance contracts and the provision of new direct insurance for such aircraft;

8. *Decides also* that all States shall:

(*a*) Reduce the level of the staff at diplomatic missions and consular posts of the Federal Republic of Yugoslavia (Serbia and Montenegro);

(*b*) Take the necessary steps to prevent the participation in sporting events on their territory of persons or groups representing the Federal Republic of Yugoslavia (Serbia and Montenegro);

(*c*) Suspend scientific and technical cooperation and cultural exchanges and visits involving persons or groups officially sponsored by or representing the Federal Republic of Yugoslavia (Serbia and Montenegro);

9. *Decides further* that all States, and the authorities in the Federal Republic of Yugoslavia (Serbia and Montenegro), shall take the necessary measures to ensure that no claim shall lie at the instance of the authorities in the Federal Republic of Yugoslavia (Serbia and Montenegro), or of any person or body in the Federal Republic of Yugoslavia (Serbia and Montenegro), or of any person claiming through or for the benefit of any such person or body, in connection with any contract or other transaction where its performance was affected by reason of the measures imposed by the present resolution and related resolutions;

10. *Decides* that the measures imposed by the present resolution shall not apply to activities related to the United Nations Protection Force, to the Conference on Yugoslavia or to the European Community Monitoring Mission, and that States, parties and others concerned shall cooperate fully with the Force, the Conference and the Mission and respect fully their freedom of movement and the safety of their personnel;

11. *Calls upon* all States, including States not members of the United Nations, and all international organizations, to act strictly in accordance with the provisions of the present resolution, notwithstanding the existence of any rights or obligations conferred or imposed by any international agreement or any contract entered into or any licence or permit granted prior to the date of the present resolution;

12. *Requests* all States to report to the Secretary-General by 22 June 1992 on the measures they have instituted for meeting the obligations set out in paragraphs 4 to 9;

13. *Decides* that the Security Council Committee established by resolution 724 (1991) shall undertake the following tasks additional to those in respect of the arms embargo established by resolutions 713 (1991) and 727 (1992):

(*a*) To examine the reports submitted pursuant to paragraph 12 above;

(*b*) To seek from all States further information regarding the action taken by them concerning the effective implementation of the measures imposed by paragraphs 4 to 9;

(*c*) To consider any information brought to its attention by States concerning violations of the measures imposed by paragraphs 4 to 9 and, in that context, to make recommendations to the Council on ways to increase their effectiveness;

(*d*) To recommend appropriate measures in response to violations of the measures imposed by paragraphs 4 to 9 and to provide information on a regular basis to the Secretary-General for general distribution to Member States;

(*e*) To consider and approve the guidelines referred to in paragraph 6 above;

(*f*) To consider and decide upon expeditiously any applications for the approval of flights for humanitarian or other purposes consistent with the relevant resolutions of the Council in accordance with paragraph 7 above;

14. *Calls upon* all States to cooperate fully with the Security Council Committee established by Security Council resolution 724 (1991) in the fulfilment of its tasks, including supplying such information as may be sought by the Committee in pursuance of the present resolution;

15. *Requests* the Secretary-General to report to the Security Council, not later than 15 June 1992 and earlier if he considers it appropriate, on the implementation of resolution 752 (1992) by all parties and others concerned;

16. *Decides* to keep under continuous review the measures imposed by paragraphs 4 to 9 with a view to considering whether such measures might be suspended or terminated following compliance with the requirements of resolution 752 (1992);

17. *Demands* that all parties and others concerned create immediately the necessary conditions for unimpeded delivery of humanitarian supplies to Sarajevo and other destinations in Bosnia and Herzegovina, including the establishment of a security zone encompassing Sarajevo and its airport and respecting the agreements signed at Geneva on 22 May 1992;

18. *Requests* the Secretary-General to continue to use his good offices in order to achieve the objectives contained in paragraph 17 above, and invites him to keep under continuous review any further measures that may become necessary to ensure unimpeded delivery of humanitarian supplies;

19. *Urges* all States to respond to the Revised Joint Appeal for humanitarian assistance of early May 1992 issued by the United Nations High Commissioner for Refugees, the United Nations Children's Fund and the World Health Organization;

20. *Reiterates* the call in paragraph 2 of resolution 752 (1992) that all parties continue their efforts in the framework of the Conference on Yugoslavia and that the three communities in Bosnia and Herzegovina resume their discussions on constitutional arrangements for Bosnia and Herzegovina;

21. *Decides* to remain actively seized of the matter and to consider immediately, whenever necessary, further steps to achieve a peaceful solution in conformity with its relevant resolutions.

Document 75

Security Council resolution approving the report of the Secretary-General recommending the enlargement of the mandate of UNPROFOR

S/RES/776 (1992), 14 September 1992

The Security Council,

Reaffirming its resolution 743 (1992) of 21 February 1992 and all subsequent resolutions relating to the United Nations Protection Force,

Expressing its full support for the Statement of Principles adopted and other agreements reached at the London stage of the International Conference on the former Yugoslavia, held on 26 and 27 August 1992, including the agreement of the parties to the conflict to collaborate fully in the delivery of humanitarian relief by road throughout Bosnia and Herzegovina,

Having examined the report of the Secretary-General of 10 September 1992 on the situation in Bosnia and Herzegovina, 1/

Noting with appreciation the offers made by a number of States, following the adoption of its resolution 770 (1992) of 13 August 1992, to make available military personnel to facilitate the delivery by relevant United Nations humanitarian organizations and others of humanitarian assistance to Sarajevo and wherever needed in other parts of Bosnia and Herzegovina, such personnel to be made available to the United Nations without cost to the Organization,

Reaffirming its determination to ensure the protection and security of personnel of the Force and of the personnel of the United Nations,

Stressing in this context the importance of air measures, such as the ban on military flights to which all parties to the Conference held in London committed themselves, whose rapid implementation could, *inter alia*, reinforce the security of humanitarian activities in Bosnia and Herzegovina,

1. *Approves* the report of the Secretary-General of 10 September 1992 on the situation in Bosnia and Herzegovina; 1/

2. *Authorizes*, in implementation of paragraph 2 of resolution 770 (1992), the enlargement of the mandate and strength in Bosnia and Herzegovina of the United Nations Protection Force, recommended by the Secretary-General in that report, to perform the functions outlined in his report, including the protection of convoys of released detainees if requested by the International Committee of the Red Cross;

3. *Urges* Member States to provide the Secretary-General, nationally or through regional agencies or arrangements, with such financial or other assistance as he deems appropriate to assist in the performance of the functions outlined in his report;

4. *Decides* to remain actively seized of the matter in particular with a view to considering, as required, what further steps might be necessary to ensure the security of the Force and to enable it to fulfil its mandate.

1/ *Official Records of the Security Council, Forty-seventh Year, Supplement for July, August and September 1992,* document S/24540.

Document 76

Security Council resolution condemning the practice of "ethnic cleansing" in Bosnia and Herzegovina

S/RES/787 (1992), 16 November 1992

The Security Council,

Reaffirming its resolution 713 (1991) of 25 September 1991 and all subsequent relevant resolutions,

Reaffirming its determination that the situation in the Republic of Bosnia and Herzegovina constitutes a threat to the peace, and reaffirming that the provision of humanitarian assistance in the Republic of Bosnia and Herzegovina is an important element in the effort by the Council to restore peace and security in the region,

Deeply concerned at the threats to the territorial integrity of the Republic of Bosnia and Herzegovina, which, as a State Member of the United Nations, enjoys the rights provided for in the Charter of the United Nations,

Reaffirming also its full support for the International Conference on the former Yugoslavia as the framework within which an overall political settlement of the crisis in the former Yugoslavia may be achieved, and for the work of the Co-Chairmen of the Steering Committee of the Conference,

Recalling the decision by the Conference to examine the possibility of promoting safe areas for humanitarian purposes,

Recalling also the commitments entered into by the parties and others concerned within the framework of the Conference,

Reiterating its call on all parties and others concerned to cooperate fully with the Co-Chairmen of the Steering Committee of the Conference,

Noting the progress made so far within the framework of the Conference, including the Joint Declarations signed at Geneva on 30 September 1992 1/ and 20 October 1992 2/ by the Presidents of the Republic of Croatia and the Federal Republic of Yugoslavia (Serbia and Montenegro); the Joint Statement made at Geneva on 19 October 1992 by the Presidents of the Republic of Bosnia and Herzegovina and the Federal Republic of Yugoslavia (Serbia and Montenegro); 3/ the Joint Communiqué issued on 1 November 1992 at Zagreb by the Presidents of the Republic of Croatia and the Republic of Bosnia and Herzegovina; 4/ the establishment of the Mixed Military Working Group in the Republic of Bosnia and Herzegovina; and the production of a draft outline constitution for the Republic of Bosnia and Herzegovina, 5/

Noting with grave concern the report of the Special Rapporteur for Yugoslavia 6,7/ appointed following a special session of the Commission on Human Rights to investigate the human rights situation in the former Yugoslavia, which makes clear that massive and systematic violations of human rights and grave violations of international humanitarian law continue in the Republic of Bosnia and Herzegovina,

Welcoming the deployment of additional elements of the United Nations Protection Force for the protection of humanitarian activities in the Republic of Bosnia and Herzegovina, in accordance with its resolution 776 (1992) of 14 September 1992,

Deeply concerned about reports of continuing violations of the embargo imposed by its resolutions 713 (1991) and 724 (1991) of 15 December 1991,

Deeply concerned also about reports of violations of the measures imposed by its resolution 757 (1992) of 30 May 1992,

1. *Calls upon* the parties in the Republic of Bosnia and Herzegovina to consider the draft outline constitution for Bosnia and Herzegovina 5/ as a basis for negotiating a political settlement of the conflict in that country

and to continue negotiations for constitutional arrangements on the basis of the draft outline, under the auspices of the Co-Chairmen of the Steering Committee of the International Conference on the former Yugoslavia, these negotiations to be held in continuous and uninterrupted session;

2. *Reaffirms* that any taking of territory by force or any practice of "ethnic cleansing" is unlawful and unacceptable, and will not be permitted to affect the outcome of the negotiations on constitutional arrangements for the Republic of Bosnia and Herzegovina, and insists that all displaced persons be enabled to return in peace to their former homes;

3. *Strongly reaffirms* its call on all parties and others concerned to respect strictly the territorial integrity of the Republic of Bosnia and Herzegovina, and affirms that any entities unilaterally declared or arrangements imposed in contravention thereof will not be accepted;

4. *Condemns* the refusal of all parties in the Republic of Bosnia and Herzegovina, in particular the Bosnian Serb paramilitary forces, to comply with its previous resolutions, and demands that they and all other concerned parties in the former Yugoslavia fulfil immediately their obligations under those resolutions;

5. *Demands* that all forms of interference from outside the Republic of Bosnia and Herzegovina, including infiltration into the country of irregular units and personnel, cease immediately, and reaffirms its determination to take measures against all parties and others concerned which fail to fulfil the requirements of resolution 752 (1992) of 15 May 1992 and its other relevant resolutions, including the requirement that all forces, in particular elements of the Croatian Army, be withdrawn, or be subject to the authority of the Government of the Republic of Bosnia and Herzegovina, or be disbanded or disarmed;

6. *Calls upon* all parties in the Republic of Bosnia and Herzegovina to fulfil their commitments to put into effect an immediate cessation of hostilities and to negotiate in the Mixed Military Working Group, continuously and in uninterrupted session, to end the blockades of Sarajevo and other towns and to demilitarize them, with heavy weapons under international supervision;

7. *Condemns* all violations of international humanitarian law, including in particular the practice of

1/ *Official Records of the Security Council, Forty-seventh Year, Supplement for October, November and December 1992*, document S/24476, annex.
2/ Ibid., document S/24704, annex.
3/ Ibid., document S/24702, annex.
4/ Ibid., document S/24748, annex.
5/ Ibid., document S/24795, annex VII.
6/ Ibid., *Supplement for July, August and September 1992*, document S/24516, annex.
7/ Ibid., *Supplement for October, November and December 1992*, document S/24766, annex.

"ethnic cleansing" and the deliberate impeding of the delivery of food and medical supplies to the civilian population of the Republic of Bosnia and Herzegovina, and reaffirms that those that commit or order the commission of such acts will be held individually responsible in respect of such acts;

8. *Welcomes* the establishment of the Commission of Experts provided for in paragraph 2 of its resolution 780 (1992) of 6 October 1992, and requests the Commission to pursue actively its investigations with regard to grave breaches of the Geneva Conventions of 12 August 1949 8/ and other violations of international humanitarian law committed in the territory of the former Yugoslavia, in particular the practice of "ethnic cleansing";

9. *Decides*, acting under Chapter VII of the Charter of the United Nations, in order to ensure that commodities and products trans-shipped through the Federal Republic of Yugoslavia (Serbia and Montenegro) are not diverted in violation of resolution 757 (1992), to prohibit the trans-shipment of crude oil, petroleum products, coal, energy-related equipment, iron, steel, other metals, chemicals, rubber, tyres, vehicles, aircraft and motors of all types unless such trans-shipment is specifically authorized on a case-by-case basis by the Security Council Committee established by resolution 724 (1991) on Yugoslavia under its "no objection" procedure;

10. *Decides also*, acting under Chapter VII of the Charter, that any vessel in which a majority or controlling interest is held by a person or undertaking in or operating from the Federal Republic of Yugoslavia (Serbia and Montenegro) shall be considered, for the purpose of implementation of the relevant resolutions of the Council, a vessel of the Federal Republic of Yugoslavia (Serbia and Montenegro) regardless of the flag under which the vessel sails;

11. *Calls upon* all States to take all necessary steps to ensure that none of their exports are diverted to the Federal Republic of Yugoslavia (Serbia and Montenegro) in violation of resolution 757 (1992);

12. Acting under Chapters VII and VIII of the Charter, *calls upon* States, acting nationally or through regional agencies or arrangements, to use such measures commensurate with the specific circumstances as may be necessary under the authority of the Council to halt all inward and outward maritime shipping in order to inspect and verify their cargoes and destinations and to ensure strict implementation of the provisions of resolutions 713 (1991) and 757 (1992);

13. *Commends* the efforts of those riparian States which are acting to ensure compliance with resolutions 713 (1991) and 757 (1992) with respect to shipments on the Danube, and reaffirms the responsibility of riparian States to take necessary measures to ensure that shipping on the Danube is in accordance with resolutions 713

(1991) and 757 (1992), including such measures commensurate with the specific circumstances as may be necessary to halt such shipping in order to inspect and verify their cargoes and destinations and to ensure strict implementation of the provisions of resolutions 713 (1991) and 757 (1992);

14. *Requests* the States concerned, acting nationally or through regional agencies or arrangements, to coordinate with the Secretary-General, *inter alia*, on the submission of reports to the Council regarding actions taken in pursuance of paragraphs 12 and 13 above to facilitate the monitoring of the implementation of the present resolution;

15. *Requests* all States to provide in accordance with the Charter such assistance as may be required by those States acting nationally or through regional agencies and arrangements in pursuance of paragraphs 12 and 13;

16. *Considers* that, in order to facilitate the implementation of its relevant resolutions, observers should be deployed on the borders of the Republic of Bosnia and Herzegovina, and requests the Secretary-General to present to the Council as soon as possible his recommendations on this matter;

17. *Calls upon* all international donors to contribute to the humanitarian relief efforts in the former Yugoslavia, to support the United Nations Consolidated Inter-Agency Programme of Action and Appeal for the former Yugoslavia and to speed up the delivery of assistance under existing pledges;

18. *Calls upon* all parties and others concerned to cooperate fully with the humanitarian agencies and with the United Nations Protection Force to ensure the safe delivery of humanitarian assistance to those in need of it, and reiterates its demand that all parties and others concerned take the necessary measures to ensure the safety of United Nations and other personnel engaged in the delivery of humanitarian assistance;

19. *Invites* the Secretary-General, in consultation with the Office of the United Nations High Commissioner for Refugees and other relevant international humanitarian agencies, to study the possibility of and the requirements for the promotion of safe areas for humanitarian purposes;

20. *Expresses its appreciation* for the report presented by the Co-Chairmen of the Steering Committee of the International Conference on the former Yugoslavia, 9/ and requests the Secretary-General to continue to keep the Security Council regularly informed of developments and of the work of the Conference;

21. *Decides* to remain actively seized of the matter until a peaceful solution is achieved.

8/ United Nations, *Treaty Series*, vol. 75, Nos. 970-973.
9/ See 3134th meeting.

Document 77

Security Council resolution demanding that the detention camps in Bosnia and Herzegovina should be closed

S/RES/798 (1992), 18 December 1992

The Security Council,

Recalling its resolutions 770 (1992) and 771 (1992) of 13 August 1992 as well as its other relevant resolutions,

Appalled by reports of the massive, organized and systematic detention and rape of women, in particular Muslim women, in Bosnia and Herzegovina,

Demanding that all the detention camps and, in particular, camps for women be immediately closed,

Taking note of the initiative taken by the European Council on the rapid dispatch of a delegation to investigate the facts received until now, 1/

1. *Expresses its support* for the initiative of the European Council;

2. *Strongly condemns* these acts of unspeakable brutality;

3. *Requests* the Secretary-General to provide such necessary means of support as are available to him in the area to enable the European Community delegation to have free and secure access to the places of detention;

4. *Requests* the member States of the European Community to inform the Secretary-General of the work of the delegation;

5. *Invites* the Secretary-General to report to the Security Council within fifteen days of the adoption of the present resolution on measures taken to support the delegation;

6. *Decides* to remain actively seized of the matter.

1/ *Official Records of the Security Council, Forty-seventh Year, Supplement for October, November and December 1992*, document S/24960.

Document 78

Declaration on the Protection of All Persons from Enforced Disappearance

A/RES/47/133, 18 December 1992

The General Assembly,

Considering that, in accordance with the principles proclaimed in the Charter of the United Nations and other international instruments, recognition of the inherent dignity and of the equal and inalienable rights of all members of the human family is the foundation of freedom, justice and peace in the world,

Bearing in mind the obligation of States under the Charter, in particular Article 55, to promote universal respect for, and observance of, human rights and fundamental freedoms,

Deeply concerned that in many countries, often in a persistent manner, enforced disappearances occur, in the sense that persons are arrested, detained or abducted against their will or otherwise deprived of their liberty by officials of different branches or levels of Government, or by organized groups or private individuals acting on behalf of, or with the support, direct or indirect, consent or acquiescence of the Government, followed by a refusal to disclose the fate or whereabouts of the persons concerned or a refusal to acknowledge the deprivation of their liberty, which places such persons outside the protection of the law,

Considering that enforced disappearance undermines the deepest values of any society committed to respect for the rule of law, human rights and fundamental freedoms, and that the systematic practice of such acts is of the nature of a crime against humanity,

Recalling its resolution 33/173 of 20 December 1978, in which it expressed concern about the reports from various parts of the world relating to enforced or involuntary disappearances, as well as about the anguish and sorrow caused by those disappearances, and called upon Governments to hold law enforcement and security forces legally responsible for excesses which might lead to enforced or involuntary disappearances of persons,

Recalling also the protection afforded to victims of armed conflicts by the Geneva Conventions of 12 August 1949 and the Additional Protocols thereto, of 1977,

Having regard in particular to the relevant articles of the Universal Declaration of Human Rights and the International Covenant on Civil and Political Rights, which protect the right to life, the right to liberty and security of the person, the right not to be subjected to torture and the right to recognition as a person before the law,

Having regard also to the Convention against Torture and Other Cruel, Inhuman or Degrading Treatment or Punishment, which provides that States parties shall take effective measures to prevent and punish acts of torture,

Bearing in mind the Code of Conduct for Law Enforcement Officials, the Basic Principles on the Use of Force and Firearms by Law Enforcement Officials, the Declaration of Basic Principles of Justice for Victims of Crime and Abuse of Power and the Standard Minimum Rules for the Treatment of Prisoners,

Affirming that, in order to prevent enforced disappearances, it is necessary to ensure strict compliance with the Body of Principles for the Protection of All Persons under any form of Detention or Imprisonment contained in the annex to its resolution 43/173 of 9 December 1988, and with the Principles on the Effective Prevention and Investigation of Extra-legal, Arbitrary and Summary Executions, set forth in the annex to Economic and Social Council resolution 1989/65 of 24 May 1989 and endorsed by the General Assembly in its resolution 44/162 of 15 December 1989,

Bearing in mind that, while the acts which comprise enforced disappearance constitute a violation of the prohibition found in the aforementioned international instruments, it is none the less important to devise an instrument which characterizes all acts of enforced disappearance of persons as very serious offences and sets forth standards designed to punish and prevent their commission,

1. *Proclaims* the present Declaration on the Protection of all Persons from Enforced Disappearance, as a body of principles for all States;

2. *Urges* that all efforts be made so that the Declaration becomes generally known and respected;

Article 1

1. Any act of enforced disappearance is an offence to human dignity. It is condemned as a denial of the purposes of the Charter of the United Nations and as a grave and flagrant violation of the human rights and fundamental freedoms proclaimed in the Universal Declaration of Human Rights and reaffirmed and developed in international instruments in this field.

2. Any act of enforced disappearance places the persons subjected thereto outside the protection of the law and inflicts severe suffering on them and their families. It constitutes a violation of the rules of international law guaranteeing, *inter alia*, the right to recognition as a person before the law, the right to liberty and security of the person and the right not to be subjected to torture and other cruel, inhuman or degrading treatment or punishment. It also violates or constitutes a grave threat to the right to life.

Article 2

1. No State shall practise, permit or tolerate enforced disappearances.

2. States shall act at the national and regional levels and in cooperation with the United Nations to contribute by all means to the prevention and eradication of enforced disappearance.

Article 3

Each State shall take effective legislative, administrative, judicial or other measures to prevent and terminate acts of enforced disappearance in any territory under its jurisdiction.

Article 4

1. All acts of enforced disappearance shall be offences under criminal law punishable by appropriate penalties which shall take into account their extreme seriousness.

2. Mitigating circumstances may be established in national legislation for persons who, having participated in enforced disappearances, are instrumental in bringing the victims forward alive or in providing voluntarily information which would contribute to clarifying cases of enforced disappearance.

Article 5

In addition to such criminal penalties as are applicable, enforced disappearances render their perpetrators and the State or State authorities which organize, acquiesce in or tolerate such disappearances liable under civil law, without prejudice to the international responsibility of the State concerned in accordance with the principles of international law.

Article 6

1. No order or instruction of any public authority, civilian, military or other, may be invoked to justify an enforced disappearance. Any person receiving such an order or instruction shall have the right and duty not to obey it.

2. Each State shall ensure that orders or instructions directing, authorizing or encouraging any enforced disappearance are prohibited.

3. Training of law enforcement officials shall emphasize the provisions in paragraphs 1 and 2 of the present article.

Article 7

No circumstances whatsoever, whether a threat of war, a state of war, internal political instability or any other public emergency, may be invoked to justify enforced disappearances.

Article 8

1. No State shall expel, return (*refouler*) or extradite a person to another State where there are substantial grounds to believe that he would be in danger of enforced disappearance.

2. For the purpose of determining whether there are such grounds, the competent authorities shall take into account all relevant considerations including, where applicable, the existence in the State concerned of a consistent pattern of gross, flagrant or mass violations of human rights.

Article 9

1. The right to a prompt and effective judicial remedy as a means of determining the whereabouts or state of health of persons deprived of their liberty and/or identifying the authority ordering or carrying out the deprivation of liberty is required to prevent enforced disappearances under all circumstances, including those referred to in article 7 above.

2. In such proceedings, competent national authorities shall have access to all places where persons deprived of their liberty are being held and to each part of those places, as well as to any place in which there are grounds to believe that such persons may be found.

3. Any other competent authority entitled under the law of the State or by any international legal instrument to which the State is a party may also have access to such places.

Article 10

1. Any person deprived of liberty shall be held in an officially recognized place of detention and, in conformity with national law, be brought before a judicial authority promptly after detention.

2. Accurate information on the detention of such persons and their place or places of detention, including transfers. shall be made promptly available to their family members, their counsel or to any other persons having a legitimate interest in the information unless a wish to the contrary has been manifested by the persons concerned.

3. An official up-to-date register of all persons deprived of their liberty shall be maintained in every place of detention. Additionally, each State shall take steps to maintain similar centralized registers. The information contained in these registers shall be made available to the persons mentioned in the preceding paragraph, to any judicial or other competent and independent national authority and to any other competent authority entitled under the law of the State concerned or any international legal instrument to which a State concerned is a party, seeking to trace the whereabouts of a detained person.

Article 11

All persons deprived of liberty must be released in a manner permitting reliable verification that they have actually been released and, further, have been released in conditions in which their physical integrity and ability fully to exercise their rights are assured.

Article 12

1. Each State shall establish rules under its national law indicating those officials authorized to order deprivation of liberty, establishing the conditions under which such orders may be given, and stipulating penalties for officials who, without legal justification, refuse to provide information on any detention.

2. Each State shall likewise ensure strict supervision, including a clear chain of command, of all law enforcement officials responsible for apprehensions, arrests, detentions, custody, transfers and imprisonment, and of other officials authorized by law to use force and firearms.

Article 13

1. Each State shall ensure that any person having knowledge or a legitimate interest who alleges that a person has been subjected to enforced disappearance has the right to complain to a competent and independent State authority and to have that complaint promptly, thoroughly and impartially investigated by that authority. Whenever there are reasonable grounds to believe that an enforced disappearance has been committed, the State shall promptly refer the matter to that authority for such an investigation, even if there has been no formal complaint. No measure shall be taken to curtail or impede the investigation.

2. Each State shall ensure that the competent authority shall have the necessary powers and resources to conduct the investigation effectively, including powers to compel attendance of witnesses and production of relevant documents and to make immediate on-site visits.

3. Steps shall be taken to ensure that all involved in the investigation, including the complainant, counsel, witnesses and those conducting the investigation, are protected against ill-treatment, intimidation or reprisal.

4. The findings of such an investigation shall be made available upon request to all persons concerned,

unless doing so would jeopardize an ongoing criminal investigation.

5. Steps shall be taken to ensure that any ill-treatment, intimidation or reprisal or any other form of interference on the occasion of the lodging of a complaint or during the investigation procedure is appropriately punished.

6. An investigation, in accordance with the procedures described above, should be able to be conducted for as long as the fate of the victim of enforced disappearance remains unclarified.

Article 14

Any person alleged to have perpetrated an act of enforced disappearance in a particular State shall, when the facts disclosed by an official investigation so warrant, be brought before the competent civil authorities of that State for the purpose of prosecution and trial unless he has been extradited to another State wishing to exercise jurisdiction in accordance with the relevant international agreements in force. All States should take any lawful and appropriate action available to them to bring to justice all persons presumed responsible for an act of enforced disappearance, who are found to be within their jurisdiction or under their control.

Article 15

The fact that there are grounds to believe that a person has participated in acts of an extremely serious nature such as those referred to in article 4, paragraph 1, above, regardless of the motives, shall be taken into account when the competent authorities of the State decide whether or not to grant asylum.

Article 16

1. Persons alleged to have committed any of the acts referred to in article 4, paragraph 1, above, shall be suspended from any official duties during the investigation referred to in article 13 above.

2. They shall be tried only by the competent ordinary courts in each State, and not by any other special tribunal, in particular military courts.

3. No privileges, immunities or special exemptions shall be admitted in such trials, without prejudice to the provisions contained in the Vienna Convention on Diplomatic Relations.

4. The persons presumed responsible for such acts shall be guaranteed fair treatment in accordance with the relevant provisions of the Universal Declaration of Human Rights and other relevant international agreements in force at all stages of the investigation and eventual prosecution and trial.

Article 17

1. Acts constituting enforced disappearance shall be considered a continuing offence as long as the perpetrators continue to conceal the fate and the whereabouts of persons who have disappeared and these facts remain unclarified.

2. When the remedies provided for in article 2 of the International Covenant on Civil and Political Rights are no longer effective, the statute of limitations relating to acts of enforced disappearance shall be suspended until these remedies are re-established.

3. Statutes of limitations, where they exist, relating to acts of enforced disappearance shall be substantial and commensurate with the extreme seriousness of the offence.

Article 18

1. Persons who have or are alleged to have committed offences referred to in article 4, paragraph 1, above, shall not benefit from any special amnesty law or similar measures that might have the effect of exempting them from any criminal proceedings or sanction.

2. In the exercise of the right of pardon, the extreme seriousness of acts of enforced disappearance shall be taken into account.

Article 19

The victims of acts of enforced disappearance and their family shall obtain redress and shall have the right to adequate compensation, including the means for as complete a rehabilitation as possible. In the event of the death of the victim as a result of an act of enforced disappearance, their dependants shall also be entitled to compensation.

Article 20

1. States shall prevent and suppress the abduction of children of parents subjected to enforced disappearance and of children born during their mother's enforced disappearance, and shall devote their efforts to the search for and identification of such children and to the restitution of the children to their families of origin.

2. Considering the need to protect the best interests of children referred to in the preceding paragraph, there shall be an opportunity, in States which recognize a system of adoption, for a review of the adoption of such children and, in particular, for annulment of any adoption which originated in enforced disappearance. Such adoption should, however, continue to be in force if consent is given, at the time of the review, by the child's closest relatives.

3. The abduction of children of parents subjected to enforced disappearance or of children born during

their mother's enforced disappearance, and the act of altering or suppressing documents attesting to their true identity, shall constitute an extremely serious offence, which shall be punished as such.

4. For these purposes, States shall, where appropriate, conclude bilateral and multilateral agreements.

Article 21

The provisions of the present Declaration are without prejudice to the provisions enunciated in the Universal Declaration of Human Rights or in any other international instrument, and shall not be construed as restricting or derogating from any of those provisions.

Document 79

Declaration on the Rights of Persons Belonging to National or Ethnic, Religious and Linguistic Minorities, adopted by the General Assembly

A/RES/47/135, 18 December 1992

The General Assembly,

Reaffirming that one of the basic aims of the United Nations, as proclaimed in the Charter, is to promote and encourage respect for human rights and for fundamental freedoms for all, without distinction as to race, sex, language or religion,

Reaffirming faith in fundamental human rights, in the dignity and worth of the human person, in the equal rights of men and women and of nations large and small,

Desiring to promote the realization of the principles contained in the Charter, the Universal Declaration of Human Rights, the Convention on the Prevention and Punishment of the Crime of Genocide, the International Convention on the Elimination of All Forms of Racial Discrimination, the International Covenant on Civil and Political Rights, the International Covenant on Economic, Social and Cultural Rights, the Declaration on the Elimination of All Forms of Intolerance and of Discrimination Based on Religion or Belief, and the Convention on the Rights of the Child, as well as other relevant international instruments that have been adopted at the universal or regional level and those concluded between individual States Members of the United Nations,

Inspired by the provisions of article 27 of the International Covenant on Civil and Political Rights concerning the rights of persons belonging to ethnic, religious or linguistic minorities,

Considering that the promotion and protection of the rights of persons belonging to national or ethnic, religious and linguistic minorities contribute to the political and social stability of States in which they live,

Emphasizing that the constant promotion and realization of the rights of persons belonging to national or ethnic, religious and linguistic minorities, as an integral part of the development of society as a whole and within a democratic framework based on the rule of law, would contribute to the strengthening of friendship and cooperation among peoples and States,

Considering that the United Nations has an important role to play regarding the protection of minorities,

Bearing in mind the work done so far within the United Nations system, in particular by the Commission on Human Rights, the Subcommission on Prevention of Discrimination and Protection of Minorities and the bodies established pursuant to the International Covenants on Human Rights and other relevant international human rights instruments in promoting and protecting the rights of persons belonging to national or ethnic, religious and linguistic minorities,

Taking into account the important work which is done by intergovernmental and non-governmental organizations in protecting minorities and in promoting and protecting the rights of persons belonging to national or ethnic, religious and linguistic minorities,

Recognizing the need to ensure even more effective implementation of international human rights instruments with regard to the rights of persons belonging to national or ethnic, religious and linguistic minorities,

Proclaims this Declaration on the Rights of Persons Belonging to National or Ethnic, Religious and Linguistic Minorities:

Article 1

1. States shall protect the existence and the national or ethnic, cultural, religious and linguistic identity of minorities within their respective territories and shall encourage conditions for the promotion of that identity.

2. States shall adopt appropriate legislative and other measures to achieve those ends.

Article 2

1. Persons belonging to national or ethnic, religious and linguistic minorities (hereinafter referred to as persons

belonging to minorities) have the right to enjoy their own culture, to profess and practise their own religion, and to use their own language, in private and in public, freely and without interference or any form of discrimination.

2. Persons belonging to minorities have the right to participate effectively in cultural, religious, social, economic and public life.

3. Persons belonging to minorities have the right to participate effectively in decisions on the national and, where appropriate, regional level concerning the minority to which they belong or the regions in which they live, in a manner not incompatible with national legislation.

4. Persons belonging to minorities have the right to establish and maintain their own associations.

5. Persons belonging to minorities have the right to establish and maintain, without any discrimination, free and peaceful contacts with other members of their group and with persons belonging to other minorities, as well as contacts across frontiers with citizens of other States to whom they are related by national or ethnic, religious or linguistic ties.

Article 3

1. Persons belonging to minorities may exercise their rights, including those set forth in the present Declaration, individually as well as in community with other members of their group, without any discrimination.

2. No disadvantage shall result for any person belonging to a minority as the consequence of the exercise or non-exercise of the rights set forth in the present Declaration.

Article 4

1. States shall take measures where required to ensure that persons belonging to minorities may exercise fully and effectively all their human rights and fundamental freedoms without any discrimination and in full equality before the law.

2. States shall take measures to create favourable conditions to enable persons belonging to minorities to express their characteristics and to develop their culture, language, religion, traditions and customs, except where specific practices are in violation of national law and contrary to international standards.

3. States should take appropriate measures so that, wherever possible, persons belonging to minorities may have adequate opportunities to learn their mother tongue or to have instruction in their mother tongue.

4. States should, where appropriate, take measures in the field of education, in order to encourage knowledge of the history, traditions, language and culture of the minorities existing within their territory. Persons belong-

ing to minorities should have adequate opportunities to gain knowledge of the society as a whole.

5. States should consider appropriate measures so that persons belonging to minorities may participate fully in the economic progress and development in their country.

Article 5

1. National policies and programmes shall be planned and implemented with due regard for the legitimate interests of persons belonging to minorities.

2. Programmes of cooperation and assistance among States should be planned and implemented with due regard for the legitimate interests of persons belonging to minorities.

Article 6

States should cooperate on questions relating to persons belonging to minorities, *inter alia*, exchanging information and experiences, in order to promote mutual understanding and confidence.

Article 7

States should cooperate in order to promote respect for the rights set forth in the present Declaration.

Article 8

1. Nothing in the present Declaration shall prevent the fulfilment of international obligations of States in relation to persons belonging to minorities. In particular, States shall fulfil in good faith the obligations and commitments they have assumed under international treaties and agreements to which they are parties.

2. The exercise of the rights set forth in the present Declaration shall not prejudice the enjoyment by all persons of universally recognized human rights and fundamental freedoms.

3. Measures taken by States to ensure the effective enjoyment of the rights set forth in the present Declaration shall not *prima facie* be considered contrary to the principle of equality contained in the Universal Declaration of Human Rights.

4. Nothing in the present Declaration may be construed as permitting any activity contrary to the purposes and principles of the United Nations, including sovereign equality, territorial integrity and political independence of States.

Article 9

The specialized agencies and other organizations of the United Nations system shall contribute to the full realization of the rights and principles set forth in the present Declaration, within their respective fields of competence.

Document 80

Security Council resolution establishing an international tribunal for the prosecution of persons responsible for serious violations of international humanitarian law committed in the territory of the former Yugoslavia since 1991

S/RES/808 (1993), 22 February 1993

The Security Council,

Reaffirming its resolution 713 (1991) of 25 September 1991 and all subsequent relevant resolutions,

Recalling paragraph 10 of its resolution 764 (1992) of 13 July 1992, in which it reaffirmed that all parties are bound to comply with the obligations under international humanitarian law, in particular the Geneva Conventions of 12 August 1949, 1/ and that persons who commit or order the commission of grave breaches of the Conventions are individually responsible in respect of such breaches,

Recalling also its resolution 771 (1992) of 13 August 1992, in which, *inter alia*, it demanded that all parties and others concerned in the former Yugoslavia, and all military forces in Bosnia and Herzegovina, immediately cease and desist from all breaches of international humanitarian law,

Recalling further its resolution 780 (1992) of 6 October 1992, in which it requested the Secretary-General to establish, as a matter of urgency, an impartial commission of experts to examine and analyse the information submitted pursuant to resolutions 771 (1992) and 780 (1992), together with such further information as the commission may obtain, with a view to providing the Secretary-General with its conclusions on the evidence of grave breaches of the Geneva Conventions and other violations of international humanitarian law committed in the territory of the former Yugoslavia,

Having considered the interim report of the Commission of Experts established pursuant to resolution 780 (1992), 2/ in which the Commission observed that a decision to establish an ad hoc international tribunal in relation to events in the territory of the former Yugoslavia would be consistent with the direction of its work,

Expressing once again its grave alarm at continuing reports of widespread violations of international humanitarian law occuring within the territory of the former Yugoslavia, including reports of mass killings and the continuance of the practice of "ethnic cleansing",

Determining that this situation constitutes a threat to international peace and security,

Determined to put an end to such crimes and to take effective measures to bring to justice the persons who are responsible for them,

Convinced that in the particular circumstances of the former Yugoslavia the establishment of an international tribunal would enable this aim to be achieved and would contribute to the restoration and maintenance of peace,

Noting in this regard the recommendation by the Co-Chairmen of the Steering Committee of the International Conference on the Former Yugoslavia for the establishment of such a tribunal, 3/

Taking note with grave concern of the report of the European Community investigative mission into the treatment of Muslim women in the former Yugoslavia, 4/

Taking note of the report of the committee of jurists submitted by France, 5/ the report of the commission of jurists submitted by Italy, 6/ and the report transmitted by the Permanent Representative of Sweden on behalf of the Chairman-in-Office of the Conference on Security and Cooperation in Europe, 7/

1. *Decides* that an international tribunal shall be established for the prosecution of persons responsible for serious violations of international humanitarian law committed in the territory of the former Yugoslavia since 1991;

2. *Requests* the Secretary-General to submit for consideration by the Council at the earliest possible date, and if possible no later than sixty days after the adoption of the present resolution, a report on all aspects of this matter, including specific proposals and where appropriate options for the effective and expeditious implementation of the decision contained in paragraph 1 above, taking into account suggestions put forward in this regard by Member States;

3. *Decides* to remain actively seized of the matter.

1/ United Nations, *Treaty Series*, vol. 75, Nos. 970-973.
2/ *Official Records of the Security Council, Forty-eighth Year, Supplement for January, February and March 1993*, document S/25274, annex I.
3/ Ibid., document S/25221, annex I.
4/ Ibid., document S/25240, annex I.
5/ Ibid., document S/25266.
6/ Ibid., document S/25300.
7/ Ibid., document S/25307.

Document 81

General Assembly resolution authorizing the participation of the United Nations in cooperation with the Organization of American States in the International Civilian Mission to Haiti (MICIVIH)

A/RES/47/20 B, 20 April 1993 1/

The General Assembly,

Having considered further the item entitled "The situation of democracy and human rights in Haiti",

Recalling its resolutions 46/7 of 11 October 1991, 46/138 of 17 December 1991, 47/20 A of 24 November 1992 and 47/143 of 18 December 1992, as well as the relevant resolutions and decisions of the Economic and Social Council and the Commission on Human Rights, in particular Commission on Human Rights resolution 1993/68 of 10 March 1993, 2/

Welcoming resolutions MRE/RES.1/91, 3/ MRE/RES.2/91, 4/ MRE/RES.3/92 and MRE/RES.4/92 adopted on 3 and 8 October 1991, 17 May 1992 and 13 December 1992, respectively, by the Ministers for Foreign Affairs of the member countries of the Organization of American States,

Also welcoming resolution CP/RES. 594 (923/92) and declarations CP/DEC. 8 (927/93), CP/DEC. 9 (931/93) and CP/DEC. 10 (934/93) adopted by the Permanent Council of the Organization of American States on 10 November 1992 and 13 January, 11 February and 5 March 1993, respectively,

Deploring the fact that, despite the efforts of the international community, the legitimate government of President Jean-Bertrand Aristide has not been re-established and that violent denial of human rights and civil and political liberties continues in Haiti,

Reiterating that the goal of the international community remains the early restoration of democracy in Haiti and the return of President Aristide, the full observance of human rights and fundamental freedoms, and the promotion of social and economic development in Haiti,

Strongly supportive of the continuing leadership by the Secretary-General of the United Nations and the Secretary-General of the Organization of American States of the efforts of the international community to reach a political solution to the Haitian crisis,

Noting with satisfaction the designation by the Secretary-General of the United Nations of a Special Envoy for Haiti and the designation by the Secretary-General of the Organization of American States of the same Special Envoy,

Welcoming the agreement which has made possible the deployment of the International Civilian Mission to Haiti by the United Nations and the Organization of American States, as described in the letter dated 8 January 1993 to the Secretary-General from President Aristide, which is contained in annex I to the report of the Secretary-General, 5/

Convinced that the work of the Mission can contribute to the full observance of human rights and create a climate propitious to the restoration of the constitutional authority,

Expressing its agreement with declaration CP/DEC.8 (927/93) of the Permanent Council of the Organization of American States that the partial elections to Parliament held by the de facto government in January 1993 would be illegitimate,

Taking note of the report of the Secretary-General on the situation of democracy and human rights in Haiti and the recommendations contained therein, 5/

1. *Approves* the report of the Secretary-General and the recommendations contained therein for United Nations participation, jointly with the Organization of American States, in the International Civilian Mission to Haiti, with the initial task of verifying compliance with Haiti's international human rights obligations, with a view to making recommendations thereon, in order to assist in the establishment of a climate of freedom and tolerance propitious to the re-establishment of democracy in Haiti;

2. *Decides* to authorize the deployment without delay of the United Nations participation in the International Civilian Mission to Haiti and requests the Secretary-General to take the steps necessary to expedite and strengthen its presence in Haiti;

3. *Expresses its full support* for the International Civilian Mission to Haiti and urges that all parties afford it timely, complete and effective cooperation;

4. *Reiterates* the need for an early return of President Aristide to resume his constitutional functions as

1/ See A/47/101/Add.2.
2/ Consequently decision 47/306, in section X.A of the *Official Records of the General Assembly, Forty-seventh Session, Supplement No. 49* (A/47/49), vol.I, becomes decision 47/306 A.
3/ Economic and Social Council decision 1993/201 of 12 February 1993; see also A/47/401/Add.1.
4/ Consequently decision 47/311, in section X.A of the *Official Records of the General Assembly, Forty-seventh Session, Supplement No. 49* (A/47/49), vol.I, becomes decision 47/311 A.
5/ A/47/107/Add.1.

President, as the means to restore without further delay the democratic process in Haiti;

5. *Strongly supports* the process of political dialogue under the auspices of the Special Envoy with a view to resolving the political crisis in Haiti;

6. *Considers* that any modifications regarding the economic measures recommended by the ad hoc meeting of the Ministers for Foreign Affairs of the member countries of the Organization of American States should be considered according to progress in the observance of human rights and in the solution of the political crisis leading to the restoration of President Jean-Bertrand Aristide;

7. *Reiterates* that any entity resulting from actions of the de facto regime, including the partial elections to Parliament in January 1993, is illegitimate;

8. *Reaffirms once again* the commitment of the international community to an increase in technical, economic and financial cooperation when constitutional order is restored in Haiti, as a support for its economic and social development efforts and in order to strengthen its institutions responsible for dispensing justice and guaranteeing democracy, political stability and economic development;

9. *Requests* the Secretary-General to make regular reports to the General Assembly on the work of the International Civilian Mission to Haiti, and in particular to report no later than September 1993 on the outcome of the comprehensive review referred to in paragraph 95 of annex III to his report;

10. *Decides* to keep open the consideration of this item until a solution to the situation is found.

Document 82

Report of the Secretary-General on the establishment of an international tribunal for the prosecution of persons responsible for serious violations of international humanitarian law committed in the territory of the former Yugoslavia since 1991

S/25704, 3 May 1993

Introduction

1. By paragraph 1 of resolution 808 (1993) of 22 February 1993, the Security Council decided "that an international tribunal shall be established for the prosecution of persons responsible for serious violations of international humanitarian law committed in the territory of the former Yugoslavia since 1991".

2. By paragraph 2 of the resolution, the Secretary-General was requested "to submit for consideration by the Council at the earliest possible date, and if possible no later than 60 days after the adoption of the present resolution, a report on all aspects of this matter, including specific proposals and where appropriate options for the effective and expeditious implementation of the decision [to establish an international tribunal], taking into account suggestions put forward in this regard by Member States."

3. The present report is presented pursuant to that request. 1/

A

4. Resolution 808 (1993) represents a further step taken by the Security Council in a series of resolutions concerning serious violations of international humanitarian law occurring in the territory of the former Yugoslavia.

5. In resolution 764 (1992) of 13 July 1992, the Security Council reaffirmed that all parties to the conflict are bound to comply with their obligations under international humanitarian law and in particular the Geneva Conventions of 12 August 1949, and that persons who commit or order the commission of grave breaches of the Conventions are individually responsible in respect of such breaches.

6. In resolution 771 (1992) of 13 August 1992, the Security Council expressed grave alarm at continuing reports of widespread violations of international humanitarian law occurring within the territory of the former Yugoslavia and especially in Bosnia and Herzegovina, including reports of mass forcible expulsion and deportation of civilians, imprisonment and abuse of civilians in detention centres, deliberate attacks on non-combatants, hospitals and ambulances, impeding the delivery of food and medical supplies to the civilian population, and wanton devastation and destruction of property. The Council strongly condemned any violations of interna-

1/ On 19 April 1993, the Secretary-General addressed a letter to the President of the Security Council informing him that the report would be made available to the Security Council no later than 6 May 1993.

tional humanitarian law, including those involved in the practice of "ethnic cleansing", and demanded that all parties to the conflict in the former Yugoslavia cease and desist from all breaches of international humanitarian law. It called upon States and international humanitarian organizations to collate substantiated information relating to the violations of humanitarian law, including grave breaches of the Geneva Conventions, being committed in the territory of the former Yugoslavia and to make this information available to the Council. Furthermore, the Council decided, acting under Chapter VII of the Charter of the United Nations, that all parties and others concerned in the former Yugoslavia, and all military forces in Bosnia and Herzegovina, should comply with the provisions of that resolution, failing which the Council would need to take further measures under the Charter.

7. In resolution 780 (1992) of 6 October 1992, the Security Council requested the Secretary-General to establish an impartial Commission of Experts to examine and analyse the information as requested by resolution 771 (1992), together with such further information as the Commission may obtain through its own investigations or efforts, of other persons or bodies pursuant to resolution 771 (1992), with a view to providing the Secretary-General with its conclusions on the evidence of grave breaches of the Geneva Conventions and other violations of international humanitarian law committed in the territory of the former Yugoslavia.

8. On 14 October 1992 the Secretary-General submitted a report to the Security Council pursuant to paragraph 3 of resolution 780 (1992) in which he outlined his decision to establish a five-member Commission of Experts (S/24657). On 26 October 1992, the Secretary-General announced the appointment of the Chairman and members of the Commission of Experts.

9. By a letter dated 9 February 1993, the Secretary-General submitted to the President of the Security Council an interim report of the Commission of Experts (S/25274), which concluded that grave breaches and other violations of international humanitarian law had been committed in the territory of the former Yugoslavia, including wilful killing, "ethnic cleansing", mass killings, torture, rape, pillage and destruction of civilian property, destruction of cultural and religious property and arbitrary arrests. In its report, the Commission noted that should the Security Council or another competent organ of the United Nations decide to establish an ad hoc international tribunal, such a decision would be consistent with the direction of its work.

10. It was against this background that the Security Council considered and adopted resolution 808 (1993). After recalling the provisions of resolutions 764 (1992), 771 (1992) and 780 (1992) and, taking into considera-

tion the interim report of the Commission of Experts, the Security Council expressed once again its grave alarm at continuing reports of widespread violations of international humanitarian law occurring within the territory of the former Yugoslavia, including reports of mass killings and the continuation of the practice of "ethnic cleansing". The Council determined that this situation constituted a threat to international peace and security, and stated that it was determined to put an end to such crimes and to take effective measures to bring to justice the persons who are responsible for them. The Security Council stated its conviction that in the particular circumstances of the former Yugoslavia the establishment of an international tribunal would enable this aim to be achieved and would contribute to the restoration and maintenance of peace.

11. The Secretary-General wishes to recall that in resolution 820 (1993) of 17 April 1993, the Security Council condemned once again all violations of international humanitarian law, including in particular, the practice of "ethnic cleansing" and the massive, organized and systematic detention and rape of women, and reaffirmed that those who commit or have committed or order or have ordered the commission of such acts will be held individually responsible in respect of such acts.

B

12. The Security Council's decision in resolution 808 (1993) to establish an international tribunal is circumscribed in scope and purpose: the prosecution of persons responsible for serious violations of international humanitarian law committed in the territory of the former Yugoslavia since 1991. The decision does not relate to the establishment of an international criminal jurisdiction in general nor to the creation of an international criminal court of a permanent nature, issues which are and remain under active consideration by the International Law Commission and the General Assembly.

C

13. In accordance with the request of the Security Council, the Secretary-General has taken into account in the preparation of the present report the suggestions put forward by Member States, in particular those reflected in the following Security Council documents submitted by Member States and noted by the Council in its resolution 808 (1993): the report of the committee of jurists submitted by France (S/25266), the report of the commission of jurists submitted by Italy (S/25300), and the report submitted by the Permanent Representative of Sweden on behalf of the Chairman-in-Office of the Conference on Security and Cooperation in Europe (CSCE) (S/25307). The Secretary-General has also sought the views of the Commission of Experts established pursuant to Security

Council resolution 780 (1992) and has made use of the information gathered by that Commission. In addition, the Secretary-General has taken into account suggestions or comments put forward formally or informally by the following Member States since the adoption of resolution 808 (1993): Australia, Austria, Belgium, Brazil, Canada, Chile, China, Denmark, Egypt,* Germany, Iran (Islamic Republic of),* Ireland, Italy, Malaysia,* Mexico, Netherlands, New Zealand, Pakistan,* Portugal, Russian Federation, Saudi Arabia,* Senegal,* Slovenia, Spain, Sweden, Turkey,* United Kingdom of Great Britain and Northern Ireland, United States of America and Yugoslavia. He has also received suggestions or comments from a non-member State (Switzerland).

14. The Secretary-General has also received comments from the International Committee of the Red Cross (ICRC) and from the following non-governmental organizations: Amnesty International, Association Internationale des Jeunes Avocats, Ethnic Minorities Barristers' Association, Fédération internationale des femmes des carrières juridiques, International Criminal Police Organization, Jacob Blaustein Institution for the Advancement of Human Rights, Lawyers Committee for Human Rights, National Alliance of Women's Organisations (NAWO), and Parliamentarians for Global Action. Observations have also been received from international meetings and individual experts in relevant fields.

15. The Secretary-General wishes to place on record his appreciation for the interest shown by all the Governments, organizations and individuals who have offered valuable suggestions and comments.

D

16. In the main body of the report which follows, the Secretary-General first examines the legal basis for the establishment of the International Tribunal foreseen in resolution 808 (1993). The Secretary-General then sets out in detail the competence of the International Tribunal as regards the law it will apply, the persons to whom the law will be applied, including considerations as to the principle of individual criminal responsibility, its territorial and temporal reach and the relation of its work to that of national courts. In succeeding chapters, the Secretary-General sets out detailed views on the organization of the international tribunal, the investigation and pre-trial proceedings, trial and post-trial proceedings, and cooperation and judicial assistance. A concluding chapter deals with a number of general and organizational issues such as privileges and immunities, the seat of the international tribunal, working languages and financial arrangements.

17. In response to the Security Council's request to include in the report specific proposals, the Secretary-General has decided to incorporate into the report specific

language for inclusion in a statute of the International Tribunal. The formulations are based upon provisions found in existing international instruments, particularly with regard to competence *ratione materiae* of the International Tribunal. Suggestions and comments, including suggested draft articles, received from States, organizations and individuals as noted in paragraphs 13 and 14 above, also formed the basis upon which the Secretary-General prepared the statute. Texts prepared in the past by United Nations or other bodies for the establishment of international criminal courts were consulted by the Secretary-General, including texts prepared by the United Nations Committee on International Criminal Jurisdiction, 2/ the International Law Commission, and the International Law Association. Proposals regarding individual articles are, therefore, made throughout the body of the report; the full text of the statute of the International Tribunal is contained in the annex to the present report.

I. The legal basis for the establishment of the International Tribunal

18. Security Council resolution 808 (1993) states that an international tribunal shall be established for the prosecution of persons responsible for serious violations of international humanitarian law committed in the territory of the former Yugoslavia since 1991. It does not, however, indicate how such an international tribunal is to be established or on what legal basis.

19. The approach which, in the normal course of events, would be followed in establishing an international tribunal would be the conclusion of a treaty by which the States parties would establish a tribunal and approve its statute. This treaty would be drawn up and adopted by an appropriate international body (e.g., the General Assembly or a specially convened conference), following which it would be opened for signature and ratification. Such an approach would have the advantage of allowing for a detailed examination and elaboration of all the issues pertaining to the establishment of the international tribunal. It also would allow the States participating in the negotiation and conclusion of the treaty fully to exercise their sovereign will, in particular whether they wish to become parties to the treaty or not.

20. As has been pointed out in many of the comments received, the treaty approach incurs the disadvantage of requiring considerable time to establish an instrument and then to achieve the required number of

*On behalf of the members of the Organization of the Islamic Conference (OIC) and as members of the Contact Group of OIC on Bosnia and Herzegovina.
2/ The 1953 Committee on International Criminal Jurisdiction was established by General Assembly resolution 687 (VII) of 5 December 1952.

ratifications for entry into force. Even then, there could be no guarantee that ratifications will be received from those States which should be parties to the treaty if it is to be truly effective.

21. A number of suggestions have been put forward to the effect that the General Assembly, as the most representative organ of the United Nations, should have a role in the establishment of the international tribunal in addition to its role in the administrative and budgetary aspects of the question. The involvement of the General Assembly in the drafting or the review of the statute of the International Tribunal would not be reconcilable with the urgency expressed by the Security Council in resolution 808 (1993). The Secretary-General believes that there are other ways of involving the authority and prestige of the General Assembly in the establishment of the International Tribunal.

22. In the light of the disadvantages of the treaty approach in this particular case and of the need indicated in resolution 808 (1993) for an effective and expeditious implementation of the decision to establish an international tribunal, the Secretary-General believes that the International Tribunal should be established by a decision of the Security Council on the basis of Chapter VII of the Charter of the United Nations. Such a decision would constitute a measure to maintain or restore international peace and security, following the requisite determination of the existence of a threat to the peace, breach of the peace or act of aggression.

23. This approach would have the advantage of being expeditious and of being immediately effective as all States would be under a binding obligation to take whatever action is required to carry out a decision taken as an enforcement measure under Chapter VII.

24. In the particular case of the former Yugoslavia, the Secretary-General believes that the establishment of the International Tribunal by means of a Chapter VII decision would be legally justified, both in terms of the object and purpose of the decision, as indicated in the preceding paragraphs, and of past Security Council practice.

25. As indicated in paragraph 10 above, the Security Council has already determined that the situation posed by continuing reports of widespread violations of international humanitarian law occurring in the former Yugoslavia constitutes a threat to international peace and security. The Council has also decided under Chapter VII of the Charter that all parties and others concerned in the former Yugoslavia, and all military forces in Bosnia and Herzegovina, shall comply with the provisions of resolution 771 (1992), failing which it would need to take further measures under the Charter. Furthermore, the Council has repeatedly reaffirmed that all parties in the former Yugoslavia are bound to comply with the obliga-

tions under international humanitarian law and in particular the Geneva Conventions of 12 August 1949, and that persons who commit or order the commission of grave breaches of the Conventions are individually responsible in respect of such breaches.

26. Finally, the Security Council stated in resolution 808 (1993) that it was convinced that in the particular circumstances of the former Yugoslavia, the establishment of an international tribunal would bring about the achievement of the aim of putting an end to such crimes and of taking effective measures to bring to justice the persons responsible for them, and would contribute to the restoration and maintenance of peace.

27. The Security Council has on various occasions adopted decisions under Chapter VII aimed at restoring and maintaining international peace and security, which have involved the establishment of subsidiary organs for a variety of purposes. Reference may be made in this regard to Security Council resolution 687 (1991) and subsequent resolutions relating to the situation between Iraq and Kuwait.

28. In this particular case, the Security Council would be establishing, as an enforcement measure under Chapter VII, a subsidiary organ within the terms of Article 29 of the Charter, but one of a judicial nature. This organ would, of course, have to perform its functions independently of political considerations; it would not be subject to the authority or control of the Security Council with regard to the performance of its judicial functions. As an enforcement measure under Chapter VII, however, the life span of the international tribunal would be linked to the restoration and maintenance of international peace and security in the territory of the former Yugoslavia, and Security Council decisions related thereto.

29. It should be pointed out that, in assigning to the International Tribunal the task of prosecuting persons responsible for serious violations of international humanitarian law, the Security Council would not be creating or purporting to "legislate" that law. Rather, the International Tribunal would have the task of applying existing international humanitarian law.

30. On the basis of the foregoing considerations, the Secretary-General proposes that the Security Council, acting under Chapter VII of the Charter, establish the International Tribunal. The resolution so adopted would have annexed to it a statute the opening passage of which would read as follows:

Having been established by the Security Council acting under Chapter VII of the Charter of the United Nations, the International Tribunal for the Prosecution of Persons Responsible for Serious Violations of International Humanitarian Law Committed in the Territory of the Former Yugoslavia since 1991 (hereinafter referred to as "the International Tribunal") shall function in accordance with the provisions of the present Statute.

II. Competence of the International Tribunal

31. The competence of the International Tribunal derives from the mandate set out in paragraph 1 of resolution 808 (1993). This part of the report will examine and make proposals regarding these fundamental elements of its competence: *ratione materiae* (subject-matter jurisdiction), *ratione personae* (personal jurisdiction), *ratione loci* (territorial jurisdiction) and *ratione temporis* (temporal jurisdiction), as well as the question of the concurrent jurisdiction of the International Tribunal and national courts.

32. The statute should begin with a general article on the competence of the International Tribunal which would read as follows:

Article 1
Competence of the International Tribunal

The International Tribunal shall have the power to prosecute persons responsible for serious violations of international humanitarian law committed in the territory of the former Yugoslavia since 1991 in accordance with the provisions of the present Statute.

A. *Competence* ratione materiae (subject-matter jurisdiction)

33. According to paragraph 1 of resolution 808 (1993), the international tribunal shall prosecute persons responsible for serious violations of international humanitarian law committed in the territory of the former Yugoslavia since 1991. This body of law exists in the form of both conventional law and customary law. While there is international customary law which is not laid down in conventions, some of the major conventional humanitarian law has become part of customary international law.

34. In the view of the Secretary-General, the application of the principle nullum crimen sine lege requires that the international tribunal should apply rules of international humanitarian law which are beyond any doubt part of customary law so that the problem of adherence of some but not all States to specific conventions does not arise. This would appear to be particularly important in the context of an international tribunal prosecuting persons responsible for serious violations of international humanitarian law.

35. The part of conventional international humanitarian law which has beyond doubt become part of

international customary law is the law applicable in armed conflict as embodied in: the Geneva Conventions of 12 August 1949 for the Protection of War Victims; 3/ the Hague Convention (IV) Respecting the Laws and Customs of War on Land and the Regulations annexed thereto of 18 October 1907; 4/ the Convention on the Prevention and Punishment of the Crime of Genocide of 9 December 1948; 5/ and the Charter of the International Military Tribunal of 8 August 1945. 6/

36. Suggestions have been made that the international tribunal should apply domestic law in so far as it incorporates customary international humanitarian law. While international humanitarian law as outlined above provides a sufficient basis for subject-matter jurisdiction, there is one related issue which would require reference to domestic practice, namely, penalties (see para. 111 below).

Grave breaches of the 1949 Geneva Conventions

37. The Geneva Conventions constitute rules of international humanitarian law and provide the core of the customary law applicable in international armed conflicts. These Conventions regulate the conduct of war from the humanitarian perspective by protecting certain categories of persons: namely, wounded and sick members of armed forces in the field; wounded, sick and shipwrecked members of armed forces at sea; prisoners of war, and civilians in time of war.

38. Each Convention contains a provision listing the particularly serious violations that qualify as "grave breaches" or war crimes. Persons committing or ordering grave breaches are subject to trial and punishment. The lists of grave breaches contained in the Geneva Conventions are reproduced in the article which follows.

39. The Security Council has reaffirmed on several occasions that persons who commit or order the commission of grave breaches of the 1949 Geneva Conventions in the territory of the former Yugoslavia are individually

3/ Convention for the Amelioration of the Condition of the Wounded and Sick in Armed Forces in the Field of 12 August 1949, Convention for the Amelioration of the Condition of the Wounded, Sick and Shipwrecked Members of Armed Forces at Sea of 12 August 1949, Convention relative to the Treatment of Prisoners of War of 12 August 1949, Convention relative to the Protection of Civilian Persons in Time of War of 12 August 1949 (United Nations, *Treaty Series*, vol. 75, No. 970-973).
4/ Carnegie Endowment for International Peace, *The Hague Conventions and Declarations of 1899 and 1907* (New York, Oxford University Press, 1915), p. 100.
5/ United Nations, *Treaty Series*, vol. 78, No. 1021.
6/ The Agreement for the Prosecution and Punishment of the Major War Criminals of the European Axis, signed at London on 8 August 1945 (United Nations, *Treaty Series*, vol. 82, No. 251); see also Judgement of the International Military Tribunal for the Prosecution and Punishment of the Major War Criminals of the European Axis (United States Government Printing Office, *Nazi Conspiracy and Aggression, Opinion and Judgement*) and General Assembly resolution 95 (I) of 11 December 1946 on the Affirmation of the Principles of International Law Recognized by the Charter of the Nürnberg Tribunal.

responsible for such breaches as serious violations of international humanitarian law.

40. The corresponding article of the statute would read:

Article 2
Grave breaches of the Geneva Conventions of 1949

The International Tribunal shall have the power to prosecute persons committing or ordering to be committed grave breaches of the Geneva Conventions of 12 August 1949, namely the following acts against persons or property protected under the provisions of the relevant Geneva Convention:

(a) wilful killing;

(b) torture or inhuman treatment, including biological experiments;

(c) wilfully causing great suffering or serious injury to body or health;

(d) extensive destruction and appropriation of property, not justified by military necessity and carried out unlawfully and wantonly;

(e) compelling a prisoner of war or a civilian to serve in the forces of a hostile power;

(f) wilfully depriving a prisoner of war or a civilian of the rights of fair and regular trial;

(g) unlawful deportation or transfer or unlawful confinement of a civilian;

(h) taking civilians as hostages.

Violations of the laws or customs of war

41. The 1907 Hague Convention (IV) Respecting the Laws and Customs of War on Land and the Regulations annexed thereto comprise a second important area of conventional humanitarian international law which has become part of the body of international customary law.

42. The Nürnberg Tribunal recognized that many of the provisions contained in the Hague Regulations, although innovative at the time of their adoption were, by 1939, recognized by all civilized nations and were regarded as being declaratory of the laws and customs of war. The Nürnberg Tribunal also recognized that war crimes defined in article 6(b) of the Nürnberg Charter were already recognized as war crimes under international law, and covered in the Hague Regulations, for which guilty individuals were punishable.

43. The Hague Regulations cover aspects of international humanitarian law which are also covered by the 1949 Geneva Conventions. However, the Hague Regulations also recognize that the right of belligerents to conduct warfare is not unlimited and that resort to certain methods of waging war is prohibited under the rules of land warfare.

44. These rules of customary law, as interpreted and applied by the Nürnberg Tribunal, provide the basis for the corresponding article of the statute which would read as follows:

Article 3
Violations of the laws or customs of war

The International Tribunal shall have the power to prosecute persons violating the laws or customs of war. Such violations shall include, but not be limited to:

(a) employment of poisonous weapons or other weapons calculated to cause unnecessary suffering;

(b) wanton destruction of cities, towns or villages, or devastation not justified by military necessity;

(c) attack, or bombardment, by whatever means, of undefended towns, villages, dwellings, or buildings;

(d) seizure of, destruction or wilful damage done to institutions dedicated to religion, charity and education, the arts and sciences, historic monuments and works of art and science;

(e) plunder of public or private property.

Genocide

45. The 1948 Convention on the Prevention and Punishment of the Crime of Genocide confirms that genocide, whether committed in time of peace or in time of war, is a crime under international law for which individuals shall be tried and punished. The Convention is today considered part of international customary law as evidenced by the International Court of Justice in its Advisory Opinion on Reservations to the Convention on the Prevention and Punishment of the Crime of Genocide, 1951. 7/

46. The relevant provisions of the Genocide Convention are reproduced in the corresponding article of the statute, which would read as follows:

Article 4
Genocide

1. The International Tribunal shall have the power to prosecute persons committing genocide as defined in paragraph 2 of this article or of committing any of the other acts enumerated in paragraph 3 of this article.

2. Genocide means any of the following acts committed with intent to destroy, in whole or in part, a national, ethnical, racial or religious group, as such:

(a) killing members of the group;

(b) causing serious bodily or mental harm to members of the group;

7/ Reservations to the Convention on the Prevention and Punishment of the Crime of Genocide: Advisory Opinion of 28 May 1951, *International Court of Justice Reports, 1951*, p. 23.

(c) deliberately inflicting on the group conditions of life calculated to bring about its physical destruction in whole or in part;

(d) imposing measures intended to prevent births within the group;

(e) forcibly transferring children of the group to another group.

3. The following acts shall be punishable:

(a) genocide;

(b) conspiracy to commit genocide;

(c) direct and public incitement to commit genocide;

(d) attempt to commit genocide;

(e) complicity in genocide.

Crimes against humanity

47. Crimes against humanity were first recognized in the Charter and Judgement of the Nürnberg Tribunal, as well as in Law No. 10 of the Control Council for Germany. 8/ Crimes against humanity are aimed at any civilian population and are prohibited regardless of whether they are committed in an armed conflict, international or internal in character. 9/

48. Crimes against humanity refer to inhumane acts of a very serious nature, such as wilful killing, torture or rape, committed as part of a widespread or systematic attack against any civilian population on national, political, ethnic, racial or religious grounds. In the conflict in the territory of the former Yugoslavia, such inhumane acts have taken the form of so-called "ethnic cleansing" and widespread and systematic rape and other forms of sexual assault, including enforced prostitution.

49. The corresponding article of the statute would read as follows:

Article 5
Crimes against humanity

The International Tribunal shall have the power to prosecute persons responsible for the following crimes when committed in armed conflict, whether international or internal in character, and directed against any civilian population:

(a) murder;

(b) extermination;

(c) enslavement;

(d) deportation;

(e) imprisonment;

(f) torture;

(g) rape;

(h) persecutions on political, racial and religious grounds;

(i) other inhumane acts.

B. *Competence* ratione personae (*personal jurisdiction*) *and individual criminal responsibility*

50. By paragraph 1 of resolution 808 (1993), the Security Council decided that the International Tribunal shall be established for the prosecution of persons responsible for serious violations of international humanitarian law committed in the territory of the former Yugoslavia since 1991. In the light of the complex of resolutions leading up to resolution 808 (1993) (see paras. 5-7 above), the ordinary meaning of the term "persons responsible for serious violations of international humanitarian law" would be natural persons to the exclusion of juridical persons.

51. The question arises, however, whether a juridical person, such as an association or organization, may be considered criminal as such and thus its members, for that reason alone, be made subject to the jurisdiction of the International Tribunal. The Secretary-General believes that this concept should not be retained in regard to the International Tribunal. The criminal acts set out in this statute are carried out by natural persons; such persons would be subject to the jurisdiction of the International Tribunal irrespective of membership in groups.

52. The corresponding article of the statute would read:

Article 6
Personal jurisdiction

The International Tribunal shall have jurisdiction over natural persons pursuant to the provisions of the present Statute.

Individual criminal responsibility

53. An important element in relation to the competence *ratione personae* (personal jurisdiction) of the International Tribunal is the principle of individual criminal responsibility. As noted above, the Security Council has reaffirmed in a number of resolutions that persons committing serious violations of international humanitarian law in the former Yugoslavia are individually responsible for such violations.

8/ *Official Gazette of the Control Council for Germany, No. 3, p. 22, Military Government Gazette, Germany, British Zone of Control, No. 5, p. 46, Journal Officiel du Commandement en Chef Francais en Allemagne, No. 12 of 11 January 1946.*
9/ In this context, it is to be noted that the International Court of Justice has recognized that the prohibitions contained in common article 3 of the 1949 Geneva Conventions are based on "elementary considerations of humanity" and cannot be breached in an armed conflict, regardless of whether it is international or internal in character. *Case concerning Military and Paramilitary Activities in and against Nicaragua (Nicaragua v. United States of America), Judgement of 27 June 1986: I.C.J. Reports 1986, p. 114.*

54. The Secretary-General believes that all persons who participate in the planning, preparation or execution of serious violations of international humanitarian law in the former Yugoslavia contribute to the commission of the violation and are, therefore, individually responsible.

55. Virtually all of the written comments received by the Secretary-General have suggested that the statute of the International Tribunal should contain provisions with regard to the individual criminal responsibility of heads of State, government officials and persons acting in an official capacity. These suggestions draw upon the precedents following the Second World War. The Statute should, therefore, contain provisions which specify that a plea of head of State immunity or that an act was committed in the official capacity of the accused will not constitute a defence, nor will it mitigate punishment.

56. A person in a position of superior authority should, therefore, be held individually responsible for giving the unlawful order to commit a crime under the present statute. But he should also be held responsible for failure to prevent a crime or to deter the unlawful behaviour of his subordinates. This imputed responsibility or criminal negligence is engaged if the person in superior authority knew or had reason to know that his subordinates were about to commit or had committed crimes and yet failed to take the necessary and reasonable steps to prevent or repress the commission of such crimes or to punish those who had committed them.

57. Acting upon an order of a Government or a superior cannot relieve the perpetrator of the crime of his criminal responsibility and should not be a defence. Obedience to superior orders may, however, be considered a mitigating factor, should the International Tribunal determine that justice so requires. For example, the International Tribunal may consider the factor of superior orders in connection with other defences such as coercion or lack of moral choice.

58. The International Tribunal itself will have to decide on various personal defences which may relieve a person of individual criminal responsibility, such as minimum age or mental incapacity, drawing upon general principles of law recognized by all nations.

59. The corresponding article of the statute would read:

Article 7
Individual criminal responsibility

1. A person who planned, instigated, ordered, committed or otherwise aided and abetted in the planning, preparation or execution of a crime referred to in articles 2 to 5 of the present Statute, shall be individually responsible for the crime.

2. The official position of any accused person, whether as Head of State or Government or as a responsible Government official, shall not relieve such person of criminal responsibility nor mitigate punishment.

3. The fact that any of the acts referred to in articles 2 to 5 of the present Statute was committed by a subordinate does not relieve his superior of criminal responsibility if he knew or had reason to know that the subordinate was about to commit such acts or had done so and the superior failed to take the necessary and reasonable measures to prevent such acts or to punish the perpetrators thereof.

4. The fact that an accused person acted pursuant to an order of a Government or of a superior shall not relieve him of criminal responsibility, but may be considered in mitigation of punishment if the International Tribunal determines that justice so requires.

C. *Competence* ratione loci (*territorial jurisdiction*) *and* ratione temporis (*temporal jurisdiction*)

60. Pursuant to paragraph 1 of resolution 808 (1993), the territorial and temporal jurisdiction of the International Tribunal extends to serious violations of international humanitarian law to the extent that they have been "committed in the territory of the former Yugoslavia since 1991".

61. As far as the territorial jurisdiction of the International Tribunal is concerned, the territory of the former Yugoslavia means the territory of the former Socialist Federal Republic of Yugoslavia, including its land surface, airspace and territorial waters.

62. With regard to temporal jurisdiction, Security Council resolution 808 (1993) extends the jurisdiction of the International Tribunal to violations committed "since 1991". The Secretary-General understands this to mean anytime on or after 1 January 1991. This is a neutral date which is not tied to any specific event and is clearly intended to convey the notion that no judgement as to the international or internal character of the conflict is being exercised.

63. The corresponding article of the statute would read:

Article 8
Territorial and temporal jurisdiction

The territorial jurisdiction of the International Tribunal shall extend to the territory of the former Socialist Federal Republic of Yugoslavia, including its land surface, airspace and territorial waters. The temporal jurisdiction of the International Tribunal shall extend to a period beginning on 1 January 1991.

D. Concurrent jurisdiction and the principle of non-bis-in-idem

64. In establishing an international tribunal for the prosecution of persons responsible for serious violations committed in the territory of the former Yugoslavia since 1991, it was not the intention of the Security Council to preclude or prevent the exercise of jurisdiction by national courts with respect to such acts. Indeed national courts should be encouraged to exercise their jurisdiction in accordance with their relevant national laws and procedures.

65. It follows therefore that there is concurrent jurisdiction of the International Tribunal and national courts. This concurrent jurisdiction, however, should be subject to the primacy of the International Tribunal. At any stage of the procedure, the International Tribunal may formally request the national courts to defer to the competence of the International Tribunal. The details of how the primacy will be asserted shall be set out in the rules of procedure and evidence of the International Tribunal.

66. According to the principle of *non-bis-in-idem*, a person shall not be tried twice for the same crime. In the present context, given the primacy of the International Tribunal, the principle of *non-bis-in-idem* would preclude subsequent trial before a national court. However, the principle of *non-bis-in-idem* should not preclude a subsequent trial before the International Tribunal in the following two circumstances:

(a) The characterization of the act by the national court did not correspond to its characterization under the statute; or

(b) Conditions of impartiality, independence or effective means of adjudication were not guaranteed in the proceedings before the national courts.

67. Should the International Tribunal decide to assume jurisdiction over a person who has already been convicted by a national court, it should take into consideration the extent to which any penalty imposed by the national court has already been served.

68. The corresponding articles of the statute would read:

Article 9
Concurrent jurisdiction

1. The International Tribunal and national courts shall have concurrent jurisdiction to prosecute persons for serious violations of international humanitarian law committed in the territory of the former Yugoslavia since 1 January 1991.

2. The International Tribunal shall have primacy over national courts. At any stage of the procedure, the International Tribunal may formally request national courts to defer to the competence of the International Tribunal in accordance with the present Statute and the Rules of Procedure and Evidence of the International Tribunal.

Article 10
Non-bis-in-idem

1. No person shall be tried before a national court for acts constituting serious violations of international humanitarian law under the present Statute, for which he or she has already been tried by the International Tribunal.

2. A person who has been tried by a national court for acts constituting serious violations of international humanitarian law may be subsequently tried by the International Tribunal only if:

(a) the act for which he or she was tried was characterized as an ordinary crime; or

(b) the national court proceedings were not impartial or independent, were designed to shield the accused from international criminal responsibility, or the case was not diligently prosecuted.

3. In considering the penalty to be imposed on a person convicted of a crime under the present Statute, the International Tribunal shall take into account the extent to which any penalty imposed by a national court on the same person for the same act has already been served.

III. The organization of the International Tribunal

69. The organization of the International Tribunal should reflect the functions to be performed by it. Since the International Tribunal is established for the prosecution of persons responsible for serious violations of international humanitarian law committed in the territory of the former Yugoslavia, this presupposes an international tribunal composed of a judicial organ, a prosecutorial organ and a secretariat. It would be the function of the prosecutorial organ to investigate cases, prepare indictments and prosecute persons responsible for committing the violations referred to above. The judicial organ would hear the cases presented to its Trial Chambers, and consider appeals from the Trial Chambers in its Appeals Chamber. A secretariat or Registry would be required to service both the prosecutorial and judicial organs.

70. The International Tribunal should therefore consist of the following organs: the Chambers, comprising two Trial Chambers and one Appeals Chamber; a Prosecutor; and a Registry.

71. The corresponding article of the statute would read as follows:

Article 11
Organization of the International Tribunal

The International Tribunal shall consist of the following organs:

(a) The Chambers, comprising two Trial Chambers and an Appeals Chamber;

(b) The Prosecutor; and

(c) A Registry, servicing both the Chambers and the Prosecutor.

A. The Chambers

1. Composition of the Chambers

72. The Chambers should be composed of 11 independent judges, no 2 of whom may be nationals of the same State. Three judges would serve in each of the two Trial Chambers and five judges would serve in the Appeals Chamber.

73. The corresponding article of the statute would read as follows:

Article 12
Composition of the Chambers

The Chambers shall be composed of eleven independent judges, no two of whom may be nationals of the same State, who shall serve as follows:

(a) Three judges shall serve in each of the Trial Chambers;

(b) Five judges shall serve in the Appeals Chamber.

2. Qualifications and election of judges

74. The judges of the International Tribunal should be persons of high moral character, impartiality and integrity who possess the qualifications required in their respective countries for appointment to the highest judicial offices. Impartiality in this context includes impartiality with respect to the acts falling within the competence of the International Tribunal. In the overall composition of the Chambers, due account should be taken of the experience of the judges in criminal law, international law, including international humanitarian law and human rights law.

75. The judges should be elected by the General Assembly from a list submitted by the Security Council. The Secretary-General would invite nominations for judges from States Members of the United Nations as well as non-member States maintaining permanent observer missions at United Nations Headquarters. Within 60 days of the date of the invitation of the Secretary-General, each State would nominate up to two candidates meeting the qualifications mentioned in paragraph 74

above, who must not be of the same nationality. The Secretary-General would forward the nominations received to the Security Council. The Security Council would, as speedily as possible, establish from the nominations transmitted by the Secretary-General, a list of not less than 22 and not more than 33 candidates, taking due account of the adequate representation of the principal legal systems of the world. The President of the Security Council would then transmit the list to the General Assembly. From that list, the General Assembly would proceed as speedily as possible to elect the 11 judges of the International Tribunal. The candidates declared elected shall be those who have received an absolute majority of the votes of the States Members of the United Nations and of the States maintaining permanent observer missions at United Nations Headquarters. Should two candidates of the same nationality obtain the required majority vote, the one who received the higher number of votes shall be considered elected.

76. The judges shall be elected for a term of four years. The terms and conditions of service shall be those of the Judges of the International Court of Justice. They shall be eligible for re-election.

77. In the event of a vacancy occurring in the Chambers, the Secretary-General, after consultation with the Presidents of the Security Council and the General Assembly, would appoint a person meeting the qualifications of paragraph 74 above, for the remainder of the term of office concerned.

78. The corresponding article of the statute would read as follows:

Article 13
Qualifications and election of judges

1. The judges shall be persons of high moral character, impartiality and integrity who possess the qualifications required in their respective countries for appointment to the highest judicial offices. In the overall composition of the Chambers due account shall be taken of the experience of the judges in criminal law, international law, including international humanitarian law and human rights law.

2. The judges of the International Tribunal shall be elected by the General Assembly from a list submitted by the Security Council, in the following manner:

(a) The Secretary-General shall invite nominations for judges of the International Tribunal from States Members of the United Nations and non-member States maintaining permanent observer missions at United Nations Headquarters;

(b) Within sixty days of the date of the invitation of the Secretary-General, each State may nominate up to two candidates meeting the qualifications set out in paragraph 1 above, no two of whom shall be of the same nationality;

(c) The Secretary-General shall forward the nominations received to the Security Council. From the nominations received the Security Council shall establish a list of not less than twenty-two and not more than thirty-three candidates, taking due account of the adequate representation of the principal legal systems of the world;

(d) The President of the Security Council shall transmit the list of candidates to the President of the General Assembly. From that list the General Assembly shall elect the eleven judges of the International Tribunal. The candidates who receive an absolute majority of the votes of States Members of the United Nations and of the non-member States maintaining permanent observer missions at United Nations Headquarters, shall be declared elected. Should two candidates of the same nationality obtain the required majority vote, the one who received the higher number of votes shall be considered elected.

3. In the event of a vacancy in the Chambers, after consultation with the Presidents of the Security Council and of the General Assembly, the Secretary-General shall appoint a person meeting the qualifications of paragraph 1 above, for the remainder of the term of office concerned.

4. The judges shall be elected for a term of four years. The terms and conditions of service shall be those of the Judges of the International Court of justice. They shall be eligible for re-election.

3. Officers and members of the Chambers

79. The judges would elect a President of the International Tribunal from among their members who would be a member of the Appeals Chamber and would preside over the appellate proceedings.

80. Following consultation with the members of the Chambers, the President would assign the judges to the Appeals Chamber and to the Trial Chambers. Each judge would serve only in the chamber to which he or she was assigned.

81. The members of each Trial Chamber should elect a presiding judge who would conduct all of the proceedings before the Trial Chamber as a whole.

82. The corresponding article of the statute would read as follows:

Article 14
Officers and members of the Chambers

1. The judges of the International Tribunal shall elect a President.

2. The President of the International Tribunal shall be a member of the Appeals Chamber and shall preside over its proceedings.

3. After consultation with the judges of the International Tribunal, the President shall assign the judges to the Appeals Chamber and to the Trial Chambers. A judge shall serve only in the Chamber to which he or she was assigned.

4. The judges of each Trial Chamber shall elect a Presiding Judge, who shall conduct all of the proceedings of the Trial Chamber as a whole.

4. Rules of procedure and evidence

83. The judges of the International Tribunal as a whole should draft and adopt the rules of procedure and evidence of the International Tribunal governing the pre-trial phase of the proceedings, the conduct of trials and appeals, the admission of evidence, the protection of victims and witnesses and other appropriate matters.

84. The corresponding article of the statute would read as follows:

Article 15
Rules of procedure and evidence

The judges of the International Tribunal shall adopt rules of procedure and evidence for the conduct of the pre-trial phase of the proceedings, trials and appeals, the admission of evidence, the protection of victims and witnesses and other appropriate matters.

B. The Prosecutor

85. Responsibility for the conduct of all investigations and prosecutions of persons responsible for serious violations of international humanitarian law committed in the territory of the former Yugoslavia since 1 January 1991 should be entrusted to an independent Prosecutor. The Prosecutor should act independently as a separate organ of the International Tribunal. He or she shall not seek or receive instructions from any Government or from any other source.

86. The Prosecutor should be appointed by the Security Council, upon nomination by the Secretary-General. He or she should possess the highest level of professional competence and have extensive experience in the conduct of investigations and prosecutions of criminal cases. The Prosecutor should be appointed for a four-year term of office and be eligible for reappointment. The terms and conditions of service of the Prosecutor shall be those of an Under-Secretary-General of the United Nations.

87. The Prosecutor would be assisted by such other staff as may be required to perform effectively and efficiently the functions entrusted to him or her. Such staff would be appointed by the Secretary-General on the recommendation of the Prosecutor. The Office of the

Prosecutor should be composed of an investigation unit and a prosecution unit.

88. Staff appointed to the Office of the Prosecutor should meet rigorous criteria of professional experience and competence in their field. Persons should be sought who have had relevant experience in their own countries as investigators, prosecutors, criminal lawyers, law enforcement personnel or medical experts. Given the nature of the crimes committed and the sensitivities of victims of rape and sexual assault, due consideration should be given in the appointment of staff to the employment of qualified women.

89. The corresponding article of the statute would read as follows:

Article 16
The Prosecutor

1. The Prosecutor shall be responsible for the investigation and prosecution of persons responsible for serious violations of international humanitarian law committed in the territory of the former Yugoslavia since 1 January 1991.

2. The Prosecutor shall act independently as a separate organ of the International Tribunal. He or she shall not seek or receive instructions from any Government or from any other source.

3. The Office of the Prosecutor shall be composed of a Prosecutor and such other qualified staff as may be required.

4. The Prosecutor shall be appointed by the Security Council on nomination by the Secretary-General. He or she shall be of high moral character and possess the highest level of competence and experience in the conduct of investigations and prosecutions of criminal cases. The Prosecutor shall serve for a four-year term and be eligible for reappointment. The terms and conditions of service of the Prosecutor shall be those of an Under-Secretary-General of the United Nations.

5. The staff of the Office of the Prosecutor shall be appointed by the Secretary-General on the recommendation of the Prosecutor.

C.   The Registry

90. As indicated in paragraph 69 above, a Registry would be responsible for the servicing of the International Tribunal. The Registry would be headed by a Registrar, whose responsibilities shall include but should not be limited to the following:

(a) Public information and external relations;

(b) Preparation of minutes of meetings;

(c) Conference-service facilities;

(d) Printing and publication of all documents;

(e) All administrative work, budgetary and personnel matters; and

(f) Serving as the channel of communications to and from the International Tribunal.

91. The Registrar should be appointed by the Secretary-General after consultation with the President of the International Tribunal. He or she would be appointed to serve for a four-year term and be eligible for reappointment. The terms and conditions of service of the Registrar shall be those of an Assistant Secretary-General of the United Nations.

92. The corresponding article of the statute would read as follows:

Article 17
The Registry

1. The Registry shall be responsible for the administration and servicing of the International Tribunal.

2. The Registry shall consist of a Registrar and such other staff as may be required.

3. The Registrar shall be appointed by the Secretary-General after consultation with the President of the International Tribunal. He or she shall serve for a four-year term and be eligible for reappointment. The terms and conditions of service of the Registrar shall be those of an Assistant Secretary-General of the United Nations.

4. The staff of the Registry shall be appointed by the Secretary-General on the recommendation of the Registrar.

IV. Investigation and pre-trial proceedings

93. The Prosecutor would initiate investigations ex officio, or on the basis of information obtained from any source, particularly from Governments or United Nations organs, intergovernmental and non-governmental organizations. The Prosecutor would assess the information received or obtained and decide whether there is a sufficient basis to proceed.

94. In conducting his investigations, the Prosecutor should have the power to question suspects, victims and witnesses, to collect evidence and to conduct on-site investigations. In carrying out these tasks, the Prosecutor may, as appropriate, seek the assistance of the State authorities concerned.

95. Upon the completion of the investigation, if the Prosecutor has determined that a *prima facie* case exists for prosecution, he would prepare an indictment containing a concise statement of the facts and the crimes with which the accused is charged under the statute. The indictment would be transmitted to a judge of a Trial Chamber, who would review it and decide whether to confirm or to dismiss the indictment.

96. If the investigation includes questioning of the suspect, then he should have the right to be assisted by counsel of his own choice, including the right to have legal assistance assigned to him without payment by him in any such case if he does not have sufficient means to pay for it. He shall also be entitled to the necessary translation into and from a language he speaks and understands.

97. Upon confirmation of the indictment, the judge would, at the request of the Prosecutor, issue such orders and warrants for the arrest, detention, surrender and transfer of persons, or any other orders as may be necessary for the conduct of the trial.

98. The corresponding articles of the statute would read as follows:

Article 18
Investigation and preparation of indictment

1. The Prosecutor shall initiate investigations ex officio or on the basis of information obtained from any source, particularly from Governments, United Nations organs, intergovernmental and non-governmental organizations. The Prosecutor shall assess the information received or obtained and decide whether there is sufficient basis to proceed.

2. The Prosecutor shall have the power to question suspects, victims and witnesses, to collect evidence and to conduct on-site investigations. In carrying out these tasks the Prosecutor may, as appropriate, seek the assistance of the State authorities concerned.

3. If questioned, the suspect shall be entitled to be assisted by counsel of his own choice, including the right to have legal assistance assigned to him without payment by him in any such case if he does not have sufficient means to pay for it, as well as to necessary translation into and from a language he speaks and understands.

4. Upon a determination that a *prima facie* case exists, the Prosecutor shall prepare an indictment containing a concise statement of the facts and the crime or crimes with which the accused is charged under the Statute. The indictment shall be transmitted to a judge of the Trial Chamber.

Article 19
Review of the indictment

1. The judge of the Trial Chamber to whom the indictment has been transmitted shall review it. If satisfied that a *prima facie* case has been established by the Prosecutor, he shall confirm the indictment. If not so satisfied, the indictment shall be dismissed.

2. Upon confirmation of an indictment, the judge may, at the request of the Prosecutor, issue such orders and warrants for the arrest, detention, surrender or trans-fer of persons, and any other orders as may be required for the conduct of the trial.

V. Trial and post-trial proceedings

A. *Commencement and conduct of trial proceedings*

99. The Trial Chambers should ensure that a trial is fair and expeditious and that proceedings are conducted in accordance with the rules of procedure and evidence and with full respect for the rights of the accused. The Trial Chamber should also provide appropriate protection for victims and witnesses during the proceedings.

100. A person against whom an indictment has been confirmed would, pursuant to an order or a warrant of the International Tribunal, be informed of the contents of the indictment and taken into custody.

101. A trial should not commence until the accused is physically present before the International Tribunal. There is a widespread perception that trials *in absentia* should not be provided for in the statute as this would not be consistent with article 14 of the International Covenant on Civil and Political Rights, 10/ which provides that the accused shall be entitled to be tried in his presence.

102. The person against whom an indictment has been confirmed would be transferred to the seat of the International Tribunal and brought before a Trial Chamber without undue delay and formally charged. The Trial Chamber would read the indictment, satisfy itself that the rights of the accused are respected, confirm that the accused understands the indictment, and instruct the accused to enter a plea. After the plea has been entered, the Trial Chamber would set the date for trial.

103. The hearings should be held in public unless the Trial Chamber decides otherwise in accordance with its rules of procedure and evidence.

104. After hearing the submissions of the parties and examining the witnesses and evidence presented to it, the Trial Chamber would close the hearing and retire for private deliberations.

105. The corresponding article of the statute would read:

Article 20
Commencement and conduct of trial proceedings

1. The Trial Chambers shall ensure that a trial is fair and expeditious and that proceedings are conducted in accordance with the rules of procedure and evidence,

10/ United Nations, *Treaty Series*, vol. 999, No. 14668, p. 171 and vol. 1057, p. 407 (proces-verbal of rectification of authentic Spanish text).

with full respect for the rights of the accused and due regard for the protection of victims and witnesses.

2. A person against whom an indictment has been confirmed shall, pursuant to an order or an arrest warrant of the International Tribunal, be taken into custody, immediately informed of the charges against him and transferred to the International Tribunal.

3. The Trial Chamber shall read the indictment, satisfy itself that the rights of the accused are respected, confirm that the accused understands the indictment, and instruct the accused to enter a plea. The Trial Chamber shall then set the date for trial.

4. The hearings shall be public unless the Trial Chamber decides to close the proceedings in accordance with its rules of procedure and evidence.

B. Rights of the accused

106. It is axiomatic that the International Tribunal must fully respect internationally recognized standards regarding the rights of the accused at all stages of its proceedings. In the view of the Secretary-General, such internationally recognized standards are, in particular, contained in article 14 of the International Covenant on Civil and Political Rights. 10/

107. The corresponding article of the statute would read as follows:

Article 21
Rights of the accused

1. All persons shall be equal before the International Tribunal.

2. In the determination of charges against him, the accused shall be entitled to a fair and public hearing, subject to article 22 of the Statute.

3. The accused shall be presumed innocent until proved guilty according to the provisions of the present Statute.

4. In the determination of any charge against the accused pursuant to the present Statute, the accused shall be entitled to the following minimum guarantees, in full equality:

(a) to be informed promptly and in detail in a language which he understands of the nature and cause of the charge against him;

(b) to have adequate time and facilities for the preparation of his defence and to communicate with counsel of his own choosing;

(c) to be tried without undue delay;

(d) to be tried in his presence, and to defend himself in person or through legal assistance of his own choosing; to be informed, if he does not have legal assistance, of this right; and to have legal assistance assigned to him, in any case where the interests of justice so require, and without payment by him in any such case if he does not have sufficient means to pay for it;

(e) to examine, or have examined, the witnesses against him and to obtain the attendance and examination of witnesses on his behalf under the same conditions as witnesses against him;

(f) to have the free assistance of an interpreter if he cannot understand or speak the language used in the International Tribunal;

(g) not to be compelled to testify against himself or to confess guilt.

C. Protection of victims and witnesses

108. In the light of the particular nature of the crimes committed in the former Yugoslavia, it will be necessary for the International Tribunal to ensure the protection of victims and witnesses. Necessary protection measures should therefore be provided in the rules of procedure and evidence for victims and witnesses, especially in cases of rape or sexual assault. Such measures should include, but should not be limited to the conduct of in camera proceedings, and the protection of the victim's identity.

109. The corresponding article of the statute would read as follows:

Article 22
Protection of victims and witnesses

The International Tribunal shall provide in its rules of procedure and evidence for the protection of victims and witnesses. Such protection measures shall include, but shall not be limited to, the conduct of in camera proceedings and the protection of the victim's identity.

D. Judgement and penalties

110. The Trial Chambers would have the power to pronounce judgements and impose sentences and penalties on persons convicted of serious violations of international humanitarian law. A judgement would be rendered by a majority of the judges of the Chamber and delivered in public. It should be written and accompanied by a reasoned opinion. Separate or dissenting opinions should be permitted.

111. The penalty to be imposed on a convicted person would be limited to imprisonment. In determining the term of imprisonment, the Trial Chambers should have recourse to the general practice of prison sentences applicable in the courts of the former Yugoslavia.

112. The International Tribunal should not be empowered to impose the death penalty.

113. In imposing sentences, the Trial Chambers should take into account such factors as the gravity of the offence and the individual circumstances of the convicted person.

114. In addition to imprisonment, property and proceeds acquired by criminal conduct should be confiscated and returned to their rightful owners. This would include the return of property wrongfully acquired by means of duress. In this connection the Secretary-General recalls that in resolution 779 (1992) of 6 October 1992, the Security Council endorsed the principle that all statements or commitments made under duress, particularly those relating to land and property, are wholly null and void.

115. The corresponding articles of the statute would read as follows:

Article 23
Judgement

1. The Trial Chambers shall pronounce judgements and impose sentences and penalties on persons convicted of serious violations of international humanitarian law.

2. The judgement shall be rendered by a majority of the judges of the Trial Chamber, and shall be delivered by the Trial Chamber in public. It shall be accompanied by a reasoned opinion in writing, to which separate or dissenting opinions may be appended.

Article 24
Penalties

1. The penalty imposed by the Trial Chamber shall be limited to imprisonment. In determining the terms of imprisonment, the Trial Chambers shall have recourse to the general practice regarding prison sentences in the courts of the former Yugoslavia.

2. In imposing the sentences, the Trial Chambers should take into account such factors as the gravity of the offence and the individual circumstances of the convicted person.

3. In addition to imprisonment, the Trial Chambers may order the return of any property and proceeds acquired by criminal conduct, including by means of duress, to their rightful owners.

E. Appellate and review proceedings

116. The Secretary-General is of the view that the right of appeal should be provided for under the Statute. Such a right is a fundamental element of individual civil and political rights and has, *inter alia*, been incorporated in the International Covenant on Civil and Political Rights. For this reason, the Secretary-General has proposed that there should be an Appeals Chamber.

117. The right of appeal should be exercisable on two grounds: an error on a question of law invalidating the decision or, an error of fact which has occasioned a miscarriage of justice. The Prosecutor should also be entitled to initiate appeal proceedings on the same grounds.

118. The judgement of the Appeals Chamber affirming, reversing or revising the judgement of the Trial Chamber would be final. It would be delivered by the Appeals Chamber in public and be accompanied by a reasoned opinion to which separate or dissenting opinions may be appended.

119. Where a new fact has come to light which was not known at the time of the proceedings before the Trial Chambers or the Appeals Chamber, and which could have been a decisive factor in reaching the decision, the convicted person or the Prosecutor should be authorized to submit to the International Tribunal an application for review of the judgement.

120. The corresponding articles of the statute would read as follows:

Article 25
Appellate proceedings

1. The Appeals Chamber shall hear appeals from persons convicted by the Trial Chambers or from the Prosecutor on the following grounds:

(a) an error on a question of law invalidating the decision; or

(b) an error of fact which has occasioned a miscarriage of justice.

2. The Appeals Chamber may affirm, reverse or revise the decisions taken by the Trial Chambers.

Article 26
Review proceedings

Where a new fact has been discovered which was not known at the time of the proceedings before the Trial Chambers or the Appeals Chamber and which could have been a decisive factor in reaching the decision, the convicted person or the Prosecutor may submit to the International Tribunal an application for review of the judgement.

F. Enforcement of sentences

121. The Secretary-General is of the view that, given the nature of the crimes in question and the international character of the tribunal, the enforcement of sentences should take place outside the territory of the former Yugoslavia. States should be encouraged to declare their readiness to carry out the enforcement of prison sentences in accordance with their domestic laws

and procedures, under the supervision of the International Tribunal.

122. The Security Council would make appropriate arrangements to obtain from States an indication of their willingness to accept convicted persons. This information would be communicated to the Registrar, who would prepare a list of States in which the enforcement of sentences would be carried out.

123. The accused would be eligible for pardon or commutation of sentence in accordance with the laws of the State in which sentence is served. In such an event, the State concerned would notify the International Tribunal, which would decide the matter in accordance with the interests of justice and the general principles of law.

124. The corresponding articles of the statute would read as follows:

Article 27
Enforcement of sentences

Imprisonment shall be served in a State designated by the International Tribunal from a list of States which have indicated to the Security Council their willingness to accept convicted persons. Such imprisonment shall be in accordance with the applicable law of the State concerned, subject to the supervision of the International Tribunal.

Article 28
Pardon or commutation of sentences

If, pursuant to the applicable law of the State in which the convicted person is imprisoned, he or she is eligible for pardon or commutation of sentence, the State concerned shall notify the International Tribunal accordingly. The President of the International Tribunal, in consultation with the judges, shall decide the matter on the basis of the interests of justice and the general principles of law.

VI. Cooperation and judicial assistance

125. As pointed out in paragraph 23 above, the establishment of the International Tribunal on the basis of a Chapter VII decision creates a binding obligation on all States to take whatever steps are required to implement the decision. In practical terms, this means that all States would be under an obligation to cooperate with the International Tribunal and to assist it in all stages of the proceedings to ensure compliance with requests for assistance in the gathering of evidence, hearing of witnesses, suspects and experts, identification and location of persons and the service of documents. Effect shall also be given to orders issued by the Trial Chambers, such as warrants of arrest, search warrants, warrants for surrender or transfer of persons, and any other orders necessary for the conduct of the trial.

126. In this connection, an order by a Trial Chamber for the surrender or transfer of persons to the custody of the International Tribunal shall be considered to be the application of an enforcement measure under Chapter VII of the Charter of the United Nations.

127. The corresponding article of the statute would read as follows:

Article 29
Cooperation and judicial assistance

1. States shall cooperate with the International Tribunal in the investigation and prosecution of persons accused of committing serious violations of international humanitarian law.

2. States shall comply without undue delay with any request for assistance or an order issued by a Trial Chamber, including, but not limited to:

(a) the identification and location of persons;

(b) the taking of testimony and the production of evidence;

(c) the service of documents;

(d) the arrest or detention of persons;

(e) the surrender or the transfer of the accused to the International Tribunal.

VII. General provisions

A. The status, privileges and immunities of the International Tribunal

128. The Convention on the Privileges and Immunities of the United Nations of 13 February 1946 would apply to the International Tribunal, the judges, the Prosecutor and his staff, and the Registrar and his staff. The judges, the Prosecutor, and the Registrar would be granted the privileges and immunities, exemptions and facilities accorded to diplomatic envoys in accordance with international law. The staff of the Prosecutor and the Registrar would enjoy the privileges and immunities of officials of the United Nations within the meaning of articles V and VII of the Convention.

129. Other persons, including the accused, required at the seat of the International Tribunal would be accorded such treatment as is necessary for the proper functioning of the International Tribunal.

130. The corresponding article of the statute would read:

Article 30
The status, privileges and immunities of the International Tribunal

1. The Convention on the Privileges and Immunities of the United Nations of 13 February 1946 shall apply to the International Tribunal, the judges, the Prosecutor and his staff, and the Registrar and his staff.

2. The judges, the Prosecutor and the Registrar shall enjoy the privileges and immunities, exemptions and facilities accorded to diplomatic envoys, in accordance with international law.

3. The staff of the Prosecutor and of the Registrar shall enjoy the privileges and immunities accorded to officials of the United Nations under articles V and VII of the Convention referred to in paragraph 1 of this article.

4. Other persons, including the accused, required at the seat of the International Tribunal shall be accorded such treatment as is necessary for the proper functioning of the International Tribunal.

B. Seat of the International Tribunal

131. While it will be for the Security Council to determine the location of the seat of the International Tribunal, in the view of the Secretary-General, there are a number of elementary considerations of justice and fairness, as well as administrative efficiency and economy which should be taken into account. As a matter of justice and fairness, it would not be appropriate for the International Tribunal to have its seat in the territory of the former Yugoslavia or in any State neighbouring upon the former Yugoslavia. For reasons of administrative efficiency and economy, it would be desirable to establish the seat of the International Tribunal at a European location in which the United Nations already has an important presence. The two locations which fulfil these requirements are Geneva and The Hague. Provided that the necessary arrangements can be made with the host country, the Secretary-General believes that the seat of the International Tribunal should be at The Hague.

132. The corresponding article of the statute would read:

Article 31
Seat of the International Tribunal

The International Tribunal shall have its seat at The Hague.

C. Financial arrangements

133. The expenses of the International Tribunal should be borne by the regular budget of the United Nations in accordance with Article 17 of the Charter of the United Nations.

134. The corresponding article of the statute would read:

Article 32
Expenses of the International Tribunal

The expenses of the International Tribunal shall be borne by the regular budget of the United Nations in accordance with Article 17 of the Charter of the United Nations.

D. Working languages

135. The working languages of the Tribunal should be English and French.

136. The corresponding article of the statute would read as follows:

Article 33
Working languages

The working languages of the International Tribunal shall be English and French.

E. Annual report

137. The International Tribunal should submit an annual report on its activities to the Security Council and the General Assembly.

138. The corresponding article of the statute would read:

Article 34
Annual report

The President of the International Tribunal shall submit an annual report of the International Tribunal to the Security Council and to the General Assembly.

Annex
Statute of the International Tribunal

Having been established by the Security Council acting under Chapter VII of the Charter of the United Nations, the International Tribunal for the Prosecution of Persons Responsible for Serious Violations of International Humanitarian Law Committed in the Territory of the Former Yugoslavia since 1991 (hereinafter referred to as "the International Tribunal") shall function in accordance with the provisions of the present Statute.

Article 1
Competence of the International Tribunal

The International Tribunal shall have the power to prosecute persons responsible for serious violations of international humanitarian law committed in the territory of the former Yugoslavia since 1991 in accordance with the provisions of the present Statute.

Article 2
Grave breaches of the Geneva Conventions of 1949

The International Tribunal shall have the power to prosecute persons committing or ordering to be committed grave breaches of the Geneva Conventions of 12 August 1949, namely the following acts against persons or property protected under the provisions of the relevant Geneva Convention:

(a) wilful killing;

(b) torture or inhuman treatment, including biological experiments;

(c) wilfully causing great suffering or serious injury to body or health;

(d) extensive destruction and appropriation of property, not justified by military necessity and carried out unlawfully and wantonly;

(e) compelling a prisoner of war or a civilian to serve in the forces of a hostile power;

(f) wilfully depriving a prisoner of war or a civilian of the rights of fair and regular trial;

(g) unlawful deportation or transfer or unlawful confinement of a civilian;

(h) taking civilians as hostages.

Article 3
Violations of the laws or customs of war

The International Tribunal shall have the power to prosecute persons violating the laws or customs of war. Such violations shall include, but not be limited to:

(a) employment of poisonous weapons or other weapons calculated to cause unnecessary suffering;

(b) wanton destruction of cities, towns or villages, or devastation not justified by military necessity;

(c) attack, or bombardment, by whatever means, of undefended towns, villages, dwellings, or buildings;

(d) seizure of, destruction or wilful damage done to institutions dedicated to religion, charity and education, the arts and sciences, historic monuments and works of art and science;

(e) plunder of public or private property.

Article 4
Genocide

1. The International Tribunal shall have the power to prosecute persons committing genocide as defined in paragraph 2 of this article or of committing any of the other acts enumerated in paragraph 3 of this article.

2. Genocide means any of the following acts committed with intent to destroy, in whole or in part, a national, ethnical, racial or religious group, as such:

(a) killing members of the group;

(b) causing serious bodily or mental harm to members of the group;

(c) deliberately inflicting on the group conditions of life calculated to bring about its physical destruction in whole or in part;

(d) imposing measures intended to prevent births within the group;

(e) forcibly transferring children of the group to another group.

3. The following acts shall be punishable:

(a) genocide;

(b) conspiracy to commit genocide;

(c) direct and public incitement to commit genocide;

(d) attempt to commit genocide;

(e) complicity in genocide.

Article 5
Crimes against humanity

The International Tribunal shall have the power to prosecute persons responsible for the following crimes when committed in armed conflict, whether international or internal in character, and directed against any civilian population:

(a) murder;

(b) extermination;

(c) enslavement;

(d) deportation;

(e) imprisonment;

(f) torture;

(g) rape;

(h) persecutions on political, racial and religious grounds;

(i) other inhumane acts.

Article 6
Personal jurisdiction

The International Tribunal shall have jurisdiction over natural persons pursuant to the provisions of the present Statute.

Article 7
Individual criminal responsibility

1. A person who planned, instigated, ordered, committed or otherwise aided and abetted in the planning, preparation or execution of a crime referred to in articles 2 to 5 of the present Statute, shall be individually responsible for the crime.

2. The official position of any accused person, whether as Head of State or Government or as a responsible Government official, shall not relieve such person of criminal responsibility nor mitigate punishment.

3. The fact that any of the acts referred to in articles 2 to 5 of the present Statute was committed by a subordinate does not relieve his superior of criminal responsibility if he knew or had reason to know that the subordinate was about to commit such acts or had done so and the superior failed to take the necessary and reasonable measures to prevent such acts or to punish the perpetrators thereof.

4. The fact that an accused person acted pursuant to an order of a Government or of a superior shall not relieve him of criminal responsibility, but may be considered in mitigation of punishment if the International Tribunal determines that justice so requires.

Article 8
Territorial and temporal jurisdiction

The territorial jurisdiction of the International Tribunal shall extend to the territory of the former Socialist Federal Republic of Yugoslavia, including its land surface, airspace and territorial waters. The temporal jurisdiction of the International Tribunal shall extend to a period beginning on 1 January 1991.

Article 9
Concurrent jurisdiction

1. The International Tribunal and national courts shall have concurrent jurisdiction to prosecute persons for serious violations of international humanitarian law committed in the territory of the former Yugoslavia since 1 January 1991.

2. The International Tribunal shall have primacy over national courts. At any stage of the procedure, the International Tribunal may formally request national courts to defer to the competence of the International Tribunal in accordance with the present Statute and the Rules of Procedure and Evidence of the International Tribunal.

Article 10
Non-bis-in-idem

1. No person shall be tried before a national court for acts constituting serious violations of international humanitarian law under the present Statute, for which he or she has already been tried by the International Tribunal.

2. A person who has been tried by a national court for acts constituting serious violations of international humanitarian law may be subsequently tried by the International Tribunal only if:

(a) the act for which he or she was tried was characterized as an ordinary crime; or

(b) the national court proceedings were not impartial or independent, were designed to shield the accused from international criminal responsibility, or the case was not diligently prosecuted.

3. In considering the penalty to be imposed on a person convicted of a crime under the present Statute, the International Tribunal shall take into account the extent to which any penalty imposed by a national court on the same person for the same act has already been served.

Article 11
Organization of the International Tribunal

The International Tribunal shall consist of the following organs:

(a) The Chambers, comprising two Trial Chambers and an Appeals Chamber;

(b) The Prosecutor, and

(c) A Registry, servicing both the Chambers and the Prosecutor.

Article 12
Composition of the Chambers

The Chambers shall be composed of eleven independent judges, no two of whom may be nationals of the same State, who shall serve as follows:

(a) Three judges shall serve in each of the Trial Chambers;

(b) Five judges shall serve in the Appeals Chamber.

Article 13
Qualifications and election of judges

1. The judges shall be persons of high moral character, impartiality and integrity who possess the qualifications required in their respective countries for appointment to the highest judicial offices. In the overall composition of the Chambers due account shall be taken of the experience of the judges in criminal law, international law, including international humanitarian law and human rights law.

2. The judges of the International Tribunal shall be elected by the General Assembly from a list submitted by the Security Council, in the following manner:

(a) The Secretary-General shall invite nominations for judges of the International Tribunal from States Members of the United Nations and non-member States maintaining permanent observer missions at United Nations Headquarters;

(b) Within sixty days of the date of the invitation of the Secretary-General, each State may nominate up to two candidates meeting the qualifications set out in paragraph 1 above, no two of whom shall be of the same nationality;

(c) The Secretary-General shall forward the nominations received to the Security Council. From the nominations received the Security Council shall establish a list of not less than twenty-two and not more than thirty-three candidates, taking due account of the adequate representation of the principal legal systems of the world;

(d) The President of the Security Council shall transmit the list of candidates to the President of the General Assembly. From that list the General Assembly shall elect the eleven judges of the International Tribunal. The candidates who receive an absolute majority of the votes of the States Members of the United Nations and of the non-Member States maintaining permanent observer missions at United Nations Headquarters, shall be declared elected. Should two candidates of the same nationality obtain the required majority vote, the one who received the higher number of votes shall be considered elected.

3. In the event of a vacancy in the Chambers, after consultation with the Presidents of the Security Council and of the General Assembly, the Secretary-General shall appoint a person meeting the qualifications of paragraph 1 above, for the remainder of the term of office concerned.

4. The judges shall be elected for a term of four years. The terms and conditions of service shall be those of the judges of the International Court of Justice. They shall be eligible for re-election.

Article 14
Officers and members of the Chambers

1. The judges of the International Tribunal shall elect a President.

2. The President of the International Tribunal shall be a member of the Appeals Chamber and shall preside over its proceedings.

3. After consultation with the judges of the International Tribunal, the President shall assign the judges to the Appeals Chamber and to the Trial Chambers. A judge shall serve only in the Chamber to which he or she was assigned.

4. The judges of each Trial Chamber shall elect a Presiding Judge, who shall conduct all of the proceedings of the Trial Chamber as a whole.

Article 15
Rules of procedure and evidence

The judges of the International Tribunal shall adopt rules of procedure and evidence for the conduct of the pre-trial phase of the proceedings, trials and appeals, the admission of evidence, the protection of victims and witnesses and other appropriate matters.

Article 16
The Prosecutor

1. The Prosecutor shall be responsible for the investigation and prosecution of persons responsible for serious violations of international humanitarian law committed in the territory of the former Yugoslavia since 1 January 1991.

2. The Prosecutor shall act independently as a separate organ of the International Tribunal. He or she shall not seek or receive instructions from any Government or from any other source.

3. The Office of the Prosecutor shall be composed of a Prosecutor and such other qualified staff as may be required.

4. The Prosecutor shall be appointed by the Security Council on nomination by the Secretary-General. He or she shall be of high moral character and possess the highest level of competence and experience in the conduct of investigations and prosecutions of criminal cases. The Prosecutor shall serve for a four-year term and be eligible for reappointment. The terms and conditions of service of the Prosecutor shall be those of an Under-Secretary-General of the United Nations.

5. The staff of the Office of the Prosecutor shall be appointed by the Secretary-General on the recommendation of the Prosecutor.

Article 17
The Registry

1. The Registry shall be responsible for the administration and servicing of the International Tribunal.

2. The Registry shall consist of a Registrar and such other staff as may be required.

3. The Registrar shall be appointed by the Secretary-General after consultation with the President of the International Tribunal. He or she shall serve for a four-year term and be eligible for reappointment. The terms and conditions of service of the Registrar shall be those of an Assistant Secretary-General of the United Nations.

4. The staff of the Registry shall be appointed by the Secretary-General on the recommendation of the Registrar.

Article 18
Investigation and preparation of indictment

1. The Prosecutor shall initiate investigations ex-officio or on the basis of information obtained from any source, particularly from Governments, United Nations organs, intergovernmental and non-governmental organizations. The Prosecutor shall assess the information received or obtained and decide whether there is sufficient basis to proceed.

2. The Prosecutor shall have the power to question suspects, victims and witnesses, to collect evidence and to conduct on-site investigations. In carrying out these tasks, the Prosecutor may, as appropriate, seek the assistance of the State authorities concerned.

3. If questioned, the suspect shall be entitled to be assisted by counsel of his own choice, including the right to have legal assistance assigned to him without payment by him in any such case if he does not have sufficient means to pay for it, as well as to necessary translation into and from a language he speaks and understands.

4. Upon a determination that a prima facie case exists, the Prosecutor shall prepare an indictment containing a concise statement of the facts and the crime or crimes with which the accused is charged under the Statute. The indictment shall be transmitted to a judge of the Trial Chamber.

Article 19
Review of the indictment

1. The judge of the Trial Chamber to whom the indictment has been transmitted shall review it. If satisfied that a *prima facie* case has been established by the Prosecutor, he shall confirm the indictment. If not so satisfied, the indictment shall be dismissed.

2. Upon confirmation of an indictment, the judge may, at the request of the Prosecutor, issue such orders and warrants for the arrest, detention, surrender or transfer of persons, and any other orders as may be required for the conduct of the trial.

Article 20
Commencement and conduct of trial proceedings

1. The Trial Chambers shall ensure that a trial is fair and expeditious and that proceedings are conducted in accordance with the rules of procedure and evidence, with full respect for the rights of the accused and due regard for the protection of victims and witnesses.

2. A person against whom an indictment has been confirmed shall, pursuant to an order or an arrest warrant of the International Tribunal, be taken into custody, immediately informed of the charges against him and transferred to the International Tribunal.

3. The Trial Chamber shall read the indictment, satisfy itself that the rights of the accused are respected, confirm that the accused understands the indictment, and instruct the accused to enter a plea. The Trial Chamber shall then set the date for trial.

4. The hearings shall be public unless the Trial Chamber decides to close the proceedings in accordance with its rules of procedure and evidence.

Article 21
Rights of the accused

1. All persons shall be equal before the International Tribunal.

2. In the determination of charges against him, the accused shall be entitled to a fair and public hearing, subject to article 22 of the Statute.

3. The accused shall be presumed innocent until proved guilty according to the provisions of the present Statute.

4. In the determination of any charge against the accused pursuant to the present Statute, the accused shall be entitled to the following minimum guarantees, in full equality:

(a) to be informed promptly and in detail in a language which he understands of the nature and cause of the charge against him;

(b) to have adequate time and facilities for the preparation of his defence and to communicate with counsel of his own choosing;

(c) to be tried without undue delay;

(d) to be tried in his presence, and to defend himself in person or through legal assistance of his own choosing; to be informed, if he does not have legal assistance, of this right; and to have legal assistance assigned to him, in any case where the interests of justice so require, and without payment by him in any such case if he does not have sufficient means to pay for it;

(e) to examine, or have examined, the witnesses against him and to obtain the attendance and examination of witnesses on his behalf under the same conditions as witnesses against him;

(f) to have the free assistance of an interpreter if he cannot understand or speak the language used in the International Tribunal;

(g) not to be compelled to testify against himself or to confess guilt.

Article 22
Protection of victims and witnesses

The International Tribunal shall provide in its rules of procedure and evidence for the protection of victims and witnesses. Such protection measures shall include, but shall not be limited to, the conduct of *in camera* proceedings and the protection of the victim's identity.

Article 23
Judgement

1. The Trial Chambers shall pronounce judgements and impose sentences and penalties on persons convicted of serious violations of international humanitarian law.

2. The judgement shall be rendered by a majority of the judges of the Trial Chamber, and shall be delivered by the Trial Chamber in public. It shall be accompanied by a reasoned opinion in writing, to which separate or dissenting opinions may be appended.

Article 24
Penalties

1. The penalty imposed by the Trial Chamber shall be limited to imprisonment. In determining the terms of imprisonment, the Trial Chambers shall have recourse to the general practice regarding prison sentences in the courts of the former Yugoslavia.

2. In imposing the sentences, the Trial Chambers should take into account such factors as the gravity of the offence and the individual circumstances of the convicted person.

3. In addition to imprisonment, the Trial Chambers may order the return of any property and proceeds acquired by criminal conduct, including by means of duress, to their rightful owners.

Article 25
Appellate proceedings

1. The Appeals Chamber shall hear appeals from persons convicted by the Trial Chambers or from the Prosecutor on the following grounds:

(a) an error on a question of law invalidating the decision; or

(b) an error of fact which has occasioned a miscarriage of justice.

2. The Appeals Chamber may affirm, reverse or revise the decisions taken by the Trial Chambers.

Article 26
Review proceedings

Where a new fact has been discovered which was not known at the time of the proceedings before the Trial Chambers or the Appeals Chamber and which could have been a decisive factor in reaching the decision, the convicted person or the Prosecutor may submit to the International Tribunal an application for review of the judgement.

Article 27
Enforcement of sentences

Imprisonment shall be served in a State designated by the International Tribunal from a list of States which have indicated to the Security Council their willingness to accept convicted persons. Such imprisonment shall be in accordance with the applicable law of the State concerned, subject to the supervision of the International Tribunal.

Article 28
Pardon or commutation of sentences

If, pursuant to the applicable law of the State in which the convicted person is imprisoned, he or she is eligible for pardon or commutation of sentence, the State concerned shall notify the International Tribunal accordingly. The President of the International Tribunal, in consultation with the judges, shall decide the matter on the basis of the interests of justice and the general principles of law.

Article 29
Cooperation and judicial assistance

1. States shall cooperate with the International Tribunal in the investigation and prosecution of persons accused of committing serious violations of international humanitarian law.

2. States shall comply without undue delay with any request for assistance or an order issued by a Trial Chamber, including, but not limited to:

(a) the identification and location of persons;

(b) the taking of testimony and the production of evidence;

(c) the service of documents;

(d) the arrest or detention of persons;

(e) the surrender or the transfer of the accused to the International Tribunal.

Article 30
The status, privileges and immunities of the International Tribunal

1. The Convention on the Privileges and Immunities of the United Nations of 13 February 1946 shall apply to the International Tribunal, the judges, the Prosecutor and his staff, and the Registrar and his staff.

2. The judges, the Prosecutor and the Registrar shall enjoy the privileges and immunities, exemptions and

facilities accorded to diplomatic envoys, in accordance with international law.

3. The staff of the Prosecutor and of the Registrar shall enjoy the privileges and immunities accorded to officials of the United Nations under articles V and VII of the Convention referred to in paragraph 1 of this article.

4. Other persons, including the accused, required at the seat of the International Tribunal shall be accorded such treatment as is necessary for the proper functioning of the International Tribunal.

Article 31
Seat of the International Tribunal

The International Tribunal shall have its seat at The Hague.

Article 32
Expenses of the International Tribunal

The expenses of the International Tribunal shall be borne by the regular budget of the United Nations in accordance with Article 17 of the Charter of the United Nations.

Article 33
Working languages

The working languages of the International Tribunal shall be English and French.

Article 34
Annual report

The President of the International Tribunal shall submit an annual report of the International Tribunal to the Security Council and to the General Assembly.

Document 83

Security Council resolution adopting the Statute of the International Tribunal for the Prosecution of Persons Responsible for Serious Violations of International Humanitarian Law Committed in the Territory of the Former Yugoslavia since 1991

S/RES/827 (1993), 25 May 1993

The Security Council,

Reaffirming its resolution 713 (1991) of 25 September 1991 and all subsequent relevant resolutions,

Having considered the report of the Secretary-General of 3 and 17 May 1993 pursuant to paragraph 2 of resolution 808 (1993), 1/

Expressing once again its grave alarm at continuing reports of widespread and flagrant violations of international humanitarian law occurring within the territory of the former Yugoslavia, and especially in the Republic of Bosnia and Herzegovina, including reports of mass killings, massive, organized and systematic detention and rape of women and the continuance of the practice of "ethnic cleansing", including for the acquisition and the holding of territory,

Determining that this situation continues to constitute a threat to international peace and security,

Determined to put an end to such crimes and to take effective measures to bring to justice the persons who are responsible for them,

Convinced that in the particular circumstances of the former Yugoslavia the establishment as an ad hoc measure by the Council of an international tribunal and

the prosecution of persons responsible for serious violations of international humanitarian law would enable this aim to be achieved and would contribute to the restoration and maintenance of peace,

Believing that the establishment of an international tribunal and the prosecution of persons responsible for the above-mentioned violations of international humanitarian law will contribute to ensuring that such violations are halted and effectively redressed,

Noting in this regard the recommendation by the Co-Chairmen of the Steering Committee of the International Conference on the Former Yugoslavia for the establishment of such a tribunal, 2/

Reaffirming in this regard its decision in resolution 808 (1993) of 22 February 1993 that an international tribunal shall be established for the prosecution of persons responsible for serious violations of international humanitarian law committed in the territory of the former Yugoslavia since 1991,

1/ *Official Records of the Security Council, Forty-eighth Year, Supplement for April, May and June 1993*, document S/25704 and Add.1.
2/ Ibid., *Supplement for January, February and March 1993*, document S/25221, annex I.

Considering that, pending the appointment of the prosecutor of the international tribunal, the Commission of Experts established pursuant to resolution 780 (1992) should continue on an urgent basis the collection of information relating to evidence of grave breaches of the Geneva Conventions 3/ and other violations of international humanitarian law as proposed in its interim report, 4/

Acting under Chapter VII of the Charter of the United Nations,

1. *Approves* the report of the Secretary-General; 1/

2. *Decides* hereby to establish an international tribunal for the sole purpose of prosecuting persons responsible for serious violations of international humanitarian law committed in the territory of the former Yugoslavia between 1 January 1991 and a date to be determined by the Security Council upon the restoration of peace and to this end to adopt the statute of the International Tribunal annexed to the report of the Secretary-General;

3. *Requests* the Secretary-General to submit to the judges of the International Tribunal, upon their election, any suggestions received from States for the rules of procedure and evidence called for in article 15 of the statute of the Tribunal;

4. *Decides* that all States shall cooperate fully with the International Tribunal and its organs in accordance with the present resolution and the statute of the Tribunal and that consequently all States shall take any measures necessary under their domestic law to implement the provisions of the present resolution and the statute, in-

cluding the obligation of States to comply with requests for assistance or orders issued by a trial chamber under article 29 of the statute;

5. *Urges* States and intergovernmental and non-governmental organizations to contribute funds, equipment and services to the International Tribunal, including the offer of expert personnel;

6. *Decides* that the determination of the seat of the International Tribunal is subject to the conclusion of appropriate arrangements between the United Nations and the Netherlands acceptable to the Council, and that the Tribunal may sit elsewhere when it considers it necessary for the efficient exercise of its functions;

7. *Decides also* that the work of the International Tribunal shall be carried out without prejudice to the right of the victims to seek, through appropriate means, compensation for damages incurred as a result of violations of international humanitarian law;

8. *Requests* the Secretary-General to implement urgently the present resolution and in particular to make practical arrangements for the effective functioning of the International Tribunal at the earliest time and to report periodically to the Council;

9. *Decides* to remain actively seized of the matter.

3/ United Nations, *Treaty Series*, vol. 75, Nos. 970-973.
4/ *Official Records of the Security Council, Forty-eighth Year, Supplement for January, February and March 1993*, document S/25274, annex I.

Document 84

Address by Secretary-General Boutros Boutros-Ghali, delivered at the opening of the World Conference on Human Rights, Vienna, 14 June 1993

A/CONF.157/22, 12 July 1993

The World Conference on Human Rights being convened today at Vienna marks one of those rare, defining moments when the entire community of States finds itself under the gaze of the world!

It is the gaze of the billions of men and women who yearn to recognize themselves in the discussions that we shall be conducting and the decisions that we shall be taking in their name. It is the gaze of all those men and women who, even now, are suffering in body and spirit because their human dignity is not recognized, or is being flouted. It is the gaze of history, as we meet at this crucial juncture!

When in 1989 the United Nations General Assembly requested the Secretary-General to seek the views of Governments and the organizations concerned on the desirability of convening a world conference on human rights, it was demonstrating remarkable historical intuition.

Two months earlier, the Berlin Wall had fallen, carrying away with it a certain vision of the world, and thereby opening up new perspectives. It was in the name of freedom, democracy and human rights that entire peoples were speaking out. Their determination, their abnegation—sometimes their sacrifices—reflected then, and still reflect, their commitment to do away with alienation and totalitarianism.

Thus preparations for today's Conference have gone hand-in-hand with an impressive acceleration of the course of history.

That conjunction of events must not be seen as pure chance or mere coincidence. It is always when the world is undergoing a metamorphosis, when certainties are collapsing, when the lines are becoming blurred, that there is greatest recourse to fundamental reference points, that the quest for ethics becomes more urgent, that the will to achieve self-understanding becomes imperative.

It is therefore natural that the international community should today feel the need to focus on its own values and, reflecting on its history, ask itself what constitutes its innermost identity—in other words, ask questions about humanity and about how, by protecting humanity, it protects itself.

The goals of the Conference faithfully reflect the following key questions:

- What progress has been made in the field of human rights since the Universal Declaration of 1948?
- What are the obstacles and how are they to be overcome?
- How can implementation of the human rights instruments be enhanced?
- How effective are the methods and mechanisms established by the United Nations?
- What financial resources should be allocated for United Nations action to promote human rights?
- And, at a deeper level, what are the links between the goals pursued by the United Nations and human rights, including the link between development, democracy and the universal enjoyment of economic, social, cultural, civil and political rights?

These are universal questions, but there is no single answer to any of them. While human rights are common to all members of the international community, and each member of that community recognizes himself in them, each cultural epoch has its own special way of helping to implement them. In this connection, a debt of thanks is owed to Member States which, at the regional level, have reminded others of this reality.

Yet this reminder must be a source of positive reflection, not of sterile misunderstanding.

Human rights, viewed at the universal level, bring us face-to-face with the most challenging dialectical conflict ever: between "identity" and "otherness", between the "myself" and "others". They teach us in a direct, straightforward manner that we are at the same time identical and different.

Thus the human rights that we proclaim and seek to safeguard can be brought about only if we transcend ourselves, only if we make a conscious effort to find our common essence beyond our apparent divisions, our temporary differences, our ideological and cultural barriers.

In sum, what I mean to say, with all solemnity, is that the human rights we are about to discuss here at Vienna are not the lowest common denominator among all nations, but rather what I should like to describe as the "irreducible human element", in other words, the quintessential values through which we affirm together that we are a single human community!

I do not want to underestimate the nature of our undertaking. Yet in such an area, this is no time to seek cautious compromise or approximate solutions, to be content with soothing declarations, or, worse still, to become bogged down in verbal battles. On the contrary, we must ascend to a conception of human rights that would make such rights truly universal!

There lies the challenge of our endeavour; there lies our work; there stands or falls this Conference in future evaluations.

An awareness of the complexities of the debate is the first step towards developing a method of debate. We should be under no illusion: a debate on human rights involves complex issues. Human rights should be viewed not only as the absolute yardstick which they are, but also as a synthesis resulting from a long historical process.

As an absolute yardstick, human rights constitute the common language of humanity. Adopting this language allows all peoples to understand others and to be the authors of their own history. Human rights, by definition, are the ultimate norm of all politics.

As an historical synthesis, human rights are, in their essence, in constant movement. By that I mean that human rights have a dual nature. They should express absolute, timeless injunctions, yet simultaneously reflect a moment in the development of history. Human rights are both absolute and historically defined.

The reason I began with these statements of principle—at the risk of appearing very abstract—is that I am convinced that there will be no appropriate solutions to any of the issues that we shall be considering in the coming days, even the most technical, unless we bear in mind the fundamental dialectical conflict between the universal and the particular, between identity and difference.

What makes our task especially urgent is the fact that with the development of communications, every day the whole world is called to witness the free enjoyment—or the violation—of human rights.

Not a day goes by without scenes of warfare or famine, arbitrary arrest, torture, rape, murder, expulsion, transfers of population, and ethnic cleansing. Not a day goes by without reports of attacks on the most fundamental freedoms. Not a day goes by without reminders of racism and the crimes it spawns, intolerance and the excesses it breeds, underdevelopment and the ravages it causes!

And what confronts those men, women and children who are suffering and dying is a reality that is more unbearable than ever; we are all similar, yet history emphasizes our differences and separates us on all sorts of grounds: political, economic, social and cultural.

We have indeed learned that it is possible to view differences as such with respect as sources of mutual enrichment; yet when differences become synonymous with inequalities, they cannot but be perceived as unjust. Today, all peoples and all nations share these feelings. That fact in itself is a step forward in the conscience of humanity.

The more so since to move from identifying inequality to rebelling against injustice is only possible in the context of a universal affirmation of the idea of human rights. Ultimately, it is this idea which allows us to move from ethical to legal considerations, and to impose value judgements and juridical constraints on human activity.

Let us not delude ourselves, however! Because judgements are based on this scale of constraints and values, it is also part of the power stakes. No doubt this is why some States seek—often and by various means—to appropriate human rights for their own benefit, even turning them into an instrument of national policy. There is no denying that some States constantly try to hijack or confiscate human rights.

Of course, in saying this, I do not mean to point a finger at any member of the international community. I only want to stress that human rights, in their very expression, reflect a power relationship.

Let us be clear about this! Human rights are closely related to the way in which States consider them; in other words, to the ways in which States govern their people; in yet other words, to the level of democracy in their political regimes!

If we bear all these problems in mind, I am positive that we shall avert the dual danger lurking ahead of us at the outset of this Conference: the danger of a cynical approach according to which the international dimension of human rights is nothing more than an ideological cover for the *realpolitik* of States; and the danger of a naive approach according to which human rights are the expression of universally shared values towards which all the members of the international community naturally aspire.

These considerations should remain present in our minds throughout our discussions, so that we may be bold in our proposals and firm in our principles.

In this regard, I should like to issue a solemn call: that this Conference should measure up to its subject matter and that it should be guided by a threefold requirement, which I shall refer to as "the three imperatives of the Vienna Conference": universality, guarantees, democratization.

Let us deal first with *the imperative of universality*. To be sure, human rights are a product of history. As such, they should be in accordance with history, should evolve simultaneously with history and should give the various peoples and nations a reflection of themselves that they recognize as their own. Yet, the fact that human rights keep pace with the course of history should not change what constitutes their very essence, namely their universality!

Secondly, there is *the imperative of guarantees*. Every day we see how discredited human rights and the United Nations itself would be, in the eyes of the world, if the declarations, covenants, charters, conventions and treaties that we draft in order to protect human rights remained dead letters or were constantly violated. Human rights should therefore be covered by effective mechanisms and procedures to guarantee and protect them and to provide sanctions.

Lastly, there is *the imperative of democratization*. In my opinion, this is essentially what is at stake as we approach the end of the century. Only democracy, within States and within the community of States, can truly guarantee human rights. It is through democracy that individual rights and collective rights, the rights of peoples and the rights of persons, are reconciled. It is through democracy that the rights of States and the rights of the community of States are reconciled.

It is on these three imperatives—universality, guarantees and democratization—that I should like you to reflect.

The imperative of universality will undoubtedly be in evidence throughout our debates. How could it be otherwise? Universality is inherent in human rights. The Charter is categorical on this score: Article 55 states that the United Nations shall promote "universal respect for, and observance of, human rights and fundamental freedoms for all without distinction as to race, sex, language, or religion". The title of the 1948 Declaration—universal, not international—reinforces this perspective.

However, this concept of universality must also be clearly understood and accepted by everyone. It would be a contradiction in terms if this imperative of universality on which our common conception of human rights is based were to become a source of misunderstanding among us.

It must therefore be stated, in the clearest possible terms, that universality is not something that is decreed, nor is it the expression of the ideological domination of one group of States over the rest of the world.

By its nature and composition, it is the General Assembly of the United Nations that is best equipped to express this idea of universality, and we should pay tribute to the human rights standard-setting in which it has been engaged for almost 50 years now.

As a result of its activities, the areas of protection have become increasingly precise: punishment of genocide, abolition of slavery, efforts to combat torture, elimination of all forms of discrimination based on race, sex, religion or belief.

Moreover, the subjects of those rights have been more clearly defined: right of peoples; protection of refugees, stateless persons, women, children, disabled persons, persons with mental illness, prisoners, victims of enforced disappearance; protection of the rights of migrant workers and their families; and protection of indigenous people. In this connection, the General Assembly is to be commended for drafting, as part of the activities relating to the International Year for the World's Indigenous People, a universal declaration for consideration next autumn.

The set of instruments resulting from this standard-setting by the United Nations General Assembly is now our common property. It has enough to satisfy all States, all peoples and all cultures, for the universality it affirms is that of the international community as a whole.

If we look closely at these instruments, and the World Conference on Human Rights affords an ideal opportunity to do so, we may be struck by, and justifiably proud of, the ceaseless efforts made by the General Assembly to develop on the very idea of universality.

While a general, abstract concept of human rights, born of liberal values, prevailed initially, as we can see from the text of the 1948 Universal Declaration, the input of the socialist States and the States of the third world helped broaden this initial vision. The 1966 Covenants bear witness to the broadening of our vision. They enable us to affirm, and I wish to emphasize this here, that civil and political rights and economic, social and cultural rights are equally important and worthy of attention.

We all know, however, that the General Assembly did not stop there: it expanded still further on the concept of universality by enunciating, after these collective rights, what I like to call rights of solidarity, rights which bring us back to a projected universality involving the joint action of all members of society both nationally and internationally. Since Article 1 of the Charter enunciated the right of peoples to self-determination, the General Assembly has proclaimed the right to a healthy environment, the right to peace, the right to food security, the right to ownership of the common heritage of mankind and, above all, the right to development.

I believe that this last right, in particular, shows just how modern the concept of universality is. The General Assembly went a long way towards recognizing this when, as early as 1979, it asserted that "the right to development is a human right" and that "equality of opportunity for development is a prerogative both of nations and of individuals who make up nations".

This idea was expressed even more clearly when, in 1986, the Assembly adopted a Declaration on the Right to Development which states that "the human person is the central subject of development and should be the active participant and beneficiary of the right to development". In that same instrument, the Assembly emphasizes the corresponding duties which this right imposes on States: the duty to cooperate with each other in ensuring development, the duty to formulate international development policies and, at the national level, the duty to ensure "access to basic resources, education, health services, food, housing, employment and the fair distribution of income".

I think that this approach to the concept of universality is the right one and that it is this course that we should follow.

We must recognize that while ideological splits and economic disparities may continue to be the hallmark of our international society, they cannot interfere with the universality of human rights.

I believe that at this moment in time it is less urgent to define new rights than to persuade States to adopt existing instruments and apply them effectively.

There are massive, ominous disparities in this essential area which must be corrected.

Some human rights conventions of which the United Nations is a depositary have been ratified by a large number of countries. For instance, as this Conference convened, the International Convention on the Elimination of All Forms of Racial Discrimination had been ratified by 135 States and the Convention on the Prevention and Punishment of the Crime of Genocide by 110 States. Of the two 1966 Covenants, the International Covenant on Economic, Social and Cultural Rights has been ratified by 121 States and the International Covenant on Civil and Political Rights by 118 States. The Convention on the Elimination of All Forms of Discrimination against Women has been ratified by 123 States. Lastly, the Convention on the Rights of the Child has been ratified by 138 States.

The level of ratification of other conventions is most unsatisfactory, however. So far, only 73 States have ratified the Convention against Torture and Other Cruel, Inhuman or Degrading Treatment or Punishment; only 55 States have ratified the International Convention against Apartheid in Sports; the Second Optional Protocol to the International Covenant on Civil and Political Rights, aiming at the abolition of the death penalty, adopted by the General Assembly on 15 December 1989, has been ratified by only 17 States; and only one country has ratified the International Convention on the Protection of the Rights of All Migrant Workers and Members of Their Families, adopted by the General Assembly on 18 December 1990.

As Secretary-General of the United Nations, I must strongly urge States to ratify all the international human rights treaties. To that end, I intend to open a dialogue with Member States to identify and try to overcome the obstacles to ratification.

I also believe that regional organizations have a positive role to play in making States increasingly aware of this problem. Regional action for the promotion of human rights in no way conflicts with United Nations action at the universal level—quite the opposite.

I understand the recent regional meetings on human rights as reflecting a concern to remain true to this concept of universality, no matter what serious problems or legitimate questions it may raise.

Important instruments exist in Latin America: the 1948 American Declaration of the Rights and Duties of Man, the 1960 Inter-American Commission on Human Rights and, lastly, the 1969 American Convention on Human Rights, now in force.

There are important instruments in Europe too, such as the 1950 European Convention on Human Rights, drawn up within the Council of Europe, or the 1961 European Social Charter.

There are important instruments in Africa: I am thinking particularly of the African Charter of Human and Peoples' Rights adopted by the OAU Summit in June 1981, which entered into force in 1986.

Regional organizations must contribute effectively to the protection of human rights, especially where they are able to set in motion mechanisms and procedures for guaranteeing human rights.

The imperative of guarantees should be the second concern of our Conference. What do human rights amount to without suitable machinery and structures to ensure their effectiveness, both internally and internationally? Here again, the Vienna Conference must not lapse into unproductive debates or futile polemics. To avoid this, the Conference must go back to the very essence of

human rights in international society, and to what is unique about them.

I am tempted to say that human rights, by their very nature, do away with the distinction traditionally drawn between the internal order and the international order. Human rights give rise to a new legal permeability. They should thus not be considered either from the viewpoint of absolute sovereignty or from the viewpoint of political intervention. On the contrary, it must be understood that human rights call for cooperation and coordination between States and international organizations.

In this context, the State should be the best guarantor of human rights. It is the State that the international community should principally entrust with ensuring the protection of individuals.

However, the issue of international action must be raised when States prove unworthy of this task, when they violate the fundamental principles laid down in the Charter of the United Nations, and when—far from being protectors of individuals—they become tormentors.

For us, this problem is a constant challenge, particularly since the flow of information and the effect of world public opinion make the issues in question even more pressing.

In these circumstances, the international community—that is to say, international organizations, whether universal or regional—must take over from the States that fail to fulfil their obligations. This is a legal and institutional construction that has nothing shocking about it and does not, in my view, harm our contemporary notion of sovereignty. For I am asking—I am asking us—whether a State has the right to expect absolute respect from the international community when it is tarnishing the noble concept of sovereignty by openly putting that concept to a use that is rejected by the conscience of the world and by the law! When sovereignty becomes the ultimate argument put forward by authoritarian regimes to support their undermining of the rights and freedoms of men, women and children, such sovereignty—and I state this as a sober truth—is already condemned by history.

Moreover, I believe all members of the international community have an interest in international action being thus defined and directed. Nothing would be more detrimental to States themselves than to leave private associations or non-governmental organizations to take sole responsibility for protecting human rights in individual States.

Yes, States must be convinced that the control exercised by the international community ultimately results in the greatest respect for their sovereignty and spheres of competence.

The Vienna Conference has therefore rightly decided to evaluate methods and machinery for guaranteeing human rights with a view to improving them. It is indeed important that all of us here be aware of the changes that have taken place, where such forms of control are concerned, at the administrative and jurisdictional levels and in the operational sphere.

At the administrative level, the number of procedures for guaranteeing human rights has been increasing for years, not only within the United Nations but also at such specialized agencies as ILO and UNESCO and at such regional organizations as the Council of Europe and the Organization of American States.

Within the United Nations, a proliferation of bodies each entrusted with monitoring implementation of a specific convention can even be noted. Some examples that come to mind are the Human Rights Committee, the Committee on Economic and Social Rights, the Committee on the Elimination of Racial Discrimination, the Committee on the Elimination of Discrimination against Women, the Committee against Torture and the Committee on the Rights of the Child.

At a more general level, the Commission on Human Rights and the United Nations Centre for Human Rights must be accorded a special place.

The Centre, in particular, has undergone profound changes in recent years.

Initially intended to carry out studies and provide information on all aspects of human rights, the Centre has gradually been called on to contribute to the implementation of conventions, and to participate in ad hoc committees of special rapporteurs set up to investigate such wide-ranging matters as summary executions, disappearances and instances of arbitrary detention.

It acts as the secretariat for the various human rights bodies and each year considers thousands of petitions, some of which lead, as a result of decisions of the Commission on Human Rights, to major investigative missions in the field.

Lastly, the Centre for Human Rights has been called upon to provide States with assistance and technical advice. Such assistance may involve preparing for elections, drafting constitutions or strengthening the judicial structures of the requesting States.

However, guaranteeing human rights also means setting up jurisdictional controls to punish any violations that occur.

In this area, regional organizations have shown the way—particularly in the context of the Council for Europe, in the form of the European Court of Human Rights, and in the Americas, in the form of the Inter-American Court.

I would draw your attention in this connection to the current efforts by the United Nations to promote both a permanent international criminal court and a special international tribunal to prosecute the crimes committed in the former Yugoslavia.

It was in February of this year that the Security Council decided to establish such a tribunal "for the prosecution of persons responsible for serious violations of international humanitarian law committed in the territory of the former Yugoslavia since 1991".

In asking the Secretary-General to consider this project, the Security Council has given itself an entirely new mandate. I believe that, the Tribunal should be established by a Council decision under Chapter VII of the Charter. Chapter VII offers the advantage of giving immediate effect to the establishment of the Tribunal, since all States are required to take the necessary steps to implement a decision adopted in this manner. The Council would thus be creating, in the context of an enforcement measure, a subsidiary organ as envisaged in Article 29 of the Charter, but one of a judicial nature.

I cannot discuss the development of measures taken by the Organization to safeguard human rights without mentioning the decisive action taken by the General Assembly in the area of humanitarian assistance.

Since December 1988, when the General Assembly adopted resolution 43/131 on humanitarian assistance to victims of natural disasters and similar emergency situations, the notion of a right to humanitarian assistance has, to a certain extent, become one of the areas in which human rights can actually be guaranteed.

We have seen this reflected in the Organization's operations in the Sudan, in Somalia, in the special case of Iraq and, today, in the former Yugoslavia.

Once again, these resolutions are not intended to justify some ostensible right of intervention, but simply to reflect one of the key ideas lying behind current efforts to safeguard human rights: the relationship between such guarantees and the imperative of democratization which the international community is rightly embracing today.

The imperative of democratization is the last—and surely the most important—rule of conduct which should guide our work. There is a growing awareness of this imperative within the international community. The process of democratization cannot be separated, in my view, from the protection of human rights. More precisely, democracy is the political framework in which human rights can best be safeguarded.

This is not merely a statement of principle, far less a concession to a fashion of the moment, but the realization that a democracy is the political system which best allows for the free exercise of individual rights. It is not possible to separate the United Nations promotion of human rights from the establishment of democratic systems within the international community.

Let me not be misunderstood nor unwittingly cause offence.

When, like so many others before me, I stress the imperative of democratization, I do not mean that some States should imitate others slavishly, nor do I expect them to borrow political systems that are alien to them, much less try to gratify certain Western States—in fact, just the opposite. Let us state, forcefully, that democracy is the private domain of no one. It can and ought to be assimilated by all cultures. It can take many forms in order to accommodate local realities more effectively. Democracy is not a model to copy from certain States, but a goal to be achieved by all peoples! It is the political expression of our common heritage. It is something to be shared by all. Thus, like human rights, democracy has a universal dimension!

To avoid misinterpretations and misunderstandings, we must all agree that democratization must not be a source of concern to some but should be an inspiration for all States! In this spirit the United Nations, in its mission to guarantee human rights, has an obligation to help States—often those that are the most disadvantaged—along the ever difficult road to democratization.

This is why we must distance ourselves from sterile polemics and act constructively to build the link between development, democracy and human rights, a link we already recognize as inescapable.

One thing is certain: there can be no sustainable development without promoting democracy and, thus, without respect for human rights. We all know that, on occasion, undemocratic practices and authoritarian policies have marked the first steps taken by some countries along the road to development. Yet, we also know that if these States do not undertake democratic reforms once they have begun to experience economic progress, they will ultimately achieve nothing more than disembodied growth, a source of greater inequity and, eventually, social unrest. Democracy alone can give development its true meaning.

This analysis must lead the developed countries to take an increasingly responsible attitude *vis-à-vis* developing States that are engaged in the democratization process. More than ever before, each one must realize its own responsibility in what is a joint undertaking. Each one must understand that development assistance contributes to the promotion of democracy and human rights. This in no way diminishes the overriding responsibility of all States, including developing countries, to promote democracy and human rights at home. This matter is of concern to the entire international community, for only through the development of each State can peace for all be ensured!

Each passing day shows that authoritarian regimes are potential causes of war and the extent to which, conversely, democracy is a guarantor of peace. We have only to look at the mandates given to United Nations forces to see the connection which the Organization is making, at the operational level and in the most concrete terms possible, between peace-keeping, the establishment of democracy and the safeguarding of human rights.

The mandate given to the United Nations operation in Namibia from April 1989 to March 1990 was an early but powerful demonstration of this evolution. Since 1991, a number of major operations have incorporated this political dimension—the safeguarding of human rights and the restoration of democracy—in their mission. We have seen this in the operations in Angola, Mozambique, El Salvador, Somalia and, of course, Cambodia.

Many States, in fact, know full how desirable it is to receive the electoral assistance which they are requesting with increasing frequency from the United Nations.

In 1989, a mission was set up to monitor the electoral process in Nicaragua. The following year, a similar mission was set up in Haiti. Requests for electoral assistance continued to increase at a steady rate, and in the autumn of 1991 the General Assembly endorsed the creation, within the Department of Political Affairs, of an electoral assistance unit, which became operational in April 1992.

Since then, equipped with this new tool, the United Nations has been better able to meet the requests for electoral assistance from many States: Argentina, Burundi, the Central African Republic, Chad, Colombia, the Congo, Djibouti, Equatorial Guinea, Eritrea, Ethiopia, Guinea, Guinea-Bissau, Guyana, Kenya, Lesotho, Madagascar, Malawi, Mali, the Niger, Romania, Senegal, Seychelles, Togo, Uganda ... the list is impressive.

Such requests fall into a variety of categories: the organization and holding of elections, their monitoring and verification, on-site coordination of international observers and with the many forms of technical assistance required for democratic elections to take place smoothly.

This is a major undertaking for the United Nations, and one whose magnitude must be stressed. We should not, however, blind ourselves to its limitations. The supervision and monitoring of elections do not in themselves constitute long-term guarantees of democratization and respect for human rights. This is borne out, unfortunately by the experiences of Angola and Haiti. The United Nations cannot guarantee that there will be enough of a sense of democracy for election results to be respected.

And so we have to do even more. We must help States change attitudes, persuade them to undertake structural reforms. The United Nations must be able to provide them with technical assistance that will allow them to adapt their institutions, educate their citizens, train leaders and set up regulatory mechanisms that respect democracy and reflect a concern for human rights. I am thinking specifically of how important it is to create independent systems for the administration of justice, to establish armies that respect the rule of law, to create a police force that safeguards public freedoms, and to set up systems for educating the population in human rights.

It is my conviction that our task is nothing less than setting up a civics workshop on a global scale.

Only by heightening the international community's awareness of human rights in this way and involving everyone in this effort can we prevent future violations that our conscience, and the law, will condemn. Here, as elsewhere, preventive diplomacy is urgently needed.

I look to the Conference to offer suggestions, innovations and proposals to give increasing substance to this human rights diplomacy!

Your Excellencies,

Ladies and Gentlemen,

Through these thoughts and illustrations I hope I have shown that the United Nations has taken a decisive turn in its history. Imperceptibly, our determination to respect human rights is now beginning to be reflected, through concrete and pragmatic efforts, in everything we do.

This has been an important lesson for us which we must bear in mind throughout this Conference: the safeguarding of human rights is both a specific and a general goal. On the one hand, it requires us to identify increasingly specific rights and to devise increasingly effective guarantees. But it also shows us that human rights permeate all activities of our Organization, of which they are, simultaneously, the very foundation and the supreme goal.

Allow me, then, by way of conclusion and at the outset of this Conference to make a final appeal:

May human rights create for us here a special climate of solidarity and responsibility!

May they serve to bind the Assembly of States and the human community!

And, finally, may human rights become the common language of all humanity!

Document 85

Vienna Declaration and Programme of Action adopted at the World Conference on Human Rights

A/CONF.157/24, 25 June 1993

The World Conference on Human Rights,

Considering that the promotion and protection of human rights is a matter of priority for the international community, and that the Conference affords a unique opportunity to carry out a comprehensive analysis of the international human rights system and of the machinery for the protection of human rights, in order to enhance and thus promote a fuller observance of those rights, in a just and balanced manner,

Recognizing and affirming that all human rights derive from the dignity and worth inherent in the human person, and that the human person is the central subject of human rights and fundamental freedoms, and consequently should be the principal beneficiary and should participate actively in the realization of these rights and freedoms,

Reaffirming their commitment to the purposes and principles contained in the Charter of the United Nations and the Universal Declaration of Human Rights,

Reaffirming the commitment contained in Article 56 of the Charter of the United Nations to take joint and separate action, placing proper emphasis on developing effective international cooperation for the realization of the purposes set out in Article 55, including universal respect for, and observance of, human rights and fundamental freedoms for all,

Emphasizing the responsibilities of all States, in conformity with the Charter of the United Nations, to develop and encourage respect for human rights and fundamental freedoms for all, without distinction as to race, sex, language or religion,

Recalling the Preamble to the Charter of the United Nations, in particular the determination to reaffirm faith in fundamental human rights, in the dignity and worth of the human person, and in the equal rights of men and women and of nations large and small,

Recalling also the determination expressed in the Preamble of the Charter of the United Nations to save succeeding generations from the scourge of war, to establish conditions under which justice and respect for obligations arising from treaties and other sources of international law can be maintained, to promote social progress and better standards of life in larger freedom, to practice tolerance and good neighbourliness, and to employ international machinery for the promotion of the economic and social advancement of all peoples,

Emphasizing that the Universal Declaration of Human Rights, which constitutes a common standard of achievement for all peoples and all nations, is the source of inspiration and has been the basis for the United Nations in making advances in standard setting as contained in the existing international human rights instruments, in particular the International Covenant on Civil and Political Rights and the International Covenant on Economic, Social and Cultural Rights.

Considering the major changes taking place on the international scene and the aspirations of all the peoples for an international order based on the principles enshrined in the Charter of the United Nations, including promoting and encouraging respect for human rights and fundamental freedoms for all and respect for the principle of equal rights and self-determination of peoples, peace, democracy, justice, equality, rule of law, pluralism, development, better standards of living and solidarity,

Deeply concerned by various forms of discrimination and violence, to which women continue to be exposed all over the world,

Recognizing that the activities of the United Nations in the field of human rights should be rationalized and enhanced in order to strengthen the United Nations machinery in this field and to further the objectives of universal respect for observance of international human rights standards,

Having taken into account the Declarations adopted by the three regional meetings at Tunis, San José and Bangkok and the contributions made by Governments, and bearing in mind the suggestions made by intergovernmental and non-governmental organizations, as well as the studies prepared by independent experts during the preparatory process leading to the World Conference on Human Rights,

Welcoming the International Year of the World's Indigenous People 1993 as a reaffirmation of the commitment of the international community to ensure their enjoyment of all human rights and fundamental freedoms and to respect the value and diversity of their cultures and identities,

Recognizing also that the international community should devise ways and means to remove the current obstacles and meet challenges to the full realization of all human rights and to prevent the continuation of human rights violations resulting thereof throughout the world,

Invoking the spirit of our age and the realities of our time which call upon the peoples of the world and all States Members of the United Nations to rededicate themselves to the global task of promoting and protecting all human rights and fundamental freedoms so as to secure full and universal enjoyment of these rights,

Determined to take new steps forward in the commitment of the international community with a view to achieving substantial progress in human rights endeavours by an increased and sustained effort of international cooperation and solidarity,

Solemnly adopts the Vienna Declaration and Programme of Action.

I

1. The World Conference on Human Rights reaffirms the solemn commitment of all States to fulfil their obligations to promote universal respect for, and observance and protection of, all human rights and fundamental freedoms for all in accordance with the Charter of the United Nations, other instruments relating to human rights, and international law. The universal nature of these rights and freedoms is beyond question.

In this framework, enhancement of international cooperation in the field of human rights is essential for the full achievement of the purposes of the United Nations.

Human rights and fundamental freedoms are the birthright of all human beings; their protection and promotion is the first responsibility of Governments.

2. All peoples have the right of self-determination. By virtue of that right they freely determine their political status, and freely pursue their economic, social and cultural development.

Taking into account the particular situation of peoples under colonial or other forms of alien domination or foreign occupation, the World Conference on Human Rights recognizes the right of peoples to take any legitimate action, in accordance with the Charter of the United Nations, to realize their inalienable right of self-determination. The World Conference on Human Rights considers the denial of the right of self-determination as a violation of human rights and underlines the importance of the effective realization of this right.

In accordance with the Declaration on Principles of International Law concerning Friendly Relations and Cooperation Among States in accordance with the Charter of the United Nations, this shall not be construed as authorizing or encouraging any action which would dismember or impair, totally or in part, the territorial integrity or political unity of sovereign and independent States conducting themselves in compliance with the principle of equal rights and self-determination of peoples and thus possessed of a Government representing the whole people belonging to the territory without distinction of any kind.

3. Effective international measures to guarantee and monitor the implementation of human rights standards should be taken in respect of people under foreign occupation, and effective legal protection against the

violation of their human rights should be provided, in accordance with human rights norms and international law, particularly the Geneva Convention relative to the Protection of Civilian Persons in Time of War, of 14 August 1949, and other applicable norms of humanitarian law.

4. The promotion and protection of all human rights and fundamental freedoms must be considered as a priority objective of the United Nations in accordance with its purposes and principles, in particular the purpose of international cooperation. In the framework of these purposes and principles, the promotion and protection of all human rights is a legitimate concern of the international community. The organs and specialized agencies related to human rights should therefore further enhance the coordination of their activities based on the consistent and objective application of international human rights instruments.

5. All human rights are universal, indivisible and interdependent and interrelated. The international community must treat human rights globally in a fair and equal manner, on the same footing, and with the same emphasis. While the significance of national and regional particularities and various historical, cultural and religious backgrounds must be borne in mind, it is the duty of States, regardless of their political, economic and cultural systems, to promote and protect all human rights and fundamental freedoms.

6. The efforts of the United Nations system towards the universal respect for, and observance of, human rights and fundamental freedoms for all, contribute to the stability and well-being necessary for peaceful and friendly relations among nations, and to improved conditions for peace and security as well as social and economic development, in conformity with the Charter of the United Nations.

7. The processes of promoting and protecting human rights should be conducted in conformity with the purposes and principles of the Charter of the United Nations, and international law.

8. Democracy, development and respect for human rights and fundamental freedoms are interdependent and mutually reinforcing. Democracy is based on the freely expressed will of the people to determine their own political, economic, social and cultural systems and their full participation in all aspects of their lives. In the context of the above, the promotion and protection of human rights and fundamental freedoms at the national and international levels should be universal and conducted without conditions attached. The international community should support the strengthening and promoting of democracy, development and respect for human rights and fundamental freedoms in the entire world.

9. The World Conference on Human Rights reaffirms that least developed countries committed to the process of democratization and economic reforms, many of which are in Africa, should be supported by the international community in order to succeed in their transition to democracy and economic development.

10. The World Conference on Human Rights reaffirms the right to development, as established in the Declaration on the Right to Development, as a universal and inalienable right and an integral part of fundamental human rights.

As stated in the Declaration on the Right to Development, the human person is the central subject of development.

While development facilitates the enjoyment of all human rights, the lack of development may not be invoked to justify the abridgement of internationally recognized human rights.

States should cooperate with each other in ensuring development and eliminating obstacles to development. The international community should promote an effective international cooperation for the realization of the right to development and the elimination of obstacles to development.

Lasting progress towards the implementation of the right to development requires effective development policies at the national level, as well as equitable economic relations and a favourable economic environment at the international level.

11. The right to development should be fulfilled so as to meet equitably the developmental and environmental needs of present and future generations. The World Conference on Human Rights recognizes that illicit dumping of toxic and dangerous substances and waste potentially constitutes a serious threat to the human rights to life and health of everyone.

Consequently, the World Conference on Human Rights calls on all States to adopt and vigorously implement existing conventions relating to the dumping of toxic and dangerous products and waste and to cooperate in the prevention of illicit dumping.

Everyone has the right to enjoy the benefits of scientific progress and its applications. The World Conference on Human Rights notes that certain advances, notably in the biomedical and life sciences as well as in information technology, may have potentially adverse consequences for the integrity, dignity and human rights of the individual, and calls for international cooperation to ensure that human rights and dignity are fully respected in this area of universal concern

12. The World Conference on Human Rights calls upon the international community to make all efforts to help alleviate the external debt burden of developing coun-

tries, in order to supplement the efforts of the Governments of such countries to attain the full realization of the economic, social and cultural rights of their people.

13. There is a need for States and international organizations, in cooperation with non-governmental organizations, to create favourable conditions at the national, regional and international levels to ensure the full and effective enjoyment of human rights. States should eliminate all violations of human rights and their causes, as well as obstacles to the enjoyment of these rights.

14. The existence of widespread extreme poverty inhibits the full and effective enjoyment of human rights; its immediate alleviation and eventual elimination must remain a high priority for the international community.

15. Respect for human rights and for fundamental freedoms without distinction of any kind is a fundamental rule of international human rights law. The speedy and comprehensive elimination of all forms of racism and racial discrimination, xenophobia and related intolerance is a priority task for the international community. Governments should take effective measures to prevent and combat them. Groups, institutions, intergovernmental and non-governmental organizations and individuals are urged to intensify their efforts in cooperating and coordinating their activities against these evils.

16. The World Conference on Human Rights welcomes the progress made in dismantling apartheid and calls upon the international community and the United Nations system to assist in this process.

The World Conference on Human Rights also deplores the continuing acts of violence aimed at undermining the quest for a peaceful dismantling of apartheid.

17. The acts, methods and practices of terrorism in all its forms and manifestations as well as linkage in some countries to drug trafficking are activities aimed at the destruction of human rights, fundamental freedoms and democracy, threatening territorial integrity, security of States and destabilizing legitimately constituted Governments. The international community should take the necessary steps to enhance cooperation to prevent and combat terrorism.

18. The human rights of women and of the girl-child are an inalienable, integral and indivisible part of universal human rights. The full and equal participation of women in political, civil, economic, social and cultural life, at the national, regional and international levels, and the eradication of all forms of discrimination on grounds of sex are priority objectives of the international community.

Gender-based violence and all forms of sexual harassment and exploitation, including those resulting from cultural prejudice and international trafficking, are incompatible with the dignity and worth of the human person, and must be eliminated. This can be achieved by legal measures and through national action and international cooperation in such fields as economic and social development, education, safe maternity and health care, and social support.

The human rights of women should form an integral part of the United Nations human rights activities, including the promotion of all human rights instruments relating to women.

The World Conference on Human Rights urges Governments, institutions, intergovernmental and non-governmental organizations to intensify their efforts for the protection and promotion of human rights of women and the girl-child.

19. Considering the importance of the promotion and protection of the rights of persons belonging to minorities and the contribution of such promotion and protection to the political and social stability of the States in which such persons live,

The World Conference on Human Rights reaffirms the obligation of States to ensure that persons belonging to minorities may exercise fully and effectively all human rights and fundamental freedoms without any discrimination and in full equality before the law in accordance with the Declaration on the Rights of Persons Belonging to National or Ethnic, Religious and Linguistic Minorities.

The persons belonging to minorities have the right to enjoy their own culture, to profess and practise their own religion and to use their own language in private and in public, freely and without interference or any form of discrimination.

20. The World Conference on Human Rights recognizes the inherent dignity and the unique contribution of indigenous people to the development and plurality of society and strongly reaffirms the commitment of the international community to their economic, social and cultural well-being and their enjoyment of the fruits of sustainable development. States should ensure the full and free participation of indigenous people in all aspects of society, in particular in matters of concern to them. Considering the importance of the promotion and protection of the rights of indigenous people, and the contribution of such promotion and protection to the political and social stability of the States in which such people live, States should, in accordance with international law, take concerted positive steps to ensure respect for all human rights and fundamental freedoms of indigenous people, on the basis of equality and non-discrimination, and recognize the value and diversity of their distinct identities, cultures and social organization.

21. The World Conference on Human Rights, welcoming the early ratification of the Convention on the

Rights of the Child by a large number of States and noting the recognition of the human rights of children in the World Declaration on the Survival, Protection and Development of Children and Plan of Action adopted by the World Summit for Children, urges universal ratification of the Convention by 1995 and its effective implementation by States parties through the adoption of all the necessary legislative, administrative and other measures and the allocation to the maximum extent of the available resources. In all actions concerning children, non-discrimination and the best interest of the child should be primary considerations and the views of the child given due weight. National and international mechanisms and programmes should be strengthened for the defence and protection of children, in particular, the girl-child, abandoned children, street children, economically and sexually exploited children, including through child pornography, child prostitution or sale of organs, children victims of diseases including acquired immunodeficiency syndrome, refugee and displaced children, children in detention, children in armed conflict, as well as children victims of famine and drought and other emergencies. International cooperation and solidarity should be promoted to support the implementation of the Convention and the rights of the child should be a priority in the United Nations system-wide action on human rights.

The World Conference on Human Rights also stresses that the child for the full and harmonious development of his or her personality should grow up in a family environment which accordingly merits broader protection.

22. Special attention needs to be paid to ensuring non-discrimination, and the equal enjoyment of all human rights and fundamental freedoms by disabled persons, including their active participation in all aspects of society.

23. The World Conference on Human Rights reaffirms that everyone, without distinction of any kind, is entitled to the right to seek and to enjoy in other countries asylum from persecution, as well as the right to return to one's own country. In this respect it stresses the importance of the Universal Declaration of Human Rights, the 1951 Convention relating to the Status of Refugees, its 1967 Protocol and regional instruments. It expresses its appreciation to States that continue to admit and host large numbers of refugees in their territories, and to the Office of the United Nations High Commissioner for Refugees for its dedication to its task. It also expresses its appreciation to the United Nations Relief and Works Agency for Palestine Refugees in the Near East.

The World Conference on Human Rights recognizes that gross violations of human rights, including in armed conflicts, are among the multiple and complex factors leading to displacement of people.

The World Conference on Human Rights recognizes that, in view of the complexities of the global refugee crisis and in accordance with the Charter of the United Nations, relevant international instruments and international solidarity and in the spirit of burden-sharing, a comprehensive approach by the international community is needed in coordination and cooperation with the countries concerned and relevant organizations, bearing in mind the mandate of the United Nations High Commissioner for Refugees. This should include the development of strategies to address the root causes and effects of movements of refugees and other displaced persons, the strengthening of emergency preparedness and response mechanisms, the provision of effective protection and assistance, bearing in mind the special needs of women and children, as well as the achievement of durable solutions, primarily through the preferred solution of dignified and safe voluntary repatriation, including solutions such as those adopted by the international refugee conferences. The World Conference on Human Rights underlines the responsibilities of States, particularly as they relate to the countries of origin.

In the light of the comprehensive approach, the World Conference on Human Rights emphasizes the importance of giving special attention including through intergovernmental and humanitarian organizations and finding lasting solutions to questions related to internally displaced persons including their voluntary and safe return and rehabilitation.

In accordance with the Charter of the United Nations and the principles of humanitarian law, the World Conference on Human Rights further emphasizes the importance of and the need for humanitarian assistance to victims of all natural and man-made disasters.

24. Great importance must be given to the promotion and protection of the human rights of persons belonging to groups which have been rendered vulnerable, including migrant workers, the elimination of all forms of discrimination against them, and the strengthening and more effective implementation of existing human rights instruments. States have an obligation to create and maintain adequate measures at the national level, in particular in the fields of education, health and social support, for the promotion and protection of the rights of persons in vulnerable sectors of their populations and to ensure the participation of those among them who are interested in finding a solution to their own problems.

25. The World Conference on Human Rights affirms that extreme poverty and social exclusion constitute a violation of human dignity and that urgent steps are necessary to achieve better knowledge of extreme poverty and its causes, including those related to the problem of development, in order to promote the human rights of the

poorest, and to put an end to extreme poverty and social exclusion and to promote the enjoyment of the fruits of social progress. It is essential for States to foster participation by the poorest people in the decision-making process by the community in which they live, the promotion of human rights and efforts to combat extreme poverty.

26. The World Conference on Human Rights welcomes the progress made in the codification of human rights instruments, which is a dynamic and evolving process, and urges the universal ratification of human rights treaties. All States are encouraged to accede to these international instruments; all States are encouraged to avoid, as far as possible, the resort to reservations.

27. Every State should provide an effective framework of remedies to redress human rights grievances or violations. The administration of justice, including law enforcement and prosecutorial agencies and, especially, an independent judiciary and legal profession in full conformity with applicable standards contained in international human rights instruments, are essential to the full and non-discriminatory realization of human rights and indispensable to the processes of democracy and sustainable development. In this context, institutions concerned with the administration of justice should be properly funded, and an increased level of both technical and financial assistance should be provided by the international community. It is incumbent upon the United Nations to make use of special programmes of advisory services on a priority basis for the achievement of a strong and independent administration of justice.

28. The World Conference on Human Rights expresses its dismay at massive violations of human rights especially in the form of genocide, "ethnic cleansing" and systematic rape of women in war situations, creating mass exodus of refugees and displaced persons. While strongly condemning such abhorrent practices it reiterates the call that perpetrators of such crimes be punished and such practices immediately stopped.

29. The World Conference on Human Rights expresses grave concern about continuing human rights violations in all parts of the world in disregard of standards as contained in international human rights instruments and international humanitarian law and about the lack of sufficient and effective remedies for the victims.

The World Conference on Human Rights is deeply concerned about violations of human rights during armed conflicts, affecting the civilian population, especially women, children, the elderly and the disabled. The Conference therefore calls upon States and all parties to armed conflicts strictly to observe international humanitarian law, as set forth in the Geneva Conventions of 1949 and other rules and principles of international law, as well as

minimum standards for protection of human rights, as laid down in international conventions.

The World Conference on Human Rights reaffirms the right of the victims to be assisted by humanitarian organizations, as set forth in the Geneva Conventions of 1949 and other relevant instruments of international humanitarian law, and calls for the safe and timely access for such assistance.

30. The World Conference on Human Rights also expresses its dismay and condemnation that gross and systematic violations and situations that constitute serious obstacles to the full enjoyment of all human rights continue to occur in different parts of the world. Such violations and obstacles include, as well as torture and cruel, inhuman and degrading treatment or punishment, summary and arbitrary executions, disappearances, arbitrary detentions, all forms of racism, racial discrimination and apartheid, foreign occupation and alien domination, xenophobia, poverty, hunger and other denials of economic, social and cultural rights, religious intolerance, terrorism, discrimination against women and lack of the rule of law.

31. The World Conference on Human Rights calls upon States to refrain from any unilateral measure not in accordance with international law and the Charter of the United Nations that creates obstacles to trade relations among States and impedes the full realization of the human rights set forth in the Universal Declaration of Human Rights and international human rights instruments, in particular the rights of everyone to a standard of living adequate for their health and well-being, including food and medical care, housing and the necessary social services. The World Conference on Human Rights affirms that food should not be used as a tool for political pressure.

32. The World Conference on Human Rights reaffirms the importance of ensuring the universality, objectivity and non-selectivity of the consideration of human rights issues.

33. The World Conference on Human Rights reaffirms that States are duty-bound, as stipulated in the Universal Declaration of Human Rights and the International Covenant on Economic, Social and Cultural Rights and in other international human rights instruments, to ensure that education is aimed at strengthening the respect of human rights and fundamental freedoms. The World Conference on Human Rights emphasizes the importance of incorporating the subject of human rights education programmes and calls upon States to do so. Education should promote understanding, tolerance, peace and friendly relations between the nations and all racial or religious groups and encourage the development of United Nations activities in pursuance of these objec-

tives. Therefore, education on human rights and the dissemination of proper information, both theoretical and practical, play an important role in the promotion and respect of human rights with regard to all individuals without distinction of any kind such as race, sex, language or religion, and this should be integrated in the education policies at the national as well as international levels. The World Conference on Human Rights notes that resource constraints and institutional inadequacies may impede the immediate realization of these objectives.

34. Increased efforts should be made to assist countries which so request to create the conditions whereby each individual can enjoy universal human rights and fundamental freedoms. Governments, the United Nations system as well as other multilateral organizations are urged to increase considerably the resources allocated to programmes aiming at the establishment and strengthening of national legislation, national institutions and related infrastructures which uphold the rule of law and democracy, electoral assistance, human rights awareness through training, teaching and education, popular participation and civil society.

The programmes of advisory services and technical cooperation under the Centre for Human Rights should be strengthened as well as made more efficient and transparent and thus become a major contribution to improving respect for human rights. States are called upon to increase their contributions to these programmes, both through promoting a larger allocation from the United Nations regular budget, and through voluntary contributions.

35. The full and effective implementation of United Nations activities to promote and protect human rights must reflect the high importance accorded to human rights by the Charter of the United Nations and the demands of the United Nations human rights activities, as mandated by Member States. To this end, United Nations human rights activities should be provided with increased resources.

36. The World Conference on Human Rights reaffirms the important and constructive role played by national institutions for the promotion and protection of human rights, in particular in their advisory capacity to the competent authorities, their role in remedying human rights violations, in the dissemination of human rights information, and education in human rights.

The World Conference on Human Rights encourages the establishment and strengthening of national institutions, having regard to the "Principles relating to the status of national institutions" and recognizing that it is the right of each State to choose the framework which is best suited to its particular needs at the national level.

37. Regional arrangements play a fundamental role in promoting and protecting human rights. They should reinforce universal human rights standards, as contained in international human rights instruments, and their protection. The World Conference on Human Rights endorses efforts under way to strengthen these arrangements and to increase their effectiveness, while at the same time stressing the importance of cooperation with the United Nations human rights activities.

The World Conference on Human Rights reiterates the need to consider the possibility of establishing regional and subregional arrangements for the promotion and protection of human rights where they do not already exist.

38. The World Conference on Human Rights recognizes the important role of non-governmental organizations in the promotion of all human rights and in humanitarian activities at national, regional and international levels. The World Conference on Human Rights appreciates their contribution to increasing public awareness of human rights issues, to the conduct of education, training and research in this field, and to the promotion and protection of all human rights and fundamental freedoms. While recognizing that the primary responsibility for standard-setting lies with States, the conference also appreciates the contribution of non-governmental organizations to this process. In this respect, the World Conference on Human Rights emphasizes the importance of continued dialogue and cooperation between Governments and non-governmental organizations. Non-governmental organizations and their members genuinely involved in the field of human rights should enjoy the rights and freedoms recognized in the Universal Declaration of Human Rights, and the protection of the national law. These rights and freedoms may not be exercised contrary to the purposes and principles of the United Nations. Non-governmental organizations should be free to carry out their human rights activities, without interference, within the framework of national law and the Universal Declaration of Human Rights.

39. Underlining the importance of objective, responsible and impartial information about human rights and humanitarian issues, the World Conference on Human Rights encourages the increased involvement of the media, for whom freedom and protection should be guaranteed within the framework of national law.

II

A. *Increased coordination on human rights within the United Nations system*

1. The World Conference on Human Rights recommends increased coordination in support of human rights and fundamental freedoms within the United

Nations system. To this end, the World Conference on Human Rights urges all United Nations organs, bodies and the specialized agencies whose activities deal with human rights to cooperate in order to strengthen, rationalize and streamline their activities, taking into account the need to avoid unnecessary duplication. The World Conference on Human Rights also recommends to the Secretary-General that high-level officials of relevant United Nations bodies and specialized agencies at their annual meeting, besides coordinating their activities, also assess the impact of their strategies and policies on the enjoyment of all human rights.

2. Furthermore, the World Conference on Human Rights calls on regional organizations and prominent international and regional finance and development institutions to assess also the impact of their policies and programmes on the enjoyment of human rights.

3. The World Conference on Human Rights recognizes that relevant specialized agencies and bodies and institutions of the United Nations system as well as other relevant intergovernmental organizations whose activities deal with human rights play a vital role in the formulation, promotion and implementation of human rights standards, within their respective mandates, and should take into account the outcome of the World Conference on Human Rights within their fields of competence.

4. The World Conference on Human Rights strongly recommends that a concerted effort be made to encourage and facilitate the ratification of and accession or succession to international human rights treaties and protocols adopted within the framework of the United Nations system with the aim of universal acceptance. The Secretary-General, in consultation with treaty bodies, should consider opening a dialogue with States not having acceded to these human rights treaties, in order to identify obstacles and to seek ways of overcoming them.

5. The World Conference on Human Rights encourages States to consider limiting the extent of any reservations they lodge to international human rights instruments, formulate any reservations as precisely and narrowly as possible, ensure that none is incompatible with the object and purpose of the relevant treaty and regularly review any reservations with a view to withdrawing them.

6. The World Conference on Human Rights, recognizing the need to maintain consistency with the high quality of existing international standards and to avoid proliferation of human rights instruments, reaffirms the guidelines relating to the elaboration of new international instruments contained in General Assembly resolution 41/120 of 4 December 1986 and calls on the United Nations human rights bodies, when considering the elaboration of new international standards, to keep those guidelines in mind, to consult with human rights treaty bodies on the necessity for drafting new standards and to request the Secretariat to carry out technical reviews of proposed new instruments.

7. The World Conference on Human Rights recommends that human rights officers be assigned if and when necessary to regional offices of the United Nations Organization with the purpose of disseminating information and offering training and other technical assistance in the field of human rights upon the request of concerned Member States. Human rights training for international civil servants who are assigned to work relating to human rights should be organized.

8. The World Conference on Human Rights welcomes the convening of emergency sessions of the Commission on Human Rights as a positive initiative and that other ways of responding to acute violations of human rights be considered by the relevant organs of the United Nations system.

Resources

9. The World Conference on Human Rights, concerned by the growing disparity between the activities of the Centre for Human Rights and the human, financial and other resources available to carry them out, and bearing in mind the resources needed for other important United Nations programmes, requests the Secretary-General and the General Assembly to take immediate steps to increase substantially the resources for the human rights programme from within the existing and future regular budgets of the United Nations, and to take urgent steps to seek increased extrabudgetary resources.

10. Within this framework, an increased proportion of the regular budget should be allocated directly to the Centre for Human Rights to cover its costs and all other costs borne by the Centre for Human Rights, including those related to the United Nations human rights bodies. Voluntary funding of the Centre's technical cooperation activities should reinforce this enhanced budget; the World Conference on Human Rights calls for generous contributions to the existing trust funds.

11. The World Conference on Human Rights requests the Secretary-General and the General Assembly to provide sufficient human, financial and other resources to the Centre for Human Rights to enable it effectively, efficiently and expeditiously to carry out its activities.

12. The World Conference on Human Rights, noting the need to ensure that human and financial resources are available to carry out the human rights activities, as mandated by intergovernmental bodies, urges the Secretary-General, in accordance with Article 101 of the Charter of the United Nations, and Member States to adopt a coher-

ent approach aimed at securing that resources commensurate to the increased mandates are allocated to the Secretariat. The World Conference on Human Rights invites the Secretary-General to consider whether adjustments to procedures in the programme budget cycle would be necessary or helpful to ensure the timely and effective implementation of human rights activities as mandated by Member States.

Centre for Human Rights

13. The World Conference on Human Rights stresses the importance of strengthening the United Nations Centre for Human Rights.

14. The Centre for Human Rights should play an important role in coordinating system-wide attention for human rights. The focal role of the Centre can best be realized if it is enabled to cooperate fully with other United Nations bodies and organs. The coordinating role of the Centre for Human Rights also implies that the office of the Centre for Human Rights in New York is strengthened.

15. The Centre for Human Rights should be assured adequate means for the system of thematic and country rapporteurs, experts, working groups and treaty bodies. Follow-up on recommendations should become a priority matter for consideration by the Commission on Human Rights.

16. The Centre for Human Rights should assume a larger role in the promotion of human rights. This role could be given shape through cooperation with Member States and by an enhanced programme of advisory services and technical assistance. The existing voluntary funds will have to be expanded substantially for these purposes and should be managed in a more efficient and coordinated way. All activities should follow strict and transparent project management rules and regular programme and project evaluations should be held periodically. To this end, the results of such evaluation exercises and other relevant information should be made available regularly. The Centre should, in particular, organize at least once a year information meetings open to all Member States and organizations directly involved in these projects and programmes.

Adaptation and strengthening of the United Nations machinery for human rights, including the question of the establishment of a United Nations High Commissioner for Human Rights

17. The World Conference on Human Rights recognizes the necessity for a continuing adaptation of the United Nations human rights machinery to the current and future needs in the promotion and protection of human rights, as reflected in the present Declaration and within the framework of a balanced and sustainable development for all people. In particular, the United Nations human rights organs should improve their coordination, efficiency and effectiveness.

18. The World Conference on Human Rights recommends to the General Assembly that when examining the report of the Conference at its forty-eighth session, it begin, as a matter of priority, consideration of the question of the establishment of a High Commissioner for Human Rights for the promotion and protection of all human rights.

B. Equality, dignity and tolerance

1. Racism, racial discrimination, xenophobia and other forms of intolerance

19. The World Conference on Human Rights considers the elimination of racism and racial discrimination, in particular in their institutionalized forms such as apartheid or resulting from doctrines of racial superiority or exclusivity or contemporary forms and manifestations of racism, as a primary objective for the international community and a worldwide promotion programme in the field of human rights. United Nations organs and agencies should strengthen their efforts to implement such a programme of action related to the third decade to combat racism and racial discrimination as well as subsequent mandates to the same end. The World Conference on Human Rights strongly appeals to the international community to contribute generously to the Trust Fund for the Programme for the Decade for Action to Combat Racism and Racial Discrimination.

20. The World Conference on Human Rights urges all Governments to take immediate measures and to develop strong policies to prevent and combat all forms and manifestations of racism, xenophobia or related intolerance, where necessary by enactment of appropriate legislation, including penal measures, and by the establishment of national institutions to combat such phenomena.

21. The World Conference on Human Rights welcomes the decision of the Commission on Human Rights to appoint a Special Rapporteur on contemporary forms of racism, racial discrimination, xenophobia and related intolerance. The World Conference on Human Rights also appeals to all States parties to the International Convention on the Elimination of All Forms of Racial Discrimination to consider making the declaration under article 14 of the Convention.

22. The World Conference on Human Rights calls upon all Governments to take all appropriate measures in compliance with their international obligations and with due regard to their respective legal systems to counter intolerance and related violence based on religion or belief, including practices of discrimination against

women and including the desecration of religious sites, recognizing that every individual has the right to freedom of thought, conscience, expression and religion. The Conference also invites all States to put into practice the provisions of the Declaration on the Elimination of All Forms of Intolerance and of Discrimination Based on Religion or Belief.

23. The World Conference on Human Rights stresses that all persons who perpetrate or authorize criminal acts associated with ethnic cleansing are individually responsible and accountable for such human rights violations, and that the international community should exert every effort to bring those legally responsible for such violations to justice.

24. The World Conference on Human Rights calls on all States to take immediate measures, individually and collectively, to combat the practice of ethnic cleansing to bring it quickly to an end. Victims of the abhorrent practice of ethnic cleansing are entitled to appropriate and effective remedies.

2. *Persons belonging to national or ethnic, religious and linguistic minorities*

25. The World Conference on Human Rights calls on the Commission on Human Rights to examine ways and means to promote and protect effectively the rights of persons belonging to minorities as set out in the Declaration on the Rights of Persons belonging to National or Ethnic, Religious and Linguistic Minorities. In this context, the World Conference on Human Rights calls upon the Centre for Human Rights to provide, at the request of Governments concerned and as part of its programme of advisory services and technical assistance, qualified expertise on minority issues and human rights, as well as on the prevention and resolution of disputes, to assist in existing or potential situations involving minorities.

26. The World Conference on Human Rights urges States and the international community to promote and protect the rights of persons belonging to national or ethnic, religious and linguistic minorities in accordance with the Declaration on the Rights of Persons belonging to National or Ethnic, Religious and Linguistic Minorities.

27. Measures to be taken, where appropriate, should include facilitation of their full participation in all aspects of the political, economic, social, religious and cultural life of society and in the economic progress and development in their country.

Indigenous people

28. The World Conference on Human Rights calls on the Working Group on Indigenous Populations of the Sub-Commission on Prevention of Discrimination and Protection of Minorities to complete the drafting of a declaration on the rights of indigenous people at its eleventh session.

29. The World Conference on Human Rights recommends that the Commission on Human Rights consider the renewal and updating of the mandate of the Working Group on Indigenous Populations upon completion of the drafting of a declaration on the rights of indigenous people.

30. The World Conference on Human Rights also recommends that advisory services and technical assistance programmes within the United Nations system respond positively to requests by States for assistance which would be of direct benefit to indigenous people. The World Conference on Human Rights further recommends that adequate human and financial resources be made available to the Centre for Human Rights within the overall framework of strengthening the Centre's activities as envisaged by this document.

31. The World Conference on Human Rights urges States to ensure the full and free participation of indigenous people in all aspects of society, in particular in matters of concern to them.

32. The World Conference on Human Rights recommends that the General Assembly proclaim an international decade of the world's indigenous people, to begin from January 1994, including action-orientated programmes, to be decided upon in partnership with indigenous people. An appropriate voluntary trust fund should be set up for this purpose. In the framework of such a decade, the establishment of a permanent forum for indigenous people in the United Nations system should be considered.

Migrant workers

33. The World Conference on Human Rights urges all States to guarantee the protection of the human rights of all migrant workers and their families.

34. The World Conference on Human Rights considers that the creation of conditions to foster greater harmony and tolerance between migrant workers and the rest of the society of the State in which they reside is of particular importance.

35. The World Conference on Human Rights invites States to consider the possibility of signing and ratifying, at the earliest possible time, the International Convention on the Rights of All Migrant Workers and Members of Their Families.

3. *The equal status and human rights of women*

36. The World Conference on Human Rights urges the full and equal enjoyment by women of all human

rights and that this be a priority for Governments and for the United Nations. The World Conference on Human Rights also underlines the importance of the integration and full participation of women as both agents and beneficiaries in the development process, and reiterates the objectives established on global action for women towards sustainable and equitable development set forth in the Rio Declaration on Environment and Development and chapter 24 of Agenda 21, adopted by the United Nations Conference on Environment and Development (Rio de Janeiro, Brazil, 3-14 June 1992).

37. The equal status of women and the human rights of women should be integrated into the mainstream of United Nations system-wide activity. These issues should be regularly and systematically addressed throughout relevant United Nations bodies and mechanisms. In particular, steps should be taken to increase cooperation and promote further integration of objectives and goals between the Commission on the Status of Women, the Commission on Human Rights, the Committee for the Elimination of Discrimination against Women, the United Nations Development Fund for Women, the United Nations Development Programme and other United Nations agencies. In this context, cooperation and coordination should be strengthened between the Centre for Human Rights and the Division for the Advancement of Women.

38. In particular, the World Conference on Human Rights stresses the importance of working towards the elimination of violence against women in public and private life, the elimination of all forms of sexual harassment, exploitation and trafficking in women, the elimination of gender bias in the administration of justice and the eradication of any conflicts which may arise between the rights of women and the harmful effects of certain traditional or customary practices, cultural prejudices and religious extremism. The World Conference on Human Rights calls upon the General Assembly to adopt the draft declaration on violence against women and urges States to combat violence against women in accordance with its provisions. Violations of the human rights of women in situations of armed conflict are violations of the fundamental principles of international human rights and humanitarian law. All violations of this kind, including in particular murder, systematic rape, sexual slavery, and forced pregnancy, require a particularly effective response.

39. The World Conference on Human Rights urges the eradication of all forms of discrimination against women, both hidden and overt. The United Nations should encourage the goal of universal ratification by all States of the Convention on the Elimination of All Forms of Discrimination against Women by the year 2000. Ways

and means of addressing the particularly large number of reservations to the Convention should be encouraged. *Inter alia*, the Committee on the Elimination of Discrimination against Women should continue its review of reservations to the Convention. States are urged to withdraw reservations that are contrary to the object and purpose of the Convention or which are otherwise incompatible with international treaty law.

40. Treaty monitoring bodies should disseminate necessary information to enable women to make more effective use of existing implementation procedures in their pursuits of full and equal enjoyment of human rights and non-discrimination. New procedures should also be adopted to strengthen implementation of the commitment to women's equality and the human rights of women. The Commission on the Status of Women and the Committee on the Elimination of Discrimination against Women should quickly examine the possibility of introducing the right of petition through the preparation of an optional protocol to the Convention on the Elimination of All Forms of Discrimination against Women. The World Conference on Human Rights welcomes the decision of the Commission on Human Rights to consider the appointment of a special rapporteur on violence against women at its fiftieth session.

41. The World Conference on Human Rights recognizes the importance of the enjoyment by women of the highest standard of physical and mental health throughout their life span. In the context of the World Conference on Women and the Convention on the Elimination of All Forms of Discrimination against Women, as well as the Proclamation of Tehran of 1968, the World Conference on Human Rights reaffirms, on the basis of equality between women and men, a woman's right to accessible and adequate health care and the widest range of family planning services, as well as equal access to education at all levels.

42. Treaty monitoring bodies should include the status of women and the human rights of women in their deliberations and findings, making use of gender-specific data. States should be encouraged to supply information on the situation of women *de jure* and de facto in their reports to treaty monitoring bodies. The World Conference on Human Rights notes with satisfaction that the Commission on Human Rights adopted at its forty-ninth session resolution 1993/46 of 8 March 1993 stating that rapporteurs and working groups in the field of human rights should also be encouraged to do so. Steps should also be taken by the Division for the Advancement of Women in cooperation with other United Nations bodies, specifically the Centre for Human Rights, to ensure that the human rights activities of the United Nations regularly address violations of women's human rights,

including gender-specific abuses. Training for United Nations human rights and humanitarian relief personnel to assist them to recognize and deal with human rights abuses particular to women and to carry out their work without gender bias should be encouraged.

43. The World Conference on Human Rights urges Governments and regional and international organizations to facilitate the access of women to decision-making posts and their greater participation in the decision-making process. It encourages further steps within the United Nations Secretariat to appoint and promote women staff members in accordance with the Charter of the United Nations, and encourages other principal and subsidiary organs of the United Nations to guarantee the participation of women under conditions of equality.

44. The World Conference on Human Rights welcomes the World Conference on Women to be held in Beijing in 1995 and urges that human rights of women should play an important role in its deliberations, in accordance with the priority themes of the World Conference on Women of equality, development and peace.

4. The rights of the child

45. The World Conference on Human Rights reiterates the principle of "First Call for Children" and, in this respect, underlines the importance of major national and international efforts, especially those of the United Nations Children's Fund, for promoting respect for the rights of the child to survival, protection, development and participation.

46. Measures should be taken to achieve universal ratification of the Convention on the Rights of the Child by 1995 and the universal signing of the World Declaration on the Survival, Protection and Development of Children and Plan of Action adopted by the World Summit for Children, as well as their effective implementation. The World Conference on Human Rights urges States to withdraw reservations to the Convention on the Rights of the Child contrary to the object and purpose of the Convention or otherwise contrary to international treaty law.

47. The World Conference on Human Rights urges all nations to undertake measures to the maximum extent of their available resources, with the support of international cooperation, to achieve the goals in the World Summit Plan of Action. The Conference calls on States to integrate the Convention on the Rights of the Child into their national action plans. By means of these national action plans and through international efforts, particular priority should be placed on reducing infant and maternal mortality rates, reducing malnutrition and illiteracy rates and providing access to safe drinking water and to basic education. Whenever so called for, national plans of action should be devised to combat devastating emergencies resulting from natural disasters and armed conflicts and the equally grave problem of children in extreme poverty.

48. The World Conference on Human Rights urges all States, with the support of international cooperation, to address the acute problem of children under especially difficult circumstances. Exploitation and abuse of children should be actively combated, including by addressing their root causes. Effective measures are required against female infanticide, harmful child labour, sale of children and organs, child prostitution, child pornography, as well as other forms of sexual abuse.

49. The World Conference on Human Rights supports all measures by the United Nations and its specialized agencies to ensure the effective protection and promotion of human rights of the girl child. The World Conference on Human Rights urges States to repeal existing laws and regulations and remove customs and practices which discriminate against and cause harm to the girl child.

50. The World Conference on Human Rights strongly supports the proposal that the Secretary-General initiate a study into means of improving the protection of children in armed conflicts. Humanitarian norms should be implemented and measures taken in order to protect and facilitate assistance to children in war zones. Measures should include protection for children against indiscriminate use of all weapons of war, especially anti-personnel mines. The need for aftercare and rehabilitation of children traumatized by war must be addressed urgently. The Conference calls on the Committee on the Rights of the Child to study the question of raising the minimum age of recruitment into armed forces.

51. The World Conference on Human Rights recommends that matters relating to human rights and the situation of children be regularly reviewed and monitored by all relevant organs and mechanisms of the United Nations system and by the supervisory bodies of the specialized agencies in accordance with their mandates.

52. The World Conference on Human Rights recognizes the important role played by non-governmental organizations in the effective implementation of all human rights instruments and, in particular, the Convention on the Rights of the Child.

53. The World Conference on Human Rights recommends that the Committee on the Rights of the Child, with the assistance of the Centre for Human Rights, be enabled expeditiously and effectively to meet its mandate, especially in view of the unprecedented extent of ratification and subsequent submission of country reports.

5. Freedom from torture

54. The World Conference on Human Rights welcomes the ratification by many Member States of the Convention against Torture and Other Cruel, Inhuman or Degrading Treatment or Punishment and encourages its speedy ratification by all other Member States.

55. The World Conference on Human Rights emphasizes that one of the most atrocious violations against human dignity is the act of torture, the result of which destroys the dignity and impairs the capability of victims to continue their lives and their activities.

56. The World Conference on Human Rights reaffirms that under human rights law and international humanitarian law, freedom from torture is a right which must be protected under all circumstances, including in times of internal or international disturbance or armed conflicts.

57. The World Conference on Human Rights therefore urges all States to put an immediate end to the practice of torture and eradicate this evil forever through full implementation of the Universal Declaration of Human Rights as well as the relevant conventions and, where necessary, strengthening of existing mechanisms. The World Conference on Human Rights calls on all States to cooperate fully with the Special Rapporteur on the question of torture in the fulfilment of his mandate.

58. Special attention should be given to ensure universal respect for, and effective implementation of, the Principles of Medical Ethics relevant to the Role of Health Personnel, particularly Physicians, in the Protection of Prisoners and Detainees against Torture and other Cruel, Inhuman or Degrading Treatment or Punishment adopted by the General Assembly of the United Nations.

59. The World Conference on Human Rights stresses the importance of further concrete action within the framework of the United Nations with the view to providing assistance to victims of torture and ensure more effective remedies for their physical, psychological and social rehabilitation. Providing the necessary resources for this purpose should be given high priority, *inter alia*, by additional contributions to the United Nations Voluntary Fund for the Victims of Torture.

60. States should abrogate legislation leading to impunity for those responsible for grave violations of human rights such as torture and prosecute such violations, thereby providing a firm basis for the rule of law.

61. The World Conference on Human Rights reaffirms that efforts to eradicate torture should, first and foremost, be concentrated on prevention and, therefore, calls for the early adoption of an optional protocol to the Convention against Torture and Other Cruel, Inhuman and Degrading Treatment or Punishment, which is intended to establish a preventive system of regular visits to places of detention.

Enforced disappearances

62. The World Conference on Human Rights, welcoming the adoption by the General Assembly of the Declaration on the Protection of All Persons from Enforced Disappearance, calls upon all States to take effective legislative, administrative, judicial or other measures to prevent, terminate and punish acts of enforced disappearances. The World Conference on Human Rights reaffirms that it is the duty of all States, under any circumstances, to make investigations whenever there is reason to believe that an enforced disappearance has taken place on a territory under their jurisdiction and, if allegations are confirmed, to prosecute its perpetrators.

6. The rights of the disabled person

63. The World Conference on Human Rights reaffirms that all human rights and fundamental freedoms are universal and thus unreservedly include persons with disabilities. Every person is born equal and has the same rights to life and welfare, education and work, living independently and active participation in all aspects of society. Any direct discrimination or other negative discriminatory treatment of a disabled person is therefore a violation of his or her rights. The World Conference on Human Rights calls on Governments, where necessary, to adopt or adjust legislation to assure access to these and other rights for disabled persons.

64. The place of disabled persons is everywhere. Persons with disabilities should be guaranteed equal opportunity through the elimination of all socially determined barriers, be they physical, financial, social or psychological, which exclude or restrict full participation in society.

65. Recalling the World Programme of Action concerning Disabled Persons, adopted by the General Assembly at its thirty-seventh session, the World Conference on Human Rights calls upon the General Assembly and the Economic and Social Council to adopt the draft standard rules on the equalization of opportunities for persons with disabilities, at their meetings in 1993.

C. Cooperation, development and strengthening of human rights

66. The World Conference on Human Rights recommends that priority be given to national and international action to promote democracy, development and human rights.

67. Special emphasis should be given to measures to assist in the strengthening and building of institutions relating to human rights, strengthening of a pluralistic

civil society and the protection of groups which have been rendered vulnerable. In this context, assistance provided upon the request of Governments for the conduct of free and fair elections, including assistance in the human rights aspects of elections and public information about elections, is of particular importance. Equally important is the assistance to be given to the strengthening of the rule of law, the promotion of freedom of expression and the administration of justice, and to the real and effective participation of the people in the decision-making processes.

68. The World Conference on Human Rights stresses the need for the implementation of strengthened advisory services and technical assistance activities by the Centre for Human Rights. The Centre should make available to States upon request assistance on specific human rights issues, including the preparation of reports under human rights treaties as well as for the implementation of coherent and comprehensive plans of action for the promotion and protection of human rights. Strengthening the institutions of human rights and democracy, the legal protection of human rights, training of officials and others, broad-based education and public information aimed at promoting respect for human rights should all be available as components of these programmes.

69. The World Conference on Human Rights strongly recommends that a comprehensive programme be established within the United Nations in order to help States in the task of building and strengthening adequate national structures which have a direct impact on the overall observance of human rights and the maintenance of the rule of law. Such a programme, to be coordinated by the Centre for Human Rights, should be able to provide, upon the request of the interested Government, technical and financial assistance to national projects in reforming penal and correctional establishments, education and training of lawyers, judges and security forces in human rights, and any other sphere of activity relevant to the good functioning of the rule of law. That programme should make available to States assistance for the implementation of plans of action for the promotion and protection of human rights.

70. The World Conference on Human Rights requests the Secretary-General of the United Nations to submit proposals to the United Nations General Assembly, containing alternatives for the establishment, structure, operational modalities and funding of the proposed programme.

71. The World Conference on Human Rights recommends that each State consider the desirability of drawing up a national action plan identifying steps whereby that State would improve the promotion and protection of human rights.

72. The World Conference on Human Rights reaffirms that the universal and inalienable right to development, as established in the Declaration on the Right to Development, must be implemented and realized. In this context, the World Conference on Human Rights welcomes the appointment by the Commission on Human Rights of a thematic working group on the right to development and urges that the Working Group, in consultation and cooperation with other organs and agencies of the United Nations system, promptly formulate, for early consideration by the United Nations General Assembly, comprehensive and effective measures to eliminate obstacles to the implementation and realization of the Declaration on the Right to Development and recommending ways and means towards the realization of the right to development by all States.

73. The World Conference on Human Rights recommends that non-governmental and other grass-roots organizations active in development and/or human rights should be enabled to play a major role on the national and international levels in the debate, activities and implementation relating to the right to development and, in cooperation with Governments, in all relevant aspects of development cooperation.

74. The World Conference on Human Rights appeals to Governments, competent agencies and institutions to increase considerably the resources devoted to building well-functioning legal systems able to protect human rights, and to national institutions working in this area. Actors in the field of development cooperation should bear in mind the mutually reinforcing interrelationship between development, democracy and human rights. Cooperation should be based on dialogue and transparency. The World Conference on Human Rights also calls for the establishment of comprehensive programmes, including resource banks of information and personnel with expertise relating to the strengthening of the rule of law and of democratic institutions.

75. The World Conference on Human Rights encourages the Commission on Human Rights, in cooperation with the Committee on Economic, Social and Cultural Rights, to continue the examination of optional protocols to the International Covenant on Economic, Social and Cultural Rights.

76. The World Conference on Human Rights recommends that more resources be made available for the strengthening or the establishment of regional arrangements for the promotion and protection of human rights under the programmes of advisory services and technical assistance of the Centre for Human Rights. States are encouraged to request assistance for such purposes as regional and subregional workshops, seminars and information exchanges designed to strengthen regional ar-

rangements for the promotion and protection of human rights in accord with universal human rights standards as contained in international human rights instruments.

77. The World Conference on Human Rights supports all measures by the United Nations and its relevant specialized agencies to ensure the effective promotion and protection of trade union rights, as stipulated in the International Covenant on Economic, Social and Cultural Rights and other relevant international instruments. It calls on all States to abide fully by their obligations in this regard contained in international instruments.

D. *Human rights education*

78. The World Conference on Human Rights considers human rights education, training and public information essential for the promotion and achievement of stable and harmonious relations among communities and for fostering mutual understanding, tolerance and peace.

79. States should strive to eradicate illiteracy and should direct education towards the full development of the human personality and to the strengthening of respect for human rights and fundamental freedoms. The World Conference on Human Rights calls on all States and institutions to include human rights, humanitarian law, democracy and rule of law as subjects in the curricula of all learning institutions in formal and non-formal settings.

80. Human rights education should include peace, democracy, development and social justice, as set forth in international and regional human rights instruments, in order to achieve common understanding and awareness with a view to strengthening universal commitment to human rights.

81. Taking into account the World Plan of Action on Education for Human Rights and Democracy, adopted in March 1993 by the International Congress on Education for Human Rights and Democracy of the United Nations Educational, Scientific and Cultural Organization, and other human rights instruments, the World Conference on Human Rights recommends that States develop specific programmes and strategies for ensuring the widest human rights education and the dissemination of public information, taking particular account of the human rights needs of women.

82. Governments, with the assistance of intergovernmental organizations, national institutions and non-governmental organizations, should promote an increased awareness of human rights and mutual tolerance. The World Conference on Human Rights underlines the importance of strengthening the World Public Information Campaign for Human Rights carried out by the United Nations. They should initiate and support education in human rights and undertake effective dissemination of public information in this field. The advisory services and technical assistance programmes of the United Nations system should be able to respond immediately to requests from States for educational and training activities in the field of human rights as well as for special education concerning standards as contained in international human rights instruments and in humanitarian law and their application to special groups such as military forces, law enforcement personnel, police and the health profession. The proclamation of a United Nations decade for human rights education in order to promote, encourage and focus these educational activities should be considered.

E. *Implementation and monitoring methods*

83. The World Conference on Human Rights urges Governments to incorporate standards as contained in international human rights instruments in domestic legislation and to strengthen national structures, institutions and organs of society which play a role in promoting and safeguarding human rights.

84. The World Conference on Human Rights recommends the strengthening of United Nations activities and programmes to meet requests for assistance by States which want to establish or strengthen their own national institutions for the promotion and protection of human rights.

85. The World Conference on Human Rights also encourages the strengthening of cooperation between national institutions for the promotion and protection of human rights, particularly through exchanges of information and experience, as well as cooperation with regional organizations and the United Nations.

86. The World Conference on Human Rights strongly recommends in this regard that representatives of national institutions for the promotion and protection of human rights convene periodic meetings under the auspices of the Centre for Human Rights to examine ways and means of improving their mechanisms and sharing experiences.

87. The World Conference on Human Rights recommends to the human rights treaty bodies, to the meetings of chairpersons of the treaty bodies and to the meetings of States parties that they continue to take steps aimed at coordinating the multiple reporting requirements and guidelines for preparing State reports under the respective human rights conventions and study the suggestion that the submission of one overall report on treaty obligations undertaken by each State would make these procedures more effective and increase their impact.

88. The World Conference on Human Rights recommends that the States parties to international human rights instruments, the General Assembly and the Economic and

Social Council should consider studying the existing human rights treaty bodies and the various thematic mechanisms and procedures with a view to promoting greater efficiency and effectiveness through better coordination of the various bodies, mechanisms and procedures, taking into account the need to avoid unnecessary duplication and overlapping of their mandates and tasks.

89. The World Conference on Human Rights recommends continued work on the improvement of the functioning, including the monitoring tasks, of the treaty bodies, taking into account multiple proposals made in this respect, in particular those made by the treaty bodies themselves and by the meetings of the chairpersons of the treaty bodies. The comprehensive national approach taken by the Committee on the Rights of the Child should also be encouraged.

90. The World Conference on Human Rights recommends that States parties to human rights treaties consider accepting all the available optional communication procedures.

91. The World Conference on Human Rights views with concern the issue of impunity of perpetrators of human rights violations, and supports the efforts of the Commission on Human Rights and the Sub-Commission on Prevention of Discrimination and Protection of Minorities to examine all aspects of the issue.

92. The World Conference on Human Rights recommends that the Commission on Human Rights examine the possibility for better implementation of existing human rights instruments at the international and regional levels and encourages the International Law Commission to continue its work on an international criminal court.

93. The World Conference on Human Rights appeals to States which have not yet done so to accede to the Geneva Conventions of 12 August 1949 and the Protocols thereto, and to take all appropriate national measures, including legislative ones, for their full implementation.

94. The World Conference on Human Rights recommends the speedy completion and adoption of the draft declaration on the right and responsibility of individuals, groups and organs of society to promote and protect universally recognized human rights and fundamental freedoms.

95. The World Conference on Human Rights underlines the importance of preserving and strengthening the system of special procedures, rapporteurs, representatives, experts and working groups of the Commission on Human Rights and the Sub-Commission on the Prevention of Discrimination and Protection of Minorities, in order to enable them to carry out their mandates in all countries throughout the world, providing them with the necessary human and financial resources. The procedures and mechanisms should be enabled to harmonize and rationalize their work through periodic meetings. All States are asked to cooperate fully with these procedures and mechanisms.

96. The World Conference on Human Rights recommends that the United Nations assume a more active role in the promotion and protection of human rights in ensuring full respect for international humanitarian law in all situations of armed conflict, in accordance with the purposes and principles of the Charter of the United Nations.

97. The World Conference on Human Rights, recognizing the important role of human rights components in specific arrangements concerning some peace-keeping operations by the United Nations, recommends that the Secretary-General take into account the reporting, experience and capabilities of the Centre for Human Rights and human rights mechanisms, in conformity with the Charter of the United Nations.

98. To strengthen the enjoyment of economic, social and cultural rights, additional approaches should be examined, such as a system of indicators to measure progress in the realization of the rights set forth in the International Covenant on Economic, Social and Cultural Rights. There must be a concerted effort to ensure recognition of economic, social and cultural rights at the national, regional and international levels.

F. Follow-up to the World Conference on Human Rights

99. The World Conference on Human Rights recommends that the General Assembly, the Commission on Human Rights and other organs and agencies of the United Nations system related to human rights consider ways and means for the full implementation, without delay, of the recommendations contained in the present Declaration, including the possibility of proclaiming a United Nations decade for human rights. The World Conference on Human Rights further recommends that the Commission on Human Rights annually review the progress towards this end.

100. The World Conference on Human Rights requests the Secretary-General of the United Nations to invite on the occasion of the fiftieth anniversary of the Universal Declaration of Human Rights all States, all organs and agencies of the United Nations system related to human rights, to report to him on the progress made in the implementation of the present Declaration and to submit a report to the General Assembly at its fifty-third session, through the Commission on Human Rights and the Economic and Social Council. Likewise, regional and, as appropriate, national human rights institutions, as well as non-governmental organizations, may present their

views to the Secretary-General on the progress made in the implementation of the present Declaration. Special attention should be paid to assessing the progress towards the goal of universal ratification of international human rights treaties and protocols adopted within the framework of the United Nations system.

Document 86

General Assembly resolution on the Third Decade to Combat Racism and Racial Discrimination (1993-2003)

A/RES/48/91, 20 December 1993

The General Assembly,

Reaffirming its objectives set forth in the Charter of the United Nations to achieve international cooperation in solving problems of an economic, social, cultural or humanitarian character and in promoting and encouraging respect for human rights and fundamental freedoms for all without distinction as to race, sex, language or religion,

Reaffirming also its firm determination and its commitment to eradicate totally and unconditionally racism in all its forms, racial discrimination and apartheid,

Recalling the Universal Declaration of Human Rights, 1/ the International Convention on the Elimination of All Forms of Racial Discrimination, 2/ the International Convention on the Suppression and Punishment of the Crime of Apartheid, 3/ and the Convention against Discrimination in Education adopted by the United Nations Educational, Scientific and Cultural Organization on 14 December 1960, 4/

Recalling also the outcome of the two World Conferences to Combat Racism and Racial Discrimination, held at Geneva in 1978 and 1983,

Welcoming the outcome of the World Conference on Human Rights, and, in particular, the attention given in the Vienna Declaration and Programme of Action 5/ to the elimination of racism, racial discrimination, xenophobia and other forms of intolerance,

Welcoming also decision 1993/258 taken by the Economic and Social Council on 28 July 1993 concerning the appointment of a special rapporteur on contemporary forms of racism, racial discrimination, xenophobia and related intolerance,

Recalling its resolution 38/14 of 22 November 1983, the annex to which contains the Programme of Action for the Second Decade to Combat Racism and Racial Discrimination,

Noting with grave concern that despite the efforts of the international community, the principal objectives of the two Decades for Action to Combat Racism and Racial Discrimination have not been attained and that millions of human beings continue to this day to be the victims of varied forms of racism, racial discrimination and apartheid,

Deeply concerned about the current trend of the evolution of racism into discriminatory practices based on culture, nationality, religion or language,

Recalling in particular its resolution 47/77 of 16 December 1992,

Having considered the report submitted by the Secretary-General 6/ within the framework of the implementation of the Programme of Action for the Second Decade,

Firmly convinced of the need to take more effective and sustained measures at the national and international levels for the elimination of all forms of racism and racial discrimination,

Welcoming the proposal to launch a third decade to combat racism and racial discrimination,

Convinced of the need to ensure and support the peaceful transition towards a democratic and non-racial South Africa,

Recognizing the importance of strengthening national legislation and institutions for the promotion of racial harmony,

Aware of the importance and the magnitude of the phenomenon of migrant workers, as well as the efforts undertaken by the international community to improve the protection of the human rights of migrant workers and members of their families,

Recalling the adoption at its forty-fifth session of the International Convention on the Protection of the Rights of All Migrant Workers and Members of Their Families, 7/

1/ Resolution 217 A (III).
2/ Resolution 2106 A (XX), annex.
3/ Resolution 3068 (XXVIII), annex.
4/ United Nations Educational, Scientific and Cultural Organization, *Records of the General Conference, Eleventh Session, Resolutions*, p. 119.
5/ *Report of the World Conference on Human Rights, Vienna, 14-25 June 1993* (A/CONF.157/24 (Part I)), chap. III.
6/ A/48/423.
7/ Resolution 45/158, annex.

Acknowledging that indigenous people are at times victims of particular forms of racism and racial discrimination,

Reaffirming the Declaration on Apartheid and its Destructive Consequences in Southern Africa, 8/ unanimously adopted by the General Assembly at its sixteenth special session, on 14 December 1989, which offers guidelines on how to end apartheid,

1. *Declares once again* that all forms of racism and racial discrimination, whether in their institutionalized form, such as apartheid, or resulting from official doctrines of racial superiority and/or exclusivity, such as "ethnic cleansing", are among the most serious violations of human rights in the contemporary world and must be combated by all available means;

2. *Decides* to proclaim the ten-year period beginning in 1993 as the Third Decade to Combat Racism and Racial Discrimination, and to adopt the Programme of Action proposed for the Third Decade contained in the annex to the present resolution;

3. *Calls upon* Governments to cooperate with the Special Rapporteur on contemporary forms of racism, racial discrimination, xenophobia and related intolerance to enable him to fulfil his mandate;

4. *Urges* all Governments to take all necessary measures to combat new forms of racism, in particular by adapting constantly the methods provided to combat them, especially in the legislative, administrative, educational and information fields;

5. *Decides* that the international community in general and the United Nations in particular should continue to give the highest priority to programmes for combating racism, racial discrimination and apartheid and intensify their efforts, during the Third Decade, to provide assistance and relief to the victims of racism and all forms of racial discrimination and apartheid;

6. *Requests* the Secretary-General to continue to accord special attention to the situation of migrant workers and members of their families and to include regularly in his reports all information on such workers;

7. *Calls upon* all Member States to consider signing and ratifying or acceding to the International Convention on the Protection of the Rights of All Migrant Workers and Members of Their Families as a matter of priority, to enable its entry into force;

8. *Also requests* the Secretary-General to continue the study on the effects of racial discrimination on the children of minorities, in particular those of migrant workers, in the fields of education, training and employment, and to submit, *inter alia*, specific recommendations for the implementation of measures to combat the effects of that discrimination;

9. *Urges* the Secretary-General, United Nations bodies, the specialized agencies, all Governments, intergovernmental organizations and relevant non-governmental organizations, in implementing the Programme of Action for the Third Decade, to pay particular attention to the situation of indigenous people;

10. *Further requests* the Secretary-General to revise and finalize the draft model legislation for the guidance of Governments in the enactment of further legislation against racial discrimination, in the light of comments made by members of the Committee on the Elimination of Racial Discrimination at its fortieth and forty-first sessions and to publish and distribute the text as soon as possible;

11. *Renews its invitation* to the United Nations Educational, Scientific and Cultural Organization to expedite the preparation of teaching materials and teaching aids to promote teaching, training and educational activities on human rights and against racism and racial discrimination, with particular emphasis on activities at the primary and secondary levels of education;

12. *Considers* that all the parts of the Programme of Action for the Third Decade should be given equal attention in order to attain the objectives of the Third Decade;

13. *Regrets* that some of the activities scheduled for the Second Decade to Combat Racism and Racial Discrimination have not been implemented because of lack of adequate resources;

14. *Requests* the Secretary-General to ensure that the necessary financial resources are provided for the implementation of the activities of the Third Decade during the biennium 1994-1995;

15. *Also requests* the Secretary-General to accord the highest priority to the activities of the Programme of Action for the Third Decade that aim at monitoring the transition from apartheid to a non-racist society in South Africa;

16. *Further requests* the Secretary-General to submit each year to the Economic and Social Council a detailed report on all activities of United Nations bodies and the specialized agencies containing an analysis of information received on such activities to combat racism and racial discrimination;

17. *Invites* the Secretary-General to submit proposals to the General Assembly with a view to supplementing, if necessary, the Programme of Action for the Third Decade;

18. *Invites* all Governments, United Nations bodies, the specialized agencies and other intergovernmental organizations, as well as interested non-governmental

---

8/ Resolution S-16/1, annex.

organizations in consultative status with the Economic and Social Council, to participate fully in the Third Decade;

19. *Invites* all Governments, intergovernmental and non-governmental organizations and individuals in a position to do so to contribute generously to the Trust Fund for the Programme for the Decade for Action to Combat Racism and Racial Discrimination, and to this end requests the Secretary-General to continue to undertake appropriate contacts and initiatives;

20. *Decides* to keep the item entitled "Elimination of racism and racial discrimination" on its agenda and to consider it as a matter of the highest priority at its forty-ninth session.

Annex
Programme of Action for the Third Decade to Combat Racism and Racial Discrimination (1993-2003)

Introduction

1. The goals and objectives of the Third Decade to Combat Racism and Racial Discrimination are those adopted by the General Assembly for the first Decade and contained in paragraph 8 of the annex to its resolution 3057 (XXVIII) of 2 November 1973:

> "The ultimate goals of the Decade are to promote human rights and fundamental freedoms for all, without distinction of any kind on grounds of race, colour, descent or national or ethnic origin, especially by eradicating racial prejudice, racism and racial discrimination; to arrest any expansion of racist policies, to eliminate the persistence of racist policies and to counteract the emergence of alliances based on mutual espousal of racism and racial discrimination; to resist any policy and practices which lead to the strengthening of the racist regimes and contribute to the sustainment of racism and racial discrimination; to identify, isolate and dispel the fallacious and mythical beliefs, policies and practices that contribute to racism and racial discrimination; and to put an end to racist regimes."

2. In drawing up suggested elements for the Programme of Action for the Third Decade, account has been taken of the fact that current global economic conditions have caused many Member States to call for budgetary restraint, which in turn requires a conservative approach to the number and type of programmes of action that may be considered at this time. The Secretary-General also took into account the relevant suggestions made by the Committee on the Elimination of Racial Discrimination at its forty-first session. The elements presented below have been suggested as those which are essential, should resources be made available to implement them.

Measures to ensure a peaceful transition from apartheid to a democratic, non-racial regime in South Africa

3. Recently, there have been signs of change in South Africa, notably the abolition of such legal pillars of apartheid as the Group Areas Act, the Land Areas Act and the Population Registration Act. Although there is reason to be hopeful that South Africa is moving into the mainstream of the international community, the transition period may prove to be difficult and dangerous. Fierce political competition between political parties and ethnic groups has in fact already lead to bloodshed.

4. The General Assembly and the Security Council should therefore continue to exercise constant vigilance with regard to South Africa until a democratic regime is installed in that country. These two bodies might, moreover, consider initiating a mechanism to advise and assist the parties concerned in order to bring apartheid to an end, not only in law but also in fact. Reference should be made to Security Council resolution 765 (1992) of 16 July 1992 urging the South African authorities to bring an effective end to the violence and bring those responsible to justice.

5. The General Assembly will continue to examine the relevant work undertaken by the established United Nations bodies in the fight against apartheid, that is, the Special Committee against Apartheid, the Group of Three and the Ad Hoc Working Group of Experts on Southern Africa.

Measures to remedy the legacy of cultural, economic and social disparities left by apartheid

6. Action will be needed to rectify the consequences of apartheid in South Africa, since the policy of apartheid has entailed the use of State power to increase inequalities between racial groups. The knowledge and experience of human rights bodies dealing with racial discrimination could be most useful in promoting equality. Assistance to the victims of the political antagonisms resulting from the process of dismantling apartheid must also be given the greatest attention, and international solidarity on their behalf should be intensified.

7. The Centre for Human Rights should offer technical assistance in the field of human rights to South Africa during and after the transition period. A cycle of seminars intended to encourage the advent of an egalitarian society should be envisaged, in cooperation with the concerned specialized agencies and units of the United Nations Secretariat, which could include the following:

(a) Seminar on measures to be taken on behalf of the disadvantaged groups in South African society in the cultural, economic and social fields ("positive discrimination");

(b) Seminar on the effects of racial discrimination on the health of members of disadvantaged groups;

(c) Training courses in human rights for the South African police force, military and judiciary.

8. In addition, in cooperation with the democratically elected Government of South Africa, the United Nations Educational, Scientific and Cultural Organization might undertake a project for the total revision of the South African educational system in order to eliminate all methods and references of a racist character.

Action at the international level

9. During the discussion at the substantive session of 1992 of the Economic and Social Council concerning the Second Decade to Combat Racism and Racial Discrimination, many delegations expressed their concern with regard to new expressions of racism, racial discrimination, intolerance and xenophobia in various parts of the world. In particular, these affect minorities, ethnic groups, migrant workers, indigenous populations, nomads, immigrants and refugees.

10. The biggest contribution to the elimination of racial discrimination will be that which results from the actions of States within their own territories. International action undertaken as part of any programme for the Third Decade should therefore be directed so as to assist States to act effectively. The International Convention on the Elimination of All Forms of Racial Discrimination 2/ has established standards for States, and every opportunity should be seized to ensure that these are universally accepted and applied.

11. The General Assembly should consider more effective action to ensure that all States parties to the International Convention on the Elimination of All Forms of Racial Discrimination fulfil their reporting and financial obligations. National action against racism and racial discrimination should be monitored and improved by requesting an expert member of the Committee on the Elimination of Racial Discrimination to prepare a report on obstacles encountered with respect to the effective implementation of the Convention by States parties and suggestions for remedial measures.

12. The General Assembly requests the Secretary-General to organize regional workshops and seminars. A team from the Committee should be invited to monitor these meetings. The following themes are suggested for the seminars:

(a) Seminar to assess the experience gained in the implementation of the International Convention on the Elimination of All Forms of Racial Discrimination. The seminar would also assess the efficiency of national legislation and recourse procedures available to victims of racism;

(b) Seminar on the eradication of incitement to racial hatred and discrimination, including the prohibition of propaganda activities and of organizations involved in them;

(c) Seminar on the right to equal treatment before tribunals and other judicial institutions, including the provision of reparation for damages suffered as a result of discrimination;

(d) Seminar on the transmission of racial inequality from one generation to another, with special reference to the children of migrant workers and the appearance of new forms of segregation;

(e) Seminar on immigration and racism;

(f) Seminar on international cooperation in the elimination of racial discrimination, including cooperation between States, the contribution of non-governmental organizations, national and regional institutions, United Nations bodies and petitions to treaty-monitoring bodies;

(g) Seminar on the enactment of national legislation to combat racism and racial discrimination affecting ethnic groups, migrant workers and refugees (in Europe and North America);

(h) Seminar on flows of refugees resulting from ethnic conflicts or political restructuring of multi-ethnic societies in socio-economic transition (Eastern Europe, Africa and Asia) and their link with racism in the host country;

(i) Training course on national legislation prohibiting racial discrimination for nationals from countries with and without such legislation;

(j) Regional seminars on nationalism, ethno-nationalism and human rights could also provide an opportunity for broadening knowledge of the causes of today's ethnic conflicts and particularly of the so-called policy of "ethnic cleansing", in order to provide solutions.

13. The General Assembly requests the Department of Public Information of the Secretariat to undertake specific activities that could be carried out by Governments and relevant national non-governmental organizations to commemorate the International Day for the Elimination of Racial Discrimination on 21 March each year. Support should be sought from artists, as well as religious leaders, trade unions, enterprises and political parties, to sensitize the population on the evils of racism and racial discrimination.

14. The Department of Public Information should also publish its posters for the Third Decade and informative brochures on the activities planned for the Decade. Documentary films and reports, as well as radio broad-

casts on the damaging effects of racism and racial discrimination, should, moreover, be considered.

15. In cooperation with the United Nations Educational, Scientific and Cultural Organization and the Department of Public Information, the General Assembly supports the organization of a seminar on the role of mass media in combating or disseminating racist ideas.

16. In cooperation with the International Labour Organisation, the possibility of organizing a seminar on the role of trade unions in combating racism and racial discrimination in employment should be explored.

17. The General Assembly invites the United Nations Educational, Scientific and Cultural Organization to expedite the preparation of teaching materials and teaching aids to promote teaching, training and educational activities against racism and racial discrimination, with particular emphasis on activities at the primary and secondary levels of education.

18. The General Assembly calls upon Member States to make special efforts:

(a) To promote the aim of non-discrimination in all educational programmes and policies;

(b) To give special attention to the civic education of teachers. It is essential that teachers be aware of the principles and essential content of the legal texts relevant to racism and racial discrimination and of how to deal with the problem of relations between children belonging to different communities;

(c) To teach contemporary history at an early age, presenting children with an accurate picture of the crimes committed by fascist and other totalitarian regimes, and more particularly of the crimes of apartheid and genocide;

(d) To ensure that curricula and textbooks reflect anti-racist principles and promote intercultural education.

Action at the national and regional levels

19. The following questions are addressed in the context of action to be taken at the national and regional levels: have there been any successful national models to eliminate racism and racial prejudices that could be recommended to States, for example, for educating children, or principles of equality to tackle racism against migrant workers, ethnic minorities or indigenous people? What kind of affirmative action programmes are there at the national or regional level to redress discrimination against specific groups?

20. The General Assembly recommends that States that have not yet done so adopt, ratify and implement legislation prohibiting racism and racial discrimination, such as the International Convention on the Elimination of All Forms of Racial Discrimination, 2/ the International Convention on the Suppression and Punishment of the Crime of Apartheid 3/ and the International Convention on the Protection of the Rights of All Migrant Workers and Members of Their Families. 4/

21. The General Assembly recommends that Member States review their national programmes to combat racial discrimination and its effects in order to identify and to seize opportunities to close gaps between different groups, and especially to undertake housing, educational and employment programmes that have proved to be successful in combating racial discrimination and xenophobia.

22. The General Assembly recommends that Member States encourage the participation of journalists and human rights advocates from minority groups and communities in the mass media. Radio and television programmes should increase the number of broadcasts produced by and in cooperation with racial and cultural minority groups. Multicultural activities of the media should also be encouraged where they can contribute to the suppression of racism and xenophobia.

23. The General Assembly recommends that regional organizations cooperate closely with United Nations efforts to combat racism and racial discrimination. Regional organizations dealing with human rights issues could mobilize public opinion in their regions against the evils of racism and racial prejudices directed towards disadvantaged racial and ethnic groups. These institutions could serve an important function in assisting Governments to enact national legislation against racial discrimination and promote adoption and application of international conventions. Regional human rights commissions should be called upon to publicize widely basic texts on existing human rights instruments.

Basic research and studies

24. The long-term viability of the United Nations programme against racism and racial discrimination will depend in part on continuing research into the causes of racism and into the new manifestations of racism and racial discrimination. The General Assembly may wish to examine the importance of preparing studies on racism. The following are some aspects to be studied:

(a) Application of article 2 of the International Convention on the Elimination of All Forms of Racial Discrimination. Such a study might assist States to learn from one another the national measures taken to implement the Convention;

(b) Economic factors contributing to perpetuation of racism and racial discrimination;

(c) Integration or preservation of cultural identity in a multiracial or multi-ethnic society;

(d) Political rights, including the participation of various racial groups in political processes and their representation in government service;

(e) Civil rights, including migration, nationality and freedom of opinion and association;

(f) Educational measures to combat racial prejudice and discrimination and to propagate the principles of the United Nations;

(g) Socio-economic costs of racism and racial discrimination;

(h) Global integration and the question of racism and the nation State;

(i) National mechanisms against racism and racial discrimination in the fields of immigration, employment, salary, housing, education and ownership of property.

Coordination and reporting

25. It may be relevant to recall that in its resolution 38/14 of 22 November 1983, in which it proclaimed the Second Decade to Combat Racism and Racial Discrimination, the General Assembly charged the Economic and Social Council with coordinating the implementation of the Programme of Action for the Second Decade and evaluating the activities. The Assembly decides that the following steps should be taken to strengthen the United Nations input into the Third Decade to Combat Racism and Racial Discrimination:

(a) The General Assembly entrusts the Economic and Social Council and the Commission on Human Rights, in cooperation with the Secretary-General, with the responsibility for coordinating the programmes and evaluating the activities undertaken in connection with the Third Decade;

(b) The Secretary-General is invited to provide specific information on activities against racism, to be contained in one annual report, which should be comprehensive in nature and allow a general overview of all mandated activities. This will facilitate coordination and evaluation;

(c) An open-ended working group of the Commission on Human Rights, or other appropriate arrangements under the Commission, may be established to review Decade-related information on the basis of the annual reports referred to above, as well as relevant studies and reports of seminars, to assist the Commission in formulating appropriate recommendations to the Economic and Social Council on particular activities, allocation of priorities and so on.

26. Furthermore, an inter-agency meeting should be organized immediately after the proclamation of the Third Decade, in 1994, with a view to planning working meetings and other activities.

Regular system-wide consultations

27. On an annual basis, consultations between the United Nations, specialized agencies and non-governmental organizations should take place to review and plan Decade-related activities. In this framework, the Centre for Human Rights should organize inter-agency meetings to consider and discuss further measures to strengthen the coordination and cooperation of programmes related to the issues of combating racism and racial discrimination.

28. The Centre should also strengthen the relationship with non-governmental organizations fighting against racism and racial discrimination by holding consultations and briefings with the non-governmental organizations. Such meetings could help them to initiate, develop and present proposals regarding the struggle against racism and racial discrimination.

29. The Secretary-General should include the activities to be carried out during the Decade, as well as the related resource requirements, in the proposed programme budgets, which will be submitted biennially, during the Decade, starting with the proposed programme budget for the biennium 1994-1995.

Document 87

General Assembly resolution on the International Year of the World's Indigenous People, 1993

A/RES/48/133, 20 December 1993

The General Assembly,

Bearing in mind that one of the purposes of the United Nations set forth in the Charter is the achievement of international cooperation in solving international problems of an economic, social, cultural or humanitarian character, and in promoting and encouraging respect for human rights and for fundamental freedoms for all without discrimination as to race, sex, language or religion,

Recognizing and respecting the value and the diversity of cultures, as well as the cultural heritage and the forms of social organization of the world's indigenous people,

Recalling its resolution 45/164 of 18 December 1990, in which it proclaimed 1993 the International Year of the World's Indigenous People, with a view to strengthening international cooperation for the solution of problems faced by indigenous communities in areas such as human rights, the environment, development, education and health,

Conscious of the need to improve the economic, social and cultural situation of the indigenous people with full respect for their distinctiveness and their own initiatives,

Appreciative of the contributions made to the voluntary fund for the Year opened by the Secretary-General,

Noting the establishment of the fund for the development of indigenous peoples of Latin America and the Caribbean as one kind of support for the objectives of the Year,

Taking note of the recommendation of the World Conference on Human Rights, held at Vienna from 14 to 25 June 1993, that an international decade of the world's indigenous people should be proclaimed, 1/

Noting the need to continue strengthening the initiatives taken as a result of the Year,

Recalling the request to the Subcommission on Prevention of Discrimination and Protection of Minorities that it should complete its consideration of the draft universal declaration on the rights of indigenous peoples,

1. *Calls upon* the United Nations system and Governments that have not yet done so to develop policies in support of the objectives and the theme of the International Year of the World's Indigenous People and to strengthen the institutional framework for their implementation;

2. *Recommends* to all thematic rapporteurs, special representatives, independent experts and working groups that they pay particular attention, within the framework of their mandates, to the situation of indigenous people;

3. *Urges* the Assistant Secretary-General for Human Rights to continue to solicit actively the cooperation of specialized agencies, regional commissions, financial and development institutions and other relevant organizations of the United Nations system for the promotion of a programme of activities in support of the objectives and the theme of the Year;

4. *Appeals* to the specialized agencies, regional commissions and financial and development institutions of the United Nations system to continue to increase their efforts to take into special account the needs of indigenous people in their budgeting and in their programming;

5. *Requests:*

(*a*) That reports of the three technical meetings, first provided for in paragraph 8 of General Assembly resolution 46/128 of 17 December 1991, be included in the final assessment proceedings provided for in paragraph 12 of the same resolution and that their conclusions be included in the report of the Coordinator for the Year to be submitted to the General Assembly at its forty-ninth session;

(*b*) That the Commission on Human Rights convene, from within existing resources, a meeting of participants in the programmes and projects of the Year, in the three days preceding the twelfth session of the Working Group on Indigenous Populations of the Subcommission on Prevention of Discrimination and Protection of Minorities, to report to the Working Group on the conclusions that can be drawn from the activities of the Year with a view to the elaboration of a detailed plan of action and the establishment of a funding plan for the International Decade of the World's Indigenous People;

6. *Stresses* the relevance for the solution of problems faced by indigenous communities of the recommendations contained in chapter 26 of Agenda 21, 2/ including their implementation;

7. *Notes with satisfaction* the holding at Manila of a Global Youth Earth-saving Summit which, by its reaffirmation of the role of traditional cultures in the preservation of the environment, underscored the right to cultural survival;

8. *Welcomes* the proposal for a gathering of indigenous youth in 1995, an "Indigenous Youth Cultural Olympics", as a follow-up to the Year, to be held in conjunction with the International Decade of the World's Indigenous People and the fiftieth anniversary of the United Nations, to reaffirm the value of traditional cultures, folk arts and rituals as effective expressions of respective national identities and as a foundation for a shared vision for peace, freedom and equality;

9. *Also stresses* that the governmental and intergovernmental activities undertaken within the context of the Year and beyond should take fully into account the development needs of indigenous people and that the Year should contribute to enhancing and facilitating the coordination capabilities of Member States for collecting and analysing information;

10. *Notes* that there is a continuing need within the United Nations system to aggregate data specific to indigenous people by means of enhancing and facilitating

1/ A/CONF.157/24 (Part I), chap. III, sect. II, para. 32.
2/ *Report of the United Nations Conference on Environment and Development, Rio de Janeiro, 3-14 June 1992* (A/CONF.151/26/Rev.1 (Vol. I, Vol. I/Corr.1, Vol. II, Vol. III and Vol. III/Corr.1)) (United Nations publication, Sales No. E.93.I.8 and corrigenda), vol. I: *Resolutions adopted by the Conference*, resolution 1, annex II.

the coordination capabilities of Member States for collecting and analysing such data;

11. *Requests* the Subcommission on Prevention of Discrimination and Protection of Minorities, at its forty-sixth session, to complete its consideration of the draft universal declaration on the rights of indigenous peoples and to submit its report to the Commission on Human Rights at its fifty-first session;

12. *Requests* the Coordinator for the Year, in the report to be submitted to the General Assembly at its forty-ninth session on the activities developed and the results achieved within the context of the Year, to include an account of the response of the United Nations system to the needs of indigenous people;

13. *Expresses its appreciation* for the work undertaken for the Year by Governments, the Coordinator for the Year, the International Labour Organisation, the Goodwill Ambassador, Rigoberta Menchú, indigenous and non-governmental organizations, the Commission on Human Rights and the Working Group on Indigenous Populations.

Document 88

General Assembly resolution creating the post of the United Nations High Commissioner for Human Rights

A/RES/48/141, 20 December 1993

The General Assembly,

Reaffirming its commitment to the purposes and principles of the Charter of the United Nations,

Emphasizing the responsibilities of all States, in conformity with the Charter, to promote and encourage respect for all human rights and fundamental freedoms for all, without distinction as to race, sex, language or religion,

Emphasizing also the need to observe the Universal Declaration of Human Rights 1/ and for the full implementation of the human rights instruments, including the International Covenant on Civil and Political Rights, 2/ the International Covenant on Economic, Social and Cultural Rights, 2/ as well as the Declaration on the Right to Development, 3/

Reaffirming that the right to development is a universal and inalienable right which is a fundamental part of the rights of the human person,

Considering that the promotion and the protection of all human rights is one of the priorities of the international community,

Recalling that one of the purposes of the United Nations enshrined in the Charter is to achieve international cooperation in promoting and encouraging respect for human rights,

Reaffirming the commitment made under Article 56 of the Charter to take joint and separate action in cooperation with the United Nations for the achievement of the purposes set forth in Article 55,

Emphasizing the need for the promotion and protection of all human rights to be guided by the principles of impartiality, objectivity and non-selectivity, in the spirit of constructive international dialogue and cooperation,

Aware that all human rights are universal, indivisible, interdependent and interrelated and that as such they should be given the same emphasis,

Affirming its commitment to the Vienna Declaration and Programme of Action, 4/ adopted by the World Conference on Human Rights, held at Vienna from 14 to 25 June 1993,

Convinced that the World Conference on Human Rights made an important contribution to the cause of human rights and that its recommendations should be implemented through effective action by all States, the competent organs of the United Nations and the specialized agencies, in cooperation with non-governmental organizations,

Acknowledging the importance of strengthening the provision of advisory services and technical assistance by the Centre for Human Rights of the Secretariat and other relevant programmes and bodies of the United Nations system for the purpose of the promotion and protection of all human rights,

Determined to adapt, strengthen and streamline the existing mechanisms to promote and protect all human rights and fundamental freedoms while avoiding unnecessary duplication,

1/ Resolution 217 A (III).

2/ See resolution 2200 A (XXI), annex.

3/ Resolution 41/128, annex.

4/ *Report of the World Conference on Human Rights, Vienna, 14-25 June 1993* (A/CONF.157/24 (Part I)), chap. III.

Recognizing that the activities of the United Nations in the field of human rights should be rationalized and enhanced in order to strengthen the United Nations machinery in this field and to further the objectives of universal respect for observance of international human rights standards,

Reaffirming that the General Assembly, the Economic and Social Council and the Commission on Human Rights are the responsible organs for decision- and policy-making for the promotion and protection of all human rights,

Reaffirming also the necessity for a continued adaptation of the United Nations human rights machinery to the current and future needs in the promotion and protection of human rights and the need to improve its coordination, efficiency and effectiveness, as reflected in the Vienna Declaration and Programme of Action and within the framework of a balanced and sustainable development for all people,

Having considered the recommendation contained in paragraph 18 of section II of the Vienna Declaration and Programme of Action,

1. *Decides* to create the post of the United Nations High Commissioner for Human Rights;

2. *Decides* that the High Commissioner shall:

(a) Be a person of high moral standing and personal integrity and shall possess expertise, including in the field of human rights, and the general knowledge and understanding of diverse cultures necessary for impartial, objective, non-selective and effective performance of the duties of the High Commissioner;

(b) Be appointed by the Secretary-General of the United Nations and approved by the General Assembly, with due regard to geographical rotation, and have a fixed term of four years with a possibility of one renewal for another fixed term of four years;

(c) Be of the rank of Under-Secretary-General;

3. *Also decides* that the High Commissioner shall:

(a) Function within the framework of the Charter of the United Nations, the Universal Declaration of Human Rights, other international instruments of human rights and international law, including the obligations, within this framework, to respect the sovereignty, territorial integrity and domestic jurisdiction of States and to promote the universal respect for and observance of all human rights, in the recognition that, in the framework of the purposes and principles of the Charter, the promotion and protection of all human rights is a legitimate concern of the international community;

(b) Be guided by the recognition that all human rights—civil, cultural, economic, political and social—are universal, indivisible, interdependent and interrelated and that, while the significance of national and regional particularities and various historical, cultural and religious backgrounds must be borne in mind, it is the duty of States, regardless of their political, economic and cultural systems, to promote and protect all human rights and fundamental freedoms;

(c) Recognize the importance of promoting a balanced and sustainable development for all people and of ensuring realization of the right to development, as established in the Declaration on the Right to Development;

4. *Further decides* that the High Commissioner shall be the United Nations official with principal responsibility for United Nations human rights activities under the direction and authority of the Secretary-General and that within the framework of the overall competence, authority and decisions of the General Assembly, the Economic and Social Council and the Commission on Human Rights, the High Commissioner's responsibilities shall be:

(a) To promote and protect the effective enjoyment by all of all civil, cultural, economic, political and social rights;

(b) To carry out the tasks assigned to him/her by the competent bodies of the United Nations system in the field of human rights and to make recommendations to them with a view to improving the promotion and protection of all human rights;

(c) To promote and protect the realization of the right to development and to enhance support from relevant bodies of the United Nations system for this purpose;

(d) To provide, through the Centre for Human Rights of the Secretariat and other appropriate institutions, advisory services and technical and financial assistance, at the request of the State concerned and, where appropriate, the regional human rights organizations, with a view to supporting actions and programmes in the field of human rights;

(e) To coordinate relevant United Nations education and public information programmes in the field of human rights;

(f) To play an active role in removing the current obstacles and in meeting the challenges to the full realization of all human rights and in preventing the continuation of human rights violations throughout the world, as reflected in the Vienna Declaration and Programme of Action;

(g) To engage in a dialogue with all Governments in the implementation of his/her mandate with a view to securing respect for all human rights;

(h) To enhance international cooperation for the promotion and protection of all human rights;

(i) To coordinate the human rights promotion and protection activities throughout the United Nations system;

(j) To rationalize, adapt, strengthen and streamline the United Nations machinery in the field of human rights with a view to improving its efficiency and effectiveness;

(k) To carry out overall supervision of the Centre for Human Rights;

5. *Requests* the High Commissioner to report annually on his/her activities, in accordance with his/her mandate, to the Commission on Human Rights and, through the Economic and Social Council, to the General Assembly;

6. *Decides* that the Office of the United Nations High Commissioner for Human Rights shall be located at Geneva and shall have a liaison office in New York;

7. *Requests* the Secretary-General to provide appropriate staff and resources, within the existing and future regular budgets of the United Nations, to enable the High Commissioner to fulfil his/her mandate, without diverting resources from the development programmes and activities of the United Nations;

8. *Also requests* the Secretary-General to report to the General Assembly at its forty-ninth session on the implementation of the present resolution.

Document 89

Security Council resolution establishing the police component of the United Nations Operation in Mozambique (ONUMOZ)

S/RES/898 (1994), 23 February 1994

The Security Council,

Reaffirming its resolution 782 (1992) of 13 October 1992 and all subsequent resolutions,

Having considered the report of the Secretary-General on the United Nations Operation in Mozambique (ONUMOZ) dated 28 January 1994 (S/1994/89 and Add.1 and 2), and *having completed* the review of the status of ONUMOZ called for in its resolution 882 (1993),

Commending the efforts of the Secretary-General, his Special Representative and the personnel of ONUMOZ in seeking to implement fully the mandate entrusted to it,

Commending also the role played by the Organization of African Unity (OAU), through the Special Representative of its Secretary-General, in the implementation of the General Peace Agreement for Mozambique (S/24635, annex),

Reiterating the importance it attaches to the General Peace Agreement, and to the timely fulfilment in good faith by all parties of their obligations under the Agreement,

Noting that the people of Mozambique bear the ultimate responsibility for the successful implementation of the General Peace Agreement,

Welcoming recent positive developments in the implementation of the General Peace Agreement, but *concerned* none the less at delays in its full implementation,

Taking note of the request by the Government of Mozambique and RENAMO concerning the monitoring of all police activities and additional tasks set out in the agreements of 3 September 1993 (S/26432), and of the agreement of both parties to the general concept for the ONUMOZ police contingent,

Stressing the necessity, in this as in other peace-keeping operations, to continue to monitor expenditures carefully during this period of increasing demands on peace-keeping resources, without jeopardizing their purposes,

Noting with appreciation in this context that the Secretary-General, in proposing the establishment of a police component as an integral part of ONUMOZ, has at the same time stated his intention to present specific proposals for the phased reduction of the military component of ONUMOZ, without prejudice to the effective discharge of its mandate, in particular the tasks of its military component,

Reaffirming its conviction that the resolution of the conflict in Mozambique will contribute to peace and security,

1. *Welcomes* the report of the Secretary-General of 28 January 1994;

2. *Authorizes* the establishment of a United Nations police component of up to 1,144 personnel as an integral part of ONUMOZ with the mandate and deployment described in paragraphs 9 to 18 of document S/1994/89/Add.1;

3. *Requests* the Secretary-General, as the police contingent is being deployed, to begin immediately preparing specific proposals for the drawdown of an appropriate number of military personnel with the objective of ensuring there is no increase in the cost of ONUMOZ without prejudice to the effective discharge of its mandate;

4. *Further requests* the Secretary-General to prepare a timetable for (a) the completion of ONUMOZ's

mandate, withdrawal of its personnel, and turnover of any remaining functions to United Nations agencies and programmes by the target date of the end of November 1994, by which time the elected government is expected to have assumed office, and in this context, for (b) the phased drawdown of military forces in the transportation corridors which should begin as soon as feasible and be completed when the new national defence force is operational, and (c) the withdrawal of military observers after demobilization is completed;

5. *Welcomes* recent positive developments in the implementation of the General Peace Agreement including the commencement of the assembly of troops and the dismantling of paramilitary forces, militia and irregular troops, the approval of the electoral law and the appointment of the National Elections Commission and of its chairperson;

6. *Expresses* its concern, however, at the continuing delay in the implementation of some major aspects of the General Peace Agreement, including the commencement of demobilization and the formation of a national defence force and calls upon the parties to work towards the elimination of further delays;

7. *Calls upon* the Government of Mozambique and RENAMO to comply with all the provisions of the General Peace Agreement, in particular those concerning the cease-fire and the cantonment and demobilization of troops, and *commends* in this respect the commitments made by both President Chissano and Mr. Dhlakama to implement the General Peace Agreement;

8. *Further calls upon* the Government of Mozambique and RENAMO to comply fully and promptly with the decisions of the Monitoring and Supervision Commission;

9. *Encourages* the Government of Mozambique to continue to fulfil its commitments in respect of the provision of logistic support and adequate food, and making outstanding payments, to the troops in the assembly areas and the training centres;

10. *Notes* the recent acceleration in the assembly of the troops of the Government of Mozambique, and *calls upon* the Government to redouble its efforts to achieve balance between the parties in the cantonment of troops and an expeditious and timely conclusion of this process as called for in the revised timetable;

11. *Underlines* the need for the troops of the Government of Mozambique and RENAMO to hand over all weapons to the United Nations at the assembly areas and for the parties to come to an immediate agreement on the transfer of all weapons to regional depots so as to ensure security in the assembly areas;

12. *Reiterates* the vital importance it attaches to the holding of general elections no later than October 1994 and to the early commencement of electoral registration and other electoral preparations, and *urges* the parties to agree promptly on a specific election date;

13. *Appeals* to the international community to provide the necessary financial assistance to facilitate the implementation of the General Peace Agreement and also to make voluntary financial contributions to the Trust Fund to be set up to support electoral activities of the political parties;

14. *Notes* the Secretary-General's decision to explore the possibility of establishing a more effective mechanism for the provision of resources, disbursement under which is subject to the scrupulous and timely implementation of the General Peace Agreement, as described in paragraph 35 of his report of 28 January 1994;

15. *Welcomes* the proposal to extend the present severance payment scheme to facilitate the reintegration of demobilizing soldiers into civil society and *encourages* the international community to provide appropriate and prompt assistance for the implementation of this scheme as a complement to the existing efforts made in the framework of the humanitarian assistance programme;

16. *Expresses* its appreciation to the United Kingdom of Great Britain and Northern Ireland, France, Portugal and Italy for their offers of assistance in military training or in rehabilitating the training centres for the new army;

17. *Notes* also with appreciation the response of the international community to the humanitarian assistance needs of Mozambique and *encourages* the international community to continue to provide appropriate and prompt assistance for the implementation of the humanitarian programme carried out in the framework of the General Peace Agreement;

18. *Urges* all parties to continue to facilitate unimpeded access to humanitarian assistance for the civilian population in need, and also to cooperate with the United Nations High Commissioner for Refugees (UNHCR) and other humanitarian agencies operating in Mozambique to facilitate the speedy repatriation and resettlement of refugees and displaced persons;

19. *Requests* the Secretary-General to ensure maximum economy in the operations of ONUMOZ, while remaining mindful of the importance of an effective discharge of its mandate;

20. *Looks forward* to the next report of the Secretary-General called for in paragraph 13 of resolution 882 (1993) on whether the parties have made sufficient and tangible progress towards implementing the General Peace Agreement and in meeting the timetable set out in paragraphs 3 and 10 of that resolution, on the basis of which it will consider the mandate of ONUMOZ;

21. *Decides* to remain actively seized of the matter.

Document 90

Security Council resolution concerning the establishment of a Commission of Experts to investigate human rights violations in Rwanda

S/RES/935 (1994), 1 July 1994

The Security Council,

Reaffirming all its previous resolutions on the situation in Rwanda,

Reaffirming, in particular, resolutions 918 (1994) and 925 (1994), which expanded the United Nations Assistance Mission for Rwanda (UNAMIR), and *stressing* in this connection the need for early deployment of the expanded UNAMIR to enable it to carry out its mandate,

Recalling the statement by the President of the Security Council of 30 April 1994 (S/PRST/1994/21) in which the Security Council, *inter alia,* condemned all breaches of international humanitarian law in Rwanda, particularly those perpetrated against the civilian population, and recalled that persons who instigate or participate in such acts are individually responsible,

Recalling also the requests it addressed to the Secretary-General in the statement by the President of the Security Council of 30 April 1994 and in resolution 918 (1994), concerning the investigation of serious violations of international humanitarian law committed in Rwanda during the conflict,

Having considered the report of the Secretary-General of 31 May 1994 (S/1994/640), in which he noted that massacres and killings have continued in a systematic manner throughout Rwanda and also noted that only a proper investigation can establish the facts in order to enable the determination of responsibility,

Welcoming the visit to Rwanda and to the region by the United Nations High Commissioner for Human Rights and *noting* the appointment, pursuant to resolution S-3/1 of 25 May 1994 adopted by the United Nations Commission on Human Rights, of a Special Rapporteur for Rwanda,

Expressing once again its grave concern at the continuing reports indicating that systematic, widespread and flagrant violations of international humanitarian law, including acts of genocide, have been committed in Rwanda,

Recalling that all persons who commit or authorize the commission of serious violations of international humanitarian law are individually responsible for those violations and should be brought to justice,

1. *Requests* the Secretary-General to establish, as a matter of urgency, an impartial Commission of Experts to examine and analyse information submitted pursuant to the present resolution, together with such further information as the Commission of Experts may obtain through its own investigations or the efforts of other persons or bodies, including the information made available by the Special Rapporteur for Rwanda, with a view to providing the Secretary-General with its conclusions on the evidence of grave violations of international humanitarian law committed in the territory of Rwanda, including the evidence of possible acts of genocide;

2. *Calls upon* States and, as appropriate, international humanitarian organizations to collate substantiated information in their possession or submitted to them relating to grave violations of international humanitarian law, including breaches of the Convention on the Prevention and Punishment of the Crime of Genocide, committed in Rwanda during the conflict, and *requests* States, relevant United Nations bodies, and relevant organizations to make this information available within thirty days of the adoption of the present resolution and as appropriate thereafter, and to provide appropriate assistance to the Commission of Experts referred to in paragraph 1;

3. *Requests* the Secretary-General to report to the Council on the establishment of the Commission of Experts, and *further requests* the Secretary-General, within four months from the establishment of the Commission of Experts, to report to the Council, on the conclusions of the Commission and to take account of these conclusions in any recommendations for further appropriate steps;

4. *Also requests* the Secretary-General and as appropriate the High Commissioner for Human Rights through the Secretary-General to make the information submitted to the Special Rapporteur for Rwanda available to the Commission of Experts and to facilitate adequate coordination and cooperation between the work of the Commission of Experts and the Special Rapporteur in the performance of their respective tasks;

5. *Urges* all concerned fully to cooperate with the Commission of Experts in the accomplishment of its mandate, including responding positively to requests from the Commission for assistance and access in pursuing investigations;

6. *Decides* to remain actively seized of the matter.

Document 91

Report of the Working Group on the Right to Development on its second session

E/CN.4/1995/11, 5 September 1994

Introduction

1. By its resolution 1993/22, the Commission on Human Rights decided to establish, initially for a three-year period, a Working Group on the Right to Development, composed of 15 experts nominated by Governments to be appointed by the Chairman of the Commission on Human Rights at its forty-ninth session, on the basis of equitable geographical representation and in consultation with the regional groups in the Commission, with the following mandate:

(a) To identify obstacles to the implementation and realization of the Declaration on the Right to Development, on the basis of information furnished by Member States and other appropriate sources;

(b) To recommend ways and means towards the realization of the right to development by all States.

2. The World Conference on Human Rights, which adopted the Vienna Declaration and Programme of Action on 16 June 1993, urged the Working Group to formulate promptly, for early consideration by the United Nations General Assembly, comprehensive and effective measures to eliminate obstacles to the implementation and realization of the Declaration on the Right to Development and to recommend ways and means towards the realization of the right to development by all States (para. II.72).

3. The Working Group, which held its first session from 8 to 19 November 1993, submitted its report on its first session to the fiftieth session of the Commission on Human Rights (E/CN.4/1994/21 and Corr.1 and 2).

4. By its resolution 1994/21, the Commission on Human Rights took note with appreciation of the report of the Working Group on the Right to Development on its first session and welcomed the efforts made by the Working Group, which were increasingly oriented towards the establishment of a permanent evaluation mechanism in the future, to follow up the implementation of the Declaration on the Right to Development. It urged the Working Group to make recommendations on the implementation of the right to development, taking into account policies at the national and international levels, particularly towards the creation of a favourable international economic climate which would be more responsive to the needs of the developing countries, as well as to give priority to the special needs of the least developed countries, and requested the Working Group to submit to the Commission at its fifty-first session a report on the progress of its work during 1994.

5. By its resolution 1994/11, the Commission on Human Rights requested the Working Group to pay particular attention in its deliberations to the social repercussions of the policies adopted to face situations of external debt on the effective enjoyment of economic, social and cultural rights.

6. By its resolution 48/130, the General Assembly welcomed the convening of the first session of the Working Group on the Right to Development and requested the Secretary-General to report to the forty-ninth session of the General Assembly on the activities of the organs, programmes and institutions of the United Nations system to implement the Declaration on the Right to Development.

7. The Working Group decided to focus its attention, during its second session, on the obstacles to the implementation of the Declaration on the Right to Development, as they relate to the work of the United Nations, its programmes and the agencies directly linked to it, as well as the work of the international financial institutions which have presented their objectives and shared their concerns and experiences with the Group.

8. The present report describes the proceedings of the second session of the Working Group on the Right to Development. It is an interim report which will be supplemented by the report on the second session, to be held in September or October 1994.

Opening and duration of the session

9. The second session of the Working Group on the Right to Development (2-13 May 1994) was held at the Palais des Nations, Geneva, and was opened by its Chairman-Rapporteur, Mr. Ennaceur. The Working Group held 17 plenary meetings 1/ and 1 restricted drafting group meeting.

10. At its second meeting, on 2 May, the High Commissioner for Human Rights, Mr. Ayala Lasso, addressed the Working Group.

11. In order to promote high-level debate on the role of the specialized bodies and agencies in the implementation of the Declaration on the Right to Develop-

---

1/ Because of 12 May being an official holiday, the Working Group could not meet on that particular day.

ment, the Working Group invited to that session senior international officials exercising or having exercised responsibilities at the head of such bodies and agencies, and a number of them responded favourably and made an appreciable contribution to the discussions. Thus it was that Mr. Blanchard, former Director-General of the International Labour Office, Mr. Radwan, Director of the Department of Technical Cooperation at the ILO, Mr. de Capitani, Director of Public-Sector Management at the World Bank, Mr. Berthelot, Executive Secretary of the Economic Commission for Europe, Mr. Fortin, Secretary-General ad interim of the United Nations Conference on Trade and Development, and Mr. Alston, Chairman of the Committee on Economic, Social and Cultural Rights participated in the meetings of the Working Group.

12. Other appreciable contributions were made by Mr. Français of the United Nations Development Programme, Mr. Robineau of the Economic Commission for Europe and Mr. Taplin of the International Monetary Fund.

13. The Working Group wishes to thank them all and hopes that it can continue to benefit from the cooperation and contributions of the specialized international bodies and agencies.

Composition of the Working Group and attendance

14. The Working Group on the Right to Development at its second session consisted of the following 15 experts: Mr. D.D.C. Don Nanjira (Kenya), Mr. Mohamed Ennaceur (Tunisia), Mr. Alexandre Farcas (Romania), Mr. Orobola Fasehun (Nigeria), Mrs. Ligia Galvis (Colombia), Mr. Stuart Harris (Australia), Mr. Stéphane Hessel (France), Mr. Serguei Kossenko (Russian Federation), Mr. Osvaldo Martínez 2/ (Cuba), Mr. Niaz A. Naik (Pakistan), Mr. Pedro Oyarce (Chile), Mr. Pan Sen (China), Mr. Allan Rosas (Finland), Mr. Haron Bin Siraj (Malaysia), and Mr. Vladimir Sotirov (Bulgaria). Mr. Hessel and Mr. Martínez joined the Group on 4 and 9 May, respectively. Mr. Sotirov attended from 2 to 6 May.

15. Observers from States members of the Commission, observers from other States members of the United Nations and representatives of United Nations bodies, specialized agencies and intergovernmental and non-governmental organizations attended the session. The list of participants can be found in Annex I.

Adoption of the agenda

16. The Working Group adopted the agenda for its second session on the basis of the provisional agenda (E/CN.4/AC.45/1994/1). The agenda as adopted is contained in Annex II.

Documentation

17. In order to perform the tasks entrusted to it, the Working Group took as a basis the documents prepared by the Secretary-General, in particular the report containing information transmitted by the specialized agencies (E/CN.4/AC.45/1994/2 and Add.1).

18. It also had at its disposal documentation prepared for the forthcoming international conferences, such as the International Conference on Population and Development (Cairo, 5-13 September 1994), the World Summit for Social Development (Copenhagen, 11-12 March 1995) and the Fourth World Conference on Women (Beijing, 4-15 September 1995).

19. The list of documents before the Working Group at its second session can be found in Annex III.

I. Follow-up to the recommendations of the first session

20. The Working Group noted the interest that the Commission on Human Rights had shown in its first report which had been submitted to the fiftieth session of the Commission (E/CN.4/1994/21 and Corr.1 and 2) and the encouragement it had received to continue and deepen its debate and reflections on the implementation of the Declaration on the Right to Development. The Working Group noted the adoption by the Commission of resolution 1994/21 entitled "The right to development" and expressed its satisfaction that the recommendations it had made at its first session had been endorsed by the Commission.

21. It equally noted Commission on Human Rights resolutions 1994/11 entitled "Effects on the full enjoyment of human rights of the economic adjustment policies arising from foreign debt and, in particular, on the implementation of the Declaration on the Right to Development", as well as resolutions 1994/12, 1994/13, 1994/14, 1994/21, 1994/22 and 1994/63.

22. The Working Group took note of the requests made by the Commission in paragraph 6 of resolution 1994/21 and paragraph 5 of resolution 1994/11, and decided to consider these at one of its next sessions.

23. The Working Group noted that the High Commissioner for Human Rights had met with members of the Administrative Committee on Coordination (ACC) at its first substantive session for 1994, where he had made certain recommendations towards enhancing the support from relevant bodies of the United Nations system to promote and protect the realization of the right to development. During that meeting, he had outlined two

2/ Mr. Jorge Lago Silva attended on 2-6 May 1994, as the alternate to Mr. Martínez.

levels of cooperation and coordination that could be envisaged to reinforce, rationalize and simplify activities to promote human rights. The first level concerned the definition and follow-up of inter-agency policy within the ACC to enable the heads of the agencies and programmes to address effectively questions of policy and implementation. The second level related to contacts through established or expanded mechanisms to ensure, on a daily basis, cooperation with the United Nations system of activities related to human rights. He also expressed his conviction that the participation of the United Nations bodies and specialized agencies in the sessions of the Working Group and their contributions would assist in the development of long-term strategies for the promotion and implementation of the right to development.

24. The Working Group welcomed the commitment which the High Commissioner had expressed to pursue personally the request made by the Commission on Human Rights to the United Nations to undertake high-level consultations with heads of State or Government, heads of multilateral financial institutions, specialized agencies, intergovernmental and non-governmental organizations on adequate measures to be implemented to find a durable solution to the debt crisis of developing countries. The High Commissioner informed the Working Group that a report on the results of the consultations would be submitted to the Commission on Human Rights at its fifty-first session.

25. The Working Group noted with interest the meeting which its Chairman had had with members of the Committee on Economic, Social and Cultural Rights during its tenth session, and shared his view that a dialogue with the other human rights bodies should be further developed and channels of communication strengthened.

26. The Working Group noted that pursuant to the recommendation contained in paragraph 107 of its report on its first session (E/CN.4/1994/21), the Assistant Secretary-General for Human Rights had invited Governments, international financial institutions, the regional economic commissions, the Commission on Social Development and the Commission on the Status of Women, as well as the relevant bodies and organizations of the United Nations system, including the Department of Humanitarian Affairs, and non-governmental organizations to provide the Working Group with the necessary additional information, taking into account, *inter alia*, the preliminary guidelines and the check-list prepared by the Working Group.

27. The Working Group welcomed the initiative of the Assistant Secretary-General who, pursuant to the recommendation contained in paragraph 112 of the report on its first session, had personally invited the Executive Secretaries of the regional economic commissions and the heads of the international financial institutions to participate actively in the sessions, of the Working Group and to contribute substantially to its work.

28. In relation to the recommendation contained in paragraph 109 of its first report, the Working Group noted that the next meeting of the Chairpersons of the treaty bodies would be held from 19-23 September 1994 in Geneva and it considered whether its third session should coincide with that meeting so that a joint consultative meeting might be arranged at that time, as recommended by the Working Group. Alternatively, it was proposed that the meeting of chairpersons postpone its meeting until next year.

29. In conclusion, the Working Group took note that consultations were under way with the Technical Services and Information Branch of the Centre for Human Rights and the Department for Public Information to discuss ways to achieve wide and effective dissemination of the provisions of the Declaration on the Right to Development.

II. Implementation of the Declaration on the Right to Development by the international organizations

(Text prepared by a drafting group and not yet considered by the Working Group)

30. At its second session, the Working Group entered into a process of consultation with the representatives of the various bodies and agencies with a twofold objective: (i) to obtain further information on the implementation of the right to development in their programmes and activities and evaluate the obstacles to its implementation; and (ii) to explore in a preliminary manner, and in cooperation with those institutions, ways and means by which they have implemented or could implement in the future the right to development.

31. The Working Group expressed its appreciation to those agencies which had contributed by their written, and even more so by their oral, statements in clarifying the problems in the implementation of the Declaration. It considered essential that the dialogue be pursued further and that it should include all other multilateral agencies concerned, at the most appropriate level, in order to make the dialogue as operational as possible.

32. A number of representatives indicated that they had, either implicitly or explicitly, taken into account the principles and objectives contained in the provisions of the Declaration on the Right to Development. The Working Group was particularly pleased that one agency, UNFPA, had already incorporated the right to development in the material it was preparing for the International Conference on Population and Development to be held

in Cairo later this year. In general, however, this recognition was confined to general principles and much more has to be done to translate it into operational reality.

33. The first major constraint on the implementation of the right to development related to insufficient transfers from multilateral, bilateral and private sources, as compared with the growing needs. In addition, the available aid is increasingly being redeployed to meet emergency needs.

34. A second constraint, one within the international agencies, was the unequal distribution of these resources, with too little being devoted to social, as distinct from primarily economic, purposes. A further constraint on the implementation of the right to development by the agencies comes from their overwhelmingly sectoral approach and the excessive emphasis on economic growth. Representatives of some agencies, such as UNDP, indicated that a reorientation of the organization's approach was under way under the influence, in particular, of a number of world conferences, notably UNCTAD VIII held in Cartagena in 1992, the Earth Summit held in Rio de Janeiro in 1992, and the World Conference on Human Rights held in Vienna in 1993. It was to be expected that these new orientations would be reinforced as a result of the forthcoming International Conference on Population and Development in Cairo in 1994, the World Summit for Social Development in Copenhagen in 1995 and the Fourth World Conference on Women in Beijing in 1995.

35. Many agencies referred to the greater level of social problems emerging in the world and the increasing difficulties facing the world in providing social protection. The trends already experienced implied that while such aspects as popular participation, democratization and strong social policies are essential for the implementation of the right to development, the means available to achieve these objectives have been greatly deficient.

36. In the case of structural adjustment programmes, the need to introduce social safety nets aimed at mitigating the negative social effects of the programmes presented the risk that, unless care was taken, they could become a substitute for global macroeconomic policies.

37. The Declaration on the Right to Development requires, *inter alia*, that the balance be preserved between economic and social development. The adoption by the World Conference on Human Rights of the concepts contained in the Declaration entails, among other things, a duty to cooperate at the international level. The concepts contained in the Declaration should therefore form, within their areas of competence, an integral part of the policies and programmes of all United Nations bodies and agencies as well as that of the Bretton Woods institutions, including the newly-established World Trade Organization. As such, the Declaration could be a guiding instrument in bridging the gap between macroeconomic policies and social objectives, as well as the gap between the institutions dealing with questions relating to human rights and social problems and those involved in areas such as finance, economic development and political and legal affairs.

38. The reports published by various United Nations bodies make clear that the objectives that the international community had in mind in framing the right to development are not being achieved for all individuals and all peoples, given the deterioration in the standard and conditions of living of large proportions of the world population and the rising social scourges, such as illiteracy, unemployment and poverty, in spite of the efforts of the multilateral agencies.

39. The multidimensional character of the right to development requires that all the United Nations bodies and agencies act together, in harmony, to achieve the common objectives. Insufficient coordination within the United Nations system is a major obstacle to the realization of the right to development. The efforts made so far to improve coordination have not yet achieved the desired results. Each of the specialized agencies, although formally linked to the United Nations system, is accountable only to its own governing body from which it derives its mandate. Furthermore, even the major programmes of the United Nations have an autonomy which is comparable to that enjoyed by the specialized agencies.

40. The existing coordinating machinery, such as the Administrative Committee on Coordination and the Consultative Committee on Programme and Operational Questions have not been allowed to address this question effectively. And the Economic and Social Council has been a weak link in the system. Strong and effective political support by member States would be required to make the concept of the right to development operational. The Working Group regarded the need for greater coordination and more transparency in the collection and allocation of resources within the United Nations system as requiring particular emphasis.

41. One of the weaknesses of the United Nations system which hindered the integration of the principles contained in the right to development in its operational activities was the tendency to separate economic development from social development and macroeconomic policies from social objectives. Moreover, the imperatives of economic growth imposed themselves on the social objectives of development. The problem was accentuated by the continuing marginalization of economic and social rights within the United Nations system.

42. Obviously, the right to development is not stated as such in the mandates of these international

organizations. In fact, one does not find in the broad structures of the programmes of these organizations the concept of the right to development either as a universal right, due to every human being and to all peoples, or as a multidimensional global right, whose economic, social, cultural and political aspects are perceived as interdependent and complementary. Moreover, international organizations had adopted only a partial and fragmented approach to human rights with the result that their implementation was carried out in a selective and hierarchical manner.

43. The Working Group felt that further wide-ranging dialogues with the agencies would clarify how they could contribute towards making the right to development more operational. Although only a few of the agencies had the opportunity to respond specifically to the Working Group's guidelines and check-list of questions, the evidence from those that did indicates that they provide a useful basis for such dialogue.

44. In the final analysis, the right to development is more than development itself; it implies a human rights approach to development, which is something new. For the right to development to be fully effective as a human right, at least two elements are required. First, minimum standards to measure progress achieved in the implementation of the Covenant by States parties have been established with respect to the International Covenant on Civil and Political Rights; this process seems to have lagged behind with respect to the International Covenant on Economic, Social and Cultural Rights. Such minimum standards should be established. In pursuing this objective, account must be taken of the practical difficulties arising from differences existing both within and between countries which are likely to lead to different minimum standards. Second, there is a need for a process of accountability. It is perhaps in this regard that close cooperation with the Committee on Economic, Social and Cultural Rights and other related bodies would be critical.

III. Obstacles to the realization of the Declaration on the Right to Development

45. The Working Group felt that for the identification of obstacles to the realization of the right to development, it should focus on specific obstacles related to the right to development as a universal human right, pertaining to all individuals and all peoples, and as a right highlighting the indivisibility and interdependence of all human rights, be they economic, social and cultural, or political or civil, as set out in the international Bill of Human Rights. This implied the existence of standards as well as a responsibility to implement the standards.

Finally, the right to development should be seen as a right which required international cooperation, in conformity with articles 3, 4 and 6 of the Declaration on the Right to Development.

46. The Working Group thought that it was particularly timely to give more attention to the new obstacles to the realization of the right to development (E/CN.4/1994/21; (para. (c)) as a result of the profound changes in the world and at the international level. These obstacles could be identified at the international, regional and national levels.

47. As the Working Group, at its first session, had not had sufficient time to consider in depth the obstacles to the implementation of the Declaration on the Right to Development, it considered it opportune to reflect further on this issue. The identification of obstacles was undertaken on the basis of the report of the Global Consultation (E/CN.4/1990/9/Rev.1, paras. 161-169) and the contributions which were received from international organizations for the preparation of the report of the Secretary-General submitted in accordance with Commission on Human Rights resolution 1993/22 (E/CN.4/AC.45/1994/2 and Add.1), as well as on the exchange of views which the members of the Working Group had with representatives of the agencies present at its second session.

Obstacles at the international level

48. The Working Group underlined that as a consequence of the globalization of the world economy, new obstacles to the right to development had emerged, such as the shrinking of the freedom of action enjoyed by governments to set their economic policies and adjust them to their development needs; less predictability in the evolution of economic conditions, which also inhibited consistency in the implementation of development strategies; and the increased marginalization of already vulnerable countries.

49. The Working Group noted that the international community, as one of the two principal actors in the realization of the right to development, was not always capable of setting rules and instituting machinery for cooperation whereby external economic obstacles to development could be eliminated, or of adopting special bilateral or multilateral measures to protect the weakest and most vulnerable countries, or of strengthening arrangements and actions designed to handle global problems—such as the environment, drug abuse, etc.—which posed an obstacle to the right to development.

50. The Working Group also thought that within the international community, States and institutions must contribute to exercising these responsibilities in the light of their resources and their importance in the world

economy. Hence, the most powerful countries would bear major responsibility in coordinating macroeconomic policies to ensure a context of a stable and predictable international environment in order to encourage, stimulate and promote human and sustainable development.

51. The Working Group felt that the system of shared responsibility for the realization of the right to development had not yet been extended to other actors, in particular to civil society, including non-governmental organizations, in order to increase their crucial role in promoting democracy and development and combating poverty. Nor had it been extended to actors in the private sector which were creators of wealth and hence agents of growth. To this effect, "ground rules" had to be laid down at the national and international levels, making it possible, *inter alia*, to combat the abuses of economic concentration and restrictive trade practices.

52. Other obstacles which the Working Group considered were the implementation of unilateral coercive measures in contradiction with the Charter of the United Nations the conditionalities which are in contradiction with principles of international law, the continued lack of self-determination and the reverse transfer of resources.

53. The Working Group also thought that the lack of adequate accountability procedures and mechanisms for the implementation of economic, social and cultural rights processes posed a major obstacle.

54. Growing disparities between developed and developing countries and between population categories were reflected in rising unemployment, a deterioration in living standards, acceleration in migratory movements, growing marginalization and an upsurge in poverty everywhere. These developments, and the burden of debt-servicing, had provoked a rise in social and political tensions and conflicts and increased inequalities in the access to the right to development. The trend was accentuated by the decline in the volume of aid flows for development, at a time when the need for such assistance was growing.

55. The pressure to compete internationally for capital, markets and labour is having a harmful effect on the realization of the right to development. The margin of manoeuvre available to States for the formulation of social, economic, monetary and fiscal policy is being reduced. In their competition to attract foreign capital, States have to be more cautious about fiscal policy in terms of redistribution and taxation and have to impose tight monetary policies to fight inflation, but with detrimental effects on employment.

56. There is a danger that "social safety nets" may, unless care is taken, become a substitute for global macroeconomic policies that should have as an integral part

the concept of the right to development as a universal and multidimensional global right where the economic, social, cultural and political dimensions are considered to be indivisible and complementary.

57. While developing countries have primary responsibility for their own economic and social development, in accordance with their priorities and plans, as well as their political and cultural diversities, developed countries have a special responsibility, in the context of growing interdependence, to create a global economic environment favourable to accelerated and sustainable development.

Obstacles at the regional level

58. The Working Group, in its effort to identify universal obstacles to the right to development, had requested the regional commissions to identify the difficulties which they have encountered in implementing the right to development. Along these lines, the Working Group took note of the contributions of ECLAC and ECE. Because of a lack of more information, the Working Group considered this part to be incomplete.

59. In its contribution, ECLAC pointed out that in its region, the main obstacles to development were poverty, unequal distribution of income, non-productive employment and social disintegration. It underlined the need for an integrated approach, which would involve economic policies that fostered not only growth, but also equity, and social policies that emphasized their effect on production and efficiency, not only equity. The integrated approach underscored elements of technical progress, productive employment and fair wages, investment in human resources and redistributive measures geared towards the most disadvantaged groups.

60. In his contribution, the representative of the ECE pointed out that its mandate was restricted to economic issues only and that so far it had not monitored the implementation of the right to development. He wished, however, to share some conceptual matters with the Group. He pointed to the ambiguity that had surrounded the concept of underdevelopment, which in the 1950s had been analysed simply as a delay in development as a result of lack of investment, which could be redressed in the way the North had done. The United Nations had to reconcile the unreconcilable approaches of the West and the East to development, with their different concepts of the role of the State and the private sector in the economy.

61. Nowadays, development was seen as a multidimensional process, bringing together progress in peace, economic growth, respect for the environment, social justice and democracy and pertinent to both the North

and the South. Actors in the field of development were considered to be States, enterprises and NGOs.

62. The Working Group discerned that the regional commissions had problems in integrating the concept of the right to development in their work, even if their mandate was not strictly economic. There was a tendency, also at the regional level, to separate the social aspects of development from macroeconomic policies.

63. The Working Group thought that also at the regional level, the lack of accountability procedures and mechanisms posed an obstacle to the right to development.

Obstacles at the national level

64. In considering national obstacles to the right to development, the Working Group paid special attention to obstacles raised in connection with the dialogue it held with representatives of intergovernmental organizations and bodies.

65. The following comments on obstacles are not exhaustive, but merely indicative of the discussions held during the second session of the Working Group.

66. The Working Group noted that States, which are the principal actors in the realization of the right to development, are responsible for guaranteeing fundamental freedoms, respect for human rights and personal security, promoting effective, honest and equitable public administration and guaranteeing the impartial operation of the courts of law. There was a need to establish a regulatory framework and economic instruments which would ensure the transparent operation of the market and correct its deficiencies; to implement policies for the development of human resources; and to achieve equity in the allocation of resources and incomes.

67. The continued discrimination against women, indigenous peoples and minorities with respect to their right of participation and their access to health care, education, work, property and other economic, social and cultural rights was seen as a major obstacle. Another major obstacle identified by the Working Group was the persistence of racism, any other form of discrimination and intolerance.

68. The Working Group noted that the implementation and enforcement of human rights required a determined and concerted effort to achieve an effective rule of law with an independent judiciary and appropriate domestic remedies. Punitive and other action was needed to combat violation of human rights and constitutional rights.

69. The Working Group also noted that many States did not fully implement economic, social and cultural rights and that although national constitutions and international treaties binding on the State could provide for economic, social and cultural rights, effective implementation was often lacking. It seemed to the Working Group that some States were limiting their responsibilities to implement these rights, e.g. in the way the privatization of health care services was carried out.

70. A number of more specific obstacles, such as illiteracy, unemployment, inequities in land and income distribution and lack of respect for the right to housing were identified by the Working Group.

71. It was also stressed that the separation between economic/financial issues and the social/humanitarian dimension at the interagency level posed an obstacle, which could be considered as an institutional obstacle. The comprehensive nature of development, including economic, social, cultural, political, environmental and other aspects was not fully understood in the planning and implementation of development strategies and policies.

72. A further obstacle was posed by the lack of good and effective governance. Corruption, mismanagement and lack of transparency and accountability continued to disrupt the implementation of the right to development.

73. Also, the lack of a clean environment, the mismanagement of natural resources and the weak implementation of relevant environmental treaties posed an obstacle.

74. A major obstacle related to the civil wars, internal conflicts and internal violence that continued to plague many States and regions. It was important to reinforce respect for human rights, tolerance and democratic structures to prevent conflicts from erupting.

75. In the final analysis, implementation of the right to development hinged on how well civil society and the contribution of each and every individual could be mobilized. A crucial obstacle identified by the Working Group was the apparent lack of participation of women, minorities and indigenous peoples and other vulnerable groups in the development process. Political and popular participation were also inadequate. There should be active involvement of real grass-roots movements at the local level and the people themselves should act as a watchdog over the implementation of national development strategies. To empower the people and prevent the exclusion of vulnerable groups, education and training in civic responsibilities, human rights and fundamental freedoms and active participation had to be made more effective.

76. Finally, the Working Group thought that indicators established by governments in accordance with their different conditions, could assist in identifying obstacles to the realization of the right to development at the individual, national, regional and international levels,

and could represent a more active approach to removing obstacles. Such indicators could also function as minimum standards for individual components of the development process or the realization of economic, social and cultural rights, as the Committee on Economic, Social and Cultural Rights has recommended to States parties.

IV. Conclusions and recommendations

77. The Working Group recommends that the international community continue its efforts towards making the right to development operational, taking into account the variety of obstacles listed in the corresponding chapter of its report, particularly in the light of some of the grave consequences caused by recent changes in the world economy.

78. It recommends that the process of consultations with international agencies, programmes and bodies of the United Nations system, Governments and other concerned agents continue on the basis of the guidelines and check-lists set out in the first report of the Working Group, and that agencies which have not responded in those terms be encouraged to do so.

79. The right to development highlights the indivisibility and universality of human rights, be they civil and political, or economic, social and cultural. In its implementation, one should therefore avoid making sharp distinctions between different categories of internationally recognized human rights.

80. The Working Group has noted that international agencies have not incorporated in their mandates the principles set out in the Declaration on the Right to Development. The Group recommends that the United Nations system take the necessary measures for the Declaration on the Right to Development to be incorporated in all their programmes.

81. In giving emphasis to the human rights aspect of development, and to make this right operational, there is a need, among other things, to encourage Governments to establish indicators by which to evaluate progress made in the realization of this right with, eventually, ways in which remedies can be sought in the event of lack of progress for particular groups. That these indicators must take into account the different conditions within individual countries, as well as differences between countries at a given stage of their development, are issues to be taken up in discussions with, among others, the treaty bodies.

82. The Working Group took note of the World Plan of Action on Education for Human Rights and Democracy adopted by the UNESCO International Congress on Education for Human Rights and Democracy (Montreal, Canada, 8-11 March 1993), and proposed that more information be requested with a view to studying the possibilities offered by the Plan of Action for the implementation of the right to development by the specialized agencies.

83. While the questions of development are approached either sectorally or thematically by a wide variety of agencies and programmes, only the Committees established under the two Covenants hold States responsible for the implementation of the rights to which they have subscribed by adhering to international treaties.

84. These international implementation procedures should be strengthened. In this context, particular attention should be paid to the International Covenant on Economic, Social and Cultural Rights. Any progress in implementing economic, social and cultural rights, and any step taken by the international community to make those rights more effective, would help to further the implementation of the Declaration on the Right to Development. The Working Group considers that greater political will should be demonstrated for the better implementation of economic, social and cultural rights.

85. The Working Group expects the High Commissioner for Human Rights to multiply efforts in order to ensure that all international agencies and bodies within the system pay the most serious attention to the need to make the right to development operational.

86. The implementation of the Declaration on the Right to Development is a collective responsibility of the United Nations system as a whole, implying greater coordination of strategies and programmes, more effective cooperation in the field, permanent consultation among the specialized agencies, and improved circulation of information between them.

87. In order to facilitate the coordination needed for concerted implementation of the Declaration on the Right to Development, it would be desirable for each agency to establish, assign special responsibility to or develop an administrative unit for that purpose.

88. Since the right to development implies an integrated approach to political, social, economic and cultural rights as a whole, care should be taken to avoid dissociating the economic and monetary aspects of development from its social aspects and to enhance the dialogue between international social and humanitarian agencies and international institutions responsible for financial and trade questions.

89. The Governments of Member States have a contribution to make to strengthening the role of the United Nations system in implementing the Declaration on the Right to Development, for which purpose they should see to it that the resolutions they have adopted in the United Nations General Assembly and the Economic and Social Council set objectives for the various specialized agencies which are at the same time global, precise and achievable.

90. It would be desirable for international financing for development to encourage the implementation of the right to development, bearing in mind the indivisibility and interdependence of its component elements. Hence the need for criteria taking account of that indivisibility and interdependence of human rights and for greater transparency in the distribution of development support funds.

91. The globalization of the economy increases the responsibility of the international community in regard to the implementation of the Declaration on the Right to Development. Ways and means of strengthening international cooperation and solidarity need to be explored. The establishment of new rules governing international trade relations cannot by itself protect the interests of the developing countries, and it is therefore necessary to enhance international dialogue to this effect. In particular, efforts should be made to ensure that developing countries do not lag behind as a result of new rules governing international trade relations.

92. The Working Group intends to pursue its exchanges of views with the Chairpersons of the various human rights treaty bodies, in order to envisage common methods for the evaluation of progress made by local, national, regional and international institutions in the implementation of the right to development.

93. The economic aspects of development seem to receive preference from funding bodies and donors over social aspects. Development assistance is not apportioned among specialized international agencies according to objective criteria related to the basic needs of individuals and population groups; the requirements of growth, production and productivity seem to win out over considerations that would make the human person "the central subject of development" as called for in article 2 of the Declaration on the Right to Development.

94. The consideration of the programmes and activities of the international institutions and specialized agencies show how far the globalization of the economy seems to be the most important change of our era, one in whose light the application of the Declaration on the Right to Development today needs to be studied. The increasingly clear consequences of this globalization of the economy are a reduction in States' room to manoeuvre and the ever more relative nature of their influence on the enjoyment of the right to development. At the same time, international cooperation seems more and more essential to the universal enjoyment of this right. The corollary to the globalization of the economy, then, is a strengthening of solid, productive international fellow-feeling: otherwise the application of the Declaration on the Right to Development will be, if not a vain, then at least an inadequate exercise.

Annex I
List of participants

Members

Mr. D.D.C. Don Nanjira (Kenya)
Mr. Mohamed Ennaceur (Tunisia)
Mr. Alexandre Farcas (Romania)
Mr. Orobola Fasehun (Nigeria)
Mrs. Ligia Galvis (Colombia)
Mr. Stuart Harris (Australia)
Mr. Stéphane Hessel (France)
Mr. Serguei Kossenko (Russian Federation)
Mr. Osvaldo Martínez/Mr. Jorge Lago Silva* (Cuba)
Mr. Niaz A. Naik (Pakistan)
Mr. H. Pedro Oyarce (Chile)
Mr. Pang Sen (China)
Mr. Allan Rosas (Finland)
Mr. Haron Bin Siraj (Malaysia)
Mr. Vladimir Sotirov (Bulgaria)

States members of the Commission on Human Rights represented by Observers

Angola	Mr. A. Parreira
Brazil	Mr. A.L. Espinola Salgado
Cuba	Mr. C. Adolfo
Hungary	Mr. S. Szapora
Japan	Mrs. M. Tomita
Malaysia	Mr. A. Ganapathy
Mexico	Mr. A. Abarca
Nigeria	Mr. C.U. Gwam, Mr. B.I.D. Oladeji
Pakistan	Mr. B. Hashmi
Peru	Mr. A. García, Mr. E. Pérez del Solar
Republic of Korea	Mr. G.W. Kim
Tunisia	Mr. M.S. Koubaa
Venezuela	Mr. W. Mendez, Mrs. L.Y. Arocha Rivaz

States Members of the United Nations represented by observers

Algeria	Mr. L. Soualem
Egypt	Mr. A. Elmoafi
El Salvador	H.E. Mr. C.E. Mendoza, Miss M. Escobar
Ethiopia	Mr. M. Alemu
Gambia	Mr. J. Johm
Ghana	Mr. J. Appiah-Kubi
Iraq	Mr. M. Salman
Israel	Mrs. T. Levy-Furman
Madagascar	Mr. J. Solo Rason
Norway	Mr. A. Lovbraek

*Alternate expert nominated in accordance with paragraph 12 of Commission on Human Rights resolution 1994/22.

Philippines	Mrs. O.V. Palala, Mrs. B. de Castro-Muller
Senegal	Mr. A.A. Ndiaye
Zimbabwe	Mr. M. Chikorowondo, Mrs. J.N. Ndaona

United Nations bodies

Committee on Economic, Social and Cultural Rights
Mr. P. Alston

Economic Commission for Europe
Mr. Y. Berthelot
Mr. P. Robineau

United Nations Centre for Human Settlements (HABITAT)
Mr. L. Ludvigsen

United Nations Childrens Fund
Ms. S. Blanchet

United Nations Conference on Trade and Development
Mr. C. Fortín
Mr. H. Ouane

United Nations Development Programme
Mr. A. Français

United Nations Environment Programme
Mr. A. Renlund
Ms. A-C. Nygard

United Nations Population Fund
Mr. R. El Heneidi
Ms. L. Lassonde

Specialized agencies

International Labour Organisation
Mr. S. Radwan
Ms. J. Hodges

United Nations Educational, Scientific and Cultural Organization
Mr. P. Malhotra

World Bank
Mr. A. Capitani

International Monetary Fund
Mr. G.B. Taplin
Mr. P. Cirillo

Intergovernmental organizations

League of Arab States
Mr. A. Harguem

Non-governmental organizations

Category I

ZONTA International
Mrs. D. Bridel

Category II

African Association of Education for Development
Mr. C.M. Eya Nchama

Friends World Committee for Consultation (Quakers)
Ms. C. Turner

International Indian Treaty Council
Mr. M. Ibarra

International Movement for Fraternal Union
among Races and Peoples
Mr. C.M. Eya Nchama

Women's International League for Peace and Freedom
Ms. J. Bruin
Ms. I. Velasquez Avieda

Annex II
Agenda

1. Adoption of the agenda.
2. Follow-up to the recommendations of the first session.
3. Procedure and methodology of work.
4. Implementation of the Declaration on the Right to Development by the international organizations.

Annex III
List of documents

Documents prepared for the session

E/CN.4/AC.45/1994/1	Provisional agenda
E/CN.4/AC.45/1994/1/Add.1	Annotations and background information to the provisional agenda
E/CN.4/AC.45/1994/2 and Add.1	Report of the Secretary-General submitted in accordance with Commission resolution 1993/22

Background and reference documents

E/CN.4/1994/21 and Corr.1-2	Report of the Working Group on the Right to Development on its first session
E/CN.4/1994/17 and Add.1	Comprehensive report of the Secretary-General prepared in pursuance of Commission on Human Rights resolution 1993/12
E/CN.4/1994/NGO/16	Written statement submitted by the Centre Europe-Tiers Monde, a non-governmental organization on the Roster
E/CN.4/1994/NGO/34	Written statement submitted by the International Federation Terre des Hommes, a non-governmental organization in consultative status (category II)
E/CN.4/1994/NGO/50	Written statement submitted by the Human Rights Advocates, a non-governmental organization in consultative status (category II)
E/1994/24-E/CN.4/1994/132	Report of the Commission on Human Rights on the fiftieth session
E/CN.4/1994/SR.12-19 and 46	Summary records of the Commission on Human Rights at its fiftieth session concerning agenda item 7, "Question of the realization in all countries of the economic, social and cultural rights contained in the Universal Declaration of Human Rights and in the International Covenant on Economic, Social and Cultural Rights, and study of special problems which the developing countries face in their efforts to achieve these human rights including: problems related to the right to enjoy an adequate standard of living; foreign debt, economic adjustment policies and their effects on the full enjoyment of human rights and, in particular, on the implementation of the Declaration on the Right to Development: (a) popular participation in the various forms as an important factor in development and in the full realization of all human rights".
A/49/24	Report of the first meeting of the Preparatory Committee for the World Summit for Social Development
A/CONF.171/PC/5	Draft programme of action of the International Conference on Population and Development: note by the Secretary-General
E/CN.6/1994/9	Preparations for the Fourth World Conference on Women: Action for Equality, Development and Peace: report of the Secretary-General

Document 92

General Assembly resolution establishing the United Nations Mission for the Verification of Human Rights and of Compliance with the Commitments of the Comprehensive Agreement on Human Rights in Guatemala (MINUGUA)

A/RES/48/267, 19 September 1994

The General Assembly,

Recalling its resolutions 45/15 of 20 November 1990, 46/109 A of 17 December 1991, 47/118 of 18 December 1992 and, in particular, 48/161 of 20 December 1993, in which it requested the Secretary-General to continue to support the peace process in Guatemala,

Welcoming the resumption in January 1994, under the auspices of the Secretary-General, of the negotiations between the Government of Guatemala and the Unidad Revolucionaria Nacional Guatemalteca, and the signing on 10 January 1994 of the Framework Agreement for the Resumption of the Negotiating Process between the Government of Guatemala and the Unidad Revolucionaria Nacional Guatemalteca, 1/

Noting that the parties decided in the Framework Agreement to request the United Nations to verify all agreements reached between them, and the support of the Secretary-General for that request, 2/

Welcoming also the signing on 29 March 1994 of the Comprehensive Agreement on Human Rights 3/ and the Agreement on a Timetable for the Negotiation of a Firm and Lasting Peace in Guatemala 4/,

Encouraged by the signing on 17 June 1994 of the Agreement on Resettlement of the Population Groups Uprooted by the Armed Conflict 5/ and, on 23 June 1994, of the Agreement on the Establishment of the Commission to Clarify Past Human Rights Violations and Acts of Violence that have Caused the Guatemalan Population to Suffer, 6/

Commending the Government of Guatemala and the Unidad Revolucionaria Nacional Guatemalteca for the flexibility demonstrated during the negotiation of the above-mentioned agreements,

Taking note of the request of the Government of Guatemala and the Unidad Revolucionaria Nacional Guatemalteca, contained in the Comprehensive Agreement on Human Rights, that the United Nations establish at the earliest possible date a mission to verify the implementation of that Agreement even before the signature of the agreement on a firm and lasting peace,

Recognizing the efforts made by the Secretary-General and the Group of Friends of the Guatemalan peace process 7/ and their constant support and contribution to the achievement of a lasting peace in Guatemala,

Wishing to contribute to the efforts to ensure adequate protection of human rights in Guatemala,

Having considered the report of the Secretary-General of 18 August 1994 on the establishment of a human rights verification mission in Guatemala, 8/

Underlining the great importance that it attaches to the early conclusion of the agreement on a firm and lasting peace as the culmination of the process of negotiated settlement of the armed confrontation in Guatemala,

1. *Welcomes* the report of the Secretary-General on the establishment of a human rights verification mission in Guatemala;

2. *Decides* to establish a Mission for the Verification of Human Rights and of Compliance with the Commitments of the Comprehensive Agreement on Human Rights in Guatemala in accordance with the recommendations contained in the report of the Secretary-General, for an initial period of six months;

3. *Emphasizes* the importance of the undertaking by the parties, contained in the Comprehensive Agreement on Human Rights, to provide their broadest support to the Mission and whatever cooperation it may need to carry out its functions, particularly with respect to the security of the members of the Mission;

4. *Calls upon* the parties to comply fully with all their other undertakings under the Comprehensive Agreement;

5. *Also calls upon* the parties to pursue a vigorous process of negotiation, as agreed by them in the Framework Agreement for the Resumption of the Negotiating

---

1/ A/49/61-S/1994/53, annex; see *Official Records of the Security Council, Forty-ninth Year, Supplement for January, February and March 1994,* document S/1994/53.

2/ See A/49/61-S/1994/53; see *Official Records of the Security Council, Forty-ninth Year, Supplement for January, February and March 1994,* document S/1994/53.

3/ A/48/928-S/1994/448, annex I; see *Official Records of the Security Council, Forty-ninth Year, Supplement for April, May and June 1994,* document S/1994/448.

4/ Ibid., annex II.

5/ A/48/954-S/1994/751, annex I; see *Official Records of the Security Council, Forty-ninth Year, Supplement for July, August and September 1994,* document S/1994/751.

6/ Ibid., annex II.

7/ The Group of Friends is composed of Colombia, Mexico, Norway, Spain, the United States of America and Venezuela.

8/ A/48/985.

Process between the Government of Guatemala and the Unidad Revolucionaria Nacional Guatemalteca and the Agreement on a Timetable for the Negotiation of a Firm and Lasting Peace in Guatemala, and to this end to cooperate fully with the Secretary-General and his representative in their efforts;

6. *Invites* the international community to support institution-building and cooperation projects in the area of human rights which could be implemented by the Mission and the relevant Guatemalan institutions and entities with the participation of United Nations organizations and programmes;

7. *Requests* the Secretary-General to conclude a status-of-mission agreement with the Government of Guatemala, to come into force no later than thirty days after the adoption of the present resolution;

8. *Also requests* the Secretary-General to keep the General Assembly fully informed of the implementation of the present resolution.

Document 93

Security Council resolution emphasizing that the practice of "ethnic cleansing" is a clear violation of international humanitarian law

S/RES/941 (1994), 23 September 1994

The Security Council,

Recalling all its earlier relevant resolutions,

Reaffirming the sovereignty, territorial integrity and political independence of the Republic of Bosnia and Herzegovina,

Taking note of the information provided by the United Nations High Commissioner for Refugees (UNHCR) and the International Committee of the Red Cross (ICRC), and that contained in other relevant reports (S/1994/265 and S/1994/674), particularly regarding grave violations of international humanitarian law affecting the non-Serb population in those areas of the Republic of Bosnia and Herzegovina under the control of Bosnian Serb forces,

Gravely concerned at the persistent and systematic campaign of terror perpetrated by the Bosnian Serb forces in Banja Luka, Bijeljina and other areas of the Republic of Bosnia and Herzegovina under the control of Bosnian Serb forces, as described in paragraphs 5 to 79 of the above-mentioned report (S/1994/265),

Emphasizing that this practice of "ethnic cleansing" by the Bosnian Serb forces constitutes a clear violation of international humanitarian law and poses a serious threat to the peace effort,

Expressing its deep concern over the continued denial by Bosnian Serb forces of prompt and unimpeded access to the Special Representative of the Secretary-General and the United Nations Protection Force (UNPROFOR) to Banja Luka, Bijeljina and other areas under Bosnian Serb control as demanded by the Security Council in its presidential statement of 2 September 1994 (S/PRST/1994/50),

Recognizing that the International Tribunal has jurisdiction over serious violations of international humanitarian law in the territory of the former Yugoslavia, and that the Council remains committed to its previous resolutions on the importance of cooperation with the Tribunal,

Determined to put an end to the abhorrent and systematic practice of "ethnic cleansing" wherever it occurs and by whomsoever it is committed,

Determining that the situation in the Republic of Bosnia and Herzegovina continues to constitute a threat to international peace and security, *reiterating* its determination to ensure the security of UNPROFOR and its freedom of movement for all its missions, and, to these ends, *acting* under Chapter VII of the Charter of the United Nations,

1. *Reaffirms* that all parties to the conflict are bound to comply with their obligations under international humanitarian law and in particular the Geneva Conventions of 12 August 1949;

2. *Strongly condemns* all violations of international humanitarian law, including in particular the unacceptable practice of "ethnic cleansing" perpetrated in Banja Luka, Bijeljina and other areas of the Republic of Bosnia and Herzegovina under the control of Bosnian Serb forces, and *reaffirms* that those who have committed or have ordered the commission of such acts will be held individually responsible in respect of such acts;

3. *Reaffirms* its support for the established principles that all declarations and actions made under duress, particularly those regarding land and ownership, are null and void, and that all displaced persons should be enabled to return in peace to their former homes;

4. *Demands* that the Bosnian Serb authorities immediately cease their campaign of "ethnic cleansing";

5. *Demands* that the Bosnian Serb party accord immediate and unimpeded access for the Special Repre-

sentative of the Secretary-General, UNPROFOR, UNHCR and ICRC to Banja Luka, Bijeljina and other areas of concern;

6. *Requests* the Secretary-General to arrange, when conditions permit, the deployment of UNPROFOR troops and United Nations monitors in Banja Luka, Bijeljina, and other areas of concern, and to intensify his efforts in this regard;

7. *Also requests* the Secretary-General to report urgently to the Council on the implementation of this resolution;

8. *Determines* to consider any further steps that it may deem necessary;

9. *Decides* to remain seized of the matter.

Document 94

Security Council resolution containing the decision to establish an international tribunal for the prosecution of persons responsible for genocide and other serious violations of international humanitarian law committed in Rwanda or in the territory of neighbouring States

S/RES/955 (1994), 8 November 1994

The Security Council,

Reaffirming all its previous resolutions on the situation in Rwanda,

Having considered the reports of the Secretary-General pursuant to paragraph 3 of resolution 935 (1994) of 1 July 1994 (S/1994/879 and S/1994/906), and *having taken note* of the reports of the Special Rapporteur for Rwanda of the United Nations Commission on Human Rights (S/1994/1157, annex I and annex II),

Expressing appreciation for the work of the Commission of Experts established pursuant to resolution 935 (1994), in particular its preliminary report on violations of international humanitarian law in Rwanda transmitted by the Secretary-General's letter of 1 October 1994 (S/1994/1125),

Expressing once again its grave concern at the reports indicating that genocide and other systematic, widespread and flagrant violations of international humanitarian law have been committed in Rwanda,

Determining that this situation continues to constitute a threat to international peace and security,

Determined to put an end to such crimes and to take effective measures to bring to justice the persons who are responsible for them,

Convinced that in the particular circumstances of Rwanda, the prosecution of persons responsible for serious violations of international humanitarian law would enable this aim to be achieved and would contribute to the process of national reconciliation and to the restoration and maintenance of peace,

Believing that the establishment of an international tribunal for the prosecution of persons responsible for genocide and the other above-mentioned violations of

international humanitarian law will contribute to ensuring that such violations are halted and effectively redressed,

Stressing also the need for international cooperation to strengthen the courts and judicial system of Rwanda, having regard in particular to the necessity for those courts to deal with large numbers of suspects,

Considering that the Commission of Experts established pursuant to resolution 935 (1994) should continue on an urgent basis the collection of information relating to evidence of grave violations of international humanitarian law committed in the territory of Rwanda and should submit its final report to the Secretary-General by 30 November 1994,

Acting under Chapter VII of the Charter of the United Nations,

1. *Decides* hereby, having received the request of the Government of Rwanda (S/1994/1115), to establish an international tribunal for the sole purpose of prosecuting persons responsible for genocide and other serious violations of international humanitarian law committed in the territory of Rwanda and Rwandan citizens responsible for genocide and other such violations committed in the territory of neighbouring States, between 1 January 1994 and 31 December 1994 and to this end to adopt the Statute of the International Criminal Tribunal for Rwanda annexed hereto;

2. *Decides* that all States shall cooperate fully with the International Tribunal and its organs in accordance with the present resolution and the Statute of the International Tribunal and that consequently all States shall take any measures necessary under their domestic law to implement the provisions of the present resolution and

the Statute, including the obligation of States to comply with requests for assistance or orders issued by a Trial Chamber under Article 28 of the Statute, and *requests* States to keep the Secretary-General informed of such measures;

3. *Considers* that the Government of Rwanda should be notified prior to the taking of decisions under articles 26 and 27 of the Statute;

4. *Urges* States and intergovernmental and non-governmental organizations to contribute funds, equipment and services to the International Tribunal, including the offer of expert personnel;

5. *Requests* the Secretary-General to implement this resolution urgently and in particular to make practical arrangements for the effective functioning of the International Tribunal, including recommendations to the Council as to possible locations for the seat of the International Tribunal at the earliest time and to report periodically to the Council;

6. *Decides* that the seat of the International Tribunal shall be determined by the Council having regard to considerations of justice and fairness as well as administrative efficiency, including access to witnesses, and economy, and subject to the conclusion of appropriate arrangements between the United Nations and the State of the seat, acceptable to the Council, having regard to the fact that the International Tribunal may meet away from its seat when it considers it necessary for the efficient exercise of its functions; and *decides* that an office will be established and proceedings will be conducted in Rwanda, where feasible and appropriate, subject to the conclusion of similar appropriate arrangements;

7. *Decides* to consider increasing the number of judges and Trial Chambers of the International Tribunal if it becomes necessary;

8. *Decides* to remain actively seized of the matter.

Annex
Statute of the International Tribunal for Rwanda

Having been established by the Security Council acting under Chapter VII of the Charter of the United Nations, the International Criminal Tribunal for the Prosecution of Persons Responsible for Genocide and Other Serious Violations of International Humanitarian Law Committed in the Territory of Rwanda and Rwandan citizens responsible for genocide and other such violations committed in the territory of neighbouring States, between 1 January 1994 and 31 December 1994 (hereinafter referred to as "the International Tribunal for Rwanda") shall function in accordance with the provisions of the present Statute.

Article 1
Competence of the International Tribunal for Rwanda

The International Tribunal for Rwanda shall have the power to prosecute persons responsible for serious violations of international humanitarian law committed in the territory of Rwanda and Rwandan citizens responsible for such violations committed in the territory of neighbouring States, between 1 January 1994 and 31 December 1994, in accordance with the provisions of the present Statute.

Article 2
Genocide

1. The International Tribunal for Rwanda shall have the power to prosecute persons committing genocide as defined in paragraph 2 of this article or of committing any of the other acts enumerated in paragraph 3 of this article.

2. Genocide means any of the following acts committed with intent to destroy, in whole or in part, a national, ethnical, racial or religious group, as such:

    (a) Killing members of the group;

    (b) Causing serious bodily or mental harm to members of the group;

    (c) Deliberately inflicting on the group conditions of life calculated to bring about its physical destruction in whole or in part;

    (d) Imposing measures intended to prevent births within the group;

    (e) Forcibly transferring children of the group to another group.

3. The following acts shall be punishable:

    (a) Genocide;

    (b) Conspiracy to commit genocide;

    (c) Direct and public incitement to commit genocide;

    (d) Attempt to commit genocide;

    (e) Complicity in genocide.

Article 3
Crimes against humanity

The International Tribunal for Rwanda shall have the power to prosecute persons responsible for the following crimes when committed as part of a widespread or systematic attack against any civilian population on national, political, ethnic, racial or religious grounds:

    (a) Murder;

    (b) Extermination;

    (c) Enslavement;

    (d) Deportation;

    (e) Imprisonment;

(f) Torture;

(g) Rape;

(h) Persecutions on political, racial and religious grounds;

(i) Other inhumane acts.

Article 4
Violations of Article 3 common to the Geneva Conventions and of Additional Protocol II

The International Tribunal for Rwanda shall have the power to prosecute persons committing or ordering to be committed serious violations of Article 3 common to the Geneva Conventions of 12 August 1949 for the Protection of War Victims, and of Additional Protocol II thereto of 8 June 1977. These violations shall include, but shall not be limited to:

(a) Violence to life, health and physical or mental well-being of persons, in particular murder as well as cruel treatment such as torture, mutilation or any form of corporal punishment;

(b) Collective punishments;

(c) Taking of hostages;

(d) Acts of terrorism;

(e) Outrages upon personal dignity, in particular humiliating and degrading treatment, rape, enforced prostitution and any form of indecent assault;

(f) Pillage;

(g) The passing of sentences and the carrying out of executions without previous judgement pronounced by a regularly constituted court, affording all the judicial guarantees which are recognized as indispensable by civilized peoples;

(h) Threats to commit any of the foregoing acts.

Article 5
Personal jurisdiction

The International Tribunal for Rwanda shall have jurisdiction over natural persons pursuant to the provisions of the present Statute.

Article 6
Individual criminal responsibility

1. A person who planned, instigated, ordered, committed or otherwise aided and abetted in the planning, preparation or execution of a crime referred to in articles 2 to 4 of the present Statute, shall be individually responsible for the crime.

2. The official position of any accused person, whether as Head of State or Government or as a responsible Government official, shall not relieve such person of criminal responsibility nor mitigate punishment.

3. The fact that any of the acts referred to in articles 2 to 4 of the present Statute was committed by a subordinate does not relieve his or her superior of criminal responsibility if he or she knew or had reason to know that the subordinate was about to commit such acts or had done so and the superior failed to take the necessary and reasonable measures to prevent such acts or to punish the perpetrators thereof.

4. The fact that an accused person acted pursuant to an order of a Government or of a superior shall not relieve him or her of criminal responsibility, but may be considered in mitigation of punishment if the International Tribunal for Rwanda determines that justice so requires.

Article 7
Territorial and temporal jurisdiction

The territorial jurisdiction of the International Tribunal for Rwanda shall extend to the territory of Rwanda including its land surface and airspace as well as to the territory of neighbouring States in respect of serious violations of international humanitarian law committed by Rwandan citizens. The temporal jurisdiction of the International Tribunal for Rwanda shall extend to a period beginning on 1 January 1994 and ending on 31 December 1994.

Article 8
Concurrent jurisdiction

1. The International Tribunal for Rwanda and national courts shall have concurrent jurisdiction to prosecute persons for serious violations of international humanitarian law committed in the territory of Rwanda and Rwandan citizens for such violations committed in the territory of neighbouring States, between 1 January 1994 and 31 December 1994.

2. The International Tribunal for Rwanda shall have primacy over the national courts of all States. At any stage of the procedure, the International Tribunal for Rwanda may formally request national courts to defer to its competence in accordance with the present Statute and the Rules of Procedure and Evidence of the International Tribunal for Rwanda.

Article 9
Non bis in idem

1. No person shall be tried before a national court for acts constituting serious violations of international humanitarian law under the present Statute, for which he or she has already been tried by the International Tribunal for Rwanda.

2. A person who has been tried by a national court for acts constituting serious violations of international humanitarian law may be subsequently tried by the International Tribunal for Rwanda only if:

(a) The act for which he or she was tried was characterized as an ordinary crime; or

(b) The national court proceedings were not impartial or independent, were designed to shield the accused from international criminal responsibility, or the case was not diligently prosecuted.

3. In considering the penalty to be imposed on a person convicted of a crime under the present Statute, the International Tribunal for Rwanda shall take into account the extent to which any penalty imposed by a national court on the same person for the same act has already been served.

Article 10
Organization of the International
Tribunal for Rwanda

The International Tribunal for Rwanda shall consist of the following organs:

(a) The Chambers, comprising two Trial Chambers and an Appeals Chamber;

(b) The Prosecutor; and

(c) A Registry.

Article 11
Composition of the Chambers

The Chambers shall be composed of eleven independent judges, no two of whom may be nationals of the same State, who shall serve as follows:

(a) Three judges shall serve in each of the Trial Chambers;

(b) Five judges shall serve in the Appeals Chamber.

Article 12
Qualification and election of judges

1. The judges shall be persons of high moral character, impartiality and integrity who possess the qualifications required in their respective countries for appointment to the highest judicial offices. In the overall composition of the Chambers due account shall be taken of the experience of the judges in criminal law, international law, including international humanitarian law and human rights law.

2. The members of the Appeals Chamber of the International Tribunal for the Prosecution of Persons Responsible for Serious Violations of International Law Committed in the Territory of the Former Yugoslavia since 1991 (hereinafter referred to as "the International Tribunal for the Former Yugoslavia") shall also serve as the members of the Appeals Chamber of the International Tribunal for Rwanda.

3. The judges of the Trial Chambers of the International Tribunal for Rwanda shall be elected by the General Assembly from a list submitted by the Security Council, in the following manner:

(a) The Secretary-General shall invite nominations for judges of the Trial Chambers from States Members of the United Nations and non-member States maintaining permanent observer missions at United Nations Headquarters;

(b) Within thirty days of the date of the invitation of the Secretary-General, each State may nominate up to two candidates meeting the qualifications set out in paragraph 1 above, no two of whom shall be of the same nationality and neither of whom shall be of the same nationality as any judge on the Appeals Chamber;

(c) The Secretary-General shall forward the nominations received to the Security Council. From the nominations received the Security Council shall establish a list of not less than twelve and not more than eighteen candidates, taking due account of adequate representation on the International Tribunal for Rwanda of the principal legal systems of the world;

(d) The President of the Security Council shall transmit the list of candidates to the President of the General Assembly. From that list the General Assembly shall elect the six judges of the Trial Chambers. The candidates who receive an absolute majority of the votes of the States Members of the United Nations and of the non-Member States maintaining permanent observer missions at United Nations Headquarters, shall be declared elected. Should two candidates of the same nationality obtain the required majority vote, the one who received the higher number of votes shall be considered elected.

4. In the event of a vacancy in the Trial Chambers, after consultation with the Presidents of the Security Council and of the General Assembly, the Secretary-General shall appoint a person meeting the qualifications of paragraph 1 above, for the remainder of the term of office concerned.

5. The judges of the Trial Chambers shall be elected for a term of four years. The terms and conditions of service shall be those of the judges of the International Tribunal for the Former Yugoslavia. They shall be eligible for re-election.

Article 13
Officers and members of the Chambers

1. The judges of the International Tribunal for Rwanda shall elect a President.

2. After consultation with the judges of the International Tribunal for Rwanda, the President shall assign the judges to the Trial Chambers. A judge shall serve only in the Chamber to which he or she was assigned.

3. The judges of each Trial Chamber shall elect a Presiding Judge, who shall conduct all of the proceedings of that Trial Chamber as a whole.

Article 14
Rules of procedure and evidence

The judges of the International Tribunal for Rwanda shall adopt, for the purpose of proceedings before the International Tribunal for Rwanda, the rules of procedure and evidence for the conduct of the pre-trial phase of the proceedings, trials and appeals, the admission of evidence, the protection of victims and witnesses and other appropriate matters of the International Tribunal for the Former Yugoslavia with such changes as they deem necessary.

Article 15
The Prosecutor

1. The Prosecutor shall be responsible for the investigation and prosecution of persons responsible for serious violations of international humanitarian law committed in the territory of Rwanda and Rwandan citizens responsible for such violations committed in the territory of neighbouring States, between 1 January 1994 and 31 December 1994.

2. The Prosecutor shall act independently as a separate organ of the International Tribunal for Rwanda. He or she shall not seek or receive instructions from any Government or from any other source.

3. The Prosecutor of the International Tribunal for the Former Yugoslavia shall also serve as the Prosecutor of the International Tribunal for Rwanda. He or she shall have additional staff, including an additional Deputy Prosecutor, to assist with prosecutions before the International Tribunal for Rwanda. Such staff shall be appointed by the Secretary-General on the recommendation of the Prosecutor.

Article 16
The Registry

1. The Registry shall be responsible for the administration and servicing of the International Tribunal for Rwanda.

2. The Registry shall consist of a Registrar and such other staff as may be required.

3. The Registrar shall be appointed by the Secretary-General after consultation with the President of the International Tribunal for Rwanda. He or she shall serve for a four-year term and be eligible for reappointment. The terms and conditions of service of the Registrar shall be those of an Assistant Secretary-General of the United Nations.

4. The staff of the Registry shall be appointed by the Secretary-General on the recommendation of the Registrar.

Article 17
Investigation and preparation of indictment

1. The Prosecutor shall initiate investigations ex-officio or on the basis of information obtained from any source, particularly from Governments, United Nations organs, intergovernmental and non-governmental organizations. The Prosecutor shall assess the information received or obtained and decide whether there is sufficient basis to proceed.

2. The Prosecutor shall have the power to question suspects, victims and witnesses, to collect evidence and to conduct on-site investigations. In carrying out these tasks, the Prosecutor may, as appropriate, seek the assistance of the State authorities concerned.

3. If questioned, the suspect shall be entitled to be assisted by counsel of his or her own choice, including the right to have legal assistance assigned to the suspect without payment by him or her in any such case if he or she does not have sufficient means to pay for it, as well as to necessary translation into and from a language he or she speaks and understands.

4. Upon a determination that a prima facie case exists, the Prosecutor shall prepare an indictment containing a concise statement of the facts and the crime or crimes with which the accused is charged under the Statute. The indictment shall be transmitted to a judge of the Trial Chamber.

Article 18
Review of the indictment

1. The judge of the Trial Chamber to whom the indictment has been transmitted shall review it. If satisfied that a prima facie case has been established by the Prosecutor, he or she shall confirm the indictment. If not so satisfied, the indictment shall be dismissed.

2. Upon confirmation of an indictment, the judge may, at the request of the Prosecutor, issue such orders and warrants for the arrest, detention, surrender or transfer of persons, and any other orders as may be required for the conduct of the trial.

Article 19
Commencement and conduct of trial proceedings

1. The Trial Chambers shall ensure that a trial is fair and expeditious and that proceedings are conducted in accordance with the rules of procedure and evidence, with full respect for the rights of the accused and due regard for the protection of victims and witnesses.

2. A person against whom an indictment has been confirmed shall, pursuant to an order or an arrest warrant of the International Tribunal for Rwanda, be taken into custody, immediately informed of the charges against him or her and transferred to the International Tribunal for Rwanda.

3. The Trial Chamber shall read the indictment, satisfy itself that the rights of the accused are respected, confirm that the accused understands the indictment, and instruct the accused to enter a plea. The Trial Chamber shall then set the date for trial.

4. The hearings shall be public unless the Trial Chamber decides to close the proceedings in accordance with its rules of procedure and evidence.

Article 20
Rights of the accused

1. All persons shall be equal before the International Tribunal for Rwanda.

2. In the determination of charges against him or her, the accused shall be entitled to a fair and public hearing, subject to article 21 of the Statute.

3. The accused shall be presumed innocent until proved guilty according to the provisions of the present Statute.

4. In the determination of any charge against the accused pursuant to the present Statute, the accused shall be entitled to the following minimum guarantees, in full equality:

(a) To be informed promptly and in detail in a language which he or she understands of the nature and cause of the charge against him or her;

(b) To have adequate time and facilities for the preparation of his or her defence and to communicate with counsel of his or her own choosing;

(c) To be tried without undue delay;

(d) To be tried in his or her presence, and to defend himself or herself in person or through legal assistance of his or her own choosing; to be informed, if he or she does not have legal assistance, of this right; and to have legal assistance assigned to him or her, in any case where the interests of justice so require, and without payment by him or her in any such case if he or she does not have sufficient means to pay for it;

(e) To examine, or have examined, the witnesses against him or her and to obtain the attendance and examination of witnesses on his or her behalf under the same conditions as witnesses against him or her;

(f) To have the free assistance of an interpreter if he or she cannot understand or speak the language used in the International Tribunal for Rwanda;

(g) Not to be compelled to testify against himself or herself or to confess guilt.

Article 21
Protection of victims and witnesses

The International Tribunal for Rwanda shall provide in its rules of procedure and evidence for the protection of victims and witnesses. Such protection measures shall include, but shall not be limited to, the conduct of in camera proceedings and the protection of the victim's identity.

Article 22
Judgement

1. The Trial Chambers shall pronounce judgements and impose sentences and penalties on persons convicted of serious violations of international humanitarian law.

2. The judgement shall be rendered by a majority of the judges of the Trial Chamber, and shall be delivered by the Trial Chamber in public. It shall be accompanied by a reasoned opinion in writing, to which separate or dissenting opinions may be appended.

Article 23
Penalties

1. The penalty imposed by the Trial Chamber shall be limited to imprisonment. In determining the terms of imprisonment, the Trial Chambers shall have recourse to the general practice regarding prison sentences in the courts of Rwanda.

2. In imposing the sentences, the Trial Chambers should take into account such factors as the gravity of the offence and the individual circumstances of the convicted person.

3. In addition to imprisonment, the Trial Chambers may order the return of any property and proceeds acquired by criminal conduct, including by means of duress, to their rightful owners.

Article 24
Appellate proceedings

1. The Appeals Chamber shall hear appeals from persons convicted by the Trial Chambers or from the Prosecutor on the following grounds:

(a) An error on a question of law invalidating the decision; or

(b) An error of fact which has occasioned a miscarriage of justice.

2. The Appeals Chamber may affirm, reverse or revise the decisions taken by the Trial Chambers.

Article 25
Review proceedings

Where a new fact has been discovered which was not known at the time of the proceedings before the Trial Chambers or the Appeals Chamber and which could have been a decisive factor in reaching the decision, the convicted person or the Prosecutor may submit to the International Tribunal for Rwanda an application for review of the judgement.

Article 26
Enforcement of sentences

Imprisonment shall be served in Rwanda or any of the States on a list of States which have indicated to the Security Council their willingness to accept convicted persons, as designated by the International Tribunal for Rwanda. Such imprisonment shall be in accordance with the applicable law of the State concerned, subject to the supervision of the International Tribunal for Rwanda.

Article 27
Pardon or commutation of sentences

If, pursuant to the applicable law of the State in which the convicted person is imprisoned, he or she is eligible for pardon or commutation of sentence, the State concerned shall notify the International Tribunal for Rwanda accordingly. There shall only be pardon or commutation of sentence if the President of the International Tribunal for Rwanda, in consultation with the judges, so decides on the basis of the interests of justice and the general principles of law.

Article 28
Cooperation and judicial assistance

1. States shall cooperate with the International Tribunal for Rwanda in the investigation and prosecution of persons accused of committing serious violations of international humanitarian law.

2. States shall comply without undue delay with any request for assistance or an order issued by a Trial Chamber, including, but not limited to:

(a) The identification and location of persons;

(b) The taking of testimony and the production of evidence;

(c) The service of documents;

(d) The arrest or detention of persons;

(e) The surrender or the transfer of the accused to the International Tribunal for Rwanda.

Article 29
The status, privileges and immunities of the International Tribunal for Rwanda

1. The Convention on the Privileges and Immunities of the United Nations of 13 February 1946 shall apply to the International Tribunal for Rwanda, the judges, the Prosecutor and his or her staff, and the Registrar and his or her staff.

2. The judges, the Prosecutor and the Registrar shall enjoy the privileges and immunities, exemptions and facilities accorded to diplomatic envoys, in accordance with international law.

3. The staff of the Prosecutor and of the Registrar shall enjoy the privileges and immunities accorded to officials of the United Nations under articles V and VII of the Convention referred to in paragraph 1 of this article.

4. Other persons, including the accused, required at the seat or meeting place of the International Tribunal for Rwanda shall be accorded such treatment as is necessary for the proper functioning of the International Tribunal for Rwanda.

Article 30
Expenses of the International Tribunal for Rwanda

The expenses of the International Tribunal for Rwanda shall be expenses of the Organization in accordance with Article 17 of the Charter of the United Nations.

Article 31
Working languages

The working languages of the International Tribunal shall be English and French.

Article 32
Annual report

The President of the International Tribunal for Rwanda shall submit an annual report of the International Tribunal for Rwanda to the Security Council and to the General Assembly.

Document 95

General Assembly resolution on the International Research and Training Institute for the Advancement of Women

A/RES/49/163, 23 December 1994

The General Assembly,

Recalling its resolution 48/105 of 20 December 1993, in which it urged the International Research and Training Institute for the Advancement of Women to continue to strengthen its activities in the areas of research, training and information aimed at mainstreaming gender in development strategies and giving women greater visibility by evaluating their contribution to social and economic development as important means of empowering women and improving their status, emphasized the unique function of the Institute as the only entity within the United Nations system devoted exclusively to research and training for the integration of women in development and stressed the importance of making its research findings available for policy purposes and for operational activities,

Recalling also its resolution 48/111 of 20 December 1993, in which it recognized the importance of adequate preparation for the Fourth World Conference on Women: Action for Equality, Development and Peace, to be held in 1995, and the role therein of the Institute,

Taking into consideration that the Economic and Social Council, in its resolution 1994/30 of 27 July 1994, reiterated the importance of maintaining the level of resources devoted to independent research and related training activities which are crucial for the situation of women,

Emphasizing that the Economic and Social Council, in its resolution 1994/51 of 3 November 1994, stressed the urgent need for appropriate leadership and staffing for the Institute so that it could continue to comply with its mandate,

Taking into account that the Economic and Social Council, in its resolution 1994/51, emphasized that the advancement of women should be an integral part of the economic and social development process within the main global issues, such as gender equality and women's participation in the peace process, in national and international governance and in sustainable development,

1. *Takes note* of the report of the Secretary-General pursuant to resolution 48/111; 1/

2. *Takes note also* of the report of the Advisory Committee on Administrative and Budgetary Questions; 2/

3. *Reiterates* the importance of maintaining the level of resources devoted to independent research and related training activities which are crucial for the situation of women;

4. *Calls upon* States, intergovernmental and non-governmental organizations to contribute, through voluntary contributions and pledges, to the United Nations Trust Fund for the International Research and Training Institute for the Advancement of Women, thus enabling the Institute to continue to respond effectively to its mandate;

5. *Urges* the Secretary-General to appoint, as expeditiously as possible, a Director of the International Research and Training Institute for the Advancement of Women and to fill the existing vacancies in order to permit the Institute to carry out its mandate;

6. *Also urges* the Secretary-General to take appropriate action for the implementation of resolution 48/111, Economic and Social Council resolutions 1994/30 and 1994/51 and the present resolution;

7. *Requests* the Secretary-General to report on this question to the General Assembly at its fiftieth session under the item entitled "Advancement of women".

1/ A/49/217-E/1994/103.
2/ A/49/365-E/1994/119.

Document 96

General Assembly resolution proclaiming the ten-year period beginning on 1 January 1995 the United Nations Decade for Human Rights Education

A/RES/49/184, 23 December 1994

The General Assembly,

Guided by the fundamental and universal principles enshrined in the Charter of the United Nations and the Universal Declaration of Human Rights, 1/

Reaffirming article 26 of the Universal Declaration of Human Rights, according to which "education shall be directed to the full development of the human personality and to the strengthening of respect for human rights and fundamental freedoms",

Recalling the provisions of other international human rights instruments, such as those of article 13 of the International Covenant on Economic, Social and Cultural Rights 2/ and article 28 of the Convention on the Rights of the Child, 3/ that reflect the aims of the aforementioned article,

Taking into account Commission on Human Rights resolution 1993/56 of 9 March 1993, 4/ in which the Commission recommended that knowledge of human rights, both in its theoretical dimension and in its practical application, should be established as a priority in education policies,

Considering Commission on Human Rights resolution 1994/51 of 4 March 1994, 5/ in which the Commission encouraged the United Nations High Commissioner for Human Rights to include among his specific objectives a plan of action for the United Nations decade for human rights education and invited the Secretary-General to submit to the General Assembly at its forty-ninth session, through the Economic and Social Council, a plan of action for a decade for human rights education,

Convinced that human rights education should involve more than the provision of information and should constitute a comprehensive life-long process by which people at all levels in development and in all strata of society learn respect for the dignity of others and the means and methods of ensuring that respect in all societies,

Convinced also that human rights education contributes to a concept of development consistent with the dignity of women and men of all ages that takes into account the diverse segments of society such as children, indigenous peoples, minorities and disabled persons,

Taking into account the efforts to promote human rights education made by educators and non-governmental organizations in all parts of the world, as well as by

intergovernmental organizations, including the United Nations Educational, Scientific and Cultural Organization, the International Labour Organization and the United Nations Children's Fund,

Convinced that each woman, man and child, to realize their full human potential, must be made aware of all their human rights—civil, cultural, economic, political and social,

Believing that human rights education constitutes an important vehicle for the elimination of gender-based discrimination and ensuring equal opportunities through the promotion and protection of the human rights of women,

Considering the World Plan of Action on Education for Human Rights and Democracy, 6/ adopted by the International Congress on Education for Human Rights and Democracy convened by the United Nations Educational, Scientific and Cultural Organization at Montreal from 8 to 11 March 1993, according to which education for human rights and democracy is itself a human right and a prerequisite for the realization of human rights, democracy and social justice,

Recalling that it is the responsibility of the United Nations High Commissioner for Human Rights to coordinate relevant United Nations education and public information programmes in the field of human rights, 7/

Taking note of the report of the United Nations High Commissioner for Human Rights, 8/ in paragraph 94 of which he declared that human rights education is essential for the encouragement of harmonious inter-community relations, for mutual tolerance and understanding and finally for peace,

Aware of the experience in human rights education of United Nations peace-building operations, including the United Nations Observer Mission in El Salvador and the United Nations Transitional Authority in Cambodia,

1/ Resolution 217 A (III).
2/ See resolution 2200 A (XXI), annex.
3/ Resolution 44/25, annex.
4/ See *Official Records of the Economic and Social Council, 1993, Supplement No. 3* (E/1993/23), chap. II, sect. A.
5/ Ibid., *1994, Supplement No.4* and corrigendum (E/1994/24 and Corr.1), chap.II, sect.A.
6/ See A/CONF.157/PC/42/Add.6.
7/ See resolution 48/141, para. 4 (*e*).
8/ A/49/36.

Bearing in mind the Vienna Declaration and Programme of Action, adopted by the World Conference on Human Rights on 25 June 1993, 9/ in particular section II, paragraphs 78 to 82 thereof,

1. *Takes note with appreciation* of the report of the Secretary-General 10/ on human rights education, submitted in accordance with the request contained in its resolution 48/127 of 20 December 1993;

2. *Proclaims* the ten-year period beginning on 1 January 1995 the United Nations Decade for Human Rights Education;

3. *Welcomes* the Plan of Action for the United Nations Decade for Human Rights Education, 1995-2004, as contained in the report of the Secretary-General, 11/ and invites Governments to submit comments with a view to supplementing the Plan of Action;

4. *Invites* the Secretary-General to submit proposals, taking into account the views expressed by Governments for the purpose indicated in paragraph 3;

5. *Appeals* to all Governments to contribute to the implementation of the Plan of Action and to step up their efforts to eradicate illiteracy and to direct education towards the full development of the human personality and to the strengthening of respect for human rights and fundamental freedoms;

6. *Urges* governmental and non-governmental educational agencies to intensify their efforts to establish and implement programmes of human rights education, as recommended in the Plan of Action, in particular by preparing and implementing national plans for human rights education;

7. *Requests* the United Nations High Commissioner for Human Rights to coordinate the implementation of the Plan of Action;

8. *Requests* the Centre for Human Rights of the Secretariat and the Commission on Human Rights, in cooperation with Member States, human rights treaty-monitoring bodies, other appropriate bodies and competent non-governmental organizations, to support efforts of the High Commissioner to coordinate the Plan of Action;

9. *Requests* the Secretary-General to consider establishing a voluntary fund for human rights education, with special provision for the support of the human rights education activities of non-governmental organizations, to be administered by the Centre for Human Rights;

10. *Invites* the specialized agencies and United Nations programmes to contribute, within their respective spheres of competence, to the implementation of the Plan of Action;

11. *Requests* the Secretary-General to bring the present resolution to the attention of all members of the international community and to intergovernmental and non-governmental organizations concerned with human rights and education;

12. *Calls upon* international, regional and national non-governmental organizations, in particular those concerned with women, labour, development and the environment, as well as all other social justice groups, human rights advocates, educators, religious organizations and the media, to increase their involvement in formal and non-formal education in human rights and to cooperate with the Centre for Human Rights in implementing the United Nations Decade for Human Rights Education;

13. *Requests* the existing human rights monitoring bodies to place emphasis on the implementation by Member States of their international obligation to promote human rights education;

14. *Decides* to consider this matter at its fiftieth session under the item entitled "Human rights questions".

9/ A/CONF.157/24 (Part I), chap. III.
10/ A/49/261-E/1994/110 and Add.1.
11/ A/49/261-E/1994/110/Add.1, annex.

Document 97

General Assembly resolution on the International Decade of the World's Indigenous People

A/RES/49/214, 23 December 1994

The General Assembly,

Bearing in mind that one of the purposes of the United Nations, as set forth in the Charter, is the achievement of international cooperation in solving international problems of an economic, social, cultural or humanitarian character and in promoting and encouraging respect for human rights and fundamental freedoms for all without distinction as to race, sex, language or religion,

Recognizing the value and diversity of the cultures and the forms of social organization of the world's indigenous people,

Recalling its resolution 48/163 of 21 December 1993, by which it proclaimed the International Decade of the World's Indigenous People, commencing on 10 December 1994,

Conscious of the need to improve the economic, social and cultural situation of the indigenous people, with full respect for their distinctiveness and their own initiatives,

Reaffirming that the goal of the Decade is to strengthen international cooperation for the solution of problems faced by indigenous people in such areas as human rights, the environment, development, education and health,

Recalling that, beginning in the first year of the Decade, one day of every year shall be observed as the International Day of Indigenous People,

Welcoming the recommendation of the Working Group on Indigenous Populations of the Subcommission on Prevention of Discrimination and Protection of Minorities of the Commission on Human Rights that the International Day be observed every year on 9 August, that date being the anniversary of the first day of the meeting of the Working Group in 1982,

Also welcoming the appointment of the Assistant Secretary-General for Human Rights as Coordinator for the Decade,

Recognizing the importance of considering the establishment of a permanent forum for indigenous people within the United Nations system in the framework of the Decade, and recalling that the Commission on Human Rights, in its resolution 1994/28 of 4 March 1994, 1/ requested the Working Group to give priority consideration to the possible establishment of a permanent forum for indigenous people,

Recalling its request to the Coordinator to coordinate the programme of activities for the Decade in full collaboration and consultation with Governments, competent bodies, the International Labour Organization and other specialized agencies, and indigenous and non-governmental organizations,

Recalling also its request to specialized agencies, regional commissions and other organizations of the United Nations system to consider with Governments and in partnership with indigenous people how they can contribute to the success of the Decade, and welcoming recommendations received in this regard,

Recognizing the importance of consultation and cooperation with indigenous people in planning and implementing the programme of activities for the Decade, the need for adequate financial support from the international community, including support from within the United Nations and the specialized agencies, and the need for adequate coordination and communication channels,

Recalling its invitation to indigenous organizations and other non-governmental organizations to consider the contributions they can make to the success of the Decade, with a view to presenting them to the Working Group on Indigenous Populations,

Taking note of Economic and Social Council decision 1992/255 of 20 July 1992, in which the Council requested United Nations bodies and specialized agencies to ensure that all technical assistance financed or provided by them was compatible with international instruments and standards applicable to indigenous people, and encouraged efforts to promote coordination in this field and greater participation of indigenous people in the planning and implementation of projects affecting them,

Convinced that the development of indigenous people within their countries will contribute to the socio-economic, cultural and environmental advancement of all the countries of the world,

Recognizing that indigenous people can and should be able through appropriate mechanisms to make their distinct contributions to humanity,

Mindful of the relevant recommendations of the World Conference on Human Rights, the United Nations Conference on Environment and Development and the International Conference on Population and Development, in particular chapter 26 of Agenda 21 2/ on recognizing and strengthening the role of indigenous people and their communities,

Welcoming the proposal for an Indigenous Youth Cultural Olympics to be held at Manila in 1995, in conjunction with the Decade and the fiftieth anniversary of the United Nations,

Determined to promote the enjoyment of the rights of indigenous people and the full development of their distinct cultures and communities,

1. *Takes note* of the preliminary report of the Secretary-General of 28 September 1994 on a comprehensive programme of action for the International Decade of the World's Indigenous People 3/ and the annexes to that report;

2. *Decides* to adopt the short-term programme of activities for 1995 contained in annex II to the report of the Secretary-General, and invites the Commission on Human Rights, at its fifty-first session, to consider the short-term programme with a view to adjusting or supplementing it if required;

3. *Invites* Governments to submit written comments to the Secretary-General, by the end of August 1995, on the preliminary report and its annexes, with a

1/ See *Official Records of the Economic and Social Council, 1994,* Supplement No.4 (E/1994/24), chap. II, sect. A.
2/ *Report of the United Nations Conference on Environment and Development, Rio de Janeiro, 3-14 June 1992* (Vol.I and Vol.I/Corr.1, Vol.II, Vol.III and Vol.III/Corr.1) (United Nations publication, Sales No. E.93.I.8 and corrigenda), vol.I: *Resolutions adopted by the Conference,* resolution 1, annex II.
3/ A/49/444.

view to the preparation of a final comprehensive programme of action for the Decade, to be submitted by the Secretary-General to the General Assembly at its fiftieth session;

4. *Decides* that the Decade will have an operational focus to implement its goals and that its theme will be "Indigenous people: partnership in action";

5. *Encourages* the Commission on Human Rights to consider the draft United Nations declaration on the rights of indigenous peoples, contained in the annex to resolution 1994/45 of 26 August 1994 of the Subcommission on Prevention of Discrimination and Protection of Minorities, 4/ with the participation of representatives of indigenous people, on the basis of and in accordance with appropriate procedures to be determined by the Commission, with a view to achieving the adoption of a draft declaration by the General Assembly within the Decade;

6. *Recognizes* the importance of considering the establishment of a permanent forum for indigenous people within the United Nations during the Decade, as recommended in the Vienna Declaration and Programme of Action, 5/ adopted by the World Conference on Human Rights at Vienna in June 1993, and requests the Commission on Human Rights to make recommendations in this regard;

7. *Recognizes* the importance of strengthening the human and institutional capacity of indigenous people to develop their own solutions to their problems, and for these purposes recommends that the United Nations University consider the possibility of sponsoring, in each region, one or more institutions of higher education as centres of excellence and the diffusion of expertise, and invites the Commission on Human Rights to recommend appropriate means of implementation;

8. *Decides* that the International Day of the World's Indigenous People shall be observed every year during the Decade on 9 August, requests the Secretary-General to support the observance of the Day, from within existing budgetary resources, and encourages Governments to observe the Day at the national level;

9. *Expresses its appreciation* for the work undertaken by the Goodwill Ambassador, Rigoberta Menchú Tum, and expresses the hope that she will continue to play an important role in promoting the Decade;

10. *Recommends* that special attention be given to improving the extent and effectiveness of the participation of indigenous people in planning and implementing the activities for the Decade, including through the recruitment, where appropriate, by relevant United Nations bodies and specialized agencies of staff from among indigenous nationals of Member States, consistent with Article 101 of the Charter of the United Nations, within

existing resources, and through consultation with Governments at the national, regional and international levels;

11. *Recommends* for this purpose that a second technical meeting on the planning of the Decade be convened immediately prior to the thirteenth session of the Working Group on Indigenous Populations, to be supported from within existing budgetary resources, and urges Governments, United Nations bodies, specialized agencies and, in particular, indigenous people's organizations to participate actively in that meeting, in accordance with agreed procedures;

12. *Decides* to consider at a later session the convening of meetings for planning and review purposes at appropriate intervals during the Decade, and urges Governments, United Nations bodies, specialized agencies and, in particular, indigenous people's organizations to participate actively in such meetings;

13. *Recommends* that the Secretary-General:

(a) Establish, during the first quarter of 1995, the Voluntary Fund for the Decade and include that Fund in the annual Pledging Conference for Development Activities held at United Nations Headquarters;

(b) Request United Nations representatives in countries where there are indigenous people to promote, through the appropriate channels, greater participation of indigenous people in the planning and implementation of projects affecting them;

(c) Urge relevant United Nations conferences convened during the Decade to promote and facilitate to the extent possible, and as appropriate, the effective input of the views of indigenous people;

(d) Ensure that information about the programme of activities for the Decade and opportunities for indigenous people to participate in those activities is disseminated in all countries and to the greatest possible extent in indigenous languages, to be financed from within existing budgetary resources;

(e) Report to the General Assembly at its fiftieth session on progress made at the national, regional and international levels in accomplishing these objectives;

14. *Requests* the United Nations High Commissioner for Human Rights to take into account the special concerns of indigenous people and the goals of the Decade in the fulfilment of his functions;

15. *Requests* the Assistant Secretary-General for Human Rights, bearing in mind the contribution that indigenous people have the capacity to make, to establish a unit within the Centre for Human Rights of the Secretariat to support its activities related to indigenous peo-

4/ See E/CN.4/1995/2 - E/CN.4/Sub.2/1994/56.
5/ *Report of the World Conference on Human Rights, Vienna, 14-25 June 1993* (A/CONF.157/24 (Part I)), chap. III.

ple, in particular to plan, coordinate and implement activities for the Decade;

16. *Invites* the Assistant Secretary-General for Human Rights to consider the appointment of a fund-raiser who could develop new sources of funding for the Decade;

17. *Requests* the Administrative Committee on Coordination, through its inter-agency process, to consult and coordinate on the Decade, with a view to assisting the Coordinator of the Decade to fulfil his function, and to report on activities of the United Nations system in relation to the Decade to the General Assembly in each year of the Decade;

18. *Invites* United Nations financial and development institutions, operational programmes and specialized agencies, in accordance with the existing procedures of their governing bodies:

(a) To give increased priority and resources to improving the conditions of indigenous people, with particular emphasis on the needs of those people in developing countries, including by the preparation of specific programmes of action for the implementation of the goals of the Decade, within their areas of competence;

(b) To launch special projects, through appropriate channels and in collaboration with indigenous people, for strengthening their community-level initiatives, and to facilitate the exchange of information and expertise among indigenous people and other relevant experts;

(c) To designate focal points for coordination with the Centre for Human Rights of activities related to the Decade;

19. *Encourages* Governments to support the Decade by:

(a) Contributing to the United Nations Trust Fund for the Decade;

(b) Preparing relevant programmes, plans and reports in relation to the Decade, in consultation with indigenous people;

(c) Seeking means, in consultation with indigenous people, of giving indigenous people greater responsibility for their own affairs and an effective voice in decisions on matters which affect them;

(d) Establishing national committees or other mechanisms involving indigenous people to ensure that the objectives and activities of the Decade are planned and implemented on the basis of full partnership with indigenous people;

20. *Also encourages* Governments to consider contributing, as appropriate, to the Fund for the Development of Indigenous Peoples of Latin America and the Caribbean, in support of the achievement of the goals of the Decade;

21. *Appeals* to Governments and intergovernmental and non-governmental organizations to support the Decade by identifying resources for activities designed to implement the goals of the Decade, in cooperation with indigenous people;

22. *Decides* to include in the provisional agenda of its fiftieth session the item entitled "Programme of activities of the International Decade of the World's Indigenous People".

Document 98

Model communication for information concerning alleged victims of human rights violations

Model communication

Date: ....

Communication to:
The Human Rights Committee
c/o Centre for Human Rights
United Nations Office
8-14 avenue de la Paix
1211 Geneva 10, Switzerland,

submitted for consideration under the Optional Protocol to the International Covenant on Civil and Political Rights.

I. Information concerning the author of the communication

Name.. First name(s) ....

Nationality............................... Profession ....

Date and place of birth ....

Present address ....

....

Address for exchange of confidential correspondence (if other than present address)

....

....

Submitting the communication as:

   (a) Victim of the violation or violations set forth below .... ☐

   (b) Appointed representative/legal counsel of the alleged
      victim(s) .... ☐

   (c) Other .... ☐

If box (c) is marked, the author should explain:

(i) In what capacity he is acting on behalf of the victim(s) (e.g. family relationship or other personal links with the alleged victim(s)):

....

(ii) Why the victim(s) is (are) unable to submit the communication himself (themselves):

....

An unrelated third party having no link to the victim(s) cannot submit a communication on his (their) behalf.

II. Information concerning the alleged victim(s) (if other than author)

Name .... First name(s) ....

Nationality .... Profession ....

Date and place of birth ....

Present address or whereabouts ....

....

III. State concerned/articles violated/domestic remedies

Name of the State party (country) to the International Covenant and the Optional Protocol against which the communication is directed:

....

Articles of the International Covenant on Civil and Political Rights allegedly violated:

....

Steps taken by or on behalf of the alleged victim(s) to exhaust domestic remedies—recourse to the courts or other public authorities, when and with what results (if possible, enclose copies of all relevant judicial or administrative decisions):

....

If domestic remedies have not been exhausted, explain why:

....

Has the same matter been submitted for examination under another procedure of international investigation or settlement (e.g. the Inter-American Commission on Human Rights, the European Commission on Human Rights)? If so, when and with what results?

....

V. Facts of the claim

Detailed description of the facts of the alleged violation or violations (including relevant dates)*

....

Author's signature: ....

---

*Add as many pages as needed for this description.

Document 99

Status of international human rights instruments; oversight bodies, international human rights instruments, basic information

The international human rights instruments of the United Nations which establish treaty bodies to monitor their implementation are the following:

(1) the International Covenant on Economic, Social and Cultural Rights (CESCR), which is monitored by the Committee on Economic, Social and Cultural Rights;

(2) the International Covenant on Civil and Political Rights (CCPR), which is monitored by the Human Rights Committee;

(3) the Optional Protocol to the International Covenant on Civil and Political Rights (OPT), which is supervised by the Human Rights Committee;

(4) the Second Optional Protocol to the International Covenant on Civil and Political Rights aimed at the abolition of the death penalty (OPT2);

(5) the International Convention on the Elimination of All Forms of Racial Discrimination (CERD), which is monitored by the Committee on the Elimination of Racial Discrimination;

(6) the International Convention on the Suppression and Punishment of the Crime of Apartheid (APAR), which is monitored by the Group of Three;

(7) the Convention on the Elimination of All Forms of Discrimination against Women (CEDAW), which is monitored by the Committee on the Elimination of Discrimination against Women;

(8) the Convention against Torture and Other Cruel, Inhuman or Degrading Treatment or Punishment (CAT), which is monitored by the Committee against Torture;

(9) the Convention on the Rights of the Child (CRC), which is monitored by the Committee on the Rights of the Child;

(10) the International Convention on the Protection of the Rights of All Migrant Workers and Members of Their Families (MWC), which was adopted by the General Assembly in 1990 and will enter into force when at least 20 States have accepted it.

The following listing of all Member States of the United Nations shows which of those States are a party (indicated by the year of entry into force or, for the Migrant Workers' Convention, the year of acceptance) or signatory (indicated by an "s") to the various United Nations human rights instruments listed. As at 1 July 1995, 180 Member States and four non-Member States were a party to one or more of those instruments and five Member States were not a party to any.

State	CESCR	CCPR	OPT	OPT2	CERD	APAR	CEDAW	CAT	CRC	MWC
Afghanistan	1983	1983	-	-	1983	1983	s	1987	1994	-
Albania	1992	1992	-	-	1994	-	1994	1994	1992	-
Algeria	1989	1989	1990	-	1972*	1982	-	1989*	1993	-
Andorra	-	-	-	-	-	-	-	-	-	-
Angola	1992	1992	1992	-	-	-	1986	-	1991	-
Antigua and										
Barbuda	-	-	-	-	1988	1982	1989	1993	1993	-
Argentina	1986	1986	1986	-	1969	1985	1985	1987*	1991	-
Armenia	1993	1993	1993	-	1993	1993	1993	1993	1993	-
Australia	1976	1980	1991	1990	1975*	-	1983	1989*	1991	-
Austria	1978	1978	1988	1993	1972	-	1982	1987*	1992	-
Azerbaijan	1992	1992	-	-	-	-	-	-	1992	-
Bahamas	-	-	-	-	1975	1981	1993	-	1991	-
Bahrain	-	-	-	-	1990	1990	-	-	1992	-
Bangladesh	-	-	-	-	1979	1985	1984	-	1990	-
Barbados	1976	1976	1976	-	1972	1979	1981	-	1990	-
Belarus	1976	1976	1992	-	1969	1976	1981	1987	1990	-
Belgium	1983	1983	1994	s	1975	-	1985	s	1992	-
Belize	-	-	-	-	-	-	1990	1987	1990	-
Benin	1992	1992	1992	-	s	1976	1992	1992	1990	-
Bhutan	-	-	-	-	s	-	1981	-	1990	-
Bolivia	1982	1982	1982	-	1970	1983	1990	s	1990	-
Bosnia and										
Herzegovina	1992	1992	1995	-	1993	1992	1992	1992	1992	-
Botswana	-	-	-	-	1974	-	-	-	1995	-
Brazil	1992	1992	-	-	1969	-	1984	1989	1990	-
Brunei Darussalam	-	-	-	-	-	-	-	-	-	-
Bulgaria	1976	1976	1992	-	1969*	1976	1982	1987*	1991	-
Burkina Faso	-	-	-	-	1978	1974	1987	-	1990	-
Burundi	1990	1990	-	-	1977	1978	1992	1993	1990	-
Cambodia	1992	1992	-	-	1983	1981	1992	1992	1992	-
Cameroon	1984	1984	1984	-	1971	1976	1994	1987	1993	-
Canada	1976	1976	1976	-	1970	-	1982	1987*	1992	-
Cape Verde	1993	1993	-	-	1979	1979	1981	1992	1992	-
Central African Rep.	1981	1981	1981	-	1971	1981	1991	-	1992	-
Chad	1995	1995	1995	-	1977	1976	1995	1995	1990	-
Chile	1976	1976	1992	-	1971*	-	1990	1988	1990	s
China	-	-	-	-	1982	1983	1981	1988	1992	-
Colombia	1976	1976	1976	-	1981	1988	1982	1988	1991	1995
Comoros	-	-	-	-	-	-	1994	-	1993	-
Congo	1984	1984	1984	-	1988	1983	1982	-	1993	-
CostaRica	1976	1976	1976	-	1969*	1986	1986	1993	1990	-
Côte d'Ivoire	1992	1992	-	-	1973	-	s	-	1991	-
Croatia	1991	1991	-	-	1991	1991	1991	1991*	1991	-
Cuba	-	-	-	-	1972	1977	1981	1995	1991	-
Cyprus	1976	1976	1992	-	1969*	-	1985	1991*	1991	-
Czech Republic	1993	1993	1993	-	1993	1993	1993	1993	1993	-
Democratic People's										
Republic of Korea	1981	1981	-	-	-	-	-	-	1990	-
Denmark	1976	1976	1976	1994	1972*	-	1983	1987*	1991	-

State	CESCR	CCPR	OPT	OPT2	CERD	APAR	CEDAW	CAT	CRC	MWC
Djibouti	-	-	-	-	-	-	-	-	1991	-
Dominica	1993	1993	-	-	-	-	1981	-	1991	-
Dominican Republic	1978	1978	1978	-	1983	-	1982	s	1991	-
Ecuador	1976	1976	1976	1993	1969*	1976	1981	1988*	1990	-
Egypt	1982	1982	-	-	1969	1977	1981	1987	1990	1993
El Salvador	1980	1980	1995	-	1979	1979	1981	-	1990	-
Equatorial Guinea	1987	1987	1987	-		-	1984	-	1992	-
Eritrea	-	-	-	-	-	-	-	-	1994	-
Estonia	1992	1992	1992	-	1991	1991	1991	1991	1991	-
Ethiopia	1993	1993		-	1976	1978	1981	1994	1991	-
Fiji	-	-	-	-	1973	-	-	-	1993	-
Finland	1976	1976	1976	1991	1970*	-	1986	1989*	1991	-
France	1981	1981	1984	-	1971*	-	1984	1987*	1990	-
Gabon	1983	1983	-	-	1980	1980	1983	s	1994	-
Gambia	1979	1979	1988	-	1979	1979	1993	s	1990	-
Georgia	1994	1994	1994	-	-	-	1994	1994	1994	-
Germany	1976	1976	1993	1992	1969	-	1985	1990	1992	-
Ghana	-	-	-	-	1969	1978	1986	-	1990	-
Greece	1985	-	-	-	1970	-	1983	1988*	1993	-
Grenada	1991	1991	-	-	s	-	1990	-	1990	-
Guatemala	1988	1992	-	-	1983	-	1982	1990	1990	-
Guinea	1978	1978	1993	-	1977	1976	1982	1989	1990	-
Guinea-Bissau	1992	-	-	-	-	-	1985	-	1990	-
Guyana	1977	1977	1993	-	1977	1977	1981	1988	1991	-
Haiti	-	1991	-	-	1973	1978	1981	-	1995	-
Holy See	-	-	-	-	1969	-	-	-	1990	-
Honduras	1981	s	s	s	-	-	1983	-	1990	-
Hungary	1976	1976	1988	1994	1969*	1976	1981	1987*	1991	-
Iceland	1979	1979	1979	1991	1969*	-	1985	s	1992	-
India	1979	1979	-	-	1969	1977	1993	-	1993	-
Indonesia	-	-	-	-	-	-	1984	s	1990	-
Iran, Islamic Rep. of	1976	1976	-	-	1969	1985	-	-	1994	-
Iraq	1976	1976	-	-	1970	1976	1986	-	1994	-
Ireland	1990	1990	1990	1993	s	-	1986	s	1992	-
Israel	1991	1992	-	-	1979	-	1991	1991	1991	-
Italy	1978	1978	1978	1995	1976*	-	1985	1989*	1991	-
Jamaica	1976	1976	1976	-	1971	1977	1984	-	1991	-
Japan	1979	1979		-	-	-	1985	-	1994	-
Jordan	1976	1976	-	-	1974	1992	1992	1991	1991	-
Kazakhstan	-	-	-	-	-	-	-	1994	1994	-
Kenya	1976	1976	-	-	-	s	1984	-	1990	-
Kuwait	-	-	-	-	1969	1977	1994	-	1991	-
Kyrgyzstan	1994	1994	1994	-	-	-	-	-	1994	-
Lao People's Dem. Rep.	-	-	-	-	1974	1981	1981	-	1991	-
Latvia	1992	1992	1994	-	1992	1992	1992	1992	1992	-
Lebanon	1976	1976	-	-	1971	-	-	-	1991	-
Lesotho	1992	1992	-	-	1971	1983	s	-	1992	-
Liberia	s	s	-	-	1976	1976	1984	-	1993	-
Libyan Arab Jamahiriya	1976	1976	1989	-	1969	1976	1989	1989	1993	-
Liechtenstein	-	-	-	-	-	-	-	1990*	s	-

State	CESCR	CCPR	OPT	OPT2	CERD	APAR	CEDAW	CAT	CRC	MWC
Lithuania	1992	1992	1992	-	-	-	1994	-	1992	-
Luxembourg	1983	1983	1983	1992	1978	-	1990	1987*	1994	-
Madagascar	1976	1976	1976	-	1969	1977	1989	-	1991	-
Malawi	1994	1994		-	-	-	1987	-	1991	-
Malaysia	-	-	-	-	-	-	-	-	1995	-
Maldives	-	-	-	-	1984	1984	1993	-	1991	-
Mali	1976	1976	-	-	1974	1977	1985	-	1990	-
Malta	1990	1990	1990	1994	1971	-	1991	1990*	1990	-
Marshall Islands	-	-	-	-	-	-	-	-	1993	-
Mauritania	-	-	-	-	1989	1989	-	-	1991	-
Mauritius	1976	1976	1976	-	1972	-	1984	1993	1990	-
Mexico	1981	1981		-	1975	1980	1981	1987	1990	s
Micronesia, Federated States of	-	-	-	-	-	-	-	-	1993	-
Monaco	-	-	-	-	-	-	-	1992*	1993	-
Mongolia	1976	1976	1991	-	1969	1976	1981	-	1990	-
Morocco	1979	1979	-	-	1971	-	1993	1993	1993	1993
Mozambique	-	1993	-	1993	1983	1983	-	-	1994	-
Myanmar	-	-	-	-	-	-	-	-	1991	-
Namibia	1994	1994	1994	1994	1982	1982	1992	1994	1990	-
Nauru	-	-	-	-	-	-	-	-	1994	-
Nepal	1991	1991	1991	-	1971	1977	1991	1991	1990	-
Netherlands	1979	1979	1979	1991	1972*	-	1991	1989*	1995	-
New Zealand	1979	1979	1989	1990	1972	-	1985	1990*	1993	-
Nicaragua	1980	1980	1980	s	1978	1980	1981	s	1990	-
Niger	1986	1986	1986	-	1969	1978	-	-	1990	-
Nigeria	1993	1993	-	-	1969	1977	1985	s	1991	-
Norway	1976	1976	1976	1991	1970*	-	1981	1987*	1991	-
Oman	-	-	-	-	-	1991	-	-	-	-
Pakistan	-	-	-	-	1969	1986	-	-	1990	-
Palau	-	-	-	-	-	-	-	-	-	-
Panama	1977	1977	1977	1993	1969	1977	1981	1987	1991	-
Papua New Guinea	-	-	-	-	1982	-	1995	-	1993	-
Paraguay	1992	1992	1995	-	-	-	1987	1990	1990	-
Peru	1978	1978	1981	-	1971*	1978	1982	1988	1990	-
Philippines	1976	1987	1989	-	1969	1978	1981	1987	1990	s
Poland	1977	1977	1992	-	1969	1976	1981	1989*	1991	-
Portugal	1978	1978	1983	1990	1982	-	1981	1989*	1990	-
Qatar	-	-	-	-	1976	1976	-	-	1995	-
Rep. of Korea	1990	1990	1990	-	1979	-	1985	1995	1991	-
Rep. of Moldova	1993	1993	-	-	1993	-	1994	-	1993	-
Romania	1976	1976	1993	1991	1970	1978	1982	1990	1990	-
Russian Federation	1976	1976	1992	-	1969*	1976	1981	1987*	1990	-
Rwanda	1976	1976	-	-	1975	1981	1981	-	1991	-
Saint Kitts and Nevis	-	-	-	-	-	-	1985	-	1990	-
Saint Lucia	-	-	-	-	1990	-	1982	-	1993	-
Saint Vincent and Grenadines	1982	1982	1982	-	1981	1981	1981	-	1993	-
Samoa	-	-	-	-	-	-	1992	-	1994	-
San Marino	1986	1986	1986	-	-	-	-	-	1991	-
Sao Tome and Principe	-	-	-	-	-	1979	-	-	1991	-

State	CESCR	CCPR	OPT	OPT2	CERD	APAR	CEDAW	CAT	CRC	MWC
Saudi Arabia	-	-	-	-	-	-	-	-	-	-
Senegal	1978	1978	1978	-	1972*	1977	1985	1987	1990	-
Seychelles	1992	1992	1992	1995	1978	1978	1992	1992	1990	1994
Sierra Leone	-	-	-	-	1969	-	1988	s	1990	-
Singapore	-	-	-	-	-	-	-	-	-	-
Slovak Republic	1993	1993	1993	-	1993	1993*	1993	1993*	1993	-
Slovenia	1992	1991	1993	1994	1992	1992	1992	1993*	1991	-
Solomon Islands	1982	-	-	-	1982	-	-	-	1995	-
Somalia	1990	1990	1990	-	1975	1976	-	1990	-	-
South Africa	s	s	-	-	s	-	s	s	1995	-
Spain	1977	1977	1985	1991	1969	-	1984	1987*	1991	-
Sri Lanka	1980	1980	-	-	1982	1982	1981	1994	1991	-
Sudan	1986	1986	-	-	1977	1977	-	s	1990	-
Suriname	1977	1977	1977	-	1984	1980	1993	-	1993	-
Swaziland	-	-	-	-	1969	-	-	-	s	-
Sweden	1976	1976	1976	1990	1972*	-	1981	1987*	1990	-
Switzerland	1992	1992	-	1994	1994	-	s	1987*	s	-
Syrian Arab Republic	1976	1976	-	-	1969	1976	-	-	1993	-
Tajikistan	-	-	-	-	1995	-	1993	1995	1993	-
Thailand	-	-	-	-	-	-	1985	-	1992	-
The Former Yugoslav Rep. of Macedonia	1991	1991	1994	1995	1991	1991	1991	1994	1991	-
Togo	1984	1984	1988	-	1970	1984	1983	1987*	1990	-
Tonga	-	-	-	-	1972	-	-	-	-	-
Trinidad and Tobago	1979	1979	1981	-	1973	1979	1990	-	1992	-
Tunisia	1976	1976	-	-	1969	1977	1985	1988*	1992	-
Turkey	-	-	-	-	s	-	1986	1988*	1995	-
Turkmenistan	-	-	-	-	1994	-	-	-	1993	-
Uganda	1987	-	-	-	1980	1986	1985	1987	1990	-
Ukraine	1976	1976	1991	-	1969*	1976	1981	1987	1991	-
United Arab Emirates	-	-	-	-	1974	1976	-	-	-	-
United Kingdom	1976	1976	-	-	1969	-	1986	1989	1992	-
United Rep. of Tanzania	1976	1976	-	-	1972	1976	1985	-	1991	-
United States of America	s	1992	-	-	1994	-	s	1994	s	-
Uruguay	1976	1976	1976	1993	1969*	-	1981	1987*	1990	-
Uzbekistan	-	-	-	-	-	-	-	-	1994	-
Vanuatu	-	-	-	-	-	-	-	-	1993	-
Venezuela	1978	1978	1978	1993	1969	1983	1983	1991*	1990	-
Viet Nam	1982	1982	-	-	1982	1981	1982	-	1990	-
Yemen	1987	1987	-	-	1989	1987	1984	1991	1991	-
Yugoslavia	1976	1976	s	-	1969	1976	1982	1991*	1991	-
Zaire	1977	1977	1977	-	1976	1978	1986	-	1990	-
Zambia	1984	1984	1984	-	1972	1983	1985	-	1992	-
Zimbabwe	1991	1991	-	-	1991	1991	1991	-	1990	-
Total number of States Parties	132	130	84	28	145	99	140	90	176	4

*Indicates that the State party has accepted the individual communications procedure (article 14 of CERD and/or article 22 of CAT).

Monitoring bodies
International human rights instruments
Basic information

	International Convention on the Elimination of All Forms of Racial Discrimination CERD	International Covenant on Economic, Social and Cultural Rights CESCR	International Covenant on Civil and Political Rights CCPR	International Convention on the Suppression and Punishment of the Crime of Apartheid	Convention on the Elimination of All Forms of Discrimination against Women CEDAW	Convention against Torture and Other Cruel, Inhuman or Degrading Treatment or Punishment CAT	Convention on the Rights of the Child CRC	International Convention on the Protection of the Rights of All Migrant Workers and Members of Their Families
Entry into force	4 January 1969	3 January 1976	23 March 1976	18 July 1976	3 September 1981	26 June 1987	2 September 1990	Pending
States parties	139	129	127	99	133	82	159	2
Optional provisions (States parties)	Article 14 (14)	None	- Article 41 (44) - First Prot. (Indiv. comm.) (77) - Second Prot. (death penalty) (23)	None	None	- Article 21 (State comm.) (29) - Article 22 (Indiv. comm.) (28)	None	- Article 76 (State comm.) - Article 77 (Indiv. comm.)
Monitoring body	Committee on the Elimination of Racial Discrimination (CERD)	Committee on Economic, Social and Cultural Rights (CESCR) (ECOSOC res. 1985/17)	Human Rights Committee	Group of Three	Committee on the Elimination of Discrimination against Women (CEDAW)	Committee against Torture (CAT)	Committee on the Rights of the Child (CRC)	Committee on the Protection of the Rights of All Migrant Workers and Members of Their Families
Number of members	18	18	18	3	23	10	10	10, then 14 (41st rat.)

	Col 1	Col 2	Col 3	Col 4	Col 5	Col 6	Col 7	Col 8
Number (length) of sessions per year	1	2 (2 wks.)	2 (2 wks.)	1 (2 wks.)	1 every 2 yrs. (1 wk.)	3 (3 wks.)	1 (3 wks.)	2 (3 wks.)
Working group	–	Yes	No	Yes (before session)	No	Yes (2 pre-sessional groups)	Yes (3 months before session)	No
Periodicity: initial report	Within 1 yr.	Within 2 yrs.	Within 1 yr.	Within 1 yr.	Within 2 yrs.	Within 1 yr.	Within 2 yrs.	Within 1 yr.
Periodicity: periodic reports	Every 5 years	Every 5 years	Every 4 years	Every 4 years	Every 4 years	Every 5 years	Every 5 years	Every 4 years (interim report every 2 years)
Country rapporteur	–	–	Country rapporteur and alternate (discussion and final comments)	–	–	Country rapporteur (list and comments)	Country rapporteur (list and final comments)	Country coordinator (discussion and conclusions)
Conclusions	–	Yes	Yes	Yes	No	Yes	Yes	Yes
List of questions	–	–	No	Yes	No	Yes	Yes	No
Time allotted for exam. of per. report (average)	–	–	1 meeting	1 meeting	1/2 meeting	3 meetings	2 meetings	1 meeting
General comments	–	General comments	–	General recommendations	–	General comments	General comments	General recommendations

Document 100

List of judgments and opinions of the International Court of Justice on the subject of human rights

1. *Corfu Channel* (Judgment of 9 April 1949): obligation to make known the existence of a danger, in this instance the presence of a minefield in Albanian territorial waters.

2. *Reparation for Injuries Suffered in the Service of the United Nations* (Advisory Opinion of 11 April 1949): right of an agent of the United Nations to the protection of the Organization.

3. *Interpretation of Peace Treaties with Bulgaria, Hungary and Romania* (Advisory Opinion of 30 March 1950): inapplicability of the so-called domestic jurisdiction reservation to the dispute settlement procedure in respect of a treaty concerning human rights.

4. *International Status of South-West Africa* (Advisory Opinion of 11 July 1950): affirmation of the right of peoples of mandated territories to obtain real protection by means of international supervision and by exercising the right of petition.

5. *Asylum (Colombia/Peru)* (Judgment of 20 November 1950): affirmation of the right to diplomatic asylum when "arbitrary action is substituted for the rule of law".

6. *Reservations to the Convention on the Prevention and Punishment of the Crime of Genocide* (Advisory Opinion of 28 May 1951): condemnation of the crime of genocide.

7. *Barcelona Traction, Light and Power Company, Limited* (Judgment of 5 February 1970): international protection of the fundamental rights of the human person.

8. *Legal Consequences for States of the Continued Presence of South Africa in Namibia* (South-West Africa)

notwithstanding Security Council Resolution 276 (1970) (Advisory Opinion of 21 June 1971): condemnation of the policy of apartheid.

9. *Western Sahara* (Advisory Opinion of 16 October 1975): affirmation of the right to self-determination of the people of Spanish Sahara.

10. *United States Diplomatic and Consular Staff in Tehran* (Judgment of 24 May 1980): condemnation of improper loss of liberty.

11. *Military and Paramilitary Activities in and against Nicaragua* (Judgment of 27 June 1986): obligation to respect international humanitarian law.

12. *Elettronica Sicula S.p.A. (ELSI)* (Judgment of 20 July 1989): definition of what is arbitrary.

13. *Applicability of Article VI, Section 22, of the Convention on the Privileges and Immunities of the United Nations* (Advisory Opinion of 15 December 1989): whether rapporteurs of the Subcommission on Prevention of Discrimination and Protection of Minorities have the status of experts on mission.

14. *Land, Island and Maritime Frontier Dispute* (Judgment of 11 September 1992): obligation to respect acquired rights in the event that a boundary is moved.

15. *Application of the Convention on the Prevention and Punishment of the Crime of Genocide (Bosnia and Herzegovina v. Yugoslavia (Serbia and Montenegro))* (Order of 8 April 1993): reaffirmation of the condemnation of the crime of genocide.

16. *East Timor (Portugal v. Australia)* (Judgment of 30 June 1995): the Court deems it cannot rule on the dispute.

V Subject index to documents

*[This subject index to the documents reproduced in this book should be used
in conjunction with the index on pages 522-536. A complete listing of the documents
indexed below appears on pages 135-141.]*

A

Accessions.
See: Signatures, accessions, ratifications.

Administration of justice.
– Documents 51-53, 58, 62-63

Advisory opinions.
– Document 11

Advisory services.
– Document 16
See also: Technical cooperation.

Africa.
– Document 47

**African Charter on Human and Peoples' Rights
(1981).**
– Document 47

African Commission on Human and Peoples' Rights.
– Document 47

Aid, humanitarian.
– Documents 74-76, 86

**American Convention on Human Rights (Pact of San
José) (1969).**
– Document 36

Americas, the.
– Document 36

Apartheid.
– Documents 25-30, 34, 39-40, 54, 86

Arbitrary detention.
– Document 37
See also: Detention camps. Juveniles deprived of
their liberty. Prisoners. Treatment of prisoners.

Aristide, Jean-Bertrand.
– Document 81

B

Banja Luka (Bosnia and Herzegovina).
– Document 93

**Basic Principles for the Treatment of Prisoners
(1990).**
– Document 67

**Basic Principles on the Independence of the Judiciary
(1985).**
– Document 53

Basic Principles on the Role of Lawyers (1990).
– Document 63

**Basic Principles on the Use of Force and Firearms by
Law Enforcement Officials (1990).**
– Document 62

Bijeljina (Bosnia and Herzegovina).
– Document 93

**Body of Principles for the Protection of All Persons
under Any Form of Detention or Imprisonment
(1988).**
– Document 58

Bosnia and Herzegovina.
– Documents 73-77, 80, 82-83, 93

Boutros-Ghali, Boutros.
– Document 84

Boycotts.
– Documents 54, 74

C

Capital punishment.
See: Death penalty.

Cease-fire agreements.
– Documents 73, 76, 89

Centre [of the United Nations] . . .
See: UN. Centre . . .

Children.
– Documents 8, 36, 60, 65, 85
See also: Juveniles.

Civil and political rights.
– Documents 8, 10, 13, 25, 32-33, 36, 61, 70, 88

**Code of Conduct for Law Enforcement Officials
(1979).**
– Document 44

D

Decade to Combat Racism and Racial
Discrimination (2nd: 1983-1992).
– Document 86

Decade to Combat Racism and Racial
Discrimination (3rd: 1993-2002).
– Document 86

Decades:
See also: International ... UN. Decade ...

Declaration of Basic Principles of Justice for Victims
of Crime and Abuse of Power (1985).
– Document 52

Declaration on fundamental human rights and
freedoms (draft).
– Document 5

Declaration on the Elimination of All Forms of
Intolerance and of Discrimination Based on Religion
or Belief (1981).
– Document 48

Declaration on the Granting of Independence to
Colonial Countries and Peoples (1960).
– Documents 21, 25, 30

Declaration on the Protection of All Persons from
Enforced Disappearance (1992).
– Document 78

Declaration on the Right to Development (1986).
– Documents 56, 91

Declaration on the Rights of Persons belonging to
National or Ethnic, Religious and Linguistic
Minorities (1992).
– Document 79

Declarations.
– Documents 5, 21, 28, 35, 48, 52, 54, 56, 65, 70,
78-79, 85, 91

Decolonization.
– Document 21
See also: Self-determination. Colonialism.

Democracy.
– Documents 8, 81, 84, 86

Deportation.
– Document 37

Detention camps.
– Document 77
See also: Arbitrary detention. Juveniles deprived of
their liberty. Prisoners. Treatment of prisoners.

Detention of juveniles.
See: Juveniles deprived of their liberty.

Development, right to.
– Documents 56, 88, 91

Diplomatic Conference on the Reaffirmation and
Development of International Humanitarian Law
Applicable in Armed Conflicts (1977).
– Document 43

Disabled persons.
– Document 85

Disappearances.
– Documents 78, 85

Discrimination.
– Documents 2, 5, 8, 10, 16, 20, 25-26, 36, 38
See also: Racial discrimination. Gender-based
discrimination.

Displaced persons.
– Documents 37, 76, 89, 93

Dispute settlement.
– Documents 72-73, 76, 92

Duties of the individual to the community.
– Document 8

E

Economic, social and cultural rights.
– Documents 8, 10, 25, 31, 36, 70, 88

Education.
– Document 16

Education, in human rights.
– Documents 26, 85-86, 88, 96

Education, right to.
– Document 8

Educational assistance.
– Document 16

El Salvador.
– Document 72

Elections.
– Document 81

Equal opportunities.
– Document 55

Equality.
– Documents 3, 8, 45, 87

Equality before the law.
– Documents 8, 10, 36, 58

"Ethnic cleansing".
– Documents 76, 86, 93

Europe.
– Documents 10, 73, 77

European Commission of Human Rights—
establishment.
– Document 10

European Communities.
– Documents 73, 77

European Convention on Human Rights (1950).
– Document 10

European Council.
– Document 77

European Court of Human Rights—establishment.
– Document 10

Evaluation of programmes.
– Document 46

Executions, extra-legal.
– Document 59

Executions, summary.
– Documents 49, 59

F

Fair trial, right to.
– Documents 8, 10, 36, 58

Families of migrant workers.
– Document 71

Family law.
– Documents 8, 10, 36

Fellowships.
– Document 16

Food availability.
– Document 74

Former Yugoslavia.
– Documents 73-74, 76, 80, 82-83

Freedom of association.
– Documents 8, 10, 36

Freedom of expression.
– Documents 8, 10, 36

Freedom of information.
– Documents 2, 5, 16, 25

Freedom of movement.
– Documents 8, 36, 93

Freedom of religion.
– Documents 8, 10, 36, 48

Freedom of the press.
– Documents 2, 5

Freedom of thought.
– Documents 8, 10, 36

G

Gender-based discrimination.
– Document 45

Genocide.
– Documents 4, 7, 11, 90, 94

Guatemala.
– Document 92

Guidelines on the Role of Prosecutors (1990).
– Document 64

Guidelines.
– Documents 64, 68

H

Haiti.
– Document 81

Health, right to.
– Documents 8, 58, 67

High Commissioner [of the United Nations]
See: UN. High Commissioner . . .

Human rights education.
– Documents 26, 85-86, 88, 96

Human rights in armed conflicts.
– Documents 43, 73-77, 80, 82-83, 93-94

Human rights institutions.
– Documents 84, 88, 92

Human rights, promotion of.
– Documents 16, 26, 55, 57, 70, 84, 88

Human rights violations.
– Documents 6, 9, 20, 26, 28-30, 34, 37-39, 80, 83, 86, 88, 90, 93-94, 98

Humanitarian aid.
– Documents 74-76, 86

I

Independence of the judiciary.
– Document 53
See also: Administration of justice.

Indigenous populations/people(s).
– Documents 85-87, 97

International Year for Human Rights (1968).
– Document 26

International Year of the World's Indigenous People (1993).
– Document 87

International years.
– Documents 26, 87

Israel.
– Document 37

J

Justice.
See: Administration of justice.

Juvenile delinquency.
– Documents 52, 68
See also: Victims of crime.

Juvenile justice.
– Documents 51, 68-69
See also: Administration of justice. Juvenile delinquency.

Juveniles deprived of their liberty.
– Document 69
See also: Prisoners.

Juveniles.
– Documents 51-52, 68-69
See also: Children.

L

Law enforcement officials.
– Documents 44, 62

Law, equality under.
– Documents 8, 10, 36, 58

Law, family.
– Documents 8, 10, 36

Law, international humanitarian.
– Document 43

Laws of war.
– Document 43

Lawyers.
– Documents 63-64

Least developed countries.
– Document 70

M

Macedonia, former Yugoslav Republic of.
– Document 82

Marriage, consent to.
– Document 23

Marriage, right to.
– Documents 8, 10, 36

Medical supplies.
– Document 74
See also: Humanitarian aid.

Medium-term plan (1980-1983)—UN.
– Document 46

Middle East.
– Document 37

Migrant workers.
– Documents 71, 85-86

Minorities.
– Documents 2, 5, 16, 20, 34, 38, 79, 85-86

Minors.
See: Juveniles.

Missions, special.
– Documents 81, 93

Missions of inquiry.
– Documents 77, 92

Mozambican refugees.
– Document 89

Mozambique.
– Document 89
See also: Refugees.

Muslim women.
– Document 77

N

Nairobi Forward-looking Strategies for the Advancement of Women (1985).
– Documents 55, 57

Nationality.
– Documents 8, 19

Natural resources.
– Document 24

Netherlands.
– Document 83

Refugees, status of.
– Document 12

Religion, freedom of.
– Documents 8, 10, 36, 48

Religious intolerance.
– Document 48

Reservations.
– Document 11

Right of assembly.
– Documents 8, 10, 36

Right to a fair trial.
– Documents 8, 10, 36, 58

Right to communication of persons under arrest.
– Documents 10, 58

Right to development.
– Documents 56, 88, 91

Right to education.
– Document 8

Right to health.
– Documents 8, 58, 67

Right to life.
– Documents 8, 10, 36

Right to marriage.
– Documents 8, 10, 36

Right to own property.
– Documents 8, 36

Right to privacy.
– Documents 8, 10

Right to vote.
– Document 8

Right to work.
– Document 8

Rights, civil and political.
– Documents 8, 10, 13, 25, 32-33, 36, 61, 70, 88

Rights, economic, social and cultural.
– Documents 8, 10, 25, 31, 36, 70, 88

Rights, human, in armed conflicts.
– Documents 43, 73-77, 80, 82-83, 93-94

Rights of the child.
– Documents 8, 36, 60, 65, 85
See also: Juveniles.

Rights, women's.
– Documents 3, 5, 8, 13, 16, 45, 55, 57, 85

Rwanda.
– Documents 90, 94

S

Safeguards guaranteeing the protection of the rights of those facing the death penalty (1984).
– Document 49

Sanctions.
– Documents 74, 76

Sarajevo (Bosnia and Herzegovina).
– Document 74

Scholarships.
– Document 16

Security, international.
– Document 1

Segregation.
– Documents 29-30, 34, 39

Self-defence.
– Document 62

Self-determination.
– Documents 21, 41-42
See also: Colonialism. Decolonization.

Settlement of disputes.
– Documents 72-73, 76, 92

Sex discrimination.
See: Gender-based discrimination.

Signatures, accessions, ratifications.
– Documents 7, 10, 26, 36, 47, 59-60, 71, 86

Slavery.
– Documents 8-10, 18, 26, 36

Slovenia.
– Document 82

Social rights.
See: Economic, social and cultural rights.

South Africa.
– Documents 28-30, 34, 39, 54, 86
See also: Apartheid.

Sovereignty, permanent.
– Document 24

Special rapporteurs.
See: UN. Special rapporteur . . .

Sports.
– Documents 54, 74, 87

V

Vienna Declaration and Programme of Action (1993).
– Documents 85-86

Vote, right to.
– Document 8

W

War, laws of.
– Document 43

War, victims of.
– Documents 43, 83

Women.
– Documents 3, 5, 8, 13, 16, 19, 25-26, 28, 45, 55, 57, 77, 85, 95

Women, advancement of.
– Documents 45, 55, 57, 95

Women, married.
– Document 19

Women, Muslim.
– Document 77

Women's rights.
– Documents 3, 5, 8, 13, 16, 45, 55, 57, 85

Work, right to.
– Document 8

Working Group
See: UN. Working Group . . .

World Conference on Human Rights (1993, Vienna).
– Documents 70, 84-85

World Conference to Review and Appraise the Achievements of the United Nations Decade for Women: Equality, Development and Peace (1985, Nairobi).
– Document 55

World Declaration on the Survival, Protection and Development of Children (1990).
– Document 65

X

Xenophobia.
– Documents 85-86
See also: Racial discrimination.

Y

Yugoslavia.
– Documents 73-74, 76, 80, 82-83

VI Index

[The numbers following the entries refer to paragraph numbers in the Introduction.]

obligations of States parties,
224, 227, 245, 249, 254, 256
periodic reports, 239, 244,
251-252, 254-257, 259
preamble, 200
provisions, 226-231
two Covenants, 220-225
International criminal jurisdiction,
111, 478
International criminal tribunal,
111, 478
former Yugoslavia, 8, 116, 478,
510-511, 515-516
competence *ratione materiae*,
511, 513
death penalty [capital
punishment], 518
Statute, 510-514, 518
Rwanda, 8, 116, 478, 515-517
death penalty [capital
punishment], 518
Statute, 516-518
International Decade of the
World's Indigenous People
(1995-2004), 440-448
International decades
Decade to Combat Racism and
Racial Discrimination
(1st: 1973-1982), 433
Decade to Combat Racism and
Racial Discrimination
(2nd: 1983-1992), 433
Decade to Combat Racism and
Racial Discrimination
(3rd: 1993-2002), 433-437
International Decade of the
World's Indigenous People
(1995-2004), 440-448
United Nations Decade for
Human Rights Education
(1995-2004), 464-465
United Nations Decade for
Women (1976-1985), 387, 389
International Development Strategy
for the Third United Nations
Development Decade, 388
International human rights court
(proposed), 243
International instruments,
141-142, 326, 410, 425, 522

obligations of States parties,
227, 254, 522-524
reservations, 113, 279, 410,
423, 427-429
supervision [monitoring and
follow-up], 260-261,
290-297, 523
reports of States parties,
272-273, 522-524
comprehensive periodic
report, 523-524
See also: Conventions.
Treaties.
initial, 263
periodic, 183-186, 239,
244, 251-252, 254-257,
259, 262-263, 371-372
procedures for submission
[Guidelines], 263-265,
371-372, 523-524
review by non-governmental
organizations, 271
review by specialized
agencies, 270
review by treaty-monitoring
bodies, 266-269
technical monitoring body, 525
International Labour Office, 246, 270
International Labour
Organization, 17, 48, 55,
118, 198
constitution, 17, 348, 398
United Nations/ILO committee
of experts on forced labour,
188
International law, 60, 428, 432
International Military Tribunal at
Nuremberg (1945), 46, 93,
111
Indictment, 93
Judgement, 93, 106-107
Statute, 98, 100, 106
International Research and
Training Institute for the
Advancement of Women,
384-386
International Women's Year
(1975), 387
International Year for Human
Rights (1968), 312

International Year of the Child
(1979), 365
International Year of the World's
Indigenous People (1993),
444-445
International years
1968 International Year for
Human Rights, 312
1975 International Women's
Year, 387
1979 International Year of the
Child, 365
1993 International Year of the
World's Indigenous People,
444-445

J

Judiciary
Basic Principles on the
Independence of the Judiciary
(1985), 338
Juvenile delinquency
United Nations Guidelines for
the Prevention of Juvenile
Delinquency (The Riyadh
Guidelines) (1990), 339

L

Law enforcement officials
Code of Conduct for Law
Enforcement Officials (1979),
337
Law, international humanitarian,
415, 509, 511, 513, 515
Law of treaties, 428
Vienna Convention on the
Law of Treaties (1969),
428
Laws of war, 415
League of Nations, 40, 53, 348
Covenant (1919), 16, 31
LON.
See: League of Nations.

M

Malawi, 471
Marriage
consent in marriage, 78, 148

Promotion of human rights, 20, 21, 23, 26, 29, 38-39, 45, 338, 353, 521, 532

Protection of human rights, 1, 6, 7, 39, 521
  role of States, 409-410, 414, 421
  role of UN, 14, 405, 408-409, 417-420
  technical cooperation, 419, 449-471

Public awareness [of human rights], 37

R

Racial discrimination, 416
  Decade to Combat Racism and Racial Discrimination (1st: 1973-1982), 433
  Decade to Combat Racism and Racial Discrimination (2nd: 1983-1992), 433
  Decade to Combat Racism and Racial Discrimination (3rd: 1993-2002), 433-437
  Declaration on the Elimination of All Forms of Racial Discrimination (1963), 150
  International Convention on the Elimination of All Forms of Racial Discrimination (1965), 164-182, 292, 294, 433
    adoption, 164
    art. 1, 166
    art. 2, 166
    art. 4, 170-171
    art. 5, 172
    art. 6, 173
    art. 7, 173
    art. 11, 292
    art. 14, 276
    definition, 166
    entry into force, 164
    individual complaints, 164, 175
    monitoring, 164, 175-181
      financing, 180
      periodic reports, 181
    philosophy, 167
    preamble, 167

programme of action, 435-436
UN. General Assembly, 166
Namibia, 433
national policies, 168
  elimination, 170, 174
  implementation, 168
  tribunals, 173
protection of groups, 169
racist propaganda, 170-171
South Africa, 165, 433
Trust and Non-Self-Governing Territories, 177
UN. Committee on the Elimination of Racial Discrimination, 175-181, 276, 292, 294
  composition, 175
  establishment, 178
  reports, 179
UN. Special Rapporteur on contemporary forms of racism, racial discrimination, xenophobia and related intolerance, 436-437
Racial groups, 99-100, 169
Racism.
  See: Racial discrimination.
Recommendations [UN], 21, 23-24, 30, 44-45, 52, 65
  obstruction [rejection], 23
Refugees, 152
  children, 374
  Convention relating to the Status of Refugees (1951), 152
  United Nations High Commissioner for Refugees, 152, 198, 383
Religious groups, 99-100, 102
Religious intolerance
  Declaration on the Elimination of All Forms of Intolerance and of Discrimination Based on Religion or Belief (1981), 335
  UN. Special Rapporteur on the implementation of the Declaration on the Elimination of All Forms of Intolerance and of Discrimination, 307

Reporting system, 263-265, 371-372, 523-524
Right of peoples to self-determination.
  See: Self-determination.
Right to a nationality, 138
Right to an adequate standard of living, 210
Right to development, 139, 341-361, 411
  Declaration on the Right to Development (1986), 341-361
    adoption, 341, 343
    principles, 347, 348
  definition, 343-344
  evaluation mechanism, 359
  international cooperation, 353
  UN. Centre for Human Rights, 361
  UN. Open-ended working group of governmental experts, 342
  UN. Working Group on the Right to Development, 342, 345, 350, 352, 354, 357-359
  UN. Secretary-General, 360-361
    reports, 348
  United Nations High Commissioner for Human Rights, 360
  United Nations system, 355, 358, 360
Right to education, 212
Right to equality, 200
Right to form trade unions, 48, 55, 207
Right to health, 211
Right to liberty, 133
Right to life, 133
Right to petition, 139
Right to protection of intellectual property, 214
Right to security of person, 133
Right to seek asylum, 133, 279, 414, 461
Right to work, 205-206
Rights, civil and political.
  See: International Covenants on Human Rights (1966).
Rights, economic, social and cultural.
  See: International Covenants on Human Rights (1966).

United Nations publications of related interest

The following UN publications may be obtained from the addresses indicated below, or at your local distributor:

An Agenda for Peace
Second edition, 1995
By Boutros Boutros-Ghali,
Secretary-General of the United Nations
E.95.I.15   92-1-100555-8   155 pp. $7.50

An Agenda for Development
By Boutros Boutros-Ghali,
Secretary-General of the United Nations
E.95.I.16   92-1-100556-6   132 pp. $7.50

Confronting New Challenges, 1995
Annual Report on the Work of the Organization
By Boutros Boutros-Ghali,
Secretary-General of the United Nations
E.95.I.47   92-1-100595-7

New Dimensions of Arms Regulation and
Disarmament in the Post–Cold War Era
By Boutros Boutros-Ghali,
Secretary-General of the United Nations
E.93.IX.8   92-1-142192-6   53 pp. $9.95

Basic Facts About the United Nations
E.95.I.31   92-1-100870-1 $7.50   forthcoming

Demographic Yearbook, Vol. 44
B.94.XIII.1   92-1-051083-6   1992   823 pp. $125.00

World's Women 1995: Trends and Statistics
Second Edition
E.95.XVII.2   92-1-161372-8 $15.95

Statistical Yearbook, 39th Edition
B.94.XVII.1 H   92-1-061159-4   1992/93
1,174 pp. $110.00

Women: Challenges to the Year 2000
E.91.I.21   92-1-100458-6   96 pp. $12.95

World Economic and Social Survey 1995
E.95.II.C.1   92-1-109130-6   245 pp. $55.00

World Investment Report 1995—
Transnational Corporations and Competitiveness
$45.00   forthcoming

Yearbook of the United Nations, Vol. 47
E.94.I.1   0-7923-3077-3   1993   1,428 pp.
$150.00

The United Nations Blue Books Series

The United Nations and Apartheid, 1948-1994
E.95.I.7   92-1-100546-9   565 pp. $29.95

The United Nations and Cambodia, 1991-1995
E.95.I.9   92-1-100548-5   352 pp. $29.95

The United Nations and Nuclear Non-Proliferation
E.95.I.17   92-1-100557-4   199 pp. $29.95

The United Nations and El Salvador, 1990-1995
E.95.I.12   92-1-100552-3   611 pp. $29.95

The United Nations and Mozambique, 1992-1995
E.95.I.20   92-1-100559-0   321 pp. $29.95

The United Nations and the Advancement of Women, 1945-1995
E.95.I.29   92-1-100567-1 $29.95

United Nations Publications
2 United Nations Plaza, Room DC2-853
New York, NY 10017
United States of America
Tel.: (212) 963-8302; 1 (800) 253-9646
Fax: (212) 963-3489

United Nations Publications
Sales Office and Bookshop
CH-1211 Geneva 10
Switzerland
Tel.: 41 (22) 917-26-13;
        41 (22) 917-26-14
Fax: 41 (22) 917-00-27

NCOMBE
MUNITY COLLEGE

3 3312 00050 6675

For Reference

Not to be taken from this room

United Nations.

The United Nations and huma
rights, 1945-1995

Printed on recycled paper